THE ROUTLEDGE HAN
PHILOSOPHY OF HU

Humility is a vital aspect of political discussion, social media and self-help, whilst recent empirical research has linked humility to improved well-being, open-mindedness and increased accuracy in assessing persuasive messages. It is also a topic central to research and discussion in philosophy, applied ethics and religious studies.

The Routledge Handbook of Philosophy of Humility is the first collection to present a comprehensive overview of the philosophy of humility, whilst also covering important interdisciplinary topics. Comprising 41 chapters by an international team of contributors, the *Handbook* is divided into seven parts:

- Theories of humility
- The ethics of humility
- The politics of humility
- Humility in religious thought
- The epistemology of humility
- The psychology of humility
- Humility: applications to the social world.

Essential reading for students and researchers in ethics, epistemology, political philosophy and philosophy of mind and psychology, this *Handbook* will also be extremely useful for those in related disciplines such as psychology, religious studies and law.

Mark Alfano is Associate Professor of Philosophy at Delft University of Technology, The Netherlands, and Associate Professor of Philosophy at Macquarie University, Australia.

Michael P. Lynch is Board of Trustees Distinguished Professor of Philosophy at the University of Connecticut, USA.

Alessandra Tanesini is Professor of Philosophy at Cardiff University, UK.

Routledge Handbooks in Philosophy

Routledge Handbooks in Philosophy are state-of-the-art surveys of emerging, newly refreshed and important fields in philosophy, providing accessible yet thorough assessments of key problems, themes, thinkers and recent developments in research.

All chapters for each volume are specially commissioned, and written by leading scholars in the field. Carefully edited and organized, *Routledge Handbooks in Philosophy* provide indispensable reference tools for students and researchers seeking a comprehensive overview of new and exciting topics in philosophy. They are also valuable teaching resources as accompaniments to textbooks, anthologies and research-orientated publications.

Also available:

The Routledge Handbook of Philosophy of Relativism
Edited by Martin Kusch

The Routledge Handbook of Metaphysical Grounding
Edited by Michael J. Raven

The Routledge Handbook of Philosophy of Colour
Edited by Derek H. Brown and Fiona Macpherson

The Routledge Handbook of Collective Responsibility
Edited by Saba Bazargan-Forward and Deborah Tollefsen

The Routledge Handbook of Phenomenology of Emotion
Edited by Thomas Szanto and Hilge Landweer

The Routledge Handbook of Hellenistic Philosophy
Edited by Kelly Arenson

The Routledge Handbook of Trust and Philosophy
Edited by Judith Simon

The Routledge Handbook of Philosophy of Humility
Edited by Mark Alfano, Michael P. Lynch, and Alessandra Tanesini

The Routledge Handbook of Metametaphysics
Edited by Ricki Bliss and JTM Miller

For more information about this series, please visit: https://www.routledge.com/Routledge-Handbooks-in-Philosophy/book-series/RHP

THE ROUTLEDGE HANDBOOK OF PHILOSOPHY OF HUMILITY

Edited by Mark Alfano, Michael P. Lynch and Alessandra Tanesini

Routledge
Taylor & Francis Group
LONDON AND NEW YORK

First published 2021
by Routledge
2 Park Square, Milton Park, Abingdon, Oxon OX14 4RN

and by Routledge
52 Vanderbilt Avenue, New York, NY 10017

Routledge is an imprint of the Taylor & Francis Group, an informa business

British Library Cataloguing-in-Publication Data
A catalogue record for this book is available from the British Library

Library of Congress Cataloging-in-Publication Data
A catalog record has been requested for this book

ISBN: 978-0-815-36411-5 (hbk)
ISBN: 978-0-367-50264-5 (pbk)
ISBN: 978-1-351-10753-2 (ebk)

Typeset in Bembo
by Deanta Global Publishing Services, Chennai, India

CONTENTS

CONTRIBUTORS

Andrew Aberdein is Professor of Philosophy in the School of Arts and Communication, Florida Institute of Technology, USA.

Mark Alfano is Associate Professor of Philosophy at Delft University of Technology, The Netherlands, and Associate Professor of Philosophy at Macquarie University, Australia.

Amalia Amaya is a British Academy Global Professor in the Law School at the University of Edinburgh, UK.

Jason Baehr is Professor of Philosophy at Loyola Marymount University, Los Angeles, California, USA.

Heather Battaly is Professor of Philosophy at the University of Connecticut, USA.

Aaron Ben-Ze'ev is Professor of Philosophy at, and Former President of, the University of Haifa (2004–2012), Israel.

Paul Bloomfield is Professor of Philosophy at the University of Connecticut, USA.

Nicolas Bommarito is Assistant Professor of Philosophy at the University of Buffalo, New York, USA.

Michael S. Brady is Head of School and Professor of Philosophy at the University of Glasgow, UK.

J. Adam Carter is Lecturer in Philosophy at the University of Glasgow, UK.

Quassim Cassam is Professor of Philosophy at the University of Warwick, UK.

Sophie Grace Chappell is Professor of Philosophy at the Open University, UK.

Ian M. Church is Assistant Professor of Philosophy at Hillsdale College, Michigan, USA.

E. M. Dadlez is Professor of Philosophy at the University of Central Oklahoma, USA.

Robin S. Dillon is the William Wilson Selfridge Professor of Philosophy and Director of Lehigh University Center for Ethics, Pennsylvania, USA.

Katherine Dormandy is Assistant Professor of Philosophy at University of Innsbruck, Austria.

Philip Fernbach is Associate Professor and Co-Director of the Center for Research on Consumer Financial Decision Making in the Leeds School of Business at the University of Colorado, Boulder, Colorado, USA.

Emma C. Gordon is Lecturer in Philosophy at the University of Glasgow, UK.

John Greco is the McDevitt Chair of Religious Philosophy at Georgetown University, Washington, DC, USA.

Allan Hazlett is Associate Professor of Philosophy at Washington University, Saint Louis, Missouri, USA.

Daniel Howard-Snyder is Professor of Philosophy at Western Washington University, USA.

Rick H. Hoyle is Professor of Psychology and Neuroscience at Duke University, North Carolina, USA.

Emily Ann Israelson is a PhD student in Political Science at Ohio State University, USA.

Casey Rebecca Johnson is Assistant Professor of Philosophy at the University of Idaho, USA.

Ian James Kidd is Assistant Professor of Philosophy at the University of Nottingham, UK.

Neil Levy is an ARC Future Fellow, the Florey Institute of Neuroscience and Mental Health, at The University of Melbourne and a Senior Research Fellow, Oxford Uehiro Centre for Practical Ethics at the University of Oxford, UK.

Nicholas Light is a PhD Student in the Center for Research on Consumer Financial Decision Making in the Leeds School of Business at the University of Colorado, Boulder, Colorado, USA.

Michael P. Lynch is Board of Trustees Distinguished Professor of Philosophy at the University of Connecticut, USA.

Elizabeth Krumrei Mancuso is Associate Professor of Psychology at Pepperdine University, California, USA.

Daniel McKaughan is Associate Professor of Philosophy at Boston College, Massachusetts, USA.

Alexus McLeod is Associate Professor of Philosophy and Asian/Asian-American Studies at the University of Connecticut, USA.

Thaddeus Metz is Humanities Research Professor at the University of Johannesburg, South Africa.

Michael A. Neblo is Professor of Political Science and Philosophy and Public Policy at Ohio State University, USA.

Nickolas Pappas is Professor of Philosophy at CUNY Graduate Center, New York, USA.

Andrew Charles Pinsent is Research Director of the Ian Ramsey Centre for Science and Religion at the Faculty of Theology and Religion, University of Oxford, UK.

Duncan Pritchard is Distinguished Professor of Philosophy at the University of California, Irvine and Professor of Philosophy at the University of Edinburgh, UK.

Robert Roberts is Distinguished Professor of Ethics, Emeritus, at Baylor University, Texas, USA.

Brian Robinson is Assistant Professor of Philosophy at Texas A&M University, Kingsville, Texas, USA.

Peter L. Samuelson is Director of Research and Evaluation at the Thrive Foundation for Youth, California, USA.

Nancy E. Snow is Professor of Philosophy and Director of the Institute for the Study of Human Flourishing at the University of Oklahoma, USA.

Carl Stauffer is Associate Professor of Justice Studies, Center for Justice & Peacebuilding, Eastern Mennonite University, Virginia, USA.

Emily Sullivan is Assistant Professor of Philosophy and Ethics at Eindhoven University of Technology, The Netherlands.

Alessandra Tanesini is Professor of Philosophy at Cardiff University, UK.

James Van Cleve is Professor of Philosophy at the University of Southern California, Dornsife, California, USA.

Sophia Vasalou is Birmingham Fellow in Philosophical Theology at the University of Birmingham, UK.

Lani Watson is a Leverhulme Early Career Fellow at the University of Edinburgh, UK.

Dennis Whitcomb is Professor of Philosophy at Western Washington University, USA.

Sarah H. Woolwine is Lecturer in Philosophy at the University of Central Oklahoma, USA.

Jennifer Cole Wright is Associate Professor of Psychology at the College of Charleston, South Carolina, USA.

ACKNOWLEDGEMENTS

The editors would like to thank all the contributors to this volume for their insightful chapters. They are especially grateful to the other founding members of the Vice Squad, Heather Battaly, Quassim Cassam, Ian James Kidd for their friendship, advice, and for embodying the true spirit of intellectual collaboration.

Finally, we would like to thank Tony Bruce and Adam Johnson at Routledge for their help and encouragement in bringing this project to its conclusion.

Research leading to this volume was partially funded by Grant No. 58942 from the John Templeton Foundation and the University of Connecticut, and by Grant DP190101507 from the Australian Research Council. Its contents are solely the responsibility of the editors and authors and do not necessarily represent the official views of the ARC, UConn or the John Templeton Foundation.

INTRODUCTION

Mark Alfano, Michael P. Lynch and Alessandra Tanesini

Philosophical research on the virtue of humility has blossomed in the last decade or so after years of relative neglect. The history of the philosophical study of humility is also characterised by intermittent interest initiated, at least in the West, by Christian traditions. Humility did not figure prominently in Greek virtue theory (but see Chappell for an account that shows that the true picture is more complex than this). Instead, it came into its own in Thomistic thought and in other religious traditions, before waning, at least in the West, under the pressure of critics such as Nietzsche. More recently, since Julia Driver's (1989, 1999) pioneering work on modesty, interest in humility has intensified and has led to interdisciplinary research, especially with psychology, but also with law, politics and peace study. This volume aims to provide a panoramic overview of the current research on humility, capturing the breadth of this work, and highlighting both its interdisciplinary nature and its social impact.

In this introduction we outline the structure of the volume, provide an overview of its contents and draw attention to some of the common themes and questions linking the varied contributions within each section. The volume consists of seven parts. Part 1 includes essays that describe theories of humility and raise questions about its classification as a virtue. Part 2 consists of chapters highlighting the moral dimension of humility, its relation to flourishing and to the moral emotions. Part 3 locates humility within a political context and addresses the contribution humility can make to public life. The chapters in Part 4 explore the role played by humility in various philosophical and religious traditions. Part 5 concerns the place of humility in people's intellectual lives. Part 6 comprises chapters that supply an overview of the psychology of humility, with a focus on those issues and areas that might be of special interest to philosophers working on the topic. Finally, Part 7 includes chapters that address questions about how humility relates to social issues such as terrorism, education and the use of social media.

Part 1: Theories of humility provides a systematic overview of humility, the various theoretical approaches that have been taken to it and the central problems that any such theory must confront. Nancy Snow's magisterial opening chapter provides a state-of-the-art guide to many of the debates in subsequent chapters. A particular focus is on the relationship between the concepts of humility and modesty, and the literatures that have examined them respectively. Readers seeking a map of the intellectual territory with regard to humility are advised to start here.

The next two chapters focus on two central issues facing any theory of humility. The first such issue, examined by Brian Robinson, is the so-called "paradox of humility": declaring (even correctly) you are humble seems to mean that you are not. Robinson argues that this apparently single problem actually turns out to be multiple problems, and theories of humility have divided over how to handle them. One kind of theory, Robinson argues, sees humble people as taking a low opinion of themselves; the other kind of theory, which Robinson champions as being able to resolve the various paradoxes of humility, sees humble people as simply not over-focussing on the self or being less ego-centric.

In the final chapter of this part, Paul Bloomfield confronts another central issue facing any theory of humility: whether or not it is a virtue. As illustrated by chapters throughout this book, many philosophers writing on the topic have assumed that it is. But drawing on certain ancient Greek philosophical conceptions of virtue, Bloomfield argues forcefully that it is not, and suggests instead that humility is better understood as a "corrective" for arrogance. In this way, Bloomfield reasons, humility is more similar to other correctives like continence.

The question of whether humility is a virtue raises its connection to morality. **Part 2: The ethics of humility** confronts the central moral questions regarding humility, collecting chapters that examine the historical roots of these questions, their contemporary relevance and the relationship that humility bears to other concepts of ethical concern.

The first two chapters focus on understanding the connections between humility and two of the most central ethical concepts: flourishing and respect. In his contribution, Robert Roberts argues that humility can come in both virtuous and vicious forms. Arguing that virtuous humility is opposed to the vices of pride—and associated diagnoses like narcissistic personality disorder—Roberts claims that virtuous humility can contribute to human flourishing by way of allowing the humble person to better exemplify the virtues of love and respect for others.

In contrast, Robin Dillon concentrates on the relationship between humility and self-respect. Drawing on Kantian and feminist philosophy, she argues that theories of humility—like Roberts'—can often overlook the serious question of whether humility can be a virtue for the oppressed or marginalised in society. In Dillon's view, the upshot of paying careful attention to these issues is that the proper opposition to arrogance is not humility but self-respect, and that humility, far from being a central virtue, can sometimes act as a vice, as when someone is inappropriately humble in the face of oppression. Similarly, in their own contribution, Whitcomb, Battaly and Howard-Snyder raise the puzzle of what they call "the puzzle of disparity"—the question of whether one should be humble in the face of those who are espousing flatly wrong or unjust views. Like Dillon, Whitcomb et al. argue that the importance of humility is limited. Nonetheless, they conclude that humility continues to have some value even in cases where one is facing someone who is clearly in the wrong.

The issues of love and self-respect continue to play a central role in the next two chapters. Nietzsche remains the most important critic of the moral value of humility in Western culture. In his chapter, Nickolas Pappas unravels Nietzsche's concern that humility essentially involves an inauthenticity in self-presentation (like the contemporary notion of the "humble-brag"); moreover, humility, Pappas argues, is fundamentally opposed to Nietzsche's own central theoretical principle of the will to power. In contrast, Aaron Ben-Ze'ev drills down into the relationship between romantic love and humility. Both are positive attitudes to other people, and both reduce the amount of what Ben-Ze'ev calls comparative concern; both encourage us to see each other non-comparatively—that is, to consider others in themselves or in virtue of their own properties.

The final two chapters in this part deal with the relation between humility and two other major ethical concepts: pride and shame. Michael Brady argues that many recent accounts of humility fail to properly understand the difference between these two attitudes. He suggests instead that the real difference lies in how pride and humility are expressed. Eva Dadlez and

Sarah Woolwine, on the other hand, and in contrast to Roberts, don't see narcissism or vanity as failures of humility; rather they are manifestations of unjustified pride. Like Dillon and Whitcomb et al., Dadlez and Woolwine explore the possible downsides of humility, drawing on David Hume's classic account of the subject. They develop aspects of Hume's account and apply them to contemporary scholarship concerning epistemic injustice and disability.

As we've already seen, many of the ethical issues raised by humility have political dimensions. **Part 3: The politics of humility**, addresses these dimensions directly.

Echoing themes suggested in Part 2, the first two chapters of this part examine the question of whether, and to what extent, we should be humble about our own beliefs and convictions. Michael Neblo and Ann Israelson start from the premise that citizens in democracy neither want to overestimate the warrant for their beliefs nor underestimate it. Neblo and Israelson argue that a bi-valent conception of humility based upon the Greek idea of the virtuous mean can be put to theoretical work in helping us to understand some of the basic principles of democracy. In his contribution, Michael Lynch explores why it is so difficult to be humble about our core convictions—because convictions, he suggests, are identity-reflecting values. Nonetheless, he claims it is possible to have intellectual humility and conviction at the same time, but that this possibility is only realisable to the extent that our political institutions encourage us to be reflective about our own biases and commitments.

In her chapter, Casey Johnson argues that intellectual humility can encourage empathy and curiosity—traits, she suggests, that tend to promote the toleration of diverse ideas, a core democratic value. Where Johnson explores the relation between toleration and humility, Carl Stauffer looks at the relation between humility and restorative justice, with particular attention paid to the social dimensions of humility, both at the individual and group level.

Heather Battaly's essay ends this part of the book by addressing the question of whether humility could be a "liberatory" virtue, or a virtue that is particularly helpful to people who are oppressed or marginalised. As such, this essay serves to bring together many of the themes explored in Parts 2 and 3. Employing her own landmark work on the "limitation-owning" account of humility, and interacting with the work of other authors in this volume, Battaly argues that there is kind of liberatory humility that involves being appropriately attentive to one's own liberatory limitations, and which is aimed at liberatory ends.

Part 4: Humility in religious thought contains chapters that, when taken together, intend to give the reader a panoramic overview of humility in diverse philosophical and religious traditions. These chapters explore humility as a kind of self-evaluation that puts the individual in relation to something bigger than her, be it a god or the community of human beings. Humility would also involve an other-regarding aspect in so far as it promotes good harmonious relations with other people and society as a whole.

In her contribution, Sophie Grace Chappell argues that there are sustained considerations and motivations in Greek ethical thought that are related to humility, even though common lists of widely recognised virtues do not include a single virtue that would clearly correspond to humility. For Chappell, humility, or something similar to it, is an archaic Greek value that is associated with godfearingness. It involves a disposition of restraint in the face of gods prepared to punish human hubris. In the Classical period, as fear of the gods diminishes, new values of cunning and greed emerge and are championed by the Sophists. In response to these, a new version of humility that is not driven by a fear of godly punishment is developed in the philosophy of Socrates, Aristotle and Plato. What emerges is a plurality of virtues, including justice, wisdom and compassion that include elements related to humility.

The chapter by Andrew Pinsent offers a defence of the Thomistic conception of humility in contemporary secular settings. He provides a detailed analysis of Aquinas' views of humility as a virtue opposed to the vice of pride which, in all of its incarnations, inhibits flourishing. Pinsent also presents Thomistic humility as a virtue that promotes good relationships and greatness in oneself.

While Pinsent provides a defence of Aquinas' views of humility, Dan Howard-Snyder and Daniel McKaughan focus in their contribution on Aquinas' notion of faith. They argue that it is not the conception of a virtue and, further, that it is be incompatible with humility, given a plausible notion of the latter which they endorse. As an alternative they propose an older Markan conception of faith, whose compatibility with humility they also defend.

In her chapter on humility in the Islamic tradition, Sophie Vasalou details the self-regarding and other-regarding nature of humility as it is conceived by a number of key Islamic philosophers. One noteworthy aspect of her account is the focus on the backward-looking nature of humility as self-evaluation and its forward-looking character as an attitude of moral commitment.

The importance of the connection of the self to humility as this is understood in the Buddhist tradition is the topic of Nic Bommarito's chapter. He argues that, in this tradition, humility could be understood as consisting in the denial of the existence of the self or at least in the adoption of an attitude of not being invested in it. So conceived, humility would involve not making oneself the focus of one's own attention.

A similar theme of humility as the adoption of an attitude to the self that is not invested in its self-importance can be found in Alexus McLeod's chapter on humility in Confucianism and early Chinese philosophy. It is this character that gives humility its foundational nature in Confucian thought. Humility would not be a virtue alongside others but instead it would be a propaedeutic for the acquisition of other virtues and an enabler of harmonious social relations.

Thaddeus Metz finds a role for humility in his chapter on the normative ethics of the Southern African philosophy of Ubuntu. He argues that humility is involved with appraisals of what we can claim from others, of our knowledge of morality and in evaluations of our own virtues.

Part 5: The epistemology of humility includes several chapters dedicated to the study of the role of humility in inquiry. Some of these chapters draw attention to how humility can contribute to good inquiry, but also to how it can be faked. Others refer to humility as the acceptance of the limitations to human knowledge in general and as drawing attention to the crucial role played by contingency in our relation to the world.

The chapter by John Greco is the first of four chapters addressing the contribution of humility to an appreciation of the limitations of one's own intellectual abilities and to the establishment of proper relations with other epistemic agents. Greco in particular contrasts humility as an appreciation of our epistemic dependence on others with intellectual pride that would be characterised by ideals of self-sufficiency.

In her contribution, Alessandra Tanesini tests the adequacy of various theories of humility by considering whether they can account for its relation to self-knowledge. She concludes that humility involves self-appraisals that are not self-centred. In this picture, hope emerges as a virtue that accompanies humility and that inoculates it against pessimism and despair.

Katherine Dormandy argues in her chapter that humility enables and supports trust in one's own abilities, but also promotes in testimonial contexts proper trust in the abilities of other epistemic agents. Finally, the chapter by Ian Church that immediately follows segues from these considerations to argue that at least some cases of testimonial injustice can be understood as failures of intellectual humility on the part of the hearer.

The chapter by Allan Hazlett explores how intellectual humility can be faked by means of insincere expressions of ignorance. These are fake forms of fallibilism and scepticism that are adopted for instance by conspiracy theorists and cause much damage to collective inquiry.

The role of humility when debating is the focus of Andrew Aberdein's chapter, which provides a detailed analysis of humility as a virtue of good argumentation. He also describes its relation to the deliberative virtues and its role in reducing the prevalence of informal fallacies.

J. Adam Carter and Emma Gordon in their contribution analyse the impact on the practice of asserting of intellectual humility as a disposition to own one's intellectual limitations. In particular, they argue that intellectual humility would reduce the prevalence of assertoric misfires and promote forbearance in assertion to avoid dominating the conversation.

The final two contributions to this part consider the role played by humility in scientific knowledge. In his contribution, Ian James Kidd explores the connections between humility and the importance of notions such as contingency and pluralism in scientific inquiry. Overall, this chapter explains the numerous ways in which humility is, or ought to be, instantiated in science.

Finally, Jan Van Cleve offers an account of Ramseyan humility as the view that any conceivable world must include non-relational properties, even though we can never know what these are. This position is compared to Humean humility and contrasted with Russellian monism.

Part 6: The psychology of humility comprises chapters on themes such as personality variables, measurement and calibration that might be especially helpful to philosophers with an interest in the psychological literature on humility.

Peter Samuelson and Ian Church provide an overview of conceptualisations of humility in positive and personality psychology. In particular, this chapter addresses the relation of humility to the so-called Big Five. It proposes that psychological accounts of the nature of humility, as of other virtues, must think of them as involving the interaction of personality and situational variables.

In their chapter on the measures of humility, Rick Hoyle and Elizabeth Krumrei Mancuso present the whole array of current approaches to psychological measures of humility, whilst highlighting the overreliance on self-reports in this literature. Their chapter also includes proposals for new ways in which humility could be measured.

Several of the chapters included in this volume (e.g., Bommarito, McLeod, Tanesini among others) highlight the role of humility as a corrective for self-centredness and self-importance. This theme is also prominent in Jen Cole-Wright's chapter, which shows how humility is a corrective for the ethical and epistemic biases caused by prevalent egocentric biases.

On a similar note, Phil Fernbach and Nick Light argue in their contribution that overconfidence and knowledge miscalibration are major obstacles to intellectual humility. Finally, they present potential interventions to increase intellectual humility.

Part 7: Humility: Applications to the social world comprises papers that reflect on social issues such as terrorism, the judicial system and education to offer an analysis of the potential offered by the cultivation of humility to address these issues.

The chapter by Quassim Cassam returns to the theme of false humility already explored by Hazlett to highlight its prevalence in studies of Middle Eastern terrorism. The chapter concludes with a discussion of what true humility would amount to.

The focus of Lani Watson's contribution are those features of education that function as obstacles to humility. She notes the pervasive negative effects of answer-oriented approaches that dominate in education and details a question-oriented alternative which, in her view, would promote more humble attitudes.

The chapter by Amalia Amaya focusses on the judiciary. She offers a detailed account of why judges serve their function better when they display attitudes that are consonant with humility.

The final three chapters in the collection consider external devices and networks in their relation to humility as an individual character trait. The contribution by Duncan Pritchard analyses the role of extended cognitive processes, including external devices, in enabling humility in general and intellectual humility more specifically. In his conclusion, Pritchard raises a word of caution about the possibility of the virtue of extended intellectual humility.

The contributions by Levy, Sullivan and Alfano raise questions about the epistemic value of intellectual humility. Thus, in his chapter Levy argues that, in on-line environments, behaviours and attitudes that are characteristic of arrogance and servility are often knowledge-conducive. Hence, if our concern is epistemic we should not promote humility as a corrective for these traits.

Sullivan and Alfano raise related concerns in the context of collective deliberation. In the context of inter-group disagreements, they argue, humility might promote tribalism. Thus, whilst humility might reduce my-side biases, it can actually increase our-side partisanship. If this is the case, humility could deepen rather than resolve inter-group conflicts.

References

Driver, J. (1989). The Virtues of Ignorance. *The Journal of Philosophy*, 86(7), 373–384. doi:10.2307/2027146.
Driver, J. (1999). Modesty and Ignorance. *Ethics*, 109(4), 827–834. doi:10.1086/233947.

PART 1

Theories of humility

1
THEORIES OF HUMILITY
An overview

Nancy E. Snow

In 1995, I published an article on humility, and observed that philosophers had neglected that virtue.[1] More than two decades later, the situation has changed dramatically.[2] A trove of books and articles can be found on religious conceptions of humility, humility in non-Western traditions, humility in the context of environmental ethics, and from psychologists and political scientists working on humility.[3] Other contributors to this volume will take up aspects of those rich resources. In this chapter, I focus on contemporary philosophical conceptions of humility, with a brief initial nod to how it was viewed in the history of Western philosophy. In addition, a large contemporary literature has emerged on modesty. In some of this work, the construct that philosophers call "modesty" is essentially the same as that which others call "humility." I will discuss a subset of this work.

1.1 A brief nod to Western history

Humility does not appear in Aristotle's list of the virtues, and seems not to have been highly regarded by the Greeks.[4] In the history of Western thought, humility rises to the fore with the advent of the Judeo-Christian tradition and has important roles in the philosophies of religious thinkers such as St. Augustine, St. Thomas Aquinas, St. Bernard of Clairvaux, and the Jewish philosopher and theologian Moses Maimonides.[5] Yet it is also recognized that these conceptions of humility contain negative elements. For example, Nadelhoffer et al. quote a Christian text, *The Cloud of Unknowing*, as stating:

> If this device [humbling oneself before God] is properly understood in its subtlety, it is nothing else but a true knowledge and experience of yourself as you are, a wretch, filth, far worse than nothing. This knowledge and experience is humility.[6]

A similar theme occurs in the writings of St. Bernard of Clairvaux:

> if you examine yourself inwardly by the light of truth and without dissimulation, and judge yourself without flattery; no doubt you will be humbled in your own eyes, becoming contemptible in your own sight as a result of this true knowledge of yourself.[7]

Maimonides, too, portrays humility in a negative light:

> When a man reflects on these things ... He will be filled with fear and trembling, as he becomes conscious of his own lowly condition, poverty, and insignificance ... He will then realize he is a vessel full of shame, dishonor, and reproach, empty and deficient.[8]

Given the negativity associated with religious conceptions of humility, it is not surprising that subsequent philosophers either did not regard it as a virtue or did not regard it as a virtue worth having.[9] Newman quotes Spinoza as stating that "Humility is not a virtue, or does not arise from Reason," and Hume as claiming that

> no one, who has any practice of the world, and can penetrate into the inward sentiments of men, will assert, that the humility, which good-breeding and decency require of us, goes beyond the outside, or that a thorough sincerity in this particular is esteem'd a real part of our duty.[10]

Among several harsh passages critical of Christianity from Nietzsche that Newman quotes, this glaringly conveys the former's disdain for humility:

> One despises the cowardly, the anxious, the petty, those who think only in terms of narrow utility; also the distrustful with their unfree glances, those who humble themselves, the doglike people.[11]

Sidgwick, too, had a dim view of humility. As Richards quotes him, Sidgwick believed that "humility prescribes low opinion of our merits" and that "it would seem just as irrational to underrate ourselves as to overrate."[12] Humility, Sidgwick thought, is not properly regulative of the opinions we form of ourselves, for in those opinions, as in others, we should aim at truth.

Other philosophers were more positive. Newman writes: "Kant argues that true humility, *humilitas moralis*, is accompanied by exaltation and self-esteem."[13] As one might expect, Kierkegaard, a Christian philosopher, believed humility to be "necessary for faith and Christian practice."[14] Finally, Sinha explains that the ideal utilitarian Hastings Rashdall offered a "love-thy-neighbor" account of humility, according to which a humble person avoids "the habitual dwelling with satisfaction" upon her merits.[15] According to Sinha, Rashdall thought we should recognize the capacities for goodness in others, and feel "sorrow and pity" instead of "contempt" or "smug self-complacency" when their capacities are not realized.[16]

The foregoing remarks provide only the briefest glimpse into the much larger topic of how humility has been viewed in Western philosophy and religions. I have not gone back to the original historical sources to "mine" this material but, instead, have accessed it from various contemporary discussions of humility. This is deliberate: I have thereby sought to illustrate how influential historical conceptions have been for many contemporary accounts. The themes that occupied our forebears still affect contemporary philosophical thinking.

1.2 Contemporary accounts of humility: an overview and discussion[17]

Three initial caveats are in order. First, my review is of secular accounts of humility, though some of these are influenced by religious theories. Second, Julia Driver's work on modesty has generated a large and focused literature, which I discuss separately in Section 1.3. Third, though

I present the views in chronological order, I have tried to highlight ongoing themes and interlocking debates where possible.

Taylor (1985) – Humility is the acceptance of one's lowly position. Taylor's account has it that: "The man who accepts his lowly position as what is due to him is the humble man, or the man who has humility."[18] Taylor furnishes an attractive starting point for our discussion, for her view can be seen as a bridge between historical and contemporary accounts of humility. This is because she draws on Aquinas to defend her view, which is then criticized by the contemporary philosopher Norvin Richards. Among other criticisms, Richards notes that restricting humility only to those who accept lowliness as their due precludes humility on the part of those who have attained a high position.[19] In work by other philosophers, Taylor's overly restrictive account has largely been left aside. Yet, she avoids a peril often associated with humility, that of self-abasement, claiming that: "The humble who occupy and accept a lowly position on some hierarchical scale may be merely poor and meek. But to be virtuously humble is not to accept meekly just any sort of inferior position."[20] Quoting Aquinas, she notes that humility restrains the mind from tending immoderately to high things. It does not imply, however, that one must be satisfied with anything lowly, such as losing one's dignity and self-respect. She contends,

> The humble will still "have their pride", still think that a certain kind of treatment is due to them, and that a certain kind of behavior on their part is due to others. They will get right what kind of treatment to give and to expect.[21]

Whether it is true that the humble will always "get right" what kind of treatment to give and to expect is an interesting question here left aside.

Richards (1988, 1992a, 1992b) – *Humility is the inclination to keep one's merits in perspective, even if stimulated to exaggerate them.* Richards rejects Taylor's account of humility, claiming instead that humility "involves having an accurate sense of oneself, sufficiently firm to resist pressures toward incorrect revisions."[22] The revisions he has in mind are to incorrectly think too highly of oneself.

Though this precludes the problem of attributing to the humble an overly low view of themselves, it still raises concerns about an overly high view, as Richards acknowledges.[23] One might have accomplishments, and so on, and resist stimulations to exaggerate, and yet still have a rather rosy view of themselves and enjoy basking in attention. In response, Richards contends that those who acknowledge their accomplishments yet reject attention can be humble.[24] What is required for humility is keeping one's accomplishments in perspective, and eschewing a variety of inflated self-regarding attitudes, such being "full of oneself," "putting on airs," etc. It seems to be about having a realistic view of, and attitude toward, one's strengths.

Snow (1995) – *Humility is the disposition to allow the awareness of and concern about one's limitations to realistically influence one's attitudes and behavior.* Unlike Richards, who focuses on the appropriate attitudes toward one's strengths, Snow is concerned with humility as having proper reactions to one's weaknesses. She develops two conceptions of humility that she calls "narrow" and "existential."[25] To have humility in the narrow sense is to be appropriately pained by, or feel sorrow or dejection because of, the awareness of one's own personal deficiencies.[26] To feel the appropriate negative emotion is to feel it commensurately with the seriousness of the failing: it is not to feel too much pain from the awareness of minor flaws, nor too little from the cognizance of major ones. To have proper existential humility "requires that your affective reaction to the cognizance of human limitations occasioned by encountering some valuable reality extending beyond the self be appropriately commensurate with the seriousness of that knowledge."[27] Narrow humility requires a focus on the self; existential humility can result from situating oneself within a broader perspective. She unifies narrow and existential humility as follows:

> To be a humble person is to recognize your limitations, to take them seriously, and thereby to foster a realism in attitudes and behavior regarding self and others. Humility can be defined as the disposition to allow the awareness of and concern about your limitations to have a realistic influence on your attitudes and behavior. At the heart of this realism is a perspective gained through accurate appraisal of your limitations and their implications for your circumstances, attitudes, and behavior.[28]

Both Richards and Snow believe that having humility can foster other good qualities. Richards thinks it can lead to an inclination to forgive, good judgment of others, and reasonable expectations of self.[29] Snow believes that, by learning through failure and being humbled yet realistic, we can develop self-confidence, self-esteem, proper pride, and autonomy.[30]

Roberts and colleagues (2003, 2007, 2017, 2018) – Humility is intelligent lack of concern for self-importance. In a series of essays, Robert C. Roberts and colleagues develop a conception of moral humility by contrasting it with a suite of vices.[31] These vices include an impressive list: arrogance, vanity, conceit, egotism, grandiosity, pretentiousness, snobbishness, impertinence (presumption), haughtiness, self-righteousness, domination, selfish ambition, and self-complacency.[32] A full and complete account of humility can be given by investigating the opposite of these vices, though in their early work, Roberts and Wood examine humility in richly textured accounts as the lack of vanity and arrogance.[33] Though the character of humility differs in its opposition to different vices on this list, it is not always only the absence of a vice. Roberts and Wood write:

> We think that in the cases in which humility is clearly a virtue, and not merely the absence of a vice, a certain kind of story can be told about the basis of the unconcern and attentiveness. We propose that in the best cases the concern for status is swamped or displaced or put on hold by some overriding virtuous concern.[34]

They give the example of Jesus Christ as the paradigm of humility. As the Son of God, he had a very high status, but he ignored this status and humbled himself in human form.[35] In later work, Roberts and his colleagues hew to essentially the same definition of humility and the manner of arriving at it.[36] Like Richards and Snow, Roberts and Cleveland think that humility can have benefits for the lives of its possessors and their families, colleagues, and acquaintances.[37] It can improve friendships, child-rearing, workplace cultures, self-understanding, and intellectual functioning.

Wielenberg (2005; 2019) – A secular account of humility. Wielenberg develops a secular account of humility that has important similarities to religious conceptions but does not require religious beliefs.[38] In his earlier work, he writes: "It is the dependence of human beings and their actions on factors beyond their control – dependence that is present whether God exists or not – that makes humility in some form an appropriate attitude to have."[39] In other words, we are not uniquely responsible for our accomplishments, good traits, advantages, and so on. In a theistic universe, we are dependent on God for our successes. In a naturalistic universe, we are dependent on luck or chance. Either way, we cannot claim full credit for ourselves, and this realization should inspire humility.

Wielenberg offers more detail in later work, claiming that:

> S has secular humility to the degree that: (i) S recognizes that she shares with all humans the important limitations of helplessness, fallibility, and moral frailty; (ii) S recognizes her relative insignificance in the grand scheme of things; and (iii) in virtue of (i) and (ii), S is (a) resistant to misplaced pride in her excellences and achievements,

> envy, and indignation at being slighted by others and (b) disposed toward forgiveness, gratitude, open-mindedness, low self-focus, and feelings of awe.[40]

Conditions (i) and (ii) are reminiscent of Snow's work, and (iii, a) of Roberts and his colleagues.

Grenberg (2005) – Kantian humility is a meta-attitude concerned with judgments valuing the self in light of moral principles. In a book developing the Kantian virtue of humility, Grenberg maintains that humility is a "meta-attitude" – a perspective or point of view – that informs every exercise of agency.[41] This results from the internalization of moral judgments and a moral disposition about the self, such that concerns of self-love are made conditional upon the satisfaction of moral demands. To achieve this disposition, one must recognize that one is corrupt and dependent, yet possessed of autonomy and self-respect before the moral law. One also recognizes that, in possessing these attributes, one is no different from other rational persons. Seeing oneself in a perspective framed by the moral law allows one a vantage point on one's strengths and weaknesses, which obviates the need to compare oneself with others in a competitive way that could foster arrogance, envy, or resentment on the one hand, or feelings of low self-worth on the other. The perspective of the moral law, which we, as rationally autonomous agents, give to ourselves, stands in or substitutes for the religious conceptions of humility according to which we must situate ourselves in a divinely ordained universe.

In common with Wielenberg, Schueler, and Ben Ze'ev (the latter two write about modesty, not humility),[42] Grenberg recognizes that humans are fallible and dependent, and acknowledges that this realization should put our accomplishments in perspective. Yet, as we'll see, she is unlike Schueler in that she attributes our achievements to our agency to at least some degree.[43]

Garcia (2006) – Humility is being unimpressed with ourselves. After a thorough review and critique of several contemporary conceptions of humility, Garcia argues that someone is:

> humble about (with respect to) her being *F* (e.g., one or more of her talents, skills, and virtues, her achievements, her possessions, her ancestors, and so on with other possible grounds of pride) if, only if, and to the extent that, she has a stable, deep-seated, and restrained disposition to play down in her own thinking, self-concept, and feelings – and therein to decenter (to place in the) background, (not to stress, focus on, make much of, relish, or delight in) – the significance of her being *F* and, because of that, similarly not to stress in her self-concept her liberties, options, entitlements, and privileges.[44]

He goes on to argue that humility is a virtue provided that it stems from appropriate mental states, i.e., someone's commitment to personal moral self-improvement or her concern that other persons and factors get due recognition for the part they play in her having *F*, also from her reasonable appreciation of the magnitude and significance of her limitations, flaws, dependencies, and so on, as well as her duties and responsibilities. This mental state, he thinks, will be reflected in her conduct.[45]

Finally, someone is humble *tout court*, "just when she is humble about enough of her (real or self-imputed) good features and is not very proud of any of them. We can then say that she is unimpressed with herself."[46]

Sinha (2012) – Humility is overriding ego-driven impulses. Inspired by the work of Hastings Rashdall, Sinha argues that "people plausibly display humility when, for the right reasons, they override their ego-driven impulses to feel good about themselves wherever they can reasonably expect those impulses to conflict with various duties – especially the duty of beneficence and the duty to pursue truth or self-knowledge."[47] Thus, humility has two dimensions – one epistemic and one agentic, giving rise to what he calls "private" and "public" humility. These two dimensions can pull apart. Privately, one might think overly well of oneself, but decline credit out of genuine concern for others' feelings. Alternatively, one could have a conservative view of one's merits, but claim credit where it is due, no matter how hurtful to others.[48] Sinha offers a key criticism of Driver: "it's likely that our use of the term 'humility' tracks agents' *attitudes towards* their merits rather than their *beliefs about* their merits."[49] Beliefs are not irrelevant, but one can have true beliefs about one's merits, which could be considerable, yet be humble in one's attitudes about them.

1.3 Modesty: a selective glimpse

Driver (1989, 1999, 2001) – Modesty is the dogmatic disposition to underestimate self-worth based on ignorance of one's self-worth. Driver is one of a group of philosophers who uses the term "modesty" interchangeably with "humility." Her work has stimulated a large body of responses, only some of which can be included here.[50]

Modesty is one of a class of virtues, which, she claims, relies on ignorance.[51] She calls her view the "underestimation" account. She argues that it is superior both to understatement and behavioral accounts, where the former entails understating one's self-worth while being fully aware of it, and the latter reduces to behavioral manifestations of modesty, such as the avoidance of boastfulness.[52] Driver regards understating one's worth while being aware of it as false modesty. Construing modesty as mere behavioral manifestations is compatible with having a high opinion of oneself, and having a high opinion of oneself is incompatible with being modest. So Driver rejects both of these views and argues instead for the underestimation approach. Underestimation is based on ignorance of self-worth, so Driver is led to claim: "Since modesty is generally considered to be a virtue, it would seem that this virtue rests upon an epistemic defect."[53] She adds that "modesty can be characterized as a dogmatic disposition to underestimation of self-worth."[54] She also regards modesty as a dependent virtue in the sense originally suggested in Michael Slote's discussion of humility, according to which humility is a virtue only when accompanied by some other virtue or desirable trait.[55] As Slote makes clear, one has to have something – some additional virtue or other good attribute – to be humble about.[56] Driver also embraces Bernard Williams' view that virtuous people typically do not act under the descriptions of specific virtues, such as justice, courage, and so on. She quotes Williams: "it is a notorious truth that a modest person does not act under the title of modesty."[57] Thus, the modest person cannot attribute that virtue to herself, though others can ascribe it to her.[58] Finally, Driver writes that: "Since modesty necessarily involves ignorance, it is also necessarily involuntary in nature."[59] Any cultivation of modesty would require cultivating beliefs about oneself that the agent takes to be false, and would require, Driver thinks, self-deception. Thus, modesty is a moral virtue only when it arises spontaneously; when cultivated, it cannot be considered a moral virtue.[60]

Driver's account is deeply at odds with Western virtue ethical traditions, both in its insistence on a class of virtues that requires ignorance, as well as on the claim that modesty (indeed, any virtue) is necessarily involuntary, and that its cultivation would require self-deception. Not surprisingly, the view has generated sustained criticism.[61] We turn now to accounts of modesty developed in response to Driver.

Flanagan (1990) – Modesty is nonoverestimation of one's accomplishments and worth. Flanagan systematically disambiguates several tangled epistemological claims that Driver makes. Central to his argument is defeating what he calls the "strong" and "weak" ignorance claims. The strong claim requires ignorance at the general level of virtue description; the weak "requires ignorance of certain facts or features of the self, others, or the world."[62] As for the strong claim, Flanagan quotes Driver as contending, "I can be modest, I cannot *know* it."[63] He points out that the statement "I am modest," is odd from a performative perspective, but it is not out of place in some contexts, for example, in communications with close friends or a therapist, in which one is brought to see and acknowledge one's modesty, or self-comprehension brought about through self-reflection. Bragging about one's modesty would undermine one's claim to being modest, but uttering the phrase, "I am modest" in contexts such as those mentioned would not. But, if so, we have no reason to think the strong ignorance claim is true, nor that there is a self–other asymmetry in ascriptions of modesty.[64]

The weak ignorance claim is that modesty requires the dogmatic disposition to underestimate one's self-worth. Flanagan criticizes this claim by comparing it with his own account, which he calls the "nonoverestimation account." On this view, the modest person can have an accurate sense of herself and her accomplishments, but she doesn't overestimate them. Flanagan argues that his view is superior to Driver's on four key points.[65] First, it avoids Driver's counterintuitive notion that there are no modest people who don't dogmatically underestimate their own worth. Flanagan writes: "The truly modest person cannot be so systematically in the dark about her own worth."[66] Second, it avoids the paradox, evident on Driver's view, that a person who accurately understands his self-worth can behave modestly (by not bragging, etc.), yet not be modest (by not being dogmatically disposed to ignorance about his self-worth). Third, another feature of Driver's view, avoided by Flanagan's, is that: "[s]ince modesty necessarily involves ignorance, it is also necessarily involuntary in nature."[67] As Flanagan rightly observes, if modesty were involuntary, it would not be open to self-cultivation.[68] He writes:

> To me, the twin ideas that the virtues of ignorance are essentially characterized by ignorance at both levels [strong and weak ignorance claims], as well as closed, in principle, to self-cultivation, are extremely implausible consequences of the underestimation account. Indeed, I take them to be a reduction of the account.[69]

Finally, the nonoverestimation account fits nicely with work from empirical psychology on self-serving attributional biases. We dramatically overestimate ourselves and tend to have unrealistically positive self-evaluations. Modesty, as the tendency not to overestimate one's abilities, accomplishments, and so on, is a useful corrective to these natural, yet erroneous, proclivities.[70]

Schueler (1997) – Modesty is not caring whether people are impressed by one for one's accomplishments. After an extensive discussion and critique of four belief-based accounts, Schueler offers his own conception, which is a desire-based account. He moves to a desire-based account after concluding that belief-based conceptions cannot make sense of three thoughts, all of which must cohere if modesty is to be a virtue:

> (1) that the modest person's beliefs (or her presentation of them) about her own accomplishments must be accurate; (2) that these beliefs (or presentations) must mean that she or her accomplishments rank low on the relevant scale; and (3) that her accomplishments must be genuine.[71]

For Schueler, the primary sense of modesty is what he calls "focused" modesty, which is about some specific accomplishment or set of accomplishments (he contrasts this with "global" modesty, or modesty *simpliciter*, which he claims to be focused modesty that takes oneself as its object).[72] Schueler contends that, since the basic concept is focused modesty "where the standard form is 'S is modest about (accomplishment) X,'" it's clear that (1)–(3) are irreconcilable.[73]

A desire-based account can explain modesty by construing the modest person as someone who "lacks a certain desire or set of desires, namely, that people be impressed by her for what she has accomplished."[74] This is not the same, he contends, as saying that she doesn't care how her accomplishments appear to people, or how they're evaluated, or what people think of her, but it is to say that she doesn't care that people (including herself) be impressed by her because of them.[75]

Schueler's account has at least some similarities to Roberts and colleagues, who think that humility is the intelligent lack of concern for one's own importance, and Garcia, who thinks that humility is being unimpressed with oneself. Schueler's view has come in for criticism.[76] For example, as Grenberg rightly notes, Schueler appeals to a secular background worldview intended to serve as a functional equivalent of religious conceptions according to which one's place in a divinely ordained order provides the perspective needed for humility. Adopting a secular worldview allows us to see the many factors – luck, upbringing, and so on, that temper the role of the self in bringing about one's accomplishments. Yet, as Grenberg recognizes, he goes too far when he writes, "none of the essential explanatory factors would be things for which one could fairly claim any credit. All would be things totally outside one's control."[77] This appears to have the effect of effacing any credit one could legitimately take for one's successes.

We can add a further worry. According to Schueler,

> on this account, a genuinely modest person will be not be someone who is trying to be or appear modest. She will, typically, not think of her actions as modest, as those that a modest person would perform, or the like.[78]

Clearly, any theory of modesty (or humility) should disqualify someone who does not care about actually being modest, but only about appearing to be modest. Here again, it seems, Schueler goes too far. As with Driver, he quotes Williams that: "it is a notorious truth that a modest person does not act under the title of modesty."[79] Consistently with Flanagan's remarks on Driver, I see no reason why this should always be true. The person whose modesty is ingrained need not consciously think of herself or her actions as modest, but someone engaged in self-reflection could come to consciously recognize that she is modest and, indeed, to extend her modest actions across different domains in her life. Additionally, the person who acknowledges the need to develop in modesty could couple self-reflection with the desire to be modest. Schueler ignores these kinds of cases, as well as others in which we think that trying to be modest does not undermine modesty, for example, those in which someone is committed to sustaining her modesty, perhaps in the face of temptations. Here, too, it seems, trying to be modest is not incompatible with genuine modesty.[80]

Ridge (2000) – Modesty is the disposition to de-emphasize one's accomplishments and traits taken to entitle one to benefits for the right reasons. Ridge's account comprises three necessary and sufficient conditions. He writes:

In sum, then, on my account, a person is modest just in case:

(a) She is disposed to de-emphasize her accomplishments and traits that are taken to entitle her to benefits.
(b) She is so disposed at least partially in virtue of not caring too much about whether she gets everything to which she is entitled.
(c) She is so disposed at least partially in virtue of caring enough that people not overestimate her accomplishments and characteristics or her responsibility for them.[81]

Several features of this account are interesting. First, there are two elements to the disposition to de-emphasize one's accomplishments:

> a disposition to refrain from going out of your way to stress the significance of your accomplishments, and … a disposition to correct others if they have an inflated conception of those accomplishments (or an inflated conception of your responsibility for them).[82]

The disposition to correct others is a new element not previously appearing in analyses of humility or modesty (when used interchangeably with "humility").

Second, Ridge links traits in particular (but also accomplishments, though his main discussion concerns traits), with being entitled to certain benefits, and suggests that not pressing for those benefits, that is, not caring too much whether one always gets them, is part of being modest.[83] This has been an unrecognized dimension of modesty/humility. For example, a star player could easily be considered immodest if he insists on being a starter in every game, even those in which the rival team can easily be defeated and the game offers an opportunity for less talented athletes to play. Similarly, one could imagine an intelligent but immodest student on a debate team or a chess team who insists on being sent to every match, not giving others a chance to participate.

The extent to which one should care about being entitled to benefits on the basis of one's traits or accomplishments raises the question of justice. If we lived in an ideally just world, conditions (a) and (b) of Ridge's conception could be adequate. But we do not live in a just world, and because of this, the clauses need to be modified. In particular, both (a) and (b) should be amended, yielding something like:

(a') She is disposed to de-emphasize her accomplishments and traits that are taken to entitle her to benefits, provided that others who possess similar traits and accomplishments are not accorded unfair recognition and entitlements to benefits.
(b') She is so disposed at least partially in virtue of not caring too much about whether she gets everything to which she is entitled, and her not caring too much is based on her experience of just distributions of the benefits of entitlements to herself and others.

(a) and (b) need to be amended in this way because of the reality of discrimination and oppression. For example, for most of the history of schooling in the United States, women's athletics were funded at far lower rates than men's. This resulted in the lack of benefits and opportunities to which women athletes would otherwise have been entitled. It would not have been modest of women athletes to de-emphasize their athletic abilities and accomplishments, nor would their not caring too much about getting the benefits to which they were entitled have been modest or praiseworthy. To the contrary, such attitudes and behavior would have displayed a lack of self-respect, the lack of a sense of justice, and the possible internalization of subordinating stereotypes about women. Similar comments can be made about other forms of discrimination, for example, on the basis of race, ethnicity, religion, sexual orientation, and disability.

In general, philosophers who write about modesty (and humility) tend to assume that people get what they deserve from others, and that modesty (humility) is good because it counteracts tendencies to exaggerate one's achievements, talents, etc. But humility has been and can be used in the service of oppression.[84] Does this mean that Ridge's condition (c), that modest people should care enough that people not overestimate their accomplishments and characteristics or their responsibility for them, also should be relaxed to take into account conditions of oppression – that the oppressed shouldn't be expected to care whether people overestimate their accomplishments, and so on? I think not. Those who have been oppressed or unfairly treated should be wary about de-emphasizing their accomplishments and traits and should be vigilant about receiving the benefits to which they're entitled. This is to ensure that they receive their due in circumstances in which justice is threatened or denied. The fact that someone has been oppressed or treated unfairly, however, does not excuse her for not caring enough about whether people overestimate her accomplishments, etc. She should get what is due to her from others – just estimation and recognition of her accomplishments and traits, and fairness in the distribution of benefits to which she's entitled – but others' overestimation of her accomplishments is not what is due to her as a matter of justice. If she corrects such mistaken views, then does she do it out of justice, modesty, or something else? With respect to the oppressed, it seems that condition (c) of Ridge's modesty conditions is also a form of justice – in correcting an exaggerated view of her accomplishments, the oppressed person ensures that others have a just opinion of her. The corrected opinion is just because it is true and it is her due. But it seems that anyone, not only the oppressed, has good reason to adhere to condition (c). But, if so, and if we accept (c) as a general condition for being modest, Ridge has identified a respect in which the virtue of modesty overlaps with the concern for justice, as well as with the concern for truth – an interesting and novel implication of his account.

Let me conclude this discussion of modesty by mentioning two recent accounts that push a discussion of that virtue well beyond the debate originating with Driver.

Bommarito (2013) – Modesty as a virtue of attention. As with other accounts, Bommarito begins with an overview and critique of the views of Driver and others who have written about modesty. Yet he takes a significant step away from that trajectory by introducing the new idea that modesty is a virtue of attention. Unlike awareness, attention is a matter of consciously focusing on something. Interestingly, modesty is, according to Bommarito, a virtue of both attention and inattention. He writes:

> Following Slote (1983, 61), it is necessary to have a good quality to be modest about. Contrary to most contemporary views, it is not necessary to underestimate the good quality nor is it necessary to have an accurate assessment. Instead, what is necessary is to direct one's conscious attention in certain ways – away from the trait or its value or toward the outside causes and conditions that played a role in developing it.[85]

He hastens to note that attending in these ways isn't sufficient for modesty; one must attend for the right reasons. One's pattern of attending must result from one's values and desires.[86] Moreover, "Modesty does not demand inattention in the sense of a total lack of attention but in the sense that one does not *dwell* on one's own good qualities."[87]

Conceptualizing modesty as a virtue of attention opens an entirely new avenue of research on modesty, as well as on other virtues.

Wilson (2014) – Modesty as kindness. Wilson offers another innovative account. He advances the idea that modesty is connected with the more fundamental virtue of kindness. He writes:

> To be modest is to be disposed to present your accomplishments/positive attributes in a way that is sensitive to the potential negative impact on the well-being of others, where this disposition stems from a concern for that well-being.[88]

One noteworthy feature of modesty as kindness is that it is consistent with the kinds of epistemic deficits that characterize Driver's view.[89] Yet it is also possible to amend the account to include the requirement that the modest person have an accurate self-assessment. This would result in a view that Wilson calls "intellectualised modesty as kindness."[90]

Wilson's view is that the non-intellectualized virtue of modesty is not doing anything special or out of the ordinary. The research agenda that he foresees is one in which philosophers examine a range of specific virtues to see whether an examination of non-intellectualized virtues, conjoined with a variety of intellectualized amendments, can add to our knowledge of the nature of virtue in general.[91] This challenges traditional intellectualized understandings of virtue, but also invites philosophers to think in more fine-grained ways about the kinds of intellectual components that specific virtues require.

Before concluding, I wish to make a criticism that applies to Driver, Bommarito, and Wilson. Driver requires that the modest person be ignorant of her accomplishments, Wilson permits ignorance but does not require it, and also allows for inaccuracy in the modest person's assessment of her accomplishments, and Bommarito allows for accurate assessments.[92] Yet, all three hold that modesty is a dependent virtue in the sense that one must have something to be modest about. I believe their openness to ignorance and/or error in assessments opens the door to problems for their accounts.

Consider two cases: the braggart and the "blow-hard." To sharpen the case, imagine that they're your undergraduate philosophy students. The braggart has philosophical talent but either doesn't know about it or inaccurately assesses it. She blows her purported acumen completely out of proportion in thinking about herself and talking with others. She is immodest. Now consider the blow-hard. He has absolutely no philosophical acumen, but mistakenly thinks he does and thinks and acts in exactly the same way as the braggart. Is the blow-hard immodest (in addition to being annoying, clueless, etc.)? Driver, Wilson, and Bommarito would have to deny that the blow-hard is immodest because, even though he thinks he has philosophical ability, he is wrong – he has nothing to be immodest about. If the braggart were to stop thinking and speaking too highly of herself, our theorists would deem her modest. That is because she has something to be modest about. Not so for the blow-hard. Were he to stop thinking and speaking too highly of himself, he would not be regarded as modest because he has nothing to be modest about.

The problem is that requiring or allowing ignorance and inaccuracy in assessment puts the braggart and the blow-hard on the same epistemic footing with respect to different ontological statuses, namely, their possession of an actual talent. If, for whatever reason that is required by the various accounts under discussion, the braggart adjusts her thinking, attention, and so on, she can rightly be said to shift from being immodest to modest. This is because her thought, patterns of attention, etc., track the truth insofar as they relate to an actual talent or ability that she possesses. But the blow-hard's shift in attention would not track the truth, for he never had anything to be modest or immodest about.

One might embrace this analysis as raising no problem for the accounts being discussed (I do not), but there is a deeper problem. Allowing ignorance and inaccuracy obscures, from a first-person perspective, the information that is necessary to ascertain whether one is truly being immodest or modest. If, as on Driver's view and consistently with Wilson's, the braggart either must have no knowledge of her talent or is allowed to have no knowledge, she is in the same epistemic situation as the blow-hard. Thus, she has no way of knowing if she is truly modest or if she is mistaken in the same way as the blow-hard. A similar first-person predicament arises on Bommarito's account, if we take his allowance of the inaccurate assessment of talents to entail being inaccurate about whether one has talent at all, or being so inaccurate in one's assessment that one trumps up a negligible ability into something much greater, and then thinks one is being modest when one is inattentive to the trumped up, yet actually quite minimal, talent. On

Bommarito's account, one can imagine the braggart having negligible philosophical ability, yet saying to herself, "I am a major philosophical star," then deciding not to pay attention to that. Bommarito would have to call her modest. I would call her self-deceived.

Consider, too, that observers are often more readily convinced of evidence of another's faults than are those who possess them. Consistently with Flanagan's critique of Driver, self-serving attributional bias can lead one to believe one has talents when one doesn't, and that one's abilities are greater than they are. This kind of bias can be difficult to correct, even in the face of evidence. Thus, I submit that allowing ignorance or inaccuracy in the mental states of agents opens the door to several kinds of problem – (1) those pertaining to whether people actually are modest or immodest, that is, whether their modesty or immodesty tracks the truth with respect to their having actual talents; (2) how people can know whether they are being modest or immodest and make reliable self-attributions of these qualities while in a state of ignorance, or while holding inaccurate beliefs; and (3) the likelihood that allowing ignorance or inaccuracy to shape their beliefs, attitudes, and emotions makes it harder to disabuse them of error because of self-serving bias.

1.4 Conclusion

Debates about humility and modesty have been ongoing and vigorous. I have offered no more than a selective theoretical overview, but it is clear that, like our historical forebears, our contemporaries continue to be engaged with these virtues, and even point to new and exciting directions for further research.

Notes

1 Snow (1995, 203).
2 This is due in no small part to the efforts of the John Templeton Foundation, which has funded three major initiatives to stimulate research on humility: at the Thrive Center of the Fuller Theological Seminary (http://thethrivecenter.org/science/); at St. Louis University (on "The Philosophy and Theology of Intellectual Humility (http://humility.slu.edu/); and at the University of Connecticut on "Humility and Conviction in Public Life" (https://humilityandconviction.uconn.edu/).
3 Religious and psychological conceptions of humility, as well as humility from non-Western perspectives, are discussed elsewhere in this volume. On humility and environmental ethics, see Gerber (2002) and Hill (1983). For work on humility in political science, see Rushing (2013), Keys (2008), and Button (2005). For work on humility from a variety of disciplinary perspectives, see Wright (forthcoming).
4 See Newman (1982, 227); but see also Roberts and Cleveland (2017, 38–39), who argue that humility is exemplified by Socrates in the *Apology* (28b–d) and the *Theaetetus*, and is found in a passage in Plato's *Laws* (4.716a–b).
5 For helpful discussions, see Wielenberg (2019), Nadelhoffer, et al., (2017), Nadelhoffer and Wright (2017), Roberts and Cleveland (2017, 38–41), Trakakis (2014), Roberts (2007, chapter 6), and Newman (1982).
6 Nadelhoffer, et al. (2017), 172; see *The Cloud of Unknowing*, trans. James Walsh (Mahwah, NJ: Paulist Press, 1981), chapter 32, 181.
7 Richards (1988, 253); see Bernard of Clairvaux, Sermon 42 on Canticle 6, trans. George Bosworth Burch in his Introduction to Bernard's *The Steps of Humility* (Cambridge, MA: Harvard University Press, 1942, 51).
8 Nadelhoffer, et al. (2017), 172; see Maimonides (Moses Ben Maimom), *A Maimonides Reader*, ed. I. Twersky (New York: Berman House, 1972).
9 See Newman (1982) and Button (2005).
10 Newman (1982, 275); see Baruch Spinoza *Ethics*, part 4, prop. 53; and David Hume, *A Treatise of Human Nature*, Book 3, part 3, section 2.
11 Newman (1982, 277); see Friedrich Nietzsche, *Beyond Good and Evil* (1966), sect. 260.

12 Richards (1988, 253); see Henry Sidgwick, *The Methods of Ethics*, 7th ed. (Chicago, IL: The University of Chicago Press, 1992), 334–335.
13 Newman (1982, 281); see also Grenberg (2005).
14 Lippitt (2017, 98).
15 Sinha (2012, 266); quoted material from Hastings Rashdall, *The Theory of Good and Evil*(Oxford, UK: Clarendon Press, 1907), 204.
16 Sinha (2012, 266); quoted material from Rashdall (1907), 207.
17 Space considerations preclude discussions of some very interesting views on humility. E.g., Kupfer (2003) argues that humility is a realistic understanding of ourselves and our relation to the world. Milligan (2007, see especially 217, 221, 224, and 226) develops a conception of humility based on Iris Murdoch's work, according to which humility is the just discernment of one's competences, including our limited moral competences, that avoids overestimation. Kellenberger (2010, 234) maintains that humility is a "polythetic" concept; that is, it "has one meaning, but that meaning allows different expressions of humility in different contexts." Different contemporary conceptions of humility, he argues, are different expressions of humility or ways of being humble. Murphy (2017, 19–32) offers interesting reflections on humility as a moral virtue. Nadelhoffer, et al. (2017) and Nadelhoffer and Wright (2017) is a collaboration between a philosopher and psychologists that advances empirical evidence for the view that humility is low self-focus and high other-focus. See also the exchange between Byerly (2014) and Garcia (2015).
18 Taylor (1985, 17); quoted in Richards (1988, 253).
19 Richards (1988, 253).
20 Taylor (1985, 51).
21 Taylor (1985, 51).
22 Richards (1988, 254); see also Richards (1992a, 578).
23 Richards (1988, 256).
24 Richards (1988, 257).
25 Snow (1995, 206–207).
26 Snow (1995, 207).
27 Snow (1995, 209).
28 Snow (1995, 210).
29 Richards (1988, 259).
30 Snow (1995, 214).
31 Roberts and Wood (2003), Roberts and Wood (2007); see also Roberts and West (2017), Roberts and Cleveland (2017), and Gulliford and Roberts (2018). Roberts and Wood (2003, 2007) investigate moral humility in order to apply their insights to intellectual humility. See Roberts (2007, chapter 6) for his work on Christian humility.
32 Roberts and Wood (2003, 258; 2007, 236).
33 Roberts and Wood (2003, 259–271; 2007, 237–250).
34 Roberts and Wood (2003, 261; 2007, 239).
35 Roberts and Wood (2003, 261–262; 2007, 239–240).
36 Roberts and Cleveland (2017, 33).
37 Roberts and Cleveland (2017, 45).
38 Wielenberg (2019, 42; 2005, 102–112).
39 Wielenberg (2005, 112).
40 Wielenberg (2019, 49).
41 Grenberg (2005, 161). See chapter 6 more generally for her discussion of humility; see also Grenberg (2007a, 622–623), and Grenberg (2007b, 645–666).
42 Though Ben Ze'ev (1993, 240) has interesting things to say about modesty, he regards humility and modesty as distinct, asserting that: "The crucial difference is that modest people do not overrate themselves, whereas humble people underrate themselves." He relies on dictionary definitions of humility to support this contention. Similarly, Nguyen (1998,101) has interesting things to say about modesty, but distinguishes it from humility: "Without further argument, I take it that humility involves an underestimation of one's achievements, or worth, taking it to a suitably low level. By contrast, I shall give an account of modesty that does not involve any underestimation."
43 See Grenberg (2005, 139–141) for a discussion of Schueler and Ben Ze'ev. She argues that Schueler commits himself to a position on which he cannot allow people to claim any credit for their accomplishments.
44 Garcia (2006, 418; italics his).

45 Garcia (2006, 418).
46 Garcia (2006, 418).
47 Sinha (2012, 260).
48 Sinha (2012, 261).
49 Sinha (2012, 269; italics his).
50 I have included accounts that are novel or that overlap with themes found in the humility literature. Other work engaging with Driver's view includes: Statman (1992, 436), who argues that modesty involves having proper respect for other human beings and a firm disposition to act accordingly; Maes (2004, 489), who contends that a self-other asymmetry in what one can say and think of oneself and others can say and think of one is essential for modesty; Sandler (2005 269), who maintains that modesty is excellence in responding to one's self-evaluations; Raterman (2006, 228), who believes that modesty is the reluctance to evaluate one's goodness, underpinned by the right normative reasons; Brennan (2007), who draws on Adam Smith's work to argue that there are two standards involved in modesty: comparison to an ideal and comparison to other people; Smith (2008), who offers an account of modesty as an Aristotelian virtue; McMullin (2010), who looks to Sartre to develop an account of modesty; Allhoff (2010, 177), who argues that modesty is not bragging or being disposed to brag; and Winter (2011, 533), who contends that modesty is having and knowing one has genuine accomplishments, yet being disposed not to put them forward.
51 Blind charity and a certain kind of refusal to hold a grudge are two others. See Driver (1989, 381–383).
52 Driver (1989, 374–375).
53 Driver (1989, 377).
54 Driver (1989, 378).
55 See Driver (1989, 378–379); Slote (1983, 61ff).
56 See Slote (1983, 61–62).
57 Williams (1985, 10), quoted at Driver (1989, 379).
58 Driver (1989, 379–380). On p. 375, she remarks on the oddity of the claim, "I am modest." Flanagan (1990, 423) points out contexts in which this statement would not be odd (see note 66). Bommarito (2013, 113–114) and Wilson (2014, 77–78) also counter this claim, as do I in discussing Schueler in the text.
59 Driver (1989, 381).
60 Driver (1989, 382–383.)
61 In addition to the views listed in note 52, see Flanagan (1990), Schueler (1997), Grenberg (2005, 166–167), Wielenberg (2005, 103–106), Garcia (2006, 422; 427–428), Raterman (2006, 222–226), Brennan (2007, 111–118), Sinha (2012, 268–270), and Roberts and Cleveland (2017, 42). See also the Driver (1999)–Schueler (1999) exchange. For a more sympathetic approach to virtues of ignorance, see Slote (2004).
62 Flanagan (1990, 423).
63 Driver (1989, 376, italics hers), quoted at Flanagan (1990, 423).
64 Flanagan (1990, 423).
65 Flanagan (1990, 424–427).
66 Flanagan (1990, 425).
67 Driver (1989, 381), quoted at Flanagan (1990, 426).
68 See Driver (1989, 382–383), where she contends that cultivating modesty would require self-deception and that when cultivated, it cannot be considered a moral virtue.
69 Flanagan (1990, 426).
70 For a critique of Flanagan (1990), see Raterman (2006, 226–227).
71 Schueler (1997, 483; see also 476–477).
72 Schueler (1997, 474). Note the similarity of focused and global modesty to Garcia (2006).
73 Schueler (1997, 477).
74 Schueler (1997, 479).
75 Schueler (1997, 479, including note 23).
76 See, for example, Grenberg (2005, 139–141), and Sinha (2012, 270–272).
77 Schueler (1997, 484); Grenberg (2005, 139–140).
78 Schueler (1997, 480).
79 Williams (1985, 10), quoted at Schueler (1997, 477).
80 Ridge (2000, 282, note 13) contends that Schueler (1999) changes his view on modesty. I am not sure this is true, though Schueler (1999, 839) does claim that "modesty is a virtue … because of what it reveals about the person who has it, namely, that her goals and purposes come from herself, not from

others." He arrives at this by asking us to imagine a person on the extreme end of immodesty, who cares so much about impressing others with her accomplishments that she adopts whatever goals and purposes they most value. It seems to me that this goes wrong in two ways. First, the extremely immodest person seems to me not immodest, but obsequious in adopting for herself goals and purposes that others value because they value them and she desires that they be impressed with her. Second, even if one held to one's own goals and purposes, one might still be immodest about them in Schueler's sense. See Ridge (2000, 282, note 13) for insights.

81 Ridge (2000, 281).

82 Ridge (2000, 277).

83 See Ridge (2000, 280-281).

84 See Snow (2003, 2004, 2015). Raterman (2006, 221–222) raises similar concerns in connection with modesty's status as a virtue. He offers a more general critique of Ridge (2000) at Raterman (2006, 227–228).

85 Bommarito (2013, 103).

86 Bommarito (2013, 103).

87 Bommarito (2013, 108).

88 Wilson (2014, 78). Wilson (2014, 84–85) raises the possibility that humility and modesty are distinct, writing that "it is possible that more work needs to be done to clarify the precise relationship between the trait of modesty and the trait of humility. It is often assumed that the two traits are one and the same" (84).

89 Wilson (2014, 86–87).

90 Wilson (2014, 81).

91 Wilson (2014, 87).

92 Bommarito (2013, 103); Wilson (2014, 81). Wilson (2014, 86–87) goes quite far in the direction of Driver's view.

References

Allhoff, Fritz. 2010. "What Is Modesty?" *International Journal of Applied Philosophy* 23(2): 165–187.

Ben Ze'ev, Aaron. 1993. "The Virtue of Modesty." *American Philosophical Quarterly* 30(3): 235–246.

Bommarito, Nicolas. 2013. "Modesty as a Virtue of Attention." *Philosophical Review* 122(1): 93–117.

Brennan, Jason. 2007. "Modesty without Illusion." *Philosophy and Phenomenological Research* LXXV(1): 111–128.

Burch, Bosworth, trans. 1942. *The Steps of Humility*. Cambridge, MA: Harvard University Press.

Button, Mark. 2005. "'Monkish Kind of Virtue'? for and against Humility." *Political Theory* 33(6): 840–868.

Byerly, T. Ryan. 2014. "The Values and Varieties of Humility." *Philosophia* 42(4): 889–910.

Driver, Julia. 1989. "The Virtues of Ignorance." *The Journal of Philosophy* 86(7): 373–384.

Driver, Julia. 1999. "Modesty and Ignorance." *Ethics* 109(4): 827–834.

Driver, Julia. 2001. *Uneasy Virtue*. New York: Cambridge University Press.

Flanagan, Owen. 1990. "Virtue and Ignorance." *The Journal of Philosophy* 87(8): 420–428.

Garcia, J. L. A. 2015. "Methods and Findings in the Study of Virtues: Humility." *Philosophia* 43(2): 325–335.

Garcia, J. L. A. 2006. "Being Unimpressed with Ourselves: Reconceiving Humility." *Philosophia* 34(4): 417–435.

Gerber, Lisa. 2002. "Standing Humbly Before Nature." *Ethics and the Environment* 7(1): 39–53.

Grenberg, Jeanine. 2005. *Kant and the Ethics of Humility: A Story of Dependence, Corruption, and Virtue*. New York: Cambridge University Press.

Grenberg, Jeanine. 2007a. "Précis of Kant and the Ethics of Humility: A Story of Dependence, Corruption, and Virtue." *Philosophy and Phenomenological Research* LXXV(3): 622–623.

Grenberg, Jeanine. 2007b. "Courageous Humility in Jane Austen's *Mansfield Park*." *Social Theory and Practice* 33(4): 645–666.

Gulliford, Liz and Robert C. Roberts. 2018. "Exploring the 'Unity' of the Virtues: The Case of an Allocentric Quintet." *Theory and Psychology*: 1–19. doi:10.1177/0959354317751666.

Hill, Jr., Thomas E. 1983. "Ideals of Human Excellence and Preserving Natural Environments." *Environmental Ethics* 5(3): 211–224.

Hume, David. 1978. *A Treatise of Human Nature*, Ed. P. H. Nidditch. New York: Oxford University Press.

Kellenberger, James. "Humility." *American Philosophical Quarterly* 47(4): 321–336.

Keys, Mary. 2008. "Humility and Greatness of Soul." *Perspectives on Political Science* 37(4): 217–222.
Kupfer, Joseph. 2003. "The Moral Perspective of Humility." *Pacific Philosophical Quarterly* 84(3): 249–269.
Lippitt, John. 2017. "Kierkegaard's Virtues? Humility and Gratitude as the Grounds of Contentment, Patience and Hope in Kierkegaard's Moral Psychology." In: *Kierkegaard's God and the Good Life*, eds. Stephen Minister, J. Aaron Simmons and Michael Strawser. Bloomington, IN: Indiana University Press, pp. 95–113.
Maes, Hans. 2004. "Modesty, Asymmetry, and Hypocrisy." *The Journal of Value Inquiry* 38(4): 485–497.
Maimonides, Moses. 1972. *A Maimonides Reader*, Ed. I. Twerksy. New York: Berman House.
McMullin, Irene. 2010. "A Modest Proposal: Accounting for the Virtuousness of Modesty." *The Philosophical Quarterly* 60(241): 783–807.
Milligan, Tony. 2007. "Murdochian Humility." *Religious Studies* 43(2): 217–228.
Murphy, Jeffrie G. 2017. "Humility as a Moral Virtue." In: *Handbook of Humility: Theory, Research, and Applications*, eds. Everett L. Worthington, Jr., Don E. Davis and Joshua N. Hook. New York: Routledge, pp. 19–32.
Nadelhoffer, Thomas and Jennifer Cole Wright. 2017. "The Twin Dimensions of the Virtue of Humility: Low Self-Focus and High Other-Focus." In: *Moral Psychology, Volume 5: Virtue and Character*, eds. Walter Sinnott-Armstrong and Christian B. Miller. Cambridge, MA: The MIT Press, pp. 309–342.
Nadelhoffer, Thomas, Jennifer Cole Wright, Matthew Echols, Tyler Perini and Kelly Venezia. 2017. "Some Varieties of Humility Worth Wanting." *The Journal of Moral Philosophy* 14(2): 168–200.
Newman, Jay. 1982. "Humility and Self-Realization." *The Journal of Value Inquiry* 16(4): 275–285.
Nietzsche, Friedrich. 1966. *Beyond Good and Evil*, Trans. Walter Kaufmann. New York: Random House.
Nuyen, A. T. 1998. "Just Modesty." *American Philosophical Quarterly* 35(1): 101–109.
Rashdall, Hastings. 1907. *The Theory of Good and Evil*. Oxford, UK: Clarendon Press.
Raterman, Ty. 2006. "On Modesty: Being Good and Knowing It without Flaunting It." *American Philosophical Quarterly* 43: 221–234.
Richards, Norvin. 1988. "Is Humility a Virtue?" *American Philosophical Quarterly* 25(3): 253–259.
Richards, Norvin. 1992a. "Humility." In: *Encyclopedia of Ethics vol. 1*, ed. Lawrence C. Becker, assoc. ed., Charlotte B. Becker. New York: Garland, pp. 577–579.
Richards, Norvin. 1992b. *Humility*. Philadelphia, PA: Temple University Press.
Ridge, Michael. 2000. "Modesty as a Virtue." *American Philosophical Quarterly* 37(3): 269–283.
Roberts, Robert C. 2007. *Spiritual Emotions: A Psychology of Christian Virtues*. Grand Rapids, MI: Wm. B. Eerdmans Publishing Company.
Roberts, Robert C. and W. Scott Cleveland. 2017. "Humility from a Philosophical Point of View." In: *Handbook of Humility: Theory, Research, and Applications*, eds. Everett L. Worthington, Jr., Don E. Davis and Joshua N. Hook. New York: Routledge, pp. 33–46.
Roberts, Robert C. and W. Jay Wood. 2003. "Humility and Epistemic Goods." In: *Intellectual Virtue: Perspectives from Ethics and Epistemology*, eds. Michael DePaul and Linda Zagzebski. Oxford, UK: Clarendon Press.
Roberts, Robert C. and W. Jay Wood. 2007. *Intellectual Virtues: An Essay in Regulative Epistemology*. Oxford, UK: Clarendon Press.
Rushing, Sara. 2013. "Comparative Humilities: Christian, Contemporary, and Confucian Conceptions of a Political Virtue." *Polity* 45(2): 198–222.
Sandler, Ronald. "Ignorance and Virtue." *Philosophical Papers* 34(2): 261–272.
Schueler, G. F. 1997. "Why Modesty Is a Virtue." *Ethics* 107(3): 467–487.
Schueler, G. F. 1999. "Why IS Modesty a Virtue?." *Ethics* 109(4): 835–841.
Sidgwick, Henry. 1992. *The Methods of Ethics*, 7th ed. Chicago, IL: The University of Chicago Press.
Sinha, G. Alex. 2012. "Modernizing the Virtue of Humility." *Australasian Journal of Philosophy* 90(2): 259–274.
Slote, Michael. 1983. *Goods and Virtues*. Oxford, UK: Clarendon Press.
Slote, Michael. 2004. "Driver's Virtues." *Utilitas* 16(1): 22–32.
Smith, Nicholas D. 2008. "Modesty: A Contextual Account." *Proceedings and Addresses of the American Philosophical Association* 82(2): 23–45.
Snow, Nancy E. 1995. "Humility." *The Journal of Value Inquiry* 29(2): 203–216.
Snow, Nancy E. 2003. "Virtue and the Oppression of Women." In: *Feminist Moral Philosophy*, ed. Samantha Brennan. Calgary, Alberta, Canada: University of Calgary Press, pp. 33–61.
Snow, Nancy E. 2004. "Virtue and the Oppression of African Americans." *Public Affairs Quarterly* 18(1): 57–74.
Snow, Nancy E. 2015. "Virtue and Oppression: A Response to Roberts." In: *Current Controversies in Virtue Theory*, ed. Mark Alfano. New York: Routledge, pp. 49–59.

Spinoza, Baruch. 1992. *Ethics: With the Treatise on the Emendation of the Intellect and Selected Letters*, 2d ed., trans. Samuel Shirley, ed. Seymour Feldman. Indianapolis, IN: Hackett Publishing Company.
Statman, Daniel. 1992. "Modesty, Pride, and Realistic Self-Assessment." *The Philosophical Quarterly* 42(169): 420–438.
Taylor, Gabriele. 1985. *Pride, Shame, and Guilt: Emotions of Self-Assessment*. Oxford, UK: Clarendon Press.
Trakakis, N. N. 2014. "The Paradox of Humility and Dogmatism." In: *Skeptical Theism: New Essays*, eds. Trent Dougherty and Justin P. McBrayer. New York: Oxford University Press, pp. 85–100.
Walsh, James, trans. 1981. *The Cloud of Unknowing*. Mahwah, NJ: Paulist Press.
Wielenberg, Erik J. 2019. "Secular Humility." In: *Humility*, ed. Jennifer Cole Wright. New York: Oxford University Press, pp. 41–63.
Wielenberg, Erik J. 2005. *Value and Virtue in a Godless Universe*. New York: Cambridge University Press.
Williams, Bernard. 1985. *Ethics and the Limits of Philosophy*. Cambridge, MA: Harvard University Press.
Wilson, Alan T. 2014. "Modesty as Kindness." *Ratio (new series)* 29(1): 73–88.
Winter, Michael Jeffrey. 2012. "Does Moral Virtue Require Knowledge: A Response to Julia Driver." *The Journal of Value Inquiry* 15(4): 533–546.
Wright, Jennifer Cole, ed. 2019. *Humility*. New York: Oxford University Press.

2

"I AM SO HUMBLE!"

On the paradoxes of humility

Brian Robinson

2.1 Introduction

Humility is a paradoxical virtue. This should come as no great surprise. It doesn't take much explanation for one to realize that if someone is boasting about how humble he is, then he probably is not humble. In fact, as we shall see, the paradoxical nature of humility has a long history, going back to at least Thomas Aquinas in the thirteenth century. While it may not be a novel claim that there exists an apparent paradox of humility, I will argue that there is more than one humility paradox, perhaps as many as five: the epistemic paradox, the paradox of self-attribution, the inculcation paradox, the agentic paradox, and the axiological paradox. All these paradoxes are distinct, yet seemingly intertwined. Upon examining them each in turn, we will be left with a Gordian knot of humility paradoxes. I will begin by discussing each paradox in turn.

To unravel this knot, it helps to consider what precisely humility is. In the past decade, a wellspring of new literature has emerged, offering new insight on this old virtue. Between older and more recent scholarship on this virtue, two differing conceptions of humility arise. All of them agree that a central aspect of humility has to do with how one regards oneself. On the first (and perhaps oldest) view, people's humility is based on *how* they assess themselves. Here humility is about having a low self-assessment (either in general or in some particular domain), whereas pride is having a high self-assessment. The second view of humility sees the trait as based not on how one views oneself, but *how often* one considers one's merit, status, or accomplishments. A humble person is inattentive (rather than inaccurate) to one's status. I will argue that this second conception of humility is able to cut the Gordian knot of the paradoxes of humility.

2.2 Paradoxes

It is generally not debated that President Trump likes to brag. One of the most fascinating things he sometimes brags about is his own humility. For example, on CBS's *Face The Nation* he said, "I do have actually much more humility than a lot of people would think" (Dickerson, 2016). On his beloved medium of Twitter, he wrote, "The new Pope is a humble man, very much like me, which probably explains why I like him so much!" (Trump, 2013).

There is something intuitively odd about these boasts. As Alfano and I argue, bragging is about trying to impress others with something about yourself (Alfano and Robinson, 2014).

Humility, regardless of its precise nature, is antithetical to trying to impress someone, either because you don't regard yourself (or the relevant aspect of yourself) as impressive, or because you are not attending to what is impressive about yourself. To humblebrag, as President Trump did in these comments, is to try to impress others with how much you don't regard yourself as impressive.

This leads us to our first paradox of humility, the **self-attribution paradox of humility**. Consider again the utterance by speaker S, "I am *so* humble!" By producing this utterance, S has (typically) generated a paradox based on what S is attributing to herself. S is bragging. Yet, if she is in fact humble, it would seem that *ipso facto* she would not brag. Hence, boasts about one's own humility are *ceteris paribus* false. By attributing humility to herself, S has indicated that she is not humble. Hume appears to recognize this problem when he states, "'Tis impossible a man can at the same time be both proud and humble" (*Treatise* 2.1.1).

This category of paradox is distinct then from paradoxes of self-reference (like the liar paradox) where the paradox is generated in part due to the sentence or utterance referring to itself. For example, "This sentence is false" is paradoxical because the sentence refers to itself. In saying "I'm humble," my utterance does not refer back to itself. Rather, I attribute a characteristic to myself that may be akin to a pragmatic contradiction (like saying, "I don't exist"); if I truly possess that characteristic, I (typically)[1] will not have made the utterance in question. In short, we can put the paradox this way: typically, anyone who says they are humble is not, and anyone who is humble will not say so.

The second paradox is the **epistemic paradox of humility**. Let's assume that knowledge is infallible: something must be true for us to know it. In that case, S cannot know that she is humble unless she is. Yet, if S is humble, then (typically) S cannot know that she is humble; her humility obscures this self-knowledge. This paradox has long been noticed, at least as far back as the sixteenth century, by the Catholic St. Teresa of Avila and the Protestant Martin Luther. Luther notes, "True humility, therefore never knows that it is humble … for if it knew this, it would turn proud from contemplation of so fine a virtue" (Luther, 1956, p. 375). Likewise, St. Teresa remarks that humility (and other virtues) "have the property of hiding themselves from one who possesses them, in such a way that he never sees them nor can believe that he has any of them, even if he be told so" (Avila, 1980, p. 77).

In addition to paradoxes regarding saying or knowing you are humble, there is a similar problem for becoming humble. The Neo-Aristotelian standard account of how one develops a virtue is through habitation (Alfano, 2016, p. 118). As Aristotle puts it,

> But the virtues we get by first practicing them, as we do in the arts. For it is by doing what we ought to do when we study the arts that we learn the arts themselves; we become builders by building and harpists by playing the harp. Similarly, it is by doing just acts that we become just, by doing temperate acts that we become temperate, by doing brave acts that we become brave.
>
> *(Nicomachean Ethics, book II. 1)*

This process of virtue inculcation through habituation requires intentionality. One must intentionally perform just acts in order to be come just. When it comes to humility, however, this process will not work. As Alfano and I argue elsewhere, one cannot intend to become humble (Robinson and Alfano, 2016, p. 439). A humble person typically does not brag, does not seek out praise from others, and demurs when praised. If one sought out praise in order to practice demurring (as a means of becoming humble), one has failed to be humble by seeking out praise from others in the first place. Likewise, someone who intentionally does not brag (knowing she could, but choosing not to) has not performed a humble act, but rather demonstrated false modesty. Humility is not something you can attain by trying. We can call this the **inculcation paradox of humility**.

So far, none of the paradoxes assume anything terribly controversial, I take it, and can be widely accepted. Not everyone, however, may be as willing to recognize the legitimacy of the next two humility paradoxes. They both make various philosophical assumptions that, while not outside the mainstream, are not universally endorsed by philosophers. Consider next the **agentic paradox of humility**. While there remains considerable debate in action theory, it is not uncommon to claim that an action must be intended by an agent in order to count as an action (Davidson, 1980). The problem for humility is that (typically) one cannot intend to act humbly and then successfully do so. You may intend to act humbly, but whatever act you then perform will *not* be a humble act. Rather, such an action would demonstrate false modesty. For example, I have just praised you for a recent accomplishment. You now intend to act humbly by demurring and saying it was "No big deal," and pointing out that it was not as noteworthy as someone else's recent achievement. Based on that intention you act accordingly, but not humbly. You tried too hard, demurring not because you in fact are humble but for some other reason, such as conforming to social expectation. Though more can be said to flesh out this claim, all that is needed at present is to note that something certainly seems paradoxical here. Different views in action theory may work out the full details of this paradox differently, but some kind of paradox will emerge out of most accounts of actions.

Lastly, we have the **axiological paradox of humility**. Humility is often considered a virtue. Virtues are good character traits for a person. Yet humility—as the name implies—requires being humbled, i.e., being brought low, brought down a peg. Being humbled does not appear to be a good state for a person to be in. Simply put interrogatively, how can it be good to be brought low? St. Aquinas noted this same problem with humility in the thirteenth century (Aquinas *ST* II-II, Q 161, A 1).[2] More recently, Baier makes the same point when she remarks,

> Humility as a virtue faces a paradox, namely that the very approval of it seems to threaten to destroy the thing approved. Pride in due pride presents no paradox, and neither does shame for shame, but pride in shame and shame for pride are at best unstable, degenerate cases of reflexivity.
>
> *(1991, p. 216)*

These paradoxes are not, I think, intractable. I follow Burge in being

> guided by the assumption that the paradoxes are best approached as resources for understanding deep and subtle features of our language and concepts, rather than as symptoms of contradiction or incoherence in them. Insofar as the paradoxes are not resolved, they are symptoms of confusion or mistakes in our assumptions about our language and concepts.
>
> *(1984, p. 7)*

2.3 Two theories of humility

Unfortunately, our problems with humility do not end with these paradoxes. There is also a lack of consensus on the basic nature of humility. For many (if not most) virtues, there is general agreement as to what the virtue essentially amounts to. Honesty is about telling the truth. Courage requires responding to danger or fear. Generosity involves giving to others. This is not to say that all the details are worked out, since they are not. How much and under what conditions truth telling, facing of danger, or giving to others are good and virtuous remain important open questions. The point, however, is that for these virtues there is agreement on a basic conceptual framework, upon which we can have these more nuanced debates. The same cannot be said for humility. Though philosophers and theologians have long considered humility, there exists a wide range of views on the nature of this trait.

One of the earliest discussions of humility as a virtue outside of the New Testament comes in the epistle 1 Clement, which was likely composed toward the end of the first century CE and has traditionally been attributed to Clement of Rome (Holmes, 2007, pp. 33–34), stating:

> For Christ belongs to those who are humble-minded, not to those who vaunt themselves over the flock. The scepter of God's majesty, the Lord Jesus Christ, did not come with an ostentatious show of arrogance or haughtiness—even though he could have done so—but with a humble mind, just as the Holy Spirit spoke concerning him.
>
> *(1 Clement 16.1–2)*

While insufficient to extrapolate a theory of morality, Clement says enough for a few points to be noteworthy. First, humility isn't mentioned per se, but being humble-minded appears to be a positive state or characteristic. Second, humility is in some way intellectual in nature, since Clement speaks of being "humble-minded." Lastly, a clear contrast is drawn with the vice of arrogance. A few centuries later, St. Augustine likewise lauded humility in several passages. While one may be able to reconstruct an Augustinian account of humility, doing so would require considerable textual exegesis and theological discussion beyond the scope of this paper. Suffice it to say, Augustine also appears to regard humility as a virtue, though (at least to this author) how precisely Augustine defined humility remains unclear.

A clearer account emerges in Aquinas (though perhaps earlier) and up through the present day. I will now briefly review some of the ancient, modern, and contemporary views on humility. Though we cannot here review in detail the historical development of theories of humility, the various accounts of humility can be, I think, grouped together into two general camps. In the rest of this section, I will canvas some of the views presented on humility, providing examples of thinkers in each group. This canvassing will by no means be an exhaustive account of all the philosophers and theologians to have discussed the virtue. Furthermore, by no means do I mean to suggest that there is unanimity regarding the nature of humility within these two groups; in fact, considerable debate continues within them to this day. Nevertheless, within each group there is consensus regarding the central aspect of what humility amounts to.

2.3.1 First theory: low self-assessment

The first, and perhaps oldest, theory of humility is that it primarily consists in accurately viewing oneself as lowly. Aquinas is one of the chief proponents of the low self-assessment view of humility. He asserts, for example, that "humility, in so far as it is a virtue, conveys the notion of a praiseworthy self-abasement to the lowest place" (*ST* II-II, Q 161, A 1, ad. 2). To be humble, as Aquinas sees it, is to see oneself as low, base, beneath God, and other humans. Others are superior, either generally or in some specific ways. This low self-assessment is not, however, some mere delusion. "It is possible, *without falsehood*" he contends, "to deem and avow oneself the most despicable of men … [and] avow and believe oneself in all ways unprofitable and useless in respect of one's own capability" (*ST* II-II, Q 161, A 6, ad. 1; emphasis mine). The humble person correctly assesses her or his lowly status in relations to others.

Not surprisingly, this view of humility is widespread and perhaps is the most common. Hume—though rejecting humility as one of the "monkish virtues" that "serve no purpose" (*EPM* 9.1)—is generally taken to regard humility in a similar manner, since he speaks of one's idea of oneself as "dejected with humility" (*Treatise* 2.1.2) and appears to think humiliation is necessary for humility (c.f., Davie, 1999, p. 146).[3]

Other contemporary theories limit the focus, shifting from one's low status in general to something more specific, such as one's limitations. Snow, for example, takes this view, arguing,

> To be a humble person is to recognize your limitations, to take them seriously, and thereby to foster a realism in attitudes and behavior regarding self and others. Humility can be defined as the disposition to allow the awareness of and concern about your limitations to have a realistic influence on your attitudes and behavior. At the heart of this realism is a perspective gained through accurate appraisal of your limitations and their implications for your circumstances, attitudes, and behavior.
>
> *(Snow, 1995, p. 210)*

Whitcomb, Battaly, Baehr, and Howard-Snyder focus on intellectual humility specifically, which the regard as "proper attentiveness to, and owning of, one's intellectual limitations" (2017, p. 12). Prima facie, these accounts of humility make it look different than Aquinas's or others in this group, since they do not require one to have a low self-assessment in comparison to someone or something else. For Aquinas, for instance, one should be humbled and humble before the greatness of God. For Whitcomb et al., however, the comparison is instead with some idealized version of oneself, one without the limitations one actually has. So according to Whitcomb et al., my humility consists primarily in recognizing that I'm not as physically strong as I might wish or that I am prone to certain errors in thinking that I might otherwise delude myself in denying. For this reason, their view of humility also falls in the low, accurate self-assessment category.

Another noteworthy variant of this view agrees that humility requires low self-assessment, but this self-assessment is mistaken. The humble person underestimates herself. Spinoza, for example, appears to espouse an inaccurate, low self-assessment view of humility. First, to establish how a humble person views herself, Spinoza says, "Humility is pain arising from a man's contemplation of his own weakness of body or mind" (*E* III, P 26). The inaccuracy of this self-assessment becomes clear when we consider what, according to Spinoza, humility gives rise to.

> We can, therefore, set down as a contrary to pride an emotion which I will call self-abasement, for as from self-complacency springs pride, so from humility springs self-abasement, which I will accordingly thus define: Self-abasement is thinking too meanly of one's self by reason of pain (*E* III, P 28, Exp – P29).

The inaccuracy and pain are precisely why Spinoza then concludes that "humility is not a virtue" (*E* IV, P 53). More recently, Driver calls modesty a virtue of ignorance, where "a modest person underestimates self-worth" (2004, p. 16). Though her theory is purportedly about modesty, "humility is closely akin to modesty," she notes (Driver, 2004, p. 114).[4]

2.3.2 Second theory: inattentive

More recently, an alternative conception of humility has begun to emerge. It is distinct from the first since it does not require one to regard oneself as lowly or limited. Rather, humility consists in being inattentive to one's own status, i.e., not engaging in self-admiration of one's merits or status or accomplishments because one does not spend much time thinking about oneself at all.

The farthest back I have been able to trace this inattentive theory of humility is to Sidgwick's *The Method of Ethics* (1874). First, he considers the low self-assessment view of humility—which he dubs the "common sense" view—and rejects it. "It seems, then, that the common account of Humility is erroneous" (1874, p. 312). We will return shortly to his reason for rejecting this view. For now, consider the conception of humility he offers instead. He writes,

> Humility is regulative of two different impulses, one entirely self-regarding and internal, the other relating to others and partly taking effect in social behaviour. The internal duty relates, strictly speaking, not to the opinions we form of ourselves (for here as in other opinions we ought to aim at nothing but Truth), but to the emotion of self-admiration, which springs naturally from the contemplation of our own merits, and as it is highly agreeable, prompts to such contemplation … . [T]he duty of Humility needs enforcing because most of us have a tendency to indulge this feeling [of self-approbation] overmuch … Humility prescribes such repression of self-satisfaction.
>
> *(Sidgwick, 1874, pp. 312–313)*

Humility, as Sidgwick understands it, is about limiting one's sense of self-satisfaction or self-admiration, regardless of one's status or merit about which one could admire.

Since Sidgwick, the inattentive view has appeared to grow in popularity. C. S. Lewis espoused it when he writes,

> [The humble man] will not be thinking about humility: he will not be thinking about himself at all. If anyone would like to acquire humility, I can, I think, tell him the first step. The first step is to realise that one is proud… If you think you are not conceited, it means you are very conceited indeed.
>
> *(Lewis, 1952, p. 71)*

More recently still, this view is endorsed by Tangney (2000), Roberts and Wood (2003, 2007), Garcia (2006), and Robinson and Alfano (2016). Similarly, Nadelhoffer et al. assert, "[B]eing humble doesn't require us to hold ourselves in low regard (or in a lower regard than is merited). Instead, humility merely requires us to avoid thinking too highly of ourselves" (2017, p. 10). They call this the "decentered and devoted" view of humility, the idea being that humble people are both not centered on themselves (and their own praiseworthiness) *and also* devoted to others. This second component is typically absent in the other inattentive views, which focus only not being centered on oneself. Whether devotion to others is a central component of humility or merely a very likely consequent of it remains an open question, but the key point is that a clear family resemblance between these views exists to warrant grouping them together despite underlying differences.

2.4 Resolving the paradoxes

Of these two different conceptions of virtue, my objective is not to reject one over the other. Christen, Alfano, and Robinson (2014, 2017) employ a psycholexical method to analyze intellectual humility and find both conceptions in how a thesaurus tracks usage of the concept. This method is meant as a proxy for folk usage, indicating that it is common to understand and talk of humility in both ways. Likewise, Alfano et al. (2017) developed and validated a psychological measure of intellectual humility that includes both views as different factors of the virtue.

Nevertheless, it can be fruitful to consider how each view handles the knot of prima facie paradoxes of humility previously discussed. This analysis is not meant to settle which of the two views is meant by 'humility,' but rather which of the two is perhaps more conceptually robust by avoiding or resolving the paradoxes.

Of the two general views on humility, the inattentive view is better equipped to handle each of these paradoxes. Sidgwick notes the shortcomings of the low self-assessment account of humility. Just before laying out his explanation of humility as inattention, he writes,

> For it is generally said that Humility prescribes a low opinion of our own merits: but if our merits are comparatively high, it seems strange to direct us to have a low opinion of them. It may be replied, that though our merits may be high when compared with those of ordinary men, there are always some to be found superior, and we can compare ourselves with these, and in the extreme case with ideal excellence, of which all fall far short: and that we ought to make this kind of comparison and not the other kind, and contemplate our faults of which we shall assuredly find a sufficiency and not our merits. But surely in the most important deliberations which human life offers, in determining what kind of work we shall undertake and to what social functions we shall aspire, we must necessarily compare our qualifications carefully with those of other men, if we are to decide rightly. And it would seem just as irrational to underrate ourselves as to overrate: and though most men are more prone to the latter mistake, there are certainly some rather inclined to the former.
>
> *(Sidgwick, 1874, p. 312)*

Sidgwick is objecting to the low self-assessment account of humility as inherently paradoxical. What exactly he considers to be the problem with this view is hard to formulate precisely, but perhaps we can help him out now that we have more clearly delineated the different paradoxes of humility. The central question is whether one's humble self-assessment must be accurate or not. As we saw, various thinkers have advocated for two versions of the low self-assessment theory, where the low self-assessment is either accurate or inaccurate. On the one hand, if one's humble self-assessment is (or must be) wrong—because one's merits are actually "comparatively high"—then we run into the epistemic paradox. One's belief, in this case, that one has low merits or status is false; therefore, one can never *know* that one has humility. Sidgwick considers this "irrational" and detrimental, since we need accurate self-assessment to determine what we should do with our lives and how to function in society. On the other hand, if one's humble self-assessment is accurate, then we run into the axiological paradox. In this case, one's self-assessment is correct, but it is unclear what is good or virtuous about being in and aware of this state. To these points, we can add an extra consideration Sidgwick does not address. Either way, the paradox of self-attribution still applies. If my self-assessment must be inaccurate to be true and I say that I am humble, then I have not inaccurately assessed my own meritorious character. Alternatively, if my self-assessment must be accurate to be true and I say that I am humble, then I am bragging about my lowliness.

Sidgwick was not alone in seeing trouble for the low self-attribution views. Nadelhoffer et al. make a similar point when they remark, "One of the driving forces behind people's unease about humility is the (we believe mistaken) assumption that being humble requires us to undervalue (even loathe) ourselves and underestimate our own capabilities" (2017, p. 8). Lewis, in his epistolary novel *The Screwtape Letters* (which contains letters from the demon Screwtape to the demon Wormwood tasked with tempting and corrupting an unnamed man), presents the problems thusly:

> Your patient has become humble; have you drawn his attention to the fact? All virtues are less formidable to us once the man is aware that he has them, but this is specially true of humility. Catch him at the moment when he is really poor in spirit and smuggle into his mind the gratifying reflection, "By jove! I'm being humble," and almost immediately pride—pride at his own humility—will appear. If he awakes to the danger and tries to smother this new form of pride, make him proud of his attempt.
>
> *(Lewis, 1942, p. 58)*

In addition to expressing the paradoxical nature of the low self-assessment views of humility, this passage also points to how the inattentive view of humility can unravel the Gordian knot of paradoxes. The key is to begin with the epistemic paradox. We will assume that humility amounts to inattention to one's merit. In that case, it is not impossible for a humble person to know that she is humble. Such a belief will not typically occur to her, so she will typically lack the *occurrent* belief that she is humble. Still, as Robinson and Alfano (2016) argue, she is disposed to believe (and know) that she is humble (since she is). This dispositional belief, however, rarely becomes occurent; it usually does not occur to her that she is humble. When this does occur to her, it typically is due to external prompting by a third party. A humble person does not typically spend much time considering her merit and praiseworthiness. If, for some reason, you are determined to convince her that she is humble and point to ample behavioral evidence of her humility, she can truthfully, occurrently believe and know that she is humble. But then she will quickly move on and go back to being merely disposed to believe she is humble (when told by others that she is). The paradox is resolved. The knowledge of one's own humility is not impossible; it just rarely occurs.

From here, the self-attribution paradox follows the same path. If a humble person does not attend to her own humility (because she is typically only disposed to believe she is humble), then she will not say that she is humble. This is not to say she never can accurately attribute humility to herself. Again, if you go to great length to prove to her that she is humble, then she can reluctantly admit that she is humble without a paradox. As Robinson and Alfano (2016) point out, however, such self-attribution usually has to be first prompted by a third party. The main point though is that for the inattentive theory of humility, this paradox is resolved. It is not that a humble person cannot truthfully attribute humility to herself; it's that she typically would not.

Two paradoxes down, three to go. The inculcation paradox raises the problem of how to train people to be humble. If they try to become humble, it would seem they would necessarily fail. This paradox, I think, remains the most problematic, but it is not intractable. Robinson and Alfano (2016) have considered this problem at length, drawing lessons from the Chinese virtue of *wu-wei*, which roughly translates as "dynamic, effortless, and unselfconscious state of mind of a person who is optimally active and effective" (Slingerland, 2014, p. 7). Almost by definition, one cannot try to achieve *wu-wei*, yet Confucian and Doaist thinkers developed several indirect strategies to achieve this virtuous state. In the same way, Robinson and Alfano (2016) argue part of the solution is to develop and promote rituals of demurring when praised by others and to encourage praising of others. Such rituals indirectly inculcate humility and simultaneously discourage false modesty by making false modesty too costly to be worth the social benefit of seeming to be humble.

Regarding the agentic paradox, it is correct that one cannot intend to be humble, just as one cannot try act humbly, just as one cannot try to try. Indeed, trying to act humbly merely results in false modesty.[5] This does not mean, however, that one therefore cannot act humbly. To act humbly, according to the inattentive account of humility, is to act in such a way that one does not attend to one's own merit or praiseworthiness, especially when one easily could do so. Acting humbly is not something you do directly. Rather, you act humbly by not doing certain actions (e.g., boasting, showing off, or flexing) because you are doing something else instead, often some other-oriented action, such as praising or helping someone else.

Lastly, we can consider perhaps the most important of paradoxes of humility, the axiological paradoxes. Why is humility good? On the low self-assessment view, we are forced to say one of three things: that it is good to have an accurate self-assessment of one's lowly status, that it is good to falsely believe one has a low status, or humility is not good. The inattentive conception of humility offers a different, non-contradictory resolution to the paradox. Humility is good because it is the inattention to our own merit or status. If we are not paying attention to ourselves and our own praiseworthiness, we are freed up to pay attention to more morally important considerations, such as the needs or praiseworthiness of others.

Notes

1 There are special cases in which a humble person can be induced to utter, "I'm humble," without producing a paradox of self-attribution. I will address these below.

2 I suspect that there may be a separate, sixth paradox regarding motivation, specifically regarding an apparent lack of motivation to be humble (or to be humbled, which appears to be necessary to be humble), even granting that humility is good or a virtue. This paradox would likely assume some form of motivational externalism. Attempts to formulate the paradox have so far, however, collapsed into standard problems with motivational externalism (and therefore are not problems unique to humility) or collapsed into one of the other five paradoxes.

3 Burch (1975) disputes this claim, arguing that Hume (at least in *An Enquiry Concerning the Principles of Morals*) considers humility to be a passion, not a character trait.

4 Driver does draw a distinction between humility and modesty. A humble person, she argues, can accurately assess his or her lowly state, while a modest person must underestimate her merit.

5 See (Robinson and Alfano, 2016) for the distinction between humility, modesty, and false modesty.

References

Alfano, M. (2016). *Moral Psychology: An Introduction*. Cambridge, MA: Polity Press. doi:10.1002/9780470696132. Chapter 5.

Alfano, M., Iurino, K., Stey, P., Robinson, B., Christen, M., Yu, F., and Lapsley, D. (2017). Development and Validation of a Multi-Dimensional Measure of Intellectual Humility. *PloS one*, *12*(8), e0182950. doi:10.1371/journal.pone.0182950.

Alfano, M., and Robinson, B. (2014). Bragging. *Thought: A Journal of Philosophy*, *3*(4), 263–272. doi:10.1002/tht3.141.

Aristotle. (1926). Nicomachean Ethics (H. Rackham, Trans.). Cambridge, MA: Harvard University Press.

Avila, S.T. (1980). *The Collected Works of St. Teresa of Avila, Vol. 2 (featuring The Way of Perfection and The Interior Castle)*, O. Rodriguez and K. Kavanaugh, (Trans.). Washington, DC: ICS Publications.

Baier, A. C. (1991). *A Progress of Sentiments: Reflections on Hume's Treatise*. Cambridge, MA: Harvard University Press.

Burch, R. W. (1975). Hume on Pride and Humility. *The New Scholasticism*, *49* (2), 177–188.

Burge, T. (1984). Epistemic Paradox. *The Journal of Philosophy*, *81*(1), 5–29.

Christen, M., Alfano, M., and Robinson, B. (2014). The Semantic Space of Intellectual Humility. *CEUR Workshop Proceedings: Proceedings of the European Conference on Social Intelligence*, *1283*, 40–49.

Christen, M., Alfano, M., and Robinson, B. (2017). A Cross-Cultural Assessment of the Semantic Dimensions of Intellectual Humility. *AI and Society*, 1–17. doi:10.1007/s00146-017-0791-7.

Davidson, D. (1980). *Essays on Actions and Events*. Oxford: Oxford University Press.

Davie, W. (1999). Hurne on Monkish Virtues. *Hume Studies*, *XXV*(1), 139–154.

Dickerson, J. (Host). (2016). Face The Nation. CBS.
Driver, J. (2004). *Uneasy Virtue*. Cambridge, UK: Cambridge University Press.
Ehrman, Bart D. (trans. and ed.). (2003). Clement 16.1–2. *The Apostolic Fathers: I Clement, II Clement, Ignatius, Polycarp, Didache*. Cambridge, MA: Harvard University Press, 62–63.
Garcia, J. L. A. (2006). Being Unimpressed with Ourselves: Reconceiving Humility. *Philosophia, 34*(4), 417–435.
Holmes, M.W. (2007). *The Apostolic Fathers: Greek Texts and English Translations* (3rd Edition). Grand Rapids, MI: Baker Academic.
Lewis, C. S. (1942). *The Screwtape Letters* (1961 Edition). New York: Touchstone.
Lewis, C. S. (1952). *Mere Christianity*. London: Geoffrey Bles.
Luther, M. (1956). *Luther's Works, Volume 21. (Sermon on the Mount and the Magnificat)*. St. Louis, MO: Concordia.
Nadelhoffer, T., Wright, J. C., Echols, M., Perini, T., and Venezia, K. (2017). Some Varieties of Humility Worth Wanting. *Journal of Moral Philosophy, 14*(2), 168–200. doi:10.1163/17455243-46810056.
Roberts, R. C., and Wood, W. J. (2003). Humility and Epistemic Goods. In: *Intellectual Virtue: Perspectives From Ethics and Epistemology*, L. Zagzebski and M. DePaul (Eds.). Oxford, UK: Oxford University Press.
Roberts, R. C., and Wood, W. J. (2007). *Intellectual Virtues: An Essay in Regulative Epistemology*. Oxford, UK: Oxford University Press.
Robinson, B., and Alfano, M. (2016). I Know You Are, But What am I? Anti-Individualism in the Development of Intellectual Humility and Wu-wei. *Logos & Episteme, 4*, 435–459.
Sidgwick, H. (1874). *The Method of Ethics*. London: Macmillan and Co.
Spinoza, B. (2018). The Ethics (R. H. M. Elwes, Trans.). New York: Dover Publications.
Slingerland, E. (2014). *Trying Not to Try*. New York: Crown.
Snow, N. E. (1995). Humility. *The Journal of Value Inquiry*, 29(2), 203–216.
Tangney, J. P. (2000). Humility: Theoretical Perspectives, Empirical Findings and Directions for Future Research. *Journal of Social and Clinical Psychology, 19*(1), 70–82. doi:10.1521/jscp.2000.19.1.70.
Trump, Donald. [@realDonaldTrump]. (2013, December 25). The New Pope Is a Humble Man, Very Much Like Me, Which Probably Explains Why I Like Him so Much! Retrieved from https://twitter.com/realdonaldtrump/status/415868924841189376?lang=en.
Whitcomb, D., Battaly, H., Baehr, J., and Howard-Snyder, D. (2017). Intellectual Humility: Owning Our Limitations. *Philosophy and Phenomenological Research*, 94(3), 509–539. doi:10.1111/phpr.12228.

3
HUMILITY IS NOT A VIRTUE

Paul Bloomfield

3.1 Introduction

There are a few concepts of folk psychology which have confounded us so much over the centuries that they have undergone significant evolutions of meaning and application.[1] Which of shame and guilt is public and which is private? "Sympathy" had different meanings for Hume and Smith. *Dignity* was once only for the noble classes, but when egalitarianism emerged in the Enlightenment, it was found that everyone had it (Waldron, 2012). More radically, "condescension" has gone through an inversion of meaning, as it was first a virtue implying, in Samuel Johnson's words, "a voluntary submission to equality with inferiors", but has since turned into a negative trait implying contempt for those "beneath" one (Appiah, 2018).[2] "Humility" is also a word with roots involving socio-economic class, and it has undergone a similar inversion of meaning, though in the opposite direction: humility has changed from being thought of as a negative trait to being a virtue. In the West, humility began to be commonly thought of as a virtue at the start of the Common Era, and it has been commonplace to think of it in that way since. Augustine even hailed humility as "the foundation of all the other virtues".

Consider, however, that while it may have been just and wise for a leader of a long-oppressed people, as Jesus was, to preach humility as a virtue to everyone who would listen (especially Romans), this does not imply that it is always equally just and wise to preach humility as virtue. It is, for example, insidiously pernicious and evil for oppressors to preach humility as a virtue to those whom they oppress: "Work sets you free", it said over the gate at Auschwitz. Or, as Frederick Douglass notes:

> I have met, at the south, many good, religious colored people who were under the delusion that God required them to submit to slavery and to wear their chains with meekness and humility. I could entertain no such nonsense as this.
>
> *(1892, p. 105)*

Humility can be a tool of moral improvement, but it can also be an instrument of subjugation, a means of social control to maintain an unjust status quo. Humility is always politically conservative. Rebellion, however well-justified, is almost impossible in a climate too rich in humility. Feeling humility is related to feeling humiliation, a horrible feeling with which oppressed people are all too familiar. Humility is indeed the overriding characteristic of the servile: they willingly accept less than their fair share, habitually defer to others, and fail to stand up for themselves. This is the worst case, but there are more frequently times when it is wrong to show humility, wrong to be deferential. Speaking truth to power, or engaging in civil disobedience more generally, should be done respectfully, but people who have the clear moral high ground have no need of moral humility, at least on that point. When speaking truth to power, one ought to look power in the eye. When Martin Luther King, Jr. (1963) responded to white, moderate clergymen by saying, "I cannot sit idly by …" and "Injustice anywhere is injustice everywhere", he did so without humility, but rather as a clarion call and with well-founded rectitude. It is hard to see humility in a thoroughly positive light given how morally inappropriate it can be. Morality does not defer to power. Were it not so, Yogi Berra couldn't have quipped, "It ain't the heat, it's the humility". Humility is often far from what is noble and fine (*to kalon*) and because it can lead us morally astray, it is wrong to think of it as a virtue.

It is cliché to point out that power corrupts and success breeds contempt. Nevertheless, this is true, and humility is needed to bring the powerful and successful back to earth, to remind people that we all began as helpless babies, that we are never more nor less than human, all too human. Compared to what is possible, we are all highly fallible, puny creatures. Almost certainly, there is too little humility in the world and everyone would be better off if there were a great deal more of it. Importantly: *arguing that humility is not a virtue is not to argue that it has no moral value or that it is always bad or a vice.* On the contrary, even among peers, humility is often of great value: it is the pin in the balloon of our egos, the deflation of our pomposity. And, in fact, many of us are in far greater need of it than we like to think or hope. But despite this paean, and however much humility may be in short supply, we ought to follow Bishop Butler's advice and see it for what it is and not another thing (1900, p. 18).

In pursuit of the thesis that humility is not a virtue, what follows is a negative program and a positive one. The negative will explain why humility is not a virtue, while the positive thesis defends an alternative account of the trait, set within a broader virtue theory, wherein *humility* naturally does the same sort of work as *continence*, which is not a virtue in the classical tradition. Thus: as continence is to incontinence, humility is to arrogance. And as temperance is the virtue toward which continence is merely an intermediary step, justice is the virtue toward which humility leads the arrogant. On this view, humility is "a corrective", something to be prescribed only to those who have already moved away from the virtue of justice and are already engaged in arrogance to one degree or another.[3]

3.2 Why humility is not a virtue

As noted at the outset, the history of humility is complicated. The word for it was originally derogatory and implied submissiveness and lack of self-reliance. "Humilitas" in Latin translates from the Greek ταπεινός, "tapeinos", which means "groveling" or "lowly"; its antonym, "kalon", was "nobility". Humility was the just and appropriate attitude to adopt for those who are "inferior" when faced with their "betters". So, at first blush, we may say that humility is originally understood as a character trait, with attending feelings or a particular phenomenology, which inhibits assertive behavior and yields deference: the humble defer to the noble.[4] It therefore had only negative connotations. And while presented in the Old Testament as the correct attitude to have toward God, who is infinitely our superior, it was not seen as a virtue to be humble before other people or nations. (Indeed, the Jewish dogma of being "the chosen people" is far from humility.) This negative view of having "humble origins" changed most dramatically when Jesus exalted the lowly in his Sermon on the Mount:

> Blessed are the poor in spirit; the kingdom of heaven is theirs.
>
> Blessed are the sorrowful; they shall find consolation.
>
> Blessed are the gentle [the humble, the meek], they shall have the earth for their possession …
>
> You have heard that they were told, 'An eye for an eye, a tooth for a tooth.' But what I tell you is this: Do not resist those who wrong you. If anyone slaps you on the right cheek, turn and offer him the other also … If someone in authority presses you into service for one mile, go with him two.
>
> *(1989, Matthew, 5: 5, 38–41)*

However reassuring this may be to the hopelessly powerless, it is striking how it contravenes ordinary notions of social justice: *do not resist those who wrong you?* (What would Jesus have said about the ancient [even in his day] slavery of Jews in Egypt? Should the Jews have built an extra pyramid? Was Moses wrong to resist?) In any case, faith in divine justice inverted the moral status of *humility*, and what was once derogatory, i.e., accepting one's inferior place, became laudatory. Humility became good because God will make it right in the end.

If God exists, then justice rightly demands humility before God. As Kant says, "We have reason to harbour a low opinion of our person … For if we compare ourselves with the holy moral law, we discover how remote we are from congruity with it" (1997, p. 129 [27:348f]).[5] This seems all the more true if one accepts the doctrine of Original Sin. But leaving God and Original Sin out of the picture, what would "humility" mean if we stripped away its theistic crust? Is there anything virtuous left? We no longer need to feel humility all the time because we are originally sinful or because we are always under the watchful eye of God. Were there inherently superior beings amongst us, it would be right and just to feel humility in front of them, but among fellow human beings, no such superior people exist. Whatever rightly inspires awe in nature, rightly leaves us feeling humility.[6] But there is nothing like this in the social or interpersonal realm. From the Enlightenment on, theists and atheists alike have wanted to justify a moral and egalitarian attitude to be shared by all human beings, and this implies a baseline equality among us, a "least common denominator". Orthogonal to theism, in contemporary times justice, human rights and the inherent dignity of humanity are founded upon the idea that we are all, fundamentally, equally deserving of respect and that no one is inherently superior to anyone else.

Since the early modern period, there have been a few critiques of humility's status as a virtue. Hume (1975) famously dismisses humility as one of the "monkish virtues", along with celibacy and mortification, among others, while Nietzsche (1989) made it a feature of "slave morality". A reasonable (though flatfooted) reading of Sidgwick (1907), taken up by Anscombe (1958), has him doubting that humility is a virtue because it requires people to underrate themselves. (James Wardle [1983] later disputes this reading of Sidgwick.) However, a more subtle, incisive, and telling critique comes from Mary Wollstonecraft, from a chapter of *A Vindication of the Rights of Women* (1995) entitled, "Modesty. – Comprehensively Considered, and Not as a Sexual Virtue", where she writes,

> [I]n defining modesty, it appears to me equally proper to discriminate that purity of mind, which is the effect of chastity, from a simplicity of character that leads us to form a just opinion of ourselves, equally distant from vanity or presumption, though by no means incompatible with a lofty consciousness of our own dignity. Modesty, in the latter signification of the term, is, that soberness of mind which teaches a man not to

> think more highly of himself than he ought to think, and should be distinguished from humility, because humility is a kind of self-abasement.
>
> *(p. 207)*

We have already noted how the idea of having "a just opinion of ourselves" is best captured by the virtue of justice, more so, quite arguably, than modesty (or humility). Importantly, however, Wollstonecraft's understanding of humility has been taken up by contemporary usage, regardless of how it is considered by philosophers and theologians. The *Oxford English Dictionary* first defines it as "The quality of being humble or having a lowly opinion of oneself", and secondly defines it in terms of "self-abasement". If we follow common usage, humility is certainly not a virtue.

Turning now to contemporary accounts of *humility*, there is much to be learned from them. Most of this literature is on intellectual humility, but there seems little reason to think that there should be any significant differences between intellectual and moral humility. The currently dominant view appears to have first been voiced by Norvin Richards (1988), who argues that humility is having a proper perspective on oneself. Nancy Snow (1995, p. 210) defines it as "the disposition to allow the awareness of and concern about [one's] limitations to have a realistic influence on [one's] attitudes and behavior". Allan Hazlett's (2017) view is that intellectual humility is excellence in attributing to oneself ignorance and other intellectual flaws, failings, or limitations, while Dennis Whitcomb, Heather Battaly, Jason Baehr, and Daniel Howard-Snyder (2015) jointly defend the claim that intellectual humility is the virtue of owning one's intellectual limitations. Presumably, moral humility is the generalization of the trait just described: the idea of knowing one's limitations, and having this knowledge affect judgment and action. For ease of reference, this view will be referred to as the "OL" view, for "owning limitations".

The start of a critique of the OL view begins with a purely analytic point: the greatest worry about the OL view is that it seems to describe half a trait while ignoring the other half. And as soon as we put both halves together, we end up with something that cannot be considered *humility* any longer. The problem is that accurately knowing one's limitations also entails accurately knowing one's strengths and competences. Analytically, there is not one without the other. It certainly does not seem virtuous to own one's limitations and yet fail at owning one's strengths. If the glass is half empty, it is apt to acknowledge the emptiness, but it makes no sense to do so without acknowledging the half which is full. We cannot know what we do not do well without being able to distinguish this from what we can do well. But if we put both parts of this self-knowledge together, we no longer have humility. "Trust me, I'm good at this" does not sound very humble. What is the virtue which informs us with an accurate picture of ourselves, including our limitations and our strengths, our weaknesses and our competences? Again, it is not humility but justice.

Try replacing the word "humility" with "justice" in the formulations of the OL view, and one ends up with a smooth and natural read. To take a few examples, first, here is a sentence of Richards with "justice" substituted for "humility": "Justice doesn't require that you take no pride at all in what you've done, but only that you take less pride than a far greater accomplishment" (1988, p. 255). Next, here are three sentences of Whitcomb, Battaly, Baehr, and Howard-Snyder, which are meant to show the plausibility of the OL view, substituting "justice" for "intellectual humility": "Justice increases a person's propensity to admit his intellectual limitations to himself and others"; "Justice reduces a person's propensity to blame and explain-away when confronting her own intellectual shortcomings"; and "Justice increases a person's propensity to defer to others who don't have her intellectual limitations, in situations that call upon those limitations"

(2015, pp. 13–14.) In the following section, more reasons will be given for thinking that these theorists have mistaken justice for humility.

Here, however, is a *reductio ad absurdum* for the view that humility is a virtue. Following tradition, as well as Martha Nussbaum (1988) and Christine Swanton (2003), let us assume that each virtue has a particular "range" or "field of action" in which it operates. So, for example, courage ranges over all dangerous situations and the courageous thing to do in any dangerous situation is the correct thing to do. Let's assume, for the sake of argument, that humility is a virtue and that the OL view of it is correct. Humility therefore ranges over all situations in which owning one's limitations becomes salient, such that the correct thing to do is to act humbly.[7] Now, consider "Tank Man", the unidentified man who stood, with food bags in hand, in front of Chinese tanks in Tiananmen Square on 5 June 1989. Let's assume that the Chinese government intended to instill humility and obedience in the protesters by sending tanks to confront them. Let's also assume that Tank Man already possessed the virtue of humility: he is well-aware of his limitations and weaknesses, he defers when apt, tempers his beliefs, etc.

Now, Tank Man finds himself in a situation in which he is (for whatever reason) uniquely well-placed to play a role in the demonstrations by walking in front of the tanks. Tank Man has no reason to think he can stop the tanks which could crush him, but thinks something like the following, "Despite my frailty in the face of this overwhelming force [acknowledging his limitations], still, the right thing to do now is speak truth to power". Let's assume that this was the morally correct and virtuous thing to do. And yet, whatever else was true of his action, there is simply no way to consider Tank Man's stepping in front of the tanks as an action motivated by humility.[8] It might be heroic, it might be reckless, it might be just or even arrogant, but it surely was not humble. Given all this, consider the following argument:

1. Humility is the virtue which ranges over all circumstances involving the owning of one's limitations. (Call these "L-situations".)
2. So, in any L-situation, the humble thing to do is the right thing to do.
3. When Chinese tanks confronted the protesters, it was an L-situation for the protesters.
4. The right to do in this L-situation was to block the tanks with one's body.
5. Blocking the path of a tank with only one's body is not being humble.
6. So, when tanks were in Tiananmen Square, the humble thing for Tank Man to have done was to not be humble (from 2 and 5). (*Reductio*).

The argument gains its purchase because there are times when it is actually wrong to act with genuine humility, even in circumstances which involve owning one's limitations.[9] Notice that structurally analogous arguments cannot be constructed for, e.g., courage or justice, as there are never situations that fall within the range of these virtues in which one ought not to be courageous or just. Virtues are supposed to always yield correct action: if they did not give this normative assurance, we would have no reason to be investigating them. Situations in which it is morally correct and virtuous to speak truth to power, such as the one Tank Man found himself within, are those in which people ought *not* to act with humility. Acting with humility in such situations is a manifestation of having "too much humility". If we accept that humility can sometimes be a virtue and sometimes not be a virtue, then we cannot rely on it for normative guidance in any particular situation: some other trait or value, besides humility, must inform us as to when humility is morally correct and when it is not. If having humility is not always the right way to be in situations in which we must own our limitations, then it is not humility itself which makes acting with humility sometimes be the virtuous action. Even if we want to say that only "appropriate humility" is virtuous, it is still not humility *per se* which determines when it is apt, and we need some other criteria to help us determine what to do, such as relying on positive outcomes. But a move such as this amounts to consequentialism and, in effect, we are no longer treating virtue ethics as its own normative theory.

Would space permit, there are other arguments that question the status of humility as a virtue. One argument concerns the acquisition of virtue and focuses on the differences in how humility is learned compared with other virtues: the basis of humility is found in making mistakes and failing, as opposed to, e.g., how learning to be courageous is modeled on learning carpentry (Aristotle, 2000, 1103a30–b2). Another argument looks into the oftentimes unpleasant phenomenology of humility, its relationship with humiliation, and how uncharacteristic such unpleasantness is for virtue. Unfortunately, space does not permit, so this concludes the negative program for why humility is not a virtue.

3.3 Humility as a corrective

Once we secularize the justification of morality, then as long as you and I socially engage with each other as free and mutually respecting equals, humility will only become desirable when our equality is breached by one of us taking an inappropriately superior attitude toward another. Humility ought to then step in and check the problem, like a palliative antidote to a social poison. Friends, real friends, like Aristotle's "virtue friends" (2000, book 8), have no use for humility in front of each other, because such friends are necessarily equals. The lesson, abstracted from this context, is that we ought not to feel humility in front of people whom we see as being no better than us. Or, to put this same point the other way around, whenever people treat each other with mutual respect and good will, when people are fair, moral, and just to each other, humility is otiose.

So, when everyone is respecting each other's equality, humility is not just superfluous but actually inappropriate. Nevertheless, we should expect any viable theory of humility to be able to explain all the praise it has received from saints and philosophers over the centuries, and this is easy to account for. For it is common to find people being inappropriately partial to themselves and/or to those they love and, given free rein (say by a ring of invisibility), most people are generally ready to arrogate as much as they can from life.[10] In Greek, this is the all-too-common vice of *pleonexia*, often translated as "greed". It is the trait associated with arrogation, or taking more than one's fair share, and contrasted to the virtue of justice, or *dikaiosunē*. Now, if arrogance were a necessary feature of human psychology, humility would then be needed by everyone, which (for reasons to be discussed below) would count in favor of it being a virtue. (Compare this with the way that everyone feels fear and to that degree everyone requires courage.) But, like all vices, arrogance is only contingent among humans (Aristotle, 2000, 1103a24–5). Nevertheless, those who become arrogant are morally in need of a corrective, a counter-balance, something which brings them back to a fair and just standing with everyone else. Secularized humility serves the important psychological purpose of keeping arrogance in check. This is not, however, sufficient to make it a virtue (also to be discussed below).[11]

One might worry that, if humility is not a virtue, any alternative account of it must be ad hoc, but this is not the case. Virtue theory already has a structure carved out into which humility naturally fits. This is to appeal to unnoticed analogies obtaining between humility and continence. But in traditional virtue theory, continence is not thought of as a virtue (Aristotle, 2000, 1145a15–17).[12] The category of trait into which continence fits was not given a name by Aristotle, but as noted above, since it is supposed to correct for incontinence, we can call it a "corrective" (see Notes 3 and 6 above). One might wonder why continence does not count as a virtue, and the answer is that, in the field of action in which continence and incontinence arises, temperance is the virtue. Continence is not an excellence, but rather more like a stop-gap measure to overcome incontinence. Incontinence is one form of intemperance, where the other is wanton self-indulgence. Incontinence is when temptation becomes too great to resist and our desires (including appetites and passions) gain mastery over us: we do what we know we ought not to do. Incontinent people are compelled by desire for what tempts them to yield to it, regardless of how misguided, inappropriate, or excessive the desire may be. Temperance is the virtue of not being tempted by what one ought not to be tempted by: temperate people distinguish good pleasures from bad ones and are not even tempted by the bad. Thus, insofar as people are temperate, they have no need of continence and are free to indulge their desires because their desires are always appropriate.[13]

Continence is employed by those who are wont to be incontinent, as a means of resisting inappropriate temptations and doing the right thing when it is difficult to do so. It is needed when a person is not "of one mind" about some X but rather both wants X and wants to not want X. Practiced to excess, continence itself can become the vice of rigid abstinence, dour bitterness, or even self-flagellating asceticism. Despite the possibility of this vice, continence can certainly be aligned with virtue if it is directed at only inappropriate desires, since continent people do what temperate people do, but they do so while fighting with themselves about it instead of acting whole-heartedly or with integrity. So, continence is not an excellent state in which to be; rather, the excellent state is the well-tempered one in which a person is "of one mind" and therefore does not need continence at all. Continence can be seen as a stepping-stone on the way to temperance: those who are not already virtuous need continence, and it is one of the ways by which we learn to be temperate. None of this should be news to people interested in virtue ethics.

What has not been noticed is the way in which an analysis of *humility* may be modeled on *continence*; notice how both involve apt self-restraint. If we understand continence as the psychological trait by which we restrain or correct for incontinence, humility is the psychological trait by which we restrain or correct for arrogance. Both are important for some people to have, while others have little or no need of them.

A Kantian picture of arrogant people suffices: those who are arrogant fail to give others the respect they are due. It may seem as if arrogant people have too much self-respect, more than is due, given how they treat others. But on Kant's account of arrogance, arrogant people do not have an excess of self-respect, but rather a deceptive way of fooling themselves into thinking that they have self-respect, when in fact they do not.[14] Kant writes:

> Arrogance [*Hochmut*] (*superbia* and, as the word expresses it, the inclination to always be *on top*) is a kind of ambition [*Ehrbegierde*] (*ambitio*) in which we demand that others think little of themselves in comparison with us … arrogance demands from others a respect it denies them.
>
> *(1996, p. 581)*

And he certainly does not underestimate the perniciousness of arrogance, calling it in one place a "source of all evil" (1998, pp. 66–7). So, arrogance occurs when we self-righteously demand more respect than we are due or when we think of ourselves as somehow deserving more respect than others.

Yet, if arrogance is a vice which is corrected for by humility, what is the virtue which manifests the appropriate and moral attitude of the self toward the self? What plays the role of temperance in the analogy of humility to continence? The answer, as indicated above, is *justice* when understood as a personal virtue, as opposed to a political or institutional virtue. The quick argument for giving justice this role goes as follows.[15] Justice is the virtue by which we make fair judgments about how much respect to accord to others, especially as compared to the (self-) respect one accords oneself. All injustice which involves a victim involves disrespect for that victim; for if the victim were adequately respected, the perpetrator would refrain from the injustice. And arrogance, the cause of much injustice, is also understood in terms of not giving others adequate respect. On the other side, when people have over-developed the trait of humility and have become servile, they disrespect themselves in a way that is also inconsistent with justice: they are unfair to themselves. So, arrogance and servility are those traits by which we accord to others either too little or too much respect, and justice is the virtue by which by which we make fair and just assessments of how much respect to accord to ourselves and others. This is backed up by Aristotle's gloss on the virtue, "justice is a mean between committing injustice and suffering it, since the one is having more than one's share, while the other is having less" (2000, 1133b30).

Justice requires that we treat like cases alike, and so we ought to judge ourselves based on the same standards by which we judge others, and so justice is also the virtue by which we make fair and just assessments of ourselves. If respecting others properly is the result of being a just person, then having proper self-respect is similarly the result of the virtue of justice, especially since we cannot genuinely have one without the other. Justice ensures that equals are treated as equals.

We may note happily that thoroughly vicious, full-blown arrogance is not too common. Still, it is all too common for people to occasionally think more highly of themselves than they deserve. Arrogance comes in degrees, and most people probably arrogate just a little at least once in a while. As Butler (1900) notes, it is natural for us to not mistrust ourselves and we are inclined to be overly partial to ourselves (and whatever we love).[16] It is not uncommon for human beings to be arrogant and so, to that degree, need to be "taken down a notch". Thus, humility ought to enter the picture. Just as it is common for people to be inappropriately tempted, and so in need of continence, it is also common for us to get a bit too full of ourselves and be in need of humility. But insofar as we succeed in embodying justice and giving ourselves and others the respect everyone is due (and no more than that), our judgment is sound, and we are not in need of correction. If so, we have no need for humility.

Humility allows us to combat what is otherwise self-aggrandizing in our nature. It is always bad to be arrogant, but that does not make it good to always have humility, for only a few of us are always self-aggrandizing and some of us never are. To see humility as a corrective is to adopt an appropriately humble theory of humility.

3.4 Conclusion

While there are many theories of what makes a character trait be a virtue, there is agreement among theorists that the virtues are character traits that are excellences of some kind. It is not possible to reliably do the right thing, at the right time, in the right way, for the right reasons, without manifesting those excellences of character which are the virtues. So, these are traits that manifest behavior which is never inapt. Humility does not fit this model. While humility is vastly important and is not to be underrated for its value in correcting arrogance, in a secular world of interaction between equals, humility's only value is this corrective function. There are times when it is simply wrong to have or feel humility, in a way that it cannot be wrong to have wisdom, courage, justice, or temperance. It therefore makes more sense to take humility "down a notch" from being considered a virtue to seeing it as a developmental phase, like continence, which one passes through on the way to virtue. Therefore, humility is not a virtue.

Notes

1 My thanks go to the following philosophers for helpful comments and suggestions: Julia Annas, Heather Battaly, Anka Finger, Mitch Green, Hanna Gunn, Raja Halwani, Allan Hazlett, Drew Johnson, Brendan Kane, Suzy Killmister, Fred Lee, Hallie Liberto, Nate Sheff, Mark Timmons, and Sam Wheeler. I'm grateful to the editors of this volume for their helpful conversations and comments on the paper, especially Alessandra Tanesini, who gave extensive comments on the paper which greatly improved it. Finally, this publication was made possible through the support of a grant from the John Templeton Foundation. The opinions expressed in this publication are those of the author and do not necessarily reflect the views of the John Templeton Foundation.

2 In Fanny Burney's novel *Evelina*, from 1778, a well-born character "thinks it incumbent upon her to support the dignity of her ancestry. Fortunately for the world in general, she has taken it into her head, that condescension is the most distinguishing virtue of high life; so that the same pride of family which renders others imperious, is with her the motive of affability".

3 My use of the word "corrective" is different from that of Philippa Foot (2002, pp. 8–12), who argues that all the virtues are "correctives", referencing Aristotle's thought that the virtues are about what is naturally difficult for people. But all agree that practicing continence does not leave one in a virtuous state, even if it gets a person to do what a truly virtuous (temperate) person would do in those circumstances. Continence is a stop-gap measure, which is far from the self-regulation of desire required for temperance.

4 The psychologist L. A. Pervin understands a character trait roughly as "a disposition to behave expressing itself in consistent patterns of functioning across a range of situations" (1994, p. 108). There are good reasons, however, to follow Christian Miller (2014, chapter 1) and normatively narrow the range of personality traits that will count as character traits. On such a view, character traits are those personality traits for which a person is responsible, and which also open a person to normative assessment.

Alessandra Tanesini (2016) refers to humility as an "attitude", using this term as it figures in psychological literature. Since "attitude" already has such an extensive use in moral philosophy, I prescind from following that terminology here. Still, despite how Tanesini refers to humility as a virtue, and as an attitude, the present account is in many ways similar to hers in spirit.

5 My thanks to Smit and Timmons (2015) for this quote.

6 Thus, I am in sympathy with Nancy Snow's (1995) discussion of "existential humility". This is reminiscent of Iris Murdoch's (1970) claim that "[h]umility is 'selfless respect for reality'". The degree to which she conceives of it as a corrective to the "fat relentless ego" is the degree to which she agrees with the present account.

One might also wonder whether we should always feel humility since we may always compare ourselves with people more virtuous than we are, or compared to the ideal of virtuous perfection, thereby always being reminded of our faults. Here, I follow Aristotle (1941), saying that the right thing to feel is "emulation":

> Emulation is pain caused by seeing the presence, in persons whose nature is like our own, of good things that are highly valued and are possible for ourselves to acquire; but it is felt not because others have these goods, but because we have not got them ourselves. It is therefore a good feeling felt by good persons, whereas envy is a bad feeling felt by bad persons. Emulation makes us take steps to secure the good things in question, envy makes us take steps to stop our neighbor having them (*Rhetoric*, Bk. II, 11, 30–8).

I learned of this helpful distinction between emulation and envy, in contexts such as these, from Smit and Timmons (2015).

7 For ease of exposition, I elide the differences between "having humility" and "being humble" in order to use the adjective "humble", since "humility" has no adjectival nor adverbial form. In fact, being humble and having humility are quite different: a person can act reliably humble in front of others and yet be quietly confident or even arrogant in his or her heart.

8 If Tank Man's action seems even possibly humble to you, please substitute in some other act of civil disobedience which is impossible to read this way. Perhaps the mass suicide of Jews at Masada in the year 73 CE will suffice. Or perhaps the way Tommie Smith and John Carlos raised their black-gloved fists when they won Olympic medals in Mexico, 16 October 1968. Or think of the famous picture, taken 9 July 2016, of Ieshia Evans as she stood in a flowing sundress in front of police wearing riot gear outside the Baton Rouge Police Department, following the killing of Alton Sterling. For the picture

of Smith and Carlos see, https://en.wikipedia.org/wiki/1968_Olympics_Black_Power_salute; and for the picture of Evans, www.reuters.com/article/us-usa-police-ieshiaevans/nurse-in-u-s-protest-photo-says-she-felt-she-had-to-face-police-idUSKCN0ZV1YJ.

9 Whitcomb, Battaly, Baehr, and Howard-Snyder (this volume) try to escape the sort of problem which the *reductio* presents by saying that humility is sometimes a virtue and sometimes is not, and to "limit its importance". This is in effect a denial of premise 1, or the idea that traits which are virtues have "fields of action" in which they are guaranteed to yield correct action. But if humility is sometimes *not* a virtue, then we cannot count on the trait of humility to tell us when to be humble or not. Humility itself can no longer give us normative guidance. I take up these themes about "virtues in excess", discussing and criticizing Gary Watson's (1984) response to the problem in my paper "Virtues are Excellences" (manuscript).

10 The idea that we are naturally partial to ourselves is, of course, not new. See for example, Plato (1993) and Butler's "Sermon on Self-Deceit" (1900).

11 To this degree, I agree with Richards (1988) and Roberts and Wood (2007), all of whom claim that humility is antagonistic to arrogance, vanity, etc. Our disagreement, however, is over whether or not humility is a virtue.

12 For a heterodox view, see Stohr (2003).

13 For more on temperance, see chapter 3 of Bloomfield (2014) and my "Temperance, Continence, Weakness, Compulsion" (manuscript).

14 For discussion, see Dillon (2004) and (2015). While I follow (Dillon on) Kant in his understanding of *arrogance*, I do not follow him in his view of *humility*, which seems to me to have too many theistic connotations. Still, I am in broad sympathy with much of Dillon's understanding of humility.

15 For further discussion, see Bloomfield (2011), (2014), and (forthcoming).

16 In a footnote labeled "(b)" in section 8 of Butler's "Sermon on Self-Deceit" (1900), he notes that not everyone tends toward self-partiality in this way: we can deceive ourselves into thinking we deserve less respect than we are due as well. For more on this idea, and the "imposter syndrome", see Kolligian and Sternberg (1990).

References

Anscombe, G. E. M. 1958. "Modern Moral Philosophy", *Philosophy* 33(124): 1–19.

Appiah, Kwame Anthony. 2018. "Thank You for 'Condescending'", *New York Times Magazine*, 1 Sept. 2018. www.nytimes.com/2018/08/28/magazine/thank-you-for-condescending.html.

Aristotle. 1941. *Rhetoric*, translated by R. McKeon. New York: Random House.

———2000. *Nicomachean Ethics*, translated by Roger Crisp. Cambridge: Cambridge University Press.

Bloomfield, Paul. Manuscript. "Virtues Are Excellences".

———Manuscript. "Temperance, Continence, Weakness, Compulsion".

———Forthcoming. "The Skills of Justice". In: *The Routledge Handbook of Skills and Expertise*, edited by Ellen Fridland and Carlotta Pavase. New York: Routledge Press.

———2011. "Justice as a Self-Regarding Virtue", *Philosophy and Phenomenological Research* 82(1): 46–64.

———2014. *The Virtues of Happiness*. New York: Oxford University Press.

Butler, Joseph. 1900. *The Works of Bishop Butler*, 2 vols., edited by J. H. Bernard. London: MacMillan.

Dillon, Robin. 2004. "Kant on Arrogance and Self-Respect". In: *Setting the Moral Compass*, edited by Cheshire Calhoun. New York: Oxford University Press.

———2015. "Humility, Arrogance, and Self-Respect in Kant and Hill". In: *Reason, Value, and Respect*, edited by M. Timmons and R. Johnson. Oxford: Oxford University Press.

Douglass, Frederick. 1892. *The Life and Times of Frederick Douglass*. Boston: DeWolf and Fisk.

Foot, Philippa. 2002. *Virtues and Vices*. Oxford: Clarendon Press.

Hazlett, Allan. 2017. "Intellectual Pride". In: *The Moral Psychology of Pride*, edited by J. A. Carter and E. C. Gordon. Lanham: Rowman & Littlefield.

Hume, David. 1975. *Enquiries Concerning the Human Understanding and Concerning the Principles of Morals*, 3rd ed., edited by L. A. Selby-Bigge. Oxford: Clarendon Press.

Kant, Immanuel. 1996. *Metaphysics of Morals*, edited and translated by Mary Gregor. Cambridge: Cambridge University Press.

———1997. *Lectures on Ethics*. Cambridge: Cambridge University Press.

———1998. *Religion With the Boundaries of Mere Reason*, edited and translated by Allen Wood and George di Giovanni. Cambridge: Cambridge University Press.
King, Jr., Martin Luther. 1963. "Letter from the Birmingham City Jail". In: *Why we Can't Wait*. Boston: Beacon Press.
Kolligian, John and Sternberg, Robert. 1990. *Competence Considered*. New Haven: Yale University Press.
Miller, Christian. 2014. *Character and Moral Psychology*. New York: Oxford University Press.
Murdoch, Iris. 1970. *Sovereignty of the Good*. Oxford: Routledge.
Nietzsche, Friedrich. 1989. *On the Genealogy of Morality*, translated by Walter Kaufmann. New York: Vintage Press.
Nussbaum, Martha. 1988. "Non-Relative Virtues: An Aristotelian Approach", *Midwest Studies in Philosophy* 13(1): 32–53.
Pervin, L. A. 1994. "A Critical Analysis of Current Trait Theory", *Psychological Inquiry* 5(2): 103–113.
Plato. 1993. *Republic*, translated by Robin Waterfield. Oxford: Oxford University Press.
Richards, Norvin. 1988. "Is Humility a Virtue?", *American Philosophical Quarterly* 25(3): 253–259.
Roberts, Robert and Woods, Jay. 2007. *Intellectual Virtues*. Oxford: Clarendon Press.
Seneca. 1995. *Moral and Political Essays*. Cambridge: Cambridge University Press.
Sidgwick, Henry. 1907. *The Methods of Ethics*, 7th ed. Indianapolis: Hackett Publishing Company.
Smit, Houston and Timmons, Mark. 2015. "Love of Honor, Emulation, and the Psychology of the Devilish Vices". In: *Kant's Lectures on Ethics: A Critical Guide*, edited by Lara Denis and Oliver Sensen. Cambridge: Cambridge University Press.
Snow, Nancy. 1995. "Humility", *The Journal of Value Inquiry* 29(2): 203–216.
Stohr, Karen. 2003. "Moral Cacophany: When Continence is a Virtue", *The Journal of Ethics* 7(4): 339–363.
Swanton, Christine. 2003. *Virtue Ethics: A Pluralistic View*. Oxford: Oxford University Press.
Tanesini, Alesandra. 2018. "Intellectual Humility as an Attitude", *Philosophy of Phenomenological Research* 96(2): 399–420.
The Revised English Bible: New Testament. 1989. Oxford: Oxford University Press.
Waldron, Jeremy. 2012. *Dignity, Rank, and Rights*. Oxford: Oxford University Press.
Wallstonecraft, Mary. 1995. *A Vindication of the Rights of Men and A Vindication of the Rights of Women*, edited by Sylvana Tomaselli. Cambridge: Cambridge University Press.
Wardle, John. 1983. "Miss Anscombe on Sidgwick's View of Humility", *Philosophy* 58(225): 389–391.
Watson, Gary. 1984. "Virtues in Excess", *Philosophical Studies* 46(1): 57–74.
Whitcomb, Denis, Battaly, Heather, Baehr, Jason and Howard-Snyder, Daniel. 2017. "Intellectual Humility: Owning Our Limitations", *Philosophy and Phenomenological Research* 94(3): 509–539.

PART 2

The ethics of humility

4

HUMILITY AND HUMAN FLOURISHING

Robert Roberts

4.1 Introduction

Popular Christianity in the Middle Ages conceived humility in such a way that it can hardly be thought to contribute to human flourishing. Saint Benedict's *Rule* (6th century) says that in the 6th step of humility the monk

> thinks himself a poor and worthless workman in his appointed tasks [and in the 7th step] a man not only confesses that he is an inferior and common wretch but believes it in the depths of his heart.[1]

Walter Hilton (14th century) advises,

> First, it behoveth thee to have humility on this manner: thou shalt in thy will and in thy feeling judge thyself unfitting to dwell among men and unworthy to serve God in conversation with His servants and as unprofitable to thy Christian brethren, wanting both skill and power to fulfil any good works of active life in help of thy neighbour, as other men and women do. And, therefore, as a wretch and an outcast and refuse of all men art shut up in a house alone, that thou shouldst not grieve nor offend man or woman by thy bad example, seeing thou canst not profit them by any well-doing.[2]

Unlike the medieval Christians, David Hume doesn't regard humility as a virtue, though he seems to pick up on their self-hatred theme when he says,

> *Pride* is a certain satisfaction in ourselves, on account of some accomplishment or possession, which we enjoy: *Humility*, on the other hand, is a dissatisfaction with ourselves, on account of some defect or infirmity.[3]

We hear an echo of this conception in the first definition of humility in the *Oxford English Dictionary*: "The quality of being humble or having a lowly opinion of oneself." According to Tara Smith, a contemporary philosopher, to be humble is to have low aspirations or a low estimate of what one can expect from life.

> Typically, the humble person does not want very much. She is content with a minimal standard of living, or job, or romance, and satisfies herself with relatively low-level needs and aims.[4]

My purpose in this chapter is to sketch how the trait of humility contributes to human flourishing—that of persons who possess the trait and of persons whose lives are touched by persons with the trait. So we need a conception of humility as a virtue. In a group of recent papers[5] I have proposed to conceive humility as an absence or low level of what I call the vices of pride, including grandiosity, conceit, envy, invidious triumph, snobbery, presumption, vanity, arrogance, hyper-autonomy, and domination. My view is that perfect humility is the complete absence of such vices, and that approximate humility is a low level of them. But I need not argue for such a strong thesis here. To see at least one major way that humility contributes to human flourishing, it will be enough to understand humility as *entailing* an absence or dearth of such vices.

The vices of pride are all basically a concern (or interest in or desire) for a false and deceptive good that I call self-importance or narcissistic enhancement. But they differ from one another in the way that that "good" is thought to be attained or possessed. For example, the snob gets self-importance by belonging to some exclusive élite, the arrogant person by having special entitlements, the domineering person by co-opting others' agency, the hyper-autonomous by minimizing his dependency on others for his achievements, the vain by soliciting others' admiration, and the envious/invidiously triumphant by besting a significant rival. A theme that seems to run through the vices of pride is invidious comparison—getting this special value by having more of some other value than others (that is, superiority in some respect). My thesis about the nature of humility is that it excludes the vices of pride. The virtuously humble person is not arrogant, not vain, not domineering, not hyper-autonomous, not snobbish, and so forth. To the extent that the vices of pride undermine such goods of human life as friendship, love, collegiality, cooperation, and knowledge, humility promotes the good life by clearing the way for these genuine goods.

4.2 Narcissism in the DSM-5

The Diagnostic and Statistical Manual[6] is an officially sanctioned reference work consulted widely in medicine and psychotherapy to identify (diagnose) what are broadly referred to as "mental" disorders. Narcissism is one of the so-called "personality" disorders, which bears a striking resemblance to the vices of pride, taken as a syndrome of related attitudes. In the case of this disorder, at least, the word "personality" can be replaced with "character," bringing out that the functional and experiential dysfunction that the disorder visits on human lives belongs as much or more to ethics than it does to medicine.[7] The havoc and unhappiness wrought by narcissism center in social relationships. Narcissism tends to render these relationships (at least secretly) adversarial, and consequently to undermine and nullify them. This chapter assumes that harmonious, mutually satisfying interhuman relationships are central to proper human functioning and happiness, and that anything that undermines them as insidiously and systematically as narcissism assaults human well-being at its core. I will here offer a philosophical commentary on the criteria presented in the DSM-5 for narcissistic personality disorder (NPD), to draw out the systematic connections among them, and render them somewhat more precise. In the present section, the words in boldface are from the DSM-5 on pages 669–670; the other words are my commentary.

Narcissism is

A pervasive pattern of grandiosity (in fantasy or behavior), need for admiration, and lack of empathy, beginning by early adulthood and present in a variety of contexts, as indicated by five (or more) of the following:

(1) has a grandiose sense of self-importance (e.g., exaggerates achievements and talents, expects to be recognized as superior without commensurate achievements)

If grandiosity (in fantasy or behavior) is "aiming at great things against right reason,"[8] then grandiosity is not, as such, a mark of narcissism. A young person might want to be a movie star, but unrealistically, because she doesn't have what it takes to become one. This unrealistic ambition might pervade her young life. But this by itself is no symptom of narcissism. The reason that the unrealistic ambition by itself doesn't amount to narcissism is that it doesn't have the target essential to narcissism. In this first criterion, the DSM notes that the target of *narcissistic* grandiosity is "self-importance."

What kind of importance of the self is self-importance? Not every desire to be important is narcissistic. I suppose that everybody wants to be important to somebody—to his mother, his family, his church, his God, perhaps even his nation. A person who feels utterly unimportant—unloved, unappreciated, worthless to all the world—has a severe life-deficit, and cannot be called happy. So people need to be important and to know themselves to be important. By contrast with this healthy kind of importance, self-importance is, from a deeply human perspective, a pseudo-value, not really importance at all: it is the kind of importance a person might feel as a result of being envied, admired as superior to others, having power over others, or having entitlements that others don't have. It's the kind of importance that the envious person is seeking when he feels frustrated and resentful of the rival who outshines him. It's the kind of importance that snobbish people feel they get from belonging to prestigious institutions and being accepted in the company of "important" people, a kind of importance that snobs take to be lacking in people who attend state universities and don't belong to any élite. Not all self-importance is individualistic. Snobbery, for example, has a "we–self" character, since it values belonging to an élite *group*. Racism can be seen as a kind of snobbery; other in-group "we–self" vices of pride are homophobia, sexism, and some forms of nationalism. If self-importance, the pseudo-value, is what persons with the vices of pride seek and value, then any concern for it whatsoever is vicious. There is no mean, no right amount or right way in which to love it. As Aristotle points out, there is no normative mean of vice.[9]

(2) is preoccupied with fantasies of unlimited success, power, brilliance, beauty, or ideal love

The comment on (1) suffices as comment on (2).

(3) believes that he or she is "special" and unique and can only be understood by, or should associate with, other special or high-status people (or institutions)

As noted above, snobbery is one of the vices of pride.

(4) requires excessive admiration

The admiration in question here is the admiration sought by the passion (vice) of vanity. It is admiration that "satisfies" the desire for the pseudo-good of self-importance. This admiration is the kind that recognizes a person as "special," that is, superior to others; it is the desire for this, in abstraction from any real excellence, that defines vanity. Whatever real excellence is admired is incidental or merely instrumental to the vain person's elevation above others. Note the basic meaning of "vain": "a. Devoid of real value, worth, or significance; idle, unprofitable, useless, worthless; of no effect, force, or power; fruitless, futile, unavailing" (OED, first definition). I'm not saying that what occasions the admiration must actually be idle, unprofitable, useless, worthless, etc. A person might be vain of something that is genuinely admirable, such as beautifully performing a piece of music, or rescuing someone from poverty, or passing significant legislation; what makes for the character trait of vanity is that the individual's chief reason or motivation for doing the admirable thing is to garner the admiration of important people and thus to be important (self-important) himself. The narcissistic passion for admiration devalues what it seeks admiration for by valuing it for a vain or empty *reason*.

It is healthy and good to enjoy admiration for genuinely admirable accomplishments. This enjoyment is a kind of fellowship with the admirer: something that you highly appreciate, something that you poured yourself into, is appreciated by another; and your common appreciation is a kind of joyful and grateful communion with a fellow human being. The narcissist, as such, is not interested in such communion, but just in the self-importance that the admiration of the admirer seems to him to project on himself. So "excessive" is perhaps not quite the right word to identify what it is about admiration that is characteristically narcissistic. The narcissist is not defined by the *amount* of admiration he "requires," but by the *kind* he seeks—namely, vain admiration, admiration as serving self-importance.

(5) has a sense of entitlement, i.e., unreasonable expectations of especially favorable treatment or automatic compliance with his or her expectations

The narcissistic concern for special entitlements goes by the name of "arrogance" or "presumption" in ordinary English (note DSM criterion (9)). As criterion (5) notes, some of the narcissist's expectations of being treated as privileged are usually unreasonable. That is, some of them are not legitimate entitlements. The reason will be that he doesn't seek entitlements just for their value as entitlements, but less discriminately, out of a narcissistic hunger for them—that is, to enhance, support, or express his self-importance. What is the legitimate value of special entitlements?

Entitlements are used to regulate social life in the interest of justice and the human good. For example, certain government officials are entitled to see classified documents that are not available to the public, because the information in them may be relevant to governing the nation. Doctors are entitled to order medicines for their patients that the patients are not entitled to buy without such prescription, because the doctor is presumed to be in a better position than the patient to know what the patient needs. And so forth for all socially legitimate special entitlements. The kind of entitlements that are designed to protect an élite, such as membership in an exclusive club, or racist entitlements that deny privileges to the non-members of a given race, are implicitly in the service of the narcissistic concern. In such manifestations, the self-importance in arrogance has a "we–self" character.

So it is perfectly rational and consistent with humility to desire the special entitlements that facilitate one's contribution to justice and the public good. The essential reason for wanting and enjoying such entitlements is to make one's special contribution. But this is not the narcissist's characteristic reason. The narcissist, as narcissist, wants such privileges because they enhance or express his self-importance. Thus, it is not essential to narcissism merely to desire and enjoy entitlements, but rather to do so for the sake of one's self-importance. The latter is what (5) expresses with "has a sense of entitlement." If a person who *has* such a sense of entitlement suffers from arrogance, a person who, perhaps with frustration, *seeks* and *longs for* such entitlements is proto-arrogant. He has the concern that defines arrogance.

I said above that, typically, "some" of the narcissist's entitlement claims are illegitimate, implying that some of them may be legitimate. Illegitimacy of entitlement claims is only an indicator of narcissism, not a necessary condition of it. A person can be narcissistic about entitlement claims that are legitimate for him. For example, a government official might experience narcissistic enjoyment of his legitimate privilege of viewing classified documents. The essential narcissistic feature is *how* he regards them; *why* entitlements interest him. To the extent that he desires and takes pleasure in having special entitlements as enhancing his self-importance, he is narcissistic, whether or not he has legitimate claim to them.

(6) is interpersonally exploitative, i.e., takes advantage of others to achieve his or her own ends

The narcissist's "ends" are typically ones that enhance or maintain his sense of self-importance: prominence, power, privilege, and wealth, for example. To be exploitative of other persons is not just to gain advantage from what others do; in any division of labor and sharing of its fruits we gain advantage from others' contributions, and we naturally and legitimately seek such advantage. The DSM uses "exploit" in this criterion to indicate that the "advantage" gained by the narcissist is *unfair* in some way. I mentioned domination as one of the vices of pride. It is the narcissist's exercise of power over others for the sake of the self-importance he feels he garners from it. It is a co-opting of another person's agency. I suppose that domination is most paradigmatic where the unfairness is objective. For example, a professor co-authors scholarship with a graduate student. The work represents almost entirely the student's creativity and labor, but the professor designates herself "first author" and in a footnote thanks the student for his "help." But narcissism doesn't require material unfairness. It is a matter of attitude, to wit, the attitude toward the "exploited" one. Narcissistic pleasure in exercising power over others, even where it is overlaid with a patina of solicitous concern for the other, will harbor an element of *disrespect*: the domineering agent in reality secretly sees the exploited one as little more than an instrument of his self-importance. This attitude is also unfair, though it is so only attitudinally. To see its moral shortcoming, think of how the "exploited" one would feel if she vividly perceived the exploiter's attitude. Among possible responses, she feels hurt if she cares about his attitude; or she "writes him off" in an effort not to care.

(7) lacks empathy: is unwilling to recognize or identify with the feelings and needs of others

Many of the vices of pride make the value of the self depend on the devaluation of the other. Examples are envy, invidious triumph, snobbery, conceit, hyper-autonomy, and self-righteousness. The vices of pride are vices, in large part, because they are self-serving while involving a false conception of the value of the self and its good; and they distort the value of the self, in large part, because of their exploitative conception of the value of the other. What makes the other good for me is his inferiority or failure relative to me—his value as an unsuccessful rival. Empathy, as it is understood in (7), is a *benevolent* feeling of the feelings of others. It is a rejoicing in the other's joys, and a sympathy with the other's sorrows; and these feelings are based on being concerned for what the other is concerned about, on behalf of the other. In empathy we track, in agreement, the other's concerns, and when we communicate such feelings to the other, she tends to feel supported, respected, and even loved. It is really a bit of an understatement to say that the narcissist lacks empathy, and that "those who relate to individuals with narcissistic personality disorder typically find an emotional coldness and lack of reciprocal interest" (DSM V, 671). This is true, but it is an understatement because so often the narcissist is not just cold to the other, but implicitly *malevolent* insofar as his exploitative attitude positively *opposes* the other's interest.

(8) is often envious of others or believes that others are envious of him or her

People are sometimes surprised that I include envy among the vices of pride. They should also be surprised that the narcissist, who supposedly has a grandiose view of his own importance, is characteristically envious. The envious person is not proud of himself, they think. To feel proud is to feel good about oneself, but to feel envy is to feel oneself to be a loser in relation to the rival and to feel bad about oneself. It is to feel frustratingly small.

It is true that envy is not a *feeling* of pride or of grandiosity. But the vices of pride are basically concerns and allied dispositions of thought, not feelings. Envy, thought of in this way, is a disposition to feel the *emotion* of envy, and this disposition is a concern to be important by besting certain others in some respect that is thought to be "enviable"—intelligence, strength, beauty, talents, skills, wealth, power, etc. When a person who has this concern and this way of thinking about his value as a person is bested by a rival, then he *feels* envy; but when the same individual bests the rival, he *feels* invidious triumph, which *is* a feeling of pride—vicious pride. Thus the disposition to envy and the disposition to invidious pride are the same *concern*, the same *disposition*, and it gives rise to one or the other *emotion* depending on the circumstances—or, more precisely, on the individual's construal of the circumstances.[10] (8) identifies both possibilities and suggests that they have the same root: to believe, with delight, that others envy you is just the flip side of believing, with pain, that others justifiably believe that you envy them.

(9) shows arrogant, haughty behaviors or attitudes

Essentially, (9) is a repetition of (5), so my comments on (5) will suffice.

4.3 The ravages of narcissism

Why should we consider narcissism a *disorder*? Why do we feel justified in judging it to be unhealthy or perverse? Why not just label it as an alternative lifestyle or perhaps a kind of religion (narcissists are self-worshipers; other religions have other gods)? Or why not say that it is just a matter of cultural difference whether we regard as "normal" the value that the DSM and I call self-importance, or, on the contrary, regard it as a false value, and regard the value that I call the real importance of persons "normal" and healthy? A general diagnostic criterion of personality disorder, according to the DSM, is "an enduring pattern of inner experience and behavior that deviates markedly from the expectations of the individual's culture."[11] It is plausible to think that self-importance is a value that is expected in our culture (and indeed promoted, say, by advertising and by the selectivity structures of institutions). If it undermines what we call friendship and love, then so much the worse for friendship and love! If it results in ignorance, let's hear it for ignorance!

I think there is a widely shared ethics or psychology, a normative anthropology, if you will, among us humans according to which love and friendship are a good thing, perhaps even close to being the meaning of human existence. Whether personality or character traits that trap one in psychic loneliness and self-ignorance and ignorance of the world are contrary to the good life is not a culturally relative matter. The ravages of narcissism are real, universal, and deplorable.

We might think that we "normal" people, who aren't at risk of being diagnosed with narcissistic personality disorder, escape from its ravages. And we do escape, to whatever extent we possess the virtue of humility. The DSM-5, recognizing that narcissistic symptoms are widespread among human beings, offers two points of guidance to distinguish people who are clinically diagnosable from the rest of us narcissists. One point is that a clinical diagnosis requires that the patient satisfy five of the nine criteria. This point is fuzzy, first, given the repetitions ((2) of (1), (9) of (5)) that our commentary has identified; second, given that each of the criteria can be satisfied in various degrees of severity; and third, given that virtually all of us satisfy all the criteria to some extent. The DSM's second point of guidance is this:

> Many highly successful individuals display personality traits that might be considered narcissistic. Only when these traits are inflexible, maladaptive, and persisting and cause significant functional impairment or subjective distress do they constitute narcissistic personality disorder.[12]

We might ask, "How inflexible, maladaptive, persistent, functionally impairing, and subjectively distressing need they be?" It would be implausible to think that narcissistic personality traits possessed by highly successful individuals leave them entirely unimpaired, while suddenly, beyond a certain threshold of inflexibility, maladaptiveness, and persistence, they cause functional impairment and subjective distress. A "highly successful" person may have no close friends (or the friendships she has may be troubled) and may suffer from ignorance attributable to her narcissism that impairs her life and her ability to contribute to her community, or even results in international disaster. It is plausible to think that *any* degree whatsoever of narcissistic traits will make one subject to *some* dysfunction and subjective distress. At least this is so if we think that friendship, love, and respect are essential ingredients in a good human life. If the essential mark of narcissism (vicious pride) is concern for the destructive pseudo-value of self-importance, then it is a disorder whether or not it is clinically diagnosable. Almost everybody is on the narcissistic *spectrum*—that is to say, almost everybody is concerned about his self-importance, a destructive object of seeking and a false value.

4.4 The well-being that unhumility compromises

If we are to be well, if our life is to be good, we human beings need both to love and to be loved, to respect our fellow humans and to be respected by them. We need to see them and to be seen by them with benevolent eyes. This style of seeing naturally evokes the corresponding style of being seen, a fellowship, a communion of souls. This responsiveness, this vector toward mutuality, seems to be built into human nature. The difference between the vain person's enjoyment of being admired and the humble person's enjoyment of being loved and respected is that the latter evokes reciprocation. Love, when received *as* love, evokes love; admiration, when received as satisfying vanity, evokes self-importance, which is not reciprocated by according importance to the admirer. Or rather, the importance of the admirer to the vain person is not the admirer's importance *as a person*, but is the admirer's importance as satisfying the vain person's appetite for self-importance. That is why there is no deep human satisfaction—no happiness, no well-being—in admiring a vain person, or, as a vain person, in being admired. When vanity becomes a settled character trait, the distortion of human nature weakens the natural vector I've identified. Then the love and respect are met, not with the happiness of returned love and respect, but with the frustrating resistance of a soul preoccupied with his or her own importance. Love can be fulfilling even when it isn't reciprocated, but the vain person's resistance is especially off-putting, perhaps because love is not just lacking, but being actively twisted, exploited, and suffocated.

The person who suffers from the vices of pride denies to his fellows the love, respect, and well-wishing (the warmth, as the DSM suggests) that they need to feel from him for their relationship to be fulfilling. And the source of his denial is his hunger for self-importance. It isn't just that he is distracted from attention to them by his concern, though that is true as well; he is in many ways (namely, in the ways the vices of pride seek self-importance: by self-display, by claiming entitlements, by denying credit to others, by dominating others, by thinking himself morally or otherwise superior) a very social animal. He doesn't just ignore his fellows, but actively (though often covertly) assaults their dignity by "putting them down," by "using" them, and by abusing them when they fail to accord him his claimed privileges. In the process, of course, the unhumble person denies to himself, as well, the happiness of reciprocal love and respect. He forsakes a real joy for the sake of a hollow one.

The habitual episodic practice of reciprocal love and respect engenders the virtues of love and respect, and to the extent that these virtues prevail in the members of the community, they dispel the interest in self-importance. The absence of the passion of self-importance is, or at least is a signal feature of, the virtue of humility. This, then, is how humility contributes to human flourishing: by constituting an absence of a main factor that spoils human life, namely, the pursuit of self-importance, and by providing room for one of the main factors that fulfills and glorifies human life, namely, love and respect. To love and respect others is to contribute to the flourishing of the human community, and this contribution expresses and constitutes the flourishing of the one who loves and respects others. To be loved and respected by others engenders the confidence and positive self-regard that are the effective basis of loving and respecting others. In this way, love and respect beget love and respect, and by doing so ground human flourishing.

4.5 Final thoughts about humility and human flourishing

Other concerns than love and respect for fellow human beings can dispel self-importance, for example, the pursuit of knowledge for its own sake, or the pursuit of excellence in an art or craft. And these passions or pursuits also contribute meaning and well-being to human life, though I think the fulfillment they provide is less universal and less fundamental than that provided by love and respect. Humility is characteristic of persons who with purity of heart seek any transcendent good, where the transcendence in question is transcendence of the persons' purely private or personal "good." To the extent that such transcendence is realized, self-importance will be excluded as an object of pursuit. So we might say that humility is a by-product of transcendence toward the good.

I mentioned earlier that in snobbery, and sometimes in arrogance, the self-importance that is aimed at has a "we–self" character. This is characteristic of racism and other invidious "isms" that undermine human flourishing. This makes possible a form of humility that is conditional on the in-group conception of self-importance. Thus, for example, within his group a white supremacist might exhibit humility: in the interest of this transcendent "good" he eschews the concern for high status and privilege, and willingly accepts a kind of social invisibility. He gladly accepts the most menial, unglorious grunt-work roles within his white supremacist community for the sake of the greater social "good." But his humility is within the parenthesis of the fundamental snobbery and arrogance of white supremacy. It seems to me that such a person does exhibit a kind of humility insofar as his transcendent "good" really appears to him to be a good. But those of us who think it is an evil and not really a good will note that outside this parenthesis the white supremacist's humility supports the vices of snobbery and arrogance.

The suggestion that humility is a by-product of transcendence toward the good raises the question what justifies assigning to humility the status of a distinct virtue. Love and respect for persons are substantive ways of caring about others and thus ways of thinking about others. And other virtues—courage, perseverance, patience, and self-control, for example—are perhaps, at least in part, self-management skills. And so they, too, have a kind of substantive, positive, psychological existence. So far, I have not identified any such positive status for humility, but I have said that it is, or at least entails, an absence of the passion for self-importance. And I have said that this absence seems to be a by-product of such passions as love and respect for others, as well as the love of knowledge or of an art or craft. Humility doesn't seem to be identical with these other virtues, yet as distinct from them we haven't identified any other positive psychological status that it might have. But even if we can't find any positive psychological status to assign to humility, I think we can still regard it as a distinct virtue.

People want their drinking water to be pure. The positive value of pure drinking water is beyond dispute. Purity is a virtue in water. But it is literally nothing in the water. If you do a chemical analysis of pure water, you won't find any substance that is the purity of the water. The great thing about pure water is that it's nothing but water. I have argued in this chapter that humility is (at least) the absence of a passion poisonous to human happiness and well-being for a pseudo-good that the American Psychiatric Association and I have called self-importance. So if it turned out that the great thing about humble love and respect is that it's nothing but love and respect, that wouldn't in the least impugn humility's status as a virtue.

Humility is not the same virtue as love and respect, because it can be displayed in connection with other concerns, such as an artistic passion or the love of knowledge. Still, it might be thought to be an *aspect* of these and any other self-transcending passions for the good. One argument in favor of thinking of humility as a distinct virtue is that it has long been regarded as such; another is that a person can try specifically to be humble upon noticing how self-importance is motivating his thought, feeling, and action, by trying specifically not to care about his self-importance. An implication of this chapter is that one of the most effective strategies for caring less about one's self-importance is to love and respect those with whom one has to do, or to train one's attention on some other transcendent object of concern.

Notes

1 *The Holy Rule of Saint Benedict*, translated by Boniface Verheyen (Grand Rapids: Christian Classics Ethereal Library, www.ccel.org/ccel/benedict/rule.html), chapter seven, pp. 13–14.

2 *The Ladder of Perfection* (Grand Rapids: Christian Classics Ethereal Library), www.ccel.org/ccel/hilton/ladder.pdf) book 1, part 1, chapter XV, p. 52.

3 *Dissertation on the Passions*, Section II. In *David Hume. An inquiry concerning human understanding. A dissertation on the passions. An inquiry concerning the principles of morals. The natural history of religion* (Bell and Bradfute. Kindle Edition), Locations 2426–2428.

4 "The Practice of Pride," *Social Philosophy and Policy* 15 (1998) 71–90, p. 78.

5 See, for example, "Learning Intellectual Humility" in Jason Baehr, editor, *Intellectual Virtues and Education: Essays in Applied Virtue Epistemology* (Routledge, 2016), pp. 184–201; "Humility from a Philosophical Point of View" with Scott Cleveland, in Everett Worthington, Joshua Hook, and Donnie Davis, editors, *Handbook of Humility* (Routledge, 2016), pp. 33–46; "Jesus and the Virtues of Pride" with Ryan West, in Adam Carter and Emma Gordon, editors, *The Moral Psychology of Pride* (Rowman and Littlefield, 2017), pp. 99–121; and "Understanding, Humility, and the Vices of Pride" in Heather Battaly, editor, *The Routledge Handbook of Virtue Epistemology* (Routledge, 2018), pp. 363–375.

6 Washington, D. C.: American Psychiatric Publishing, 2013.

7 In saying that narcissism is as much a character defect as a personality disorder, I may seem to be *blaming* the narcissist for his mental *illness*. This seems inappropriate. But the vices of pride have a long history of being regarded as vices while being pretty obviously contrary to individual and social well-being, and thus health. Here I follow the Christian tradition, which has allowed for the idea of inherited sin. You can hardly be blamed for what you inherited without your consent, and yet sin is inherently blameworthy. In a similar way, we do blame people for the nasty and destructive behaviors and attitudes that are rooted in their envy, arrogance, conceit, and vanity, even though we also think that such traits are a kind of sickness of the spirit. And then, if pushed, we admit that they seem to be characteristic of human nature and can often be at least partially explained by reference to people's unhealthy upbringing and current social environment. I thank Mark Alfano for raising this question.

8 Thomas Aquinas, *Summa Theologiae* 2a2ae, Q161, art.1, reply to objection 3.

9 See *Nicomachean Ethics*, translated by W. D. Ross, edited and revised by J. L. Ackrill and J. O. Urmson (Oxford: Oxford University Press, 1980), 2.6, 1107a22–27, pp. 39–40.

10 For the fuller account of the nature of emotions as concern-based construals, see my *Emotions in the Moral Life* (Cambridge U. P., 2013), chapters 3–5. Sara Protasi identifies a kind of "envy" that lacks the concern to be more important than the "envied" one ("Varieties of Envy" *Philosophical Psychology 29* (2016): 535–549). In "emulative envy" the subject focuses on the good at which the other person outshines the subject, and feels the other's superiority as an incentive to emulate the other's excellence rather than to put her down. Whether it is right to call this emotion a kind of *envy* is a matter of linguistic intuition, but it is clear that emulative envy is not a vice of pride or a symptom of narcissism.

11 DSM IV Quick Reference, p. 275.

12 p. 672.

5

HUMILITY AND SELF-RESPECT

Kantian and feminist perspectives[1]

Robin S. Dillon

In a culture increasingly shaped by the conviction that high self-esteem is unquestionably valuable, advocating humility might seem hopelessly old-fashioned and misguided. In an age increasingly dominated by narcissistic self-absorption, egotistic self-promotion, and arrogant disregard of other persons, humility might seem to be precisely what is needed to counteract self-valuing gone awry. Contemporary philosophical accounts of humility take the second position, holding that by opposing "vices of pride"[2] such as arrogance, humility both rectifies the tendency to make too much of oneself and is appropriate self-valuing.

Yet few of these accounts discuss humility in relation to what are arguably the most important perspectives on self-worth and the morally appropriate relation to other persons, namely, self-respect and respect for others.[3] If self-respect is morally proper self-valuing, then it would seem that it, and not humility, is what is needed to correct misguided self-valuing. Indeed, humility seems to be in tension with, if not opposed to, the self-respect one morally ought to have in virtue of being a person equal in dignity and moral status with all other persons. If that is the case, perhaps humility is itself a form of misguided self-valuing.

Most contemporary accounts assume, however, that humility is a virtue,[4] a trait that it is good for all persons to have, that makes whomever possesses it a good person, that contributes to individual and collective flourishing, that every person has the strongest reason to develop in ourselves and encourage in others. Yet few accounts consider the value of or need for humility in contexts of oppression. Few ask whether arrogance is actually a vice afflicting all humans for which a universal prescription of humility is apt, whether humility actually is a virtue for subordinated people as well as for members of dominant groups.[5]

For Kant and feminist theorists, self-respect and respect for other persons are morally central and enormously powerful, both theoretically and motivationally; they shape a distinctive approach to understanding and evaluating humility that is critical of both contemporary and traditional accounts. The aim of this chapter is to employ insights from Kant and feminist ethics to explore connections between humility and self-respect, and assess claims about the virtuousness of humility.

Kant regards arrogance as a serious vice. But he doesn't treat humility as a cure for arrogance, nor does he think it is a virtue.[6] And although he gives it a role to play in the moral life, he regards it as a threat to moral agency. It is self-respect—a self-regard at the heart of Kant's account of the morally good person living a morally good life—that is the virtue opposing arrogance.

At best, humility is a servant of self-respect; at worst, it is as serious a vice as arrogance, indeed, an aspect of it. In contrast to both the unjustified and inordinate self-valuing of arrogance and the possibly justified but potentially agency-undermining self-valuing of humility, self-respect is the commitment to appropriate self-valuing that precludes some forms of humility, includes but constrains other forms, properly opposes arrogance and all other forms of misguided self-valuing, and makes possible and expresses vibrant moral agency.

Feminist ethics draws attention to ways in which character traits, attitudes, beliefs, and stances can take on differential moral valences in contexts of oppression.[7] Thus, what might be a virtue for members of dominant groups can be a vice for members of subordinate groups, and vice versa.[8] From a feminist perspective, arrogance is not a vice that afflicts all humans; it is a vice of only some humans, especially members of dominant groups.[9] While humility can be useful in dislodging arrogance in dominants, it is not something that is good for all persons to develop. Indeed, calls for subordinates to develop humility are morally objectionable inasmuch as humility reinforces subordination. Self-respect and respect for all other persons are the morally valuable stances that inform the identification of traits as virtues or vices, that constrain liberatory activity, and towards which such activity ought to aim.[10]

5.1 Traditional and contemporary accounts of humility

There is a plethora of accounts of the nature and value of humility, forwarded from a range of perspectives, including religious and secular, philosophical and psychological, individual and social, ethical and epistemological. I'm going to focus primarily on philosophical accounts of humility as, putatively, a morally significant characteristic of individuals. Some of those accounts take a religious perspective, some a secular one.

Let me begin, though, with a peek at the dictionary. The *O.E.D.* defines humility as "the quality of being humble or having a lowly opinion of oneself; meekness, lowliness, humbleness: the opposite of pride or haughtiness." To be humble is to have "a low estimate of one's importance, worthiness, or merits," to lack "self-assertion or self-exaltation … [and] pride." To humble someone is to "to cause [them] to think more lowly of [themselves]; to bring [them] low or abase [them]." *The American Heritage Dictionary* concurs: to be humble is to be "marked by meekness or modesty in behavior, attitude, or spirit; not arrogant or prideful; low in rank, quality, or station;" to humble someone is "to curtail or destroy the pride of" that person, or "to give a lower condition or station to [them]; to abase [them]." The definitions highlight the etymological root (from L. *humilis*: low, lowly; from *humus*: the ground).[11]

For the ancient Greeks, humility was not a virtue. Indeed, what the dictionaries describe is what Aristotle would have called the vice of "pusillanimity," underestimating or having too low a regard for one's worth. But for the early and medieval Christians, a low opinion of one's worth was precisely the appropriate opinion. From their perspective, humility was a very important virtue, for it combatted what they regarded as the deadliest of the deadly sins, namely, arrogance, which they called *superbia*, the sin of pride.[12] In the deadly sins tradition, arrogance is making too much of oneself, one's worth or importance, abilities, or entitlements vis-à-vis God or other people. The virtue of humility involves viewing the self as nothing, worthless, even contemptible in light of the majesty of God; or being oblivious to or even annihilating the self; or restraining one's ambition for excellence; or declaring one's inferiority to everybody else.[13] Self-abasement is thus the essence of humility.

Nor is this view merely a quaint feature of bygone times. A humility that combats arrogance through acknowledging one's relative unimportance and unworthiness is an important virtue in traditional and contemporary Christianity, Islam, Judaism, Hinduism, and Buddhism, which all agree that only the humble individual has the right view of themselves, which orients them properly to God (or transcendent reality) and other persons and makes right living and other virtues possible.[14]

This view, however, strikes many contemporary non-religious thinkers as objectionable: self-abasement cannot be what makes humility a virtue. Kant would agree, since from his perspective, it is false that the self is nothing or worthless; concern for self-worth is of the greatest moral importance; self-abasement is opposed to the moral duty to respect oneself as a being with dignity; all persons are equal in dignity so that none should be valued more highly than others; and we have a moral duty to strive for moral excellence. Feminists would also agree: regarding oneself and one's activity as worthless or unimportant, affirming one's inferiority, and constraining ambition are objectionable because they recapitulate and reinforce subordination.

Contemporary theorists take it for granted that humility is a virtue. But because they eschew theism and reject the assessment of humans as essentially worthless and undeserving of any credit for what we do, they are left with the task of developing a secular account of a virtue that would be appropriate even for, as Richards (1992) puts it, "the rather splendid among us." Most of the accounts are revisionary, since they either reject the idea that humility is essentially a matter of having a lowly opinion of oneself, or treat lowliness as a distortion or excess of humility.[15]

Although there is significant disagreement about how to redefine humility,[16] there is general agreement about its conceptual shape: humility is almost universally regarded as a virtue that is or involves beliefs, attitudes, emotional responses, or stances regarding one's worth or importance, or the worth or significance of one's qualities or deeds. On many accounts, humility also is, involves, or results in various positive attitudes towards morally appropriate relations with other persons; but the evaluative perspective on the self is generally treated as the *sine qua non* of humility. The main concern humility is supposed to address is the tendency to think too highly of oneself and make too much of oneself in other ways. And the accounts seem to assume that humility is the virtue of appropriate self-valuing.[17]

On contemporary accounts, humility is variously defined as a matter of awareness of the smallness and limitations of the human condition;[18] being ignorant of, underestimating, not overestimating, or having an accurate sense of one's abilities and achievements,[19] or being unconcerned or unimpressed with them or not giving them much thought or attention;[20] sharing credit with others for one's accomplishments;[21] having a realistic view of one's flaws and limitations and owning or being at ease with them;[22] restraining one's self-aggrandizing ambitions or claims, or not being concerned with the "ego-exalting potency" of one's entitlements;[23] not being enamored with oneself,[24] regarding self-worth as unimportant,[25] or being unconcerned with others' opinions of one's worth;[26] or decentering or transcending the self.[27]

These accounts have been subjected to much criticism, which I'm not going to rehearse. I want instead to identify what I regard as problematic dimensions of these accounts. Before doing that, however, let me admit to being old-fashioned when it comes to defining humility: I am satisfied that the *O.E.D.* has it right, that humility is a matter of having a lowly opinion of one's worthiness or importance, or the worthiness of one's qualities, abilities, and accomplishments. Nevertheless, a low self-estimate need not involve regarding oneself or one's deeds as wholly without worth or importance, nor holding oneself inferior to other humans; nor do we have to equate a low self-estimate with the humiliation of being treated as if one were nothing or worse than nothing. Properly understanding and assessing humility requires properly understanding the various forms of self-valuing and how humility might be related to each.

If we accept the idea that the *sine qua non* of humility is the lowly self-estimate, then one striking feature of the contemporary accounts that reject this idea is that humility is not conceptually continuous with the cognates "to humble," "humiliate," and "humiliation."[28] To be sure, humiliating someone is morally objectionable when it assaults self-respect.[29] But the conceptual connection ought not to be denied. It is also striking that few of the contemporary accounts discuss bad forms of humility, such as servility, submissiveness, aquiescence in subordination, obsequiousness, groveling, and self-denigration. These are morally problematic, to be sure, but their close relation to good humility (if there is such a thing) also shouldn't be denied. At the same time, we are owed an explanation of how the putative virtue of humility is distinct from and not liable to degenerate into these other forms.

If the core of humility is lowly self-assessment, then it is hard to see many contemporary accounts as accounts of humility rather than something else. For example, where is the lowliness in having an accurate or realistic view of one's worth, good qualities, or accomplishments; or in ignoring, being unconcerned with, or not paying attention to them; or in sharing credit for achievements with other contributors? Of course, having a realistic sense of one's flaws and limitations and owning them could be understood in terms of a low self-estimate. But it is not at all clear why this stance is anything more than, or has moral value other than, honesty and integrity. It is also hard to see anything virtuous about regarding one's real merits or moral worth as unimpressive or unimportant, or viewing the self as less valuable than it is or as something to be unconcerned with, or being at ease with flaws that one might correct.

Furthermore, the claim that humility is the foe of arrogance is puzzling, since humility doesn't preclude arrogance;[30] someone can be arrogant about some aspects of themselves and humble about others, or arrogant in some contexts and humble in others, and it makes perfect sense to speak of arrogant humility, as Proust does in mocking the Princesse de Parme (Proust 1934: 1023).

Grenberg (2005) identifies another problem. Once contemporary theorists reject a theistic view in which God's supreme excellence provides the standard for self-assessment, they need to find some other standard. They turn to interpersonal comparison. But their reliance on self–other comparisons "inadvertently give[s] approbation to just those excesses and distortions of humility they are trying to avoid" (Grenberg 2005: 112). As we'll see, Kant regards arrogance and humility that are grounded in self–other comparisons as two sides of the same bad penny.

Finally, from a feminist perspective, the prescribing of humility that is part of calling it a virtue is highly problematic. For members of oppressed groups whose life experience is one of constraint and devaluation, humility about their place, merits, abilities, ambitions, entitlements, worth, or importance would seem to reinforce their subordination and undermine possibilities for flourishing. Self-expansion, embracing merits, downplaying limitations, even self-aggrandizement and arrogance could be more life-enhancing for them.[31] Humility may be a corrective for a tendency, engendered and reinforced in certain social positions, to be possessed by an inflated sense of self, just as a strict diet may be a corrective to pervasive temptations to overeat. But just as not everyone is overweight and many are even starving, so not every human is self-aggrandizing or claims inordinate self-importance, and some have too low a sense of self-worth and importance.

I suspect that what happens with contemporary accounts is that, although they reject one aspect of the traditional account of humility, they accept without question the other three aspects: (1) humility is a virtue, (2) humility is the, i.e., the only, opposite of the vice of arrogance, and (3) the liability to arrogance infects everyone. Abandoning the core sense of humility and the theistic framework in which the other aspects are most at home, they redefine humility so as to make it both a virtue and the opposite of arrogance, however arrogance is understood. But this move ignores the possibility that the appropriate and non-arrogant stance toward the self, or the inhibitor or cure for arrogant self-importance, is something else, such as self-respect or respect for others, and that developing a certain kind of humility is but a means (perhaps only one way for some but not all people in some but not all circumstances) to be self-respecting.

The problematic aspects of contemporary accounts raise the following questions. What is the best way to understand what humility is? Since it is possible to be both humble and arrogant, is humility really the cure for arrogance? Is humility genuinely a human virtue, a trait that is good for all persons to have; or is it instead a characteristic that might be useful only for certain people in certain contexts; or, worse, is it, like arrogance, morally objectionable because it is incompatible with respect for ourselves as persons? If humility is indeed compatible with self-respect, how are the two related? If it is indeed a virtue, might at least a part of its value derive from connections to self-respect? Kant provides valuable answers.

5.2 Kant on the vices of humility

Kant's account of humility has the virtue of defining it as a lowly opinion of oneself. But an individual's opinion of herself might be justified or unjustified. Most of what Kant has to say about humility concerns unjustified forms of it, chief among which is servility.

In *The Metaphysics of Morals* (1996c) Kant identifies servility as one of the vices opposed to duties all persons have to themselves, contrasting it with both self-respect and arrogance (6: 434–437).[32] His discussion begins by emphasizing the dignity, the unsurpassable and unconditional moral worth, that persons have simply as persons, that is, as rationally autonomous moral agents. Each person has dignity, and so the authority to "exact *respect* for himself from all other rational beings in the world" (6: 435). Each of us also has a duty to respect ourselves, i.e., a duty to not disavow our dignity but to act always with consciousness of our status and worth as equal persons. Servility is deliberate self-abasement: "the disavowal of all claim to any moral worth in oneself" that is "contrary to one's duty to oneself since it degrades one's personality" (6: 436).

As Hill (1991) has usefully argued, servility is the absence of a certain kind of self-respect, which I call "interpersonal recognition self-respect."[33] This is the reflexive form of the respect that each person is owed and "exacts" from every person. Interpersonal recognition respect is the practical acknowledgement of a person as a being with dignity and the moral status of an equal among equals. Recognition respect for persons is a categorical moral duty: the End in Itself formulation of the Categorical Imperative, on my reading of it, declares that our fundamental moral obligation is to respect persons.[34]

Interpersonal recognition self-respect involves understanding and valuing oneself as an equal person among persons with the moral authority to demand from all others, and the right to be accorded, the same practical acknowledgement of one's dignity and moral status that all persons are owed, as well as a categorical duty to acknowledge one's worth and status in relation to others' actions and attitudes, and living in light of this self-understanding and self-valuing. Individuals with interpersonal recognition self-respect regard certain attitudes and forms of treatment from others as their due as a person, and other attitudes and forms of treatment as degrading and beneath the dignity of persons; and, other things equal, they are not willing to be regarded or treated by others in ways that mark them as less than a person.

Interpersonal recognition respect and self-respect are core concerns to feminists inasmuch as they justify and can motivate liberatory struggle against all forms of unjust hierarchies in which the dignity and equality of all persons is denied.

The servile person disavows his dignity and invites others to regard him as a being with the status of moral inferior. The low opinion of self-worth and status that servility involves makes it clear that it is a kind of humility;[35] the deliberate discounting of one's dignity makes it clear that it is a vice. Two features make servility deeply bad. First, servility is "false humility" (6: 436), in that its invitation to others to regard one as a being of a lesser sort reflects a false view, both of one's own moral status and worth and also of the moral status and worth of all persons. In its denial that one is an equal member of the moral community with the same dignity and right to respect as every other member, servility conveys the false view that the moral community is not a relation of equals but, rather, a hierarchy of two moral castes, one composed of beings with higher moral status and greater fundamental worth, and the other, to which one belongs, of beings with lower status and less worth who are entitled to much less, maybe nothing, in the way of consideration and respect.

The false picture is reiterated in sociocultural contexts of domination and subordination. Servile subordinates are meekly submissive, acquiescing in their inferiorization. Their servility also encourages members of dominant groups to view social subordinates as inherently inferior and themselves as inherently superior, which bleeds easily from social contexts into attitudes about what is morally appropriate regarding each group. False humility thus reinforces oppression.

Kant objects to servility for a second reason: it is also "lying humility." The servility with which Kant is concerned is not a matter of the possibly blameless misunderstanding of one's worth and status that might, for example, cause someone raised in a racist or sexist society to believe she is inherently inferior to others. Rather, the servile person lies about his moral status, worth, and rights; and his lies are motivated, as lies typically are, by desires for something. It's not that the servile person doesn't care at all about worth; rather, he trades in his dignity in order to "acquire a borrowed worth" or "as a means to acquiring the favor of another" (6: 435–436). Instead of exacting the respect that is his due as a person, the servile individual seeks to "borrow" worth from the value that others ascribe to him for qualities such as his submissiveness, usefulness, or flattering dependence. The servile person, that is, wants others to value him so that he can value himself in reflection. He thus sacrifices his interpersonal recognition self-respect for another form of valuing: self-esteem. Self-esteem is a self-approving attitude, "thinking well of oneself" or "feeling good about oneself," that, according to psychologists, need not be grounded in anything about oneself that is morally significant and typically derives from how one is regarded by others.[36]

In letting the desire for self-esteem determine his self-valuing, the servile individual makes himself, as Kant says, "a plaything of the mere inclinations and hence a thing" (6: 420). Through its willingness to let one's choices be determined by inclinations rather than by reason, servility degrades that which, on Kant's view, is most truly one's self: the rationality that makes one a person. Servility is thus a violation of self-respect and a deeply serious vice.

In contrast with servility, which waives all claims to moral worth and invites others to deny one the respect one is owed, arrogance "demands from others a respect it denies them" (6: 465). As Kant explains, "arrogance (*superbia* and, as the word expresses it, the inclination to be always *on top*) is a kind of *ambition* (*ambitio*) in which we demand that others think little of themselves in comparison with us" (6: 465). Just as servility disrespects oneself by denying one's own dignity and moral status, so arrogance disrespects other persons by denying that they have dignity and the status of equality with oneself. It involves viewing other persons, and demanding that they view themselves, as beings of a lesser kind with lower worth and no right to interpersonal recognition respect. Arrogance is thus "a vice opposed to the respect that every human being can lawfully claim" (6: 465).

Arrogance, Kant says, is the inclination to think highly of oneself, but it asks "not what one is worth, but how much more one is worth than another"; the arrogant person "already believes in his own worth, but he esteems it solely by the lesser status of other people" (Kant 1997; 27: 241). Because the arrogant person falsely believes that the only worth all persons have is comparative, he regards neither himself nor others as beings with dignity unconditionally deserving respect. Indeed, Kant says, the arrogant person is always "*mean* in the depths of his soul," for he knows that "were his fortune suddenly to change, he himself would not find it hard to grovel and to waive any claim to respect from others" (6: 466). Significantly, the "meanness" that is prepared to waive all claims to respect is the same self-abasement that characterizes servility. That is, the arrogant are servile at heart.

Both servility and arrogance are false and lying stances toward the self. They rest on interpersonal comparisons: one has either more or less worth, a higher or lower status, more or fewer rights than others. They share the same hierarchical view of the moral community, differing only with regard to where one locates oneself—at least for now, for the two stances are but alternative ploys in the competition for comparative worth. The view of relative status and comparative value that they share lies about the incomparable, unconditional, and equal dignity of all persons. They both sacrifice interpersonal recognition self-respect in order to boost self-esteem.

Now, Kant makes it clear that servility is not the only false form of humility. Indeed, all humility that involves comparing oneself to other human beings and valuing oneself less is false (6: 435; 27: 349). It is important to recognize that Kant's objection applies to interpersonal comparisons on any value dimension, including merits, accomplishments, personal qualities, social position, likeability, etc. It is thus specious to identify virtuous humility as involving any beliefs about one's lesser worth or importance relative to others.

What's more, Kant regards interpersonal humility as morally dangerous because it inevitably becomes competitive. For "when a human being values his own worth according to others, he seeks either to raise himself above others or to diminish the value of others" (Kant 2007; 9: 491). Interpersonal humility is thus just another arena for competition, as one tries to "equal or surpass others in [being humble] ... believing that in this way one will gain even greater inner worth" (6: 435). Interpersonal comparison always gives rise to competition, and competitors always seek to win, to come out on top: *ambitio et superbia*. Thus even in the humility arena, interpersonal arrogance is at work: the individual who takes others as the measure of his own worth and holds a low opinion of himself is, as Kant says, "actually proud thereby" (27: 349).

Interpersonal humility, then, is at bottom just arrogance in disguise, as arrogance is just humility in waiting. Interpersonal humility not only does not correct interpersonal arrogance, but leads to or expresses it and involves the same false view of the worth of persons. They are the same kind of violation of one's categorical moral duty of interpersonal recognition self-respect. Interpersonal humility is not a virtue, but as serious a vice as interpersonal arrogance.

5.3 Kant on true humility

Not all humility, however, is vicious. Because humility involves a low estimation of one's worth, it necessarily involves a comparative judgment. Interpersonal humility and arrogance take the wrong standard for comparison and wrongly traffic in worth. But what Kant calls "true humility" employs the only genuine standard of worth, namely, the moral law. True humility is "the consciousness and feeling of the insignificance of one's moral worth *in comparison with the law*" (6: 558) that "follows unavoidably from our sincere and exact comparison of ourselves with the moral law" (6:436) and "presupposes a *correct estimation* of self" (27: 39).

The moral worth referred to here is not unconditional dignity but, rather, a conditional, scalar worth that individuals have to earn through goodness of will and can lose through acting wrongly, acting rightly for the wrong reasons, or having a weak or bad character. Given, on the one hand, our ineluctable imperfection and inevitable failings and, on the other, the high standards for conduct and character set by the moral law, it is reasonable to suppose that an accurate assessment of one's moral worth would yield humility.

True humility contrasts not only with servility but also with a form of arrogance that is "a conviction of the greatness of one's moral worth, *but only from failure to compare it with the law*" (6:435; emphasis mine).[37] The last part indicates that arrogance is not only a matter of unjustifiable claims to superiority over others but also of claiming any worth for oneself independently of the moral law. This is not, however, the conceit that results from poor assessment skills; it is the refusal to acknowledge the moral law as the supreme condition of all worth of persons. The arrogance here involves a failure of another kind of self-respect, which I call "agentic recognition self-respect." True humility plays its important moral role in relation to this kind of self-respect.

Whereas interpersonal recognition self-respect is properly acknowledging and valuing oneself as a person among persons, agentic recognition self-respect is properly acknowledging and valuing oneself as a moral agent. Someone who respects herself as a moral agent takes her responsibilities seriously, especially her responsibilities to honor her dignity as a person, to govern herself fittingly, and to make of herself and her life something she can with good reason believe to be good and worthy. For Kant, the most vital of the responsibilities each moral agent has is to actualize one's capacity for moral valuing and autonomous agency by choosing to act through rational motives, i.e., from respect for the moral law. When one acts as one's reason sincerely says it is right to act, rather than doing what one wants regardless of whether it is right or wrong, one acts like the rational being one is and honors one's dignity as a being with the capacity to act on reason. When one acts otherwise, one betrays one's dignity and fails to respect oneself as a moral agent.

The arrogance that claims moral worth independently of the moral law involves just this kind of failure to respect oneself. What makes it morally objectionable is the source of the unjustified claiming of great moral worth: one's desires arrogate the moral authority to determine worth, which belongs to reason's moral law alone. As with the arrogance that lords it over others, this kind of arrogance is motivated by a particular desire: it exchanges honest self-assessment for the more easily obtained enhancement of self-esteem. The arrogant individual wants to think well of himself, but rather than striving to earn moral merit, he arranges his judgments and interpretation of the moral law's demands to declare himself to be admirable. In doing so, he subordinates his rationality to desire and so makes himself a "plaything of the inclinations," debasing his dignity as a rational being and disrespecting his moral agency.

This form of arrogance is the psychological source of all modes of making too much of oneself, all of the vices of pride (and all other vices as well). Kant identifies it as the deepest source of evil in human nature, in which "the mind's attitude is corrupted at its root" (Kant 1996d; 6: 30), because of its denial of the supremacy of the moral law and of reason over mere desires. It must therefore be eliminated to make possible morally justified employment of our agency. Here is where true humility comes in.

True humility is the recognition of the insignificance of our worth that arises inexorably when we honestly and accurately compare ourselves with the exacting standards of the moral law. It curbs the too-high assessment of worth to which we are enticed or pushed by the desire for self-esteem, thus, as Kant says, "confining self-esteem in its legitimate bounds" (27: 636). When we honestly hold ourselves up to the standard of the moral law, we realize that any opinion of our moral worth (or, for that matter, any worth except dignity)[38] other than a low opinion is unjustified. When we realize this, our pretentious self-conceit is, as Kant says in the second *Critique*, "struck down" as the moral law "unavoidably humiliates" our unjustified claims of moral worthiness (Kant 1996a; 5: 73–4). This humiliation is part of the subjective experience that constitutes the "incentive of pure practical reason," i.e., the effect that the moral law has on our motivational system as soon as we recognize it. The humiliating recognition of unworthiness sweeps away the self-importance that otherwise blocks us from directing the abilities and efforts of our agency toward making morally appropriate choices, acting rightly, and improving ourselves morally.

There is a danger here, however. For if humility is all we are left with upon self-evaluation, we are quite liable to lose all moral motivation, sinking into despair, "despondency" and "timorousness" (27: 350). When we focus on the inevitably long list of our flaws, deficiencies, inadequacies, and failures, we can come to "doubt as to man's capacity for ever attaining the moral law," and so "give up all effort to approach it" (27:611). We may come to believe that we will never amount to anything, morally speaking, that we can't even hope to be the good persons that we believe we should be; and then "inertia arises [and we] venture to do nothing at all" (27: 350). There is a real possibility, that is, that true humility will undermine moral agency. Thus, even true humility is as much in need of constraint as is the desire to think well of ourselves, and as morally dangerous without it.

Luckily, however, the experience of humiliation and the ensuing appropriately low assessment of worth that is true humility are not the only results of comparing ourselves sincerely to the moral law. For at the same time as we recognize our failure to live up to the law, we recognize ourselves as its author and are conscious of our "sublime predisposition" for moral self-governance and virtue. We also understand that it is "only through the noble predisposition to the good in us" that we judge ourselves as lacking worth (6: 441). The result of these realizations is "an exaltation of the highest self-valuation," which is respect for our dignity as persons (6: 436). In this way, arrogance is replaced by self-respect. The low self-assessment of humility is thus not an independent or defining attitude about self-worth, but only the first stage in a complex response to ourselves and our worth. And Kant's emphasis in discussing this response throughout the ethical works is not on lowly humility, but on the elevated respect for ourselves that proper assessment of worth inevitably produces.[39]

True humility is the knowledge of one's limitations and deficiencies judged in comparison with self-given moral law. But it is not a Kantian virtue, although it can be part of one.[40] The virtue lies in dealing properly with this knowledge,[41] which is what agentic recognition self-respect involves.

Like interpersonal recognition self-respect, agentic recognition self-respect is a duty we have to ourselves. It is also a virtue, because the acknowledgment of one's dignity that is the motivational core of one's self-conception, and the self-defining considered resolve to live in ways that honor one's dignity as a moral agent and a person among persons, are what make one a good person living a morally appropriate life.

The life-shaping commitment to honor one's dignity as a person involves a commitment to "strive with all one's might" to live up to the standards of the moral law, and so a commitment to moral self-improvement. And that requires honest self-assessment. The judgment of true humility provides important information that helps guide self-improvement. But the central purpose of comparison with the law and accepting its judgment is not to show us how unworthy we are, but rather to remind ourselves of the work yet to be done and to motivate renewed striving to be good and do right. Because what is important to the agentically self-respecting person is not thinking highly of herself, but knowing whether she is living in accord with her moral commitments, true humility does not yield despair, nor does it motivate efforts to boost self-esteem by fiddling with her moral score or giving higher weight to scores based on comparative accomplishments, abilities, or social standing. The self-respecting person puts true humility to work in "a firm determination" to the "tenacious pursuit" of her principles in "dutiful obedience to the law" (27: 610). Humility thus has an important role to play, but its proper place and value is in service to the commitment to respect oneself as a moral agent.

From Kant's perspective, to think that virtuous humility is a matter of being oblivious to, unconcerned about, or unimpressed with self-worth, or of underestimating one's real worth, or of restraining one's ambition for moral excellence, to think that its value lies chiefly in freeing one to pay attention to more important things or in preventing or curing arrogance, is not only to misunderstand what humility is and how it matters morally. It is also to deeply misunderstand both the relation of humility to arrogance and self-respect, and the significance of self-respect to properly valuing the moral dimensions (which is to say, all dimensions) of human life and to effectively motivating morally appropriate living.

From a feminist perspective, agentic recognition respect is a powerful motivation for liberatory struggle. For it adds to the understanding of the inherent injustice of domination and subordination that interpersonal recognition self-respect involves the further understanding that one morally owes it to oneself, and others just like oneself, to resist unjust attempts to constrict freedom and deny agency. And what effective resistance requires is not discounting one's abilities, acknowledging one's limitations and flaws, constraining one's ambitions, or minimizing one's importance; it requires the kind of commitment to oneself as worthy of freedom, worthy of equality, worthy of agency, which is at the heart of self-respect. But for members of dominant groups whose arrogant assumptions of great personal and interpersonal worth underwrite their false and lying beliefs in the rightness of their superior social position, cultivating true humility and even experiencing appropriate humiliation can be the corrective needed to become self-respecting and just.

Humility thus has an important role to play, but only in service to the commitment to respect oneself as a moral agent and an equal person among persons. Humility that is not anchored in and constrained by interpersonal recognition self-respect and agentic recognition self-respect is liable both to agency-undermining servility and despair and to interpersonal comparisons of self-worth that misvalue the self and lead to arrogance. A humility worth having is at best (a) an ancillary virtue, by which I mean that it is of moral value only when it is subsumed by self-respect; (b) a contextual virtue, good only in some contexts but not in all; and (c) an instrumental virtue, one that can serve as a corrective for dispositional deficiencies, especially those that can infect members of dominant groups, but not in itself partially constitutive of human excellence or a flourishing life. Self-respect, not humility, is the primary, absolute, and intrinsic virtue of self-valuing.

Notes

1 This chapter draws significantly from Dillon (2015).
2 I take the term "vices of pride" from Roberts and Wood (2003), where humility is defined as the absence of the vices of pride. All of these vices, I have argued, are dimensions of arrogance (Dillon 2003), so I will focus on arrogance.
3 Exceptions include Richards (1992), Grenberg (2005), Louden (2007), and Dillon (2015).
4 Bloomfield (this volume) is one of the few exceptions.
5 Exceptions include Battaly (this volume) and Bloomfield (this volume).
6 Here I disagree with Grenberg (2005), who argues that humility is the core virtue for Kant. I develop this disagreement below.
7 See Dillon (2017).
8 I develop this position in Dillon (2012) and Dillon (in press).
9 See Dillon (in press).
10 See Dillon (2012).
11 To be meek (from an Old Norse word meaning "soft") is to be "submissive and easily imposed on," "unresentful under injury or reproach" (*O.E.D.*). Here we can begin to see why encouraging humility for oppressed people is problematic.

12 See, for example, Gregory (1850).
13 See, for example, Aquinas (1921: II–II); Benedict (1875); Bernard (1929); and Eckhart (1981).
14 See Porter et al. (2017); Weil (2002); Carlson (1944); Warren (2002).
15 Snow (1995) and Driver (2001) are exceptions.
16 The *Stanford Encyclopedia of Philosophy* entry on "Modesty and Humility" (Bommarito 2018) has an overview of the differences.
17 I say "seems" because the claim is rarely asserted. But the failure even to mention self-respect as appropriate self-valuing strongly suggests it.
18 See Snow (1005) on "existential humility."
19 See, for example, Ben-Ze'ev (1993); Driver (2001); Flanagan (1990); Richards (1992).
20 Garcia (2006); Bommarito (2013); Nadelhoffer et al. (2016).
21 Nuyen (1998).
22 Snow (1995); Grenberg (2005); Whitcomb et al. (2017); Andre (2015).
23 Roberts and Wood (2003).
24 Nadelhoffer, et al. (2016).
25 Roberts (2009).
26 Roberts and Wood (2003).
27 Taylor (2006).
28 One exception is Snow (1995), which explicitly connects humility with being humbled.
29 See Margalit (1996).
30 Whitcomb et al. (2017) notes that one can be both humble and arrogant at the same time: humble about limitations, arrogant about strengths.
31 I have argued for this in Dillon (in press).
32 Citations from Kant's texts refer to volume and page numbers in the Akademie edition (Kant 1900). All quotations are from specified volumes of *The Cambridge Edition of the Works of Immanuel Kant*.
33 I borrow the term "recognition respect" from Darwall (1977).
34 I follow Wood (1999) in this reading of the End in Itself formulation.
35 Richards (1992) argues that what he calls humility ("having an accurate sense of oneself, sufficiently firm to resist pressures … to think too much of oneself" (5) and "having oneself in proper perspective" (36)) is not incompatible with self-respect. The discussion makes it clear that he is contrasting servility and interpersonal recognition self-respect, thus vaguely echoing Kant.
36 The literature on self-esteem is vast. But see Rosenberg (1965); Coopersmith (1967); Owens, Stryker, and Goodman (2001); Mruk (2006); and Kernis (2006).
37 See Dillon (2003) for analysis of two kinds of arrogance.
38 I take Kant's assertion that "nothing can have a worth other than that which the [moral] law determines for it" (1996b; 4: 436) to mean every kind of valuing of absolutely everything.
39 In reversing the significance of these two moments of humility and self-respect, Grenberg (2005) misrepresents Kant's views of both the moral value of true humility and its place in the moral life. Here I agree with Louden (2007).
40 In the *Lectures* Kant says that "proper self-esteem" comprises humility ("for if we compare ourselves with the holy moral law, we discover how remote we are from contiguity with it") and "true noble pride" ("but in regard to our humanity we should think highly of ourselves") (27:349). (Kant treats "self-esteem" and "self-respect" as synonyms.)
41 Swanton (2011) distinguishes humility as knowledge and as the disposition to deal appropriately with it.

References

Andre, Judith. 2015. *Worldly Virtue: Moral Ideals and Contemporary Life*. Lanham, MD: Lexington Books.

Aquinas, Thomas. 1921. *Summa Theologica I–II*, Literally translated by the Fathers of the English Dominican Province. London: Burns Oates and Washborne.

Augustine. 1996. *The City of God Against the Pagans*, Translated by Phillip Levin. Loeb Classical Library, London: William Heineman LTD and Cambridge, MA: Harvard University Press.

Battaly, Heather. 2020. "Can Humility Be a Liberatory Virtue?" In: Mark Alfano, Michael P. Lynch and Alessandra Tanesini (Eds.) *Handbook on the Philosophy of Humility*. New York: Routledge.

Benedict. 1875. *The Rule of Our Most Holy Father St. Benedict*, Edited by Fathers of St. Michaels. London: Washbourne.

Ben-Ze'ev, Aaron. 1993. "The Virtue of Modesty." *American Philosophical Quarterly* 30: 235–246.
Bernard of Clairvaux. 1929. *The Twelve Degrees of Humility and Pride*, Translated by Barton R.V. Mills. London: MacMillan.
Bloomfield, Paul. 2020. "Humility Is Not a Virtue." In: Mark Alfano, Michael P. Lynch, and Alessandra Tanesini (Eds.) *Handbook on the Philosophy of Humility*. New York: Routledge.
Bommarito, Nicolas. 2013. "Modesty as a Virtue of Attention." *Philosophical Review* 122(1): 93–117.
Bommarito, Nicolas. 2018. "Modesty and Humility." In: Edward N. Zalta (Ed.) *The Stanford Encyclopedia of Philosophy* (Winter 2018 Edition). https://plato.stanford.edu/archives/win2018/entries/modesty-humility/. Accessed June 3, 2019.
Carlson, Sebastian. 1944. "The Virtue of Humility." *The Thomist: A Speculative Quarterly Review* 7(2): 135–178, 363–414.
Coopersmith, Stanley. 1967. *The Antecedents of Self-Esteem*. Palo Alto, CA: Consulting Psychologists Press.
Darwall, Stephen. 1977. "Two Kinds of Respect." *Ethics* 88(1): 34–49.
Dillon, Robin S. 2003. "Kant on Arrogance and Self-Respect." In: Cheshire Calhoun (Ed.) *Setting the Moral Compass: Essays by Women Philosophers*. New York: Oxford University Press.
Dillon, Robin S. 2012. "Critical Character Theory: Toward a Feminist Theory of 'Vice'." In: Sharon Crasnow and Anita Superson (Eds.) *Out From the Shadows*. New York: Oxford University Press.
Dillon, Robin S. 2015. "Self-Respect and Humility in Kant and Hill." In: Mark Timmons, and Robert Johnson (Eds.) *Reason, Value, and Respect: Kantian Themes from the Philosophy of Thomas E. Hill, Jr.* New York: Oxford University Press.
Dillon, Robin S. 2017. "Feminist Virtue Ethics." In: Ann Garry, Serene J. Khader, and Alison Stone (Eds.) *Routledge Companion to Feminist Philosophy*. New York: Routledge.
Dillon, Robin. In press. "Self-Respect, Arrogance, and Power." In: Richard Dean and Oliver Sensen (Eds.) *Respect for Persons*. New York: Oxford University Press.
Driver, Julia. 2001. "The Virtues of Ignorance." In: J. Driver (Ed.) *Uneasy Virtue*. London: Cambridge University Press.
Eckhart, Meister. 1981. "On Humility" and "On Detachment." In: *The Essential Sermons, Commentaries, Treatises, and Defense*, Translated by Edmund Colledge and Bernard McGinn. New York: Paulist Press.
Flanagan, Owen. 1990. "Virtue and Ignorance." *The Journal of Philosophy* 87(8): 420–428.
Garcia, J. L. A. 2006. "Being Unimpressed with Ourselves: Reconceiving Humility." *Philosophia* 34(4): 417–435.
Gregory The Great. 1850. *Morals on the Book of Job*, vol. 4. Oxford: John Henry Parker, and London: F. and J. Rivington.
Grenberg, Jeanine. 2005. *Kant and the Ethics of Humility: A Story of Dependence, Corruption and Virtue*. Cambridge: Cambridge University Press.
Hill, Thomas E., Jr. 1991. "Servility and Self-Respect." In: T. E. Hill (Ed.) *Autonomy and Self-Respect*. Cambridge: Cambridge University Press.
Kant, Immanuel. 1900. *Kants gesammelte Schriften*. Königlichen Preußischen (later Deutschen), Edited by Akademie der Wissenschaften. Berlin: Georg Reimer (later Walter De Gruyter).
Kant, Immanuel. 1996a. *Critique of Practical Reason*. In: I. Kant, *Practical Philosophy. The Cambridge Edition of the Works of Immanuel Kant*, Translated and edited by Mary Gregor. Cambridge: Cambridge University Press.
Kant, Immanuel. 1996b. *The Groundwork of the Metaphysics of Morals*. In: I. Kant, *Practical Philosophy. The Cambridge Edition of the Works of Immanuel Kant*, Translated and edited by Mary Gregor. Cambridge: Cambridge University Press.
Kant, Immanuel. 1996c. *The Metaphysics of Morals*. In: I. Kant, *Practical Philosophy. The Cambridge Edition of the Works of Immanuel Kant*, Translated and edited by Mary Gregor. Cambridge: Cambridge University Press.
Kant, Immanuel. 1996d. *Religion Within the Boundaries of Mere Reason*, Translated by George di Giovanni. In: I. Kant, *Religion and Rational Theology. The Cambridge Edition of the Works of Immanuel Kant*, Edited by Allen W. Wood and George di Giovanni. Cambridge: Cambridge University Press.
Kant, Immanuel. 1997. *Lectures on Ethics: The Cambridge Edition of the Works of Immanuel Kant*, Translated by Peter Heath, Edited by Peter Heath and Jerome Schneewind. Cambridge: Cambridge University Press.
Kant, Immanuel. 2007. *Lectures on Pedagogy*, Translated by Robert B. Louden. In: I. Kant, *Anthropology, History, and Education. The Cambridge Edition of the Works of Immanuel Kant*, Edited by Gunter Zoller and Robert B. Louden. Cambridge: Cambridge University Press.
Kernis, Michael H. (Ed.). 2006. *Self-Esteem Issues and Answers: A Sourcebook of Current Perspectives*. New York: Psychology Press.

Louden, Robert B. 2007. "Kantian Moral Humility: Between Aristotle and Paul." *Philosophy and Phenomenological Research* 75(3): 632–639.
Margalit, Avashai. 1996. *The Decent Society*. Cambridge, MA: Harvard University Press.
Mruk, Christopher J. 2006. *Self-Esteem Research, Theory and Practice*, 3rd edn. New York: Springer Publishing Company.
Nadelhoffer, Thomas, Jennifer Cole Wright, Matthew Echols, Tyler Perini, and Kelly Venezia. 2016. "Some Varieties of Humility Worth Wanting." *Journal of Moral Philosophy* 14(2): 1–32.
Nuyen, A. T. 1998. "Just Modesty." *American Philosophical Quarterly* 35: 101–109.
Owens, Timothy J., Sheldon Stryker, and Norman Goodman. 2001. *Extending Self-Esteem Theory and Research: Sociological and Psychological Currents*. New York: Cambridge University Press.
Porter, Steven L., Anantanand Rambachan, Abraham Vélez de Cea, Dani Rabinowitz, Stephen Pardue, and Sherman Jackson. 2017. "Religious Perspectives on Humility." In: Everett L. Worthington, Jr., Don E. Davis, and Joshua N. Hook (Eds.) *Handbook of Humility: Theory, Research, and Applications*. New York: Routledge.
Proust, Marcel. 1934. *Remembrance of Things Past*. Translated by C.K. Scott Moncrieff. New York: Random House.
Richards, Norvin. 1992. *Humility*. Philadelphia, PA: Temple University Press.
Roberts, Robert C. 2009. "The Vices of Pride." *Faith and Philosophy* 26(2): 119–133.
Roberts, Robert C., and Jay Wood. 2003. "Humility and Epistemic Goods." In: Michael DePaul and Linda Zagzebski (Eds.) *Intellectual Virtue: Perspectives from Ethics and Epistemology*. Oxford: Clarendon Press.
Rosenberg, Morris. 1965. *Society and the Adolescent Self-Image*. Princeton, NJ: Princeton University Press.
Snow, Nancy E. 1995. "Humility." *The Journal of Value Inquiry* 29(2): 203–216.
Swanton, Christine. 2011. "Kant's Impartial Virtues of Love." In: Lawrence Jost and Julian Wuerth (Eds.) *Perfecting Virtue*. Cambridge: Cambridge University Press.
Taylor, Gabrielle. 2006. *Deadly Vices*. London: Oxford University Press.
Warren, Rick. 2002. *The Purpose Driven Life*. Grand Rapids, MI: Zondervan.
Weil, Simone. 2002. *Gravity and Grace*, Translated by Emma Craufurd. London: Routledge.
Whitcomb, Dennis, Heather Battaly, Jason Baehr, and Daniel Howard-Snyder. 2017. "Intellectual Humility: Owning Our Limitations." *Philosophy and Phenomenological Research* 94(3): 509–539.
Wood, Allen W. 1999. *Kant's Ethical Thought*. New York: Cambridge University Press.

6
THE PUZZLE OF HUMILITY AND DISPARITY

Dennis Whitcomb, Heather Battaly, Jason Baehr and Daniel Howard-Snyder

True story: when the female members of a colleague's research lab learned of his plans to study humility, they remarked: "Humility is exactly what you need more of, *if you're a white male*!" Subtext: humility is uncalled for when you're oppressed. Frederick Douglass observed something similar with respect to the horrific source of oppression that was American slavery:

> With a book in my hand so redolent of the principles of liberty, and with a perception of my own human nature and of the facts of my past and present experience, I was equal to a contest with the religious advocates of slavery, whether white or black; for blindness in this matter was not confined to the white people. I have met, at the south, many good, religious colored people who were under the delusion that God required them to submit to slavery and to wear their chains with meekness and humility. I could entertain no such nonsense as this…
>
> *(Douglass 1892, 104–105)*

Humility seems the last thing the enslaved need. More generally, and to put it mildly, humility seems to be an inappropriate response for the oppressed toward their oppressors. It seems inappropriate elsewhere too. If you find yourself accosted by a neo-Nazi who advocates reinstating the Final Solution, humility seems like the wrong response, just as it does when you're evangelized by a flat-earther. In sum, humility seems inappropriate as a response in a variety of contexts. But how can this be? If humility is a virtue, and if to act virtuously is to act well, how can it ever be inappropriate to act humbly?

To sharpen this puzzle, we'll use the phrase "contexts of disparity" to capture interactions in which people differ dramatically along a normative dimension, where some are in the right and others are in the wrong. If you're an oppressed person interacting with your oppressor, or if you're buttonholed by neo-Nazis or flat-earthers, you are in a context of disparity. In each case, you differ dramatically from others along a normative dimension—*social power* in the case of oppression, *moral credentials* in the case of neo-Nazism, and *epistemic credentials* in the case of flat-earthism—and you are in the right and they are in the wrong. To be sure, there are important differences across different "contexts of disparity." For instance, the oppressed are harmed systematically (and often horrifically) whereas those who face wielders of heinous or ridiculous views may be harmed in one-off ways or even not harmed at all. In terms of *harm*, then, some contexts of disparity are utterly unimportant compared to others. Nonetheless, the concept of "contexts of disparity" captures something important these interactions all share: due to a dramatic normative difference, humility seems to *mis*advise those who are in the right about how to respond to those who are in the wrong.

Again we wonder: how can this be? Is it because humility is not a virtue, as Hume (1751/1975) argued? Or is it instead that genuine virtues sometimes misadvise us? Or, if they never misadvise us, are they nonetheless sometimes unimportant or irrelevant or silent? Or might it so happen that humility gives us correct advice after all, even when we are in the right in contexts of disparity? This thicket of questions entangles us; what follows is our attempt to work through it.

6.1 First lesson: the importance of humility is limited

Contexts of disparity reveal that the importance of humility is limited in several ways. First, it is limited because it is limited for in-the-right parties in contexts of disparity *relative to in-the-wrong parties* in those contexts. The in-the-wrong parties in these contexts should be *much* more concerned with humility than the in-the-right parties. *Theirs* are the thinking, sentiments, and behavior that blatantly manifest humility's lack; *theirs* is the primary responsibility to increase humility's exercise.[1] Second, the importance of humility is limited because it is limited for in-the-right parties in contexts of disparity *relative to other virtues* for those parties in those contexts. More than humility, those parties should draw on self-respect, self-trust, courage, and perseverance.[2] Perhaps most centrally, they should draw on *pride*: an attentiveness to and ownership of their *strengths* (Whitcomb et al., 2017, 528–532). Third, virtues *in general,* humility included, are plausibly at least sometimes *less important than certain other things* when it comes to contexts of disparity—less important in perhaps several senses, including (at least) the sense that our ameliorative efforts should focus on those other things before focusing on the cultivation of virtues. For instance, *social structures*—such as laws against slavery, or integrated educational systems, or social media content feed algorithms reducing the spread of false information—are plausibly at least sometimes more important when it comes to contexts of disparity than are *any* virtues, humility included. Our efforts should, at least sometimes, focus on improving such social structures before they focus on improving peoples' statuses as virtuous.

There is a fourth way, too, in which contexts of disparity reveal limits of the importance of humility. In order to explain this one, we'll need to first explain our theory of the nature of humility. In Whitcomb et al. (2017), we argued that the trait of *intellectual* humility consists in being both attentive to and owning one's *intellectual* limitations, such as cognitive mistakes, gaps in knowledge, deficits in cognitive skills, intellectual character flaws, and so forth. On our view, the trait of humility *per se* consists in being both attentive to and owning a much broader range of one's limitations, such as moral mistakes (e.g., breaking a promise), affective shortcomings (e.g., lacking a sense of humor), deficits in general skills (e.g., being a terrible cook or an awful driver), flaws in moral character (e.g., being cowardly or rash), and so on.

For the humble to be *attentive* to their limitations is for them to be disposed in such a way that their limitations come to mind routinely, in contrast with being oblivious to them. So a person who is completely inattentive to their limitations cannot be humble. However, someone can be attentive to their limitations while also being flagrantly complacent about them, systematically attempting to conceal them from others, or responding defensively whenever they are brought to light. They would not be humble either. Accordingly, the humble also own their limitations.

For the humble to *own* their limitations is for them to be so disposed that, when their limitations come to mind, they respond in such a way that excludes flagrant complacence, systematic concealment, chronic defensiveness, and the like. More generally, owning one's limitations characteristically involves dispositions to (i) believe and accept that one has them, (ii) admit and acknowledge them, (iii) care about them and take them seriously, and (iv) feel regret or dismay about them. Owning one's limitations tracks familiar ways of thinking and speaking, as when we tell a friend it is high time for them to "own their shit," or when we encourage a loved one to "own their addiction," or when a losing team "owns its poor play."

That is our theory of the trait of humility, roughly. If it is correct, then (among other things) the humble will be more likely than the non-humble to admit their limitations to others, defer to others, seek help from others, and have a low concern for status, and they will be less likely to set unattainable goals and disrespect others. (See Whitcomb et al., 2017, 13–26).

Note that someone can possess the trait of humility while lacking the *virtue* of humility, for at least two reasons.

First, someone might be disposed to attend to and own their limitations but at the *wrong* time, toward the *wrong* people, or in the *wrong* way. If this disposition is entrenched in their psychology, they might be humble; however, their humility would not be a virtue since they might be excessively humble or foolishly so. For the trait of humility to be a virtue in someone, they must possess *phronesis* (or something similar), i.e. good practical judgment, whereby they know *when*, toward *whom*, and *how* to attend to and own their limitations.

Gary Watson makes a similar point about benevolence: "the word 'benevolence' names both a general concern for others (which may be excessive, and lead to bad action) and the qualified and informed concern that constitutes the virtue" (1984, 68). Watson's point applies widely. Just as an excess of the trait of benevolence can cause one to donate without considering an organization's merit, an excess of the trait of open-mindedness can cause one to engage perspectives that aren't helpful in reaching the truth (Baehr 2011), an excess of the trait of intellectual perseverance can cause one to stick with projects that are ill-fated (Battaly 2017), and—pertinently—an excess of the trait of humility can cause one to defer without considering the epistemic or moral credentials of the view or person one is deferring to. More generally, an excess of the trait of humility can cause one to be overly attentive to, or to over-own, one's limitations. If you constantly attend to your limitations, or you routinely over-emphasize them, over-attribute negative outcomes to them, or care too much about them, or they regularly overwhelm you, then you lack the virtue of humility, even though you possess the trait. You are humble to a fault. We call this excess *servility*, which tends to be vicious (see also Tanesini 2018). On our view, then, the *virtue* of humility lies in a mean between the vice of servility and a corresponding vice of arrogance, which involves deficient attentiveness to, and under-owning of, one's limitations.

Second, someone disposed to attend to and own their limitations at the right time, toward the right people, and in the right way, might nevertheless be disposed to do so for the *wrong reason*, in which case they will have the trait but not the virtue of humility. For example, a power-hungry faculty member who aims to be elected department chair, but whose department values humility, might set out to cultivate a settled disposition to attend to and own their limitations at the right time, in the right way, and so on. Even if they succeed, they do not possess the virtue of humility since the motives that underlie their humility do not make them better as a person (Baehr 2011, chapter 6; Battaly 2015, chapter 3).

On our view, the *virtue* of humility is a disposition to *appropriately* attend to and own one's limitations. We can't emphasize strongly enough that the *form* this takes can *vary significantly* across situations. For instance, in some cases it may call for one to explicitly acknowledge one's limitations to someone else, e.g., when you've callously offended them, while in other cases it might call for one simply to admit the limitation to oneself, e.g., when you realize that you're not as gifted as you thought. Another example: compare owning one's struggle with abstract reasoning with owning one's tendency to irresponsibly gossip. If you can't do anything about the first but you can do something about the second, then appropriately owning the first might involve little more than accepting it, while appropriately owning the second might involve resolving to get rid of it.

Applying these views to contexts of disparity, we can delineate a fourth way in which the importance of humility is limited, to wit: if it is the *trait* we are talking about, then in contexts of disparity humility *does indeed* sometimes misadvise those who are in the right. *Douglass was right* about the *trait* that is humility. For the trait can be excessive, thus amounting to servility. In such cases, the trait can advise in-the-right parties to engage in such inappropriate acts as deferring to neo-Nazis or flat-earthers, or (in the slavery case) refraining from resisting one's owners. A trait that sometimes yields inappropriate actions such as these is thereby of limited importance.

To recapitulate: humility's importance is limited because it is limited for those in the right in contexts of disparity in at least four ways. Limitations-owning itself has its limits.

6.2 Second lesson: humility *is* important, even for those in the right in contexts of disparity

We've argued that the importance of humility is limited. Some readers might conclude, with apologies to Larry David and the Templeton Foundation, that we should curb our enthusiasm about it. But that would be a mistake. For, despite its limits, humility—that is, the *virtue* of humility—*does* play several important roles, even for those who are in the right in contexts of disparity. Or so we'll argue.

It is with some unease that we will share these arguments. W.E.B. Du Bois observes that slaveholders encouraged slaves to be humble: "The long system of repression and degradation of the Negro tended to emphasize the elements of his character which made him a valuable chattel: courtesy became humility, moral strength degenerated into submission" (1903/1994, 121). Following suit, Nancy Snow observes that slaveholders encouraged "certain traits or 'virtues'" in slaves, including "docility … shame, gratitude, loyalty … [and] humility," since the humble and docile were easier to control (2004, 60). These passages make us worry that our arguments might generate grist for the mill of those who would abuse the language of humility to keep oppressed people down. But we'll share those arguments nonetheless, for two reasons. First, while there are no doubt cases where theorizing should remain unshared due to its potential for abuse, the downside risk must be weighed against upside potential. In the current case the upside potential is non-trivial, because (we'll argue) a proper understanding of the virtue of humility reveals that it is *not* demeaning, submissive, or degrading, *but instead* enables informed, forceful, and courageous moral and intellectual action. Second, although there is a heartening current trend in the opposite direction, moral theorizing among academic philosophers has long failed to pay sufficient heed to conditions of oppression. The current trend in the opposite direction ought to continue and expand. We offer our arguments with the goal of contributing to that continuation and expansion. Without further ado then, we'll argue that there are at least five important roles the virtue of humility can play, even for those in the right in contexts of disparity.

6.2.1 Ambition

The virtue of humility helps us balance our ambition, both by tempering it and by bolstering it. As for tempering, the virtue of humility sometimes keeps us from biting off more than we can chew (Helgevold 2013, 127; Whitcomb et al., 2017, 522). That's because, when we own our limitations, we are more apt than we otherwise would be to temper our ambitions and set achievable goals. This does *not* mean that our goals aren't *difficult*; rather, it means that they aren't *too* difficult given our limitations. For instance, suppose a flat-earther confronts you. Thinking too highly of your powers of persuasion, you might endeavor to convince them on the spot that they are wrong, to produce a disquisition so incisive that they see the light and immediately recant. The virtuously humble are more apt to acknowledge that this goal is beyond reach. In the service of other virtues, like charity or curiosity, the virtue of humility can help one set *appropriately* difficult goals with respect to the flat-earther. One such goal might be to understand what motivates this person's belief. And another, if one is especially charitable, might be to formulate and enact a several-step plan in light of that motivation such that, once those steps are implemented, the flat-earther may begin rethinking his view. In this way, the virtue of humility can play a supporting role in relation to the virtues of charity or curiosity—it can help us set goals that are appropriately difficult instead of goals that are too difficult.

The black musician Daryl Davis (1958–) may be a case in point. He has gradually convinced several KKK members to leave the Klan. In a documentary film about his efforts, he compares changing the mind of a Klan member to losing weight. He says:

> Y'all see this fine figure right here [indicating his ample mid-section]? I didn't put this on overnight. I want to lose it. I'm not going to lose it by tomorrow. But, if I work on it over time, it will shrink down. When you are engrained in this stuff [white supremacy], you are not going to shut it off overnight.
>
> *(Ornstein 2016, 13:58)*

Davis owns his inability to immediately change the minds of Klan members; so he tempers his ambitions, thereby removing obstacles to drawing on charity, inviting Klan members to conversations and meals, with some success.

The virtue of humility also helps keep us from biting off *less than we should*. Imagine someone who *over*-owns his limitations by paying too much heed to them, attributing too many shortcomings to them, and so on. Such a person might refrain from resisting racism at all, in any way, because he (wrongly) judges that he is poorly equipped for the task. Or imagine a person who incorrectly thinks his powers of interpersonal pedagogy are so limited that he can't knock even the tiniest chip away from the worldview of a flat-earther. Such a person, taking himself to be unable, might refrain from trying to make *any* progress with the flat-earther. In cases such as these, people refrain from setting appropriately ambitious goals *not* because their goals are *too* ambitious, but because their goals aren't ambitious *enough*. Their failures to set appropriately ambitious goals manifest the vice of servility, of *over*-owning one's limitations. The virtue of humility corrects for such failures by bolstering our ambitions. It does so by keeping us from over-owning our limitations, keeping us balanced in the mean of appropriate owning, between the extremes of excessive and deficient owning.

6.2.2 Belief

The virtue of humility also tempers and bolsters belief. With respect to tempering, it helps us to refrain from forming beliefs that outstrip our evidence, by making us aware of ways in which our evidence supports only a limited range of claims to a limited extent (Whitcomb et al., 2017, 525). For example, humility might make us aware that our evidence does not support the conclusion that in-the-wrong parties are irredeemable monsters or hopeless dolts and, having owned that fact, enable us to overcome the temptation to draw it. As a result, we are freed to draw on intellectual virtues like fairmindedness and moral virtues like justice to help us follow the often-difficult advice of Martin Luther King (1963, 45):

> [W]e must recognize that the evil deed of the enemy-neighbor, the thing that hurts, never quite expresses all that he is. An element of goodness may be found even in our worst enemy … . When we look beneath the surface, beneath the impulsive deed, we see within our enemy-neighbor a measure of goodness and know that the viciousness and evilness of his acts are not quite representative of all that he is.

That is, humility can help us recognize that in-the-wrong parties are not monsters but rather humans, who may even occasionally, or in some domains of their lives, do things that are morally or intellectually appropriate. Humility can help us recognize that our interlocutors may not possess moral and intellectual vices across all domains, though they may possess those vices and/or perform vice-characteristic actions in some domains.

Interestingly, the virtue of humility can also help oppressed people resist internalizing the perspective of the oppressor. Since humility tends to keep us from forming beliefs that outstrip our evidence, it might help prevent oppressed people from believing they are inferior or worthless. Just as humility can keep us from jumping to the conclusion that an in-the-wrong party is a monster or a dolt, it can keep oppressed people from jumping to the conclusion that *they* are inferior or worthless, or at least slow the process of internalization.

The virtue of humility doesn't only *temper* belief by keeping us from *under*-owning our limitations; it also *bolsters* belief by keeping us from *over*-owning our limitations. Over-owning the limitations of your evidence or reasoning powers, you might refrain from believing that Klan members or neo-Nazis or flat-earthers are making serious mistakes; for you might think your evidence and reasoning abilities do not quite justify such beliefs. In such a scenario you would manifest the vice of servility. The proper corrective would be the virtue of humility, the virtue through which you own your limitations *appropriately* instead of excessively or deficiently.

6.2.3 Emotion

In the passage quoted above, MLK also claims that "there is some good in the worst of us and some evil in the best of us. When we discover this, we are less prone to hate our enemies" (1963, 45). This suggests that the virtue of humility can also help us temper our emotions. It helps, first, by alerting us to our tendencies toward excess, e.g., to respond to flat-earthers with disgust or rage, and second, by enabling us to own them and so to respond appropriately, e.g., by taking steps to retrain our emotions (Coplan 2010). Sometimes, in contexts of disparity, anger is called for but white-hot rage is not; sometimes antipathy is called for but unrelenting hatred is not; sometimes dislike is called for but revulsion is not. By alerting us to our tendencies to excessive emotion and enabling us to own them, humility allows us to draw on a range of other virtues in contexts of disparity, including what Aristotle (350BCE/1998) calls "good-temper," which involves avoiding excessive anger, i.e. being "angry at the right things and with the right people, and … as we ought, when we ought, and as long as we ought" (NE.1125b32–33, ungendered).

We can't emphasize strongly enough that, in contexts of disparity, the virtue of humility helps temper our emotions *when such tempering is called for*. We claim, not that the virtue of humility *always* calls for such tempering, but rather that it *sometimes* does. So then: when, exactly, does the virtue of humility call for the tempering of emotion in contexts of disparity? This is a difficult question to which we have no complete answer. But we can say this much.

Tempered emotion is called for in one-off interactions with flat-earthers, when one has a tendency to respond with loathing and rage rather than dismay and frustration. Perhaps, tempering is even called for in some one-off interactions with neo-Nazis and Klan members, though these cases will be more complex since the normative dimension will have shifted from epistemic ridiculousness to massive moral heinousness and one's social identity might justify a less-than-tempered response. Here, intense rage and loathing may be appropriate, even if hardened, merciless, and terrifying rage or dehumanizing hatred would be excessive.

The really difficult case, though, is horrific oppression. Might tempered emotion be called for on the part of the oppressed in the face of their oppressors? Tessman argues that an unsurpassable level of unrelenting rage and hatred is an appropriate affective response to proponents of systematic racism, in which case tempering is not called for (2005, 115–117, 124). In the same vein, bell hooks writes: "Many African Americans feel uncontrollable rage when we encounter white supremacist aggression. That rage is not pathological. It is an appropriate response to injustice" (1995, 26). In contrast, MLK, Jesus, Ghandi and others (e.g., Silvermint 2017) advise against hatred and the sort of hardened resolve against one's oppressors that leads to dehumanization. We do not feel well-positioned to resolve this dispute.[3] But we do think that even if tempering anger and hatred has no place in contexts of horrific oppression, it will still be relevant in other contexts of disparity.

Crucially, the virtue of humility not only tempers but also *bolsters*—with emotion as well as ambition and belief. Just as it brings us to appropriately own and thus manage the limitations which are our tendencies to *excess* emotion, it also brings us to appropriately own and thus manage the limitations which are our tendencies to *deficient* emotion. When what is called for is *more* anger or fear or disgust or dismay, so that we are limited in *not having enough* of these things, the virtue of humility brings us to attend to and appropriately own, and thus manage, these emotional limitations. For instance, suppose that you are no longer angry with Klan members, having been numbed to them over the years. The virtue of humility would bring you to attend to and own this emotional deficiency. It would thereby set the stage for proper management. Frequently this management would consist in retraining your emotions to make them stronger, though in some cases it might consist in coming to peace with them while continuing to recognize them as deficient. Similar points apply in other cases of deficient emotion such as insufficient dismay with flat-earthers.

6.2.4 Seeking and accepting assistance

In contexts of disparity, the virtue of humility can help us seek and accept assistance when (and only when) we need it (Whitcomb et al., 2017, 524). Moreover, it can help us appropriately manage our affective responses to receiving or avoiding this assistance.

For one example, the virtue of humility can help people seek and accept assistance in their efforts to survive or resist oppression. It can help them, first, to recognize the limitations of their ability to respond to oppression alone and, second, to own the need for outside assistance, e.g., by mitigating the effects of debilitating feelings of guilt about needing and receiving assistance.[4] In this manner, the virtue of humility might pave the way for other virtues involved in surviving or resisting oppression, e.g., courage, perseverance, and justice.[5]

For another example, imagine being challenged by a flat-earther to give them, on the spot, your evidence for why you think that the earth is round. You haven't thought about the matter since high school, and you don't remember much about it. Humility can help you to own your failure to remember, keep you from trying to fake a response, check your rising embarrassment and/or frustration with yourself. With these impediments nullified by humility, other virtues can kick in if the matter is important enough to you to pursue, e.g., curiosity, fairmindedness, and thoroughness as you throw yourself into the requisite research. In these ways, the virtue of humility helps us seek and accept assistance when we should do those things. It does this by keeping us from *under*-owning our limitations.

Are there also cases in which one is *too* inclined to seek and accept assistance or *too* emotionally at ease with doing so? And, if there are, can the virtue of humility help in these cases?

Analyses of the virtue of autonomy will tell us whether and when one can be excessively inclined to seek and accept assistance, and whether and when it is appropriate to exercise one's own agency.[6] When the virtue of autonomy calls for exercising one's own agency, the virtue of humility can play a supporting role by keeping us from *over*-owning our limitations. People with the virtue of humility don't pay their limitations excessive heed, and so *won't* (at least not *via* such heed) refrain from exercising their own agency in cases where that is appropriate.

6.2.5 Engaging the Other

Believing that in-the-wrong parties are monsters, or hating them with a resolve that hardens us against their humanity, can lead us to *disengage* with them, to leave them to their own devices away from our clean hands. While disengagement is surely sometimes called for, surely other times it is not. Virtues such as civility, charity, and respect for others can guide us here. When they advise engagement, the virtue of humility can assist them through tempering and bolstering.

Start with tempering. Virtues such as civility, charity, and respect sometimes advise engagement with in-the-wrong others. When they do so, the virtue of humility, through limitations-owning, can assist by tempering our uncivil, uncharitable, and disrespectful beliefs, behavior, and emotions, making disengagement less likely. By way of illustration, return to Frederick Douglass. In the decades preceding the Civil War, some abolitionists advocated the secession of the Free States and forming a new country in which slavery was illegal, one dissociated with the remaining slave-holding United States. They rallied under the motto "no union with slaveholders." Douglass (1855, 32–33) rejected this position, arguing that it

> leads to false doctrines, and mischievous results … It condemns … our Savior, for eating with publicans and sinners … [moreover,] to dissolve the Union, as a means to abolish slavery, is about as wise as it would be to burn up this city, in order to get the thieves out of it …. We hear the motto, "no union with slaveholders", and I answer it … "*No union with slaveholding*". I would unite with anybody to do right; and with nobody to do wrong.

Douglass argued that those in the wrong, even those heinously and ridiculously in the wrong, are not beneath our engagement. We suspect that humility helped him make this argument by tempering his ambitions, beliefs, and emotions. In any case, Douglass *did* engage with his oppressors, in his context of disparity. Even if humility did not in fact support him in this respect, it would have been apt to do as much.

Douglass has an unlikely ally in Megan Phelps-Roper, who left the cult-like Westboro Baptist Church in 2012, an anti-Semitic and anti-gay hate group comprised almost entirely of the Phelps-Roper family. She credits her departure to others outside the Church who engaged her. In her Ted talk, she encourages such engagement:

> My friends on Twitter didn't abandon their beliefs or their principles, only their scorn. They channeled their infinitely justifiable offense and came to me with pointed questions tempered with kindness and humor … . They approached me as a human being and that was more transformative than two full decades of outrage.
>
> *(Phelps-Roper 2017)*

Here we see the tempering of belief, behavior, and emotion that humility can provide, curtailing unrelenting rage and hatred toward people like Phelps-Roper, helping us to avoid jumping to the conclusion that she is a monster, and enabling suitable engagement.[7]

The virtue of humility not only *tempers* belief, behavior, and emotion by keeping us from *under*-owning our limitations, but also *bolsters* those things by keeping us from *over*-owning limitations. The bolstering, no less than the tempering, can help us engage in-the-wrong others in cases where virtues like charity and civility call on us to do as much. This is because over-owning one's limitations, no less than under-owning them, can make one disinclined to engage. People who over-own their limitations might be disinclined to engage in-the-wrong others because they mistakenly fail to be angry or dismayed with those in-the-wrong others, or because they mistakenly think they can't make a worthwhile difference and fail to set appropriately ambitious goals. The virtue of humility blocks these kinds of failures to engage because, keeping us from over-owning our limitations, it bolsters our beliefs and emotions.

6.3 Answering some worries

In keeping with the worries from Du Bois and Snow above (page 75), Robin Dillon argues that "to laud humility for its usefulness to others borders on sinister, given the long history of casting it as a virtue of subordinated peoples—how much easier to dominate those who believe that submissiveness makes them good" (2015, 45). Here, Dillon understands humility as a kind of "lowliness, submissiveness, degradation of position or value, abasement" (2015, 45).[8]

Humility, understood like *this*, is no doubt inappropriate in contexts of disparity. However, the expressions of humility sketched above are not like this. For instance, someone who owns their moral and intellectual limitations, and who thereby makes way for charity to prevent them from unduly vilifying flat-earthers and neo-Nazis, does not manifest lowliness, submissiveness, degradation, or abasement. On our theory, lowliness is an excess of the *trait* of humility and not a manifestation of the *virtue*; it is a kind of servility, of over-owning one's limitations, and it is often vicious. It causes inappropriate actions and emotions in contexts of disparity. Far from *exemplifying* the virtue of humility for those in the right in contexts of disparity, lowliness, submissiveness, degradation, and abasement *are incompatible with* the virtue of humility for those people in those cases. Thus we agree with Hannah Gadsby, who in her remarkable standup routine *Nanette* (2018) says

> I built a career out of self-deprecating humor … . And I don't want to do that anymore. Because do you understand what self-deprecation means when it comes from somebody who already exists in the margins? It's not humility, it's humiliation. I put myself down in order to speak, in order to seek permission to speak, and I simply will not do that anymore … If that means that my comedy career is over, then, so be it.

Hear hear. Humility is not humiliation. Though an excess of the *trait* of humility can bring one to humiliate oneself, the *virtue* of humility enables informed, forceful, and courageous moral and intellectual action of the sort Gadsby here exemplifies.

Another worry is that humility is inappropriate in contexts of disparity because it involves *deference* and deferring, e.g., to a flat-earther or a neo-Nazi, is inappropriate; or because it involves *low concern for status*, which is "implausible with respect to members of oppressed groups" who "must be very concerned … about how others perceive them (especially the powerful)" (Daukas 2019, 381). We agree that deferring to a flat-earther or a neo-Nazi is inappropriate, and that it is appropriate for the oppressed to be concerned with status. On our theory, deferring and low concern for status are characteristic manifestations of the virtue of humility in *some* contexts, e.g., in contexts of privilege. But in contexts of disparity, deferring and low concern for status are characteristic manifestations of the vice of servility instead of the virtue of humility.

Let's unpack this a bit. On our theory, people with the *trait* of humility characteristically defer to others and even have a low concern for status. Indeed, on our theory, these are also characteristic of the *virtue* of humility *in privileged contexts*, contexts in which people do not differ dramatically along some normative dimension like social power or moral status or epistemic credentials, with some in the right and others in the wrong. To illustrate, imagine an academic giving a talk at a department colloquium, and now *add* that this is *not* a context of disparity. Relative to this context, audience members with the virtue of humility who lack knowledge about the speaker's topic will be aware of this gap in their knowledge, own it, and so likely defer to the speaker on a range of points. They will also be relatively unconcerned with their professional status, and thus won't grandstand or play games of "one-up-man-ship" in the Q&A. Rather, they will ask questions that they don't already know the answers to and they will not pretend expertise on the speaker's topic. If the speaker also has the virtue of humility, they will likely admit when they don't know the answer to a question or have no reply to an objection.

However, on our theory, in contexts of disparity, it is *not* appropriate to defer to in-the-wrong parties; moreover, in such contexts, concern for status *is* appropriate for in-the-right parties. Deferring and lack of concern manifest the vice of servility in such contexts. Consider severe cases of oppression in which one needs to be concerned with one's status in order to survive. This is not, of course, a concern for one's professional status (as above); it is a concern for one's status as a person. Now, consider what it would be like to be in this context and to limitations-own in such a way that one comes to have a low concern for one's status as a person—one no longer cares about one's entitlements as a person or about being seen and treated as property. Relative to this context, low concern for status is characteristic of the vice of servility, rather than the virtue of humility. Next, consider someone who limitation-owns in such a way that they come to defer to the neo-Nazi or the flat-earther. Imagine a person who is so focused on their own limitations that they don't trust their own views, or don't trust their ability to figure out what is wrong with the views of the flat-earther or the neo-Nazi, and so they defer. This, too, is characteristic of the vice of servility, rather than the virtue of humility.

6.4 Future work

Many relevant questions remain. Do similar puzzles apply to other virtues such as honesty or courage? Would arguments analogous to ours help resolve *those* puzzles? On the puzzle of humility and disparity in particular, does the limitations-owning theory do *better* than other theories of humility might? More generally, how do the numerous theories of humility compare to one another concerning their success in solving this puzzle? Do contexts of epistemic disparity such as those involving flat-earthers connect to the epistemology of disagreement? Are those contexts usefully theorized as featuring *extreme non-peer disagreement*? Do contexts of disparity involving heinous views and social power connect to liberatory epistemology, for instance to work on epistemic injustice and white ignorance? Do our arguments about contexts of disparity apply equally to interactions with climate-deniers or dogmatic Trump-supporters? Do they tell us anything about humility and political polarization? We have yet to explore these matters.[9]

Notes

1 Responsibility can also extend to bystanders with privilege.
2 On courage, see Tessman (2005, 125); on self-respect, see Dillon (2015); on self-trust, see Jones (2012).
3 See Cherry (2017) on some of the difficulties involved in trying to do so.
4 Thanks to June Tangney and Robert Emmons for suggesting these ideas about seeking and accepting assistance. Also, compare Helgevold (2013, 148): "humility is not simply about restraint; it is about being

disposed to hope for the right kinds of excellence (those that are actual possibilities) in the right kinds of ways (i.e., those that reflect an awareness of the influences of others)." La Guardia-Lo Bianco (2018) addresses the relationship between the ill, humility, and seeking assistance.

5 In a similar vein, Tessman advocates cultivating virtues that involve a "self-reflective understanding (and perhaps acceptance) of the limitations of the moral health of a self under oppression" (2005, 31; cf. 94), virtues that can help one recognize and come to terms with, e.g., limitations in one's capacities to survive or resist. Clearly, humility is one of these virtues.

6 Grasswick (2019) addresses epistemic autonomy in the context of oppression.

7 Douglass and Phelps-Roper highlight a key point: we should not conflate humility with open-mindedness. Even when it is appropriate to manifest humility in one's interactions with in-the-wrong parties, this need not—and in many cases should not—involve an open-minded consideration of their reprehensible actions, beliefs, or sentiments. Rather, humility clears obstacles to appropriate engagement.

8 Elsewhere, Dillon says humility involves an awareness of one's moral limitations (2015, 65). She argues that, so understood, it can be a virtue, when in the service of self-respect; but if we understand it as lowliness, it is a vice.

9 For help, we thank Alex Arnold, Jamie Aten, Nathan Ballantyne, Teresa Blankmeyer Burke, David Briggs, Ryan Byerly, Michael Byram, Fabiana Cardetti, Charlie Crerar, Kim Cameron, Don Davis, Robert Emmons, Jorge Garcia, Peter Hill, Josh Hook, Frances Howard-Snyder, Peter Howard-Snyder, Rick Hoyle, Hud Hudson, Christian Lee, Tracy Llanera, Michael Lynch, Elizabeth Krumrei Mancuso, Dan McKaughan, Johann Neem, Bradley Owens, Michael Pace, Dee Payton, Sara Protasi, Wade Rowatt, Steve Sandage, Paul Shoemaker, Sandra Sirota, Barbara Stock, June Tangney, Neal Tognazzini, Kirk VanGilder, Manuela Wagner, and Ryan Wasserman, and audiences at Gallaudet University and the University of Connecticut. Work on this paper was supported by John Templeton Foundation Grant 60622, "Developing Humility In Leadership."

References

Aristotle. 350BCE/1998. *Nicomachean Ethics*, trans. W. D. Ross. New York: Oxford University Press.

Baehr, Jason. 2011. *The Inquiring Mind*. New York: Oxford University Press.

Battaly, Heather. 2015. *Virtue*. Cambridge: Polity Press.

Battaly, Heather. 2017. "Intellectual Perseverance." *Journal of Moral Philosophy* 14(6): 669–697.

Cherry, Myisha. 2017. "The Errors and Limitations of Our 'Anger-Evaluating' Ways." In: eds. M. Cherry and O. Flanagan, *The Moral Psychology of Anger*. New York: Rowman and Littlefield, pp. 49–65.

Coplan, Amy. 2010. "Feeling without Thinking: Lessons from the Ancients on Emotion and Virtue-Acquisition." In: ed. H. Battaly, *Virtue and Vice, Moral and Epistemic*. Malden, MA: Wiley-Blackwell, pp. 133–151.

Daukas, Nancy. 2019. "Feminist Virtue Epistemology." In: ed. H. Battaly, *The Routledge Handbook of Virtue Epistemology*. New York: Routledge, pp. 379–391.

Dillon, Robin. 2015. "Humility, Arrogance, and Self-Respect in Kant and Hill." In: eds. M. Timmons and R. N. Johnson, *Reason, Value, and Respect*. Oxford: Oxford University Press, pp. 43–69.

Douglass, Frederick. 1855. *The Anti-Slavery Movement: A Lecture Before the Rochester Ladies' Anti-Slavery Society*. Rochester, New York: Press of Lee, Mann, & Co. https://babel.hathitrust.org/cgi/pt?id=inu.30000005087683;view=1up;seq=40 (accessed 12/26/2018).

Douglass, Frederick. 1892. *The Life and Times of Frederick Douglass*. Boston, MA: DeWolfe and Fisk. https://docsouth.unc.edu/neh/dougl92/dougl92.html (accessed 12/20/2018).

Du Bois, W. E. B. 1903/1994. *The Souls of Black Folk*. Mineola, New York: Dover.

Grasswick, Heidi. 2019. "Epistemic Autonomy in a Social World of Knowing." In: ed. H. Battaly, *The Routledge Handbook of Virtue Epistemology*. New York: Routledge, pp. 196–208.

Helgevold, Abbylynn. 2013. *Humility, Oppression, and Human Flourishing: A Critical Appropriation of Aquinas on Humility*. Ph.D. Dissertation. University of Iowa.

Hooks, Bell. 1995. *Killing Rage*. New York: Holt.

Hume, David. 1751/1975. *An Enquiry Concerning the Principles of Morals*. In: ed. L. A. Selby-Bigge, Hume's *Enquiries Concerning Human Understanding and Concerning the Principles of Morals*, 3rd ed. revised by P. H. Nidditch. Oxford: Clarendon Press.

Jones, Karen. 2012. "The Politics of Intellectual Self-Trust." *Social Epistemology* 26(2): 237–251.

King, Martin Luther. 1963. *The Strength to Love*. New York: Harper and Row.
La Guardia-Lo Bianco, Alycia. 2018. *Suffering and Self-Sabotage in Ethical Life*. Ph.D. Dissertation. University of Connecticut.
Olb, Jon and Madeleine Parry. 2018. *Hannah Gadsby: Nanette*. Netflix.
Ornstein, Matthew. 2016. *Accidental Courtesy: Daryl Davis, Race, & America*. Sound and Vision.
Phelps-Roper, Meghan. 2017. www.ted.com/talks/megan_phelps_roper_i_grew:up_in_the_westboro_baptist_church_here_s_why_i_left (accessed 12/26/2018).
Silvermint, Daniel. 2017. "Rage and Virtuous Resistance." *The Journal of Political Philosophy* 25(4): 461–486.
Snow, Nancy. 2004. "Virtues and the Oppression of African Americans." *Public Affairs Quarterly* 18(1): 57–74.
Tanesini, Alessandra. 2018. "Intellectual Servility and Timidity." *Journal of Philosophical Research* 43: 21–41.
Tessman, Lisa. 2005. *Burdened Virtues*. Oxford: Oxford University Press.
Watson, Gary. 1984. "Virtues in Excess." *Philosophical Studies* 46(1): 57–74.
Whitcomb, Dennis, Heather Battaly, Jason Baehr and Daniel Howard-Snyder. 2017. "Intellectual Humility: Owning Our Limitations." *Philosophy and Phenomenological Research* XCIV(3): 509–539.

7

HUMILITY AND TRUTH IN NIETZSCHE

The humblebrag of the lambs

Nickolas Pappas

When the author of the Letter to the Ephesians addresses slaves and masters, humility is at stake for both.[1]

> Slaves, obey those who are your masters [*kurioi*] according to flesh … being the slaves [*douloi*] of Christ … knowing that each one, if he does good, will receive the same from the Lord [*para kuriou*] … And masters [*kurioi*], do the same to them, refraining from threats, knowing that the master [*kurios*] of both them and you is the master in heaven, and there is no respect of personages in him.[2]

Slaves have something to do under this new dispensation: to obey not merely as they must but wholeheartedly, aware that they are demonstrating their obedience to God. Masters should treat their slaves well in the awareness that God serves as master to all.

Somewhere in this combination of how things are, how they should be, and what they are called, we will find humility in the full and exact sense. For when humility is known as a virtue and prized, one asks where the humility is to be achieved, in one's nature or behavior or self-description. This virtue entails deliberate underestimation of oneself, so it seems to be a virtue one has to be conscious of, thus something beyond low standing alone.

Likewise possibly where humility is sneered at and barred from the company of the virtues, one may have to ask where it goes wrong, or what you want to say is wrong about a humble person. Do we blame that person's actual low or weak condition, or the works of humility suited to that condition? Or is it something in the language by which the humble know themselves to be humble?

The home may be ever so humble without thereby possessing the virtue of humility. What accounts for the difference?

What Nietzsche condemns the humble for raises questions like the ones I am asking. His attitude seems straightforward. In fact the less you know about Nietzsche the more straightforward it will appear. Proud self-assertion is healthy, and the herd's morality tames the proud, and humility sins against human greatness. But these are closer to sound bites than ruminative chews. The reader who wants more than a commonplace about humility from its most pitiless critic will wonder what self-assertion is like; or who should care when those who are objectively not great call themselves in all humility, or truthfully, "not great."

Does the offense (for instance) in the life of humility described in Ephesians consist in the *falseness* of the caution that its author recommends to masters? Denying a divine cause for caution makes Nietzsche no more original than any other atheist, who'd likewise respond to this Epistle that there is no master up above in heaven.

Maybe asking about a document from the Christianizing Roman world starts the story too late. Nietzsche drew on pre-Christian Greece, and as far as possible on Greek antiquity before Socrates, when he sought words for his opposition to a morality enfeebled by Christian and Platonic pieties. I will mainly be looking at *On the Genealogy of Morals*, because that book (henceforth *GM*) contains Nietzsche's most sustained and greatest discussion of ethical phenomena; and it is informed throughout by Nietzsche's reading of Greek antiquity. We will have an easier time understanding *GM*'s revulsion toward humility if we imagine as Nietzsche does the reaction that a very early un-Pauline time would have exhibited to the sight of humility.

7.1 Humility as falsehood

It suits Nietzsche's description of the masters' antiquity, and of noble morals as a long-lost inheritance, that appearances of humility in classical writings sometimes meet with bafflement and surprise – not as threat, not with enmity – as if a Greek uncorrupted by decadent moralizing could not have recognized this trait as even a putative virtue. This is the innocence against which Nietzsche measures morality's long fall. This is directness in description that describes power as power manifests itself. The nobles or masters call themselves "good" and "beautiful" with unmediated self-regard.[3]

Aristotle, who in some distinctive ways reflects an ethos predating Plato's, likewise associates frank talk with political dominance. Aristotle's apparent coinage for the other kind of talk, *metaphora*, understands metaphor as transfer (which is what *metaphora* means) or exchange, one word's being replaced by another word related to it.[4] Although the account of metaphor as substitution or transfer ought to make its alternative be something like "language that stays where it is," Aristotle only occasionally refers to a word's literal sense as *oikeion* "fitting, at home," from *oikos* "home, household." More typically he spoils his own contrast by calling the literal word *kurion* "strict, authoritative, controlling, master."[5] Mixing his metaphors for the contrast between metaphorical and literal, Aristotle makes ordinary straight diction *kurion* or masterly, using the word that we find not only in such later documents as the Letter to the Ephesians, but already and without fanfare in Aristotle's own *Politics* naming the powerful element in a constitution.[6] Metaphors are words that travel and literal words are the ones in charge.[7]

(The closest parallel in English to Aristotle's *kurios* might be the expression "strictly speaking" to signal a word's literal application; as if metaphors were other than strict, even shirking the task set to them by language, even on a holiday.)

Against masterly straight talk comes humble talk, and the masters can't make sense of it. The confusion and the surprise among ancients when confronted with manifestations of humility may express themselves as the suspicion that someone is lying, even up to something. That is the response we find in Thrasymachus, one of Plato's two most uncompromising (and most non-Socratic, and most grandly drawn) characters, when he hears the familiar line from Socrates: "Teach me, I'm ignorant."

"Here is that *eirôneia* of Socrates!" Thrasymachus says, using the Greek word from which "irony" derives, but that meant something harsher and more fixed than irony; mendacity, rather than the playful indeterminacy of utterance.[8]

Thrasymachus means: What a fraud! Socrates says he wants to learn from others, but he's obviously lying. He is playing dumb in order to get a definition of justice out of his co-

conversationalists and then turn around and best them by refuting it. Humility can only mean hypocrisy.

In the antagonistic setting of *Republic* Book 1, Thrasymachus's words for Socrates are accusatory and dismissive at once. Socrates must be playing dumb for a strategic purpose. Why else would he understate his talents? Real men in politics, like those "stronger" ones whom Thrasymachus describes as bending justice to their will, do not hang back and parry definitions. They take what advantages them and call it right, with that communicative immediacy that Nietzsche attributes to masters and that Aristotle associates with the master sense of a word. So, besides being mendacious, Socrates is doomed to remain inefficacious. He brought a logical razor to a gunfight.

Aristotle too has the Socratic personality in mind when he speaks of the type he calls the *eirôn* "ironic one," but he describes that type more charitably than Thrasymachus did. *Nicomachean Ethics* 4.7 contrasts the *eirôn*, at one end of the spectrum of self-presentation, with the boastful type at the spectrum's other end. Boastful people claim more about themselves than is true, while dissembling or ironic people say less. We might describe the latter as humble; and Aristotle allows for merit in them. In fact, this is almost the only place in his corpus that looks at *eirôneia* with indulgence. But that he continues to find misrepresentation in their presentation, as Thrasymachus found in Socrates, is evident from Aristotle's contrast of both extremes with the mean or best value of truthfulness. As it features in ethics, speaking with humility means speaking untruly, and therefore not in the manner that one most virtuously speaks.[9]

Nietzsche sometimes extends himself to giving a fair hearing to Socrates.[10] In such moods he might echo the Aristotle of this *Nicomachean Ethics* passage. More often Nietzsche sounds like Thrasymachus smelling a lie, or shouting back as the jurors did at the trial of Socrates (as reported by Plato). There was little humility in Socrates when he proposed the sentence of free meals for life. His story about the Delphic oracle's pronouncement that there is "no one wiser than Socrates" was hardly tempered by the report that he considered this oracular news impossible. That reply "But I know nothing" only makes the anecdote a humblebrag, the pretense of humility for the purpose of boasting.[11] No wonder Socrates had to tell the angry jury to quiet down.[12]

As effective stratagems go, the Socratic plea of ignorance leaves something to be desired. Thrasymachus sneers and jurors convict. But Nietzsche does pick up some of their response. He attributes strategic thinking to the resentful – which does not mean he credits them with real success – as when he calls the man of *ressentiment* adept at "temporarily abasing and humbling himself" in the far-seeing plan to get even with the masters.[13] Humbling yourself temporarily must mean humbling yourself as a game or an act.

It is in the same spirit that *GM* complains about the New Testament's advocacy of humility. Nietzsche speaks sarcastically of the slave-revolt weaklings "so humble [demüthig] about everything." He sums up the Christian Scripture: "Humility and pomposity [Demuth und Wichtigtheuerei] right next to each other."[14] Nietzsche's Zarathustra will warn his friends that "nothing is more vindictive" than the priests' humility, which in his warning sounds like a false humility.[15]

We know what Nietzsche is talking about in passages like these. We've seen Uriah Heep present himself as "so humble," then show his true opinion of himself when he maneuvers to marry Agnes Wickfield. The condemnation is a familiar one, even too familiar, not to mention that it arrives from Nietzsche a quarter-century after *David Copperfield*. It does not say much for Nietzsche (or for the way he smirks at English psychologists)[16] that he has let Dickens get the drop on him. In any case, the accusation of hypocrisy returns the inquiry to those Christian values that Nietzsche claims to have overcome.[17] And we have come to expect more and deeper from Nietzsche than the fun of exposing sanctimonious hypocrisy, a kind of fun that must rank among the most fleeting, most spurious.

The telling consideration against reading Nietzsche as Thrasymachus appears in *GM*'s third essay. In search of asceticism's true meaning Nietzsche takes up the figure of the philosopher. The philosopher behaves in every respect as ascetics do but is no such thing. All an act! In philosophers' hands, ascetic virtues like chastity and humility serve a purpose: advance the philosophical work: grant the truly original thinker an escape from distractions. Philosophers avoid marriage not because they consider sex wrong but to keep up the energy that counts, as jockeys do when abstaining before a race. Chastity is "not a virtue" for philosophers but a practical discipline, and so is the humility-behavior that lets a philosopher avoid publics and recognition. As philosophical chastity has nothing to do with prudishness, philosophical humility is not about undervaluing oneself.[18] Humility specifically helps to bring about the solitude necessary for true independence of mind.[19]

Nietzsche's own character Zarathustra can say: "Was trug nicht schon das Fell meiner Demuth."[20] What hasn't already worn away at the hide of my humility? The precision and play of Nietzsche's German here are hard to reproduce, but any translation should note Zarathustra's word "Fell," the hide or fur that is the humility he wears, which is the humility that endures the assaults he suffers. Whichever way you parse the sentence, Zarathustra's humility belongs on his outside and protects him, is skin deep, and even (as with the stitch known as a "fell" in English) works to conceal. Zarathustra's humble wrapping does not register as hypocritical, and it never seems to cross Nietzsche's mind in *GM* that a philosopher's self-presentation might read that way either.

7.2 The smallness in humility

Aristotle comes upon something resembling humility from another direction, when mapping out the spectrum whose mean he calls "greatness of soul." Aristotle measures all human types against what each one is *axios* "worthy" of, what honor or how much respect each deserves. Those who are great of soul deserve great honor and also affirm that they deserve it. The boastful or vain assert themselves to be worthier than they are. But more matters than accuracy, because deserving little and esteeming yourself accordingly only qualifies you as temperate. Just as physically small people may be nicely proportioned without being beautiful, Aristotle says, so too those with the right sense of how little they're worth cannot attain greatness.[21]

In the vocabulary of virtues we might call Aristotle's self-aware unworthies humble without ascribing humility to them. They view themselves correctly, and they get credit for their correctness, but the moral credit they earn for their humility is discounted because of their lesser worth.

Something closer to complete humility emerges with the type that Aristotle calls "small-souled," his name for those who value themselves as *less* than they are worth. Regardless of your true value, you could value yourself beneath that value, thus exhibiting humility whether or not you are actually ordinary or humble. To ears that are accustomed to hearing humility called a virtue this sounds closer, because it bespeaks an effort to aim below what the evidence seems to show. Those who deserve little and say they deserve little could be no more than guileless or naïve. People with real humility are doing something more.

This difference between accurate self-estimation and underestimation is not quite as sharp as the words for the two behaviors might suggest. Given the human propensity for thinking more highly of yourself than you should, it takes some work at under-assessing yourself even to esteem yourself truly. I suppose that (unlike Aristotle) I am looking at the ongoing effort at rating oneself lower, not at the rating that results.

For Aristotle, the act of underselling yourself makes you worse the better you actually are. He proposes this valuation in the form of a puzzle. "Most of all," i.e. smallest-souled of all, "would the one worthy of much seem to be," if that person claims a lower worth than is true. "For what would he do if he were not even worth *that*?"[22] There seems to be no self-disrespect to which this kind won't sink. The humility strikes Aristotle as mysterious.

Aristotle's reaction to humility sounds a Nietzschean note in that *GM*, too, finds something puzzling about Christian virtues at large and about self-effacement specifically, what Zarathustra – now sounding like an Aristotle launched on a tirade – calls "submission and modesty and shrewdness and diligence and considerateness and the long and-so-on of little virtues."[23] Self-denial seems to be at work in self-effacement, and the third essay of *GM* will come to a halt and turn its inquiry in a new direction with the comment that self-denial makes no sense. "Such a self-contradiction … 'life *against* life' is – this much is obvious right away – simple nonsense [Unsinn] when understood physiologically and not only psychologically."[24] Contradictions and nonsense don't prove that ascetic behavior fails to occur, but they do show that it eludes simple explanation. Those who wear a hair shirt may constantly want to scratch their bodies. Philosophers who watch those people can only scratch their heads.

But *GM*, polemic that it is, battles the self-effacing virtues in a way that would have bemused Aristotle. People sell themselves short; these kinds of people evidently make mistakes, and the mistakes make them look bad. To Aristotle, it looks like peculiar behavior but nothing to get exercised about. You would need to say more about humility, or more about what causes that self-underestimation, to account for the difference between Nietzsche's reaction and Aristotle's.

7.3 Humility as mass domestication

The other grandiose anti-Socratic character in Plato is Callicles, in the *Gorgias*, who gripes about morality in language reminiscent of Nietzsche's. Callicles is an aristocratic type like Thrasymachus and similarly impatient with Socrates. Where Thrasymachus scoffed at Socrates' interrogative method, Callicles withdraws from their conversation, so that Socrates has to pose his questions to himself and answer them alone. Callicles can barely acknowledge that common people exist, let alone the pedestrian elements of their lives. When he says that he admires the great type's "having more" than lesser people do, Socrates asks whether this means asking for big shoes to wear, and the vulgarity of the example exasperates Callicles.[25] The good life should address itself to finer things.

But Callicles really sounds Nietzschean when he goes on a tear against morality. When E. R. Dodds prepared a Greek edition of the *Gorgias* in 1959, he added an appendix outlining the obvious parallels. Sixty years ago, Nietzsche's works were less widely known among Anglophone readers, but even so these parallels stood out. Life's heroes (Callicles argues) find themselves shackled by morality, until a man comes along who possesses "enough of a nature" to free himself from "our writings and tricks and incantations and laws, all of which are against nature,"[26] as if human society had magical forces available to it powerful enough to outdo nature's order.[27]

Exceptional humans aside, morality succeeds in its efforts at humbling heroes. And this is the meaning of humility: law's uncanny victory over nature. It looks like humiliation. The dictum that humility is a virtue (and that virtue must be humility) turns the man who's big enough to fill the natural world into a citizen content with occupying his social niche. Now humility is not only false but widespread, standing everywhere as a sign of falsehood. And far from being a strategy for losers, humility has taken on a magical efficacy.

Several beyond-the-law figures turn up in *GM* reminiscent of Callicles' hero naturally strong enough to escape convention. We have the man who has earned the right to make a promise;

the oppressors who create new states, heedless of nonsense about "social contract"; the "beasts of prey" who relax with rape and arson, never feeling a moment's remorse.[28] The complaint that a tyrannizing social order keeps such types from acting in accord with their natures seems to have traveled straight from the *Gorgias* through *Crime and Punishment*, whose Raskolnikov has written an article that voices the same complaint.[29] Even without going back to Plato, Nietzsche could have inherited the Calliclean theory through Dostoevsky.

Humility understood as an oppressed condition, therefore a sign of how slave morality has conquered natures nobler than its own, would account for the disparaging language that Nietzsche saves for this erstwhile virtue. And *GM* does acknowledge the motives that people have for suppressing the nobler natures. Contemplating "sickly" and "weak" human specimens of the present from whom the powerful type needs to be protected, Nietzsche speaks of "the conspiracy of those who suffer against those who are successful and victorious." Those enfeebled conspirators slander the healthy. "How much sugared, slimy, humble humility [demüthige Ergebung] swims in their eyes!"[30]

The first essay of the book has already announced itself as revealing how the "slave revolt in morality" began.[31] Assuming the slaves are shrewd enough, their revolt succeeds, and their humility becomes the law of the land.

As close as Nietzsche's frustration comes to Callicles', reading *nomos* as Callicles and Raskolnikov do misses something about Nietzsche's lament over modern morality. Those two follow the social-contract argument in discovering the imprisoning effects of convention everywhere. Society as such enslaves, just by virtue of being society. Callicles after all represents the "tragic age of Greece," as Nietzsche calls that era, therefore moral thinking in its least contaminated condition. He can't be criticizing the morality that Socrates introduced to Europe and that Christianity nurtured. On Callicles' argument, everyone who lives among other people must choose between a domesticating morality and no morality at all. We would have to call the Nietzsche who held such a view an anarchist, as one astonishing assessment of his thought did call him when Nietzsche was still alive, after he had lost the capacity to set the record straight.[32]

Nietzsche would have had good reason to correct the reading of him that makes humility the effect of social organization as such, and so a feature of all morality. That reading plays into the hands of the modern morality that Nietzsche resists, and resists specifically for its claim to represent the only possible moral values. Nietzsche sees something that he suspects modern civilization of having forgotten. Another option existed once, the morality of the masters, still a code and principle and value even if no longer (or not yet) available. The way of the masters is a morality, not amorality. Callicles' heartlessness is in the right place, but his complaint about *nomos* and petty virtue undoes the basis that Nietzsche offers for criticizing those virtues, namely that these examples fail as virtues rather than because all virtue fails. The petty virtues fail, that is, by comparison with the traits of those long-ago fine people that deserved the name of virtue. Human society as such does not have to make humility a virtue, for look at the marvelous societies that never did so.

Callicles differs from Thrasymachus and Aristotle in smelling conspiracy and power behind the forces for humility. This is also the point at which Nietzsche parts ways with Callicles, despite his own comments about the triumph of slave morality.[33] Callicles announces the conspiracy of the weak in order to alert the strong and shield them; Nietzsche expects the participants in the slave revolt to be the ones wounded by his analysis, and he presents his analysis with them as his audience, for the purpose of wounding them. They conspired, if you want to put it that way, without having told themselves about the plan.

Regarding humility, Nietzsche would say what neither Callicles nor Raskolnikov would dream of saying, that the really puzzling aspect of humility derives not from humble people's shrewd and sly secretiveness about their motives, but the opposite: that they have rendered themselves unintelligible to themselves; that they are repeating rumors about their inward states until they believe the rumors might be on to something; that they cling to a self-interpretation as if it were a fact, and then imagine that non-fact to demonstrate their moral superiority. They call on themselves to esteem themselves as less than they are worth, thereby somehow simultaneously dishonoring themselves and honoring their effort at undervaluing themselves.

7.4 The moral rhetoric of the lambs

Humility, and what that name refers to, and what moral authority the humble may claim, all come up together in section 13 of *GM*'s first essay. It is an unforgettable passage that pivots the essay in a new direction, as the 13th section does in each of the book's 3 essays. Not a surprise that Nietzsche would use the unluckiest number in Christendom when communicating his own revelation.

The first essay's section 13 begins with a fable, building to a "moral" that diagnoses errors about free will. Lambs deplore the way that a bird of prey is wont to swoop down and eat them. They call the bird evil, inferring from its evil nature that whatever is as little as possible a bird of prey and as much like its opposite as possible must be good. It follows that lambs are good! Fair enough, Nietzsche remarks, but understand that the bird might answer that it loves tasty little lambs.[34]

He almost sounds sympathetic. You should not expect the intended dinner to welcome the sound of the dinner bell. The joke in the fable is that the lambs can say anything they like and it won't affect the bird. The genre of fable lets all animals speak, and here they speak grammatical German, yet the two sides aren't talking to each other. The bird does not pick up the lambs' extension of the concept "good"; birds grasp many things but not metaphors. The literal early bird that gets the worm wants that worm to be a wriggling invertebrate, and the fable's bird – restrained in its language, even modest – contents itself with calling one of the little lambs good when it is soft and fatty, as opposed to when it's thoughtful and meek.

Only as a joke would you say that the bird has adopted the lambs' valuation, as it would only be joking to think that a lifetime criminal who is fond of good sushi has begun reforming, and might thereby get on the track to more goodness.

A children's movie might give the fable a happy ending, with a hawk that learns to bleat and chew grass and line up with the sheep to be shorn, and with the farmer's understated praise (clippers in hand), "That'll do, Hawk." In the exchange that Nietzsche reports, the bird of prey couldn't understand such a thing. Its talk contains no imagination, let alone figures of speech.

Clearly this bird plays the role of *kurios*. "What is *kurios* is what has executive power or the power to compel," C. D. C. Reeve writes explaining Aristotle's use of the word in *Physics*, "so that a general is *kurios* over his army." Thus, when Aristotle identifies the *kurios* meaning of a word, he means its *chief* sense.[35] The lords are not the fancy talkers; for deep souls, seek a slave.[36]

Compared to the good in a bird's "good lamb," the goodness that the sheep claim for themselves is a euphemizing metaphor. The powerless pledge not to rape or attack, nor to retaliate after being attacked. In plain words all this amounts to is the prudential avoidance of any act beyond the powerless person's capacity.

Thrasymachus correctly heard something false in the humility that Socrates affected, and Aristotle was right to find something inexplicable or mystifying in self-underestimation – only not (says Nietzsche supplying what they missed) for the reason that humility misrepresents facts or that it deceives the lordly types. No one has concocted a conspiracy. The language of humility, operating as metaphors operate, has its origins in a true statement but translates that truth into a new lexicon. The powerless pledge not to exert the power they lack. Thus they misdescribe as a virtue what had only ever been a fact, as if an oyster took itself to be sitting still out of prudence and patience rather than because it lacked limbs. As Nietzsche writes in *Daybreak*:

> The same drive evolves into the painful feeling of *cowardice* under the impress of the reproach custom has imposed upon this drive: or into the pleasant feeling of *humility* if it happens that a custom such as the Christian has taken it to its heart and called it *good*.[37]

Morality's descriptions permit facts to generate self-approval.

Some virtues have to know themselves as virtues to deserve that name, and a humility that differs from the factually humble state must be one. But in this case we get a self-description both true and false.

As he does in every section 13 in *GM*, Nietzsche urges his reader to mistrust language.[38] In I.13 the fault lies with the subject-predicate structure of sentences, because that structure tempts us to read natural action as conscious choice. This "moral of the story" that Nietzsche has to offer is explaining what the lambs got wrong about their behavior and the bird's.[39] Because we describe lightning with the sentence "Lightning flashes," we mistakenly deduce that a thing named lightning had already been there, and then came in and worked its flashing work. It's a harmless way of thinking about the weather, but when thinking about human action the habit of mind has insidious effects. The facts that aggressors dominate and predators prey – that the strong exhibit strength – emerge from the prism of language refracted into a subject of a certain kind and the action, distinct from that subject, that the subject happens to perform and so might also choose to refrain from doing. Nietzsche says there is no such complex to be analyzed. Being strong means quite simply working that strength, typically by overpowering anyone weaker. Dominators dominate; which is to say, domination takes place.

The story goes that the philosopher Sidney Morgenbesser heard B. F. Skinner argue for behaviorism and asked him, "Are you telling me it's wrong to anthropomorphize *people*?" What Skinner said back we can only guess. But if Morganbesser had come to Nietzsche with that question he may well have answered, "What you want to do is not anthropomorphize, it's spiritualize. And yes, all wrong."

Everyday language about choice does describe selections among available possibilities. I took the bus to work because of the rain, not because I am essentially a bus-rider. Poetically: the wind picked that moment to blow through our yard and scatter the papers. Some ancestors of giraffes decided to stretch out their stubby necks so they could reach the leaves on higher branches – the language of choice now entertainingly re-describing natural realities.

With the same transfer of choice-vocabulary out of its accustomed place into new territory, one speaks of character and disposition as if they too were objects of choice for all subjects. As the forces that produced a long-necked ruminant are metaphorically transformed into that animal's yearning and forethought, the impotence of the weak and enslaved finds poetical new names if we conceive it as chosen, becoming prudence, meekness, and humility.

Euphemistic metaphors now represent the weak to themselves as virtuous, and not merely virtuous for being weak but virtuous inasmuch as weak. "Lies are turning weakness into an *accomplishment* … timid baseness is being turned into 'humility,'"[40] deflecting the mean fact into language of excellence and effort.

Later in *GM* Nietzsche asks "What do they really want?" and answers himself: "to *represent* justice, love, wisdom, superiority," to exemplify those traits. "The will of the sick to appear superior in *any* way …where can it not be found, this will to power of precisely the weakest!"[41]

Though newly and perversely reconfigured, the motive at work is the same force that drives everyone: the impulse toward domination and mastery. Neither good nor bad but present everywhere, will to power is a principle of life that always takes positive impulse form. Nietzsche counts it as his achievement to have unveiled positive life force in a domain in which even he had been tempted to find only reactive or negative energy.[42]

The self-assertion that exists among "the sick" takes involuted form. They are in fact unworthy and they declare themselves unworthy, and so far what they say in that declaration is true, except that it's presented as an expensive purchase when it cost them nothing. Thanks to the metaphorical choices they credit themselves with, the sheep can literally make a virtue of necessity. In fabulous language: the animal can now call itself a sheep in sheep's clothing, as if it had elected to be sheepish.

7.5 The metaphor and the riddle

The euphemistic names that circulate among the humble come from metaphorical transfers of words. Euphemisms in general might begin as acronym (WC) or circumlocution. Where humility is concerned, Nietzsche finds it acquiring its nicer name through resemblance, as metaphors do. The behavior of humility resembles the behavior of weakness and unimportance.

If we want to look to Aristotle for a sign of what the euphemizing might cost, his words on diction specify what metaphors do and overdo. On the one hand, language that uses only *kurioi* forms, literal language, is *tapeinê* "flat, pedestrian, humble."[43] Aristotle doesn't mean that the masters of a language have something lowly about them, although he might well agree with Nietzsche that personages with power speak direct unvarnished truths.

Foreign words and metaphors enliven the flat prose. On the other hand, excessive borrowing from other languages or dialects goes wrong, making your speech foreign. People who say "Cela m'est égal" in conversation have crossed over from the use of a French word to speaking French. Within a language, the clarity of literal prose is threatened by overdone metaphor. One substitution colors the diction. A string of them, Aristotle says, create an *ainigma* "puzzle, enigma, mystery." Sometimes metaphor enhances learning; taken too far it obscures and perplexes.[44]

Aristotle had the right instincts when he spoke as if humility were mystifying, and he provided the tools for explaining why. To possess the virtue of humility, which means understanding yourself as possessing that virtue, is to report on yourself to yourself in metaphors that make you a riddle to yourself. The holders of certain other virtues might not need to represent themselves to themselves as having their virtue. Depending on your account of virtue, you might find true generosity, for instance, in a quite unselfconscious and unaware liberality of spirit. But humility demands self-representation in order to distinguish itself from lowness.

In recognizing your actual humble condition and calling it humble, you had imagined yourself to attain moral and psychological transparency. In fact, you disguised the weak condition as a powerful achievement, deriving pleasure from what you might otherwise have seen as cowardice. That is the last temptation posed by slave morality, and nearly all its proponents have succumbed to it.

One danger in representing Nietzsche's point in terms of language and metaphor is that the debased morality he sets himself against comes to look like a mistake. We do not scream correcting the child who asks "What if the lightning didn't strike?" and Nietzsche should not make a fuss over modern morality. What is so bad about humility that he needs to mock and abuse it as he does?

Partly the answer can come from thinking about the obfuscation in metaphor as such, but more than that from the worldview implied by these metaphors.

That metaphor in general inspires Nietzsche's tough talk comes out when he justifies his strong language "Ausschweifung des Gefühls" – "excess of feeling" in Carol Diethe's recent translation, "orgies of feeling" in Walter Kaufmann and R. J. Hollingdale's more aggressive rendering.[45] Kaufmann and Hollingdale's dramatic instinct is probably closer to the mood of the passage: "Ausschweifung" can mean debauchery and loose living, and Nietzsche's digression acknowledges that there might be something to temper in the language, as one might not have to temper the word "excess." "Obviously," Nietzsche says,

> it would sound more pleasant and sound better on the ears if I were to say "the ascetic priest has made use of the *enthusiasm* that lies in all strong affects." But why caress the effeminate ears of our modern weaklings?

He rejects the available euphemism. This "verbal tartuffery" has gone on for too long already and it is past time for direct diction.[46] Metaphors about enthusiasm and energy will only continue to hide the sexual excitement behind asceticism, and above all they will hide that excitement from the ones who are sexually excited.

An aside in *Beyond Good and Evil*, written not long before *GM*, contains something close to the most overt joke in Nietzsche's writings. "A curiosity like mine is still the most pleasant vice of all" – then he corrects himself "Sorry! I meant to say: the love of truth finds its reward in heaven and even on earth."[47] First he gives the fact, then the metaphorical version so gussied up for piety's sake that it wouldn't even recognize itself in the mirror.

Elsewhere in *Beyond Good and Evil* Nietzsche asks: "Do you have to salt your truth to the point where it doesn't quench thirst anymore?"[48] That a few tough kernels of truth disrupt our sleep as much as they do proves that we have spent thousands of years padding the bed with soft metaphors.

But we need more to say than that about Nietzsche's tone and aggressivity, which are the effects not only of the soft condition modern ears have gotten into but of the animus in him. Nietzsche is not just speaking frankly and happening to ruffle feathers. Often enough he has feather-ruffling on his mind. His words scream because he screams them.[49]

The metaphor that lies behind the euphemisms "humility," "patience," and the others, which is the metaphor of choosing one's own nature as if from a subject or soul's standpoint, encourages a worse error than Christians' complacent self-regard. Nietzsche has diagnosed the distorted self-representation of "the sick" as a manifestation of will to power. Their will to power hardly gushes, in fact is hardly a trickle, but Nietzsche gladly escapes the antinomies regarding inner conflict that have thus far bedeviled philosophers (and even find their way into *GM*'s psychological speculations).[50] The will to power drives the strong to overcome and dominate and motivates the weak to convince themselves they are the ones really on top.

When you call humility a virtue, thus a state that one achieves, you are distinguishing it from humbleness. As virtue and accomplishment humility calls for claiming and doing less on your own behalf than you would be normally inclined to claim or do. You can countermand the will to power. Humility that has the right to call itself a virtue denies what *GM* I.13 proclaims, namely that "a quantum of force is just such a quantum of drive, will, action."[51]

Humility is therefore not only false here and there, as hypocrites' virtues are, but false to nature. Humility *qua* virtue implies that the will to power can hold itself back, and that domination can exist as an unexpressed capacity – unexpressed not for the moment in the interests of later domination, nor deferred in one sphere of activity for the purpose of achieving domination in another sphere, but unexpressed completely and forever, never moving from potential to act. The will to power stops itself; the judging soul chooses *not* to act out what it might act out. This riddling account of freedom and self-restraint speaks as if it were a new and truest-of-all theory of moral psychology.

Imagine the will to power as Nietzsche's surrogate for Holy Spirit, which the Christian creed says is *kurion* "master, lord" and *zôopoion* "life-making," and *lalêsan dia tôn prophêtôn* "spoke through the prophets." The will to power is master too. It *accounts* for mastery. If not life-producing, it pertains to the essence of life. It speaks through everyone, but most of all finds voice in Nietzsche its great spokesman. In Christianity, blasphemy against the Holy Spirit is the unpardonable sin: denying the goodness and efficacy of the Spirit.[52] But it appears that Christianity has now bad-mouthed the will to power, and for that, for Nietzsche, there can be no forgiveness either. This disrespect for the will to power is what makes its prophet scream.

Notes

1 I am grateful for the comments I have received about this paper, from Mark Alfano who read an early draft, and from the members of a Nietzsche workshop at Fordham University (March 2019): Michael Begun, Preston Carter, Mateo Duque, Pedro Mauricio Garcia Dotto, Sara Pope, and Nicholas Smyth.

2 Ephesians 6.5–9. All translations from Greek are my own. I should acknowledge that when this letter was written, and by whom, have been topics of debate. But the authorship makes no difference to my discussion here, so I will not weigh in on the question.

3 Nietzsche, *On the Genealogy of Morals,* I.2, I.4, I.5. For example Nietzsche pictures "the origin of language itself as a manifestation of the power of the rulers: they say 'this *is* so and so,' they set their seal on everything and every occurrence with a sound" (I.2). Similarly: "in most cases [the nobles] might give themselves names which simply show superiority of power (such as 'the mighty,' 'the masters,' 'the commanders') or the most visible sign of this superiority" (I.5). See Nietzsche, *On the Genealogy of Morality*, translated by Carol Diethe (Cambridge: Cambridge University Press, 2006). Unless otherwise indicated, references to *GM* will be to this translation.

4 Aristotle, *Poetics*, chapters 21–22 1457a31–1459a16.

5 Aristotle: literal language *oikeion*, *Rhetoric* 3.2 1404b35; the literal *kurion*, *Rhetoric* 3.2 1404b35, 33; 3.10 1410b12–13; *Poetics* 21 1457b1, 3.

6 Aristotle, *Politics*: those in Sparta and elsewhere who command serfs are *kurioi*, 2.9 1269b10; in any state the supreme power is *kurios*, 3.6 1278b10–12; king as *kurios*, 3.15 1286b25; the majority in democracy is, 4.4 1292a5; the supreme authority generally, 6.8 1322b12–15; also see 2.11 1272b41; 4.4 1292a10.

7 G. E. R. Lloyd, more extensively than any other author I am aware of, has investigated the metaphorical vocabulary with which Aristotle describes metaphor, despite Aristotle's reluctance to credit metaphorical language with accuracy and precision. In this discussion Lloyd touches on the metaphors of *metaphora* and *kurios*. See "The Metaphors of *Metaphora*," in *Aristotelian Explorations* (Cambridge: Cambridge University Press, 1996), pp. 205–229; and p. 211 on the particular metaphors at work. Also see Paul Crittenden, "Philosophy and Metaphor: The Philosopher's Ambivalence," *The Journal of the Sydney Society of Literature and Aesthetics* 13.1 (2003): 27–42. As a rule I find that although commentators regularly remark on Aristotle's use of metaphor to practice philosophy, as with the words *kurios* and *metaphora*, they don't ask why ordinary talk should be branded master language.

8 Plato, *Republic* 1.337a. On the word as it appears in Plato see Gregory Vlastos, "Socratic Irony," *The Classical Quarterly* 37.1 (1987): 79–96.

9 Aristotle, *Nicomachean Ethics*: the ironic type, 4.7; association with Socrates, 1127b25; contrast with truthfulness, 1127a31, b10; and *Eudemian Ethics* 3.7 1234a3. For some discussion see P. W. Gooch, "Socratic Irony and Aristotle's *Eirôn*: Some Puzzles," *Phoenix* 41.2 (1987): 95–104. For the more typically negative presentation of *eirôneia* in Aristotle see *Rhetoric* 2.5 1382b21. Aristotle "almost always assesses it negatively," says Gooch (98).

10 Thus *The Wanderer and his Shadow* section 86; for recent discussions and elaborations of the problem see Alexander Nehamas, *The Art of Living: Socratic Reflections from Plato to Foucault* (Berkeley: University of California Press, 1998), pp. 128–156; James I. Porter, "Nietzsche and 'The Problem of Socrates,'" in Sara Ahbel-Rappe and Rachana Kamtekar (eds.) *A Companion to Socrates* (Sussex: Blackwell Publishing, 2009), pp. 406–425.

11 Mark Alfano and Brian Robinson explicate the structural relationship between humblebragging and bragging in "Bragging," *Thought: A Journal of Philosophy* 3.4 (2014): 263–272.
12 Plato, *Apology*: meals for life, 36e–37a; oracle, 21a; impossible, "for I am ignorant," 21b; jury's noise, 20e, 21a.
13 Nietzsche, *The Genealogy of Morals*, I.10.
14 Nietzsche, *Genealogy of Morals*: "so humble," I.15; "humility and pomposity," III.22. Michael Begun has made the point to me that the German word "demüthig," which is the one I am most often rendering "humble" here, includes a deference toward others that is not necessarily implied by the English "humble." And it is true that I will be emphasizing the individualized kind of humility: what you really are (are like, are worth), not where you stand relative to someone else. But I don't see that the difference between the German and English words will affect my conclusions. Human worth is almost always relational: what you are worth compared to someone else, what recognition you demand from the other or else grant to the other.
15 Nietzsche, *Thus Spoke Zarathustra* II.4, "On the Priests."
16 See Nietzsche, *Genealogy of Morals*, I.1.
17 It is often noted that the word *hupokritês* meant nothing more than "respondent" or "actor" before its transformation in Biblical Greek into "dissembler." The first appearances of the word meaning "hypocrite" are the Septuagint translation of Job 34.30 and then the Greek text of Matthew 23.13.
18 Nietzsche, *Genealogy of Morals*, III.8. Note that in this passage Nietzsche *cannot* mean humility in relational terms. This passage sees the faux humility of the philosopher as shyness and withdrawal, which do not imply or require deference toward others.
19 On humility and solitude see Mark Alfano, *Nietzsche's Moral Psychology* (Cambridge: Cambridge University Press, forthcoming). In section 10.2 "Solitude in virtue theory and Nietzsche scholarship," Alfano draws out the connection between solitude and humility: "it's worth noting that on the few occasions when Nietzsche speaks positively about humility, he does so in the context of solitude." Alfano cites *Daybreak* 449, *Gay Science* 283.
20 Nietzsche, *Thus Spoke Zarathustra*, II.22 "The Quietest Hour."
21 Aristotle, *Nicomachean Ethics* 4.3: *megalopsychia* "greatness of soul," 1123a36–1125a35; comparison to small people, 1123b5–7.
22 Aristotle, *Nicomachean Ethics* 4.3 1123b13.
23 Nietzsche, *Thus Spoke Zarathustra*, IV.13.3 "On the Higher Humans." Translation my own.
24 Nietzsche, *Genealogy of Morals*, III.13. Translation my own.
25 Plato, *Gorgias*: Callicles withdraws, 505c–d; Socrates asks and answers questions, 506c–e; on having more versus asking for big shoes, 490a–e.
26 Plato, *Gorgias*: Callicles on morality's shackles, 483b–484c; the natural force who can overcome law, 484a. E. R. Dodds, *Plato: Gorgias* (Oxford: Clarendon Press, 1959), pp. 387–391.
27 Kristian Urstad spells out other similarities between Callicles and Nietzsche in "Nietzsche and Callicles on Happiness, Pleasure, and Power," *Kritike* 4.2 (2010): 133–141. Given the purpose of that article it naturally seeks out the points of resemblance between their ethics; I find it notable that Urstad focuses on moral psychology and individual *ethos*, and observes distinct differences in the two men's social and political theories. Special thanks to Sara Pope for recommending this reading to me and pointing out where it touches my argument.
28 Nietzsche, *Genealogy of Morals*: man who can promise, II.2; oppressors, II.17; beasts of prey, I.11.
29 I have argued for the continuity between Callicles and Raskolnikov in "*Crime and Punishment* Rereading and Rewriting Plato's *Gorgias*," *Journal Mundo Eslavo* 16 (2017): 192–198.
30 Nietzsche, *Genealogy of Morals* III.14.
31 Nietzsche, *Genealogy of Morals* I.10.
32 Heinrich Goebel and Ernest Antrim, "Friedrich Nietzsche's Uebermensch," *The Monist* 9.4 (1899): 563–571, at 570.
33 See e.g. Nietzsche, *Genealogy of Morals*, I.7–I.9.
34 Nietzsche, *Genealogy of Morals*, I.13.
35 C. D. C. Reeve, *Aristotle Physics* (Indianapolis: Hackett Publishing, 2018), pp. 244–245. Reeve is explaining *Physics* 3.3 202b20–21, with reference to *Nicomachean Ethics* 3.8 1116a29–b2 and 6.13 1144b1–32.
36 See e.g. *Genealogy of Morals* I.6 on the more interesting quality of the human after the slave revolt.
37 Nietzsche *Daybreak: Thoughts on the Prejudices of Morality*, edited by Maudemarie Clark and Brian Leiter; translated by R. J. Hollingdale (Cambridge: Cambridge University Press, 1997), section 38.

38 This might be a commonplace about the book but I haven't come across it. In II.13 Nietzsche resists the assumption that a noun like "punishment" means any single thing ahistorically, and in III.13 will unravel the preposition "against" in the phrase "life against life," to show that it conceals a very different relationship. No longer is the word the beginning.
39 Nietzsche, *Genealogy of Morals*, I.13.
40 Nietzsche, *Genealogy of Morals*, I.14; compare I.13.
41 Nietzsche, *Genealogy of Morals*, III.14. Emphases in original.
42 Nietzsche, *Genealogy of Morals* III.13.
43 Aristotle, *Poetics* 22 1458a20, 32.
44 Aristotle: too many foreign words, *Poetics* 22 1458a20-31; metaphors making *ainigma*, *Poetics* 22 1458a24–26; metaphor enhancing learning, *Rhetoric* 3.10 1410b8–14.
45 Nietzsche, *Genealogy of Morals*, III.19. See Nietzsche, *On the Genealogy of Morals*, translated by Walter Kaufmann and R. J. Hollingdale (New York: Random House, 1967).
46 See also *Beyond Good and Evil*, section 249: "Every people has its own tartufferies, and calls them its virtues." *Beyond Good and Evil*, translated by Judith Norman (Cambridge: Cambridge University Press, 2002), p. 140.
47 Nietzsche, *Beyond Good and Evil*, p. 44 (section 45). See my "Morality Gags," *The Monist* 88 (2005): 52–71.
48 *Ibid.*, p. 60, section 81.
49 I use the verb "scream" in recognition of Heidegger's acute description of Nietzsche – more psychologically sensitive than we might expect Heidegger to be – as shy yet forced to scream. See *Was heisst Denken?* [What is Called Thinking?], Lecture 5.
50 See *GM* II.16 on instincts' being turned back in the kind of inner conflict that Essay III will refuse. Self-punishment begins with a punishing self and one being punished, hence with the paradox of "life against life."
51 Nietzsche, *Genealogy of Morals*, I.13.
52 Mark 3.28–30.

8
THE COMPARATIVE CONCERN IN HUMILITY AND ROMANTIC LOVE

Aaron Ben-Ze'ev

Humility and romantic love are two major positive attitudes toward other people. Humility expresses a *general* attitude toward *all* people, while romantic love is a *unique* attitude toward a *specific* person (or several people). A central issue in both attitudes is how to treat people properly despite significant differences among them.

Both attitudes reduce the weight of the comparative concern while increasing the weight of a noncomparative framework. There is a difference, however: the beloved has a unique, preferable status that is hardly comparable with other people. Within the framework of judging the beloved, we find two major scales. One is a *nonrelational* scale, which evaluates the beloved's properties, such as appearance, wisdom, wealth, and sense of humor. These qualities stand on their own, independent of interactions with the lover. The second scale is a *relational* scale, which refers to the suitability of the beloved to the lover; for example, their conflicts, communication, and ability to bring out the best in each other.

As in the case of humility, the noncomparative scale measuring suitability is of greater importance than the comparative one. Nevertheless, in light of the greater sensitivity of romantic love to personal and environmental factors, its comparative concern has a certain role as well. Comparison in love is not everything, and it is not even the most important thing. But, comparison is not completely valueless—it has some impact upon us.

8.1 Humility

The terms "humility," or "modesty," which for the purpose of this discussion I treat as interchangeable, have various senses. In my view, humility is rooted in one's (implicit or explicit) primary normative framework which assumes that one's fundamental human worth is similar to that of other people; in this sense, humility involves a type of *egalitarian* approach. This global evaluation rests on a belief in the common nature and fate of human beings, and on the assumption that this commonality dwarfs other differences. In this profound sense, the humble person perceives every person as entitled to have an equal status and autonomy (Ben-Ze'ev, 1993).

Humility does not oblige anyone to deny her superior comparative position within a secondary framework. This refers, for instance, to professional standing, external appearance, or various accomplishments. Hence, there is no conflict between humility and accurately perceiving reality. Humility just requires us not to exaggerate the value of the comparative secondary framework when considering one's overall value as a human being. Einstein, for example, was a humble person who recognized his exceptional accomplishments in physics. His humility was indeed based upon the assumption that our personal talents and accomplishments are of less importance when related to our role and place in the universe. Considering each human being's marginal place in the universe, or for some people, perceiving the greatness of God, the comparative differences among individual human beings become insignificant. Humility thus requires a realization of the fundamentally similar noncomparative worth of all human beings within the primary framework, and the evaluation of this similarity as more significant than the personal differences evaluated in the secondary framework referring to traits and accomplishments of different human beings (Ben-Ze'ev, 1993; 2000, 518–525; Statman, 1992).

The psychologist Don Davis and colleagues (2011, 2016) speak about "relational humility," which consists of three major measurable components: global humility, a trait that is other-oriented; a lack of a sense of superiority; and an accurate view of the self. My characterization of humility mainly refers to global humility, with which a lack of sense of superiority and an accurate view of the self are typically associated.

The profound noncomparative worth of all human beings also does not mean that we see everyone as important to us as our children or spouses. I can be a humble person and still love my spouse and children more profoundly than I love other people. We see this attitude in a Talmudic saying about giving charity: "The poor of one's own city take precedence." If this is true of the poor of my city, it is even more obvious in the case of my family members. Such love complements, rather than opposes, the basic attitude underlying humility, as it requires investing time and resources on top of those associated with humility. We can say that everyone deserves such love and care, but these things cannot be given by one person to all people.

We can be humble in the sense of respecting other human beings, and still be proud, for example, of our comparative accomplishments. Here, the humble person simply does not view such accomplishments as changing the profound similar worth of all people. Humility does not require us to hide our achievements—just not to display them in contexts that may cause our listeners to feel uncomfortable. Constant bragging is an indication that one is not humble.

Humility is often understood as a preventive measure for not insulting other people. Although this function is indeed important, humility also involves the more profound function of nurturing the other, that is, promoting and sustaining the growth and development of someone. Nurturing often refers to developing the other's capacities, talents, tolerances, and friendships. Humility, which assumes the equal human worth of all people, provides a favorable atmosphere and circumstances for such mutual nurturing. This is particularly so in close relationships, where the two people know each other and feel that their ongoing interactions are meaningful.

We can shed light on the idea of humility by thinking about the difference between being "the best" and being "optimal." Being the best is a comparative measure: you are better than anyone else is. Being optimal is being as good as possible within the given circumstances. No external comparison with other people is necessary here. Moreover, being the best is a constantly moving target that is only minimally in one's own hands: others can always improve and do better than you. Thus, even if one is "the best," it is usually only for a moment. Being optimal, by contrast, mainly depends on you, and hence its experience can last for a long time—if you adapt yourself to the changing circumstances.

Humility is not a developing attitude with various degrees. There are no degrees of the profound value underlying humility; either you believe in the fundamental noncomparative worth of people or you do not. There are various ways of expressing humility, but the attitude itself is equivalent among humble people.

Being humble does not mean being average or thinking low of oneself. Having an egalitarian evaluation concerning the fundamental worth of people does not imply that all human beings are equal in their traits or accomplishments. Humility involves the realization of similar human worth despite these obvious differences. No contradiction exists in being humble and in being the best, average, or even worst in certain activities (and knowing this). In the same manner that humble people do not consider others with low accomplishments as inferior to them in the profound human sense, they do not consider themselves inferior in this sense when their accomplishments are lower.

In their professional work, humble people are typically not motivated by the desire to be the best in the world (since they attach less significance to the comparative concern), but by the desire to improve their work and their satisfaction from it. These people may be achievement-oriented, but they are less likely to be competitive. Humble people usually conceive of their work as an end in itself and not as a means for arriving at material or social benefits. These benefits, no doubt, may be quite useful and humble people may enjoy them, but in light of their overall values, they will not overrate their significance (Ben-Ze'ev, 2000, 520–521).

Genuine humility, like other genuine forms of positive attitudes such as love, gratitude, compassion, generosity, and forgiveness, requires investing time and effort in other people. This is a rare commodity in our highly competitive, achievement-oriented society. Hence, these attitudes are not high on the list of cherished attitudes in our society (Ben-Ze'ev, 2019; Rinofner-Kreidl, 2018).

The importance of humility in human relations is evident when humiliation, which in some respects is the opposite of humility, is present. Humiliation refers to injuring someone's self-esteem, often by making the individual feel inferior. Thus, humiliation does not adopt two evaluative frameworks in which the noncomparative one assumes the fundamental similar worth of all humans. In humiliation, all evaluations are collapsed into meritocracy considerations: a person is evaluated on the basis of her comparative accomplishments alone, without any account taken of her unique personality and circumstances. In such a case, a single failure can have a devastating impact on one's self-esteem and what others think of her or him (Miller, 1993).

The attitudes of open-mindedness and taking oneself lightly are vital to the good life. Underlying both is humbleness and respect toward other people. Such humbleness can be cognitive—as in open-mindedness, or evaluative—as in taking oneself lightly. Both attitudes affirm the complexity and diversity of human life, which accounts for their essential role in the good life.

To sum up, humble people assume a fundamental noncomparative worth of all human beings, while recognizing comparative differences in traits and accomplishments among various people. They can be proud of their achievements, but this does not diminish the value they attribute to other people. Humble people do not consider comparison with other people as essential to their wellbeing, but they still can be highly motivated to improve their achievements. Humiliation, which disregards the basic value underlying humility, is lethal to any human relationship.

8.2 Romantic love

Romantic love is probably the most complex of all emotions. Unlike other emotions, which often involve only the person herself, romantic love involves the dynamic connection between two people. This complexity is expressed in a more multifaceted system of evaluative frameworks and scales. I use the term "framework" as referring to a system of principles that you use when you are forming your decisions and judgments; and "scale" refers to measurements within a particular system (*Macmillan Dictionary*).

The two major frameworks refer to (1) the overall value of the beloved in relation to other people, and (2) the scales determining this overall value. In the first framework, the beloved receives a far higher value than other people get. The second framework is composed of two subscales: the comparative, nonrelational scale that measures the value of the beloved's properties as they stand on their own, and the noncomparative, suitability scale that refers to features determining the quality of the relationship between the two partners.

It is clear that romantic love attaches greater value to the beloved than to other people. This value does not conflict with humility, but rather complements it, since it refers to realms requiring investment of time, efforts, and resources that one person cannot spread much beyond those who are very close to him/her. This does not mean that such weight overcomes all considerations concerning other people.

At the basis of romantic love, there is a global, noncomparative, positive evaluation of the beloved. By making this evaluation, lovers do not necessarily distort reality nor are they completely blind to the beloved's faults; they simply do not consider many, but not all, of such faults to be significant and sometimes they even perceive them to be charming. The psychological mechanism underlying love does not merely evaluate the object's characteristics as good or bad, but also gives each characteristic a relative weight. This relative weight expresses the significance we attribute to each characteristic and accordingly establishes the order of priority underlying the emotional experience. Hence, a woman may say that she perceives her partner to be as handsome as she did when she first fell in love with him, but this no longer matters to her since the weight of his other (negative) characteristics has become so great that she no longer loves him (Ben-Ze'ev and Goussinsky, 2008).

There are psychological findings supporting this conceptualization of love. Lisa Neff and Benjamin Karney proposed a model of global adoration and specific accuracy in love, whereby spouses demonstrate a positive bias in global perception of their partners, such as being "wonderful," yet are able to display greater accuracy in their perception of their partners' specific attributes, such as being not punctual. In this model, spousal love may be conceived as a hierarchically organized experience giving different relative weight to the global characteristic than to the specific ones. Spouses appear to rate the positive perceptions of their partners as more important for the relationship than their negative perceptions. In this manner, an accurate perception of a partner's specific traits and abilities would not interfere with the global belief that one's partner is a wonderful person (Neff and Karney, 2003, 2005). Since importance is a matter of degree, the impact of specific negative perceptions upon the positive global one depends upon many personal and contextual features.

A related significant difference between humility and romantic love concerns the fact that humility is a stable attitude that is not so sensitive to specific circumstances and changes and does not always have immediate behavioral implications. Romantic love is quite different—it is an ongoing attitude highly sensitive to specific circumstances and changes and involves ongoing processes of development (or deterioration). Accordingly, whereas humble people are likely to remain humble for the rest of their lives, lovers often replace their beloveds. Changes in lovers or their beloveds, as well as changes in life circumstances, can end love; in this sense, life often wins over love. However, this does not imply that the initial love was not genuine. In the beautiful words of Edna St. Vincent Millay: "After all, my erstwhile dear, My no longer cherished, Need we say it was not love, Just because it perished?"

The case of humility is different. Life can hardly change one's humility, since humility is much less sensitive to life circumstances. Thus, people will not stop being humble in light of their significant successes or failures, or the successes and failures of those around them. Hence, we would usually say that it was *not* humility, if it perished. Indeed, while it is rare to find a humble person who stops being so, it is common to find a lover who replaces his or her beloved with someone else.

8.3 The comparative concern

When it comes to acute intense emotions, which are generated by a significant change in our situation, meanings is mainly comparative—the new situation is compared with the previous one. However, when it comes to enduring emotions, such as profound love, development, and dynamic stability, rather than external change, are at the basis, enabling a long-term profound love. This does not mean that comparisons and changes are meaningless in profound romantic love—it just means that they are of a lesser weight.

Iddo Landau (2017) distinguishes between two meaningful attitudes toward life: (1) aspiring to be the best, and (2) aspiring to improve. He criticizes the first attitude, which is often associated with over-competitiveness, involving an endless, unproductive search for "the best," and praises the second, which is associated with meaningful development.

As indicated above, the humble person aspires to improve, but not to be the best. The reduced value of the comparative concern relates to the egalitarian assumption concerning the fundamental similar worth of all humans. I believe that genuine lovers, too, have a similar aspiration: improving their relationship with their beloved, but not searching for the "best" person.

Being romantically meaningful in the first sense of aspiring to find the best, "perfect" lover depends on comparison with factors that are external to the connection between the two lovers. In the second sense of aspiring to improve, love depends mostly on the connection between the two lovers, and especially on their joint activities and experiences. Improving the connection between the two romantic partners, rather than finding the perfect person with the best nonrelational properties, is the most meaningful task of romantic profundity. If romantic flourishing mainly involves improvement, achieving it is in the hands of the two lovers. If, however, romantic meaning mainly concerns achieving the best, lovers will always be restless, consumed with the comparative concern about missing the "perfect" person, or perhaps the younger, the richer, or the more beautiful one. As Saurabh Sharma nicely puts it: "If you have an old habit of competing and comparing yourself with others, then you are still living your life like a sperm. GROW UP!!"

Another difficulty in considering the comparative concern as central in romantic love is related to the comparative benchmark. The comparison is likely not to be concerned with the average partner, but with extreme ideals presented by romantic ideology and deeply imbedded in our culture (Ben-Ze'ev and Goussinsky, 2008). This will result in being dissatisfied with one's partner.

A similar issue is why people believe they are above average but are not especially happy about it. Shai Davidai and Sebastian Deri (2019) argue that this is so since, although people do indeed believe that they are above average, they also hold themselves to standards of comparison that are well above average; people tend to compare themselves with others who are high on a given domain of comparison. The high comparative benchmark in both love and happiness prevents us from being satisfied with our lot.

Being married to someone who is not perfect but is still a caring and loving partner is not necessarily a compromise. In fact, that partner might be the optimal choice. We can have an (almost) perfect loving relationship with an imperfect lover. The ability to notice and cope with both negative and positive aspects of the beloved expresses emotional complexity and is valuable for profound love. One might even say that an imperfect partner is more likely to have a better love relationship with another imperfect partner than with a "perfect" partner. This is so because the difference between the "perfect" and "imperfect" lovers may hinder the development of the relationship.

8.4 The suitability and nonrelational scales

In addition to the framework proving a preferential value to the beloved compared with other people, there is another framework evaluating the beloved. This framework consists of two major scales: the *nonrelational* scale, which is a general measure of people, and the *relational* scale of *suitability*, which measures a unique connection.

The comparative, nonrelational scale of romantic love measures the value of the beloved's properties as they stand on their own, such as intelligence, outward appearance, and affluence. This sort of measure has two advantages—it is easy to use, and most people would agree about the assessments. The noncomparative, suitability scale is more complex, since it depends on personal and contextual factors, and no consensus is relevant here.

As in the case of humility, in love, too, the primary framework is based on a non-comparative (or less comparative) value. However, while humility concerns what is common to all humans, romantic love entails the unique connection between two specific lovers. The secondary framework in love measures the quality of the connection between the two lovers. Within this framework, the relational scale assessing the uniqueness of the bond and the suitability between the two partners is the primary scale. The secondary scale is the comparative, nonrelational scale. Unlike in humility, in love the comparative scale is nevertheless of some value, though still not the crucial one. This difference stems from romantic love being concerned with actual ongoing processes that change over time.

In accordance with the above considerations, dictionary definitions of "perfect" have two major meaning (a) *flawless*: being entirely without fault or defect; and (b) most *suitable* (or optimal): being as good or correct as it is possible to be, and completely appropriate for someone. While the first meaning focuses on the negative aspect, the second meaning centers on the positive one.

The view that regards the beloved as the perfect person, in the sense of being without faults, has a strong comparative push; it considers the beloved's main characteristics to be flawless, nonrelational, and easily discoverable (by others as well). This comparative approach takes a static view of romantic love in which love is essentially fixed, while occasionally moving from one point of comparison to another.

The view that considers the beloved to be a perfect partner in the sense of being most suitable (or optimal) emphasizes the uniqueness of the relationship. It sees the beloved's most important qualities as relational and sees confirmation of many of them during interactions. The uniqueness approach offers a dynamic kind of romantic love over time. Such love involves intrinsic development that includes bringing out the best in each other. Both the comparative and uniqueness approaches describe important aspects of long-term robust love; it seems, however, that the odds of establishing such love are better in the second of these.

For many people, the quest for the perfect person, instead of the perfect (in the sense of most suitable) partner, is a major obstacle to an enduring, profound, loving relationship. Since life is dynamic and people change their attitudes, priorities, and wishes over time, achieving such romantic compatibility is not a onetime accomplishment but an ongoing process. In a crucial and perhaps little-understood switch, perfect compatibility is not necessarily a precondition for love; it is love and time that create a couple's compatibility (Ben-Ze'ev, 2019).

As it turns out, we can tell precious little about how someone will be as a partner by knowing how he or she rates as a person. It is far from obvious that the higher your partner is on the comparative, nonrelational scale, the better the connection between you will be. In this context, the following friendly interchange comes to mind. Woman: "Why is it that the people I fall in love with are never interested in me, whereas the ones who do fall in love with me are never the ones I care about?" Coworker: "You're an 8 constantly chasing after 10s, and constantly being chased by 6s" (Frank, 2006). The noncomparative, relational scale measures suitability to an actual person, not to people in general. This scale analyzes the general overall romantic value in terms of a specific partner.

At the initial stage of romantic relationships, enduring profound suitability is not a critical issue. After all, information about such suitability is not yet available. This information comes from interactions between the two partners and a loving attitude becomes more knowledge-based. As time goes by, the issue of suitability gains greater importance, and the gap between the two scales could grow.

The two scales are updated and refined over time, often without our conscious awareness or any deliberative process. With time, changes in each scale relate mainly to the *weight* given to each trait, and attribute lesser value to the absolute *score* of that trait on each scale. A woman whose spouse is not particularly sensitive might say that, over time, his lack of sensitivity disturbs her less (she assigns it less weight), since she finds that his other traits compensate for it. However, she might also say that he seems to her a little bit more sensitive than she initially thought. This is a kind of trait adaptation.

In hedonic adaptation, something beautiful or ugly becomes less so with time. In trait adaptation, some of the partner's characteristics, which were initially seen as very positive or very negative, come to be evaluated more moderately. Romantic breakups are often traceable to properties that have a low score on the noncomparative suitability scale that become more evident with time rather than to properties that have a low score on the comparative nonrelational scale, which people may adapt to (Ben-Ze'ev, 2019).

The two scales raise interesting issues about the nature of long-term romantic love. One of these is the possibility of predicting the success of love. As others can assess the comparative, nonrelational scale quite well, this assessment is possible even before the partners meet. The noncomparative, relational scale, however, is different. There, many traits cannot be assessed by others, and most of this evaluation must wait until the partners meet and interact. Because reciprocal interactions are so important, the main traits can only be reliably assessed after such interactions. Indeed, the renowned expert on marital stability, John Gottman, who is immensely successful in predicting the likelihood of divorce, bases his judgments on partners' interactions during conflicts in verbal communication (Gottman, 1995).

The relational suitability scale assesses the suitability of the partner's nonrelational traits to the individual. In principle, one can compare the suitability of one's partner with another possible partner. However, this suitability is much harder as mutual suitability is something that is developed over time and is difficult to identify without ongoing interactions. Both nonrelational and relational traits can enhance romantic love. Although there is no direct positive correlation between the two groups, they often correlate.

As the possibility of lasting love draws heavily on the connection between the two lovers, relational traits are far more important in the long term. Nonrelational traits have greater impact at the beginning of the romantic relationship, when the relational traits are not yet apparent. As the two lovers become more familiar with each other, the impact of their noncomparative, relational traits increases. There also seem to be qualities that are probably bad for both the relational and the non-relational desirability. Bitterness, impatience, aggression, inconsistence, indecisiveness, etc. make one a bad partner, but also probably a person who is less successful in the general non-relational world.

A high positive evaluation of one's nonrelational qualities is significant—but it is no guarantee of profound romantic love. This is because it does not take into account the partners' connection, which is vital for maintaining this kind of enduring love. We admire the traits of many people with whom we are definitely not in love. And we would not criticize someone who loves her partner profoundly, just because we think she could have found a person with better qualities (Brown, 1987, 24–30; Frankfurt, 1987). This is not true when the gap between the two partners prevents the development of a profound connection. Thus, someone can adore her partner's relational attitudes, such as sensitivity and kindness, and still not love him, because, say, he is not intelligent or wealthy enough or has a low social status. So, a lack of high nonrelational traits can be significant—especially when the absence of these traits can prevent the lover's and the couple's togetherness from flourishing.

Being a person who has good nonrelational qualities does not make you a good partner—and it is only with a good partner that you can nurture an intimate, flourishing connection. People often search for the ideal partner by focusing on the qualities that make a perfect, flawless person. The problem is that this quest fails to focus on the connection between the would-be couple. Romantic relationships benefit from nonrelational traits in a kind of backhanded way; they offer better circumstances in which to enhance relational traits—and, therefore, the connection. Being married to an optimistic person, for example, can upgrade the couple's relational activities because a sense of optimism can improve dialogue. At the end of the day, though, the value of the relational traits on the noncomparable, suitability scale is what counts most (Ben-Ze'ev, 2019).

Along these lines, Paul Eastwick and Lucy Hunt (2014) show that when people are picking partners, they focus more on relational characteristics than consensual, nonrelational traits, especially over time. They found that although there was a lot of agreement on desirable (nonrelational) qualities at first, this agreement was weaker than participants' tendency to see one another as uniquely desirable or undesirable over time. Eastwick and Hunt conclude that despite the unbalanced distribution of desirable nonrelational traits among people, "mating pursuits take place on a more-or-less even playing field, in which most people have a strong chance of being satisfied with their romantic outcomes" (Eastwick and Hunt, 2014, 729).

8.5 Concluding remarks

Both humility and romantic love give less weight to the comparative concern, thereby implying that some values in human behavior are beyond mechanistic comparisons. In humility, which is a general attitude toward all people, individual differences are of lesser weight. They matter merely for specific circumstances, such as the professional arena, where meritocracy gives preference to those with particular accomplishments. In romantic love, whose essence is the connection between two specific lovers, the main concern is the relational one, namely, the suitability of the partners to each other. In light of the complex interactions between the lover and the beloved, the attitude of romantic love is based upon two scales measuring the value of the beloved: a comparative nonrelational scale and a relational scale whose main task is assessing the suitability of the beloved to the lover. The comparative concern in the suitability scale is of lesser weight.

The similarity between humility and profound romantic love in giving less weight to the comparative concern indicates that humility, like other positive attitudes toward the partner such as commitment, forgiveness, generosity, gratitude, and respect, is good for romantic relationships. Empirical studies confirm that humility, in the sense of a global attitude toward other people, positively affects the satisfaction and stability of romantic relationships, and is related to greater commitment and forgiveness. Humility enables people to prioritize their partner or the relationship above their individual needs. Perceived humility in your partner is an active relational factor in its own right and not merely a function of a gracious outlook toward others (Davis, et al., 2016; Dwiwardani, et al., 2018).

It seems, then, that humility has not only a significant moral value, but an important romantic one as well.

References

Ben-Ze'ev, A. (1993). The virtue of modesty. *American Philosophical Quarterly*, *30*, 235–246.
Ben-Ze'ev, A. (2000). *The Subtlety of Emotions*. Cambridge, MA: MIT Press.
Ben-Ze'ev, A. (2019). *The Arc of Love: How Our Romantic Lives Change over Time*. Chicago, IL: University of Chicago Press.
Ben-Ze'ev, A., and Goussinsky, R. (2008). *In the Name of Love: Romantic Ideology and Its Victims*. Oxford: Oxford University Press.
Brown, R. (1987). *Analyzing Love*. Cambridge: Cambridge University Press.
Davidai, S., and Deri, S. (2019). The second pugilist's plight: Why people believe they are above average but are not especially happy about it. *Journal of Experimental Psychology: General*, *148*(3), 570–587.
Davis, D. et al. (2011). Relational humility: Conceptualizing and measuring humility as a personality judgment. *Journal of Personality Assessment*, *93*(3), 225–234.
Davis, D. et al. (2016). Relational humility. In: E. L. Worthington Jr, D. E. Davis, and J. N. Hook (Eds.), *Handbook of Humility* (pp. 105–118). New York: Routledge.
Dwiwardani, C., et al. (2018). Spelling HUMBLE with U and ME: The role of perceived humility in intimate partner relationships. *The Journal of Positive Psychology*, *13*(5), 449–459.
Eastwick, P. W., and Hunt, L. L. (2014). Relational mate value: Consensus and uniqueness in romantic evaluations. *Journal of Personality and Social Psychology*, *106*(5), 728–151.
Frank, R. H. (2006). When it comes to a search for a spouse, supply and demand is only the start. *New York Times*, 21/12/2006.
Frankfurt, H. G. (1987). Equality as a moral ideal. *Ethics*, *98*(1), 21–43.
Gottman, J. (1995). *Why Marriages Succeed or Fail*. London: Bloomsbury.
Landau, I. (2017). *Finding Meaning in an Imperfect World*. Oxford: Oxford University Press.
Miller, W. I. (1993). *Humiliation*. Ithaca, New York: Cornell University Press.
Neff, L. A., and Karney, B. R. (2003). The dynamic structure of relationship perceptions: Differential importance as a strategy of relationship maintenance. *Personality and Social Psychology Bulletin*, *29*(11), 1433–1446.
Neff, L. A., and Karney, B. R. (2005). To know you is to love you: The implications of global adoration and specific accuracy for marital relationships. *Journal of Personality and Social Psychology*, *88*(3), 480–497.
Rinofner-Kreidl, S. (2018). Gratitude. In: H. Landweer, and T. Szanto (Eds.), *Handbook of Phenomenology of Emotions*. London: Routledge.
Statman, D. (1992). Modesty, pride and realistic self-assessment. *The Philosophical Quarterly*, *42*(169), 420–438.

9
PRIDE AND HUMILITY

Michael S. Brady

Humility is held to be more valuable, more morally praiseworthy, than pride. Some make this point in terms of virtues – that humility counts as virtuous, whilst pride, if not a vice, fails to be a virtue. There are of course those who disagree with such a ranking – Aristotle is one notable example of someone who seems to have had an opposing assessment of the value of these states – but on the whole philosophers and common sense opinion converge in thinking better of those who are humble than they do of those who are proud. This raises a puzzle, however. For there are considerable similarities between pride and humility. Both, for instance, involve a relation to something that is good or valuable; both have an 'appraisal structure' that reflects this relation; and both function to communicate this relation to others, and so have an essentially social nature. Given this, those who think humility is virtuous whilst pride is not are faced with a problem – namely, the problem of explaining this difference in our aretaic rankings of them, by appealing to some other feature or condition that suffices to distinguish the two. In this paper, I'll argue that a number of recent attempts to explain what humility is, and in so doing explain why humility is virtuous, fail on this account. In the final section, I'll suggest that a more plausible solution can be found if we locate the relevant difference in how these emotions are expressed, and in particular in the respective *demands* that such expressions make on us. We'll see that, whereas the communication of pride requires us to make a particular response – to esteem and give deference to the proud person – the communication of humility permits, but does not require, such an attitude. Because of this, humility allows us to bestow *gifts* of esteem on the humble person, in a way which we find agreeable, but also in a way that itself expresses respect for our freedom. As a result, we not only find humility more agreeable than pride; it also seems to embody a more valuable (because more respectful) motive. Or so, at least, I'll argue.

9.1 Preliminaries

(i) We talk of pride and humility as *episodes*, and also as *traits*. Thus someone might experience feelings of pride in a particular instance – when she's receiving her degree certificate, say; and the same person might experience instances of humility or modesty – when she's asked afterwards about her achievement, for example.[1] We also talk of humble or modest people, and mean by this those who are disposed to be humble or modest in the right circumstances. Things are a little more complicated when we talk of proud people – which might be one reason why the latter is often regarded as of dubious value. For calling someone a proud person seems to imply that they have an overly rigid, and perhaps exaggerated, view of their own standing and qualities. We sometimes say that people are too proud to do manual labour, or too proud to be seen in that pub or with those people, or too proud for their own good, and so on. Our puzzle would easily be solved if we pointed out the difference between the modest person, and someone who is proud in this kind of way. But the puzzle remains, I think, when we focus on *episodes* of pride and humility. To avoid complications associated with pride as a (potentially dubious) long-standing character trait, therefore, I'll focus on the former: cases where, for instance, a tennis player is proud of his victory, or a musician is humble or modest about her performance.

(ii) Pride and humility are, in the episodic sense, *emotions*. We talk easily of feelings of pride, and equally of feeling humble(d), and so the episodes have associated affective elements.[2] As we'll see, pride and humility have a particular appraisal structure: they involve evaluations of the world and of oneself, they embody ways of seeing or perceiving value. Pride and humility have effects on attention and other cognitions. They incline us towards certain behaviours. And they have associated facial and bodily expressions. Since emotions are standardly characterized just in terms of this collection of elements or components, it is plausible to think that pride and humility are also emotional.[3]

(iii) Pride and humility need to be distinguished from their respective close relations. Pride should be distinguished from *arrogance* (which is associated with being unpleasantly or overbearingly proud) and *self-aggrandizement* (which is associated with aggressively promoting one's own power and accomplishments). Again, it would be too easy a solution to our puzzle to castigate pride by aligning it with one of these vices. But if one *is* tempted by this argumentative line, note that we can do the same with humility: for we can equally well distinguish humility from *timidity* (which is associated a lack of courage or confidence) and *self-deprecation* (which is associated with belittling and disparaging oneself). These are vices, too, but it is no strike against humility that it can be mistakenly associated with such things.

With these preliminaries in mind, let us outline the nature of pride and humility, and highlight the important similarities between them, similarities which generate the problem of distinguishing them in terms of their value.

9.2 Similarities between pride and humility

There are many different accounts of pride. But what most have in common is a certain 'appraisal structure'. Roughly, pride involves an appraisal or assessment of an object or event as (i) valuable, and (ii) as related in some way to oneself. A prominent and plausible account of pride is due to Gabriele Taylor, who writes:

> [A] person who experiences pride believes that she stands in the relation of belonging to some object (person, deed, state) which she thinks desirable in some respect. This is the general description of the explanatory beliefs. It is because (in her view) this relation holds between her and the desirable object that she believes her worth to be increased, in the relevant respect. This belief is constitutive of the feeling of pride. The gap between the explanatory and identificatory beliefs is bridged by the belief that her connection to the thing in question is itself of value, or is an achievement of hers.[4]

On this view, there are three 'conditions' for pride. First, pride is *dependent*: we feel pride as a response to some object or event that, in our eyes at least, constitutes a positive value. Second, we must regard the valuable object or event as standing in some relation to us. As Jeremy Fisher puts it, "experiencing the emotion of pride requires that we view ourselves as standing in some special relation to the object of our emotion".[5] In Taylor's terms, this relation can be a broad one, such as 'belonging'. Taylor writes: "It is in virtue of belonging to the same family, the same country or institution that people are proud of their ancestors, countrymen, or colleagues".[6] Third – and this will be important as we go on – the proud person must regard her standing in this relation as something that is itself valuable, as a source of self-worth or esteem. It is not simply the fact that one stands in a relation of belonging to something of value that suffices for pride; I might, after all, not feel pride about my family's mansion, despite its value and my relation to it, since I regard such ostentatious displays of wealth to be immoral. The proud person must therefore regard the fact that she is in a relation with something of value as bearing positively on her worth. Together, these three beliefs – or perhaps cognitions that fall short of beliefs – make up the complex appraisal that is distinctive of pride, and without these three beliefs our feeling would fail to be an instance or episode of pride. What, then, of humility?

As with pride, there are a variety of different accounts of humility. We'll see some recent accounts shortly. What (nearly) all accounts of humility seem to have in common is something noted by Michael Slote, namely that humility is also dependent upon some other good, and so, like pride, is a relational state. As Nicolas Bommarito puts it, "being modest requires some other good quality for us to be modest *about*".[7] We might capture this dependent or relational aspect of modesty by proposing that it too has a particular appraisal structure. Humility, like pride, must involve thinking or believing that one stands in a relation to some good or value. As with pride, the good or value might not be something that the person themselves has brought about. People *are* often humble or modest about their own qualities and achievements, but this need not be the case: I can be modest about the achievements of my children, or the prestige of my university. This means that the first two conditions for pride are mirrored for humility: we feel humility in relation to some valuable object or event or quality, and we regard the object (etc.) as standing in some relation to us. Following Taylor, we might think that this is once again a relation of 'belonging'. To this point, then, we've not encountered any real difference between pride and modesty, at least at the level of appraisal *structure*. Both involve thinking about the relation between oneself and something of value in a particular way.

What of the third condition? Do pride and humility differ here? Some might be tempted to think so, and maintain that whereas pride requires the thought or belief that the relation in question bears positively on one's standing, humility doesn't involve any such appraisal. Indeed, some might go further and claim that humility *cannot* involve thinking of the relation in this way: that it is a necessary condition on being modest or humble that one does not have this belief. This would be a version of an 'ignorance' account of the concept. As Bommarito states, such accounts "explain modesty by appeal to states that are epistemically defective in some way; the modest person either lacks certain beliefs about their own goodness or has false beliefs that involve underrating themselves".[8] So on this view, the modest person must be ignorant of the fact that her standing in a relation to something of value speaks well of her, enhances her standing in the eyes of others.

There are a couple of problems with this line, however. First, it seems unduly restrictive: there seems little reason, other than adherence to the theory, to suppose that the modest person *cannot* have a belief about of how the relation in question enhances her standing. Consider: it is at least possible (indeed, reasonably likely, given how he conducts himself in interviews) that Andy Murray is a modest person. But he is surely aware of how his tennis prowess and achievements are viewed by his fellow Scots. Modesty surely cannot require Andy Murray to be puzzled when he keeps winning awards and public acclaim, for instance. Second, it is not at all obvious how lacking the belief in question makes the modest person better or more virtuous than someone who is proud of his achievements, and so who *is* aware of how the relation bears positively on his standing. Whatever the reason we prefer those who are modest to those who are proud, clearly lack of the relevant belief isn't it. If so, it's plausible to suppose that pride and modesty have the same kind of appraisal structure, at least to the extent that they share the three 'conditions' explained above. How, then, might we explain the difference in the evaluative status that pride and humility have? In the next section, I'll examine some recent ways of answering this question, and argue that none of them are convincing.

9.3 Modesty as hedonic indifference, kindness, and inattention

Suppose we move away from 'doxastic' accounts, which focus on some putative epistemic difference between the states, and look to some non-doxastic element to solve our puzzle. In this section I'll examine accounts which appeal to differences in pleasure, kindness, and attention, in attempting to show why humility, but not pride, counts as virtuous.

(i) Even if pride and humility share a certain appraisal structure, one rather obvious difference between them is at the level of hedonics. This is because pride would seem to involve a subject's taking *pleasure* in the fact that the relevant relation bears positively on their standing, whilst the humble subject does not. In support of the former, note that the typical facial expression of pride is one in which the subject seems pleased with herself and her achievement.[9] Pride and pleasure seem very closely linked, therefore. Not so with humility, which some want to characterize in terms of a *lack* of any pleasure. Indeed, a number of accounts of humility highlight precisely that it involves an indifference to the fact that one's relation to some good bears positively on one's standing.[10] On this account, it is the fact that one *fails* to take pleasure in the relevant fact that makes the person virtuous; conversely, those who are proud fail to be virtuous precisely because they take pleasure in the fact of their relation to some good.

Does this solve our puzzle? Not really. For one thing, the pleasure that pride involves is often entirely fitting from a moral perspective. Suppose that Lucy has just been made captain of the school football team; Lucy, and others, would expect Lucy's parents to be *beaming* with pride at this achievement. This is not just an expectation, reflective of how parents tend to react in cases like this. There would be something morally and normatively amiss if Lucy's parents *didn't* take pleasure in this fact. So taking pleasure in achievement that is suitably related to one cannot be the reason why we think pride isn't virtuous. Indeed, there is theoretical backing for this intuitive take on Lucy's situation. Consider Thomas Hurka's work on the nature of virtue. In his book *Virtue, Vice, and Value*, Hurka proposes and defends a 'recursive characterization' of good and evil.[11] This characterization involves a number of clauses. For our purposes, two are particularly important. The first is a recursion clause "about the intrinsic goodness of a certain attitude to what is good, namely, loving it, or, more specifically, *loving for itself what is good*, (LG): If x is intrinsically good, loving x (desiring, pursuing, or taking pleasure in x) for itself is also intrinsically good".[12] He supplements this with a clause about indifference to goods: "(IG) If x is intrinsically good, being indifferent to x (neither loving nor hating x when, given one's cognitive states, one could do so) for itself is intrinsically evil".[13] Hurka claims, further, that "The moral virtues are those attitudes to goods and evils that are intrinsically good, and the moral vices are those attitudes to goods and evils that are intrinsically evil".[14] On this view, then, it is virtuous to take pleasure in something that is good, and vicious to be indifferent to something that is good. On the assumption that enhancement in social standing *is* a good, it would follow from Hurka's recursive account that pride is virtuous precisely on the grounds that it involves pleasure.

Hurka is not alone in taking virtue to be a way of favouring what is good. Robert Adams holds something similar, claiming: "I identify virtue with persisting excellence in being for the good".[15] Linda Zagzebski also holds that virtues involve positive attitudes towards goods and negative attitudes towards evils, embodied in the emotional responses that constitute the 'motivational components' of virtue.[16] Indeed, virtue theorists in general – no doubt influenced by Aristotle to some extent – deny that taking pleasure in (virtuous) activity in any sense undermines the virtue-status of that activity. If so, it is difficult to see how pride falls short of virtue on hedonic grounds. The appeal to pleasure as a differentiating element fails to answer our puzzle, therefore.

(ii) A different approach appeals, not to pleasure, but to kindness. Consider, in this light, Alan Wilson's 2014 paper 'Modesty as Kindness'.[17] Wilson thinks that accounts of modesty which restrict themselves to "features internal to an agent",[18] such as beliefs about their own abilities or comparisons with others, allow "for the agent to be both proud and obnoxiously boastful about some ability that they possess".[19] For Wilson, "What is needed is an external requirement – a restriction of how the truly modest agent will behave in their interactions with other people". (Ibid.) Wilson's own requirement invokes kindness. He writes:

> My suggestion is that the trait of modesty ought to be considered as closely related to the more fundamental virtue of kindness. It is at least part of the nature of kindness that the kind agent will be concerned to protect and promote the well-being of others. The modest agent is one who shares this concern and who is influenced by it in the way that they present themselves. … To be modest is to be disposed to present your accomplishments/positive attributes in a way that is sensitive to the potential negative impact on the well-being of others, where this disposition stems from a concern for that well-being.[20]

Wilson thinks that this allows us to explain why modesty is virtuous. Part of the explanation here is that the modest person, being kind, will be concerned not to undermine the esteem of others, and so will avoid "bragging and boasting about their achievements". As a result, the humble person "is unlikely to provoke envy and dislike in others", and so will maintain cordial social relations. Since this is a good end, then modesty will be reliably connected with this end. But the main reason for viewing modesty in a positive light is because of a close relation to an overarching virtue. Wilson writes: "The modest agent is concerned to protect and promote the well-being of others through their self-preservation, and so will be likely to also possess the virtue of kindness".[21] This helps us to explain the value of episodes of modesty as well, in so far as particular instances of modesty will express the feelings that the kind and therefore virtuous person is disposed to have. Episodes of modesty count as virtuous for this reason.

There is a lot that is attractive about Wilson's account. Unfortunately, it suffers from a couple of problems. First, it seems to be too narrow in its focus on the potential negative impact on the well-being of others. Consider Andy Murray again. I take it that Andy can be modest when he is motivated to downplay his impressiveness, even in situations where there is little or no chance of negative impact on the well-being of others. Suppose, for instance, he is at a dinner celebrating Grand Slam winners since 2010. Surely it's possible for him to be modest, and yet rightly unconcerned with the effect that his talking about his accomplishments might have on the well-being of Serena Williams and Novak Djokovic. So his motivation to downplay his achievements here cannot be kindness to them.

Second, and importantly, the appeal to kindness doesn't really help us to solve our puzzle. This is because *pride* can equally fit Wilson's definition: the proud person can also be disposed to present her accomplishments or positive attributes in a way that is sensitive to the potential impact on the well-being of others, where this disposition stems from a concern for that well-being. For the proud person might sometimes be disposed to display pride *because* of the positive impact this will have on the well-being of others: think again of Lucy's proud parents being sensitive to the benefit such an emotional expression brings to their daughter, or sensitive to the harm that their failure to express pride in Lucy's achievements might cause. This point is not simply restricted to cases where someone is proud of a family member or another in a relation of 'belonging'. Olympic athletes on the winners' podium might rightly display pride out of sensitivity to the sacrifices that their trainers have made, or the financial support of their funding bodies, or the applause and adulation of the crowd and indeed the nation. (Failure to display pride in such cases would be evidence of mean-spiritedness or a lack of public concern, a kind of churlishness.) A disposition to feel pride, no less than modesty, can therefore express kindness and a sensitivity to the well-being of others. As a result, an appeal to kindness gets us no further to solving our puzzle.

(iii) A third recent approach, due to Nicolas Bommarito, grounds the value of modesty in "certain patterns of attention".[22] Like Wilson, Bommarito thinks that "a good theory will … provide a framework that helps us see what is good about modesty and what is bad about immodesty".[23] He thinks that "what is essential to modesty is that we direct our attention in certain ways", and that as a result modesty is a virtue of attention.[24] In particular, he claims that the modest person will direct her attention "away from the trait or its value or toward the outside causes and conditions that played a role in developing it".[25] So a modest person might not attend to the fact that she is a skillful driver, or to the value of her architectural work; or she might instead focus on the vital role that others have played in enabling her to fulfil her talent and achieve what she does. But these patterns of attention are not sufficient for modesty; instead, the modest person's attention must be directed in one of these ways "for the right reasons … [as] a result of their values or desires". (Ibid.) In the case of someone who attends to external factors and their role in enabling her to exhibit her skill, attention is governed by her concern for the importance of family, friends, and society; so her attention seems virtuous as a result. By the same token, someone might be inattentive to her abilities, or to the value of these, because she lacks certain morally problematic (e.g. narcissistic) desires or concerns. It is the *absence* of negative values or desires that makes inattention in these cases virtuous. And it is this feature which also helps to explain why modesty is a virtue: namely, that it manifests morally good or valuable desires and concerns, or a lack of morally bad desires. Immodesty, on the other hands, expresses and manifests 'egocentric vices', and as such counts as morally criticizable.[26]

This, too, is a rich and initially attractive account of the nature of modesty and its value. However, it is problematic for much the same reason as Wilson's – namely, it doesn't do enough to distinguish (the value of) modesty from pride, and so fails to address our puzzle. Modesty and pride might very well differ in terms of their patterns of attention – with the proud person being more attentive to their own qualities or the value of these qualities than the modest person, and less attentive to the role that external factors have played with respect to the value in question. But none of these differences need evince morally problematic desires or concerns on the part of the proud person. Indeed, the case can be made that dispositions to attend to one's abilities can reliably express virtuous dispositions themselves. The proud Olympian might reliably attend to her abilities and their value because she thinks that inattention to her talents would be neglectful or sinful: she pays attention to them and to their value because she regards them as a gift, and, as with other gifts, attention (rather than inattention) seems apt as a form of *gratitude*. By the same token, she might be less attentive to the role that external factors have played with respect to her achievements precisely because external factors *have* had little to do with her success. Instead, any external factors she has faced have been ones that she has had to overcome: poverty, lack of parental support, indifference of funding bodies, the sexist or racist attitudes of the selection committees and fans and broadcasters, the jealousy of her team-mates; and so on. The notion, therefore, that relative inattention to help from others belies a morally problematic attitude would seem to be unfounded. Indeed, it might even be the case that those who are inclined to pay attention to the help they received from others are often more *privileged* than those who are not, precisely because the latter group of people didn't receive much help in the first place. It is not obvious, therefore, that paying attention to the help one received from others manifests a morally better attitude than paying attention to one's own abilities and the value of one's own achievements. It is therefore not clear why modesty is a virtue of attention whilst pride is not.

The lesson to be learnt from this discussion is that attempts to explain the difference in value between pride and humility that focus solely on the features of the subjects involved – whether doxastic elements like beliefs (inaccurate or accurate), hedonic elements like pleasure (or indifference), or virtues associated with kindness and attention – seem to fail. If we are to answer our puzzle, we should look elsewhere. In the final section, I'll make the case that we should shift focus to the reactions of others to those who display pride and humility. I'll suggest that those who are proud are less highly regarded than those who are humble, because pride requires or demands esteem from us, whilst humility makes esteem a gift that we can bestow. This is the case even if pride and humility each express or manifest virtues associated with kindness or attention.

9.4 Pride as demanding, humility as permissive

We can better answer our question if we turn our attention away from what pride and humility are, and focus instead on what pride and humility *do*. In short, I want to argue that pride signals that one merits esteem and a raised social standing, in such a way that these are demanded or required from others. Humility, conversely, does not. This is because the humble person's lack of concern with their enhanced public standing allows or permits the observer to be equally unconcerned. For if the humble person doesn't care about being esteemed, then it's difficult to see how esteeming her is required of others. Nevertheless, humility allows the observer to give a *gift* of esteem – to do something that isn't required, but expresses generosity on the observer's part. The basic thought is that we prefer expressions of humility to expressions of pride because the former allow us to be better, because more generous, people. Moreover, in allowing us to give the gift of esteem, humility also seems to express a valuable and virtuous motive – a form of respect, precisely for our freedom – and one that isn't expressed by pride, which demands our esteem. As a result, we don't just find humility more agreeable; it arguably embodies a more valuable and more virtuous motive.

To see this line in more detail, let's look at a recent and plausible social-functionalist account of pride developed in a paper from 2010 by Jessica Tracy, Azim Shariff, and Joey Cheng.[27]

On their account, "pride is a psychologically important and evolutionarily adaptive emotion" that has "evolved to serve specifically social functions".[28] In particular, they argue that pride has evolved "to help individuals transform culturally valued achievements into higher social status".[29] Tracy and her colleagues note that pride enhances status through "its universally recognized nonverbal expression, which may function to inform observers (other social group members) of the proud individual's achievement, indicating that he/she deserves higher status"[30]. The authors support this with their own research: "Using the Implicit Association Test … we found that the pride expression is rapidly and automatically perceived as a signal of high status".[31] Such signals can be of value to the subject displaying pride, and thus who is perceived to be of high status as a result, since they then "receive increased resources, attention, and other status-related benefits".[32] But such signalling and display can also benefit *observers*: those who observe the high-status subjects can then "more effectively navigate the status hierarchy by showing appropriate deference, knowing whom to emulate, forming productive alliances, and facilitating their own status jockeying".[33] So there is practical pressure for us to automatically show deference to those who display pride. Of course, we might ultimately come to reject these automatic impulses; we might, for instance, reflectively reject the idea that the proud person merits esteem (perhaps they are basking in reflected glory), and/or decide not to show deference to such people. Our quick and automatic perceptions of our evaluative landscape might prove to be inaccurate, and our quick and automatic tendencies to esteem others and show deference might turn out to be unfounded. Nevertheless, it is not implausible to suppose that pride expressions instinctively *call for* a way of seeing the proud person – namely, as one who has high status – and equally a behavioural response to the proud person – namely, of esteeming and showing appropriate deference to them. Such evaluative and behavioural responses are, at least *prima facie*, demanded or required of us.

It is plausible to think that humility can also play an important social role, *via* its facial and bodily expression. For there seem to be standard facial and bodily expressions associated with humility or modesty too: lowered gaze, turning away, blushing.[34] And it might be argued that humility counts as virtuous as a result of these facial and bodily manifestations. As Bommarito notes, humility is sometimes regarded as virtuous in "combating jealousy and making social interactions run more smoothly".[35] Whatever such things signal, it isn't primarily that the person is associated with some achievement; nor are such expressions automatically taken to be a mark of high esteem and enhanced social standing. One reason for this is that similar expressions are associated, not with achievements, but certain forms of failure: those associated with shame, guilt, and embarrassment, for instance. As a result, facial and bodily expressions associated with modesty don't seem to call for any particular response; at least, they don't call for or demand the kind of evaluative and behavioural responses as those automatically elicited by pride expressions.

If this is the case, then we can explain the difference in the aretaic status of humility and pride by appealing, not to anything central to the evaluative structure of these emotions, nor to differences in their valence or effects on attention, but instead to a difference in what expressions of these emotions demand of us as observers. For if the above is correct, pride expressions call for particular appraisals, viz. that someone merits esteem, and particular actions, viz. of esteeming that person. As noted, such requirements are only *prima facie*: they can be overridden by other considerations, and undermined if it turns out that the person isn't suitably related to something of value or worth. But they are requirements nonetheless. As a result, observing someone displaying pride has mandatory *costs*, in terms of appraising someone as having higher standing, and in showing due deference to them. And the fact that paying these costs can nevertheless benefit us doesn't mean that they are not demanded from us. The same is true of moral requirements, after all: although we benefit in the long run if we abide by the demands of morality, they are still demands.

Things are different when it comes to humility. Expressions of humility call for neither appraisals nor behaviour on the part of the observer. Although humility requires a relation to something of value, and although we might recognize the relevant facial and bodily expressions for what they are, humility doesn't demand that anyone actually esteem the humble person in light of this relation, or show due deference to them. To see this, note that if the modest person seems indifferent or inattentive to her success or achievement – if she doesn't seem to take pleasure in this, but lowers her gaze and turns away, directs conversation elsewhere or to the achievements of others, as per the accounts of humility explained earlier – then it is clear that *we* are permitted to do likewise. Consider: if your neighbour, glowing with pride, shows you pictures of his grandchildren, then there is some normative pressure on you to respond appropriately. Even if you don't think that they are the most adorable children on the planet, you are required to make the right kind of noises in response. Failure to do so would be at best rude, but more plausibly unkind. If, on the other hand, your neighbour never draws your attention to valuable objects to which he's related – grandchildren, new car, holiday in Cuba – then it seems that you are under no normative pressure to esteem him for such relations, nor show any deference to him on this account. "If he doesn't care about these things", you might well say to yourself, "then I'm not required to". Humility, unlike pride, doesn't therefore demand or require some normative response.

This doesn't mean that such a response wouldn't in fact be appropriate or fitting; if someone is related to some valuable object, and if this isn't (say) a source of shame to them, then it seems perfectly acceptable to mention this fact, to esteem them for it, and to show due deference to them as a result. Although such responses are not required, they therefore seem permissible. This means that if we do esteem or show deference to the humble person, it is something in our *gift*, rather than a cost that is demanded from us. There might be many reasons why we would want to esteem the humble person: as an expression of gratitude, perhaps, or because (in the case of public acknowledgement) we think it important that others are aware of the humble person's achievements, or because such esteem and deference accurately reflects their social standing. Because of this, esteeming the modest or humble person is something that it is entirely fitting and appropriate to do. But this is something that humility allows us the *freedom* to do.

This helps to explain why we are inclined to value expressions of pride and humility differently – and why, as a result, we might think that the latter express a virtuous motive whilst the former do not. We find expressions of humility much more agreeable than pride because they allow us the freedom to act in an appropriate way, rather than demanding this from us: they allow us to make a gift of esteeming and showing deference to another person. But because such expression gives us the freedom to esteem and show deference to another, we might think that humility also expresses a measure of respect for us: respect for our capacity to freely show esteem, to freely render unto others what they are due. So expressions of humility both allow us the freedom to esteem others, and thus strike us as more agreeable than expressions of pride; at the same time, they express respect for our capacity to esteem others, and thus strike us as expressing virtuous motives. It is not kindness that humility and modesty express, therefore, but respect for the freedom of others to show esteem and deference as they wish. And whilst pride can, as we saw, express kindness, pride nevertheless demands that others esteem or show deference to us, and so does not itself express respect for the capacity of others to give us the gift of esteem. As a result, expressions of pride strike us as less worthy or less valuable motives, because they fail to express respect for our freedom in this way.

We started with a puzzle – to explain the difference in our aretaic assessments of pride and humility. If I'm right, this puzzle can best be solved by reflecting on what pride and humility demand, or permit, us to do. This helps us to explain a difference in how agreeable we find these expressions and traits, and so helps to explain the difference in ranking along Humean lines. But it also helps to explain a difference in the value of the attitudes expressed themselves: humility expresses respect for our freedom to esteem, in a way that pride does not. Because of this, we are inclined to think that the motives expressed in humility are more valuable, and more virtuous, than those expressed in pride.

Notes

1 I will, throughout, treat humility and modesty as referring to the same kind of quality. This is, I take it, in line with what most philosophers think about this issue, although there are some dissenters. For this paper, I'll go with the majority view. It's not obvious that anything of importance rests upon this issue, given the arguments to come.
2 Alessandra Tanesini suggested to me that it's doubtful whether we can feel humble, as opposed to feel humbled – by one's situation, by nature, by some other person's qualities or performance, etc. I'm not so sure that we can't feel humble, however. I might enter my boss's office feeling humble, in a situation where I'm going to ask for a raise, without it being true of me that I'm feeling humbled by the situation. (I might, after all, think it likely that I'll get the raise I'm asking for.) So, too, in cases where I've achieved something great – I can feel humble without feeling humbled in such situations.
3 Many contemporary philosophers and psychologists regard emotions as clusters of components. For more on this, see Prinz, J. (2004), chapter 1.
4 Taylor, G. (1985), *Pride, Shame, and Guilt: Emotions of Self-Assessment*, New York: Oxford University Press, p. 41.
5 Fisher, J. (2017), 'Pride and Moral Responsibility', *Ratio* 30(2), p. 182.
6 Taylor, G (1985), p. 30.
7 Bommarito, N. (2013), 'Modesty as a Virtue of Attention', *Philosophical Review* 122(1), p. 94.
8 Bommarito, N. (2018).
9 See Tracy, J. L., Robins, R. W., and Schriber, R. A. (2009). Development of a FACS-verified set of basic and self-conscious emotion expressions. *Emotion, 9*, 554–559.
10 For this line, see Roberts, R., and Wood, J. (2003), 'Humility and Epistemic Goods', in M. DePaul and L. Zagzebski (eds.), *Intellectual Virtue: Perspectives from Ethics and Epistemology*, Oxford: Clarendon Press.
11 Oxford University Press (2001).
12 p. 13.
13 p. 63.
14 p. 20.
15 Adams, R. (2006), *A Theory of Virtue*, Oxford: Oxford University Press, p. 11.
16 Zagzebski, L. (1996), *Virtues of the Mind*, Cambridge, UK: Cambridge University Press.
17 Wilson, Alan T., 2014, "Modesty as Kindness", *Ratio*, 29(1): 73–88.
18 p. 76.
19 p. 77.
20 p. 78.
21 pp. 78–79.
22 'Modesty as a Virtue of Attention', *Philosophical Review* (2013), 122(1), p. 93.
23 p. 95.
24 p. 99.
25 p. 103.
26 p. 115.
27 Tracy, J., Shariff, A. and Cheng, J. (2010), 'A Naturalist's View of Pride', *Emotion Review 2(2)*: 163–177.
28 p. 164.
29 p. 168.
30 p. 169.
31 Ibid.
32 Ibid.

33 pp. 169–170.
34 See Darwin, C. (1890/2009), *The Expression of the Emotions in Man and Animals*, Cambridge: Cambridge University Press, pp. 353–354.
35 Bommarito, N. 'Modesty and Humility', *The Stanford Encyclopedia of Philosophy* (Winter 2018 Edition).

References

Adams, R. (2006), *A Theory of Virtue*, Oxford: Oxford University Press.
Bommarito, N. (2013), 'Modesty as a Virtue of Attention', *Philosophical Review*, 122(1): 93–117.
Bommarito, N. (2018), 'Modesty and Humility'. In: *The Stanford Encyclopedia of Philosophy* (Winter 2018 Edition), Edward N. Zalta (ed.). https://plato.stanford.edu/archives/win2018/entries/modesty-humility/.
Darwin, C. (1890/2009), *The Expression of the Emotions in Man and Animals*, Cambridge: Cambridge University Press.
Fisher, J. (2017), 'Pride and Moral Responsibility', *Ratio*, 30(2): 181–196.
Hurka, T. (2001), *Virtue, Vice, and Value*, Oxford: Oxford University Press.
Roberts, Robert, and Wood, Jay (2003), 'Humility and Epistemic Goods'. In: *Intellectual Virtue: Perspectives from Ethics and Epistemology*, M. DePaul and L. Zagzebski (eds.). Oxford: Clarendon Press.
Taylor, G. (1985), *Pride, Shame, and Guilt: Emotions of Self-Assessment*, New York: Oxford University Press.
Tracy, J., Shariff, A., and Cheng, J. (2010), 'A Naturalist's View of Pride', *Emotion Review*, 2(2): 163–177.
Tracy, J. L., Robins, R. W., and Schriber, R. A. (2009), 'Development of a FACS-Verified Set of Basic and Self-Conscious Emotion Expressions', *Emotion*, 9(4): 554–559.
Wilson, Alan T. (2014), 'Modesty as Kindness', *Ratio*, 29(1): 73–88.
Zagzebski, L. (1996), *Virtues of the Mind*, Cambridge, UK: Cambridge University Press.

10
ASHAMED OF OUR SELVES
Disabling shame and humility

E.M. Dadlez and Sarah H. Woolwine

Humility, as opposed to pride, is generally accounted a virtue, particularly in Christian religious traditions which label pride one of the seven deadly sins. In today's political climate, humility is often regarded as a worthwhile anodyne to narcissism, overweening vanity, and unwarranted self-confidence. However, the vices just referred to need not be interpreted as the consequences of a deficiency in humility. We could instead see them as manifestations of the wrong kind of pride: unjustified or excessive pride, or pride over things for which one isn't in fact responsible. When considered as a Humean emotion, humility can similarly be felt toward or about the wrong things, or for the wrong reasons. As a disposition, it can involve the inculcation of inappropriate habits. And the account which makes contentions about there being a downside to humility most apparent is that ventured in Book II of David Hume's *Treatise of Human Nature*. We will argue that disability becomes interesting within the context of this account, because Hume discusses the experience of being humbled by alterations in one's physical capacity in terms of its power to shape one's overall disposition. With this argument in place, we shall demonstrate that the relations among disability, humility, and disposition suggested in Hume's writing gain greater clarity and nuance when interpreted from the standpoint of recent scholarship in disability studies and on the topic of epistemic injustice.

10.1 Hume on humility and disablement

It should be noted from the outset that Hume makes a clear case against humility being regarded as always and invariably a virtue, and against pride always being thought of as a vice. Vices and virtues themselves are things we can be humbled by or proud of, after all:

> There may, perhaps, be some, who being accustom'd to the style of the schools and pulpit … may here be surpriz'd to hear me talk of virtue as exciting pride, which they look upon as a vice; and of vice as producing humility which they have been taught to consider as a virtue. But … by *pride* I understand that agreeable impression, which arises in the mind, when the view either of our virtue, beauty, riches or power makes us satisfy'd with ourselves: And that by humility I mean the opposite impression. 'Tis evident the former impression is not always vicious, nor the latter virtuous. The most

> rigid morality allows us to receive a pleasure from reflecting on a generous action; and 'tis by none esteem'd a virtue to feel any fruitless remorses upon the thoughts of past villainy and baseness.
>
> *(2.1.7.8, SBN 297–298)*

First, as indicated above, it is important to stress that Hume treats pride and humility as indirect passions rather than outright behavioral dispositions, though it seems clear in what he writes that the tendency to experience such sentiments is expected to give rise to habits of action. Feelings of pride and smugness would be expected to give rise to preening and bragging. Feelings of humility would be expected to give rise to self-effacing or modest behavior. There is a clear difference, of course, between humility considered as an emotional response (to some perceived personal deficit) and as a trait of character. Humility as a virtue in the best, non-religious sense, involves the kind of apprehension of one's own limitations that prevents one's undertaking tasks one isn't suited to perform. A properly humble person acknowledges her fallibility, is unpretentious, and does not indulge in wishful thinking when engaging in self-assessment. Humility should ideally lead to realistic evaluations of the strengths of others, and realistic estimations of one's own corresponding weaknesses. But there can be excessive, misdirected, or otherwise inappropriate humility: a self-mistrust that always leads to second-guessing oneself or paralyzes action; a failure to act caused by unrealistically low estimates of one's own competence; an inappropriate deference to others; the constant assumption of one's own inferiority; subservience; an inability to stand up for oneself or what one believes is important.

An emotion, on the other hand, if we consider the Humean sentiment, is not a behavioral disposition, though it comprehends more than the unanalyzable sensation at the heart of Hume's analysis. These sensations are bracketed by cognitions. First, the indirect passions of pride and humility, even according to a non-cognitivist like Hume, are intentional. They have specific objects that the individual experiencing them will evaluate in particular ways. Both pride and humility have the self as object (T 2.1.3.2, SBN 280). That is, pride and humility are paradigmatically self-directed, the first accompanied by pleasure, the second accompanied by pain. They are *about* us and our perceived advantages and deficits. Considered as an emotion or passion, humility is the unpleasant sentiment we feel when we contemplate some trait, action, or object affiliated closely with ourselves that we find wanting or defective or flawed:

> To begin with the causes of pride and humility we may observe, that their most obvious and remarkable property is the vast variety of *subjects*, on which they may be plac'd. Every valuable quality of the mind … [can be] the cause of pride; and the opposite of humility Nor are these passions confin'd to the mind, but extend their view to the body likewise. A man may be proud of his beauty, strength, agility … and of his dexterity in any manual business or manufacture. But this is not all. The passions looking farther, comprehend whatever objects are in the least ally'd or related to us … any of these may become a cause either of pride or of humility.
>
> *(T 2.1.2.5, SBN 278–279)*

Humility as a passion involves unpleasant sentiments: shame, mortification, guilt, embarrassment, self-reproach, self-hatred, humiliation. It is the painful emotional apprehension of a personal deficit. The causes (and Hume would say the subjects) of humility are always things associated with the self that are disvalued. Disagreeable objects related to ourselves produce humility (T 2.1.6.1). So one can be embarrassed about a personal failure, a lack of talent or prowess, weakness, clumsiness, or ineptitude. One can be ashamed of some previous despicable action, of one's poverty, of the shabbiness of one's car, of the bad behavior of one's child, or of one's prominent ears. These are not all things about which we *should* feel humble or ashamed, any more that the objects of someone's pride or vanity are always appropriate. Hume is here writing about what people actually feel or are inclined to feel, not what they should feel. He simply expects that most people will be humbled by what they regard as personal deficits most of the time, though he leaves plenty of room to question what might legitimately count as a deficit and how misapprehension about such things might lead to a pride or a humility that was inappropriate.

Our bodies and our personal appearance are prime targets for pride and humility:

> Thus the beauty of our person, of itself, and by its very appearance, gives pleasure, as well as pride; and its deformity, pain as well as humility. … [I] take it for granted at present … that every cause of pride, by its peculiar qualities, produces a separate pleasure, and of humility a separate uneasiness.
>
> *(T 2.1.5.1, SBN 285)*

It is important to remember that objects of humility need not be things for which the agent is responsible. Morally charged words like "shame" and "guilt"—the words that signify emotions which are most closely associated with humility—also carry with them a sometimes-inapplicable connotation of personal responsibility. However, humility—when read as an emotion—is any unpleasant feeling produced by the apprehension of some personal flaw or failure, or some deficiency in one's circumstances, property, or affiliations. It can be a feeling of inferiority. It is sometimes an apprehension of being beleaguered or desperately placed:

> For the same reason, that riches cause pleasure and pride, and poverty excites uneasiness and humility power must produce the former emotions, and slavery the latter. Power or an authority over others makes us capable of satisfying all our desires; as slavery, by subjecting us to the will of others, exposes us to a thousand wants, and mortifications.
>
> *(T 2.1.10.11, SBN 315)*

There are a great many self- and situation-deprecating sentiments that fit under the umbrella of humility, just as vanity, smugness, over-confidence, and self-respect fit equally under the aegis of pride. And there are a great many entirely objective reasons for, say, judging one's abilities as being inferior to those of another, or not up to a professional standard. The apprehension of such a deficit or inferiority is never pleasurable. But, more to the point, it often concerns something we couldn't possibly rectify and for which we're not in the least responsible. The case is the same for humility in the case of slavery or poverty. Humility can be a pained awareness that one's circumstances are not good. It should be remembered that Hume is making a plausible psychological observation about our being pained by personal and situational shortfalls of one sort or another, not prescribing distressful feelings about them.

There is room in Hume, moreover, to challenge what should count as a shortfall or deficit in the first place. Socio-cultural standards and customs and norms may promote notions of deficiency and inferiority that are false or pernicious, and these can govern our shame and sense of inferiority, just as they can motivate improper pride:

> *general rules* have a great influence upon pride and humility as well as on all the other passions. Hence we form a notion of different ranks of men, suitable to the power or riches they are possest of; and this notion we change not upon account of any pecu-

> liarities of the health or temper of the persons … . This may be accounted for from the same principles, that explain'd the influence of general rules on the understanding.
>
> Custom readily carries us beyond the just bounds in our passions, as well as in our reasonings.
>
> *(T 2.1.6.8, SBN 293)*

So, for instance, I may notice that you have a far nicer home than I do. Objectively, it is better appointed, located in a nicer neighborhood, and equipped with the VR system of my dreams in a basement that has sensors mounted on the walls. I may feel envy (Hume is canny with respect to examples such as these, and classifies envy as an indirect passion as well), but feeling humility, inferiority, or mortification about my own perfectly adequate VR-free home isn't fitting. It suggests that I have adopted standards of worth based exclusively on the predilections of the yacht-owning, mansion-acquiring classes. We could probably devise standards for minimal adequacy in homes, but these couldn't be purely comparative. Likewise, there are probably standards that tell us when someone is and is not a competent pianist, but the simple fact that some people play better shouldn't be sufficient, by itself, for the ascription of a defect, or everyone but the best pianist in the world would be justified in feeling mortified. Proper pride and proper humility arise, roughly, from correct ascriptions of one's worth, and of the worth of the things with which one is affiliated. Improper pride and humility occur on account of incorrect ascriptions of worth—incorrect because exaggerated or involving invidious comparisons or simply because they are false.

Hume has a lot to say about pride and shame in physical appearance:

> *beauty* of all kinds gives us a peculiar delight and satisfaction; as *deformity* produces pain, upon whatever subject it may be plac'd … . If the beauty or deformity, therefore, be plac'd upon our own bodies, this pleasure or uneasiness must be converted into pride or humility … The beauty or deformity is closely related to self, the object of both these passions. No wonder, then, our own beauty becomes an object of pride, and deformity of humility.
>
> *(T 2.1.8.1, SBN 298)*

Hume doesn't think that one is usually proud of or embarrassed by something true of everybody, since that would not usually count as an advantage or as disadvantage. It would be ridiculous to announce pride or mortification on account of being embodied, for instance, or on account of possessing lungs, unless, of course, one were the happy recipient of a recent transplant. Similarly, the bare fact of having a cold, or of being healthy, isn't sufficient for humility or pride unless such advantages or liabilities were mainly due to one's own endeavors or recklessness. However,

> wherever a malady of any kind is so rooted in our constitution, that we no longer entertain any hopes of recovery, from that moment it becomes an object of humility; as is evident in old men, whom nothing mortifies more than the consideration of their age and infirmities. They endeavour, as long as possible, to conceal their blindness and deafness, their rheums and gouts; nor do they ever confess them without reluctance and uneasiness.
>
> *(T 2.1.8.8, SBN 302–303)*

Here the perceived disadvantage is connected to the inescapability of the condition, to the recollection of its absence, and to the presence of others who are not (at least not as yet) afflicted by it. Again, however, the point isn't that people ought to feel humbled by age, but that they very often do. The same point can be made, perhaps even more emphatically, about disability. Hume would expect the disabled to be humbled by their disability in the same way he expects the elderly to be humbled by geriatric afflictions. One need not infer from this, however, that Hume believes the disabled *should* be humble, that this is requisite for any acquaintance with something that one regards as a personal limitation. Moreover, while Hume criticizes conceit and vanity and thereby endorses a clearheaded acquaintance with one's own deficiencies, he does manage to suggest that humility is not always what it is cracked up to be, and that all aspects of pride are not necessarily vicious. Each, in other words, can be proper or improper, appropriate or inappropriate.

To the extent that humility represents a realistic awareness of one's limitations, it seems respectable and unproblematic. Indeed, it seems positively beneficial in that it will prevent one from undertakings at which one is bound to fail (#AmericanIdolAudition). The best case for humility, one that most philosophers would cheerfully endorse, is the laudable acknowledgement of fallibility. But this carries with it no stigma or negative self-evaluation. The recognition that one isn't omniscient is rather unlikely to prove a source of dejection. Sloppy and illogical thinking are and probably should be causes of embarrassment or dejection, of course, but the acknowledgement of fallibility is not, since everyone is fallible to one degree or another.

Emotional humility would arise from actual mistakes and shame over having made them. An acknowledgement of fallibility is an acknowledgement that one might not always get things right, not that an error has occurred.

As suggested earlier, many attempts to venture an argument in support of humility focus on what humility is *not* rather than on what it is. The humble will not brag, or exaggerate their accomplishments, or consider themselves superior to everyone else. They will not have such a high opinion of their intellectual prowess that they'll assume themselves capable of any feat. Instead, they will acknowledge their intellectual fallibility. But this simply assumes that the humble individual is not proud in the pejorative sense. Presumably, it is also possible not to be proud (in the sense of conceit and self-aggrandizement), and to acknowledge fallibility as well, without on that account being humble. What is the distinctive thing about humility itself that leads many to consider it a virtue?

We fear that what distinguishes humility from improper pride, and distinguishes it again from the very attractive position of neutrality just now outlined, is pain. Humility, particularly when considered as an affective state rather than a behavioral disposition, is painful. That is, if we regard humility as an emotion, that emotion is an unpleasant one. "Humility and shame deject and discourage us," according to Hume (T 2.2.10.6, SBN 391). For some cases, it is clear that distressful feelings can quite convincingly be held to be useful or character-improving. Guilt and shame over specific actions may prevent their repetition. Mortification over poor performance might lead to new endeavors and greater striving. It shows a realization of how one has erred and an acknowledgement that one has done so. Embarrassment over some shortfalls might lead to their rectification. Negative reinforcement can stimulate or inspire improvements. If humility involves the unhappy awareness of a personal deficiency, the unhappiness may act as a spur to reformation.

But to the extent that humility must involve feeling bad about the kinds of limitations one can do absolutely nothing about, it seems worse than useless as an adjunct to self- betterment or character-building, especially humility with respect to physical characteristics like age and disability where, provided the neutral stance regarding realistic beliefs about physical limitations is taken, negative emotional experiences are likely to do much more harm than good. Consider the preceding examples where deficit was ascribed solely on the basis of comparison. I am mortified by the quality of my house, not because I live in a state of squalor, not because my home has been condemned, but only because yours (and the mayor's, and that of my friend with the VR setup in the basement) is better. It is perfectly possible to acknowledge some houses are better than mine without generating the kind of humility tied to negative emotion. Indeed, there seems to be something wrong with allowing oneself to be made unhappy on account of such an acknowledgement. One's house isn't defective or flawed simply because others are better.

Being humbled by one's physical condition—being mortified or ashamed of it—when one's personal decisions or conduct aren't the cause of it, and when there is nothing that can be done to ameliorate or alter it, is problematic in a similar way. Having less mobility or less youth than others and acknowledging this need not be regarded as the acknowledgement of a flaw. One can acknowledge physical limitations, even incapacities, without considering them as instances of outright deficiency. The tenor of ageist and ableist thinking in this regard has almost always characterized such bodily conditions as defective and undesirable. Hume's claim that custom can carry us "beyond the just bounds" of passions like humility, and of reason as well, is very much to the point here (T 2.1.6.8, SBN 293). A limitation or incapacity, a lack evident only via comparison, is not always an appropriate subject or cause for an emotional response of humility. Acknowledgements of limitation of this kind very often produce shame and mortification, but there are many circumstances in which they ought not to do so. There are, after all, many cases of unjustified smugness on account of inherited wealth or due to a gross overestimation of one's talents and capacities. People's proud feelings very frequently arise from such causes, but it seems entirely correct to suggest that they ought not to do so either. It is usually a mistake to base one's self-assessment exclusively on the suppositions of others in any case. Socio-cultural beauty standards, attractiveness standards, and wholeness standards have always aroused criticism, and for good reason. Reasoned injunctions against subscribing to such standards wholesale are familiar to us all. No sensible person believes that a physical inability to live up to such standards should arouse a shame or mortification quite likely to prove self-destructive.

More recent investigations into humility can be informed by and expand on Hume's nuanced account, which could serve as a template for further analyses. Humility is not, then, always a virtue, as the case of disability makes especially apparent. It can serve one very ill. And to fail to see that is at the same time to overlook the sometimes subtle but important respects in which humility can (again, sometimes) authentically prove virtuous.

10.2 Humility, disablement, and the effects of testimonial injustice

We argue that the foregoing connections among disability, humility, and disposition suggested in Hume's writing raise an important question upon which the work of Jose Medina and Miranda Fricker may be brought fruitfully to bear. Namely, how might the experience of being humbled by and/or ashamed of one's disability influence the development of one's habits of thought and character—whether for better or for worse? On a Humean account, shame felt over one's disability amounts to an unfounded negative assessment of oneself in comparison with others. It is usually unfounded in at least two senses. In the first place, this feeling of shame implies the typically groundless notion that one bears some degree of personal responsibility for the disability in question. Secondly, the sense of personal inferiority felt on account of the disability often has its source in arbitrary standards of beauty and normalcy. As we discussed previously, an account of humility like Hume's suggests that this type of baseless, negative self-assessment can have damaging repercussions for a person's habits and overall disposition. Thus, if Hume is correct, there is reason to think that persistent shame over one's disability can potentially harm one in the development of one's character. Medina (2013) and Fricker (2007) also discuss feelings of shame as they arise in response to identity prejudice, and the potential effects of these feelings upon character. But, for them, these effects are taken to be aspects of injustice in their own right.

Fricker and Medina agree that social injustice goes hand in hand with unjust knowledge practices, the latter of which serve to perpetuate and further entrench unfair balances of power. Medina states, "Social injustices breed epistemic injustices; or rather, these two kinds of injustice are two sides of the same coin, always going together, being mutually supportive and reinforcing each other" (2013, p. 27). Prejudicial assumptions about the moral and intellectual capabilities of oppressed groups, for example, tend to undermine the impartiality of our judgments about them and what they attempt to tell us about their experiences. Think of the woman who reports being raped only to be interrogated about what she was wearing or how much she had had to drink at the time of the attack. This exemplifies a phenomenon Fricker has labeled "testimonial injustice," a kind of injustice wherein "prejudice causes a hearer to give a deflated level of credibility to a speaker's word" (2007, p. 1). Interestingly, and as Fricker and Medina have argued, subjection to testimonial injustice appears to instill problematic epistemic practices with oneself.

Medina contends that racist and sexist attacks upon an individual's credibility can cause that person to develop chronic deficiencies in confidence and self-trust that can destroy the motivation necessary for learning and self-cultivation. And, as Fricker avers, it is the feelings of shame and inferiority often aroused by those attacks which factor most importantly into the development of such deficiencies. She argues that the experience of having one's credibility undermined owing to identity prejudice demeans one not only as a potential giver of knowledge but also in one's very humanity. This is because those who are so treated suffer the symbolic meaning of that treatment. As she writes, "Such a dehumanizing meaning, especially if it is expressed before others, may make for a profound humiliation, even in circumstances where the injustice is in other respects fairly minor" (2007, p. 44). If humiliation is an apprehension of oneself as defective, as less than human, then clearly it has pernicious effects (unless, of course, some voluntarily performed error or wrongdoing is being exposed). Echoing Medina's point about the influence of identity prejudice on our epistemic habits, Fricker argues that this kind of humiliation leads to the inculcation of certain tendencies such as backing away from well-founded convictions and failing to see projects through to completion (2007, pp. 49–50). The upshot, for our purposes, is that feelings of lowliness engendered by normative conceptions of oneself as inferior because of some feature of one's identity can be compounded and reinforced through knowledge practices that are humiliating in their own right, such as having one's credibility called into question. Moreover, this amplification of shame over one's person can influence one's own epistemic habits in complex ways.

While there is much discussion of the foregoing issues in the contexts of gender and race, little has been written on epistemic injustice as it is experienced by the disabled. Elizabeth Barnes (2016) has recently addressed the topic, but her focus lies with the tendency of the non-disabled to disbelieve disabled people who claim to be proud of their bodies, rather than the ways in which our epistemic practices may perpetuate and even worsen feelings of inferiority arising from prejudicial assumptions about those with disabilities. As Barnes (2016) argues, many disabled people are happy with their bodies and do not wish to become non-disabled despite the widely held, ableist belief that it is always better to be able-bodied. Yet there is little doubt that disability remains a stigmatized and stigmatizing identity, and that one of the potential difficulties of being disabled is dealing with ableist stereotypes and assumptions. These include, but are of course not limited to, the idea that disabled bodies are inherently flawed, that disabled people are burdensome to society, that their physical characteristics are outward manifestations of hidden moral failings, that they are possessed of overwhelming envy and hatred of the able-bodied, that they would be better off never having been born, and that they should not reproduce. On the flip-side, successful disabled people are often depicted as being possessed of transcendent qualities of personal strength and inner fortitude by reason of which they are believed to be moral exemplars for the able-bodied. Our point is that ableist stereotypes and assumptions provide ample occasion for the disabled to develop feelings of shame not only over their disabilities, but over *who they are as people* because they are disabled.

How might instances of epistemic injustice work to compound these feelings? To provide an especially insidious example of epistemic injustice in a disability context, consider that people with disabilities are more likely than the non-disabled to be sexually assaulted *and* disbelieved when they report instances of assault. One commonplace way of discrediting their testimony is to claim that disabled individuals cannot be assaulted, either because they lack sexuality or that they must have been solicitous of and/or grateful for what was done to them. The disability rights activist, Nidhi Goyal, has discussed this issue at length as it pertains to disabled women and girls living in India. She has said that a disabled woman who reports an assault in India is unlikely to be believed because "She is considered asexual, unattractive, or on the other extreme: desperate and only wanting sex (www.cnn.com/2018/04/05/health/india-disabled-sexual-assault-survivors-intl/index.html)." Having one's testimony discredited in this manner can, of course, destroy confidence in one's ability to understand the events in question, and contribute to an overall sense of uneasiness about the accuracy of one's judgments of the world. As Fricker states,

> When you find yourself in a situation in which you seem to be the only one to feel tension between received understanding and your own intimated sense of a given experience, it tends to knock your faith in your own ability to make sense of the world.
> *(2007, p. 163)*

The painful feelings of inferiority a person may develop because of their disability can be engendered by the epistemic interactions to which they are subjected *and* the demeaning stereotypes according to which they are depicted. This underscores the complexity and degree to which these feelings may often feature in the experiences of those who have disabilities. Furthermore, it suggests that the effects of such feelings upon habits of thought and action can directly contribute to a person's situation of social disempowerment by decreasing the likelihood that they will trust their own perception of their situation as unjust. For all of these reasons, we think the afore-stated question about disability, humility, and disposition that arises from humility as construed in the Humean sense remains as significant as ever. But how, more precisely, might the emotions Hume associates with humility occasioned by losses or differences in one's bodily capacity come to shape one's disposition?

It is just here that Medina's recent work on the epistemic virtues and vices characteristic of stigmatized groups is especially helpful. As we indicated previously, Medina recognizes along with Fricker that the humbling experiences characteristic of oppressed minorities can so erode confidence in one's capabilities that one is unmotivated to learn, cultivate oneself, or explore possibilities for transforming one's situation for the better. However, he also argues that the epistemic humility manifested by oppressed individuals can be virtuous in the sense that it increases the likelihood one will be able to engage successfully in all three of these activities. He states,

> When it does not undermine one's confidence and erode one's character (that is, when it does not become pathological), epistemic humility can afford great benefits. Having a humble and self-questioning attitude toward one's cognitive repertoire can lead to many epistemic achievements and advantages: qualifying one's beliefs and making finer-grained discriminations; identifying one's cognitive gaps and what it would

> take to fill them; being able to formulate questions and doubts for oneself and others; and so on.
>
> *(2013, p. 43)*

Medina goes on to link proper epistemic humility with other virtues including open-mindedness and diligence. Such virtues are grounded in the kind of "ego-skepticism" often engendered in one by a situation of oppression, according to Medina; however, they are also virtues that can be of assistance in becoming properly critical of one's situation and help one determine effective methods of resisting it (2013, 43). So, while he thinks we should avoid romanticizing the humbling vantage points on the world that oppression creates, he believes it is worthwhile to think through the ways in which those vantage points can help people form habits that make them better thinkers who are, on that account, more capable of resisting their subjugators than they otherwise would be. For example, and as Medina goes on to elaborate,

> Oppressed subjects tend to feel the need of being more attentive to the perspectives of others. They have no option but to acknowledge, respect, and (to some extent) inhabit alternative perspectives, in particular the perspective(s) of the dominant other. They are often encouraged and typically even forced to see reality not only through their own eyes, but also through the eyes of others whose perspectives and social locations matter more. In this way oppressed subjects accomplish the epistemic feat of maintaining active in their minds two cognitive perspectives simultaneously as they perform various tasks ... The epistemic perspective of oppressed subjects often exhibits a characteristic kind of hybridity, inclusiveness, and open-mindedness, whereas the cognitive functioning of privileged elites tends to be more parochial and one-sided, often operating in complete disregard of alternative standpoints.
>
> *(2013, p. 44)*

As Medina points out, this phenomenon is what is known in race theory as "double-consciousness." Ultimately, the epistemic perspective made possible by double consciousness is one of greater lucidity regarding oneself and one's environment (2013, pp. 44–45).

To provide an example of how this multi-faceted epistemic perspective can potentially arise in the context of ableism, consider the well-known phenomenon of passing for able-bodied. Many disabled people face significant pressure to conceal and deflect attention from their disabilities so as to appear as "normal"—especially in professional situations. They are often shamed into passing, not only because their bodies are seen to fall short of the able-bodied ideal, but because disabled people are viewed as burdensome to those around them. As Tobin Siebers has argued, passing is a psychologically complex act that involves anticipating what others are likely to need to perceive for it to be successful. He describes this psychic complexity in the following manner:

> Disability passing involves playing roles, but its essential character is less a matter of deception than of an intimate knowledge of human ability and its everyday definition. Those who pass understand better than others the relation between disability and ability in any given situation. As careful strategists of social interaction, they know what sightedness looks like, though they may be blind; they know what conversation sounds like, though they may be deaf. Passers are skillful interpreters of human society.
>
> *(2008, pp. 117–18)*

In short, anyone who routinely passes for abled spends significant time and energy imaginatively inhabiting the perspectives of those in positions of relative privilege—namely, the able-bodied—alongside their own experiences of the world. Though there are practical reasons to engage in passing such as the protection of one's job, it is very often the shame of stigma that motivates the development of habits such as anticipatory watchfulness and sympathy with other perspectives which make it possible to pull off a performance of able-bodiedness. If Medina's account of epistemic virtue can be accepted, such habits may at times prove instrumental in the formation of intellectual humility. But this seems to be dependent upon a necessary degree of moderation, such that the patterns of feeling and thought by which we recognize such humility are not taken to extremes. We take it that the intellectual modesty of which Medina writes is indeed a virtue, thereby placing it beyond the ambit of our critique of humility as an emotion.

We conclude, then, that the connections among disability, humility, and disposition that are emergent in Hume's writing are rendered more intelligible when interpreted from the standpoint of recent scholarly discussions of epistemic injustice and ableism. Hume's recognition of these connections was surely accurate; however, it is important to understand that the effects of humility upon one's disposition may be seen to be outcomes of social and epistemic forms of injustice.

References

Barnes, Elizabeth. (2016), *The Minority Body: A Theory of Disability*, Oxford: Oxford University Press.

Fricker, Miranda. (2007), *Epistemic Injustice: The Power and Ethics of Knowing*, Oxford: Oxford University Press.

Hume, David. (1978), *Treatise of Human Nature*, ed. L.A. Selby-Bigge, Oxford: Clarendon Press.

Medina, Jose. (2013), *The Epistemology of Resistance: Gender and Racial Oppression, Epistemic Injustice, and Resistant Imagination*, Oxford: Oxford University Press.

Siebers, Tobin. (2008), *Disability Theory*, Ann Arbor: The University of Michigan Press.

PART 3

The politics of humility

11
A HUMBLE FORM OF GOVERNMENT
Democracy as the politics of collective experience

Michael A. Neblo and Emily Ann Israelson

> Democracy … is the sole way of living which believes wholeheartedly in the process of experience as end and as means.
>
> *John Dewey, from* Creative Democracy

11.1 Introduction

Democracy, for Dewey, is a humble form of government in that both its inputs and its outputs are rooted in quotidian experience. Everyday life tells us where the shoe pinches, and what has relieved the chaffing. In a democracy, moreover, the relevant experiences come from the humble of society just as much as the exalted. Equality in having our interests served, as well as judging how they have been served, forms the foundation of democratic politics (Neblo, 2015).

Yet, there is also a kind of hubris in democracy. Everyday experience provides a notoriously myopic lens through which to view the good of the commonwealth. Those of a more aristocratic bent have long claimed that the common person tends toward avidity for immediate and personal gain at the expense of the long-term flourishing of all. T. S. Eliot, no democrat in his politics, cautions us against myopia toward both the past and the future. In the *Four Quartets* he writes that there is "only a limited value / In the knowledge gained from experience… The only wisdom we can hope to acquire / Is the wisdom of humility: humility is endless." Like Burke before him, Eliot believes that we tend to overestimate our ability to innovate ways to realize our future goals reliably, and to underestimate the past as a guide to what we really should want and how best to get it.

Juxtaposing Dewey and Eliot like this puts one in mind of the useful cliché attributed to Churchill that democracy is the worst form of government, except for all the others. The juxtaposition, however, also puts us in a better position to see why democracy is so allegedly bad, and how we might hedge against its badness. Attending carefully to the role of humility in democracy, then, can help us improve on its advantages over "all the others"—hopefully rendering the currently resurgent attractions of non-democratic regimes less tempting.

We first identify key distinctions between types of democracy, humility, and actors. The three models of democracy discussed here require differing levels of humility from different democratic actors, but deliberative models place particular expectations on citizens themselves.

To soften the apparent implications of these demands, we discuss the virtue of *sophrosyne* as a governor of just and humble discourse. Finally, we propose that a more complicated model of humility can provide plentiful room for further study regarding its relationship with efficacy and democratic innovation.

11.2 Distinctions

Both "humility" and "democracy" are multifaceted terms, so it behooves us to clarify the concepts and how we will be using them throughout this essay. The first such distinction relevant to applying humility to democracy hinges on what we might call "cognitive" versus "conative" humility. By "cognitive" we mean humility in forming, individually relying upon, and endeavoring to spread one's beliefs. By "conative" we mean humility in forming, pursuing, and especially claiming social priority for the fulfilment of one's desires. We can further distinguish the object of our cognitive and conative humility. We most naturally think of humility toward others: cognitive (or intellectual) humility vis-a-vis our epistemic superiors or even peers; conative humility toward others affected by the way that we pursue our goals (among further specifications of "others" pursued below). On certain virtue theories, though, we might also be humble with respect to ourselves, critically reflecting on our own beliefs and the pursuit of our desires, even when these do not importantly affect others. Finally, we add a temporal dimension to "others:" that is, humility toward the past when it comes to our beliefs and humility toward future generations when it comes to pursuing our desires (Burke again).

On the heels of these distinctions, we should also note that we will be treating "humility" as a bi-valent term. That is, we will understand humility as a virtue that admits of corresponding vices of excess and deficiency (Church and Samuelson, 2016). This choice is not obvious since one prominent theoretical and ordinary-language meaning of humility treats it as univalent: a person is either humble and virtuous, or arrogant and blameworthy. Eliot, a devout Christian, follows an important tradition according to which we are radically fallen creatures who should be maximally humble: that "humility is endless." One might also use humility to anchor one end of a dichotomy and claim, pace Eliot, that the virtuous characteristic is to be found somewhere in the middle.

Instead, we will treat "humility" as the virtuous mean between two vicious extremes. In the case of cognitive (or intellectual) humility, the vice in which we are insufficiently humble is "arrogance," and the vice in which we are overly humble is "diffidence." Correspondingly, for conative humility, the vice in which we are insufficiently humble is "greed," and the vice in which we are overly humble is "abnegation." The virtuous mean of conative humility might also be described as knowing and asserting our proper self-worth (Neblo, 2007a).

Similarly, "democracy" is a capacious concept that means many things to different people. For our purposes, we will *not* insist on a single, encompassing definition, but rather distinguish between three ideal-typical notions of democracy, and then examine the role of humility in them separately. We do not necessarily mean that humility is required in each of these understandings of democracy in order for them to self-perpetuate, but that for each system to provide desirable goods, some form of humility must be present somewhere in the process. These goods include improvements in the epistemic dynamics of deliberation and the power dynamics of democratic decision making. Desirable epistemic dynamics require that the right people assert and defer in the proper contexts, while desirable power dynamics emerge when people humbly adhere to their roles. We shall focus on three broad theoretical genera of democracy, further distinguishing species under them only as it seems necessary (Neblo, 2007b). We call the three main theories we will analyze as follows: competitive-elitist democracy, liberal democracy, and deliberative democracy.[1]

Competitive-elitist theories of democracy focus on securing peaceful transitions of power between elites elected by the masses at semi-regular intervals. These are sometimes called "deflationary" theories because they are relatively unambitious regarding the standards that they apply for policy success. Such theories generally disavow notions of a common good, or at a least reliable means of knowing and securing such a common good, should it exist. Weber, Schumpeter, Riker, and, more recently, Achen and Bartels fall under this category. In between elections, average citizens play a minimal role in forming policy, and can only be intermittently and imperfectly relied upon to turn elites out of power if they fail to please the electorate.

Calling the next group "liberal" theories invites some confusion because the concept of liberalism is at best oblique to democracy. That said, as an empirical matter, the combination (liberalism paired with democracy) co-occurs often enough to treat it as a sort of genus. The "liberal" part of liberal democracy tends to focus on pluralism, individual rights, limited government, the separation of powers—that is, limits or at least inflections on what democratic majorities can accomplish. Some variants are skeptical of singular notions of the common good, though many would acknowledge a finite number of competing notions of the good. Others countenance the idea of a common good but counsel caution, arguing that liberal constraints conduce toward it (or at least hedge against grave deviations). Madison and, more recently, Brennan (2009) typify this latter approach.

Deliberative theories of democracy embody more ambitious standards for forming and judging policy decisions than the other two theories, and non-elites generally play a more important role in deliberative theories as well (Neblo et al., 2018). Though only a few embrace a strong, singular theory of the common good, they almost all have some robust notion of better and worse arguments in favor of prospective policy choices, and in judging their consequences after the fact (Neblo, 2005). Habermas, Mansbridge, Cohen, Dryzek, Fishkin, as well as Gutmann and Thompson have all proposed theoretical variants on the deliberative model (Bächtiger et al., 2010).

Finally, we distinguish between the kind and degree of humility required by the various roles that one might play in an actually functioning democracy. One tends to think of citizens (or perhaps all those subject to the political power of a given jurisdiction) as the obvious agents who relate to each other in terms of humility, arrogance, and diffidence, or greed and abnegation. Nearly all modern democracies, however, are representative democracies. So we must distinguish between the officials who make and enforce law and policy, and those subject to those laws and policies, but, being subject to them, typically elect their representatives (Minozzi et al., 2015). In addition to being representative, modern democracies are also typically large, complex states, governing a wide array of policy areas. Thus the role of policy experts in democracies has grown dramatically in the modern era; below, we will discuss the pattern of virtues necessary for the proper functioning of democracy according to each model as broken out by citizens, officials, and experts (Goold et al., 2012).

11.3 Competitive-elitist democracy

Citizens: in competitive-elitist models of democracy, average citizens play a minimal and highly indirect role in influencing policy. Political entrepreneurs (usually parties) package policy bundles and compete for votes and other forms of political support. As a relative matter, voters do not need to be highly informed in order to choose among those vying for their vote and, by extension, they do not have to display a high degree of cognitive humility in order for the system to run reasonably well by its own standards. Just so long as votes are not systematically perverse vis-a-vis relatively good policy (and voters do not empower authoritarians so that democracy itself fails), competitive-elitism can satisfy their theoretical and practical requirements. That said, citizens do have to evince a degree of conative humility in not empowering authoritarians or (what amounts to almost the same) in supporting democratically empowered elites who refuse the peaceful transfer of power upon electoral losses. We can construe such conative humility in self-referential terms (being a virtuous person), interpersonally (being a good democratic citizen), and vis-a-vis history (recognizing that sacrificing short-term authoritarian advantage to long-term democratic goods is generally a poor strategy).

Officials: since elected officials are the first movers in competitive-elitist theories, they play a nearly determinative role in forming policy. They are broadly constrained by what they can sell voters, of course, but they stage political conflict in a way that sets the terms of debate. As such, the production of desirable deliberative and power dynamics in this system relies on them possessing more than a modicum of intellectual virtue, prominently cognitive humility. That said, the role of conative humility looms larger. Politicians willing to sacrifice social goods in the quest for a short- or even long-term hold on power have a lot of rope to hang all of us under this model of democracy. There need not exist a single common good in order for politics to realize all manner of (near) consensually bad outcomes. While this system would be self-sustaining in that elites need not consider any public goods in order to replicate it, the competitive-elitist system of democracy could hardly produce fair decision-making dynamics without the presence of humility. Conative humility toward future generations, in particular, would seem to be a desideratum of officials in competitive-elitist models of democracy.

Experts: since competitive-elitism places so few cognitive burdens on citizens, and only moderate ones on officials, it falls to experts to carry most of the cognitive weight of inputs into forming good public policy. As such, they would seem to need a higher degree of cognitive humility, depending on the structure of competition among policy experts. Similarly, since other democratic actors are not in a good position to challenge their cognitive contributions to the policy process, they would need a higher degree of conative humility in order not to exploit the slack in the system to their personal or collective advantage (again, conditional on the structure and degree of competition among elites—e.g., whether there is an overarching community of scientific experts, or whether they divided into think-tanks that roughly mirror the structure of partisan competition). Such exploitation is antithetical to the good democratic decision-making that humility is intended to buy us.

11.4 Liberal democracy

Citizens: the cognitive burden placed on average citizens under most liberal models of democracy are more extensive than under the competitive-elitist account, but, as we will see, less than that on the modal deliberative account. On a Madisonian account, for example, their main function is to select leaders with sound judgment, not just those whose policy packages promise the most payoff for one personally. Rather than staging all political conflict (constrained only by the broadest sense of public sentiment), leaders on the liberal model should, in the words of Federalist 10, "refine and enlarge the public views." Note that, here, members of the public are, in a sense, the first actors, in contrast to the competitive-elitist view.

Under pluralism, most citizens are members of sub-groups that have more or less coherent values and interests. As such, they must articulate those values and interests, and thus need corresponding levels of cognitive humility so as not to under or even oversell their individual views. While they ought to be open to the possibility of being factually wrong, they also ought not to be so preoccupied with doubt that their views are not heard and enlarged by their representatives. Unlike in the competitive-elitism model, citizens must only select among representatives rather than among policy bundles, so they have a greater risk of their interests not being met if they are not appropriately articulating those interests. What cognitive humility gives us is a fairer epistemic dynamic in citizens' expression of their choices, such that personality is not predicting who is heard. But citizens are not generally responsible for wisely balancing and reconciling those values and interests against other groups. Hence the demands on both their cognitive and conative humility are more specific and less intense than those expected of their elected representatives. They are less intense in that there is a backstop against their arrogance and greed (i.e., the presumably more virtuous representatives). They are more specific in that their conative humility need not apply so much to their desire for first-order political goods, just so long as it does not extend to punishing elected officials who wisely and fairly sacrificed some of those first-order goods to the just demands of others and the commonweal more generally.

Officials: on the liberal model, elected officials are empowered by selection, but are more constrained than on the competitive model, where they stage almost all political conflict. Thus they need a middling level of cognitive humility. As with the elitist model, cognitive humility is required for parties to peacefully transfer power to others when the majority and minority balance changes. If each party is appropriately aware of the justifications for their beliefs and open to the possibility that they might be wrong, it will be easier to pass the torch to another ideological group than if they inappropriately overvalue the positive epistemic status of their beliefs. In addition, however, on the liberal model they must also attempt to "refine and enlarge the public views" by making reasonable trade-offs between social groups.

Conative humility is important for representatives on a Madisonian understanding of liberal democracy for similar reasons. The peaceful transfer of power and reasonably balancing group interests are only possible when officials understand that their desires do not warrant more attention than the desires of other elected officials, since they were all chosen by the same selection process and represent plural worldviews and interests. Even if the quality of representatives differs such that some do a better job encapsulating the interests of their districts and some do worse, this would still not warrant officials discrediting the desires of others on this basis. Not only would other officials not know the quality of other officials' representation unless they were well acquainted with another official's constituents, but the selection model of liberal democracy does not require that representation be good as long as the official has the legitimacy of having been elected. Ultimately, epistemic virtue on a liberal model depends on the ability of incumbent representatives to exercise self-restraint, since they are in a position to achieve their desires if they believe they are deserving (Neblo, 2004). In theory, if they recognize that their own knowledge is limited, then they are more likely to acknowledge that government itself ought also to be limited (Kober, 1997).

Experts: since on the liberal model officials are presumed to have some of the knowledge and judgment allocated to experts on the elitist model, their need for both cognitive and conative humility is correspondingly less, though that is not to say negligible. At the cognitive level, they need to avoid confusing their own desires with their expertise, and, at the conative level, they need to avoid exploiting their superior knowledge against elected officials (and, to a lesser extent, the public). Which is to say that they need both types of humility to a moderate degree.

11.5 Deliberative democracy

Citizens: theorists have developed many variants on the basic deliberative model, but for all of them the cognitive burden placed on citizens is generally at least somewhat higher than on the liberal and competitive-elitist models. The distinction between proceduralist and epistemic interpretations of deliberative theory does not really change this burden all that much, since the quality of procedures includes criteria like the informedness and reasoning of the deliberators (Neblo, 2006). That said, some have overestimated the cognitive demands on the deliberative account. The idea is not that average citizens should quit their day jobs and spend all of their time deliberating about all the issues of the day. The main claim is only that the quality of the reasoning processes feeding into the policy process (as they are broadly understood) matter for judging the quality of the outcomes (Lazer et al., 2015). Since, on most deliberative accounts, the line between average citizens and officials is at least somewhat blurred, their need for both cognitive and conative humility increases accordingly. Moreover, worries over vices of excess loom larger on the deliberative account. Denigrating one's cognitive status and legitimate conative claims is more likely to lead to injustices on the deliberative model than on the other two (Wu, 2011). When citizens themselves have the responsibility of seeing their interests heard and prioritized rather than leaving most of these demands up to officials, the interests of the too-humble citizen are more likely to be ignored in favor of the interests of the more assertive.

Officials: since, on the deliberative model, citizens, officials, and experts are all responsible for the quality of debate, the cognitive demands on officials is somewhat less (in *relative* terms) than on the other two models. Rather than officials being first movers (as with the competitive-elitist theory) or second movers (as with liberal theories), the deliberative model imagines a much more recursive and cooperative process cycling through the larger political system (Lazer et al., 2011). Both cognitive and conative humility, then, are importantly and somewhat distinctively directed *among* civil society, formal government actors, and expert communities.

Experts: as with elected representatives and governmental officials more generally, experts bear a bit less of the relative cognitive burden of forming good policy on the deliberative model because their cognitive status is something akin to first-among-equals, rather than constituting a qualitative break in deliberative capacity regarding policy. Jasanoff (2003), for example, argues for "technologies of humility" vis-a-vis scientific expertise in democracy. As such, experts' need for both cognitive and conative humility, while still substantial, is less acute than on the other two models. Given that the deliberative model requires more humility on the part of the average citizen than the other models, we need to analyze such demands in practice to see how democratic citizens might practicably realize such virtue.

11.6 *Sophyrosyne* and deliberative democracy

Skeptics of deliberative conceptions of democracy often point to the rather demanding expectations imposed on citizens in the deliberative account. With some justice, critics argue that it is utopian to believe that sufficient numbers of citizens in mass democracy will dramatically improve their knowledge about politics and sophistication in reasoning about policy. We argue that the key characteristic required of deliberative democratic citizens is not so much political knowledge, sophistication in reasoning, or, in their absence, humility as it is narrowly understood. Rather, the key trait to develop is something akin to what the ancients called *sophrosyne*, a conceptual cousin to humility, but whose broader connotations are remarkably apt for fostering good democratic—and especially deliberative democratic—citizenship (Neblo, 2011).

The Greek word has an unusually wide range of translations, but it is often rendered as temperance, moderation, sobriety, self-control, and sound-mindedness. *Sophrosyne* is alone among the ancient cardinal virtues in lacking a clear modern referent, and it has been relatively neglected in updated accounts of politics and the virtues. Yet, we argue that *sophrosyne* is a particularly needful virtue in the citizenry if a deliberative conception of democracy is to fulfill its purpose of allowing us to steer between technocratic elitism, vulgar populism, and an anomic politics-as-market. Unlike producing vast increases in information and political sophistication, fostering *sophrosyne* in the context of democratic deliberation is a plausible goal. Thus, it should be regarded as a kind of low-hanging fruit for hopes of democratic reform.

In his underappreciated dialogue *Charmides*, Plato runs through four definitions of *sophrosyne* (quietness, modesty, minding one's own business, and knowledge of what one knows and does not know). Despite the aporetic ending of the dialogue, these definitions, taken together, sketch a syndrome of deliberative habits that is remarkably well tailored to ameliorating the main vulnerabilities of deliberative politics in an imperfect world. The main barriers to deliberation are not rooted in individuals being ignorant or naïve, but rather in mobilizing the knowledge and judgment latent in varying sectors of the public appropriately.

Each of the definitions bear some connection to our broad notion of humility as it relates to democratic politics. Quietness is necessary for listening to others, a precondition for cognitive humility, and an enactment of conative humility insofar as one is not trying to win the debate by any means. Obviously one must not be too quiet, which is one of the reasons that Socrates rejects quietness as an adequate definition. That said, even if humility is a bi-valent concept, most people are, as a general matter, more apt to both cognitive and conative assertiveness than their opposites (though, in a political context, this may be less true of women and under-represented minorities). Thus urging a bit more quietness is wise counsel for most of us, most of the time. Plato's second definition, modesty, seems to be almost constitutive of humility (again, on the presumption that more people tend toward assertiveness than self-effacement more often than not). The dialogue's third definition, "minding one's own business," is crucial for finding the virtuous mean: we should be more assertive when we are relative experts and our well-being is most at stake, and less so when the reverse is true (Minozzi et al., 2012). Finally, "knowledge of what one knows and does not know," is a kind of second-order knowledge that is again necessary for properly sorting cases where we should be deferent versus those where assertiveness would be appropriate.

Thus, if we want to correct the vulnerabilities of deliberation, we have a duty as citizens to foster reasoned discourse about public matters in a manner congruent with *sophrosyne*. Many people, however, treat political choices like impulsive consumer choices and political discourse like a call-in show on sports radio. If we are going to use our political power to pass laws affecting our fellow citizens, though, we owe each other reasoned explanations in a way that we do not about what sports teams we support or what toothpaste we buy. Political choices are different from consumer choices and sports loyalties because laws are enforced by people with guns.

That said, discourse governed by *sophrosyne* is not the same as polite, unemotional discourse. Democracies sometimes need passionate protest, and civil disobedience can actually be a duty in extreme cases (Neblo, 2003). The tricky part is knowing the difference between gross injustices that cry out for redress, and deep but reasonable disagreements that people in a diverse society cannot avoid. Who is to decide which is which? The first amendment to the U.S. constitution, wisely, says that it cannot be the government itself—the people with guns. So the only ones left to decide are you and me and our fellow citizens. That is one of the main reasons why *sophrosyne* is so important to good deliberative citizenship, and usefully augments standard accounts of the role of humility in democratic politics. As a sibling virtue to humility, *sophrosyne* adds needed dimensions to our understanding of democratic virtues, but cannot replace humility. We can certainly argue, then, that humility understood this way not only relates to how citizens epistemically evaluate conclusions and prioritize goals, but also to whether or not they are confident in their societal goals and can reasonably expect them to be accomplished.

11.7 Humility and political efficacy

Empirically oriented political scientists conceptualize and measure a widely studied construct they call political "efficacy." Efficacy comes in distinct "internal" and "external" varieties.

External political efficacy measures people's beliefs that they can influence the political system—e.g., that elected officials will listen and respond to their input. Internal political efficacy measures people's sense of competence to participate in politics—e.g., that the policy process is not too complicated for a person like them to understand. In principle, the two concepts can swing independently of each other as an empirical matter: e.g., one might believe that government officials *should* be responsive to me because I am politically competent, and yet believe that such officials will not, in fact, be responsive.

Obviously internal political efficacy is related to cognitive humility vis-a-vis democratic citizenship. Heretofore, there has been some confusion in the literature because political scientists have assumed that humility is univalent—those who are cognitively humble do not think of themselves as especially competent, and hence there would be a negative relationship between cognitive humility and internal efficacy. But on the bi-valent conception of cognitive humility, the relationship becomes more complex. Presumably one should express levels of internal political efficacy appropriate to one's actual level of political competence. If so, then the relationship between humility and efficacy is open to further exploration, and may even exhibit "unfolding" properties—i.e., rather than relating in a linear fashion, the relationship would follow an inverted U shape, since one might be inappropriately matched in either direction: excess or deficiency.

Additionally, most political science literature casts high levels of political efficacy as a good thing. Democratic legitimacy hinges on reasonable levels of external political efficacy, and democratic engagement relies on people believing that they are competent to participate (Neblo et al., 2010). But given the augmentation of humility with *sophrosyne*, one should generally "mind one's own business" and remain vigilant about "what one knows and does not know," rather than assuming more self-confidence is always a good thing. This divergence might result from modern politics reversing which vice is more common: whereas in most cases people have too high an opinion of themselves (e.g., 90% of people believe that they are above average drivers), in modern mass politics, many people feel disempowered and overwhelmed by the complexity of the policy process. Conditional on entering the process they may tend toward over-assertiveness, but many are hesitant to begin in the first place.

In the empirical literature, Grönlund et al. (2010) hypothesized that deliberation would increase both kinds of political efficacy by increasing people's political knowledge. Instead, they found that deliberation led to a slight decrease in internal political efficacy, though Morrell (2005) and Nabatchi (2010) found positive effects. Esterling et al. (2011) found that deliberation between elected officials and members of the public increased external political efficacy for the public, but did not affect internal political efficacy either way (though this null finding might be a result of people more appropriately estimating their political competence—i.e., that those who were excessively high on internal political efficacy were humbled somewhat, and those who were excessively low experienced a better sense of their potential). Interestingly, Himmelroos et al. (2017) found that "enclave" deliberation—i.e., among like-minded people—significantly increased internal political efficacy among marginalized groups with few political resources. This discussion of political efficacy suggests potential reforms of standard democratic practices as well.

11.8 Humility and delegative democracy

Recently there has been a surge of interest in a novel form of governance called "delegative" (or sometimes "liquid") democracy (Blum and Zuber, 2016). The idea is that voters have the option of delegating their voting power to others. They can always vote themselves, or vote on some issues but not others, or revoke or change their delegated authority. Some think of delegative democracy as a compromise between direct and representative democracy, but this view does not do justice to the potential flexibility of delegative democracy in that it could generate a variation on either of those pure theories, rather than standing as an alternative per se. For example, one could imagine a system of representative democracy in which votes for one's representatives were subject to delegation. Similarly, one could imagine a system of direct democracy in which some people voted directly, while others delegated, or people mixed the topics that they delegated or engaged directly on. Several experiments in delegative democracy have been undertaken; for example, in Argentina, with the Democracia en Red initiative.

Delegative democracy is of special interest to those concerned about the role of humility in democracy because the entire system would seem to hinge on the virtuous exercise of both cognitive and conative humility. Knowing one's own strengths and limits vis-a-vis different issues, as well as whom to trust as a delegate would be essential for delegative democracy to function properly. Further theoretical and empirical research on humility in such democratic innovations is well warranted.

11.9 Conclusion

Although humility is sometimes understood as univalent such that one can never be too humble, this understanding can be more harmful than helpful for understanding its role in democracy. Although citizens ought to overestimate neither their epistemic conclusions nor the level of priority that should be attributed to their societal goals, it is also important that they not underestimate these. For this reason, we examine a bi-valent concept, where the ideal is a virtuous mean between extremes.

We have outlined several advantages to this approach. Since we have identified that deliberative models in particular place a high virtuous burden on citizens, this conception of humility taken alongside the Greek virtue of *sophrosyne* allows us to more clearly identify how citizens in a deliberative model ought to behave. This approach shifts the focus away from democracy as a consumer choice and toward democracy as a reasoned discourse regarding what is just or unjust. Aside from these normative advantages, our concept of humility also has practical benefits. Treating humility as bi-valent gives us space to explore how humility and political efficacy relate from one problematic extreme to the other. Additionally, we can use humility to help us understand innovations in democracy and deliberation.

Our hope is that humility will be a useful lens through which to see how democracy might be improved and its advantages made more attractive. Democracy itself incorporates both the modesty of the average citizen's everyday experiences as well as the hubris of narrow self-interest in people's views and demands. Exploring how individuals can balance themselves between diffidence and arrogance may give us insight as to how government might do the same.

Note

1 In the discussion below, we have been informed by, but freely modify the taxonomy and analyses in, Kelly (2012: 44–58).

References

Bächtiger, A., Niemeyer, S., Neblo, M., Steenbergen, M.R., and Steiner, J., 2010. Disentangling diversity in deliberative democracy: Competing theories, their blind spots and complementarities. *Journal of Political Philosophy*, *18*(1), pp.32–63.

Blum, Christian, and Zuber, Christina Isabel, 2016. Liquid democracy: Potentials, problems, and perspectives. *Journal of Political Philosophy*, *24*(2), pp.162–182.

Brennan, Jason, 2009. Polluting the polls: When citizens should not vote. *Australasian Journal of Philosophy*, *87*(4), pp.535–549.

Church, Ian, and Samuelson, Peter, 2016. *Intellectual Humility: An Introduction to the Philosophy and Science*. Bloomsbury Publishing.

Esterling, K.M., Neblo, M.A., and Lazer, D.M., 2011. Estimating treatment effects in the presence of noncompliance and nonresponse: The generalized endogenous treatment model. *Political Analysis*, *19*(2), pp.205–226.

Goold, S.D., Neblo, M.A., Kim, S.Y., Vries, R.D., Rowe, G., and Muhlberger, P., 2012. What is good public deliberation? *The Hastings Center Report*, *42*(2), pp.24–26.

Grönlund, Kimmo, Setälä, Maija, and Herne, Kaisa, 2010. Deliberation and civic virtue: Lessons from a citizen deliberation experiment. *European Political Science Review*, *2*(1), pp.95–117.

Himmelroos, Staffan, Rapeli, Lauri, and Grönlund, Kimmo, 2017. Talking with like-minded people—Equality and efficacy in enclave deliberation. *The Social Science Journal*, *54*(2), pp.148–158.

Jasanoff, Sheila, 2003. (No?) Accounting for expertise. *Science and Public Policy*, *30*(3), pp.157–162.

Kelly, Jamie Terence, 2012. *Framing Democracy: A Behavioral Approach to Democratic Theory*. Princeton University Press.

Kober, Stanley, 1997. The spirit of humility. *The Cato Journal*, *17*, p.235.

Lazer, D., Neblo, M., and Esterling, K., 2011. The internet and the madisonian cycle: Possibilities and prospects for consultative representation. In: *Connecting Democracy: Online Consultation and the Flow of Political Communication*, eds., Price, V., Chadwick, A., Åström, J., Grönlund, Å., Balla, S.J., Hwang, S., Wright, S., Gibson, R., Schneeberger, A.I., Monnoyer-Smith, L., and Lubbers, J.S. MIT Press, pp.265–285.

Lazer, D.M., Sokhey, A.E., Neblo, M.A., Esterling, K.M., and Kennedy, R., 2015. Expanding the conversation: Multiplier effects from a deliberative field experiment. *Political Communication*, *32*(4), pp.552–573.

Minozzi, W., Neblo, M.A., Esterling, K.M., and Lazer, D.M., 2015. Field experiment evidence of substantive, attributional, and behavioral persuasion by members of Congress in online town halls. *Proceedings of the National Academy of Sciences of the United States of America*, *112*(13), pp.3937–3942.

Minozzi, William, and David A. Siegel, 2010. A theory of deliberation as interactive reasoning. *Annual Meeting of the Midwest Political Science Association*, Chicago, IL.

Morrell, Michael E., 2005. Deliberation, democratic decision-making and internal political efficacy. *Political Behavior*, *27*(1), pp.49–69.

Nabatchi, Tina, 2010. Deliberative democracy and citizenship: In search of the efficacy effect. *Journal of Public Deliberation*, *6*(2), p.8.

Neblo, M.A., Forthcoming. Impassioned democracy: The roles of emotion in deliberative theory. *American Political Science Review*.

Neblo, M.A., 2004. Motive matters: Liberalism & insincerity. In: *Annual Meeting of the Midwest Political Science Association*, Chicago, IL.

Neblo, M., 2005. Thinking through democracy: Between the theory and practice of deliberative politics. *Acta Politica*, *40*(2), pp.169–181.

Neblo, M.A., 2006. *Change for the Better? Linking the Mechanisms of Deliberative Opinion Change to Normative Theory*. Paper presented to the Midwest Political Science Association Annual Meeting, Chicago, IL.

Neblo, M.A., 2007a. Philosophical psychology with political intent. In: *The Affect Effect: Dynamics of Emotion in Political Thinking and Behavior*, ed., Crigler, Ann N. University of Chicago Press, pp.25–47.

Neblo, M.A., 2007b. Family disputes: Diversity in defining and measuring deliberation. *Swiss Political Science Review*, *13*(4), pp.527–557.

Neblo, M.A., 2011. The virtue of deliberation: Sophrosyne & epistemic democracy. In: *APSA 2011 Annual Meeting Paper*, Seattle, WA.

Neblo, Michael A., 2015. *Deliberative Democracy Between Theory and Practice*. Cambridge University Press.

Neblo, M.A., Esterling, K.M., Kennedy, R.P., Lazer, D.M., and Sokhey, A.E., 2010. Who wants to deliberate—and why? *American Political Science Review*, *104*(3), pp.566–583.

Neblo, M.A., Esterling, K.M., and Lazer, D.M., 2018. *Politics with the People: Building a Directly Representative Democracy* (Vol. 555). Cambridge University Press.

Wu, Kevin Chien-Chang, 2011. Deliberative democracy and epistemic humility. *Behavioral and Brain Sciences*, *34*(2), pp.93–94.

12
CONVICTION AND HUMILITY

Michael P. Lynch

12.1 The problem

Can we be intellectually humble about our own convictions? Should we be? These are the two questions I want to examine in this chapter.

These questions, while overtly philosophical, have a personal and a political relevance in our lives. Most people have, at one point or another, felt the anxiety-producing tension between recognizing that their convictions may be improvable on the one hand, and wishing to hold fast to their principles on the other. This tension can arise whenever we find our convictions challenged or even queried. Most of us desire to not appear dogmatic, but we also find it uncomfortable to question those ideas we hold most dear. Doing so seems to raise the prospect that we might not be as committed as we wish to be.

Politically speaking, this tension manifests itself as a familiar conflict between two democratic ideals. One ideal is that of the committed, engaged public—citizens with convictions who are willing to lobby and vote for them. Democracies strive for this ideal because an apathetic electorate is an obviously ineffective electorate. Yet it is also an ideal that citizens should listen to, and deliberate about, each other's convictions. But that can be politically difficult, as any politician can tell you. It is often politically unwise to appear willing to listen to the other side.

Most people, and most democracies, tend to operate on the assumption that the tensions just sketched can be relieved, or at least lived with. I agree, or at least hope, that this is true. But in order to relieve this tension we must first understand its elements. To this task I now turn.

12.2 Conviction

What is a conviction? It is not just a strongly held belief. I strongly believe I am writing on a computer at the moment but that isn't a conviction of mine. I suggest instead that convictions are identity-reflecting commitments.[1]

Let's expand on these points. As Wittgenstein famously opined, sometimes reasons just run out, and "our spade is turned" on bedrock. That is how we often think of our deepest convictions—as the ground on which our worldview stands. They become part of the landscape, our frame of reference, our "picture of the world" that is the very "background against which [we] distinguish between what is true and what is false" (Wittgenstein, 1969, §94). As a result, convictions feel certain. But not everything we feel certain about is a conviction. I don't *need* conviction for anything I'm absolutely or *logically* certain about. Just as the belief that I'm writing on a computer is not a conviction of mine, neither is the belief that two and two is four.

This may be because convictions are often formed in a context of actual or potential disagreement. Unlike logical certainties like two and two make four, we are aware that our convictions can be doubted and challenged, even if we ourselves just cannot imagine that they are false. This is why Wittgenstein seems on the right track: What *makes* a conviction a conviction is not its logical certainty or how well supported it is. It is not the content of the conviction that matters; what matters is its connections, or its perceived connections, to our way of life and to what matters to us. Moreover, a conviction isn't just a bare belief. It typically involves a belief (or beliefs), but it is primarily a commitment to action; it is action-guiding.

Most importantly, convictions signify to others what kind of person we take ourselves to be. They reflect, and partly compose, our self-identity. It is this fact that makes a conviction feel certain to us, whether or not it really is. By "self-identity" I mean my aspirational self, or what is sometimes called my self-image (Flanagan, 1996, Frankfurt, 1988, Lynch, 2019). This aspect of my overall identity is determined by several other factors, chief among them an interplay of my social-identity and my values. The kind of person I aspire to be, in other words, is partly determined by which social groups I actually belong to, my ethnicity, my race, my gender, my sexual preference, and the role that I play in my social life. What kind of job I have, what sort of love life I enjoy, and how I interact with others all affect who I am and how I see myself. But these social facts, while helping to determine my self-identity, don't exhaust it. That's because the kind of person I want to be is also a factor of what I care about, my values, and deepest commitments. Caring about something means identifying with it, investing in it to the point that I thrive when it flourishes and suffer when it is diminished (Frankfurt, 1988).

By virtue of the fact that they reflect our self-identities, our convictions carry authority over our lives. Most obviously, they have authority over our actions; they obligate us to do some things and grant us permission to do others. A religious conviction, for example, can give believers the moral permission to blow themselves up, or cause them to engage in nonviolent protest in support of civil rights. Even a personal conviction can play this role—by excusing us, for example, from other moral demands. If one of your convictions is to put family before work, then it will make sense for you to skip a late meeting to make it to your kid's soccer game. Or, if you missed the last one, you might feel obligated to make the next one. We may not live up to such obligations, but we feel them just the same.

But convictions don't just carry moral authority. They also carry a kind of subjective epistemic authority over what we believe. Once something becomes a real conviction, it is difficult for us, from a psychological standpoint, to doubt. That's because to doubt it would be to doubt our deepest commitments, to doubt that we are who we say we are. As a result, our own self-interest motivates us to hold convictions that are fixed, and willing to make all sorts of sacrifices on their behalf. We often are willing to explain away contrary evidence, even if doing so flies in the face of the facts or logic itself. And we do that precisely because of the authority we give convictions over our life by virtue of their connection to our self-identity. That's why I am so reluctant to give them up, and why I may feel bad or guilty for not having the courage to live up to them. It is because they are commitments central to my self-identity that giving up a conviction can feel like an act of self-betrayal and a betrayal of one's tribe. And of course the tribe may well agree. Hence, as the Yale psychologist Dan Kahan (2013) has emphasized, it can actually be pragmatically rational to end up ignoring the evidence and sticking to your convictions come what may. No one wants to crush their self-image and be voted off the island.

12.3 Intellectual humility

Let's turn now to the other element of the tension we are investigating: intellectual humility.

As the various discussions in this volume indicate, intellectual humility is a concept that is still very much under negotiation.[2] But the psychological phenomenon it describes has been widely discussed in philosophy. Michel de Montaigne and David Hume recommended that inquiry be guided by it. The American philosopher John Dewey would have called it open-mindedness; the educational establishment sometimes calls it critical thinking. Moreover, it has very deep roots in philosophy. Its core elements are clearly highlighted by two central Socratic lessons—first, that the wise person recognizes what they don't know, and second, that wisdom can be gained by listening to others and engaging in dialogue with them.

The first of these lessons arises from Socrates' famous retort, upon being declared the wisest man in all of Athens by the Oracle of Delphi, that he only knew that he knew nothing. One has to acknowledge one's epistemic limitations, but there is arguably more to it than that. Mere recognition of one's limitations is not sufficient to be intellectually humble; the real point of the Socratic lesson is that we must own those limitations and be ready to act and respond in ways that are consistent with that fact. As Whitcomb et al. put it, "owning an intellectual limitation consists in a dispositional profile that includes cognitive, behavioral, motivational, and affective responses to an awareness of one's limitations" (2015, 10). In other words, it is not enough to simply abstractly note one's flaws and then pass on unperturbed. One must be motivated to do something about it to the extent that one can.

This first aspect of intellectual humility, note, is self-directed. It concerns "knowing thyself" so to speak. But recent discussions of the subject have also pointed out that another key feature of intellectual humility is other-directed (Priest, 2017). In particular, it involves a willingness to learn from others through our interactions with them. This, too, can be seen as a central Socratic lesson—to seek knowledge through dialogue. This second aspect of intellectual humility—the other-directed aspect—is a disposition *to see your worldview as open to epistemic improvement from new evidence via the testimony of others* (Lynch, 2018b).

This second aspect of intellectual humility is as important as the first. What it tells us is that being intellectually humble means more than admitting when you don't know, more than just owning your limitations. That could be done, after all, in isolation. The extremely intellectually arrogant person might admit they've made a mistake but think that they alone can rectify it. In contrast, having intellectual humility involves the realization that others might have something to teach you, that there may be something to gain from the experience of other people. The intellectually humble person is willing to show basic epistemic respect to others—to see them as fellow participants in a game of giving and asking for reasons as it is sometimes put (Lynch, 2019). And that is also what makes intellectual humility so important for democracy. As Dewey argued throughout his career, successful democratic politics requires constant work. We must work at mutual respect, and to do that we must work at listening and learning—to try to be open-minded, to be free "from prejudice, partisanship, and other such habits that close the mind and make it unwilling to consider new problems and entertain new ideas".[13]

To sum up, intellectual humility can be understood as having two components, self-regarding and other-regarding. A person is intellectually humble to the extent that she

1. owns her epistemic limitations;
2. recognizes that her worldview can be epistemically improved in light of evidence supplied by others and is motivated to make those improvements.

Intellectual humility is clearly a psychological phenomenon. But of what kind? Alessandra Tanesini (2016) has influentially argued that intellectual humility is best understood as a complex psycho-social attitude. An "attitude" in this context is a directed mental state with a positive or negative orientation. It is, as we might say, a kind of mental orientation. Intellectual humility, and its contrasting attitude, intellectual arrogance, are in this sense like neighboring attitudes such as contempt, appreciation or resentment. What makes intellectual humility especially interesting for our purposes, however, is that, like curiosity, it is a properly epistemic attitude. That's because it is, at least in part, directed at our beliefs and their epistemic position.

Like any attitude, intellectual humility is internally related to a network of other attitudes and mental states. As a properly epistemic attitude, it necessarily involves caring about believing what's true. As such, and as our Socratic allusions suggest, it is an attitude that is at the heart of science and philosophy. Perhaps more surprisingly, it is also an attitude that requires *confidence*. Intellectual humility is not timidity in belief. And it is not the attitude of skepticism—at least, where that is understood to mean doubting that you know anything at all. In order to adopt Socratic humility, you can't be overly concerned about your ego. But that doesn't mean you lack an ego; you just don't put your ego before truth. To be open to learning from others, you need to be confident enough to realize what you know, and what you don't.

Neither is intellectual humility the same as intellectual servility. It isn't a matter of abasing yourself or seeing yourself as lower than others. It is not about giving up your convictions just because others, or the majority, think you must. As Socrates's own life makes plain, the pursuit of truth and the combating of arrogance often put you into conflict with those in power, simply because those in power are often the ones most resistant to challenging their convictions.

And that, of course, raises the uncomfortable questions at the heart of this essay. What we have to confront is whether intellectual humility is also an attitude we can have toward our *own* convictions.[3]

12.4 Convictions with humility

As we noted at the outset, we are concerned with two questions. The first is modal: whether passionate conviction is even *possible* for a person who is intellectually humble. The second is normative: whether we should be intellectually humble about our convictions. Having defined our terms, we can now confront these in turn.

Our first question itself conceals two separate issues: whether we can we be intellectually humble and *have* convictions and whether we can be intellectually humble *about* our convictions.

With regard to the first issue, the answer is a clear "yes". Indeed, there are reasons to think one could not be intellectually humble without convictions.

Here's why. Convictions, I've argued, both reflect and compose our self-identity—the kind of person we aspire to be. It is an open question whether and how human beings can fail to possess a self-identity. It is certainly logically possible, and it seems to also be psychologically possible. To fail to have a self-identity would be to fail to have any cares or commitments; it would mean not identifying with anything or anyone—even one's self-interest (after all, self-absorption is still a self-identity). Such people may well exist, and if they do, they lack convictions. But as a result, they will also lack the capacity to care about either their limitations or improving their worldview via the evidence. Nor, presumably, would they be particularly wedded to their own opinions. They wouldn't be arrogant; but neither could they be intellectually humble.

What all this tells us is that intellectual humility is not an opponent of just having convictions. To be open to improvement you must have a base to improve on. As Dewey remarked, this kind of attitude is "very different from empty-mindedness. While it is hospitality to new themes, facts, ideas, questions, it is not the kind of hospitality that would be indicated by hanging out a sign: 'Come right in; there is nobody at home'" (Dewey, 1986, 136).

We will return to this point below. But for now let's turn to the second, and harder, question: whether we can be intellectually humble *about* our convictions. This is a variant of a puzzle sometimes raised about open-mindedness and full belief. As Wayne Riggs introduces it:

> It would seem that only a lack of full confidence in one's beliefs could lead one to spend any time or effort considering views that conflict with one's own. Indeed, full confidence in one's beliefs would seem to render the attitude of open-mindedness irrational.
>
> *(Riggs, 2010, 177)*

Intuitively, the same problem appears to arise with regard to intellectual humility as well. How can one regard one's worldview as open to epistemic improvement from others' views while still remaining committed to that worldview?

One thought right off the bat is that one might be intellectually humble about one's worldview without thinking that a specific commitment within it needs revision. Thus, as Adler has suggested, we might see intellectual humility as involving a second-order "doubt about the perfection of one's believing, not a doubt about the truth of any specific belief" (2004, 310). Applied here, the thought is that the intellectually humble person, with respect to her beliefs, is much like the inspector at a factory, who checks the widgets that come down the line, not because he has any particular doubts about any specific widget, but because of a general policy to check the widgets. He may be fully convinced, prior to inspection, that a given widget will be error-free.

But we must be careful about the analogy. For much depends on why our faithful inspector (a) is convinced that a particular widget will be blemish-free; and (b) why he thinks that he should nonetheless inspect that widget. Much depends on the former because our inspector might think that a given widget must be blemish-free because he thinks God tells him that every third widget he sees on Tuesdays always will be, and that's the widget he happens to be examining at the moment. Much depends on the latter because our inspector may nonetheless carry on inspecting because, well, it is the company's policy—and he always follows the policy.

Analogously, a person who holds a belief irrationally or dogmatically in the first place may be doing so only because he is intellectually arrogant about his beliefs with regard to some subject, and so unwilling to consider seriously anyone else's opinions. If so, then questions of intellectual humility are by the board in any event. And he might only be willing to carry on taking objections seriously only because he has been convinced to do so for political reasons.

Now, I'm all for people being convinced for political reasons to take objections seriously. I wish more people were more convinced of the importance of political tolerance and the political value of the space of reasons. But if that is the *only* reason (as opposed to one among many) you are motivated to take objections seriously, then you are not acting out of intellectual humility, because you lack an epistemic motivation.

In order for the analogy to succeed, we must therefore think of the inspector as having a particular motivation. We must see him as following the policy to inspect the widgets at least partly because he knows that the assembly line is not perfect. Hence, he regards *the plurality of widgets that are produced by this particular line* (as opposed to any particular one widget) as possibly flawed in some way or other. Similarly, then, with intellectual humility. Intellectual humility, as we noted above, is intrinsically connected to a commitment to believing what's true. As such, one who has that attitude toward some aspect of their worldview is disposed to consider beliefs that fall under that aspect as open to epistemic improvement, and thus also possibly flawed, or the product of biases or limitations on his part. To be so disposed is to regard a *plurality of commitments held by a particular epistemic agent* as fallible, not to regard any particular commitment as unjustified or possibly false.

So it seems plausible that one can be intellectually humble about one's convictions considered as a plurality. But can we be intellectually humble about a particular conviction? Here, I think, we already have our answer: it is possible, but it will normally signal that the agent in *question is already in, or about to enter, a reflective state about their self-identity*. And such reflection, in turn, may well signal that the agent is shifting from treating the issue as a matter of conviction to treating it as a matter of belief.

As I noted above, to the extent that one's commitment to a proposition is a full conviction, and therefore reflective of one's self-identity, to that extent it will be psychologically extremely difficult to see *it* as open to revision. A conviction is not merely a confident belief that some proposition is true. Convictions are so deeply embedded into who and what we are that doubting them, or even seeing them as improvable, is to reveal oneself as less than fully committed, and thus to doubt your very self-identity. But of course, it is not impossible to change one's convictions. We all know this, if not personal experience, then from experience with the human condition in general. But changing your convictions also means modifying one's vision of oneself, it means modifying your self-identity. That is a process required if one is to change and grow, morally or otherwise, but it is also a process that normally takes time. It can, and often does happen gradually over the course of living, adopting new customs, moving to a new place, speaking a different language or falling in love. The gradual nature of these processes can mean that changes in our self-identity happen largely without explicit conscious attention. But not wholly so. No change in our aspirational vision of what kind of person we are can be wholly without an impact, on our conscious decisions about how to represent ourselves to both ourselves and others. And such decisions require some level of conscious awareness, as when one realizes one can, after college, no longer support all the same values one had adopted during your earlier life.

This raises the difficult further question of the relationship between reflection about our convictions and intellectual humility (see Williams, 1985). It may be, for example, that being intellectually humble about a particular conviction (or convictions) is a *precursor* to reflection; or it may be that it is, in other cases, a *by-product*. Both possibilities seem plausible, but I will not explore them further here. Instead, I will now turn to the question of when such reflection, and intellectual humility about one's convictions, is warranted, and when it is not.[4]

12.5 The limits of intellectual humility

We have reached, then, our second question. Should one strive to always be intellectually humble about one's convictions—especially one's *particular* convictions?[5]

Even so roughly framed, there are at least two reasons to think the answer is no. First, there are straightforward epistemic reasons as we've already noted, intellectual humility is not the only value that informs being a responsible believer and knower. Responsible epistemic agents are not so open-minded that their brains just fall out. They are not simply ambivalent nor are they outright skeptics. And thus, in a particular situation, with regard to a particular commitment/conviction, the extent to which one should be intellectually humble about that commitment will depend on factors such as the following:

(i) whether the target commitments are justified by the evidence or the product of reliable faculties, or both;

(ii) whether one has reason to think they are;
(iii) whether one has reason to think that there is little chance that further testimony or investigation will present any defeaters to one's justification for those commitments.

To the degree that these epistemic considerations are in place, to that degree it may be all things considered better, *from the epistemic point of view*, for her to be less intellectually humble about particular commitments. Thus, for example, a climate scientist with overwhelming evidence for her belief that climate change has been accelerated by human activity can be epistemically responsible without being motivated to respond to every objection—no matter how strange—to this belief. And the same holds if the scientist holds this belief with the force of conviction.[6]

Moreover, one's epistemic agency has a social aspect. It is partly a product of the community that one is within. How one is situated within that community, and in particular, the degree to which one is the victim of marginalization and testimonial injustice may affect whether one is being responsible epistemically.[7] Consider, for example, a black woman who is frequently told by white people that she is exaggerating racist incidents or seeing bias where it doesn't exist, when in fact her experiences in this regard are perfectly veridical. In such a context, it is more valuable, all things considered, that she stick to her convictions, not only because seeing them as possibly flawed would undermine her self-identity as a possible knower, but because they also provide vital evidence from which others may learn. In such a case, being less intellectually humble may indeed be the *most* responsible attitude from the social-epistemic perspective. And the reverse also seems true: the more one's worldview reflects that of the politically and culturally advantaged within a given context, the more intellectually humble one should be. Here, at least, it is with intellectual humility as it is with humility proper: it is most appropriately a demand on the powerful. The meek may inherit the earth, but they will need the courage of their convictions to do so.

What these points demonstrate is that intellectual humility, while valuable, is a *pro tanto* value. All other things being equal, it is good. But things are not always equal. This does not distinguish intellectual humility from most values. Your mom no doubt taught you that honesty is the best policy. But policies have exceptions. When the Nazis are at the door looking for the Jews hidden in your attic, deceit is your only real option. Likewise with the case just outlined above; sometimes it may not be the best overall outcome to be intellectually humble in situations where, for both moral and epistemic reasons, it is crucial to have one's voice heard.

In other cases, intellectual humility itself may demand not being open to certain types of testimony. You don't need to thoughtfully reconsider your views about racism when talking to the white supremacists on your doorstep. And one reason you don't has to do with the core meaning of intellectual humility. It means, in part, being open to the evidence supplied by the experience and testimony of others. But "evidence" here is key; just because someone comes up to you and says the Earth is flat doesn't mean you have to take that statement seriously. So intellectual humility's value is *pro tanto*.

Nonetheless, it must be admitted that these points, while correct, are of limited practical value. Suggesting that you forego humility whenever "your convictions are justified" seems less than helpful. Indeed, adopting an attitude of intellectual humility is important precisely because we can be, and often are, *wrong about when we are justified. We are often wrong, in other words, about whether we are meeting conditions (i)–(iii).* The evidence for this is both scientific and personal. Even when we aren't completely wrong that we have a good evidential base for some belief or commitment, we very often overestimate the level of credence we should assign to the commitment or belief given that base. And because of bias and other cognitive limitations, humans are notoriously bad about knowing whether they can learn something new about a topic they think they know something about. Of course, that is, one might think, just why intellectual humility is important for us as individual epistemic agents. To the extent that individual citizens adopt the attitude of intellectual humility, then, *other things being equal*, they are, to that extent, more epistemically responsible.

Yet focusing just on the individual epistemic agent would be a mistake. That's because intellectual humility's highest impact on our convictions—may emerge not at the individual level but at the social level. In particular it may emerge at the connection point between our epistemic and democratic norms.

One reason to think so is that the social-epistemic practices that help to sustain democracy arguably embody intellectual humility as a regulative norm. Naturally, *which* practices do so is a question that goes beyond what can be said here (nonetheless, see Lynch, 2018a). But the practices I see as most relevant for the present discussion are explicitly what Goldman called social-epistemic—they are those crucial for the acquisition and distribution of knowledge and hence for epistemic trust (Goldman, 1999). Without such trust, the ideals of democracy are difficult to meet (Lynch, 2019). The social practices that seem most relevant include those embedded in historical and scientific inquiry (archival techniques, experimental replication, peer review); journalistic standards (using more than one source); dialogue techniques (having empathy, giving everyone a chance to speak, listening) and legal investigation (appealing to reliable evidential techniques, examining the motivation of witnesses).

These sorts of practices exist *partly because we recognize that our individual epistemic assessments are so often flawed* (Allen and Lynch, 2020). Biases are hard to spot—that is why they are biases, and appeal to informational checks and balances is a way to compensate for that fact (Lynch, 2019). In following practices like these, and in forming beliefs and reasons by doing so, we are encouraged to see ourselves as capable of knowing more than we do now, capable of responding to reasons.

Arguably, therefore, certain social epistemic practices can be understood as embodying intellectual humility as a key regulative norm. A social practice embodies an attitudinal orientation as a regulative norm just when the activities constitutive of that practice are guided by the idea that participants ought to adopt that attitude (Lynch, 2019). Consider, for example, the practice of peer review. Participants within the practice ought to be willing to *improve their beliefs based on the open-minded assessment of new evidence from others.* They may often fail to do so—just as a firefighter may fail to have grit or courage—but the practice is guided by the norm that they should. Indeed, the guidance is arguably essential: if you aren't willing, either as an author or as a reviewer, to learn and improve your opinions as a result of the process of the review, you aren't participating in the practice but just going through the motions. Similarly, with the institutions of grant assessment, experimental replication, journalistic inquiry, and basic civil and criminal legal inquiry—elements of each practice are aimed at improving participants' beliefs via responsiveness to evidence, as opposed to prestige, wealth, or power. That aim is not often met, but the practice embodies the norm just the same.

By engaging in social practices that embody intellectual humility, we are, to some extent, like the inspector at the widget factory. We are abiding by rules meant to correct for our own fallibility. And like the inspector, we should follow such rules, even if, and especially when, we passionately believe that our convictions are unimpeachable. For such procedures exist to compensate for our biases, to force us to be responsive to reasons, and thus implicitly encourage us to take a more reflective view, to improve our worldview from the evidence and experience of others. By giving and asking for reasons that emerge from such practices, we sustain and participate in the democratic space of reasons itself—a space that remains open to dialogue, even when we are not.[8]

Notes

1 For more on convictions and their nature, see (Pianalto, 2011) (Skitka, et al., 2005), (Williams, 1985).
2 See, e.g. chapters by Alfano, Battaly, Whitcomb, et al. Greco and Church.
3 For further discussion of intellectual humility, see Alfano et. al (2017); Lynch (2018b, 2019) Hazlett (2012), Christen et al. (2019), Whitcomb et al. (2015), Church (2016), Kidd (2016), and Tanesini (2016).
4 My thinking on this matter was greatly aided by comments by Mark Alfano.
5 Note, however, that both intellectual humility and conviction are psychological states which come in degrees. One can be more or less humble and one can be more of less committed in one's convictions. Keeping this in mind as we proceed is wise.
6 This is not to deny that the same scientist should remain willing to improve her view about all manner of other more specific and particular beliefs about climate change—its rate of increase, how it exactly effects particular aspects of the climate, and so on.
7 For more on these issues see Fricker (2007) and Medinda (2012).
8 Thanks to conversations and comments from A. Tanesini, P. Bloomfield, T. Allen, H. Gunn, T. Napoleatano, and most especially Mark Alfano.

References

Adler, J. (2004). Reconciling Open-Mindedness with Belief. *Theory and Research in Education*, 2(2), 127–142.

Alfano, M., Iurino, K., Stey, P., Robinson, B., Christen, M., Yu, F. and Lapsley, D. (2017). Development and Validation of a Multi-Dimensional Measure of Intellectual Humility. *PloS one*, 12(8), e0182950.

Allen, T. and Lynch, M. P. (2020). Can We Be Reasonable? In: *Reason, Bias, and Inquiry: New Perspectives from the Crossroads of Epistemology and Psychology*. In N. Ballantyne and D. Dunning (Eds.)Oxford: Oxford University Press.

Christen, M., Alfano, M. and Robinson, B. (2019). A Cross-cultural assessment of the semantic dimensions of intellectual humility. *AI and Society*. 34, 785–801.

Church, I. M. (2016). The Doxastic Account of Intellectual Humility. *Logos and Episteme*, 7(4), 413–433.

Dewey, J. (1986). *The Later Works: 1925–1953*.Vol. 8. Carbondale, IL: Sothern Illinois University Press.

Flanagan, Owen (1996). *Self Expressions: Mind, Morals, and the Meaning of Life*. New York: Oxford University Press.

Frankfurt, Harry (1988). *The Importance of What We Care About*. Cambridge: Cambridge University Press.

Fricker, Miranda (2007). *Epistemic Injustice: Power and the Ethics of Knowing*. Oxford: Oxford University Press.

Goldman, A. (1999). *Social Epistemology*. New York: Oxford University Press.

Hazlett, A. (2012). Higher-Order Epistemic Attitudes and Intellectual Humility. *Episteme*, 9(3), 205–223.

Kahan, D. (2013). Ideoloogy, Motivated Reasoning and Cognitive Reflection: An Experimental Study. *Judgment and Decision Making*, 8(4), 407–24.

Kidd, I. J. (2016). Intellectual Humility, Confidence, and Argumentation. *Topoi*, 35(2), 395–402.

Lynch, M. P. (2018a). Epistemic Arrogance and the Value of Political Dissent. In: C. R. Johnson (Ed.). *Voicing Dissent: The Ethics and Epistemology of Making Disagreement Public* (pp. 129–139). New York: Routledge.

Lynch, M. P. (2018b). Arrogance, Truth, and Public Discourse. *Episteme*, 15(3), 283–296.

Lynch, M. P. (2019). *Know-It-All Society: Truth and Arrogance in Political Culture*. New York: Norton.

Medina, José (2012). *The Epistemology of Resistance: Gender and Racial Oppression, Epistemic Injustice, and the Social Imagination*. New York: Oxford University Press.

Pianalto, M. (2011). Moral Conviction. *Journal of Applied Philosophy*, 28(4), 381–395.

Priest, M. (2017). Intellectual Humility: An Interpersonal Theory. *Ergo*, 4, 463–480.

Riggs, Wayne (2010). Open-Mindedness. *Metaphilosophy*, 41(1), 172–188.

Skitka, Linda J., Bauman, Christopher W. and Sargis, Edward G. (2005). Moral Conviction: Another Contributor to Attitude Strength or Something More? *Journal of Personality and Social Psychology*, 88(6), 895–917.

Tanesini, A. (2016). Intellectual Humility as an Attitude. *Philosophy and Phenomenological Research*, 96(2), 399–420.

Whitcomb, D., Battaly, H., Baehr, J. and Howard-Snyder, D. (2015). Intellectual Humility: Owning Our Limitations. *Philosophy and Phenomenological Research*, 94(3), 509–539.

Williams, B. (1985). *Ethics and the Limits of Philosophy*. Cambridge: Harvard University Press.

Wittgenstein, Ludwig (1969). *On Certainty*. Oxford: Basil Blackwell.

13
HUMILITY AND THE TOLERATION OF DIVERSE IDEAS

Casey Rebecca Johnson

In an interview with Fox News in December 2016, Donald Trump said, "You know, I'm, like, a smart person. I don't have to be told the same thing and the same words every single day for the next eight years. It could be eight years — but eight years. I don't need that" (Nelson, 2016). President Trump said this in order to explain why he would only attend to intelligence briefings when he "needs it". Whatever else one might think of President Trump, his policies, or his character, this statement clearly fails to display much in the way of humility. Without delving into President Trump's virtues and vices, I want to consider a similar kind of statement in a thought experiment.

Imagine a leader who considered himself too smart to need briefings, a leader who considered his views and beliefs the very best, and who did not see the need to reach out to those with whom he disagreed. Imagine a leader who would not tolerate questions that suggested disapproval or disagreement, and who showed little interest in, let alone tolerance for the perspectives or positions of those not entirely aligned with him in values or vision. Now imagine a leader who said something similar to the Trump quote above. What would we expect of that leader? How would we expect him to relate to others? In particular, would we expect him to be at all empathetic? Perhaps with those with whom he identified – but what about those who are different from himself? Would we expect him to be at all curious? Why should he be curious, when he takes his own view to be the very best? When a person shows no humility, the way our imagined leader does, we expect that person to also fail to be empathetic and curious.

In this paper, I want to suggest that humility, particularly intellectual humility, facilitates the development of empathy and curiosity. Having these three traits, in turn, makes it more likely that an agent will be open to a diversity of views. To argue for this, I'll first give some detail about humility, and then I'll explore each of these attitudes in turn. The goal is to illuminate the connection between humility and tolerance by way of each of these discussions.

13.1 Humility

It is familiar from Aristotelian ethics to conceive of humility as a virtue. Indeed, Aristotle says, "with regard to honor and dishonor, the mean is proper pride, the excess is known as a sort of empty vanity, and the deficiency is undue humility" (Aristotle, 1999, p. 29). Proper pride, which we might also understand as proper (or due) humility, is the virtuous golden mean between vices of deficiency and excess. As one would expect, there has been much philosophical discussion of Aristotle's understanding of humility. Many of the more recent discussions of humility have focused on *intellectual* humility. That is, humility regarding one's intellectual or epistemic standing. For the purposes of this paper, I'll take this kind of humility as my focus.

Intellectual humility is a concept in progress. Philosophers and psychologists are in the process of defining and coming to understand what intellectual humility is and what place it has in our theories (Church and Samuelson, 2016; Hazlett, 2012; Kidd, 2016; Lynch, 2018a; Whitcomb, Battaly, Baehr, and Howard-Snyder, 2017).[1] Robert Roberts and Jay Wood, for example argue that intellectual humility is or involves a disposition to be unconcerned with the social status that results from the recognition of one's epistemic prowess (Roberts and Wood, 2007). Ian Church and Peter Samuelson, on the other hand, argue for what they call the *doxastic account*. According to the doxastic account, the intellectually humble person accurately tracks what she could non-culpably take the positive epistemic status of her beliefs to be (Church and Samuelson, 2016). The precise nature of intellectual humility is contentious, but it is widely agreed that it involves, or is closely related to, a recognition of the limits of one's own knowledge and experience.

A third prominent view, defended by Whitcomb et al., holds that we must *own* our limitations, rather than simply recognize them (Whitcomb et al., 2017). Owning one's own limitations involves a complex set of attitudes. As Whitcomb et al. put it, "owning an intellectual limitation consists in a dispositional profile that includes cognitive, behavioral, motivational, and affective responses to an awareness of one's limitations" (Whitcomb et al., 2017, p. 518). The intellectually humble person is disposed to believe that she has limitations, to admit those limitations to herself and others, to care about those limitations when relevant, and to affectively respond to her limitations as appropriate in various contexts. Intellectual humility, on this account, is a fairly complex psychological disposition. Knowing someone is intellectually humble puts us in a position to anticipate various behaviors and attitudes she might also hold. Because this account involves more than mere recognition of limitations, but also responses to those limitations, we have greater understanding of the intellectually humble person. For these reasons, this is the account of intellectual humility that I will take on board for the purposes of this chapter. However, my conclusions should follow, *modulo* some changes, for at least some other accounts of intellectual humility.[2]

We might come to own our limitations in the ways necessary for intellectual humility from learning about cognitive biases, like confirmation bias, implicit bias, and various aliefs[3] (Gendler, 2011). It might come from the realization that we are prone to rate ourselves as much less biased than we in fact are (Uhlmann and Cohen, 2007).[4] Or it might come from comparing one's own experience with testimonial evidence of the experiences of others (Johnson, 2017).

An intellectually humble person, then, would reflect on her own epistemic position and would own both the strengths and the limitations of that position. She would also weigh those strengths and weaknesses appropriately. She would also be more likely to have other related attitudes and responses. In particular, we would expect her to have certain attitudes toward others. If an agent is aware of her limitations, and is disposed to care about them, and react affectively to them as appropriate, then we'd expect her exchanges with others to go in particular ways. Being intellectually humble would make her more likely to be empathetic with those with whom she has deep disagreement, as well as more curious about the positions of those whose views are different from her own. I'll argue for each of these in the next two sections.

13.2 Intellectual Humility and Empathy

Many theorists who study discourse, from journalists to linguists to political scientists, agree that empathy is important for fruitful dialogue (Jorgensen, 2002; Morrell, 2007; Ryfe, 2003).

Empathy helps interlocutors to overcome biases, to be more reciprocal in conversations, and to decrease egocentric behavior. There is good reason to think that these effects are helpful in producing fruitful dialogue, especially between interlocutors who don't antecedently agree. Just what empathy is, however, is contentious.

Some hold that affect matching (or affect approximation) is necessary for empathy (De Vignemont and Jacob, 2012; De Vignemont and Singer, 2006; Snow, 2000). Affect matching occurs when the empathetic agent feels the emotions of the target agent in a particular way.[5] If affect matching is necessary for empathy, then an agent who does not feel what the target agent feels fails to be empathetic. If affect matching is sufficient for empathy, then all an empathetic agent needs to do is to feel (exactly or approximately) what her target feels (I am not aware of anyone who holds this view, but it is available in logical space). Others argue that a cognitive component is necessary or sufficient (Goldie, 1999; Rameson and Lieberman, 2009). This cognitive component involves taking on the perspective of the target agent, and making inferences in light of their values (Ickes, 2003). If this is necessary, then agents must share perspectives with their target to be empathetic. If it is sufficient, then this is all they must do. Whether one or the other (or both of these) is necessary, whether either is sufficient, or whether they are jointly sufficient is one point of contention.[6]

Despite this disagreement, most views agree that empathy typically or at least often involves, among other things, taking on or sharing the perspective of another. Indeed, when we want to train people to be more empathetic, we train them to imagine what it would be like from the others' point of view (Ançel, 2006; Webster, Bowers, Mann, and Marshall, 2005). So, one ingredient that helps one person to be empathetic with another is for her to assume that other's perspective.[7]

It can be quite difficult to assume the perspective of someone whose viewpoint you take to be limited, or whose perspective differs greatly from your own. In many cases, I will have a hard time imagining what it would be like to experience something from the perspective of someone radically different from myself. L. A. Paul's work has deep and thorough discussions of this phenomenon (Paul, 2014). It is, she argues, very hard to imagine having drastically different values. I cannot, prior to having a child, imagine what it would be like to have the values that parents have. The experience of becoming a parent so alters one's values, on her account, that if I am childless, I cannot imagine my way into the parent perspective. Insofar as one's values are part of one's perspective, then, it will be difficult to imagine having someone else's perspective. And, because taking on someone else's perspective is necessary for one kind of empathy, it will be very difficult to empathize with someone whose values are drastically different from my own. This makes having dialogue with them difficult. However, I want to suggest that humility – in particular intellectual humility – may be able to mitigate against the impact of this problem.

Remember that for an agent to have intellectual humility, as we're understanding it, that agent must own the limitations of her epistemic state. If she can own her own limits, she might be able to imagine what it would be like to have a perspective that was limited, but in different ways. That is, if an agent is able to realize the limits of her experience, and of her epistemic state, she can then assume the perspective (to some extent) of someone else that she takes to also be limited. By owning her own intellectual limitations, she can to some extent empathize with someone who she takes to be limited in (somewhat) similar ways. The agent can empathize with someone she takes to be limited by realizing that they have intellectual and experiential limits in common.

An example might help here. Consider a middle-class white woman who disagrees with a poor white man about some matter of feminist politics. This woman might consider her interlocutor's perspective to be limited, and so find it difficult to immediately empathize with him on the basis of shared values. If, however, she reflects on her own limitations – she might consider, for example, that she's not experienced discrimination on the basis of class – she can identify corresponding limitations in her interlocutor's perspective. Owning her own particular limitations allows her to imagine what it would be like to be limited in the ways she takes her interlocutor to be. Thus, intellectual humility facilitates empathy.

Three objections might arise, here. First, this strategy seems to suggest that to empathize with someone you disagree with, you should focus on their intellectual limits. But surely in the target cases, fruitful discourse isn't thwarted because the interlocutors who disagree fail to see each other as intellectually limited. Surely, in other words, emphasizing our disagreeing interlocutors' limits won't help.

This objection, however, gets the strategy a bit backwards. The idea is not that realizing our own limits allows us to see new limits in our interlocutors. The idea is, rather, that when we see our interlocutor as limited, and then can see and own analogous limits in ourselves, we gain some insight into their perspective. We can empathize with them precisely because we see *their* limits as analogous to limitations in *our own perspectives*. I'll call this kind of empathy *negative empathy*.

Negative empathy isn't negative because it is bad, or because it is focusing on negative characteristics. Negative empathy is negative because it involves aligning the gaps in one's experience, evidence, and rationality with analogous gaps in one's interlocutor.

The second objection is that the strategy I described above won't be available to one subset of the population: people who have never experienced systematic subordination. That is, there will be people who, because of their social identities, won't have the relevant experiences from which to draw the kinds of analogies that might help them realize their own limitations. And we might worry that people who have never experienced social or political subordination are the most in need of a strategy for developing empathy.

This is a reasonable concern, and it would be a serious problem for my view if the strategy I've outlined were unavailable to many or most people. Fortunately, for the strategy to be entirely out of reach for an agent that agent would a) have to be maximally socially privileged and b) have to never have realized a gap in their own experiences. I think there are probably very few such agents. All an agent really needs to take advantage of this strategy is to have had an experience that demonstrates his or her limited perspective. Experiences of comparative social subordination can help highlight an agent's intellectual limits, but they are not necessary for intellectual humility, or for empathy by analogy. I suspect that there are comparatively few agents who have never had such an experience. I admit, though, that for those agents who do, the strategy is out of reach.

The third objection is that intellectual humility doesn't get us terribly far in terms of either empathy or productive discourse. Even if intellectual humility can help an agent take on the perspective of her interlocutor, perspective sharing is only one part, or – depending on one's preferred model – one kind of empathy. In other words, at best, perspective taking only gets us as far as cognitive empathy. Nothing about intellectual humility seems to help much with affective empathy. Further, the objection might continue, it seems that cognitive empathy won't take us as far as productive discourse. Many other steps will need to be taken before my father and the religious conservative can have a fruitful conversation.

This, too, is a reasonable concern, but it is not an objection to the reasonability of the hypothesis I've suggested. I've been offering a strategy to move agents toward empathy. Many theorists claim that empathy is *necessary* for fruitful discourse. Neither I, nor those theorists, claim that it is *sufficient* for fruitful discourse. Even if the strategy helps to enable empathy in deeply different agents, many other conditions may be necessary before discourse between them can be fruitful.

Despite not being concerned with these objections, it is important to be clear that the extent to which intellectual humility helps facilitate the development of any kind of empathy is an empirical matter. We'd want work from psychologists testing the relationship between the two traits. Preliminary work from psychologists working on intellectual humility suggests that having the trait does contribute to empathy (Krumrei-Mancuso, 2017), however, more work is needed. So far, my claim remains, at best, a reasonable and attractive hypothesis.

13.3 Intellectual humility and curiosity

In addition to making it more likely that an agent is empathetic with deeply different persons, humility also facilitates the development of curiosity. Curiosity has received recent attention in moral psychology and virtue epistemology (Inan, 2013; Inan, Watson, Whitcomb, and Yigit, 2018). Curiosity, like humility, is conceived as an intellectual virtue (Ross, n.d.; Watson, n.d.).

Following Lani Watson's treatment of curiosity, let us understand curiosity as involving motivation to acquire epistemic goods (Watson, 2018). A virtuously curious person, then, has the proper motivation to acquire epistemic goods. We would expect her to ask good questions and seek salient, well-justified information. A deficiently curious person might lack interest or be blissfully ignorant. We would expect her to rarely ask questions, or to only ask redundant questions affirming what she already knows. An excessively curious person would then be nosy or prying. Her questions would likely be inappropriate or ill-conceived. My claim is that intellectual humility facilitates proper curiosity.

Intellectual humility has already been linked with curiosity. In their study of the semantic dimensions of intellectual humility, Christensen et al. performed a psycholexical analysis of ordinary speakers' associations with intellectual humility. This analysis demonstrated that curiosity, and a cluster of related concepts like *inquiry*, and *learning*, were associated with intellectual humility. These concepts weren't at the core, however, the authors took their results to be, "representative of the notion that an intellectually humble person will be open and responsive to new ideas and information" (Christen, Robinson, and Alfano, 2014, p. 5).

My conjecture, though, is that this relationship plausibly goes beyond conceptual association. As I've said, it seems likely that being intellectually humble could facilitate curiosity. Here's how that would go: imagine Annie, who is a total novice regarding, say, floriculture. If Annie is intellectually humble, she will own her own epistemic limitations. If Annie owns her own epistemic limitations, she will be aware that there is a distance between her epistemic position with respect to floriculture and the epistemic position of a floriculture expert. Annie's awareness of this distance, and the motivation she is disposed to have regarding her limitations, makes her better able to ask questions, when presented with an expert in the right context. What she doesn't know will be salient to her, allowing her to properly pursue knowledge – allowing her to be curious.

To see this more clearly, contrast Annie's case with two others: consider Bev, who is intellectually arrogant, and Cal, who is intellectually servile. Bev is not sufficiently aware of her epistemic limitations. This means that she fails to ask relevant questions, fails to attend to information that could improve her epistemic position, and fails to acquire epistemic goods. She is not curious because she fails to identify relevant lacunae in her belief set. Bev's intellectual arrogance keeps her from attending to her limitations, so keeps her from being curious.

Cal, on the other hand, takes himself to be far more epistemically limited than he is. So while he might be highly motivated to seek information, at least some of the information he seeks will be confirmation of beliefs he already holds or information he's already had access to. He doubts his own beliefs, or the justification for them, and so his motivation to seek information is not properly directed – he fails to be motivated to acquire epistemic goods, as he is motivated to re-cover the same ground.

Annie, because she is intellectually humble, is better positioned than either Bev or Cal to be properly motivated to seek epistemic goods. Her intellectual humility facilitates her virtuous curiosity.

Several objections might arise here. First, it might be argued that Annie might be intellectually humble but still not motivated to seek epistemic goods. It is, after all, perfectly coherent for Annie to be aware that she doesn't know much about floriculture, be in a context in which floriculture is relevant, and yet still not be motivated to acquire floriculture information. This might be because Annie is distracted, or tired, or simply not that interested in floriculture. She might hope never to be in a similar context again. In this case she is intellectually humble, but not virtuously curious.

Similarly, one might argue that Cal and Bev, despite failing to be intellectually humble, are still able to be virtuously curious. Bev could still be unmotivated to acquire epistemic goods even despite being aware of her limitations. Indeed, she might seek new information and then respond, "oh, I already knew that", or "that was just obvious". We've all met people who respond to novel information in this way, and they are paradigmatically, intellectually arrogant. These arrogant responses to new information don't, in principle, keep Bev from being properly curious. She might be deeply and overly confident in her own epistemic prowess, but still be appropriately motivated to seek new information. Cal, too, could be properly curious, but fail to own his own abilities and epistemic qualifications. Indeed, Cal might happen to (by accident) only inquire about those areas in which he is in fact epistemically limited. He overestimates or is overly concerned with his own limitations, but nonetheless, happens to be appropriately curious.[8]

I agree that these are perfectly possible cases, however, they are not counter examples to my claim. Intellectual humility is not the same as curiosity, nor does it guarantee that an agent will be curious. It further is not necessary for proper curiosity. My claim is only that owning her own limitations better positions an agent to be motivated to seek further epistemic goods. And we would have to do some empirical work to see if this claim could be fortified by data.

As with the above discussion of empathy, my claim is, to some extent, empirical. We would want to have more data from psychologists working on characteristics like intellectual humility and curiosity. Until then, my claim can be, at best, a going hypothesis. It is an attractive hypothesis, however, given that we are interested in cultivating tolerance of diverse ideas. In the next section, I will explore the connection between the virtues I've been discussing so far and tolerance of diverse ideas.

13.4 Empathy, curiosity, and diverse ideas

There are a variety of reasons that we might value diverse ideas and points of view: interacting with those with whom we disagree can help us to check our assumptions, improve our inquiry (Elgin, 2018; Longino, 2002), know we are justified (Mill, 1966), and meet democratic ideals (Landemore, 2017; Lynch, 2018b), to name just a few. And it is important, when we interact with those with whom we disagree, that we can identify and voice our disagreements, in at least some contexts (Johnson, n.d.). To do this, and to achieve these valuable goals, we have to tolerate viewpoints and positions that differ from our own. Intellectual humility, if it helps us to be more empathetic and curious, can help us to tolerate diverse viewpoints.

It is key that, by hypothesis, intellectual humility helps us to be empathetic *and* curious. This is because neither curiosity nor empathy alone helps us to be tolerant of diverse viewpoints in a productive way. To see this, we'll consider agents that have one but not the other trait as compared with an agent who has both.

First, consider Edward. Edward is empathetic in both ways outlined above: he is both affectively and cognitively empathetic. This means that when Edward encounters Sarah, he is able to both feel what Sarah feels and make inferences based on her values. This will, by hypothesis, make Edward better able to relate to and have productive dialog with Sarah. However, this relies on Edward encountering Sarah. If Edward is not curious, his interactions will be limited. And, since we know that people tend to interact with those with whom they antecedently agree, Edward will likely only interact with those whose views are similar to his own (Badger, 2017; Baumgaertner, 2014; Nguyen, n.d.). Because of this, despite being empathetic, Edward will only encounter (and so be in a position to tolerate) diverse ideas by accident and in a limited way.

Next consider Cate. Cate is virtuously curious: she is properly motivated to acquire epistemic goods. Cate asks questions, seeks new information. In particular, we can imagine that Cate is curious about people who are different than she is. However, she is curious without being empathetic. This means that when she encounters Sean, who holds deeply different political beliefs she asks him questions, but is horrified, put off, or judgmental of the answers. She might be fascinated precisely because Sean's views seem so weird, or exotic. She seeks to know his views, not to assume or even understand his perspective, but as a kind of detached empirical exercise. And, unless she's very good at hiding the nature of her interest and her reactions to Sean's answers, she's unlikely to achieve much in the way of productive interaction with him.

We can see from the cases of Edward and Cate that neither curiosity nor empathy alone puts agents in a good position to tolerate diverse beliefs. However, if we imagine that Edward had some of Cate's curiosity, or that Cate were a little more empathetic, then they might each be better positioned to encounter and to tolerate diverse beliefs. And, if I'm right in what I've argued in the above, both curiosity and empathy are facilitated by intellectual humility. Being intellectually humble, then, may improve the chances that agents are both curious and empathetic, thereby improving the chances that they tolerate diverse ideas.

Notes

1 Research for much of this work has been funded by the Templeton Foundation.

2 There is not room, here, to canvas all of the changes that would be needed for my account under each understanding of intellectual humility. Nonetheless, we can begin to see the kinds of changes needed for some accounts: for the Roberts and Wood account, the lack of concern with recognition for intellectual achievement would make a person more likely to be open to engage with someone who fails to recognize that achievement – such a person would not be defensive of their epistemic position, or reluctant to admit other thinkers hold reasonable views. This, in turn, could facilitate empathy and curiosity. Additional dispositions or traits might be necessary on this view, but nonetheless, for most going views of intellectual humility, the account should go through.

3 I mean to be inclusive in my use of *alief* of all the sorts of automatic habits of thought or attitudes that are in tension with our explicit or avowed beliefs.

4 (Hazlett, 2012) has some discussion about how awareness of these could help us be intellectually humble. This discussion, though useful, is beyond the current scope.

5 (De Vignemont and Jacob, 2012) offers a helpful and empirically based explanation of the variety of ways in which an agent might experience the affective state of another, only some of which are rightly called empathetic.

6 (Michael, 2014) offers a really helpful exposition of the conflict detailed in this section.

7 Notice that imaginatively taking on another's perspective can be instrumental in either affective or cognitive empathy. I might be imagining what it would feel like to be in my target's position, or I might be imaging having the same prior commitments or beliefs as that person. The claim, here, is that

when psychologists want to encourage empathy, they ask their subjects/patients to imagine being in the position of the target of that empathy.

8 In these cases in which Cal and Bev happen to be curious, my inclination is to think that their servility and arrogance, respectively, aren't quite sincere. I can imagine an agent who feigns arrogance to cover up her insecurity. Such an agent would then be highly motivated to find out more information in order to shore up her show of arrogance. Similarly, if Cal is curious only about those areas where he is *in fact* limited, then I would guess that he *is* really aware of his limitations but is feigning servility. In both of these cases, the agent in question is not acting fully virtuously, but the failure is less clearly one of intellectual humility. Nonetheless, I admit that cases like Cal and Bev's above are possible.

References

Ançel, G. (2006). Developing empathy in nurses: An inservice training program. *Archives of Psychiatric Nursing, 20*(6), 249–257.

Aristotle. (1999). *Nichomachean Ethics*, W. D. Ross, Ed. Ontario: Kitchener.

Badger, E. (2017). Political migration: A new business of moving out to fit. *The New York Times*.

Baumgaertner, B. (2014). Yes, no, maybe so: A veritistic approach to echo chambers using a trichotomous belief model. *Synthese, 191*(11), 2549–2569.

Christen, M., Robinson, B., and Alfano, M. (2014). The semantic space of intellectual humility. In: A. Herzig, and E. Lorini (Eds.), *Proceedings of the European Conference on Social Intelligence*. IRIT-CNRS, Toulouse University, France, pp.40–49.

Church, I., and Samuelson, P. (2016). *Intellectual Humility: An Introduction to the Philosophy and Science*. New York: Bloomsbury Publishing.

De Vignemont, F., and Jacob, P. (2012). What is it like to feel another's pain? *Philosophy of Science, 79*(2), 295–316.

De Vignemont, F., and Singer, T. (2006). The empathic brain: How, when and why? *Trends in Cognitive Sciences, 10*(10), 435–441.

Elgin, C. Z. (2018). Reasonable disagreement. In: C. R. Johnson (Ed.), *Voicing Dissent* (18–29). New York: Routledge.

Gendler, T. S. (2011). On the epistemic costs of implicit bias. *Philosophical Studies, 156*(1), 33.

Goldie, P. (1999). How we think of others' emotions. *Mind and Language, 14*(4), 394–423.

Hazlett, A. (2012). Higher-order epistemic attitudes and intellectual humility. *Episteme, 9*(3), 205–223.

Ickes, W. (2003). *Everyday Mind Reading: Understanding What Other People Think and Feel*. New York: Prometheus Books.

Inan, I. (2013). *The Philosophy of Curiosity*. New York: Routledge.

Inan, I., Watson, L., Whitcomb, D., and Yigit, S. (2018). *The Moral Psychology of Curiosity*. London: Rowman & Littlefield.

Johnson, C. R. (2018). Just say "no": Obligations to voice disagreement. *Royal Institute of Philosophy Supplements, 84*, 117–138.

Johnson, C. R. (2017). Intellectual humility and empathy by analogy. *Topoi*, 1–8. doi:10.1007/s11245-017-9453-0.

Jorgensen, K. W. (2002). Understanding the conditions for public discourse: Four rules for selecting letters to the editor. *Journalism Studies, 3*(1), 69–81.

Kidd, I. J. (2016). Intellectual humility, confidence, and argumentation. *Topoi, 35*(2), 395–402.

Krumrei-Mancuso, E. J. (2017). Intellectual humility and prosocial values: Direct and mediated effects. *The Journal of Positive Psychology, 12*(1), 13–28.

Landemore, H. (2017). Beyond the fact of disagreement? The epistemic turn in deliberative democracy. *Social Epistemology, 31*(3), 277–295.

Longino, H. E. (2002). *The Fate of Knowledge*. Princeton: Princeton University Press.

Lynch, M. P. (2018a). Arrogance, truth and public discourse. *Episteme, 15*(3), 283–296.

Lynch, M. P. (2018b). Epistemic arrogance and the value of political dissent. In: C. R. Johnson (Ed.), *Voicing Dissent* (137–147). New York: Routledge.

Mill, J. S. (1966). On liberty. In: Robson, J. M. (Eds), *A Selection of His Works*. London: Palgrave.

Morrell, M. E. (2007). Empathy and democratic education. *Public Affairs Quarterly, 21*(4), 381–403.

Nelson, L. (2016). Trump: I don't need daily briefings (online). *Politico*, 11 December.

Nguyen, C. T. (2018). Echo chambers and epistemic bubbles. *Episteme*, 1–21.

Paul, L. A. (2014). *Transformative Experience*. Oxford: Oxford University Press.
Rameson, L. T., and Lieberman, M. D. (2009). Empathy: A social cognitive neuroscience approach. *Social and Personality Psychology Compass*, *3*(1), 94–110.
Roberts, R. C., Wood, W. J., and Wood, W. J. (2007). *Intellectual Virtues: An Essay in Regulative Epistemology*. Oxford: Oxford University Press on Demand.
Ross, L. (n.d.). The virtue of curiosity. *Episteme*, 1–16. doi:10.1017/epi.2018.31.
Ryfe, D. M. (2003). The principles of public discourse: What is good public discourse. *Public Discourse in America*, 163–177.
Snow, N. (2000). Empathy. *American Philosophical Quarterly*, *37*(1), 65–78.
Uhlmann, E. L., and Cohen, G. L. (2007). "I think it, therefore it's true": Effects of self-perceived objectivity on hiring discrimination. *Organizational Behavior and Human Decision Processes*, *104*(2), 207–223.
Watson, L. (n.d.). Educating for curiousity. In: I. Inan (Ed.), *The Moral Psychology of Curiousity*. London: Rowan and Littlefield.
Watson, L. (2018). Curiosity and inquisitiveness. In: H. Battaly (Ed.), *The Routledge Handbook of Virtue Epistemology* (155–166). New York: Routledge.
Webster, S. D., Bowers, L. E., Mann, R. E., and Marshall, W. L. (2005). Developing empathy in sexual offenders: The value of offence re-enactments. *Sexual Abuse: A Journal of Research and Treatment*, *17*(1), 63–77.
Whitcomb, D., Battaly, H., Baehr, J., and Howard-Snyder, D. (2017). Intellectual humility: Owning our limitations. *Philosophy and Phenomenological Research*, *3*(94), 509–539.

14

HUMILITY, FORGIVENESS, AND RESTORATIVE JUSTICE

From the personal to the political

Carl Stauffer

14.1 Introduction

Humility is an elusive idea. The mystery of humility lies in the fact that we can intuit the sense of it inwardly, yet when it is externalized and articulated outwardly it becomes difficult to ascertain its authenticity. Research conducted by Weidman, Cheng, and Tracy (2018) indicates that there are two distinct forms of humility – "*appreciative*", which infers a positive self-esteem and strong sense of worthiness, and "*self-abasing*", which infers the opposite. In past societies governed by pseudo-religious norms and rituals, the self-abasing form of humility was dominant, however, with the dawn of secularized philosophy and values in Western democracies the appreciative form of humility has gained considerable traction.

In the current context, it is important to differentiate between the notions of humility (self-imposed) and humiliation (other-imposed). While they share the same grammatical roots, they should not be confused or conflated as is often done in contemporary public discourse. Humiliation refers to "*actual or perceived feelings of devaluation, shame, and rejection [intentionally inflicted] by others*" (Chancellor and Lyubomirsky, 2013, p. 828). Humility, on the other hand, according to researcher and author Steven Sandage, refers to a: "*Realistic self-awareness of one's strengths and limitations, the capacity to regulate emotions of shame and pride, and a concern for others*" (Barlow, 2017, p. 2).

The research challenge has been to find ways to legitimately and effectively measure *what* humility is, and *how* it influences the way we think and act, both as individuals and collectively. Researchers Davis and Hook (2013) maintain that there is enough evidence to make five positive claims with relative assurance about the functions and impact of humility. These are: 1.) Humility is accurately judged under strain, 2.) Humility is more easily observed in others than in one's self, 3.) Humility strengthens relational and social bonds, 4.) Humility optimizes competitiveness while simultaneously keeping relationships intact, and 5.) Humility is connected to better health outcomes (Davis and Hook, 2013, pp. 2–3).

14.2 Defining the contours and pathways of humility

Humility is both a virtue and a science. The English word humility comes from the Latin word, *humilis*, "meaning *low or humble, from the earth, not proud or haughty, not pretentious, unassuming, and insignificant*" (Merriam-Webster Dictionary, 2004, p. 350). This traditional definition explains why for centuries the concept and exercise of humility was left to devout religious communities who were concerned with the virtues of self-depreciation, self-denial, and personal sacrifice as sacred practice. However, in the recent decades, humility research has become an important social and psychological science. With the multiplication of research, the conception of humility, its values, benefits, and outcomes, has deepened and widened significantly.

Neilson and Marrone (2018, p. 807) define humility as a: "*Relatively stable trait that is grounded in a self-view that something greater than the self exists*". The authors note the attributes of humility as both "expressed" through external action, and "experienced" through internal reflection (Neilson and Marrone, 2018, p. 809). Table 14.1 summarizes the key components of humility as described by the authors.

Neilson and Marrone's research (2018, p. 813) focuses on individual and organizational humility and dives in-depth to name the "antecedents" to humility, the "moderators" and "mediators" of humility, and finally the "outcomes" of humility. The organizational outcomes of humility are categorized into four levels: *Self-outcomes* – (pro-social/relational, emotional well-being, and learning/performance), *follower-outcomes – (engagement and psychological freedom), team and organizational-outcomes – (performance and innovation)*.

Wright et al. (2017, p. 4) define the core of humility as a: "*Particular psychological positioning of oneself – namely, one that is both epistemically and ethically aligned*". The authors develop their research of humility on two elements that seem to frame most significant studies in the subject matter; that of *low self-focus* and *high other-focus* as key descriptors exhibited by humble people. Table 14.2 extrapolates this theory further.

Chancellor and Lyubomirsky (2013), provide an alternative perspective that delineates humility as a '*state of being*' as opposed to a set of attributes, actions or outcomes alone. By this, the authors differentiate between "*Dispositional*" humility which focuses attention on "traits" or characteristics, and "*Situational*" humility which is predisposed to understand humility as contextual; an experience of feeling humble in a particular moment in time and/or location in space (Chancellor and Lyubomirsky, 2013, p. 821). In an effort to combine elements of both dispositional and situational humility, the authors outline what they term the five hallmarks of humility: 1.) Secure, accepting identity, 2.) Freedom from distortion, 3.) Openness to new information, 4.) Other-focus, and 5.) Egalitarian beliefs (Chancellor and Lyubomirsky, 2013, pp. 823–827). It is in this list of 'humility hallmarks' that one can find a possible integration of *personal* traits and *communal* attitudes and actions that represent a whole expression of humility.

Table 14.1 Summary of the key components of humility

Major (higher scoring) components:	*Minor (lower-scoring) components:*
• Accurate self-awareness • Appreciation of others and their strengths and contributions • Openness to feedback and 'teach-ability' • Transcendence and a larger life perspective (worldview or cosmology)	• Self-transcendent pursuit • No desire for control • Recognition of luck and good fortune • Relational/collective orientation • Lack of concern for superiority

(*Neilson and Marrone, 2018, p. 808*)

Table 14.2 Summary of humility descriptors

Low Self-Focus: (epistemically aligned)	**High Other-Focus:** (ethically aligned)
"The understanding and experience of oneself as a finite and fallible being that is but an infinitesimal part of a vast universe, and so has a necessarily limited and incomplete perspective or grasp on the 'whole', which is infinitely larger and greater than oneself".	"The understanding and experience of oneself as only one among a host of other morally legitimate beings, whose interests are foundationally as legitimate, and as worthy of attention and concern, as one's own (a state of extended compassion)".
• Low self-prioritization	• Increased orientation of oneself outwards
• Low self-importance	• Concern for needs, interests, and benefits for other's well-being
• Reduced sense of ego	• Increased appreciation for the value of others
• Reduced attachment to self and its products and capacities	• Increased sense of connection to others

(Wright et al., 2017, pp. 4–5)

14.3 The forgiveness factor

Not unlike humility, forgiveness resides in a place of paradox. Beyond the obvious problematic of whether to respond to personal or corporate violations with mercy or revenge, forgiveness presents a more complex predicament – the fact that one's psychological release and healing are intertwined with a seemingly free gift of unconditional mercy being offered to the person/people who have caused the harm. While one would like to be convinced that the victim-survivor's liberation is a separate process altogether from the emancipation of the offender or the offending institution, it is not. The 'harmed' and the 'harm-doers' are inextricably connected through the shared trauma experiences of the past. After meeting the man who murdered his mother ten years earlier, one courageous young man exclaimed, "*For ten years this man lived in my head rent-free, today through meeting him I was able to finally evict him*".[1] If the wronged are unable or unwilling to 'let go' of the traumatic memories of personal and collective hurt, they will continue to be controlled by their history. Forgiveness becomes an essential process in order to keep the past from invading the present in its waking and sleeping hours, daily emotions, and the sustainability of socio-political compacts that require trust and must be continually negotiated in order to live together for the sake of the common good (e.g. deliberative democracy).

On the other hand, forgiveness is not without critique, and it would be negligent not to mention the downside to this complex process. To do this, it may be useful to explore "grudge theory" as an explanatory framework for why people don't forgive. According to Baumeister, Exline, and Sommer (1998, pp. 90–97), people hold grudges for at least five broad reasons: 1.) Claims on rewards and benefits, 2.) To prevent recurrence, 3.) Because of continued suffering, 4.) Pride and revenge, and 5.) Principled refusal usually in pursuit of justice. While "grudge theory" provides a window into the utilitarian logic of not forgiving, it would be important to also outline the distortions of the forgiveness process itself. First and most obvious is the damage that occurs when force or coercion is utilized in attempting to obtain forgiveness. Not only will this not bring about the desired outcomes, it is actually detrimental to the individuals involved. Luchies et al. (2010) make the argument that obligatory forgiving can erode self-respect and self-concept clarity. Second, premature forgiveness can circumvent critical steps of emotional grieving and loss (e.g. anger) that are essential to the healing process (Kubler-Ross, 1969). Third, when forgiveness is held up as the singular ideal response, it can feed the polarizing notion of 'good victim' (forgiving) and 'bad victim' (angry) which is often played out in the media and public discourse (Grier and Cobbs, 2000). Fourth, when forgiveness is enacted at a macro collective level it can function to silence truth-telling. The unintended consequence of pronouncing corporate forgiveness too early lies in the embedded assumption that forgiveness entails a forward-moving process, and as a result it is often considered no longer necessary (or even harmful) to continue to interrogate past harms (Smedes, 1998, pp. 343–350; Bartel, 2018).

However, the question still remains – how are people (from a personal to a collective level) able to free themselves from the pain of the past? With the massing of quantitative and qualitative research on forgiveness over many decades (Enright, Gassin, and Wu, 1992; Worthington, 1998; Henderson, 2009) it has become clear that forgiveness does offer humankind a pathway to freedom from the 'ghosts of our past'. It is not an easy path to follow, in fact, by all estimations it is an arduous journey that may take a lifetime, but it offers genuine liberation along the way. After experiencing the harrowing murder of his 76-year-old mother, academic researcher and practitioner, Everett Worthington Jr., spent the rest of his professional career studying forgiveness. His five-fold path of forgiveness, the acrostic REACH (Worthington, 2001), has given guidance to many on the forgiveness journey:

1.) **R – Recall the hurt** – Psycho-social trauma research has long determined that suppression of memory inhibits forgiveness, healing, and reconciliation. Truth-telling in the process of healing is essential, however just knowing the *what*, or understanding the *why* of a painful event is not enough. The key question is what is *done* with the memory and how is it *acted* upon once the truth is exposed?
2.) **E – Empathy awakened** – In this phase a person(s) intentionally seek to understand why others would choose to hurt them. They work through a process of role-reversal and ask the question: *If I had been born and raised in the same circumstances of life as the one who committed the violation, could I have committed the same violence?* In the words of the great Russian writer and poet, Alexander Solzhenitsyn, "*The battle-line between good and evil runs through the heart of every man*".
3.) **A – Altruistic gift** – Ultimately, if a person(s) are genuinely pursuing forgiveness, they will come to a place where they realize they will need to make a choice to unconditionally forgive regardless of the response of the other. It is in this space of making a principled decision of the will that a person(s) can release the other and themselves from the 'closed loop' cycle of memory-revenge.
4.) **C – Commitment to process** – The prior three stages could all be worked out internally, however, research indicates that the resolve to forgive is greatly strengthened when a person(s) are willing to talk to others about it. Not only is it vital to externalize this process (publicly speak about it), but it is equally import to solicit the support of a community of people who will hold the survivor(s) accountable to their commitment.
5.) **H – Hold on** – Finally, the pathway of forgiveness has many minefields along the way. There will be many voices of well-meaning relationships, influences of societal norms, and potentially "triggering" experiences that will push a person(s) to renounce forgiveness and embrace revenge. Worthington's longitudinal research discovered that many people have had to walk themselves through this five-fold model multiple times in their lives in order to stay in the space of forgiveness.[2]

When applying humility to the process of forgiveness, it is certainly not hard to see the pro-social linkages present. For instance, not only does the research connect humility directly to empathic responses and forgiveness, many of the other qualities of humility are also driving the forgive-

Table 14.3 Qualities and characteristics of humility that buttress the forgiveness process

Worthington's 5-stage model of forgiveness	*Recall hurt*	*Empathize*	*Altruistic Gift*	*Commitment*	*Hold on*
Descriptive values and positive benefits of humility derived from empirical research	+Openness to new information +Freedom from distortion +Teach-ability	+Secure, accepting identity +Compassion +Admitting mistakes +Moral Identity +Relationship bonding	+Other focus +Egalitarian beliefs +Generosity +Benevolence +Cultural humility +Gratitude	+Cooperation +Helpfulness +Social Justice Commitment	+Flexibility +Integrity +Pro-social

(*Nielson and Marrone, 2018; Wright et al., 2017; Chancellor and Lyubomirsky, 2013*)

ness process. Table 14.3 takes Worthington's five-stage model of forgiveness and highlights the qualities and characteristics of humility that need to be present for forgiveness to go forward.

While multiple positive links between humility and forgiveness are encouraging, there is clear research to indicate that the opposite is also true; that people with less humility tend to subscribe to negative or destructive behaviors that discourage forgiveness. Wright et al. (2017) uncovered a significant connection between people with low humility scores and higher manifestations of manipulation, displaced aggression, vengefulness/retaliation, social dominance, and hierarchy-oriented values (Wright et al., 2017, p. 7). These research linkages raise important questions around the process of socialization and how certain cultural mores, socio-political ideologies, and religious norms may assist in forming humble citizens and others may not.

14.4 Defining restorative justice

There have been many attempts to define Restorative Justice throughout the decades. Tony Marshall (1999) in his report on Restorative Justice prepared for the British home Office described it as follows: "*A process whereby all parties with a stake in a particular offence come together to resolve collectively how to deal with the aftermath of an offence and its implications for the future*". Dr. Howard Zehr built on this definition with his own version:

> Restorative Justice is a process to involve, to the extent possible, those who have a stake in a specific offence and to collectively identify and address harms, needs and obligations, in order to heal and put things as right as possible.
>
> (*Zehr, 2002*)

A more comprehensive definition that has a closer affinity to the idea of Restorative Justice as a social movement comes from Suffolk University:

> [A] broad term which encompasses a growing social movement to institutionalize peaceful approaches to harm, problem-solving and violations of legal and human rights. Rather than privileging the law, professionals and the state, restorative resolu-

> tions engage those who are harmed, wrongdoers and their affected communities in search of solutions that promote repair, reconciliation and the rebuilding of relationships. Restorative justice seeks to build partnerships to reestablish mutual responsibility for constructive responses to wrongdoing with our communities. Restorative approaches seek a balanced approach to the needs of victim, wrongdoer and community through processes that preserve the safety and dignity of all.
>
> *(Suffolk University, 2019)*

One of the best ways to understand Restorative Justice in theory and practice is to identify the elemental values that drive its applications. For instance, both Sharpe (2011) and Zehr (2002) discuss critical concepts like democracy, responsibility, safety, healing, dignity, respect, and belonging as essential components of the vernacular of Restorative Justice. Authors Van Ness and Heetderks Strong (1997) use an umbrella framework that encompasses four cross-cutting values and principles of practice: *Inclusion*, *Encounter*, *Amends*, and *Reintegration*.

Inclusion: By inclusion it is meant that Restorative Justice is invitational, not coercive. It acknowledges that all stakeholders in a situation of harm have unique perspectives, interests, and responsibilities to work to repair the harm that has been or is being done. Inclusion recognizes that when all the affected parties to a violation are brought into a Restorative Justice process, constructive alternatives for repairing and healing the wrong-doing are more likely to occur.

Encounter: The concept of encounter refers to the facilitated interactions of affected parties – either meeting face-to-face or virtually. A guided interface allows for the participants to speak and be listened to without being silenced. It provides an opportunity for all stakeholders to increase their levels of empathy, and to re-narrate the negative emotions of the original "conflict-saturated stories" (Monk and Winslade, 2000, pp. 72–82; 155–156) and replace them with hopeful narratives laced with positive change and growth for the future. It entails gaining new understanding and agreement, as well as restoring the balance of power between all stakeholders involved.

Amends: Another word for amends is reparations. Reparations can come in intangible (symbolic) or tangible (material) forms. Symbolic reparations may come in the form of apology, commitment to changed behavior, memorialization, and/or forgiveness, and relational reconciliation (although the latter are not forced). Tangible reparations may come in the form of restitution given in terms of money, in-kind contributions, time and expertise resources, or positional and public recognition. The need for reciprocity; to honor human dignity, restore equity, and to show responsibility and generosity are the values driving the processes of amends.

Reintegration: The idea here is to counter the division, marginalization, and isolation that often accompanies serious harms. Reintegration as opposed to degradation, marginalization or isolation involves garnering community assets and resources in support of those who have been harmed and those who have caused harm. It means acknowledging human worth, providing material assistance for basic human needs, and offering safety, healing, and moral or spiritual direction in order to prevent further harm and address future intentions of all parties affected.

These four Restorative Justice 'process-principles' are particularly strategic because of their value to assist in both micro- and macro-level transformation. They are not only good protocol for interpersonal engagements around harm, but they can also guide the policies, procedures, and human resources of an organization or workplace, and they can serve as the framing for legislation, good governance, and public participation in political decision-making. They provide useful leads for changing hierarchical structures, redistributing ownership and resources in a community, and accompanying whole groups of people through war-to-peace transitions of justice and healing.

Table 14.4 How Restorative Justice practices and processes provide the container for humility value-outcomes:

Van Ness and Heetderks Strong, 1997	*Inclusion*	*Encounter*	*Amends*	*Reintegration*
Descriptive values and positive outcomes of humility derived from empirical research	+ Group status acceptance + Egalitarian + Openness + Moral Identity + Cooperation + Equality + Non-hierarchy	+ Relational-bonding + Non-hierarchy + Empathy + Connection + Openness + Admitting mistakes + Equality + Egalitarian	+ Helpfulness + Generosity + Social Justice Commitment + Forgiveness + Benevolence + Compassion + Gratitude + Admitting mistakes	+ Forgiveness + Civic Responsibility + Humanitarian concern + Integrity + Cooperation + Moral Identity + Group status acceptance

(*Nielson and Marrone, 2018; Wright et al., 2017*)

In considering the operationalization of humility in the practice of Restorative Justice, it is important to note how necessary it is to possess humility in order to carry out these process-principles. However, not only is humility a prerequisite, but it is also a by-product of these process-principles being facilitated with skill and expertise. Table 14.4 presents the integration of humility as both a value to, and positive outcome of, Restorative Justice work. Note that there are certain 'value-outcomes' that are repeatedly listed to show the important synergies between humility and Restorative Justice.

The above integration chart is significant because there is now evidence that humility can be taught. Wright et al., (2017, pp. 8–9) undertook a research project using a writing therapy approach that they called the "semantic signature of humility". What these researchers discovered is that people can be influenced through education on how to write about themselves, their lives, work and accomplishments in more-humble and less-humble ways. Therefore, as people can learn how to *write* with humility, it seems appropriate to imagine that people can learn how to *act* with humility also. In short, Restorative Justice appears to offer the experiential container for teaching people humility should they choose to engage it its processes.

14.5 Restorative Justice: social service, paradigm shift, or social justice movement?[3]

In this essay, Restorative Justice has been referred to as a social justice movement. However, this designation is contested and does not by any means share consensus among everyone who espouses Restorative Justice. The contemporary beginnings of the field of restorative justice were pragmatic. For the most part, the term 'Restorative Justice' referred to a values-based practice that was honed out of necessity in a time period (1970s) when strong impulses to find alternatives to the current criminal legal system were calling for innovation. And, as such, the first few decades of Restorative Justice growth could be characterized by the efforts to mold a technical, relational skill-set that was hoped to be universal, standard, and carefully accredited in order to find its way into the echelons of other professional development and ***social service*** provision. In short, the primary focus of the restorative justice field in its early years was to repair the interpersonal relationships of the parties most directly affected by the harms of crime; with the needs of family, community or structural transformation as secondary concerns.

With the advent of the seminal work by Dr. Howard Zehr (1990; 2002), a new vision was given language and credence. Zehr introduced the idea of Restorative Justice as providing the philosophical values and principled practices to lay the foundation for a ***paradigm shift*** in the whole western legal system. This 'shift' was away from the reliance on retribution and punishment, to the priority of reconstruction and repair. At that time, the notion of a paradigm shift (Kuhn, 1962) was often imagined as requiring a mammoth task of designing an entirely new system with a detailed blueprint that would guide a full methodical overhaul of the current legal system. For some people, this was idealistic and impossible, for others it meant working for comprehensive legislation, for others it meant building a critical mass, one case and one non-profit organization at a time, and for others still it meant resisting the criminal legal system and advocating for its abolishment. A resulting split between those who believed change required *incrementalism* and those who believed that change required *transformation* developed among the proponents of Restorative Justice. Incrementalism suggests that change occurs over time, in small steps, and as a part of a slow shift of the values and structures that internally undergird the system. Transformation, on the other hand, suggests a dismantling of oppressive structures and a rechanneling and/or reconstruction of new formations. This debate between Restorative Justice 'reformists' and 'revolutionaries' continues to this day.

In the last two decades, an iterative turn has taken place in the language and application of Restorative Justice morphing from containment of a professional field of study and praxis, to a ***social justice movement*** (Van Gelder, 2016). A social movement assumes a number of important markers – namely, it needs a clear political opportunity, a visible increase in the mobilization of human and material resources, and a mass popular framing message (Moyer et al., 2001). Restorative Justice as a movement currently seems to exhibit all these identifying elements. With regards to **political opportunity**, there has been a global ground-swell of restorative justice local organizing and advocacy in response to increased authoritarian governance, cultural hate speech, social polarization, racial/ethnic violence, and many other political threats to the values and principles of the 'common good' that shapes a shared humanity of co-existence (Dashman et al., 2019; Stauffer and Turner, 2018).

There has also been a substantial increase in the **mobilization of human and material resources** around Restorative Justice. Firstly, there are widespread applications of Restorative Justice beyond the criminal legal system and reaching into a myriad of public sectors (Lewis and Stauffer, 2019). Secondly, formerly marginalized and disenfranchised voices of indigenous peoples and communities of color are engaging the Restorative Justice movement and calling for the transformation of structures of racial/ethnic violence and cultural oppression across the Globe (Llewellyn, 2008; Hoffman, 2008). Thirdly, in the US, there is a national movement calling for truth-telling and healing of the historical harms of Native-American genocide and the enslavement of African people in the founding of the nation (DeWolf and Geddes, 2019; Davis, 2019). Finally, the structures that are emerging for this work are both de-centralized and de-institutionalized, and yet widespread in societal impact (Stauffer, Shah and King, 2017).

Restorative Justice as a **framing message** for a social justice movement has given reformist and activist groups a shared peacemaking framework in which to hold dialogue and build partnerships that bring together the key pillars of human justice: Truth-telling, accountability, repair, healing, and reintegration. Multiple authors are delineating the theory and building the applied practice that makes up the scaffolding for an effective restorative justice social movement to go forward (Hooker and Czajkowski, 2012; Hooker, 2016).

In summary, this section has explored the momentum of Restorative Justice as a global social movement to influence the potential shift in cultural attitudes and actions away from punishment and toward restoration. For this Restorative Justice cultural shift to happen, however, this essay argues that a parallel shift toward a 'culture of humility' would need to occur simultaneously.

14.6 Humility and oppressive structural power – a critique

To date, a majority of the research around the concept of humility has been focused on the personal psychology of humility with little attention given to the dynamics of humility in the face of oppressive structural power. Oppression is characterized by a totalizing system that enforces control. It maintains a uniform, dominant socio-political narrative that benefits an elite group of people and subjugates all other counter-narratives. Oppressive structures consolidate ownership in the hands of a few, manipulate political decision-making, and control the distribution and redistribution of public communication, power, position, and resources throughout society. Oppressive systems refuse to tolerate any resistance that question its totalizing existence and actively work to eliminate, incapacitate, or silence any dissenting voices.

The question than arises, what is the place of humility in the face of oppressive power; whether direct or structural? On a surface level, it seems that humility would be susceptible to being 'taken advantage of', or being more easily manipulated and violated. Many might think that when confronted with direct or structural violence, humility has little to offer and would likely fold or capitulate. In other words, by its very nature humility might appear to prefer to avoid or accommodate oppression, as opposed to confront it. And often when oppressed people are told to show more humility what is required of them is self-abasement. For example, patriarchy attempts to maintain its dominance through the enforcement of gendered norms of modesty and femininity. These arguments could cause some people to dismiss humility as having little value in resisting and changing structural harms. However, as outlined in the below section on 'Recommendations for Future Research', this essay would argue otherwise.

14.7 Recommendations for future research

1.) **Humility studies**: ***organizational analysis*** – Through the cursory glance of humility taken in this essay, it is clear that the current research is primarily measuring interpersonal manifestations of humility and are mostly descriptive in nature. What is missing is a focus on the applied practice of humility. While Neilson and Marrone's (2018) research aimed to measure the role and function of humility in organizational structure, it assumes that the location of humility in an organizational setting originates from the individuals that inhabit positions in the organization. In contrast, what if one were to locate humility in the environmental 'DNA' of the workplace structure and therefore, by necessity, it would either be embedded in the legislation, policies, and procedures of the organizational culture or not. To take the work of Chancellor and Lyubomirsky (2013) and their proposed 'hallmarks' of humility further, one might want to ask, how can an organization move in the direction of being more 'free from distortion', 'open to new information', 'other-focused', and 'egalitarian'? Could these proposed hallmarks be measured as foundational to an organizational climate or culture of humility? And, if so, could this lead to identifying and comparing both humble and non-humble organizations? These and other questions are yet to be fully hypothesized or researched in a comprehensive manner.

2.) **Forgiveness and humility studies**: ***collective analysis*** – A plethora of material has been written and published on forgiveness from an interpersonal perspective. Like humility however, what is less clear is the idea of 'collective forgiveness'. With the rise of the field of transitional justice (including truth and reconciliation commissions), there has been a claim that whole nations, societies, people-groups, or communities can experience corporate forgiveness, healing, and reconciliation (Shriver, 1995; Hartwell, 1999; Tutu, 2000; and Helmick and Peterson, 2001). And, if this were so, it would also take a 'culture of humility' to intentionally enact these processes. However, can these collective emotions be assumed to be true? Do masses of people have a shared psyche? If so, what would corporate processes of forgiveness and humility look like and feel like in the public domain? Trudy Govier in her seminal work on macro-forgiveness processes states that to make the claim of the existence of collective forgiveness, three aspects would need to be proven: 1.) That groups can be agents responsible for wrong-doing, 2.) That groups can suffer wrongful harm, and 3.) That groups can have – and can amend – feelings, attitudes, and beliefs about harms they have suffered at the hands of others (Govier, 2002, p. 87). All three of Govier's standards for macro-forgiveness would also apply to measuring the existence, role, and function of cultural or group humility.

3.) **Restorative justice and humility studies**: ***structural power analysis*** – The intra- and inter-personal linkages between the 'value-outcomes' of both humility and Restorative Justice are quite self-evident. What is less apparent, is if there are power-structural connections between humility as a cultural force and Restorative Justice as a social movement. It could be argued that for humility to be understood as a powerful collective phenomenon it needs to be activated and expressed in public spaces. This argument then raises the question: Does the movement of Restorative Justice offer a bounded structure necessary for the applied practice of corporate humility to become manifest in the political domain? Gaventa (2006) proposes a multi-dimensional 'Power Cube' model that provides a more nuanced differentiation of the various forms of power: 1.) Places of Power – *household, local, national, and global*, 2.) Types of Power – *visible, hidden, and invisible*, and 3.) Spaces of Power – *claimed, invited, and closed*. Applying these categorizations to a power analysis of the Restorative Justice social movement, the idea of collective humility, and the potential synergies that they generate for social change could prove to be a useful research agenda.

4.) **Group humility and nonviolent strategic action studies** – It is too simplistic to equate humility with meekness or weakness alone. To understand the power of humility as a response to the threat of force or violation, a complex and nuanced conceptual view of humility must be investigated. In order to keep fidelity to the true meaning of humility, it needs to be comprehended as a paradoxical, yet powerful, balance between self and other, strength and sensitivity, truth and mercy, and risk and protection. Potentially, one could hypothesize that the activation and expression of group humility may function as a forerunner to prepare the way and cast the back-drop for the application of nonviolent strategic action (Sharp, 2005; Ackerman and DuVall, 2000; Chenoweth and Stephan, 2011; and Vinthagen, 2015). A sample of questions arising from this thread of research are: Does the exercise of group humility, open up options to apply individual agency and collective will? Does the application of group humility provide an array of creative choices that could surprise the oppressive "powers that be?" (Wink, 1999). And, in a world where punitive violence dictates the "rules" of conflict and war, might the posture of group humility change these "rules of the game" (Conflict Management Group, 1994), and thereby offer a formidable opponent to oppressive structural powers?

Notes

1 This is a paraphrased quote taken from an HBO video focusing on Victim-Offender Mediation cases in the early 1990s. The video is no longer available.
2 While the 5 steps of forgiveness outlined here are from Worthington's REACH model (2001), the descriptions of each of them represent my own verbiage and understanding of them.
3 This section is a paraphrased summary of the idea of Restorative Justice as a social movement adapted from three of my previous collaborative publications: *Restorative Justice Listening Project – Final Report* (2017); *The next generation of restorative justice* (2018), and *Restorative Justice: Taking the Pulse of a Movement* (2019) – (see all citations in Reference List).

References

Ackerman, P., and DuVall, J. (2000) *A Force More Powerful: A Century of Non-Violent Conflict*. London: St. Martin's Griffin Press.

Barlow, R. (2017) 'Studying the benefits of humility'. *BU Today*. Boston, MA: Boston University, May 27. Available at: www.bu.edu/today/2017/studying-the-beneifts-of-humility/#comments. (Accessed: 8 February 2019).

Bartel, R. (2018) 'Confession and the anthropology of forgiveness: Reflections on Colombia's process of transitional justice'. *The Journal of Latin American and Caribbean Anthropology*, 24(1), pp. 145–161.

Baumeister, R., Exline, J., and Sommer, K. (1998) 'The victim role, grudge theory, and two dimensions of forgiveness'. In: Worthington, Jr., E. (ed.), *Dimensions of Forgiveness – Psychological Research & Theological Perspectives*. Philadelphia, PA and London: Templeton Foundation Press.

Chancellor, J., and Lyubomirsky, S. (2013) 'Humble beginnings: Current trends, state perspectives, and hallmarks of humility'. *Social and Personality Psychology Compass*, 7(11), pp. 819–833.

Chenoweth, E., and Stephan, M. (2011) *Why Civil Resistance Works: The Strategic Logic of Nonviolent Conflict*. New York: Columbia University Press.

Conflict Management Group. (1994) *Dealing with a Difficult Negotiator* (A Principled Negotiation Training Manual). Cambridge, MA: Harvard Negotiation Project.

Dashman, M., Culberg, K., Dean, D., Lemler, A., Lyubansky, M., and Shackford-Bradley, J. (2019) 'Bringing a racial justice consciousness to the restorative justice movement: A call to white practitioners'. In: Lewis, T. and Stauffer, C. (eds.), *Listening to the Movement: Essays on New Growth and New Challenges in Restorative Justice*. Eugene, OR: Wipf & Stock Publishers.

Davis, F. (2019) *The Little Book of Race and Restorative Justice: Black Lives, Healing, and US Social Transformation*. New York: Good Books, an imprint of Skyhorse Publishing, Inc.

Davis, Jr., D., and Hook, J. (2013) 'Measuring humility and its positive effects'. *Observer*, Association for Psychological Science, October. Available at: www.psychologicalscience.org/observer/measuring-humility-and-its-positive-effects. (Accessed: 8 February 2019).

DeWolf, T., and Geddes, J. (2019) *The Little Book of Racial Healing: Coming to the Table for Truth-Telling, Liberation, and Transformation*. New York: Good Books, an imprint of Skyhorse Publishing, Inc.

Enright, R., Gassin, E., and Wu, C. (1992) 'Forgiveness: A developmental view'. *Journal of Moral Education*, 21(2), pp. 99–114.

Gaventa, J. (2006) 'Finding spaces for change: A power analysis'. *IDS Bulletin*, 37(6), pp. 23–33. Institute for Development Studies, November. [Online]. Available at: www.powercube.net/wpcontent/uploads/2009/12/finding_spaces_for_change.pdf. (Accessed: 26 February 2019).

Govier, T. (2002) *Forgiveness and Revenge*. London and New York: Routledge Press.

Grier, W., and Cobbs, P. (2000) *Black Rage*. Eugene, OR: Wipf & Stock Publishers.

Hartwell, M. (1999) 'The role of forgiveness in reconstructing society after conflict'. *The Journal of Humanitarian Assistance*, Article 1819, May. [Online]. Available at: www.jha.ac/articles/a048.htm (Assessed: 8 February 2019).

Helmick, R., and Peterson, R. (eds.) (2001) *Forgiveness and Reconciliation: Religion, Public Policy, and Conflict Transformation*. Philadelphia, PA and London: Templeton Foundation Press.

Henderson, M. (2009) *No Enemy to Conquer: Forgiveness in an Unforgiving World*. Waco, TX: Baylor University Press.

Hoffman, E. (2008) 'Reconciliation in Sierra Leone: Local processes yield global lessons'. *The Fletcher Forum of World Affairs*, 32(2), Summer, pp. 129–141. [Online]. Available at: www.fambultok.org/wp-content/uploads/2009/12/Hoffman_32-21.pdf. (Accessed: 27 February 2019).

Hooker, D. (2016) *The Little Book of Transformative Community Conferencing: A Hopeful, Practical Approach to Dialogue*. New York: Good Books, an imprint of Skyhorse Publishing, Inc.
Hooker, D., and Czajkowski, A. (2012) 'Transforming historical harms (A training manual)'. *Coming to the Table (CTTT)*. [Online]. Available at: http://comingtothetable.org/wp-content/uploads/2013/10/01-Transforming_Historical_Harms.pdf. (Accessed: 27 February 2019).
Kübler-Ross, E. (1969) *On Death and Dying*. New York: The MacMillan Company.
Kuhn, T.S. (1962) *The Structure of Scientific Revolutions*. Chicago, IL: University of Chicago Press.
Lewis, T., and Stauffer, C. (eds.) (2019) *Listening to the Movement: Essays on New Growth and New Challenges in Restorative Justice*. Eugene, OR: Wipf & Stock Publishers.
Llewellyn, J. (2008) 'Bridging the gap between truth and reconciliation: Restorative justice and the Indian residential school truth and reconciliation commission'. In: Brant-Castellano, M., Archibald, L. and DeGagne, M. (eds.), *From Truth to Reconciliation: Transforming the Legacy of Residential Schools*. Ottawa: Aboriginal Healing Foundation. Available at SSRN: https://ssrn.com/abstract=2109508. (Accessed: 26 February 2019).
Luchies, L., Finkel, E., McNulty, J., and Kumashiro, M. (2010) 'The doormat effect: When forgiving erodes self-respect and self-concept clarity'. *Journal of Personality and Social Psychology*, 98(5), pp. 734–749.
Marshall, T. (1999) *Restorative Justice – An Overview*. A Report by the Home Office - Research Development and Statistics Directorate. London.
Monk, G., and Winslade, J. (2000) *Narrative Mediation: A New Approach to Conflict Resolution*. San Francisco, CA: Jossey-Bass, Inc., Publishers.
Moyer, B., MacAllister, J., and Soifer, M.L. (2001) *Doing Democracy: The Map Model for Organizing Social Movements*. Canada, British Columbia: New Society Publishers.
Nielson, R., and Marrone, J. (2018) 'Humility: Our current understanding of the construct and its role in organizations'. *International Journal of Management Reviews*, 20(4), pp. 805–824.
Sharp, G. (2005) *Waging Nonviolent Struggle: 20th Century Practice and 21st Century Potential*. Boston, MA: Porter Sargent Publishing.
Sharpe, S. (2011) *Walking the Talk: Developing Ethics Frameworks for the Practice of Restorative Justice*. Langley, British Columbia: Fraser Region Community Justice Initiatives Association.
Shriver, D. (1995) *An Ethic for Enemies: Forgiveness in Politics*. Oxford: Oxford University Press.
Smedes, L. (1998) 'Stations on the journey from forgiveness to hope'. In: Worthington, Jr., E. (ed.), *Dimensions of Forgiveness – Psychological Research & Theological Perspectives*. Philadelphia, PA and London: Templeton Foundation Press.
Stauffer, C., and Shah, S. (2019) 'Restorative justice: Taking the pulse of a movement'. In: Lewis, T. and Stauffer, C. (eds.), *Listening to the Movement: Essays on New Growth and New Challenges in Restorative Justice*. Eugene, OR: Wipf & Stock Publishers.
Stauffer, C., Shah, S., and King, S. (2017) 'Restorative justice listening project – final report, a publication of the *Zehr Institute for Restorative Justice*, at the center for justice & peacebuilding of Eastern Mennonite University, Harrisonburg, Virginia, USA'. [Online]. Available at: http://zehr-institute.org/publications/. (Accessed: 26 February 2019).
Stauffer, C., and Turner, J. (2018) 'The new generation of restorative justice'. In: Gavrielides, T. (ed.), *Routledge International Handbook of Restorative Justice*. Oxford: Routledge, pp. 442–461.
Suffolk University. (2019) *What is Restorative Justice?* [Online]. Available at: www.suffolk.edu/cas/centers-institutes/center-for-restorative-justice/what-is-restorative-justice. (Accessed: 19 February, 2019).
Merriam-Webster, Inc. (2004) The *Merriam-Webster Dictionary 11th Edition*. (Springfield, MA: Merriam-Webster, Incorporated.
Tutu, D. (2000) *No Future without Forgiveness*. New York: Doubleday Publishing Group.
Van Gelder, S. (2016) 'The radical work of healing: Fania and Angela Davis on a new kind of civil rights activism'. *YES!* [Online]. Available at: www.yesmagazine.org/issues/life-after-oil/the-radical-work-of-healing-fania-and-angela-davis-on-a-new-kind-of-civil-rights-activism-20160218. (Accessed: 26 February 2019).
Van Ness, D., and Heetdricks-Strong, K. (1997) *Restoring Justice – An Introduction to Restorative Justice*. 5th edition. New York: Routledge.
Vinthagen, S. (2015) *A Theory of Nonviolent Action – How Civil Resistance Works*. London: ZED Books.
Weidman, A.C., Cheng, J.T., and Tracy, J.L. (2018) 'The psychological structure of humility'. *Journal of Personality and Social Psychology*, 114(1), pp. 153–178.
Wink, W. (1999) *The Powers That Be: Theology for a New Millennium*. New York: Doubleday Publishing Group.

Worthington, E. (ed.) (1998) *Dimensions of Forgiveness: Psychological Research & Theological Perspectives*. Philadelphia, PA and London: Templeton Foundation Press.
Worthington, E. (2001) *Five Steps to Forgiveness: The Art and Science of Forgiveness*. Manhattan, New York: Crown Publishing Company.
Wright, J., Nadelhoffer, T., Perini, T., Langville, A., Echols, M., and Venezia, K. (2017) 'The psychological significance of humility'. *The Journal of Positive Psychology*, 12(1), pp. 3–12.
Zehr, H. (1990) *Changing Lenses – A New Focus on Crime and Justice*. Scottdale, PA: Herald Press.
Zehr, H. (2002) *The Little Book of Restorative Justice*. Intercourse, PA: Good Books.

15

CAN HUMILITY BE A LIBERATORY VIRTUE?

Heather Battaly

Humility is an unlikely candidate for liberatory virtue. It seems to be the last thing that could help an oppressed person, since humility in interacting with one's oppressors arguably reinforces and sustains, rather than subverts, one's oppression (Whitcomb et al. 2020). As Vrinda Dalmiya explains: "humility … is a peculiar resource to deploy for feminist purposes … one can argue that [epistemic] humility is a symptom of oppression, and its inculcation can only entrench exploitative structures that require deference to centers of power" (2016: 133). In short, humility seems to be a better candidate for liberatory vice than liberatory virtue.

The chief aim of this chapter is to explore whether the above view is correct. Is humility a liberatory vice for oppressed persons, or is there space for it to be a liberatory virtue? The chapter ultimately argues that humility can be a liberatory virtue for oppressed persons, though this runs counter to our intuitions. Section 1 uses feminist virtue theory to sketch an analysis of liberatory virtue. Section 2 endorses the notion of humility as limitations-owning, distinguishing the virtue of humility from the virtue of pride and both of these from servility and arrogance (Whitcomb et al. 2017). It then explores what is needed to convert this notion of humility into a liberatory virtue. Section 3 evaluates the trail-blazing arguments of Vrinda Dalmiya (2016) and Robin Dillon (in press). Dalmiya offers an account of humility, what she calls 'historicized relational humility,' as a liberatory virtue primarily for the privileged. Dillon argues that arrogance, specifically 'unwarranted claims arrogance,' can be a liberatory virtue for the oppressed. Both warn against treating humility as a virtue for the oppressed in interactions with oppressors. I explore whether there might, nevertheless, be a role for such humility. I make a case for humility as a liberatory virtue in interactions with one's oppressors, on the assumption that liberatory virtues will ultimately aim at "flourishing-apt societies" (Silvermint 2017: 470)—at making flourishing more possible for all people, oppressed and oppressors alike.

15.1 Liberatory virtue: a sketch

Liberatory virtues are, at minimum, dispositions to respond appropriately to conditions of oppression. But, not every disposition to respond appropriately to conditions of oppression is a specifically *liberatory* virtue. The category needs narrowing. This section attempts to home in on an analysis of liberatory virtue by exploring four main questions.

(1) What is liberatory about liberatory virtue?
(2) What is virtuous about liberatory virtue?
(3) Whose virtues are the liberatory virtues—are they restricted to oppressed persons?
(4) Can liberatory virtues be traits that also count among the traditional virtues?

15.1.1 What is liberatory about liberatory virtue?

In her groundbreaking book, *Burdened Virtues* (2005), Lisa Tessman argues that some dispositions to respond appropriately to conditions of oppression will contribute to resisting it, while others will not. For instance, on Tessman's view, hardened rage against one's oppressors is an appropriate response to oppression that contributes to resisting it. But, there will be other appropriate responses to oppression that either help us survive it, or help us choose options that are the least bad, without motivating us to resist it. Here, compartmentalization comes to mind (2005: 166), as does the aptly named virtue of 'sensitivity to others' suffering in moderation' (2005: 90). Tessman argues that nearly all virtues in conditions of oppression—including hardened rage, compartmentalization, and moderate sensitivity to suffering—are 'burdened': they are "traits that while practically necessitated for surviving oppression or morally necessitated for opposing it, are also costly to the selves who bear them" (2005: 107). But, only some virtues in conditions of oppression contribute to resisting it. I suggest that we restrict the category of 'liberatory' virtues to those that contribute to *resisting* oppression and achieving liberation. This seems to fit with standard usage. It reflects Tessman's distinction between virtues that help one resist oppression (2005: 165) and those that help one survive it (2005: 166), and it answers Dillon's call to explore traits that foster "resistance to oppression and emancipation" (2012: 83).

What kind of oppression do liberatory virtues resist—for instance, do they resist social oppression, or epistemic oppression? And, further, what kind of change do liberatory virtues engender? Do they engender changes in unjust structures (in laws, policies, and other institutions) or changes in unjust individuals (in actions, motives, and awareness)? I will assume that 'liberatory virtue' is a broad category in these respects. It can include traits that contribute to resisting either social oppression or epistemic oppression (or both), and that engender either structural or individual changes (or both). The aim of this chapter is to explore whether humility could be a liberatory virtue for oppressed persons, whose oppression is primarily (though not exclusively) social. Accordingly, this chapter will focus on liberatory virtues that contribute to resisting *social* oppression and achieving *social* liberation. Note that, even if humility is one such virtue for oppressed persons, it won't be the most important—we can expect justice to be paramount. Nor will humility engender changes on its own, though it can, as limitations-owning, be an initial spark for change in individuals, and can support virtues like justice in engendering structural changes.

15.1.2 What is virtuous about liberatory virtue?

Thus far, we have narrowed our focus to virtues that contribute to resisting social oppression and achieving social liberation. In other words, we have sketched what makes them liberatory. Let's now sketch what makes them *virtues*. Will every trait that contributes to resisting social oppression and achieving social liberation be a virtue? If not, why not, and what further restrictions are needed? Moreover, what does it mean for a trait to 'contribute' to an end?

Let's begin with some distinctions from traditional virtue theory. Traditional virtue theorists develop their analyses of virtue with *ideal* conditions in mind. Though traditional virtue theory is itself diverse—encompassing consequentialist, sentimentalist, and Aristotelian analyses of virtue—it is united in conceiving of virtues as *excellences*. For traditionalists, that virtues are excellences is not in dispute. What is in dispute are the features needed for excellence and, thus, for virtue. Accordingly, some have argued that virtues make us excellent by enabling us to produce a preponderance of good effects (Driver 2001). Virtues, as it is sometimes put, require reliable success in producing goods. Others have argued that for virtues to make us excellent, they must involve good motives and need not produce good effects (Slote 2001). A third camp combines these criteria, arguing that for virtues to make us excellent, they must both produce a preponderance of good effects and involve good motives (Zagzebski 1996). My own pluralist view argues that there is more than one way to be excellent, and more than one kind of virtue (Battaly 2015). One can be excellent by producing good effects, or having good motives, or both.

How do these traditional distinctions help us home in on liberatory virtues? Do they even translate to conditions of oppression? In some ways, they do not, since excellence may be out of reach in conditions of oppression. Tessman has argued that oppression produces 'dirty hands' cases and tragic dilemmas "in which there are no good choices" (2005: 108). If this is correct, liberatory virtues won't be traits that make one excellent, so much as they will be traits that make "the best of bad circumstances" (2005: 30). In other words, they won't be traits that produce good effects, or involve good motives. Rather, when the only effects and motives on offer are bad, they will be traits that produce or involve the least bad.

But, in other ways, these traditional distinctions do translate to conditions of oppression. We can explore whether liberatory virtues require producing the least bad *effects*, or possessing the least bad *motives*, or *both*. More generally, we can ask whether success in producing liberatory effects is sufficient, or whether liberatory virtues also require liberatory motives. Silvermint (2017: 470), for instance, seems to emphasize success in producing liberatory effects, while Dalmiya (2016: 139) seems to think liberatory virtues also require "the motivation to intervene in unjust institutional structures." This distinction likewise captures three ways in which a trait might 'contribute' to an end: by producing the end, or having the end as a motive, or both.

Whichever analysis of 'contribute' one adopts, a trait won't be a liberatory *virtue* unless it contributes to a liberatory end that is *appropriate* (the least bad even if not good). Under-specifying this end can cause us to count too many traits as virtues, to misidentify some *vices* as virtues. With this in mind, we can ask whether the end of resisting social oppression and achieving social liberation is still too broad. Will every trait that contributes to this end be a virtue? Or, will some traits that contribute to it be vices? Consider, for instance, traits that facilitate the killing of oppressors or taking revenge. Such traits might contribute to the end of resisting social oppression and achieving social liberation for oppressed persons. But we shouldn't count them as virtues. As Tessman observes: "There is a danger … of glorifying traits that, while purportedly aimed at liberation, facilitate morally horrifying actions" (2005: 165). In an effort to exclude such traits, she defines the virtues of resistance as aiming not just at liberation, but at human flourishing.[1] On her view, such virtues aim at "eventually making flourishing lives more possible overall" (2005: 165)—at eventually making flourishing more possible for the person who is resisting, for oppressed persons, and (as she sometimes puts it) for all members of our "inclusive social collectivity" (2005: 76). Though Silvermint and Tessman disagree over the details, he likewise defines virtues of resistance in terms of human flourishing.[2] In Silvermint's words (2017: 475):

> There's nothing inherently virtuous about simply seizing power from those that have abused it previously, if doing so harms one's fellow victims and partially complicit allies, or if retribution for oppression spirals into the kind of revenge or future mistreatment that preserves barriers to flourishing in society.

To be a virtue of resistance, a trait must resist oppression in ways that facilitate "flourishing-apt societies," those characterized by "an absence of systematic social barriers to everyone's flourishing, not just an absence of barriers for the beneficiaries of resistance" (2017: 475). In a similar spirit, the Black Lives Matter movement lists as one of its guiding principles: "work[ing] vigorously for freedom and justice for Black people and, by extension, all people."[3]

In short, the end of resisting social oppression and achieving social liberation is too broad to ground an analysis of liberatory virtues, since it 'lets in' traits that are vices. To exclude such traits, we can follow Tessman, Silvermint, and BLM in refining this end. We can understand liberatory virtues to be traits that contribute not just to resisting social oppression and achieving liberation, but also to making flourishing more possible for all persons, formerly oppressed and former oppressors alike. We have left the analysis of 'contribute' open, acknowledging that there is room for debate on this score.

15.1.3 Whose virtues are the liberatory virtues?

Who can possess the liberatory virtues? Is the possession of liberatory virtues restricted to oppressed persons? Or can privileged persons also have liberatory virtues?[4] Readers should note that my language here oversimplifies—due to intersectionality, people are rarely 'oppressed' or 'privileged' *simpliciter*. Many persons will be oppressed along one axis of their social identity but privileged along others. Keeping this qualification in mind, let's return to brass tacks for a moment: liberatory virtues are, at minimum, supposed to help persons who are *oppressed* along some axis resist oppression and make progress toward liberation. Thus, at a fundamental level, it is assumed that liberatory virtues are the sorts of traits that can be possessed by oppressed persons. What is at issue here is whether liberatory virtues extend to persons who are privileged.

There are several reasons to think that liberatory virtues can and should extend to the privileged.[5] First, the burden of resisting oppression, achieving liberation, and making flourishing more possible for all shouldn't fall solely on oppressed persons. Indeed, since oppressors are the ones in the wrong, and privileged persons have benefitted from oppression, one might argue that the burden of change should fall predominantly on them. Second, if Miranda Fricker (2007) is correct, we are all at risk of possessing qualities like testimonial injustice, whether we are oppressed or privileged. Accordingly, we can all benefit from the liberatory virtue of testimonial justice—it would be absurd to suggest that only oppressed persons should have this liberatory virtue! Finally, if the trait of humility turns out to be a liberatory virtue, then liberatory virtues had better be the sorts of traits that can be possessed by the privileged. Privileged persons need the liberatory virtue of humility, and need it badly.

15.1.4 Can liberatory virtues be traits that also count among the traditional virtues?

Relatedly, if the trait of humility is to be a liberatory virtue, traditional virtues and liberatory virtues cannot be mutually exclusive. So, we need to ask: will some of the same traits count as both liberatory virtues and traditional virtues? In other words, will these two categories intersect? And, will humility be one of the traits in their intersection?

Let's first consider an argument for answering in the negative. Why might one think that liberatory virtues *won't* be traditional virtues? For starters, traditional virtues are identified and analyzed with ideal conditions in mind. Case in point: neo-Aristotelians often argue that the virtues of the *phronimos* are ideals that we can get closer to achieving if we put in the work. But, oppressive conditions are 'non-ideal' (Norlock 2018; Mills 2018). Indeed, oppressive conditions may be so starkly different from ideal conditions that we are "forced to recommend different character traits, dispositions, and aims for each."[6] To put the argument differently, when we analyze virtues with *oppressive* conditions in mind, we should expect to home in on an entirely different set of traits: traits that do not count as virtues in ideal conditions, and might even count as vices. Tessman (2005: 165) argues that some virtues of resistance, such as hardened rage, fit this description.[7] But, do *all* liberatory virtues fit this description? Does this argument for a stark separation between liberatory and traditional virtues succeed? Does it show that these categories are mutually exclusive?

We can say this much. Beginning with oppressive conditions allows for the possibility of expanding beyond the traditional virtues—it allows for the possibility that a trait might be a liberatory virtue even if it isn't a traditional one. But, there is a problem with the argument above. On its own, beginning with oppressive conditions doesn't guarantee mutual exclusivity. It doesn't preclude the possibility that some traits will be both liberatory and traditional virtues. Indeed, it's hard to see how it could, since the trait of justice seems to contribute to resisting social oppression, achieving liberation, and making flourishing more possible for all, while also being a paradigm of traditional virtue. Silvermint acknowledges this much and more. In arguing for a "unified account of political agency" (2017: 462), he contends that the very same traits will be political virtues in ideal and oppressive conditions. The claim under consideration here—that *at least some* of the same traits will be virtues in ideal and oppressive conditions—is weaker than Silvermint's contention that *all* of the same traits will be (political) virtues in ideal and oppressive conditions.

15.2 Traditional humility and liberatory humility

Still, humility is not justice. One might argue that even if some traits will be both liberatory and traditional virtues, the prospects for humility falling in this intersection seem bleak—humility is unlikely to be a liberatory virtue. To explore this, we first need an analysis of humility. Let's assume that the analysis below is traditional, in the sense that humility was identified, and analyzed, as a virtue with near-ideal conditions in mind.

15.2.1 Traditional humility

Let's begin with the trait of humility. The *trait* of humility consists in an attentiveness to and owning of one's limitations (Whitcomb et al. 2017; Whitcomb et al. 2020). Intellectual humility is one kind of humility, whereby one is attentive to and owns one's intellectual limitations—one's cognitive mistakes, deficits in cognitive skills, etc. Humility-in-general is broader in scope, and applies to limitations of all kinds, including one's moral mistakes (e.g., breaking a promise), deficits in general skills (e.g., being a terrible cook), flaws in moral character (e.g., being dishonest), and affective shortcomings (e.g., being irascible). It consists partly in an *attentiveness* to one's limitations—a disposition to be aware of them, rather than oblivious to them—and partly in *owning* one's limitations rather than denying them. Roughly, owning one's limitations characteristically involves dispositions to: (i) believe and accept that one has them; (ii) admit and acknowledge them; (iii) care about them and take them seriously; and (iv) feel regret or dismay about them. Owning limitations does not entail having control over them or being responsible (blameworthy) for their acquisition.

The trait of humility is not always a *virtue*. For the trait to be a virtue, one must own one's limitations for the right reasons (one's motivations must be good rather than bad). But, more importantly, one must also own one's limitations at the right times and in the right ways. This requires good judgment (*phronesis*). Without good judgment, there is nothing to prevent limitations-owning from going overboard—nothing to prevent the trait of humility from being excessive. Excessive humility causes one to be overly attentive to, and to over-own, one's limitations. It causes one to obsess about one's limitations, defer to others at every opportunity, and fail to trust oneself. The person who is constantly aware of her limitations, over emphasizes them, or cares too much about them does not have the *virtue* of humility. She has an excess of the *trait* of humility—she is humble to a fault. This excess is servility, and it is a vice. The virtue of humility lies in a mean between this vice of servility and a corresponding vice of arrogance, which involves deficient attentiveness to, and under-owning of, one's limitations. In short, to have the *virtue* of humility, one must be appropriately attentive to, and appropriately own, one's limitations—one must have good judgment, which enables one to avoid both servility and arrogance—and one must do so with the right motives.

Pride is related to, but distinct from, humility (Whitcomb et al. 2017). The trait of pride consists in being attentive to and owning one's *strengths*. To be a virtue, this trait likewise requires good motives and, pertinently, good judgment. Excessive pride causes one to be overly attentive to, and to over-own, one's strengths. Thus, the person who over emphasizes her strengths, or cares too much about them does not have the *virtue* of pride. She has an excess of the *trait* of pride. This excess is a second way to have the vice of arrogance, this time with respect to one's *strengths*. The virtue of pride lies in a mean between this vice of arrogance and a corresponding version of the vice of servility, which involves deficient attentiveness to, and under-owning of, one's strengths. In short, to have the *virtue* of pride, one must be appropriately attentive to, and appropriately own, one's strengths—one must have good judgment which enables one to avoid both arrogance and servility—and one must do so with the right motives.

Putting all of this together, **humility** as a trait is a disposition to be attentive to and own one's limitations. One can have the *trait* of humility to excess, in which case one does not have the *virtue* of humility, but instead has the vice of servility. The virtue of humility consists in appropriate attentiveness to and owning of one's limitations; it requires good judgment and right motives.

Pride as a trait is a disposition to be attentive to and own one's strengths. One can have the *trait* of pride to excess, in which case one does not have the *virtue* of pride, but instead has the vice of arrogance. The virtue of pride consists in appropriate attentiveness to and owning of one's strengths; it too requires good judgment and right motives.

Servility is both a vice of excess and a vice of deficiency. It is a vice of excess with respect to humility—it is a vicious way of having the trait of humility. As such, it is a disposition to be overly attentive to or over-own one's limitations. Servility is also a vice of deficiency with respect to pride. It is a lack of the trait of pride—it is a general unwillingness or inability to be attentive to or own one's strengths. It is likewise a lack of the virtue of pride; it includes the disposition to be insufficiently attentive to one's strengths and to under-own them.

Arrogance is also a vice of deficiency and a vice of excess. It is a vice of deficiency with respect to humility. It is a lack of the trait of humility—it is a general unwillingness or inability to be attentive to or own one's limitations. It is likewise a lack of the virtue of humility; it includes the disposition to be insufficiently attentive to one's limitations and to under-own them. Arrogance is a vice of excess with respect to pride—it is a vicious way of having the trait of pride. As such, it is a disposition to be overly attentive to or over-own one's strengths.

15.2.2 Liberatory humility

Liberatory virtues are traits that contribute to resisting social oppression, achieving liberation, and making flourishing more possible for all persons. Does the traditional virtue of humility, understood as appropriate limitations-owning, contribute to these ends? In other words, is appropriate limitations-owning a liberatory virtue?

Recall from 1.2 that we left the definition of 'contribute' open. 'Contributing' to liberatory ends might mean: producing liberatory effects, or having liberatory motives, or both. Now, some of the arguments in Whitcomb et al. 2020 suggest that the traditional virtue of humility, as appropriate limitations-owning, can help *produce* liberatory effects. For instance, it can help produce liberatory effects by countering servile over-owning—by bolstering goals, beliefs, and emotions that are crucial for acts of resistance. But, notice two things about those arguments. First, we assume (with few exceptions) that the virtue of humility only helps to produce liberatory effects when some other virtue (like justice) is on the scene supplying liberatory motives. Humility, as appropriate limitations-owning, does not itself supply liberatory motives, nor is it constituted by any specifically liberatory content. By itself (with few exceptions), the virtue of humility won't help to produce liberatory effects—it needs some other virtue to point it in that direction. Second, we assume that even when some other virtue *is* on the scene supplying liberatory motives, the virtue of humility (usually) only *helps* to produce liberatory effects—it plays a supporting role. Appropriate limitations-owning enables one to identify and own one's shortcomings in resisting oppression, but it doesn't (typically) produce acts of resistance all by itself. Other virtues (like justice) typically take the lead in producing acts of resistance. Thus, it would be a stretch to claim that appropriate limitations-owning, traditionally conceived, is a liberatory virtue. It isn't a liberatory virtue *yet*.

Can we adapt our analysis of appropriate limitations-owning so as to convert it into a liberatory virtue? If so, what needs to change in our analysis of appropriate limitations-owning? It will need some additional and revised features.[8] Here, we can follow Nancy Daukas (2019), who recommends building liberatory content into our analyses of the individual liberatory virtues. Daukas points out that feminist virtue epistemologists have already reconceptualized the virtues of intellectual autonomy (Code 2006) and intelligence (Braaten 1990) along such lines. She likewise recommends an analogous reconceptualization of humility (Daukas 2019: 389). Following this general advice, what might the virtue of liberatory humility look like?

Here is a sketch. We can think of the virtue of **liberatory humility** as consisting in a motivation to pursue liberatory ends, and a disposition to be appropriately attentive to and own one's liberatory limitations.

To explicate, the virtue of liberatory humility will involve several motivations. It will involve an awareness of oppression and the motivation to resist it, as well as the motivations to make progress toward liberation and future flourishing for all. The aforementioned motivations will be shared by all liberatory virtues (liberatory humility, liberatory autonomy, liberatory pride, etc.). They will also generate a motivation that is distinctive of liberatory humility, namely, the motivation to be attentive to and own the limitations that prevent one from resisting and from making progress toward liberation and future flourishing. They will generate this humility-specific motivation when combined with the belief that owning such limitations will get one closer to achieving one's liberatory goals.[9]

The virtue of liberatory humility will also involve a disposition to be appropriately attentive to and own one's liberatory limitations. These limitations prevent one from resisting oppression, and from making progress toward liberation and future flourishing. They include, for instance, particular types of ignorance (e.g., of one's privilege and accompanying unjust benefits), affective shortcomings (e.g., not being angry enough to resist), cognitive shortcomings (e.g., assigning credibility deficits to persons of color and credibility excesses to white people), and character flaws (e.g., apathy). Arguably, these limitations must belong to the agent—they must be *hers* and not merely in her environment—in order for her attentiveness to them and owning of them to qualify as virtuous liberatory humility. To take a simple case, the agent's attentiveness to and owning of *her* particular identity prejudices (e.g., assigning credibility deficits to persons of color) will manifest virtuous liberatory humility, but her attentiveness to and owning of prejudices in the environment that differ from hers (e.g., explicit transphobia), will not. Agents do not manifest the virtue of liberatory humility when they are attentive to and own prejudices *that do not belong to them.*[10]

That said, we need further analysis of exactly when a liberatory limitation belongs to an agent and when it instead belongs to her environment. Oppressive conditions highlight the need for such analysis. To drive home the point, what should we say of the limitation of being a woman in an environment that is rife with gender prejudice? Or the limitation of being gay in a society where homosexuality is criminalized? Do these limitations belong to the agent, or to the environment, or to the-agent-in-the-environment? Must an agent's limitations be indexed to her effectiveness in an environment? If so, what would that mean for oppressed agents? Would being attentive to and owning the aforementioned limitations manifest the virtue of liberatory humility, or the vice of liberatory servility, or some other quality?[11] What might owning the aforementioned limitations look like, and would all such owning be over-owning? I flag these as questions that a complete analysis of liberatory humility will need to answer.

Whatever account we give of limitations, the above analysis of liberatory humility acknowledges that differently situated people may be prone to different limitations—privileged persons may be at greater risk for some limitations, while oppressed persons are at greater risk for others.[12] Appropriate attentiveness to and owning of one's liberatory limitations will likewise involve good judgment that steers clear of the liberatory vices of arrogance and servility. Note the use of 'contribute' on my analysis: liberatory humility contributes to liberatory ends through its motives. Whether it also contributes by producing liberatory effects is left unanswered. For now, we can say that liberatory humility contributes through its motives *even if* it ends up playing a merely supporting role in producing liberatory effects.

This analysis builds an awareness of sociopolitical realities and liberatory motives into the virtue of liberatory humility. It *adds* liberatory features to the traditional conception of appropriate limitations-owning, and thus *revises* its backdrop of near-ideal conditions. It adapts the traditional conception of humility to our sociopolitical reality, which includes oppression. But, nothing I have said entails binning the traditional conception altogether—relegating it to the philosophical scrap-heap;[13] and for that reason, some critics of ideal theory may think my analysis hasn't gone far enough. Still, I have argued that the traditional conception of humility, as appropriate limitations-owning, is not a liberatory virtue. Accordingly, we can now answer one of the questions of section 1.4 in the negative: the traditional virtue of humility does not fall in the intersection of traditional and liberatory virtues because it is not liberatory. Likewise, the virtue of liberatory humility does not fall in this intersection because it is not traditional. It revises the backdrop of near-ideal conditions. Liberatory humility is a kind of appropriate limitations-owning, but it is a specifically liberatory kind.

15.3 Oppressed persons and the virtue of liberatory humility

We have carved out conceptual space for a virtue of liberatory humility, which consists in liberatory motives and a disposition to be appropriately attentive to and own one's liberatory limitations. We can now ask this concept to prove its worth. *Who* is this *virtue* for? Is the virtue of liberatory humility designed solely for privileged persons? Or, can it also be a virtue for oppressed persons? Below, I suggest that it can be a virtue for privileged persons *and* for oppressed persons, even in interactions with oppressors. I briefly evaluate two alternatives: Dalmiya's (2016: 147) worry that the virtue of liberatory humility is "unproductive" for oppressed persons in interactions with their oppressors, and Dillon's (in press) argument that arrogance can be a liberatory virtue for oppressed persons in interactions with oppressors.

15.3.1 Dalmiya on liberatory humility

Dalmiya contends that liberatory humility is a virtue for privileged persons, but warns against claiming that it is a virtue for oppressed persons in their interactions with the privileged. Though Dalmiya and I disagree about this (and some other details), our two analyses of liberatory humility enjoy significant overlap.

On Dalmiya's view, 'relational humility' involves both a humility component, i.e., an awareness of one's own limitations and ignorance, and a relational component, i.e., an awareness of the strengths and knowledge of other people. In her words, it involves "other-regard … because of a realistic self-regard" (2016: 119). Dalmiya argues that although relational humility on its own is not a liberatory virtue, *historicized* relational humility is a liberatory virtue. Historicized relational humility includes (1) an awareness of one's own, and others' limitations and strengths. It also involves (2) understanding that one's own, and others' limitations and strengths are embedded historically—they are influenced by the social location of one's group and the unequal distribution of social power. In short, it involves understanding that one's location as privileged or oppressed plays a role in producing the limitations and strengths that one has, and that the limitations and strengths of the privileged can differ from those of the oppressed (2016: 144). Dalmiya likewise recognizes that for historicized relational humility to be a liberatory virtue, it must be accompanied by (3) motivations to resist social injustice. Without those motivations, the awareness and understanding described above won't engender liberatory change (2016: 148).

Dalmiya intends historicized relational humility to be a liberatory virtue that is for the privileged, and for the oppressed in their interactions with other oppressed persons. On her view, it is important to recommend liberatory virtues for privileged persons since "stability of reform require[s] reworking the dispositional apparatus of those in power so that they accept … change and not push back" (2016: 146). Agreed: liberatory humility is a virtue for privileged persons. Is it also a virtue for oppressed persons? In carving out space for an affirmative (albeit qualified) answer, Dalmiya rightly points out that humility is neither diffidence nor humiliation (2016: 146). Here, too, we agree: the virtue of humility is not the vice of servility. Dalmiya likewise recommends humility for oppressed persons in their interactions with peers "who are differently located within the periphery" (2016: 147). But, she warns against recommending it for oppressed persons in interactions with the privileged, suggesting that "we should be mindful of *who* we are being relationally humble towards … It could well be unproductive for the marginalized to defer to the knowledge of those at the center" (2016: 147).

Though Dalmiya and I agree about much, here, we part ways. Below, I suggest that liberatory humility can be a virtue for oppressed persons in interactions with oppressors. First and foremost, the virtue of liberatory humility enables oppressed persons to avoid servility in these interactions and can help them stay on the path of resistance. It wards off, rather than entails, deference. Where applicable, it also enables oppressed persons to avoid arrogance in these interactions and keep striving for the flourishing of all.

Avoiding servility. The liberatory vice of servility is, roughly, a disposition to over-own one's liberatory limitations and, in so doing, to subvert one's ability to contribute to liberatory ends, including the end of resisting oppression. Simply put, over-owning limitations can make it harder for one to resist.

Oppressed persons are susceptible to over-owning their limitations. This is no accident—interactions with oppressors (and with dominant culture) encourage oppressed persons to focus on and over-emphasize their own weaknesses, to distrust their own abilities, and even to dehumanize themselves. To explicate, it is easier to dominate people who over-own their limitations, particularly liberatory limitations which already hamper their resistance.

Consider an oppressed person whose liberatory limitations include gaps in confidence, which themselves result from oppression, and which impede her resistance to some extent (they slow it down or make it harder). Now, add the susceptibility to over-owning. Oppressed persons who constantly focus on, over-emphasize, and care too much about such gaps in confidence over-own them and thereby manifest servility (non-culpably). Arguably, oppressed persons who are servile in this way will be even less likely to resist oppression and less likely to flourish in the future, since servility further erodes their confidence.

The virtue of liberatory humility can help oppressed persons appropriately attend to and own gaps in confidence when interacting with oppressors, and to that extent can help them stay on the path of resistance. Recall that the virtue of liberatory humility involves the motivation to resist oppression and the disposition to be appropriately attentive to and own the limitations that prevent one from resisting it. Accordingly, oppressed persons with this virtue will be aware of their liberatory limitations—e.g., their gaps in confidence—without being overly focused on them or overwhelmed by them. And, they will own these limitations by admitting them to themselves, and perhaps also by trying to change them. For instance, one might own these limitations by initiating a plan to counteract them—to develop higher levels of confidence by (say) meeting with allies. Where possible, one might even own these limitations by trying to change the oppressive conditions that produced them in the first place. In short, appropriately owning one's gaps in confidence might help one stay engaged in projects of resistance, and might even spark an effort to narrow those gaps and strengthen one's confidence. Appropriate owning does not yield despondency. Nor does it yield deference to oppressors. Deferring to oppressors is characteristic of servility, not the virtue of liberatory humility. While over-owning one's limitations can make one disposed to defer, the virtue of liberatory humility reins in such over-owning (Whitcomb et al. 2020).

Arguably, oppressed persons are at greater risk for servility than arrogance, since their servility is systematically encouraged. We can thus expect the virtue of liberatory humility to be especially important for oppressed persons in reigning in servility. Privileged persons are correspondingly at greater risk for arrogance than servility. Accordingly, we can expect liberatory humility to be especially important for them in combatting arrogance. That said, the virtue also has a role to play in combatting arrogance, when it arises, in oppressed persons.

Avoiding arrogance. The liberatory vice of arrogance is, roughly, a disposition to under-own one's liberatory limitations and, in so doing, to subvert one's ability to contribute to liberatory ends, including the end of making flourishing more possible for all. Simply put, under-owning one's limitations can make it harder for one to contribute to the future flourishing of the formerly oppressed and former oppressors alike.

Consider a particular oppressed person who tends to jump to the conclusion that her oppressors are inhuman monsters, or whose anger at them is hardened against their humanity (Whitcomb et al. 2020). These tendencies are liberatory limitations insofar as they impede a future society in which flourishing is more possible for all, formerly oppressed and former oppressors alike. Think long-term: imagine that resistance movements make significant progress in shifting power to the formerly oppressed. Such tendencies would then risk perpetuating further cycles of oppression (of former oppressors). Arrogance exacerbates this risk. Suppose that our agent acknowledges that she has these tendencies, but doesn't recognize that they are problematic, doesn't care that she has them, and doesn't try to change them. In short, she under-owns them and thereby manifests arrogance. Arguably, arrogance with respect to these tendencies makes her even more likely to oppress her former oppressors.

The virtue of liberatory humility enables agents to appropriately own such tendencies, and, to that extent, can keep them striving toward 'flourishing-apt societies.' An agent who has the virtue of liberatory humility will recognize that her tendencies to dehumanize her oppressors are limitations that impede progress toward the future flourishing of all. She will also appropriately own these limitations by acknowledging them to herself and trying to change them. This does not mean that she won't be angry at (former) oppressors, or won't believe that they are vicious, or won't endorse punishment for their crimes! It merely means that she will try to prevent her beliefs from outstripping her evidence—she can believe that (former) oppressors are vicious and should be punished for crimes, while simultaneously resisting the temptation to conclude that they are inhuman and should be treated as such. She will likewise take steps to prevent her anger toward oppressors from being dehumanizing, though she can do so while being extremely and intensely angry. This brings us to Dillon's argument that arrogance can be a liberatory virtue.

15.3.2 Dillon on arrogance

Dillon conceives of humility as a kind of lowliness and submissiveness, what I have called 'servility.' She argues that humility as lowliness is not a virtue for anyone, least of all for oppressed persons (2015: 45), and she takes self-respect, rather than humility (as lowliness), to be the virtue opposed to arrogance (2015: 43). For Dillon, humility is not a liberatory virtue, but arrogance can be. She argues that an oppressed person's 'unwarranted claims arrogance' will sometimes manifest or facilitate respect for the self. When it does, it is a liberatory virtue.

Let's begin with some background. Dillon's analysis of arrogance is inspired by both Kantianism and feminism. 'Unwarranted claims arrogance' is a disposition to claim rights or entitlements for oneself that are in fact unwarranted, based on an inaccurate and inflated view of one's own importance, knowledge, and abilities (Dillon 2004: 198). Though Dillon's analysis of arrogance differs from the analysis in section 2.1, they are correlated: the person with unwarranted claims arrogance will under-own limitations and over-own strengths. On Dillon's view, unwarranted claims arrogance usually undermines 'agentic recognition self-respect,' which entails appropriately valuing oneself as a moral agent and committing oneself to live in accordance with the moral law (2004: 206). But, Dillon (in press) argues that arrogance doesn't always undermine self-respect. Unwarranted claims arrogance in interactions with one's oppressors will sometimes manifest or facilitate agentic recognition self-respect.

Dillon uses the examples of Antigone and Sethe (from Toni Morrison's *Beloved*) to argue that unwarranted claims arrogance can enable oppressed persons to protest injustice, refuse subordination, and carve out space for agentic self-respect. She contends that Antigone, the protagonist of the eponymous play by Sophocles, manifests both unwarranted claims arrogance and agentic self-respect in her interactions with Creon (in press). In burying her brother, Antigone violates an edict issued by Creon, the ruler of Thebes, which expressly prohibits his burial. Upon discovering this violation, Creon accuses Antigone of hubris—of aspiring beyond her station and unwarrantedly claiming the role of 'the man'—and condemns her to death.

Let's assume that in refusing to defer to Creon's edict, Antigone is manifesting self-respect. The problem, I submit, is that she is not manifesting arrogance. Instead, she is manifesting the virtue of pride and, perhaps also, the virtue of humility. In refusing to defer, Antigone avoids servility. She does not under-own her strengths, e.g., her knowledge, agency, and abilities. She appropriately owns them—she manifests the virtue of pride. Perhaps, she also avoids seeing limitations in herself where there are none, and avoids internalizing Creon's inaccurate view of her. Perhaps, she has an accurate picture of her limitations, and manifests the virtue of humility. Nor, importantly, is she claiming entitlements that are *un*warranted; she is, after all, right about her knowledge, agency, and abilities, and she is right to protest Creon's unjust edict. In these ways, Antigone avoids servility, while also avoiding arrogance.

What we have, in the case of Antigone, is misperceived arrogance rather than actual arrogance. Creon incorrectly perceives Antigone's pride and self-respect as arrogant. Dillon doesn't take this tack,[14] though she has argued to similar effect elsewhere (2004: 210): "what is in fact self-respect can seem like arrogance to those whose moral outlook is itself perverted by arrogance, and so to some, virtues of self-respect will appear to be vices of arrogance." When arguing in that vein, Dillon contends that persons who are both privileged and arrogant are likely to misperceive the self-respecting acts of oppressed persons engaged in liberatory struggles. She cites, for instance, the inclination to label Black Lives Matter as arrogant and uppity (in press). Dillon is right about the ways in which pride and self-respect in oppressed persons can be misperceived. She is also right that pride and self-respect, misperceived as arrogance, can contribute to resistance and be liberatory virtues. But, what we need to know for present purposes is whether actual arrogance is a liberatory virtue.

Dillon likewise contends that Sethe, the lead character in *Beloved*, gains a sense of her own agency through the arrogant action of killing her daughter. By way of background: Sethe had escaped slavery with her children. When they were all confronted with recapture, Sethe attempted to kill her children in order to prevent them from returning to the horrors of slavery. She succeeded in killing her daughter, insisting that she was justified in doing so.

This case is difficult to judge. Let's assume that Sethe's actions are arrogant. Do they carve out space for agentic self-respect, as Dillon argues? Sethe's actions violate Kantian moral law, and to that extent undermine agentic self-respect. But, more importantly, we might worry that the tragic dilemma Sethe faces will impede, rather than facilitate, her ability to develop self-respect. In this vein, Tessman (2005: 89) has argued that tragic dilemmas can haunt one, ruining one's life and impeding one's character. Relatedly, we might wonder whether Sethe's actions contribute to, or detract from, the liberatory goals of resisting oppression, making progress toward liberation, and making flourishing more possible for all. We might worry that Sethe's actions are not liberatory.

Whatever we conclude about the examples above, Dillon is onto something. It is worth considering whether occasional arrogant actions can help oppressed persons resist the vices that oppression would have them develop. Perhaps, the occasional under-owning of limitations and over-owning of strengths can help an oppressed person resist servility and make progress toward the virtues of humility and pride. Oppressed persons are systematically pressured to develop servility. Given that downward pressure, it is important to explore whether occasional over-correction could help oppressed persons make eventual progress toward the mean. In Aristotelian language, combatting servility might involve "dragging" oneself "to the contrary extreme" (Aristotle 1998: NE.II.9.1109b5). This brings us to Dillon's final claim: that arrogant actions can be used strategically by oppressed persons to combat vices in the privileged; they can be used in the service of liberatory motives, to shock the privileged into recognizing their own arrogance. This, too, is worth exploring.

To be clear, I am not recommending that oppressed persons develop arrogance as a stable disposition, since *consistent* under-owning of liberatory limitations will subvert, rather than support, liberatory ends. In the short term, consistent under-owning will lead to unsuccessful acts of resistance (one won't realize or won't care that one, e.g., lacks key pieces of knowledge that are needed for successful resistance). In the long term, once power has shifted to the formerly oppressed, it could result in further cycles of oppression, and in any case, would be difficult to dislodge as a stable disposition. Rather, the argument suggests that *occasional* arrogant acts, in interactions with oppressors, might serve liberatory ends. It recommends that oppressed persons occasionally and knowingly act the same way an arrogant person would act—i.e., mimic the actions of an arrogant person. It does not recommend that oppressed persons develop a disposition to act this way, nor does it recommend that oppressed persons develop the cognitive, affective, or motivational dispositions of an arrogant person. In short, it does not recommend that oppressed persons become arrogant. It merely acknowledges that occasional under-owning of limitations and over-owning of strengths might serve liberatory ends, even though the stable disposition of arrogance will not.

Where does this leave us? I have argued that liberatory humility can be a virtue for oppressed persons in interactions with oppressors. It enables oppressed persons to avoid servility and stay on the path of resistance and, where applicable, avoid arrogance and keep striving toward flourishing for all. But, I have likewise acknowledged that occasional arrogant acts might serve the liberatory motives of oppressed persons. This means that: (i) it is appropriate for oppressed persons to have the virtue of liberatory humility, which is hard enough to get on its own, and (ii) it is simultaneously appropriate for them to be ready to occasionally perform arrogant acts, which can make it even harder to acquire the virtue of liberatory humility. I wish my conclusions were more optimistic. My hope is that the analyses in this chapter have provided a map for the further exploration of liberatory virtue, liberatory humility, and the liberatory vices of servility and arrogance.[15]

Notes

1 She argues that lying and manipulation are "not virtues; they are failures of other-regarding virtues" (2005: 69).

2 Silvermint emphasizes the eventual *production* of human flourishing (2017: 470), whereas Tessman emphasizes the *motive* for flourishing (2005: 165).

3 https://blacklivesmatter.com/about/what-we-believe/.

4 We should also consider whether groups can have liberatory virtues.

5 Though we shouldn't expect liberatory virtues to look exactly the same in oppressed and privileged persons. Because context matters, a single liberatory virtue can (and often will) call for different actions from oppressed persons and privileged persons.

6 Silvermint (2017: 462) is describing a view that he rejects.

7 But, she acknowledges that there are other virtues of resistance, such as pride and perseverance, that are virtues in ideal conditions (2005: 115).

8 Kwong (2015) might disagree.

9 On the motivational component of the intellectual virtues, see Zagzebski 1996: 176.

10 Arguably, they manifest the vice of liberatory servility, at least insofar as such attentiveness and owning involves misattributing those prejudices to themselves.

11 Would it manifest the quality of humbling oneself, where this is distinct from humility and involves taking on a limitation that does not belong to one in order to be effective in an oppressive environment? See Baehr (ms).

12 Tessman (2005: chapter 3) argues that privileged persons are at greater risk for callousness and cowardice, whereas oppressed persons are at greater risk for hopelessness and vindictiveness.

13 It helps us envision flourishing-apt societies.

14 She argues instead that it is reasonable for Creon, from within his own socio-moral perspective, to regard Antigone as arrogant. She acknowledges that, from our perspective, Antigone is not arrogant. But, she suggests that since there is no view from nowhere, we theorists cannot assume that our perspective is authoritative.

15 Thanks to Mark Alfano, Jason Baehr, Nora Berenstain, Teresa Blankmeyer Burke, Paul Bloomfield, Charlie Crerar, Nancy Daukas, Heidi Grasswick, Raja Halwani, Allan Hazlett, Dan Howard-Snyder, Tracy Llanera, Michael Lynch, Heather Muraviov, Gregory Peterson, Louise Richardson-Self, Barbara Stock, Alessandra Tanesini, Lisa Tessman, Kirk VanGilder, Dennis Whitcomb, Chase Wrenn, and audiences at the Bled Epistemology Conference, South Dakota State University, Syracuse University, and the University of Connecticut. Work on this paper was supported by John Templeton Foundation Grant 60622, "Developing Humility in Leadership."

References

Aristotle. 1998. *Nicomachean Ethics*, trans. D. Ross. New York: Oxford University Press.
Baehr, Jason. Manuscript. "Two Views of Intellectual Humility."
Battaly, Heather. 2015. *Virtue*. Cambridge: Polity Press.
Black Lives Matter. https://blacklivesmatter.com/about/what-we-believe/. Accessed. 2.25.2019.
Braaten, Jane. 1990. "Towards a Feminist Reassessment of Intellectual Virtue." *Hypatia* 5(3): 1–14.
Code, Lorraine. 2006. *Ecological Thinking*. New York: Oxford University Press.
Dalmiya, Vrinda. 2016. *Caring to Know*. Oxford: Oxford University Press.
Daukas, Nancy. 2019. "Feminist Virtue Epistemology." In: Heather Battaly (ed.), *The Routledge Handbook of Virtue Epistemology*. New York: Routledge, pp. 379–391.
Dillon, Robin. 2004. "Kant on Arrogance and Self-Respect." In: Cheshire Calhoun (ed.), *Setting the Moral Compass*. New York: Oxford University Press, pp. 191–216.
Dillon, Robin. 2012. "Critical Character Theory." In: Sharon L. Crasnow and Anita M. Superson (eds.), *Out from the Shadows*. Oxford: Oxford University Press, pp. 83–114.
Dillon, Robin. 2015. "Humility, Arrogance, and Self-Respect in Kant and Hill." In: M. Timmons and R. N. Johnson (eds.), *Reason, Value, and Respect*. Oxford: Oxford University Press, pp. 43–69.
Dillon, Robin. In press. "Self-Respect, Arrogance, and Power." In: Richard Dean and Oliver Sensen (eds.), *Respect for Persons*. New York: Oxford University Press.
Driver, Julia. 2001. *Uneasy Virtue*. Cambridge: Cambridge University Press.
Fricker, Miranda. 2007. *Epistemic Injustice*. Oxford: Oxford University Press.
Kwong, Jack M. C. 2015. "Epistemic Injustice and Open-Mindedness." *Hypatia* 30(2): 337–351.
Mills, Charles W. 2018. "Through a Glass, Whitely: Ideal Theory as Epistemic Injustice." *Proceedings and Addresses of the American Philosophical Association* 92: 43–77.
Norlock, Kathryn J. 2018. "Perpetual Struggle." *Hypatia*. doi:10.1111/hypa.12452.
Silvermint, Daniel. 2017. "Rage and Virtuous Resistance." *The Journal of Political Philosophy* 25(4): 461–486.
Slote, Michael. 2001. *Morals from Motives*. Oxford: Oxford University Press.
Tessman, Lisa. 2005. *Burdened Virtues*. New York: Oxford University Press.
Whitcomb, Dennis, Heather Battaly, Jason Baehr, and Daniel Howard-Snyder. 2017. "Intellectual Humility: Owning Our Limitations." *Philosophy and Phenomenological Research* XCIV(3): 509–539.
Whitcomb, Dennis, Heather Battaly, Jason Baehr, and Daniel Howard-Snyder. 2020. "The Puzzle of Humility and Disparity." In: Alessandra Tanesini, Mark Alfano and Michael Lynch (eds.), *The Routledge Handbook of the Philosophy of Humility*. New York: Routledge.
Zagzebski, Linda. 1996. *Virtues of the Mind*. Cambridge: Cambridge University Press.

PART 4

Humility in religious thought

16
HUMILITY AMONG THE ANCIENT GREEKS

Sophie Grace Chappell

> Perhaps the most notorious passage in Aristotle's *Ethics* is [NE 1123a33–1125a17] where he describes the *megalopsychos*, or great-souled, or magnanimous man—sometimes [as by Ross] translated as 'the proud man'. These are some of the things that Aristotle says about him: the magnanimous man thinks himself worthy of great things and *is* worthy of them. The greatest thing is honour [actually NE 1123b18, 1124a17 says only that honour is the greatest of the external goods] and it is therefore with this that the magnanimous man is most concerned. Magnanimity is a sort of crown of the virtues [1124a1] (and the magnanimous man is great in each of the virtues); therefore it is hard to be truly magnanimous. The magnanimous man does not run into trifling dangers, nor is he fond of danger, because he honours few things; but he will face great dangers, and when he is in danger he is unsparing of his life, knowing that there are conditions on which life is not worth having. And he is the sort of man to confer benefits, but he is ashamed of receiving them; for the one is a mark of a superior, the other of an inferior. He is open in his hate and in his love; he does not flatter. He does not make his life revolve around anyone, unless it be a friend; for this is slavish, and for this reason all flatterers are servile and people lacking in self-respect are flatterers. He is one to possess beautiful and profitless things rather than profitable and useful ones; for this is proper to a character that suffices to itself. Further, a slow step is thought appropriate to the magnanimous man, a deep voice and a level utterance; for the man who takes few things seriously is not likely to be hurried, nor the man who thinks nothing great to be excited, while a shrill voice and a rapid gait are the results of hurry and excitement.
>
> (John Casey, Pagan Virtue 199–200)

> The New Testament not only praises virtues of which Aristotle knows nothing—faith, hope, and love—and says nothing about virtues such as *phronesis* which are crucial for Aristotle, but it praises at least one quality as a virtue which Aristotle seems to count as one of the vices relative to [*megalopsychia*], namely humility. Moreover since the New Testament quite clearly sees the rich as destined for the pains of Hell, it is clear that

> the key virtues cannot be available to them; yet they *are* available to slaves ... Aristotle would certainly not have admired Jesus Christ and he would have been horrified by St Paul.
>
> (Alasdair MacIntyre, After Virtue 182, 184)

16.1

In the West we are the inheritors of two main virtue-ethical traditions, the Christian tradition and the pagan[1] Greek tradition. Both traditions are flourishingly alive today, both in our individual psyches and in our lives together. It is often said (as suggested by my two epigraphs) that one major difference between them is that the Christian tradition recognises, and the pagan tradition does not, a virtue of humility. One of the concerns that motivate this essay is the historical question whether and in what sense this commonplace might be true, in particular of the Greek tradition from Homer to Aristotle. Another (though I won't have space to say much about it here) is the philosophical question whether we *should* recognise a virtue of humility, and if so, what that virtue should look like here and now.

I say "whether *we* should recognise" it, and I say "here and now", because in investigating any virtue, humility included, we must always keep in mind that real virtues are not timeless essences but sociological and psychological realities. Virtues are nodes and concentrations[2] of disposition, belief, attitude, response, vision, and expectation, actually present in real agents (individual or joint), in real and particular social settings.

This point narrows the gap that I may seem to have just opened up, between my historical and my philosophical question. All the way back to Socrates, philosophers have tended to hunt for ahistorical and abstract accounts of the virtues, allegedly captured in counterexample-proof iff-definitions, and relativised to nothing except an equally timeless abstraction called "human nature".

Now certainly, there is such a thing as human nature. But real human nature is neither timeless nor abstract, as we know from science; obviously from evolutionary science, but from anthropological, ethological, sociological, historical, and psychological science too. As we actually see it, human nature is always and essentially *socialised*, and that means socialised in some historically specific way. We might even say, with an echo of Pico della Mirandola (and indeed of Sartre), that *homo sapiens* is the animal whose nature is to have *no* nature that is not also a culture.[3]

Equally certainly, our understanding of the virtues should have some sort of dependence on our account of human nature. So given the historical variety of socialisations of human nature, there must be a corresponding variety of understandings of the virtues. (To say so is not to espouse the dubious thesis of relativism; it is to recognise the obvious fact of relativisation.) Our understanding of the virtues here and now needs to be grounded in the history of that variety, and seen as a continuation of that history. Understanding a virtue by way of an iff-definition can be useful, where such a definition is available. But quite often it is at least equally useful to see why no such definition is available, or why, even if it is, that formula in itself radically underdetermines what counts as a realisation of it in any particular society or psychology. Either way we need to engage with the messiness of history.

In the case of humility, it is particularly obvious that this sort of historical inquiry will be more useful than the standard iff-definitional approach. For even if we are historically minded, we are enough the heirs of Socrates to want to start our inquiry into humility by saying, at least at an intuitive level, what humility *is*. But this is not easy, because intuitively, and philosophically too, we say and think such a dizzying variety of things about humility that it is most unlikely that any unitary definition could make good sense of them all. So for instance, in the common thinking of our society, "humble" can be taken straightforwardly as a descriptive adjective, meaning not much more than "poor". Another word that can also mean something close to "poor" is "modest"; and it is widely thought, too, both by philosophers and by non-philosophers, that modesty is pretty much the same thing as humility. To my ear at least, modesty is about how you present yourself to others; humility is about how you see yourself irrespective of others. But even if my ear is right, such nuances of distinction often go missing. Or humility can be praised as a refreshing lack of side, a pleasing down-to-earth-ness—and appropriately enough, given the word's etymology. (It comes from the Latin *humilitas*, cp. *humus* "earth".[4] Two other Latin words that also seem to derive from *humus* are *humor*, "humour", and *homo*, "human"—cp. Hebrew *adam*, which means both "earth" and "man/human".)

Sometimes we also view humility with puzzlement, as a kind of amiably bumbling, absent-minded blindness to one's own merits, as arguably exhibited (relative particularly to his own *intellectual* virtues) by Socrates in dialogues like the *Symposium*. So viewed, humility seems to involve a kind of self-forgetfulness; but "humility" can also name a disposition that is all about *focusing* on myself, constant self-monitoring to make sure I don't get too uppity. On that sort of view, humility can seem as puzzling a virtue as faith. Those who take faith to be "Believing whole-heartedly what you know isn't true" may well likewise take humility to be a "virtue of ignorance" (as Driver argues modesty is, JP 1989) or even self-deception, and/or deliberately fostering a false low opinion of yourself. (So Sidgwick 1907: 334: "humility prescribes a low opinion of our merits: but if our merits are comparably high, it seems strange to direct us to have a low opinion of them".) People may also see humility simply as low self-esteem, and so as a symptom of poor mental health; perhaps even, as Hume proposes, as a vice.[5] Or again, more darkly, humility can be seen as a pious humbug of the Uriah Heep variety, a smarmy pretence of self-effacement that—none too successfully—masks the inner rancour, *ressentiment*, and relentless will-to-power of a small and ugly soul. (Is there a more Nietzschean character than Heep in all Dickens?)

Given all this diversity, it is not easy to follow Socrates' advice, and start from a *definition* of humility. Very probably, the attempt to find one will itself drive us back to the historical question where all that diversity came from; to which I now turn.

16.2

The commonplace of recent ethics that the pagan Greeks had no virtue of humility is evidenced at least to this extent: it's certainly true that, if you look at classical Greek philosophers' tables or lists of virtues, a virtue called humility does not appear in them. In Plato and Aristotle, it is not even clear what the word for "humility" would be. Moreover, one of Aristotle's virtues is, famously or notoriously, *megalopsychia*, a quality of character that some modern commentators (Sir David Ross, for example) think Anglophones should call *pride*. (Another of Aristotle's virtues is *megaloprepeia*, which perhaps stands to *megalopsychia* as I have suggested modesty stands to humility, the one being external, about how one presents oneself, and the other internal, about how one sees oneself. More about *megalopsychia*, and about pride, in due course.)[6]

However, the fact that Plato and Aristotle say little or nothing directly about any such virtue does not mean that humility is not an important value in their society. The opposite is true, and obviously true as soon as we look more widely in classical antiquity than just at the best-known and best-preserved philosophers—something which quite a few self-described "Aristotelian ethicists" perhaps do not do quite as much as they should.

For every classical Greek thinker from Homer to Socrates, it is an essential requirement for humans that they should know their place in the cosmos, and avoid *hybris*, overstepping the mark, seeking to rival the gods and thereby, perhaps, attracting their fatal attention. Socrates himself is a case—as we shall see, a special case—of this careful avoidance of *hybris*: that is precisely the point of his famous claim to know nothing, and likewise of his taking to heart of the Delphic injunction "Know thyself".

A century before Socrates, Heracleitus applies the same principle of keeping within our bounds not only to men, but to the cosmic order as well, all the way up to the sun ("the sun will not overstep its marks, *metra*, or *dike* will find it out", DK22 B94). For Heracleitus, indeed, everything in the universe is governed by the notion of *metron*, measure or limit. And for Heracleitus as for every other ancient Greek, *hybris* is "outrage", i.e. going beyond (French *outre*) the limits set by nature.

It is also in the spirit of avoiding rivalry with the gods that the Chorus of sea-nymphs in the Aeschylean *Prometheus Vinctus* deplore Io's *mésalliance* with Zeus, precisely on the grounds that such divine dalliances are certain to lead to disaster—in Io's case, the rather farcical disaster of being turned into a cow by the jealous Hera.

> A wise man he, a wise man he indeed,
> who first weighed in his mind and spoke this truth:
> that love of like to like most answers need,
> that a poor man's love of a rich bride breeds—reproof,
> that the slave should never seek the hand of her master,
> that a god's seed mixed with a mortal's brings disaster.
>
> Never then, O never, Fates, bestow
> on me the trembling glory of Zeus' concubine.
> No bridegroom high for me who am below,
> for my slight self no Olympian lord divine.
> For look at Io, barren, lost, unmanned,
> unwombed, unhoused by Hera's hard command.
>
> *([Aeschylus], Prometheus Vinctus 889–903)*[7]

No one, the nymphs tell their audience, should reach too far above their station in the world. And often that thought is naturally manifested in a superstitious fear of attracting nemesis by crowing too much over one's successes. The same fear lingers to this day in the southern Mediterranean, in the superstition of the "evil eye" and indeed in the very word "envy" (Latin *invidia,* from *in-videre*, "to look on with hostility"). This is partly why, in Herodotus, Solon advises Croesus to "call no man happy until his life is completed" (*Histories* 1.56; cp. Euripides, *Troiades* 510, Ovid *Metaphorphoses* 3.131–152).

The same formula comes at a key moment in Aeschylus' *Oresteia*, the moment that spells Agamemnon's ruin. This is the point where Clytaemestra succeeds in cajoling him, despite his pious reluctance, to tread the gorgeously dyed tapestry that, *not* like Penelope, she in his absence has woven. "No, do not make me walk this envious way", pleads Agamemnon,

> and draw the waiting wrath down from Above.
> These things are honours for the gods, not men.
> The man who walks and soils such silken gear—
> a fool does this; a twice-fool, with no fear.
> I am no god. Give me a human's due.
> This sheening scarlet broidure-web I call
> no footpath for my trampling to tear through.

God's greatest wisdom-gift is we not fall
into false wisdom we mistake for true.
Living by this thought only quells our fears:
"Call no man happy till he end with happy years".

(Aeschylus, Agamemnon 921–930)

Despite these words he quickly yields to her, and Clytaemestra sees his *hybris*, and in the quiet and deadly ironies of her extraordinary *estin thalassa* speech, celebrates his coming death as a thing now inevitable (*Agamemnon* 958–971).

Or take Sophocles' *Antigone*, where the central question is whether Antigone by seeking the same decent burial for both her dead brothers, or Creon by seeking to prevent her from equally honouring the "loyal" Eteocles and the "traitor" Polyneices, is overstepping the bounds set by their place in the world. The *Antigone* is not, *pace* some distinguished readers including Hegel and Nussbaum, a drama which pits "the value of the political" against "the value of the personal". The statement that Antigone wishes to make is *both* personal and political, and the catastrophic loss that Creon endures during the play is both personal and political too. For both Antigone and Creon, the question is how to respond to demands that are at once personal and political; and for both of them, the question is how to do this in a way that does not overstep humanity's ethical bounds.[8]

Antigone is also, in some crucial respects, an instance of that key class of afflicted ones in the ancient world, the *suppliant*. Suppliants are everywhere in classical Greek literature, from Homer on: the *Iliad* begins and ends with a suppliant.[9] And from Homer on we see that among the most familiar appeals that a suppliant can make is to rouse their vanquisher's fear of overstepping the human limits. Such an appeal can certainly be overridden, and in the bleak and brutal war-world of the *Iliad*, it usually is. But even when it is overridden, it addresses to the vanquisher a demand that he must respond to somehow. In the most famous supplication scene in the whole poem, *Iliad* 21.64–137, Lycaon's main plea to Achilles is that because this is the second time that Achilles has captured him in battle, there must be some special tie of Fate between them, which Achilles will avoid *hybris* only by respecting. "Feel *aidos* towards me" (shame), Lycaon implores, "and have pity" (σὺ δέ μ' αἴδεο καί μ' ἐλέησον, *Iliad* 21.74).

Pity, mercy on the suppliant, is close here conceptually to its etymological near-neighbour, piety: to see that I have reason to spare my victim is to see both him and myself in the light of our shared vulnerability to the gods. Thus the shame that Lycaon means to arouse is not (as a Nietzschean might suppose) an embarrassment felt by Achilles at Lycaon's helplessness, but a willingness in Achilles to recognise the constraints that should inhibit even the most exalted mortal, given that he is, permanently and unavoidably, as helpless before the gods as his suppliant is before him. Achilles' unbending reply is that since Patroclus' death he no longer wants to spare *any* Trojans, and that *aidos* no longer gives him any reason to be inhibited by his own vulnerability; for the gods have doomed him already. Yet Lycaon's pleas do demand *some* answer; Achilles cannot just kill him and say nothing. He has to justify his action in killing a suppliant, however stark his justification may be. This is a kind of limiting case of the recognition that even heroes stand under the ethical demand that they keep within the bounds that are set for mortals; only so can they avoid *hybris*.

What then, in the conceptual scheme of early classical Greek ethics, is the virtue that restrains a person from *hybris*, overstepping, not knowing your place, in the multifarious forms that, as we have now seen, it can take? In Homeric and archaic Greek thought, such restraint falls within the remit of a virtue that is usually called *sophrosune*, "self-control" (literally "healthiness of judgement"): that, apparently, is what Agamemnon lacked, in being too easily persuaded—and moreover by a woman—to trample over the triumphal tapestry. But alternatively, and equally possibly in the right contexts, such restraint can be seen as the work of the virtue called *dikaiosune*, "justice" (literally "doing what is indicated": *deiknumi*, cognate with German *zeigen* and Latin *in-dic-are* and English "digit"): it is justice that Antigone and Creon are disputing about, and their conflict, as I have argued, is both ethical and political—and theological too.[10] Or again, the virtue that avoids *hybris* may be called *hosiotes,* piety (literally "holiness"). It is this virtue that Lycaon vainly begs Achilles to display, and it is piety that Io lacks in allowing herself to be seduced by Zeus—not that she had any choice, but fate can be pitiless. Agamemnon also lacks piety, despite a few fine words: "I am no god. Give me a human's due", he piously says—then tramples over the silk.

Whatever the manifestations or particular forms of *hybris*-avoiding virtue, there is always something close to our humility in it, and when we seek to translate the Greek terms for this sort of virtue into our own English vocabulary, the language of humility can easily be—sometimes should be—the one that we reach for.

Something rather like our humility *is*, then, an important part of the ethics of early classical Greece.[11] But along with that first-order conclusion comes the methodological point that there can be very different ways of listing the virtues or dividing up their domains—and that nonetheless very similar particular verdicts about how to feel, how to respond, and how to act can derive from these diverse lists.[12] Thus what we typically think of as one unitary virtue of humility, the archaic Greeks regarded as a requirement to keep within human bounds that they distributed across and found within a whole range of different virtues.[13]

16.3

It is a familiar point in classical history of ideas that the archaic Greek outlook, the one represented, in their different ways, by both Homer and Aeschylus, both Sophocles and Heracleitus, had broken down by the time of Plato and Socrates. The story of how and why it broke down is, centrally, the story is one of what we would call *secularisation*.

Between Hesiod's time and Socrates', traditional theological conceptions lost at least some of their cultural and psychological grip. This matters to the historian of humility, insofar as the central motivating thoughts of archaic Greek humility were "Remember you are mortal" and "Do not provoke the jealousy of the gods". It is no accident that the main critics of the traditional theology in sixth- and fifth-century-BC Greece were also critics of the traditional "quiet"[14] virtues of restraint, discretion, moderation, fairness, pity, and indeed humility that are dictated by that theology. When a person begins to think that, if there is a God at all, then that God can be nothing like the Zeus of Homer, then he naturally begins also to question the traditional notion that we should fear the envy or spite (or justice) of a Homeric Zeus. What people will say is permitted to them, in the absence of theological sanctions, is familiar from the "sophists"—professional savants whose ethical teaching seems usually to have had very little theological content, and was often strikingly revisionist. For Thrasymachus, Callicles, or Polus, the message does not even seem to have been the Dostoyevskian "If God does not exist, then anything is permitted". Their message, rather, is simply "Anything is permitted"—provided only you are strong enough and shameless enough to get away with it.[15]

> To those who were princes from the start, or to those who were men enough by nature to achieve some kind of rule or kingship or dynastic power on their own—to people like that, what could be more contemptible, more pernicious, than *temperance* and *justice*? If it is open to you to enjoy the good things of life without anyone to

> hinder you, why should you impose upon yourself the control of herd morality, herd reasoning, herd disapproval? ... Justice and happiness means luxury, intemperance, and libertinism, backed up by brute force. All the rest—those man-made conventions that run contrary to nature—is nothing but a fine pretence; it is worthless drivel.
>
> (Callicles, at Gorgias 492b2–c8)

Amoralist sophists like Callicles were hybristic god-defiers. On the empirical ground that typically the wickedness of the wicked is *not* punished by Zeus but rewarded by circumstances, these sophists advocated a life quite free from fear of the gods. Their leading idea—which Nietzsche endorses—is that the natural life, for anyone who is strong enough to achieve it, is a life of luxury won by ruthlessness and unimpeded by the scruples, the humility, and the shame (*aidos*) that god-fearingness gives rise to. Their ethics was perceived as an outrage upon traditional Greek values, and that is what they meant it to be.

Nietzsche, then, had things back to front when he argued, in *Twilight* and *Genealogy* (and elsewhere), that Socrates was the great opponent of the Greeks' traditional values—a rationalist decadent whose "knife-thrust of the syllogism" was the assault of the resentful mob upon the noble and anti-moralistic aristocrats, whose true values men like Callicles represented. On the contrary, in Socrates' time—as the *Meno, Gorgias*, and other dialogues all demonstrate—sophistical amoralism was a historically recent innovation, and the sophists who went around advocating it were decidedly looked down upon by real aristocrats. Moreover, to charge traditionalist aristocrats with holding sophistical values was a scandalous charge; for sophistical amoralism was, and was meant to be, a shocking and iconoclastic heresy.

This much is clear from the reactions to it of so many characters in Plato's dialogues: Anytus in the *Meno*, for example, or Glaucon and Adeimantus in the *Republic*. Glaucon's famous challenge to Socrates[16], at the beginning of *Republic* II, is to answer the question "Why be just?" without reference to the traditional rewards and punishments—divine or human. The whole point of the question is that Glaucon is looking for an answer to sophistical amoralism that will vindicate traditional Greek values. Given the waning of the older religious orthodoxy, it will not help for this answer to appeal to the vengeance of Zeus. But fundamentally—*pace* Nietzsche—what Glaucon is asking Socrates to do is not to replace traditional values, but to rescue them by providing them with a new and a philosophical justification.

Whether those values *can* be rescued in this way, whether they are still the same values at all if they are re-presented on the completely new basis that Plato wants to give them, is a standing question for every reader of Plato. One familiar aspect of this question is salient for present purposes insofar as what we call humility falls, as I have described, within the scope of what the Greeks called justice, *dikaiosyne*. This is the celebrated question whether there is a fallacy of equivocation about justice in Plato's *Republic* (Sachs 1963)—that is, whether what the *Republic* calls *dikaiosyne* is anything like the same thing as what Plato's contemporaries had traditionally meant by the word. But then, if there is this question about *dikaiosyne* in the *Republic*, there is clearly a parallel question about the *Republic*'s other three principal[17] virtues—courage, wisdom, and again *sophrosyne*.

Something that gets less attention, but which is at least as relevant when we are thinking about pagan Greek humility, is the discussion of *sophrosyne*, temperance, that is staged in the *Charmides*. As in the other "Socratic" dialogues, Plato's characters do not succeed in defining the target quality of *sophrosyne* (which, significantly or not, is never quite called a virtue in the *Charmides*: Levine 2016). But they do along the way review five interesting candidate definitions: (1) That *sophrosyne* is quietness, the almost Thucydidean *hesychiotes* (159b). (2) That it is "shame" or modesty, *aidos* (160e). (3) That it is "doing your own business" (161b). (4) That it is self-knowledge (164d), a formula perhaps offered because, *inter alia*, of Socrates' endorsement of the Delphi *gnothi seauton*. And (5) that it is knowledge of the kinds of knowledge and of itself—which means that *sophrosyne* is also knowledge of knowledge *and of ignorance* (166e); a formula perhaps proffered in allusion to Socrates' reputation, whether or not earned, for saying "All I know is that I know nothing".[18]

The dialogue's official line is that none of these formulae can possibly be correct. For temperance to be a good to us, it needs to be knowledge *of the good*, but Socrates professes that he cannot see what kind of good *sophrosyne* would be the knowledge of (175a). But as so often in the Socratic dialogues, we should look beyond the official line. The *Charmides* itself is a rich source of possible answers to that question, some of them in the last paragraph. With an eye on 160e, *sophrosyne* might be defined—and, modulo the deficiencies of any simple formula, really rather plausibly defined—as the knowledge when it is right or fitting to be ashamed, and when not. Or picking up on 161b, we might say—again, pretty plausibly—that *sophrosyne* means understanding what *is* your own business, and what isn't. Such a view of *sophrosyne* would be very close to the definition of it that Plato's Socrates explicitly advocates at *Republic* 432a–b—that *sophrosyne* is an agreement between the parts of the city, or soul, about which of them should make it its business to rule; and even closer to the *Republic*'s definition of *dikaiosyne*—as, precisely, "doing your own business", *to ta hautou prattein*.

One last intriguing feature of the *Charmides*, taken as a text on the pagan-Greek conceptions that are closest to our notion of humility, is that it contains at least two anticipations of the modern idea that there is something paradoxical about humility; that if it is a virtue, it needs to be what some (following Roy Sorensen) have called a *blindspot* virtue, or what others (following Driver 1989) have called a *virtue of ignorance*.

One of the two passages I have in mind here is 158c–d, where Socrates asks the beautiful young Charmides whether he, Charmides, "already has a sufficient share of *sophrosyne*, or is lacking in it". To answer this, Charmides needs to know not only how much temperance he has, but also (as it were) how much temperance he *hasn't*—at what points and in what ways Charmides' disposition falls short of temperance. This paradox we will come back to below. The problem that is more immediately obvious to Charmides himself is—he tells Socrates, and blushes with shame as he says it (158c5)—more like a social dilemma facing any young gentleman of good manners:

> "For," he said, "if I say I am *not* temperate, that is both an absurd accusation to make against myself, and also me giving the lie to Critias and many others, who by his account think I *am* temperate. But if on the other hand I say I *am* temperate, and sing my own praises, then that seems repellent behaviour. So I don't know what I should reply to you."
>
> *(158c9–d7)*

If *sophrosyne* is a virtue of self-restraint, then if I claim to have it, that might just seem to show that I don't; no genuinely self-restrained person needs to *say* that she is self-restrained. A wide variety of arguably virtuous dispositions show something similar—we may call it a *blindspot* feature: no one can talk (or not much) about her own ability to keep silent, no one can plan to be spontaneous, no one can spend their lives focusing on making themselves focused on others. How exactly its blindspot shows up for any blindspot disposition depends on the particular disposition in question. But, most relevantly here, it seems obvious that it is self-defeating to boast about your own modesty or humility; it may even be contrary to humility just to *believe* that you are humble. In which case, it is a necessary condition of being humble that you not believe that you are humble; which makes humility, in Driver's terminology, a "virtue of ignorance".

The other passage is 167b–169c, in which Socrates argues—in a refutation of Critias that makes Critias too blush with shame, 169c8—that temperance cannot be knowledge of knowledge and of ignorance, because, he says, "There cannot be knowledge of ignorance". To see Socrates' point, read it as the claim that "You cannot know the answer to the question: 'What true propositions are there that I do not know?'"; or as the claim that "You cannot know the answer to the question: 'What false propositions are there that I believe?'"; or indeed as both claims. Those two claims are plainly true; and they seem to threaten the whole idea of knowing what you don't know or understanding what you don't understand, an idea that, as Plato points out, is often taken to be at least part of what humility involves. As Wittgenstein says in the Preface to the *Tractatus*: "In order to set a limit to thought, we would have to find both sides of the limit thinkable".

16.4

There is much in Plato's mindset—and, one speculates, in the historical Socrates' before him—that equipped him to question a central feature of the ethical tradition that he inherited that is of the first importance in thinking about pagan Greek humility: namely the honour-code, the aristocrats' preoccupation with the winning of glory (*kudos*) and the protection of honour (*timê*).—On one reading of the *Iliad*—a reading which to me seems unquestionably right, and which is canonically expressed in our era by Simone Weil in her famous essay "L'*Iliade* ou le poème de la force"—the destructive power of this preoccupation is a key moral lesson of Homer.

But Homer is a great poet, and great poets may *show* moral lessons, but they never *tell* them; they are always ambiguous; the greater they are, the *more* ambiguous they are (Tolstoy, for example, comes close to ruining *War & Peace* by a *lack* of ambiguity). The *Iliad* can also be read, and often has been, as a celebration of the aristocratic honour-code. If it were such a celebration, it would not follow that it was also an implicit dismissal of any kind of positive evaluation of humility; honour and humility coexist as ideals in plenty of other places, for instance in the mediaeval Christian-courtly aristocratic romance-cycle that we know as Thomas Malory's *Morte d'Arthur*. Nonetheless, that Plato read Homer as implicitly celebrating, not questioning, the honour-code, and as thereby rejecting values like justice, restraint, and humility as Plato understood them, is obviously one of the reasons for his emphatic rejection of Homer. We may surmise that Plato's rejection of Homer was driven, too, by the way contemporary sophists such as Ion were using Homer to reinforce their own exaltations of force and violence. Socrates of Alopece, the humble maker of clay statues, was a teacher and friend of the very aristocrats who most upheld the Athenian honour-code—people from noble families like Plato's. Yet he stood out as someone who questioned and opposed and often plain ridiculed that code, and thereby made space for a more extended notion of *sophrosyne* as including many elements of what we call humility. And in this Plato followed Socrates.

Like Socrates and unlike Plato, Aristotle appraised the ethos of the aristocracy of classical Athens as an outsider; but a different kind of outsider. During the years he lived at Athens (367–347 BC, and intermittently thereafter till his death in Euboea in 322 BC) he had the half-citizen status of a resident alien, a *metoikos* or "metic", someone whose home (*oikos*) was with (*meta*) the Athenians and who had the protection of their laws, but no right to vote or stand for office. Aristotle seems to have been an admirer both of Plato and of the Athenian society that Plato so fiercely criticised; his central methodological dictum was always the broadly conservative and deeply anti-Platonic *tithenai ta phainomena* (NE 1145b2–7), "preserve as much as possible of our already-established understanding of the world"; and he was famously tutor to the one man above all in whom the Calliclean or Thrasymachean vision of a proud life of *kudos* and *timê* won by extreme violence actually came true—Alexander the Great. It is then perhaps unsurprising that Aristotle offers a quite different response from Plato's to the tradition of the honour-code—and, especially in the *Eudemian Ethics*,[19] seems in fact to be something like a defender of that code.

My thesis so far has been that the pagan-Greek ethical concept closest to our concept of humility is the concept of avoiding *hybris*, overreaching or overstepping one's bounds, which (I have argued) is an important part of the content of at least three of their virtues—*hosiotes*, *sophrosyne,* and *dikaiosyne.* But we come now to an obvious objection to describing the avoidance of *hybris* as humility in anything like our sense. This is that whether a person counts as humble by not overreaching his bounds depends, after all, on what his bounds *are.* But Aristotle's "man of virtue" is the *megalopsychos*, the great-souled man. And the whole point about the *megalopsychos* is that, for him, the bounds of what he can do without *hybris* are far more extensive than for other people: "he claims great things, and is entitled to them" (NE 1123b1–4). Perhaps surprisingly to us, for Aristotle truthfulness turns out to be a matter of self-assessment, and a mean between "boastfulness" (*alazoneia*) and "self-deprecation" (*eironeia*) (NE IV.7); thus the *megalopsychos* has a high opinion of himself, *and is right to* (Curzer 1990, Curzer 2012). The bounds that the *megalopsychos* must not overstep are different from those that apply to other mortals.

Perhaps, indeed, there is at least one place where there are no bounds *at all* on the *megalopsychos*, namely when he is engaging in *theôria*. It is not clear that, in this context, anything he could do would count as *hybris* or overstepping. Instead, at least as Aristotle advises, he should simply disregard the usual advice to "remember that he is a mortal", and should rather, *eph' hoson endekhetai, athanatizein* ("seek to be, as far as possible, divine", NE 1177b36). It matters here that in Aristotle's schema the "intellectual virtues" do not, unlike the "virtues of character", lie in a mean.

On Aristotle's character-sketch of the *megalopsychos*, John Casey comments (*Pagan Virtue* 200):

> The magnanimous (or "proud") man has not proved to be the most durably popular of Aristotle's ethical portraits ... The kindest thing that now seems to be said about the *megalopsychos* is that he is a crystallization of an aristocratic ethic prevalent in Aristotle's time, which Aristotle is not able to transcend.

But if people do say that, they are surely missing something. Why would Aristotle not be "able to transcend" the prevalent aristocratic ethic? The idea that he couldn't suggests that that ethic had never then been questioned, so that it could not have crossed his mind to go beyond it. But this suggestion is obviously false: Aristotle had spent twenty years studying with the main philosopher who *did* put in question the aristocratic ethic, and along with it the ideas of Greek racial supremacy, of male superiority, and of anything like a natural division between slaves and free men, namely Plato. Behind Plato stood the even more radically questioning and (as Nietzsche pointed out) decidedly proletarian figure of Socrates. Alongside both Plato and Socrates, throughout Aristotle's time and before it, the aristocratic ethic had been subjected to open questioning and disruption by the Athenian dramatists for over 100 years. Before them all, there is—as Simone Weil and others have shown—a marked strain in Homer himself of spiritual, but not political, egalitarianism: of the idea that there are deep commonalities to all human lives, that being a king like Odysseus rather a swineherd like Eumaeus, or a Greek rather than a Trojan, or a man rather than a woman, or even a free man rather than a slave, is a relatively shallow division of natures compared with what those natures have in common. In the Attic dramatists as in (for instance) Shakespeare, the artistic imagination could and did make good sense—and great art—of all these ways of being human. If Aristotle refused the vision of Andromache's humanity, or Ion's, or Atossa's, or Hecuba's, or Alcestis', that was indeed a *refusal* on his part; it was not that he was never offered the vision in the first place.

So *pace* Casey, it was hardly that, by some accident of history, Aristotle was "not able to transcend" the aristocratic ethic. He chose not to transcend it. Like Plato in the *Republic* before him, Aristotle sought new foundations for a revisionary version of social elitism. His notion of the *megalopsychos* is part of this project, and what it shows is that Aristotle was much more willing than the Plato of the *Republic* to accommodate Calliclean and Thrasymachean thoughts about the naturally superior man. Plato's deep scepticism about ordinary opinions, and his inheritance of Socrates' at-least-in-practice egalitarianism, made him prepared to advance a theory of human nature and the ordering of society that was radically at odds with how things actually were in contemporary Athens. Aristotle, by contrast, works as we have seen on the basis that there is always *something* in the views of "the many and the wise"; moreover, for at least part of his career he was tutor to a prince who turned into a world-dictator. Perhaps it is not altogether surprising that Aristotle turns out to be the proponent of a revisionary defence of the aristocratic ethic that is also, by way of a compromise, very happy to follow sophists like Callicles and Thrasymachus at least some of the way, in setting up "the great man" as an ideal to which there is reason to aspire for all those who can (not that there are so many of them). So understood, Aristotle's idealisation of the *megalopsychos* stands in parallel with his effort to find arguments for racial and gender supremacy. In the context of his background culture, his project is an eccentric and, in the strict sense of the word, a reactionary project (Chappell 2010).

16.5

Clearly Aristotle is no great friend of any substantive virtue of humility. He does, like all other ancient Greek thinkers—and indeed the idea is close to truism—hold that each of should avoid overreaching or overstepping the bounds that are proper to us. But that is not saying much when he also believes that the proper bounds can vary radically for different people.

Here too we see the close connection between the ethical concept of humility, as we have it, and the ethical concept of *equality*. (As noted, again, by John Casey: "It goes without saying that he is directly opposed to Christian humility. But modern dislike of him extends far beyond the ranks of believing Christians. He offends that spirit of equality—partly rooted, of course, in Christianity—which few of us can escape even if we try": *Pagan Virtue* p.200.)

To think that each of us is right to have the modest self-assessment that is a key part of substantive humility is already to think that each of us alike occupies a rather small place in the world. On any sober and realistic account of humans' place in the cosmos, that thought is surely both true and salutary. But there is at least a tendency in the pagan Greek honour-code, as indeed in any honour-code, to ignore, sideline, or simply reject that true thought: to think instead, for instance, that nothing matters more than winning political glory here and now. On any sober and realistic assessment, such a thought is straightforwardly insane. Though maybe, as Douglas Adams suggests, a true sense of our cosmic smallness might also be a challenge to our sanity:

> Trin Tragula ... was a dreamer, a thinker, a speculative philosopher or, as his wife would have it, an idiot. And she would nag him incessantly about the utterly inordinate amount of time he spent staring out into space, or mulling over the mechanics of safety pins, or doing spectrographic analyses of pieces of fairy cake. "Have some sense of proportion!" she would say, sometimes as often as thirty-eight times in a single day.

> And so he built the Total Perspective Vortex just to show her. And into one end he plugged the whole of reality as extrapolated from a piece of fairy cake, and into the other end he plugged his wife: so that when he turned it on she saw in one instant the whole infinity of creation and herself in relation to it. To Trin Tragula's horror, the shock completely annihilated her brain; but to his satisfaction he realized that he had proved conclusively that if life is going to exist in a Universe of this size, then the one thing it cannot afford to have is a sense of proportion.
>
> (Douglas Adams, The Restaurant at the End of the Universe, ch.11; accessed online at https://hitchhikers.fandom.com/wiki/Trin_Tragula)

Much of our ordinary, self-interested life is—as Adams' satire brings out—precisely about failing to see ourselves in true relation to the hugeness of things; and the thoughts that the honour-code encourages, about glory and success and honour here and now among others similarly pre-occupied, are thoughts that take us in absolutely the opposite direction from facing such realities. To his credit Aristotle does not always go along with such thoughts: see the visible deities remark in (NE 1141b1), and Aristotle's rejection of honour as an aim for life in (NE 1095b27-30). But sometimes he does, and the reasons why are not hard to see: because he gets caught up in a cult of the great man that, for the tutor of Alexander, was perhaps only too tempting.

We move one step closer to our own substantive conception of humility when we get to the age of the Stoics, whose "cosmopolitan" ideal is a vision of a universe in which all humans are both small and also equal, and where each individual is called upon to work together with others for the common good. That is a step in the direction of our notion of humility, even if, in practice, the Stoic vision was often put on hold, and the actual living of actual Stoics, like that of Epicureans such as the Roman poet Horace (see e.g. *Odes* 2.10), was not so much a life of humble and equal cooperative striving for the good, but rather a kind of ironic distancing from *all* society's corrupt concerns.

We get closer again to the modern notion of humility when, at the coming of Christianity, we add to this cosmopolitanism both the markedly and sometimes studiedly demotic social tone of the actual Christian communities—at least one early opponent of Christianity, Celsus, pointed to the disproportionately lowly demographics of Christianity as a reason to reject it (Origen, *Against Celsus* 3.44, 59, 64)—and also the idea that there is something in each of us that biases us away from a true self-assessment and a true humility, from seeing ourselves truly as *small in the world*, and that needs to be broken into pieces before we can see and choose straight, and without that bias. We might call this bias, for want of a better word, what Iris Murdoch called it, the "fat relentless ego"; or again what the Bible calls it, sin.

It is not wrong to see this addition to our ethical understanding as a distinctively Judaeo-Christian achievement, and to link it directly to the Psalms' and the New Testament's praise of self-abasement (*tapeinosis*, Philippians 2.3, 2.8) and abasement of mind (*tapeinophrosyne*, 1 Peter 5.5–6, James 4.6).[20] Yet, if the basic Christian idea is that spiritual homecoming and true and humble self-knowledge is only possible for us after long, painful, and degrading expiation through battles and wanderings, neither is it wrong to think that Homer himself would agree.[21]

Notes

1 "Pagan" here is neither an ameliorative nor a pejorative. It does not mean "superstitious backwoods rustic" (as *paganus* often did). Nor do I mean the contemporary sense of "paganism", as, roughly, Celtic druidism plus Californian pantheism (and minus human sacrifice). "Pagan" here is neutrally descriptive; it just means "follower of traditional pre-Christian Greek religion in its various forms".

2 Corollary: possession of a virtue is a matter of degree; there are vague and borderline cases of "X has V".

3 See della Mirandola, *Oratio de Hominis Dignitate* (1487), paragraphs 18-23, where God tells Adam that he has made him with no definite nature except to be the *creator* of his own nature: "Nec te celestem nec te terrenum, neque mortalem neque immortalem fecimus, ut tui ipsius quasi arbitrarius honorariusque plastes et factor, in quam malueris tu te formam effingeris" (22). Also Alasdair MacIntyre, *After Virtue* p.161: "Man without culture is a myth. Our biological nature certainly places constraints on all cultural possibility; but man who has nothing but a biological nature is a creature of whom we know nothing". (Thanks to Ben Colburn for the Pico reference. Sarah Broadie reminds me that there is something similar in Protagoras' myth.)

4 "Humble?" said Charlotte. "'Humble' has two meanings. It means 'not proud,' and it means 'near the ground.' That's Wilbur all over. He's not proud and he's near the ground". I am grateful to Mary Keys, "Humility and Greatness of Soul", *Perspectives on Political Science*, 37:4, 217–222, for reminding me of this passage from one of my favourite children's books, *Charlotte's Web* (White 1980, 140).

5 Hume's polemic is well-known, but also irresistibly quotable (*Enquiry concerning the Principles of Morals,* p.73 in Beauchamp's 1998 edition): "[A]s every quality, which is useful or agreeable to ourselves or others, is, in common life, allowed to be a part of personal merit; so no other will ever be received, where men judge of things by their natural, unprejudiced reason, without the delusive glosses of superstition and false religion. Celibacy, fasting, penance, mortification, self-denial, humility, silence, solitude, and the whole train of monkish virtues; for what reason are they everywhere rejected by men of sense, but because they serve to no manner of purpose; neither to advance a man's fortune in the world, nor render him a more valuable member of society; neither qualify him for the entertainment of company, nor increase his power of self-enjoyment? We observe, on the contrary, that they cross all those desirable ends; stupefy the understanding and harden the heart, obscure the fancy and sour the temper. We justly, therefore, transfer them to the opposite column, and place them in the catalogue of vices; nor has any superstition force sufficient, among men of the world, to pervert entirely these natural sentiments".

This denunciation of the "monkish virtues" begins from a list that is not in fact a list of virtues, not even on Hume's own almost uselessly capacious definition of "virtue". But perhaps it is not meant to be: perhaps "and the whole train of monkish virtues" introduces a further item beyond those already listed. The grammar is ambiguous. It is also ambiguous whether Hume can be convicted here of describing celibacy, fasting, etc., as *qualities*, which would certainly be odd.

6 Thus Ross's Oxford translation (1935) of NE 1123a30 ff. John Casey comments (*Pagan Virtues,* n.3 on p.199) that "pride" is "closer to an interpretation than a translation", and prefers "magnanimity" for *megalopsychia.*

7 Unless I say otherwise, all translations are my own.

8 For more on the *Antigone*, see Chappell 1999.

9 As Simone Weil famously pointed out, and as Michael Morris reminds me.

On the role and relation of suppliant see e.g. F.S.Naiden, *Ancient Supplication* (OUP 2006); John Gould, "*Hiketeia*", Journal of Hellenic Studies 1973; on *aidos* see Douglas Cairns, *Aidos* (OUP 1992). (My thanks to Gillian Clark and Stephen Clark.)

10 For the theological significance of *dikaiosyne* and *dike* see *MacIntyre After Virtue* (London: Duckworth 1981), p.134: "'*Dike* means basically the moral order of the universe,' wrote Hugh Lloyd-Jones (1971, 161): and the *dikaios* is the man who respects and does not violate that order. At once the difficulty in translating *dikaios* by 'just' is clear; for someone in our culture may use 'just' without any reference to or belief in a moral order in the universe". Cp. *After Virtue*'s famous opening "disquieting suggestion".

11 And Rome too; see e.g. Horace, Odes 2.10, and Ovid, *Tristia* 3.4.25–26: Crede mihi, bene qui latuit bene vixit, et intra/ Fortunam debet quisque manere suam. ("Believe me: he has lived well who has well concealed himself; everyone ought to keep within the bounds of his fortune".) The middle phrase of this sentence was, according to some, chosen by Descartes as his epitaph.

12 On listing the virtues see my papers "Utrum ..." and "Lists of the virtues".

13 Aquinas' view is an interesting contrast here with what I am characterising as the common classical Greek view. According to Aquinas too (ST 2a2ae.161.4) humility is a subpart of another virtue—but only one other virtue; namely temperance.

14 For the competitive/ active vs the cooperative/ quiet virtues, see Adkins, *Merit and Responsibility,* with A.A. Long's critical commentary in JHS 1970.

15 On Thrasymachus—and on the differences between his thesis and Callicles'—see Chappell 1993.

16 In this essay, "Socrates" always refers to Plato's character of that name.

17 The principal virtues were later, e.g. in Aquinas's discussion, to be named the cardinal virtues—the virtues on which everything else hinges (Latin *cardo*, a hinge; it seems to have been St Ambrose who invented the term "virtus cardinalis").

18 The theme of specifically *epistemic* humility in ancient Greek thought would be a fascinating discussion in its own right, and would necessarily have much to say about Socrates and the *Charmides*—if I had room for it.

19 On differences in doctrine between the *Eudemian* and *Nicomachean Ethics*, see Chappell 2010. In sum: the EE is more aristocratic in tone, the NE more egalitarian; and the NE seems to be later, because it expands or develops points that the EE merely states or hints at.

20 *Tapeinophrosune, tapeinotes* is a Christian notion: see LSJ on these and associated words. The vocabulary hardly ever occurs in the ancient world in other contexts, and when it does (e.g. Aristotle NE 1125a2, *hoi tapeinoi kolakes;* Arrian's *Diatribes of Epictetus* 3.24.56, Josephus *The Jewish Wars* 4.9.2), it is clearly pejorative—it means meanness of mind, not so much self-abasement as baseness. The contrast with the characteristic Christian attitude is obvious in e.g. Lk 16.15: "What is exalted among men is an abomination before the Lord".

At Romans 12.3 St Paul says something more consistent with a notion of humility not as thinking *lowly* of oneself, but as thinking *rightly* of oneself: "For I say, through the grace given unto me, to every man that is among you, not to think of himself more highly than he ought to think; but to think soberly, according as God has dealt to every man the measure of faith". It would of course be a mistake to see this as anything like Aristotle's subsumption of humility into simply *right* opinion of oneself.

In Aquinas ST 2a2ae.161 there is a deep and rich discussion of humility as a virtue, with particular reference to the relation between *low* opinion of oneself and *true* opinion of oneself. Given that Aquinas was educated in large part by Cistercians, it is perhaps particularly interesting that he expounds and defends quite a lot of St Bernard of Clairvaux' rules for humility; but as several commentators have pointed out, it is even more interesting what part of those rules he leaves out.

21 For discussion and criticism, I am grateful to Sarah Broadie and to Mark Alfano. Both disagree with the views of this essay, for which neither of them is responsible.

References

Douglas Adams, *The Hitchhikers' Guide to the Galaxy: Box Set* (5 Volumes). London: Penguin, 2002.
Arthur Adkins, *Merit and Responsibility*. Oxford: Oxford University Press, 1960.
Aeschylus, *Aeschyli Tragoediae*, ed. D.L. Page. Oxford: Clarendon, 1970.
Aquinas, *Summa Theologiae*. Accessed Online at https://dhspriory.org/thomas/summa/.
Aristotle, *Ethica Nicomachea*, ed. I. Bywater. Oxford: Clarendon, 1891.
Douglas Cairns, *Aidos*. Oxford: Oxford University Press, 1992.
T. Chappell, "The virtues of Thrasymachus", *Phronesis*, 38(1) 1993, 1–17.
T. Chappell, "Socrates and Antigone: Two ways not to be martyred", *Prudentia* (Online Supplement), 1999.
T. Chappell, "Ethical blindspots: Why Socrates was not a cosmopolitan", *Ratio*, 2010, 17–33.
T. Chappell, "Aristotle", In: Thomas Angier, ed., *Key Ethical Thinkers* (Continuum). London: Bloomsbury, 2012.
S.G. Chappell, "Lists of the virtues", In: Alessio Vaccari, ed., *Ethics and Politics: Special Edition* on Virtue Ethics, 2015.
S.G. Chappell, "Utrum sit una tantum vera enumeratio virtutum moralium", In: Michel Croce, ed., Special Issue of *Metaphilosophy* on Connecting Virtues, 2018.
Howard Curzer, "Greatness of soul", *Canadian Journal of Philosophy*, 1990.
Howard Curzer, "Truthfulness and integrity", In: H. Curzer, ed., *Aristotle and the virtues*. Oxford: Oxford University Press, 2012.
H. Diels, W. Kranz, *Die Fragmente der Vorsokratiker*. Berlin: Weidmannsche buchhandlung, 1903.
Julia Driver, "Virtues of ignorance", *Journal of Philosophy*, 1989, 373–384.
Euripides, *Euripidis Fabulae*, ed. James Diggle. Oxford: Clarendon, 1994.
John Gould, "Hiketeia", *The Journal of Hellenic Studies*, 1973, 74–103.
Herodotus, *Herodoti Historiae*, ed. N.G. Wilson. Oxford: Clarendon, 2015.
Homer, *Iliad*, Accessed Online at www.perseus.tufts.edu/hopper/text?doc=Perseus:text:1999.01.0133.
Horace, *Odes*, Accessed Online at www.perseus.tufts.edu/hopper/text?doc=Perseus:text:1999.02.0024.
Hugh Lloyd-Jones, *The Justice of Zeus*. Oxford: Oxford University Press, 1971.

A.A. Long, "Morals and values in Homer", *The Journal of Hellenic Studies*, 1970, 121–139.
Alasdair MacIntyre, *After Virtue*. London: Duckworth, 1981.
Thomas Malory, *Le Morte d'Arthur*, Accessed Online at www.gutenberg.org/files/1251/1251-h/1251-h.htm.
F.S. Naiden, *Ancient Supplication*. Oxford: Oxford University Press, 2006.
Ovid, *Metaphorphoses*, Accessed Online at www.thelatinlibrary.com/ovid.html.
Pico della Mirandola, *Oration*, Accessed Online at www.andallthat.co.uk/uploads/2/3/8/9/2389220/pico_-_oration_on_the_dignity_of_man.pdf.
Plato, *Platonis Opera*, ed. John Burnet. Oxford: Clarendon, 1863–1928.
Sir David Ross, *Aristotle's Complete Works in Translation*. Oxford: Clarendon, 1935.
David Sachs, "A fallacy in Plato's *Republic*", *The Philosophical Review*, 1963, 141–158.
Henry Sidgwick, *The Methods of Ethics*. Cambridge: Cambridge University Press, 1907.
Sophocles, *Sophoclis Fabulae*. Oxford: Oxford University Press, 1990–1992.
Leo Tolstoy, *War and Peace* (1869), Translated Rosemary Edmonds. London: Penguin, 1957.
Simone Weil, "L'*Iliade* ou le poème de la force". 1941, Accessed Online at http://teuwissen.ch/imlift/wp-content/uploads/2013/07/Weil-L_Iliade_ou_le_poeme_de_la_force.pdf.
Ludwig Wittgenstein, *Tractatus Logico-Philosophicus*. 1922, Accessed Online at www.gutenberg.org/files/5740/5740-pdf.pdf.

17

AQUINAS ON HUMILITY AND RELATIONAL GREATNESS

Andrew Charles Pinsent

17.1 The orphaned virtue of humility

Humility occupies an anomalous position in contemporary society and virtue ethics, to the point that there is some doubt over whether it should be regarded as a virtue at all. The attributes that are often associated with humility, such as being low, deferential, and submissive, are rarely considered praiseworthy and go against the grain of a world in which it is proclaimed that we can be whatever we want to be. Moreover, it is challenging to find exemplars of humility, given the suspicion that if someone is prominent enough to be considered as an exemplar, that very prominence would seem to refute being humble. Given also that the path to humility is associated with humiliation, one of the least desirable experiences of life, why then should anyone bother with humility at all? Expressed in rhetorical terms, in the spirit of Nietzsche, shoudn't we reach for the stars rather than crawl in the dust?

The effects of these dire connotations are compounded by the lack of a wholly satisfactory account of humility within many influential accounts of virtue ethics. Humility is notoriously absent from Aristotle's *Nicomachean Ethics*, which MacIntyre has described as the canonical text of the Western tradition of virtue ethics,[1] and it has proved difficult to retrofit humility into an Aristotelian framework as a mean between two vicious extremes. After all, in what sense is humility a virtuous mean, given that humility conveys the sense of an *extravagance* of self-giving or self-emptying? And the notion of a disposition to self-giving or self-emptying raises the additional question of how humility is conducive to the fullness and completion associated with human flourishing, the traditional goal of the most influential kinds of virtue ethics. But it is also challenging to see how humility fits in with most alternative approaches to virtue ethics, such as agent-based, exemplarist, or target-centred accounts.

One partial exception to the orphaning of humility might be virtue ethics in the Platonic tradition, insofar as this tradition emphasizes the way in which good agency presupposes the contemplation of the Form of the Good.[2] Given the focus on a relationship to that which is supremely good, humility in relation to this supreme good might then be regarded as a disposition that is proper to human perfection. For this reason, it should not come as a surprise that one of the few classical references to humility is not to be found in the Aristotlelian corpus but in the following passage from Plato's *Laws* IV, 716a–b, a text that can also be found in citations by Christian authors in the early patristic era[3]:

ATHENIAN. Now, then, our address should go like this: 'Men, according to the ancient story, there is a god who holds in his hands the beginning and end and middle of all things, and straight he marches in the cycle of nature. Justice, who takes vengeance on those who abandon the divine law, never leaves his side. The man who means to live in happiness latches on to her and follows her with meekness and humility (*tapeinotês*). But he who bursts with pride, elated by wealth or honors or by physical beauty when young and foolish, whose soul is afire with the arrogant belief that so far from needing someone to control and lead him, he can play the leader to others – there's a man whom God has deserted. And in his desolation he collects others like himself, and in his soaring frenzy he causes universal chaos. Many people think he cuts a fine figure, but before long he pays to Justice no trifling penalty and brings himself, his home and state to rack and ruin. Thus it is ordained. What action, then, should a sensible man take, and what should his outlook be? What must he *avoid* doing or thinking?'

CLINIAS. This much is obvious: every man must resolve to belong to those who follow in the company of God.[4]

According to this text, which mentions *tapeinotês* ('humility') explicitly in relation to God, the person who bursts with pride, and who thinks that he has no need of someone to control and lead him, is deserted by God, losing friendship with God.[5] Such persons play the leader to others, produce chaos, and swiftly bring ruin on themselves, their families, and cities. On this account, humility is a necessary concomitant of human flourishing, insofar as it protects against the personal and social ruination caused by pride.

Plato in this passage emphasizes some significant dangers from a lack of humility, but his emphasis on the loss of divine favour underlines another important point about humility, namely that it is theological texts, or at least theological themes in philosophical texts, that have typically championed humility. This association is reinforced by the frequency with which humility is mentioned in key texts of revealed theology. For example, Jesus in the Gospel of Matthew says, "*Take my yoke upon you, and learn from me; for I am gentle and humble in heart, and you will find rest for your souls*" (Matthew 11:29 NRSV),[6] which not only underlines the importance of humility in relation to God, but makes the utterly unintuitive assertion that God incarnate is also humble, and in an exemplary fashion. The First Letter of Peter says, "*Humble yourselves therefore under the mighty hand of God, that in due time he may exalt you*" (1 Peter 5:6), and the Letter of James reminds us that, "*God opposes the proud, but gives grace to the humble*" (James 4:6). A similar emphasis runs through the whole Christian tradition, with the texts of patristic authors, scholastic theologians and doctors of the church replete with references to the value and indispensability of humility for Christian life and salvation.

The ubiquity of humility in the theological tradition does not, however, necessarily commend humility in the contemporary and more secular world. Indeed, the close association of humility with theological faith, and its decline along with faith, can in fact be interpreted as lending support to a fairly standard critique, along Nietzschean lines, that humility is bound up with Judeo-Christian "slave morality" and lacks the nobility of the strong-willed. On such an account, humility has been orphaned by the decline of faith and, as the life of faith fades, perhaps also humility deserves to fade and be forgotten.

Before dispensing with humility, however, it is at least prudent to examine what its most able defenders have to say. In this chapter, I examine the work of St Thomas Aquinas (d. 1274), who incorporated humility within his most mature and detailed account of virtue ethics in his *Summa theologiae* (*ST*) II–I.55–89 and II–II.1–170. I analyse humility and its opposing vice of pride, and I conclude by examining briefly the prospects for a secular transposition of Aquinas' account.

17.2 Humility and pride

Within the vast account of *ST* II–II.1–170, with its 815 articles, Aquinas devotes 5 questions (qq.161–165) comprising 22 articles on humility and its opposing vice of pride. Aquinas' principal treatment of humility is covered in the six articles of q.161, followed by pride in general in q.162, and pride in the special case of the first sin in qq.163–165.

In article q.161 Aquinas argues, first, that humility is a virtue (a.1); that humility principally moderates the movement of the appetite rather than the judgment of reason (a.2); that by humility, a person ought to be subject to every neighbor, in respect of that which the latter has that is of God (a.3); and that humility is part of the virtue of temperance since it suppresses impetuous tendencies (a.4). He then ranks humility, placing it after the theological virtues, intellectual virtues, and after justice, especially legal justice, but before all other virtues (a.5). Finally, he interprets and validates an ancient guide to humility, namely the 12 degrees of humility in the Rule of St Benedict (a.6).

Aquinas' descriptions of humility in itself do not seem to contain anything unusual or particularly insightful, but the broader context does present some surprises. For example, although Aquinas describes the virtue of humility in terms of a praiseworthy self-abasement to the lowest place (q.161, a.1), he argues in *ST* II–II.129–133 that there is also a Christian virtue of greatness, namely magnanimity, which he describes using language drawn largely from Aristotle. There is also, of course, a vice associated with certain attitudes toward greatness, namely pride, the details of which highlight the value of humility.

What is pride and why is it a problem, if it is a problem? The latter question is not rhetorical, given that there are at least some instances in which pride describes something commendable, as in the case of someone saying to parents who are watching their child excel, "You must be so proud!" Moreover, it has become standard practice to translate μεγαλοψυχία (*megalopsychia*) in the *Nicomachean Ethics* IV.3 as 'pride', in which context it is hailed as a virtue concerned with great things.[7] In this context, Aristotle describes the proud person as someone who thinks himself worthy of great things, and who is, in fact, worthy of them (*NE*.IV.3.1123b1–2). The proud man, he states, although extreme in respect of the greatness of his claims, does in fact observe the proper mean of virtue, insofar as what he claims is in accordance with his merits (*NE*.IV.3.1123b13–15).

On this account, pride is a virtue of greatness, and the proud man must be good in the highest degree, and the truly proud man must be good. Given that pride, in this context, is understood as a superlative good, in what sense or senses can it be a moral failing?

The task of shedding light on this question is made easier by considering what, precisely, is meant by pride when it is analyzed as a vice. Aquinas in *ST* II–II.162.4 defines four kinds of pride, drawing from a list set down in the patristic era by Pope St Gregory I. The following statements make use of these definitions but modify the wording slightly to highlight the connections of pride, relatedness and gift:[8]

P1 Ascribing an excellence to oneself that one does not possess.
P2 Thinking that one has acquired for oneself some excellence that one has received as a gift.
P3 Thinking that some excellence that one has received as a gift is due to one's own merits.
P4 Thinking that some excellence that one possesses is greater insofar as others do not have it.

One striking point from this list is that there is nothing in these definitions that excludes one from actually being great, or from knowing genuinely that one is great. This consideration leads to a first and important conclusion, namely that being proud in the Aristotelian sense does not necessarily mean that one is proud in Aquinas' sense of having one or more of the four species of pride listed above.

On what grounds, then, are P1–P4 to be considered as vices? On the basis that virtues conduce to flourishing and vices are defined as such as dispositions which impede that flourishing, it is important to examine in what senses, if any, the various species of pride might impede personal flourishing.

As a first example, P1 pride involves misjudging one's own excellences, which is itself a serious flaw insofar as it marks a lack of intellectual development. Moreover, choices made on the basis of an exaggerated and unwarranted estimate of personal excellence risk going awry. In extreme cases this may even prove destructive to one's person, family or society, as in the case of the skier who overestimates her ability on a dangerous ski slope, or the military general whose self-belief is exaggerated to the point of ignoring all views contrary to his own. More subtly, a person who thinks she *already* has some particular excellence will not strive for it for herself or from others. The person who believes erroneously he is already a great pianist or philosopher will not be ready to receive instruction from others and strive for improvement. One can therefore consider that P1 pride is unwise even from the point of view of enlightened self-interest, given that it will tend to impede personal flourishing.

The other species of pride have similar drawbacks. P2 pride involves a recognition of genuine excellence, but fails to recognize the correct cause. A person with P2 pride may actually consider himself the cause of a particular excellence, as when a person delights in a scientific breakthrough he has made when the seminal idea really came from someone else. More subtly, even when he does not actively think he has caused his own excellence, he may simply delight in the excellence but be forgetful of the person who has brought this about. Whatever else may be said, that kind of misattribution and forgetfulness makes it less likely that the person with P2 pride will be a recipient of further gifts in future which, once again, is detrimental to the attainment of further excellence.

The person with P3 pride acknowledges a personal excellence and its cause correctly but will tend to regard herself as at least the cause of the cause of her own excellence. Of course, for some kinds of excellence this assessment may be correct in part, as in the many kinds of sports and activities that require dedicated practice. But there are also many kinds of excellences or causes of excellence that are more in the manner of undeserved gifts, such as the loving care that is usually given to children by their parents, or the divine gifts that are generally regarded as necessary for a successful outcome of the Christian life.[9] In such cases, it is inappropriate to think of these gifts as things one deserves or that are owed to oneself. Indeed, if one persistently treats undeserved gifts as if they are owed to oneself in the manner of a contract, the person with P3 pride is once again unlikely to be the recipient of further gifts in future, which is once again detrimental to the attainment of greater excellence.

P4 pride involves thinking that some excellence that one possesses is greater insofar as others do not have it, which is closely linked to what is today called *schadenfreude*, that is, taking pleasure, joy, or self-satisfaction from the troubles, failures, or humiliation of others. Schadenfreude is frequently described as a secret or guilty pleasure, implying an inherent awareness that enjoying this kind of pleasure reflects badly on oneself. But whatever else may be said about P4 pride, it does at least involve the misjudgment that one's own success, at least to some degree, is measured by the failures of others, like taking an extra-large slice of a shared cake. By contrast, if the good one seeks is a virtuous life, then the failures of others are in fact likely to be detrimental to this goal. After all, it is typically easier to be a virtuous person in a society of other virtuous persons, compared to being virtuous in a society of the vicious. On this account, the failures of others desired by P4 pride are, in fact, detrimental to oneself in an absolute sense, whatever the short-term advantage one gains over others in a relative sense.

In summary, all of these species of pride involve some kind of misjudgment of truth, a misjudgment that is itself an anomaly in a fully formed life. But if the desired good of such a life is some kind of superlative greatness, then what is also striking is that all four kinds of pride will, in various ways, tend to frustrate the attainment of that greatness. On this account, it is not only possible to be great and to be aware of one's own greatness without being proud in the senses meant by Aquinas, but these various dispositions of pride will in fact tend to inhibit genuine personal greatness. What follows is not only the compatibility of pride in the Aristotelian sense with an absence of pride in Aquinas' sense, but that the absence of the latter may actually be a precondition of the former.

17.3 Second-person consequences of pride

The section above considered the harm of pride to oneself, understood in terms of the four species listed by Aquinas, but it is commonly understood that pride has second-person as well as first-person consequences, insofar as it has an impact on relationships with other persons.

As a first example, P1 pride, to ascribe an excellence to oneself that one does not possess, implies a self-admiration that is excessive and beyond reason, corresponding to the dictionary definition of narcissism.[10] As is well known and is now well documented, persons who are obsessed with themselves in a narcissistic fashion are less likely to be capable of any genuine love of others, and there is an extensive and growing literature on the toxicity of narcissism for relationships.[11]

P2 pride is also damaging to relationships insofar as it prevents a person from acknowledging that a gift *is* a gift, or the relationship of the gift with a giver, or the giver as a giver. This failure will scarcely be appreciated by the giver, and is unlikely to be helpful to the relationship. Therefore, as in the case of P1 pride, which has the characteristic of self-satisfied closure, P2 pride is also 'cold' in the sense that it is deleterious to relationships or fails to establish or acknowledge a relationship that should exist.

P3 pride, thinking that some excellence that one has received as a gift is due to one's own merits, which can imply that what one has received is, in effect, owed to oneself because of what one is or what one has done. If one thinks of the relationship in this way, then the gift is received in the manner of a contractual transaction. As a consequence, there is also a kind of 'coldness' about P3 pride, as in the case of a marriage in which the spouses have been reduced to bickering about the distribution of rights and responsibilities. Although a relationship exists, it lacks the characteristics of genuine love in the sense of friendship, in which the twofold desires for the good of the other and for union with the other are not conditional upon receiving some good *from* the other, even though some minimal good from the other, namely openness to the friendship, is earnestly desired. P3 pride therefore acknowledges only an *inadequate* relationship, akin to a contractual relationship rather than friendship.

P4 pride also damages relationships, but principally because the person with P4 pride fails to understand the nature of the gift in the relationship with a giver. Perhaps the clearest illustration of a failure to grasp this point can be seen in one of the parables of Jesus, the story of the Pharisee and the tax collector:

> Two men went up into the temple to pray, one a Pharisee and the other a tax collector. The Pharisee stood and prayed thus with himself, 'God, I thank thee that I am not like other men, extortioners, unjust, adulterers, or even like this tax collector. I fast twice a week, I give tithes of all that I get.' But the tax collector, standing far off, would not even lift up his eyes to heaven, but beat his breast, saying, 'God, be merciful to me a

sinner!' I tell you, this man went down to his house justified rather than the other; for every one who exalts himself will be humbled, but he who humbles himself will be exalted.

(Luke 18:10–14)

In this parable, the Pharisee acknowledges God as the cause of what he has and thanks God for his gifts, but part of his delight is not just that he has these gifts but that others lack them. But given that being right with God is not something that diminishes by being shared with others, the Pharisee's attitude shows that he does not really understand the nature of the divine gifts to which he aspires. Moreover, the fact that the Pharisee secretly takes delight in the apparent relative failure of the tax collector shows that he is not, in fact, aligned with the desire of God that all should be saved, and hence is not in that harmony with God that corresponds to a state of divine friendship. Hence Jesus warns that it is not the Pharisee but the tax collector, who simply begs for God's mercy, who goes home justified.[12]

17.4 Relational greatness

The considerations above underline how pride, understood in terms of the four species listed by Aquinas, has the potential both to inhibit any greatness that one would want for oneself and is toxic for one's relationships with others. But the dangers of pride are compounded when these two sets of goods coincide, in other words when the greatness that one seeks consists principally in the flourishing of a relationship. The coincidence is central to Aquinas' own account of human flourishing, outlined in *ST* II–II.1–170, which is entirely ordered by and toward *caritas* or divine love, which Aquinas describes in terms of friendship (*ST* II–II.23.1), first and principally with God but also with other persons.

Given that pride is toxic to friendship, for the reasons highlighted above, pride is wholly antipathetic to human flourishing in Aquinas' account. Moreover, pride will also tend to impede even the first steps toward the goal of flourishing since, as I have argued extensively elsewhere, Aquinas' entire account of virtue ethics is built around what psychologists today have called 'joint attention', in which one permits oneself to be moved by a second person to align psychologically with that second person.[13] Given that, in a state of pride, one resists being moved at all to align with another person, pride not only inhibits friendship but also the second-person relatedness[14] that is a precondition of and oriented toward friendship. On this account, pride leaves one cold, isolated, and unable to grow in virtue.

Given the toxicity of pride for flourishing in Aquinas' highly relational account of virtue ethics, one can perceive why humility has a natural and important place in his account of virtue ethics, given that humility specifically protects the second-person relatedness that is the means to continue and develop in virtue as well as the friendship or divine love that is the goal or fruition of virtue.

What, then, does Aquinas think about the Aristotelian virtue of μεγαλοψυχία (*megalopsychia*) often translated today as 'pride'? As noted previously, nothing in the four species of the vice of pride prevents persons from being great or knowing that they are great. Moreover, as noted previously, in *ST* II–II.129–133, Aquinas specifically defends this virtue of greatness, not under the name of 'pride' but 'magnanimity' from the Latin *magnanimitās*, from *magna* "great" and *animus* "soul, spirit", which is a transliteration of the Greek word *megalopsychia* (μεγαλοψυχία). It is this Greek word of which Aristotle writes in *NE*.IV.3.1123b1–2, "Now a person is thought to be great-souled if he claims much and deserves much" (δοκεῖ δὴ μεγαλόψυχος εἶναι ὁ μεγάλων αὑτὸν ἀξιῶν ἄξιος ὤν).

The introduction of a good pride, magnanimity, helps to avoid some linguistic confusion and it is notable that Aquinas follows Aristotle in describing magnanimity as being about honor (*ST* II–II.129.1), and specifically about great honor (129.2). He further argues that magnanimity is a virtue (129.3), and since honor is a reward of every virtue, magnanimity is about doing great deeds in the actions associated with every virtue. On this account, magananimity pertains to every virtue, making their actions greater and worthy of great honor (129.4 ad 3). Hence Aquinas can and does defend the disposition to greatness, using descriptions drawn largely from Aristotle, while also opposing the fourfold vice of pride.

Despite this apparent resolution, however, it must be admitted that there is some reluctance to translate *megalopsychia* as magnanimity today, and to deny that the Christianized virtue of magnanimity captures what Aristotle meant by *megalopsychia*. The reason, I think, is that some of the characteristics of Aristotle's great-souled person, which are also defended by Aquinas, do seem to clash with Christian ideals, including in particular: being unmindful of favors; being remiss and slow of action; employing 'irony' (*eironia*) toward many; being unable to associate with others; holding on to barren things rather than to those that are fruitful;[15] considering oneself worthy of great honors, and yet despising such honors; not being cast down by dishonor, and despising such dishonor, because it is undeserved;[16] having complete confidence in achieving greatness; being perfectly free from fear; making use of goods of fortune, but neither being uplifted much by having them, nor downcast much by losing them.[17] At first glance, such characteristics convey the impression that the magnanimous person is aloof, disdainful and arrogant, contrary to humility and love.

The Aristotelian attributes of *megalopsychia* as described above could, it must be admitted, be ascribed to someone who is viciously proud. Such a person, with a distorted assessment of the first person at the heart of his or her world, may well act with aloofness, disdain, and arrogance. But at the heart of Aquinas' virtue ethics is the relationship with God in the manner of a second person, and it is this second person who is at the heart of the Christian life. On this interpretation, many of the Aristotelian attributes of *megalopsychia* can be given an alternative reading, not in terms of isolated arrogance but in terms of confident second-person dependence, as I have written elsewhere as follows,

> a child that is confident in her parent is not going to be over-anxious about what she possesses herself in order to complete some difficult task, and can afford to hold to 'barren' things, for their own sake, rather than those that are 'fruitful'. Such a person can also be free from fear and make use of goods of fortune, but neither being uplifted much by having them, nor downcast much by losing them. Being remiss or slow of action and 'irony' can also be understood in terms of confidence that is second-personal, rather than a first-personal confidence that depends on one's own resources, efforts and time. With regard to honor, such a person can consider herself worthy of great honours while treating the actual bestowal of such honours, or dishonours, lightly, since the approval sought is not from civic society but God. Similarly, 'being unable to associate with others' can be interpreted as a different mode of relationship with God which may set a person apart, at least from certain other associations. Even being 'unmindful of favours' can be accommodated within a second-personal account, if being mindful of favours is interpreted as implying a balance sheet approach to giving and receiving favours, an approach that is pertinent to a third person or contractual approach to favors rather than freely given gifts.[18]

In other words, while one can read Aristotelian *megalopsychia* in terms of first-person arrogance, which is perhaps a typical reading today, one can also interpret it in terms of the second-person confidence of a beloved child with a parent, stemming from the security of a relationship with God made possible through love, humility, and the divine gifts of grace. On this account, whatever Aristotle's own views on this matter, it is possible to incorporate his claims into an account of magnanimity that is both compatible with and dependent upon humility with respect to the divine source of all that is good.

17.5 The secular transposition

For Aquinas, the principal second person to whom we are meant to relate in the life of grace is God, with whom joint attention is made possible thanks to certain divine gifts, and human flourishing is organized around the principle of friendship with God. But can this account of theological flourishing retain any validity if it is transposed to a more contemporary and secular context?

The answer, I think, is straightforwardly affirmative. Just as the metaphor of human relationships is used to understand the theological principles of the life of grace, so also some of the lessons of flourishing in the theological life of grace can be applied back to human development. In particular, it has been argued that joint attention with other human persons, starting with simple shared actions like pointing, gaze following, and turn-taking games, plays an important role in child development, including the acquisition of language and character formation.[19] Moreover, many parents will also be familiar with moral struggles of their own children, especially when children face a choice between aligning with their parents' will to do some good thing and their tendency to resist aligning with their parents' will, as in the familiar case of a child refusing to say sorry after doing something wrong. The drama and appropriate virtues of the relationship with God, played out throughout Scripture, therefore have clear parallels with the more conventional and everyday drama of human development and relationships.

These considerations suggest that humility, although achieving prominence especially in a theological context, is scarcely restricted to relating to God as to a second person, as 'I' to 'you'. On the contrary, the commonsense view that it is proper and good for human persons to relate to other persons as second persons, and the damage to relationships from the species of pride, underline how humility is also valuable in a more general and secular sense. Hence Aquinas' arguments that humility is inherently important and a prerequisite of greatness is not limited to the theological context. On the contrary, the point that G. K. Chesterton expresses in the following passage is broadly applicable:

> If a man would make his world large, he must always be making himself small. Even the haughty visions, the tall cities, and the toppling pinnacles are the creations of humility … For towers are not towers unless we look up at them, and giants are not giants unless they are larger than we are.[20]

Chesterton's observations, as well as what has been written above, suggest that pride leads at most to a false, narrow, and petty superiority. By contrast, humility strengthens the possibility of true friendship and greatness insofar as it opens us to relate personally with what is greater than ourselves.[21]

Notes

1 Alasdair MacIntyre, *After Virtue: A Study in Moral Theory, Third Edition*, 3rd ed. (Notre Dame, IN: University of Notre Dame Press, 2007), 147.

2 Timothy Chappell, *Knowing What To Do: Imagination, Virtue, and Platonism in Ethics* (Oxford; New York: OUP Oxford, 2014), 295.
3 See, for example, Clement of Rome, *Stromata*, II, 22; Origen, *Against Celsus*, VI, 15.
4 Plato, *Laws*, IV, 716a-b, trans. Trevor J. Saunders, in *Plato: Complete Works*, ed. John M. Cooper and D. S. Hutchinson, (Indianapolis, IN: Hackett Publishing Company, 1997), p. 1402. First published by Penguin Books Ltd., 1970.
5 The connection between Plato's conception of humility and being a friend of God is also made clear in the subsequent paragraph, *Laws* IV, 716c–d. "On this principle the moderate man is God's friend, being like him, whereas the immoderate and unjust man is not like him and is his enemy", ibid.
6 Citations from Scripture are taken from the Revised Standard Version (RSV) unless marked 'NRSV', indicating the New Revised Standard Version. For this passage, the NRSV has been used since it translates *tapeinos* explicitly as 'humble'.
7 An influential example of the translation of *megalopsychia* as 'pride' is that of W. D. Ross and J. O. Urmson in Jonathan Barnes, *Complete Works of Aristotle, Volume 2: The Revised Oxford Translation* (Princeton, NJ: Princeton University Press, 1998), 1173–1776.
8 I have drawn these definitions, and some of the subsequent analysis, from my earlier work, Andrew Pinsent, "Humility", in *Being Good: Christian Virtues for Everyday Life*, ed. Michael W. Austin and Douglas Geivett (Grand Rapids, MI: Eerdmans, 2012), 250–255.
9 P2 pride, in the context of the goal of salvation, corresponds to the ancient heresy of Pelagianism, that one can gain salvation through one's own efforts; while P3 pride maps onto semipelagianism, that one can merit the grace required for salvation in some way.
10 "Narcissism, n.", in *OED Online*, Oxford English Dictionary (Oxford: Oxford University Press), accessed June 10, 2019, www.oed.com/view/Entry/125088.
11 See, for example, Jean Twenge and W. Keith Campbell, *The Narcissism Epidemic: Living in the Age of Entitlement* (New York London Toronto Sydney New Delhi: Atria Books, 2010); Brandon Grey, *Narcissistic Relationship: Ultimate Guide to Torture a Narcissist. Recovery from the Epidemic Narcissism, Emotional Abuse and Personality Disorder. The Revenge for Lovers (Also for Parents).* (Independently published, 2019).
12 I note, in passing, that Rebecca Konyndyk De Young has argued that humility is a disposition to consider oneself small in relation to God and magnanimity as a virtue of 'acknowledged dependence' on God. See Rebecca Konyndyk de Young, "Aquinas's Virtues of Acknowledged Dependence: A New Measure of Greatness", *Faith and Philosophy* 21, no. 2 (2004): 219. This solution is consistent with the rejection of P1 and P2 pride, but does not, I believe, fully explain the rejection of P3 and P4 pride, since, for example, the Pharisee in the parable acknowledges dependence on God but still suffers from P4 pride.
13 Andrew Pinsent, *The Second-Person Perspective in Aquinas's Ethics: Virtues and Gifts* (New York; Abingdon, UK: Routledge, 2012), 31–63. For an introduction to the psychology of joint attention, see, for example, Naomi Eilan et al., eds., *Joint Attention: Communication and Other Minds: Issues in Philosophy and Psychology* (Oxford: Clarendon Press, 2005).
14 I use the term 'relatedness' rather than 'relationship' so as not to exclude short-term and momentary interactions in which one aligns with second persons. I am grateful to advice from Peter Hobson for this practice.
15 In *ST* II–II.129.3 arg 5. In his response to this objection, Aquinas claims that such characteristics, with certain qualifications, call not for blame but for very great praise, insofar as they belong to a magnanimous person. Note that 'irony' here denotes the Greek *eironia*, namely dissimulation of one's own good; cf. *ST* II–II.113.1 arg 1.
16 *ST* II–II.129.2 ad 3.
17 *ST* II–II.129.6, 7, 8.
18 Pinsent, *The Second-Person Perspective in Aquinas's Ethics*, 82.
19 See, for example, Peter Hobson, *The Cradle of Thought: Exploring the Origins of Thinking* (New York: Oxford University Press, 2003).
20 Gilbert K. Chesterton, *Orthodoxy*, (London: Bodley Head, 1908), chapter III.
21 As noted in the text, I have drawn some of the material of this chapter from two earlier publications, namely Pinsent, "Humility", 242–264.; and Pinsent, *The Second-Person Perspective in Aquinas's Ethics*, 77–83. I am especially grateful for feedback and advice from Eleonore Stump for the preparation of these earlier works.

Bibliography

Barnes, Jonathan. *Complete Works of Aristotle, Volume 2: The Revised Oxford Translation*. Princeton, NJ: Princeton University Press, 1998.

Chappell, Timothy. *Knowing What to Do: Imagination, Virtue, and Platonism in Ethics*. Oxford; New York: OUP Oxford, 2014.

Chesterton, Gilbert K. *Orthodoxy*. London: Bodley Head, 1908.

Eilan, Naomi, Christoph Hoerl, Teresa McCormack, and Johannes Roessler, eds. *Joint Attention: Communication and Other Minds: Issues in Philosophy and Psychology*. Oxford: Clarendon Press, 2005.

Grey, Brandon. *Narcissistic Relationship: Ultimate Guide to Torture a Narcissist. Recovery from the Epidemic Narcissism, Emotional Abuse and Personality Disorder. The Revenge for Lovers (Also for Parents)*. Independently Published, 2019.

Hobson, Peter. *The Cradle of Thought: Exploring the Origins of Thinking*. New York: Oxford University Press, 2003.

"Narcissism, n." In: *OED Online*. Vol. Oxford English Dictionary. Oxford: Oxford University Press. Accessed June 10, 2019. www.oed.com/view/Entry/125088.

Pinsent, Andrew. "Humility." In: *Being Good: Christian Virtues for Everyday Life*, edited by Michael W. Austin and Douglas Geivett. Cambridge, UK: Grand Rapids, Michigan, Eerdmans, 2012.

———. *The Second-Person Perspective in Aquinas's Ethics: Virtues and Gifts*. New York; Abingdon, UK: Routledge, 2012.

Twenge, Jean, and W. Keith Campbell. *The Narcissism Epidemic: Living in the Age of Entitlement*. New York London Toronto Sydney New Delhi: Atria Books, 2010.

Young, Rebecca Konyndyk de. "Aquinas's Virtues of Acknowledged Dependence: A New Measure of Greatness." *Faith and Philosophy* 21(2) (2004): 214–227.

18

FAITH AND HUMILITY

Conflict or concord?

Daniel Howard-Snyder and Daniel J. McKaughan

In some circles, faith is said to be one of three theological virtues, along with hope and agape. But not everyone thinks faith is a virtue, theological or otherwise. Indeed, depending on how we understand it, faith may well conflict with the virtues. In this chapter, we will focus on the virtue of humility. Does faith conflict with humility, or are they in concord?

In what follows, we will, first, sketch a theory of the virtue of humility. Second, we will summarize a common view of faith, arguably shared by Thomas Aquinas among others, and we will argue that faith, so understood, is not an intellectual virtue and that it conflicts with humility in the domain of inquiry. Third, we will plump for an older view of faith, one that predates Aquinas by at least 1500 years. Fourth, we will argue that, on that older view, faith is an intellectual virtue and it is in concord with humility in the domain of inquiry. Fifth, we will contrast the two views of faith both in relation to humility and in the domain of personal relationships.

18.1 The limitations-owning theory of the virtue of humility

Theorists think of virtue in different ways. We will presuppose the *personal worth theory* (Baehr 2011; Battaly 2015). On the personal worth theory, virtues are excellences of persons, among which are character traits. A *character trait* of someone is a trait grounded in their motivations and values, both of which are relatively stable.

Not all character traits are virtues, however. Someone's character trait is a *virtue* only if it makes them better as a person, and it makes them better as a person only if they are a good judge of when, toward whom, and how they exercise it, and only if it is grounded in good motivations and values. To illustrate, consider someone stably disposed to give liberally but at the wrong time, toward the wrong people, or in the wrong way. They might have the trait of generosity but lack the virtue since, for example, they tend to give too much and they tend to give to scams, cons, and fraudulent charities. Or imagine someone stably disposed to give liberally at the right time, toward the right people, and in the right way, but who developed that disposition just to look good in the eyes of others, and thereby extend their power over them. They might have the trait of generosity but lack the virtue since what grounds their disposition is bad.

Theorists also think of humility in different ways. We will presuppose the *limitations-owning theory* (Whitcomb et al. 2017). On that theory, the trait of humility consists in being both attentive to and owning one's limitations. *Limitations* are, roughly, the bad or not-so-good things about oneself: cognitive mistakes, e.g., errors in grading exams; gaps in knowledge, e.g., the economics of American slavery; deficits in cognitive skills, e.g. ignorance of statistical analysis; intellectual character flaws, e.g. onesidedness; moral mistakes, e.g., speaking harshly to a student; affective shortcomings, e.g., lacking empathy; deficits in general skills, e.g., housecleaning; or flaws in moral character, e.g., being judgmental—among many other things. Someone is *attentive* to their limitations when they are so disposed that their limitations come to mind regularly, in contrast with being oblivious to them. So someone completely inattentive to their limitations is not humble. However, someone can be attentive to their limitations while also being flagrantly complacent about them, systematically concealing them from others, responding defensively when they are brought to light, and the like. They are not humble either. The humble own their limitations. Someone *owns* their limitations when they are so disposed that, if their limitations come to mind, they do not respond routinely with complacency, concealment, defensiveness, and the like. More generally, owning one's limitations *characteristically* involves cognitive, behavioral, motivational, and affective dispositions to (i) believe or accept that one has them, (ii) admit and acknowledge them, (iii) care about them, and (iv) feel regret or dismay about them. (NB: characteristically, but not always; see the paragraph after next.) If the limitations-owning theory is correct, then, among many other things, the humble will be more likely than the non-humble to admit their limitations to others, defer to others, seek help from others, and have a low concern for status, and they will be less likely to set unattainable goals and disrespect others (Whitcomb et al. 2017, 13–26).

As we said, not all character traits are virtues. The same goes for humility. Someone might be stably disposed to attend to and own their limitations but at the *wrong* time, toward the *wrong* people, or in the *wrong* way; and someone might be stably disposed to attend to and own their limitations at the right time, toward the right people, and in the right way, yet be disposed to do so for the *wrong reason*, i.e., bad motivations or values ground their disposition. Either way, they will have the trait of humility but not the virtue of humility. On the limitations-owning theory, the *virtue* of humility is a disposition to *appropriately* attend to and *appropriately* own one's limitations.

We can't emphasize strongly enough that the ways in which one appropriately attends to and appropriately owns one's limitations can both *vary significantly* across situations and *differ from* their characteristic manifestations. For example, in some cases appropriate owning may call for one to acknowledge one's limitations to someone else, e.g., when you've wronged them, while in other cases it might call for one simply to admit the limitation to oneself, e.g., when we acknowledge our unhealthy sedentariness. Or compare owning one's inability to play basketball with owning one's chronic tardiness. If you can't do anything about the first, say, because you're old and decrepit, but you can do something about the second, say, because you can routinely set your alarm five minutes earlier, then appropriately owning the first might not involve feeling regret or dismay but rather coming to peace with it, while appropriately owning the second might involve feeling regret or dismay and resolving to get rid of it. (The last three paragraphs draw on Whitcomb et al. 2020.)

18.2 Thomistic faith

Aquinas's view of faith is well-trod territory. In what follows, we will not get embroiled in scholarly textual disputes about it. Rather, we will articulate a view that has a significant, even if disputable, basis in Aquinas's writings and that is recognizably Thomistic, in the way that a view might be recognizably Augustinian, Cartesian, or Humean, even though it has a significant but disputable basis in their writings.

According to Aquinas, the object of faith is God but, since we have no immediate awareness of God, the object of faith is, strictly speaking, propositions about God, such as the proposition that God exists or the proposition that Jesus is God incarnate (ST II–II. q.1. a.1–2). Faith, then, is an act of intellectual assent to propositions about God. Many contemporary commentators call this act of intellectual assent "belief"; we will follow suit. Notably, Aquinas says that faith shares important features with both (i) high-grade knowledge (*scientia*), such as a mathematician's knowledge of first principles and their knowledge of theorems based on demonstrations from those principles, and (ii) mere opinion, suspicion, and doubt (*opinione, suspicione et dubitatione*), such as our mere opinion that Trump's campaign conspired with the Russians, our suspicion that there is extra-terrestrial sentient life, and our doubt about whether the number of kayakers on Pearrygin Lake this century will be even. Like knowledge, faith requires psychological certainty, and so no doubt, a view echoed by, among others, *The Catholic Encyclopedia*: "doubt cannot coexist with faith … ; faith and doubt are mutually exclusive". Like mere opinion, suspicion, and doubt, the evidence for faith is inadequate for belief, in two ways. First, the evidence for faith is causally inadequate to move someone's intellect to belief since the evidence for faith is only enough to move their intellect to mere opinion, suspicion, or doubt (ST II–II. q.4. a.1). Second, the evidence for faith is justificatorily inadequate for belief since the evidence for faith is only enough to justify intellectual acts such as mere opinion, suspicion or doubt and not belief. Nevertheless, someone can have faith that a proposition about God is true since they might be so attracted to its being true that their will moves their intellect to believe it is true even though their intellect alone could not be moved by the evidence to believe it (ST II–II q.1 a.4; cf. Hebrews 11:1, #558, and QDV q.14, a.2). And that is what faith is, says Aquinas: believing a proposition about God, on inadequate evidence, by an act of will due to an attraction to its being true.

Aquinas also distinguishes virtuous faith from faith lacking virtue. On his view, if someone is attracted to the truth of a religious proposition out of a love (*caritas*) of God or a love of what is in fact the goodness of God, then, if they believe it by an act of will, their faith is virtuous; otherwise, it is not (ST II–II. q.4. a.3–5). But this isn't quite right since, by Aquinas's lights, faith is virtuous only if what evidence one has for it is testimonial, e.g. hearing the word of God (ST II–II. q.4. a.8). Finally, a person can be saved, says Aquinas, only if they have virtuous faith. (For extended discussion of the relationship between faith and salvation, see Stump 2003, chapters 12 and 15.) So, for example, if Valerie is attracted to the truth of the basic Christian story out of love of God or the goodness of God presented in the basic Christian story, then, if she believes it by an act of will, her faith is virtuous and so salvific, whereas if Victor is attracted to the truth of the basic Christian story solely out of a desire to avoid hell, then, if he believes it by an act of will, his faith is not virtuous and so not salvific.

We have several objections to Aquinas's view about what faith is and when it is virtuous. As for what faith is, we deny that faith can only take God or religious propositions as objects. Obviously enough, spouses, friends, children, and one's self, among other non-religious things, can be objects of faith, as can propositions that are not about God. Moreover, even if the will and an attraction to the truth of a proposition figure in faith somehow, one can have faith that it is true even if one's faith is not caused by an act of will due to an attraction to its truth. As for when faith is a virtue, one's faith in relations to one's intimates can be virtuous even if what evidence one has to go on is non-testimonial, as when a mother puts her faith in her son or two friends have faith that their friendship will endure a crisis. Further, if you put your faith in someone else, you may well be attracted to them coming through for you with respect to what you've put your faith in them. But, in order for your faith in them to be virtuous, your attraction need not be motivated by love (caritas) of them or their goodness; any number of other positive motivations might do. For example, if we put our faith in Dr. Huber as a dentist, we may well be attracted to her coming through for us as a dentist, but our faith in her can be virtuous even if our attraction is motivated solely by a desire for a healthy doctor–patient relationship, one that need not involve love of her or anyone or anything else.

It's little wonder, then, that all the details of Aquinas's view of faith have found little traction in contemporary pistology. Even so, the core of the view has found some traction. It is this core that we will call

> *Thomistic faith.* For someone to have faith is for them to believe something with certainty on inadequate evidence.

Others agree that this is what faith is. According to the New Atheists, "faith is belief in the absence of evidence", or "believing something without good reasons", or "belief in spite of, even perhaps because of, the lack of evidence" (Rosenberg 2013; Pinker 2006; Dawkins 1992). Sam Newlands says: "A lot of people think of faith as having a kind of belief commitment that something is going to be certain, or that something is going to be probable, that maybe outstrips the evidence" (2017). According to Robert Pasnau: "To hold a belief on faith is to hold it firmly and to attach a high credence to it even though one does not suppose that the evidence warrants such confidence"; those with faith, "adhere to their firm convictions even while maintaining a self-consciously grown-up awareness of how poor the evidence is" (2017, 135). It seems, then, that Thomistic faith has some purchase on thinkers as diverse as these.

Notice that Thomistic faith is a cognitive attitude, not a character trait; when instantiated, it takes a specific proposition as its object, not all or nearly all propositions with respect to which one has faith, as we would expect of a trait. Even so, we can ask what character trait would correlate with it. On the personal worth theory we presuppose in this paper, it would be this:

> *Thomistic faith as a character trait.* For a person to have faith as a character trait is for them to be disposed to consistently believe things with certainty on inadequate evidence, and to do so because of their stable motivations and values.

Two questions arise. Could such a character trait be a virtue? How would it relate to humility?

It is difficult to see how Thomistic faith as a character trait could be an *intellectual* virtue. A character trait is an intellectual virtue only if it is grounded in a strong desire for epistemic goods such as truth, knowledge, understanding, and justified belief. But anyone with a strong desire for such goods will be ill-served by such a trait. That's because a disposition to consistently believe things with certainty on inadequate evidence lends itself to falsehood, ignorance, misunderstanding, and unjustified belief. Thomistic faith as a character trait, therefore, conflicts with the motivations and values appropriate to intellectual virtue.

Thomistic faith as a character trait would conflict with the virtue of humility in the domain of inquiry, for at least two reasons.

First, we are often in no position to settle a matter that's important to us because our cognitive powers are not up to the task or we have yet to exercise them to gain enough evidence to form a reasonable opinion. The virtue of humility counsels us to be appropriately attentive to, and to own, our intellectual limitations, including a lack of evidence, and so to refrain from believing in such cases. Not so with Thomistic faith as a character trait. If we are stably disposed to consistently believe on inadequate evidence, then we will be less likely to be attentive to our intellectual limitations including our lack of evidence or, when we are attentive to them, we will be less likely to own them and respond appropriately by not believing, and so less likely to avoid falsehoods.

Second, Thomistic faith as a character trait stably disposes us not just to *believe* on inadequate evidence but to believe *with certainty*. Beliefs accompanied by certainty are more difficult to dislodge. Thus, if we have this disposition, once having believed something, it will not only have made it more likely that we believe a falsehood, it will make it more likely that we *retain* a falsehood. Since we frequently meet inadequate evidence in our inquiries, and since we sometimes err and believe on inadequate evidence, we will be stably disposed to crowd our minds with difficult-to-dislodge falsehoods. Not so with the virtue of humility. If we are stably disposed to appropriately attend to and own our intellectual limitations, then, if we believe something on inadequate evidence, we will be more likely to be aware of it, and we will be more likely to change our minds rather than dig in with certainty.

In light of these two points, the inquirer with both the character trait of Thomistic faith and the virtue of humility would be pulled in incompatible directions. They would be pulled toward believing on inadequate evidence and not; and, when believing on inadequate evidence, they would be pulled toward believing with certainty and not.

Thomistic faith as a character trait, therefore, is not an intellectual virtue and, in the domain of inquiry, it conflicts with humility as a virtue. Later we will argue that it is not a relational virtue either and that, in the domain of personal relationships, it conflicts with humility as a virtue.

18.3 Markan faith

We turn to an older account of faith, one rooted in ancient Greco-Roman thought and practice, as well as ancient Jewish and early Christian thought and practice (Morgan 2015; McKaughan 2017). We could name it any number of things, but we will call it *Markan faith* because the characters of *The Gospel According to Mark* exhibit it so well; e.g., Jairus, the friends of the paralytic, blind Bartimaeus, the hemorrhaging woman, the Syrophoenican woman, the woman at Bethany, the father of the demon-possessed son, and Jesus, especially in his relationship with the 12 disciples, as well as in his prayer in Gethsemane and his cry of dereliction on Golgotha (Howard-Snyder 2017). However, before we introduce the account, we must draw an important distinction.

Sometimes we have faith *that* something is true, as when a father has faith that his daughter will flourish in adulthood, despite adolescent evidence to the contrary. Call this *propositional faith*. On other occasions, we put or maintain faith *in* someone, or some property or event involving them, as when a man puts his faith in a woman, as his wife, or soldiers put their faith in another, as their commander. Call this *relational faith*. Relational faith paradigmatically inaugurates and perpetuates a relationship of mutual faith and faithfulness between people, one in which someone puts or maintains faith in another, as a thus-and-so, and the other responds with faithfulness to them, as a thus-and-so (and vice versa). We say "as a thus-and-so" because relational faith is relative to some things but not others, e.g., you might have faith in your children, as students, but not as horticulturalists. We distinguish propositional faith from relational faith because the older account of faith is, first and foremost, an account of relational faith, which will be our focus.

We will introduce the older account by contrast with what some experts regard as Aquinas's view of relational faith (Stump 2003, 439–440; Swinburne 2005, 138–141). On this view, relational faith is a kind of *propositional belief*, something like the belief that the person in whom you have put your faith will deliver or come through for you with respect to what it is you have put your faith in them. We call this view

> *Belief-Only*. For you to put or maintain faith in someone, as an *x*, is for you to *believe* that they *will* come through as an *x*.

On Belief-Only, for you to put your faith in Dr. Huber, as your dentist, is for you to believe that she will come through for you as a dentist. Notice that, unlike Thomistic faith, Belief-Only wisely removes the idea of believing with certainty on inadequate evidence. Even so, four concerns remain.

First, you can believe that someone will deliver as an *x* even if you do not want them to and you think it is undesirable or bad that they do; but you lack faith in that case. That's why you would never put your faith in Timothy McVeigh, as a terrorist, even if you believed that he will deliver as one. That's why you would never have faith in Satan, as a devil, even if you believed that he comes through all too well on that score. You are against terrorism and devilry; you regard them as undesirable or bad. Faith involves a *positive conative-evaluative posture* toward its object.

Second concern: you can believe that someone will deliver as an *x*, and even want them to and think it's a good thing, without being disposed to rely on them as an *x*; but you lack faith in that case. In this connection, imagine Jesus calling someone to follow him. Suppose they regard following him as desirable, and they even want to follow him. Yet, due to the demands of discipleship—e.g., relinquishing attachment to wealth, status, power, autonomy, and the like—they are conflicted and so, perhaps due to weakness of will, they walk away. They lack faith in Jesus *as Lord* since they are not disposed to rely on him *as Lord*. Another illustration: you might well believe that your neighbor is a fine wife, and you might even be for it and think it's a good thing; however, you do not have faith in them *as a wife* since you are not disposed to rely on them *as a wife*, in contrast with their husband. In short, if you have faith in someone, as an *x*, then you will be *disposed to rely on them*, as an *x*.

To set up our third concern, we submit that to theorize about what faith is we might usefully reflect on what makes faith valuable, notably the role that it plays in forming and maintaining relationships of *mutual faith and faithfulness*. Ryan Preston-Roedder (2018) observes three sources of value. First, when you put your faith in someone, as a spouse, or a friend, or the like, you are more likely to see and appreciate their potential and value in these capacities. Second, when you put your faith in someone, in a certain capacity, they are more likely to live up to your favorable view of them because your approval of and reliance on them gives them additional reason to come through for you in that capacity. Third, when you put your faith in someone, there's a sense in which you cast your lot with them; you make yourself vulnerable to them and you rely on them to respond faithfully. If they do respond faithfully, the result is a sort of solidarity, a solidarity that can increase when they reciprocate the faith you have put in them by putting their faith in you, and you respond faithfully. These observations make sense of Teresa Morgan's claim that, in the ancient Greco-Roman world, faith played a crucial role in forming and maintaining relationships of mutual faith and faithfulness "at every socio-economic level", "relationships of wives and husbands, parents and children, masters and slaves, patrons and clients, subjects and rulers, armies and commanders, friends, allies, fellow-human beings, gods and worshippers, and even fellow-animals" (2015, 120).

Now to our third concern. Putting your faith in someone can help to promote and sustain valuable relationships in these three ways *only if* it is at least somewhat resilient in the face of challenges of various sorts. By way of illustration, unless the faith you put in your spouse can withstand the strains of marriage, your faith in them won't make these valuable things more likely. If you are disposed to pack your bags and head out the door at the first sign of them not delivering as a spouse, your "faith" in them will not make it more likely that you will see them as a spouse favorably, or that they will see themselves as a spouse favorably and act accordingly, or that you both experience marital solidarity. Nor will the relationship benefit from ways that resilient reliance itself contributes to stability and security (McKaughan 2017).

Fourth concern: you can put your faith in someone, as an *x*, even if you lack belief that they will deliver as an *x*. That's not to say that you can *dis*believe it and still have faith. Faith involves a more positive cognitive attitude than that. Still, faith need not involve *belief* that they *will* deliver as an *x*, for at least two reasons (cp. Howard-Snyder 2019).

The first reason begins with the observation that, according to Belief-Only, you have faith in someone, as an *x*, only if you *believe* that they will deliver as an *x*. No other type of attitude will do. Not seeming, not credence, not trust, not acceptance, not beliefless assuming. Only belief is allowed. Moreover, according to Belief-Only, when belief is the positive cognitive attitude that you have while you have faith in someone, as an *x*, the content of that belief must be that they *will* deliver as an *x*. No "thinner" content will do: not that *it's likely that* they will deliver, not that *it's more likely than not*, not that *there's a good enough chance to risk putting your faith in them*, and so on for a long list of ineligible "thinner" propositions. Only the "thick" proposition that they *will* deliver is allowed. The sheer implausibility of requiring exactly one attitude-type and exactly one content counts against Belief-Only, especially since other attitude-types and "thinner" contents can sustain the role of faith in a well-lived life.

The second reason begins with the observation that the role of faith in a well-lived life is to render you resilient in the face of challenges to relying on those in whom you repose faith, and faith serves this role partly by responding to new evidence against their not coming through. While new counterevidence might induce doubt about whether they will come through, faith tends to help keep you from being deterred or disheartened into inaction, it tends to help keep you behaviorally on track. By way of illustration, consider a case of faith *in oneself*. Imagine "a first-generation college student—a child of Mexican immigrants—who discovers, upon entering college, that many of her classmates and teachers hold rather dim views of Hispanic students' drive and intellectual ability" (Preston-Roedder 2018, 175). Suppose these dim views constitute new counterevidence to her belief that she will succeed as a student, and suppose it is strong enough to induce belief-cancelling doubt about the matter. If she has sufficient faith in herself, as a student, her resilience in the face of this counterevidence might help her to overcome the otherwise debilitating effects of her doubt, e.g., by helping her to keep her nose in the books, by motivating her to say "no" to extracurricular temptations, etc., rather than throwing in the towel. Her faith in herself, as a student, would not help her in this way if it required her to *believe* that she *will* succeed. Due to its stringent belief-condition, Belief-Only cannot account for faith's role when counterevidence produces belief-cancelling doubt.

If we wish to avoid these four concerns about Belief-Only in our theorizing about faith, we will be led to

> *Markan faith*. For you to put or maintain faith in a person, as an *x*, is for you to have a positive conative-evaluative posture and a positive cognitive attitude toward their coming through as an x, and for you, in light of your posture and attitude, to be disposed to *rely* on them to come through and to be *resilient* in the face of challenges to relying on them as an x.

How does Markan faith differ from trust? On every theory of trust in the literature, trust is either unnecessary or insufficient for Markan faith; notably, faith and not trust necessarily involves resilience (cf. McKaughan and Howard-Snyder unpublished).

Markan faith is a complex attitude, not a character trait; when someone instantiates it, it takes a specific person as its object, not all or nearly all of those in whom one reposes faith, as we would expect of a trait. Even so, we can ask what trait would correlate with it. It would take us too far afield to explain our answer to this question and so, without argument, we identify *resilient reliance* as the central defining feature of Markan faith. We will understand resilience as a disposition to overcome challenges to relying on those in whom we repose faith (Battaly 2017; King 2014). Thus we have:

> *Markan faith as a character trait.* For someone to have faith as a character trait is for them to be disposed to overcome challenges to relying on those in whom they repose faith, and to do so because of their stable motivations and values.

This view fits well with Teresa Morgan's repeated observation that, in the Greco-Roman world, faith was a "social virtue" drawn on in times of crisis because it enabled people to overcome the "fear, doubt, and skepticism" that threatened their relationships of mutual faith and faithfulness (Morgan 2015, 7, 117, 120, 121). Moreover, it helps explain why the Greeks and Romans deified faith as *Pistis/Fides*. Furthermore, it fits well with faith as understood and practiced in the early churches, and as exhibited in *The Gospel According to Mark*, about which Christopher Marshall—the foremost expert on the theme of faith in that Gospel—wrote: "Without doubt, the leading characteristic of Markan faith is sheer dogged perseverance" (1989, 237).

Now, as we said earlier, not all character traits are virtues, and Markan faith is no exception, for the following two reasons.

First, someone might be stably disposed to overcome challenges to relying on those in whom they repose faith but lack the virtue of faith because they lack good judgement. Imagine a spouse suffering in an abusive marriage who maintains great faith in their partner, consistently overcoming challenges to relying on them in a variety of ways—when they shouldn't, contrary to good judgment. If this disposition generally characterizes the faith they put in others, they lack the virtue of faith. You might say they have too much faith, faith to a fault, faith in excess. They don't give up when they should. As a result, the trait of faith in them exhibits intransigence. For most of us, however, intransigence is not a problem. Rather, we are prone to give up too readily, give up when we shouldn't. Our friend doesn't return our calls; our neighbor lets their dog out too early in the morning; our religious congregation questions a policy we favor strongly—and so, contrary to good judgement, we withdraw, we no longer rely on them for friendship, neighborliness, and community. If this disposition generally characterizes the faith we put in others, we lack the virtue of faith. You might say we have too little faith, a deficiency of faith. As a result, our faith exhibits irresolution. The trait of Markan faith is a virtue only if you are neither *over*disposed nor *under*disposed to overcoming challenges to relying on those in whom you repose faith, neither disposed toward intransigence nor disposed toward irresolution.

Second, someone might be stably disposed to overcome challenges to relying on those in whom they repose faith and regularly exercise good judgment, but lack the virtue of faith because their disposition is grounded in bad motivations and values. Imagine an ambitious young priest who learns that archbishops must have faith as a trait, and so they embark on a regimen to gain it. In due course, they succeed, and they also develop good judgment about who to put faith in, and when and for what. Even though they have the trait of faith, they lack the virtue since their stable disposition to overcome challenges to relying on others in whom they repose faith is grounded in hunger for ecclesiastical power and its privileges.

Upshot: as a *virtue*, Markan faith is a disposition to *appropriately* overcome challenges to relying on those in whom one reposes faith, as the context demands.

18.4 Markan faith and humility in the intellectual domain

Earlier we asked whether Thomistic faith as a trait could be an intellectual virtue and how it would relate to the virtue of humility in the domain of inquiry. We now ask, and answer, the same two questions about Markan faith.

Markan faith as a trait can be an intellectual virtue since anyone who values epistemic goods will be well-served by it, provided they use good judgement in its exercise.

In this connection, consider the project of human inquiry, which aims to gain truth, knowledge, and understanding about the world, ourselves, and our place in the world. We participate in this project well only when we work together. That's because it is no easy task to achieve its aims, especially regarding matters we care about deeply, matters related to the STEM disciplines as well as the human sciences, the humanities, the arts, and the law, among other things. Inquiry is demanding. Success is more likely if we work together—learning from each other and our predecessors, teaching the next generation, collaborating on projects, critiquing and improving each other's work, and so on—all of which requires a disposition to rely on each other as fellow inquirers. Of course, our fellows can let us down. But unless we are at least somewhat disposed to stick with them even when they let us down, we will be less likely in the long run to achieve our goal. This does not mean that if a researcher, research group, or even an entire discipline *regularly* lets us down, e.g., by routinely falsifying data or routinely excluding feasible viewpoints, we should stick with them come hell or high water. We need to exercise good judgment. But absent any disposition to *appropriately* overcome challenges to relying on our fellow inquirers, we will be less likely to achieve the epistemic goods at which we aim by participating in the project of human inquiry.

Of course, we care about epistemic goods in domains other than the project of human inquiry. Take, for example, journalism. We want to know the truth about important current affairs, at home and abroad. Clearly enough, we rely on others to be informed—editors, investigators, reporters, photographers, eyewitnesses, technicians, etc.—and, clearly enough, absent any disposition to overcome challenges to relying on them for information, we will be less likely to achieve the truth we seek. This does not mean that we should ignore challenges to the reliability of certain journalists and media outlets; rather, it means that we should exercise good judgement in deciding who to stick with, for what, and for how long. Something similar can be said about governmental administrations, healthcare, the judicial system, the military, meteorology, finance, real estate, wilderness management, and many other domains of human life.

As for the second question, it seems that Markan faith as a virtue would relate well to the virtue of humility in the domain of inquiry.

First, in general, Markan faith as a virtue facilitates the successful exercise of other intellectual virtues. Consider curiosity, for example, a disposition to wonder, ponder, and ask questions with an eye toward gaining understanding. Or consider intellectual autonomy, a disposition to think things through for oneself; or fairmindedness, a disposition to consider the merits of opposing views with equanimity; or intellectual carefulness, a disposition to avoid errors and foster accuracy; or intellectual thoroughness, a disposition to investigate broadly and deeply in the quest for understanding. For each of these virtues, you can exercise it only if you *rely on* the cognitive abilities that constitute it; furthermore, unless you are appropriately *resilient* in the face of challenges to relying on those constitutive abilities, you will be less likely than you otherwise would be to gain the epistemic goods at which the virtue aims.

And the same goes for humility. You can exercise humility only if you *rely on* the cognitive abilities that constitute it, both the ability to perceive your limitations and the ability to own your limitations. Furthermore, unless you are appropriately *resilient* in the face of challenges to relying on those abilities, you will be less likely than you otherwise would be to gain the truth, knowledge, and understanding at which humility aims. Having faith in yourself, as an intellectually humble person, facilitates the successful exercise of humility. More generally, having faith in yourself, as an intellectually virtuous person, facilitates the exercise of your intellectual virtues.

Next, consider two other ways in which Markan faith as a virtue would relate well to the virtue of humility in the domain of inquiry. First, humble people will be aware of their intellectual limitations and, for some of them, such awareness will reveal *many* limitations. If they have faith in themselves, as inquirers, it can help buck them up in the face of an otherwise daunting host of limitations; it can help direct their minds to their many strengths as inquirers and past successes in inquiry; it can help invigorate an "I can do this!" attitude. Second, when you put your faith in someone, it's typically someone *else* you put your faith in. Thus, when humility reveals your limitations, faith would typically direct you to rely on others with resilience to help you fill in the gaps in your knowledge, to lend a technical hand, to add or hone a skill, and the like.

18.5 Thomistic faith, Markan faith, and humility in the domain of personal relationships

Markan faith as a trait would also relate well to the virtue of humility in the domain of personal relationships, whether human–human or divine–human.

As for human–human relationships, not infrequently, we find ourselves needing to rely on others to come through for us on matters of importance to us, especially in areas of our lives where we recognize our own deficiencies.

By way of illustration, consider a marriage in which each partner brings different strengths and limitations to the relationship. Suppose one partner is incompetent at managing finances, while the second is competent. If the first partner is virtuously humble, they will be disposed to recognize and own this limitation of theirs, and if they have faith in their partner, they will be disposed to rely on them, as a financial manager, and to appropriately overcome challenges to relying on them in this capacity, e.g., continuing to rely on them despite a minor mistake in the budget or a penalty from an unpaid bill. Further, suppose the second partner is significantly less able than the first to provide the empathy, perspective, and emotional support that their teenage child needs. If the second partner is virtuously humble, they will be disposed to recognize and own this limitation of theirs, and if they have faith in their partner, they will be disposed to rely on them, as the more emotionally switched-on parent, and appropriately overcome challenges to relying on them in this capacity, e.g., when they occasionally fail to meet their teenager's emotional needs. Of course, there are many other ways in which limitations-owning can dovetail with resilient reliance to enhance a marriage and family life. To the extent that each partner virtuously owns their limitations and virtuously relies on the other, and the other comes through with respect to that which they rely on them for, a successful marriage and family life seems more likely than it otherwise would be.

Also, in human–human relationships, appropriately relying on someone can be an aid to becoming more virtuously humble. By way of illustration, when you put your faith in a partner, friend, or therapist, as a confidant, and in doing so you rely on them for honesty about defects in your deep self, you rely on them to be discrete and to hold you accountable. By providing you with a safe, supportive relationship for you to work through your deficiencies, you may well be more likely to recognize and own your laziness, narcissism, selfishness, and other vices, so as to enhance the process of personal growth needed to help you flourish as an individual and in your other relationships.

We suspect that these two observations generalize. Generally speaking, humility and faith, virtuously exercised, make human–human relationships more likely to flourish. What holds for marriage and family life, and for therapeutic relationships, also holds for a wide variety of other relationships between parents, children, lovers, colleagues, neighbors, business partners, commanders and soldiers, leaders and citizens, employers and employees, and many other worthwhile social relationships.

How might Thomistic faith as a character trait fare in the domain of human–human relations, and how might it relate to humility? There are many ways in which a tendency to believe something with certainty on inadequate evidence will not serve relationships well. For example, if our first marriage partner described above forms and persists in the belief that they are a competent financial manager, despite their evidence, and if the second one forms and persists in the belief that they are an emotionally switched-on parent, despite their evidence, and if both of them are stably disposed to believe with certainty on inadequate evidence in other ways pertinent to their marriage and family life, then they are more likely to misrepresent their relationship with each other and with their child in ways that would worsen those relationships. Furthermore, just like in the domain of inquiry, a stable disposition to believe with certainty on inadequate evidence and a stable disposition to own limitations relevant to a personal relationship pull in different, incompatible directions. When we think about someone in a personal relationship *and hold the first disposition fixed in our thinking about them*, they would at best only sporadically own their limitations since they would be stably disposed to misrepresent themselves to themselves.

Let's now turn to humility and faith in a divine–human relationship. Any attempt to explain how they would relate to each other will be tradition-bound. We choose Abrahamic religion. On that tradition, humans tend to fail in multiple ways: we don't live up to our own moral ideals, we seek our own power and interest over the general good, we squander our natural and God-given talents, we neglect to steward creation well, and by acts of commission and omission we undermine the establishment of a peaceful, just, and harmonious global community. These and other failures are at odds with God's purposes. Consequently, we are alienated from God, and we are alienated from each other. At our best, we are aware of our failings and we own them, with regret and an intention to improve. But improvement is difficult, fraught with setbacks, uncooperativeness, greed, malaise, disrespect, and a thousand other impediments. Left to our own devices, failure is not only our past, it is our future as well. Fortunately, God has not left us to our own devices. God has provided a way to be reconciled with God and, as a consequence, a way to be reconciled with each other. Different Abrahamic traditions tell different stories about what that way is. But the stories share in common the idea that human beings individually and collectively can align themselves with God's way by maintaining faith in God, relying with resilience on God and God's way, to help us undo the alienation that characterizes our relationship with God and our relationships with each other. On Abrahamic religion, therefore, humility enables us to see and own our failures and alienation, while faith enables us to align ourselves with God's way of reconciliation. Humility dovetails with Markan faith.

It is difficult to see how Thomistic faith would fit well into this general picture. Just one illustration. Suppose we were generally stably disposed to believe with certainty on inadequate evidence. In that case, we would be more likely to incorrectly view our failings, either by believing that we are worse off than the evidence warrants or by believing that we are better off than the evidence warrants. Moreover, having formed these false beliefs, we would hold them with certainty, and so we would be more likely to retain them. As a consequence, we would be less likely to see ourselves aright, and so more likely not to own them appropriately, whether by being too disheartened by an overly negative view of ourselves or by being too unperturbed by an overly positive view of ourselves. Either way, a precondition of God's way of reconciliation—namely, our seeing ourselves aright—would be less likely to be satisfied. So it is that Thomistic faith would be at odds with humility, and how humility serves God's purposes in reconciliation.

18.6 Conclusion

We acknowledge that in this chapter we have focused selectively on (i) how resilient reliance dovetails with limitations-owning to promote the aims of inquiry and personal relationships, and on (ii) how believing on inadequate evidence with certainty is at odds with limitations-owning in the domains of inquiry and personal relationships. What we offer thus falls short of a full evaluation of the comparative merits of Markan faith and Thomistic faith. Nevertheless, we invite the friend of Thomistic faith to exhibit (i) how resilient reliance is at odds with limitations-owning in the domains of inquiry and personal relationships, and (ii) how believing on inadequate evidence with certainty dovetails with limitations-owning to promote the aims of inquiry and personal relationships. Until the friends of Thomistic faith accept our invitation, and deliver on it, we tentatively conclude that while Thomistic faith conflicts with humility, Markan faith is in concord with it.[1]

Note

1 We thank audiences at the Free University, Amsterdam, and the University of Arkansas. We especially thank Frances Howard-Snyder, Alessandra Tanesini, and Dennis Whitcomb for their extensive and critically constructive conversation and comments. This publication was supported by a grant from The John Templeton Foundation. The views expressed in it are those of the authors and do not necessarily reflect those of The John Templeton Foundation.

References

Aquinas, Thomas. 1265–74/1981. *Summa Theologiae, Part II–II (Secunda Secundae)*. Translated by Fathers of the English Dominican Province. London: Burns, Oates, and Washbourne. Reprinted by New York: Benziger 1947–48 and Westminster, MD: Christian Classics. www.newadvent.org/summa.

Aquinas, Thomas. 1256-59/1951-54. *Truth (Quaestiones Disputatae De Veritate)*, q. 14 ("On faith"). Translated by Robert W. Mulligan, J. V. McGlynn, and R. W. Schmidt, 3 vols., Chicago, IL: Henry Regnery Company. https://dhspriory.org/thomas/QDdeVer14.htm.

Aquinas, Thomas. 1272-73/2012. *Commentary on the Letter of Saint Paul to the Hebrews (Super Epistolam B. Pauli ad Hebraeos lectura)*. Translated by F. R. Larcher, O. P., edited by J. Mortensen and E. Alarcón. Lander: Aquinas Institute.

Baehr, Jason. 2011. *The Inquiring Mind*. New York: Oxford.

Battaly, Heather. 2015. *Virtue*. Malden, MA: Polity.

Battaly, Heather. 2017. "Intellectual Perseverance". *Journal of Moral Philosophy* 14(6): 669–697.

Dawkins, Richard. 1992. "A Scientist's Case against God". *The Independent*, April 20.

Howard-Snyder, Daniel. 2017. "Markan Faith". In: Rebekah Rice, Daniel McKaughan, and Daniel Howard-Snyder (eds) *Approaches to Faith*. New York: Springer, pp. 31–60.

Howard-Snyder, Daniel. 2019. "Three Arguments to Think that Faith Does Not Entail Belief". *Pacific Philosophical Quarterly* 100(1): 114–128.

King, Nathan. 2014. "Erratum to: 'Perseverance as an Intellectual Virtue'". *Synthese* 191(15): 3779–3801.

Marshall, Christopher. 1989. *Faith as a Theme in Mark's Narrative*. New York: Cambridge.

McKaughan, Daniel J. 2017. "On the Value of Faith and Faithfulness". In: Rebekah L. H. Rice, Daniel J. McKaughan, and Daniel Howard-Snyder (eds) *Approaches to Faith*. New York: Springer, pp. 7–29.

McKaughan, Daniel J., and Daniel Howard-Snyder. Unpublished. "How Does Trust Relate to Faith?"

Morgan, Teresa. 2015. *Roman Faith and Christian Faith: Pistis and Fides in the Early Roman Empire and the Early Churches*. New York: Oxford.
Newlands, Samuel. 2017. "Faith and Hope are Two Different Philosophical Mindsets". www.youtube.com/watch?v=-b5Hiijc4bU.
Pasnau, Robert. 2017. *After Certainty*. New York: Oxford.
Pinker, Steven. 2006. "Less Faith, More Reason". *The Harvard Crimson*. www.thecrimson.com/article/2006/10/27/less-faith-more-reason-there-is.
Preston-Roedder, Ryan. 2018. "Three Varieties of Faith". *Philosophical Topics* 46(1): 173–199.
Rosenberg, Alex. 2013. "Is Faith in God Reasonable? Debate: Alex Rosenberg vs. William Lane Craig". http://open.biola.edu/resources/is-faithin-god-reasonable.
Stump, Eleonore. 2003. *Aquinas*. New York: Routledge.
Swinburne, Richard. 2005. *Faith and Reason*, 2nd edition. New York: Oxford.
Whitcomb, Dennis, Heather Battaly, Jason Baehr, and Daniel Howard-Snyder. 2017. "Intellectual Humility: Owning Our Limitations". *Philosophy & Phenomenological Research* 94(3): 509–539.
Whitcomb, Dennis, Heather Battaly, Jason Baehr, and Daniel Howard-Snyder. 2020. "The Puzzle of Humility and Disparity". In: Mark Alfano, Michael Lynch, and Alessandra Tanesini (eds) *The Routledge Handbook of Philosophy of Humility*. New York: Routledge, pp. 72–83.

19
HUMILITY IN THE ISLAMIC TRADITION

Sophia Vasalou

A commonplace view of how many religions approach the right relationship to self-worth is that the less we have of it, the better off we are. The virtuous attitude to the self requires thinking poorly of one's merits, and this attitude constitutes the virtue we call humility. This was the view implicitly taken by David Hume when he defended the importance of a "steady and well-establish'd pride and self-esteem" in human life and expressed his expectation that this would draw the animus of a "great many religious declaimers," who typically placed their loyalties in the "monkish" virtue of humility instead (Hume 1978: 599–600, Hume 1975: 270). In framing this point, Hume had primarily Christian attitudes in mind. What about Islamic attitudes?

This chapter attempts to answer this question by a selective survey of the approaches taken by a number of key contributors to the discourse on character in the Islamic world. While this "commonplace view" contains an element of truth when applied to the Islamic tradition, it is a blunt instrument for capturing Islamic thinking on the subject. As Muslim thinkers articulate the virtue of humility, it possesses two distinct (though related) dimensions. On the first, humility concerns attitudes to self-worth and self-assessment, which many philosophers and also non-philosophers would consider the proper field of this virtue. On the second, by contrast, humility has a forward-looking or conative quality, and is tied to an attitude of moral commitment that is ultimately co-extensive with the virtue of religious obedience. One of the most distinctive aspects of the approaches to humility and pride in the Islamic tradition, as I will suggest, is the central role played by temporal concepts. Virtuous attitudes to the self look to the past, but, even more importantly, they also look to the future: to as-yet uncertain future outcomes which underline the fragility of virtue. Despite the emphasis on the underestimation of self-worth that shapes these approaches, there is also a more positive attitude to self-worth that can be read out of Islamic works on the virtues.

19.1 The ethics of virtue in a scriptural paradigm

Islamic views of the virtues were moulded inside a cadre of overlapping intellectual frameworks, which included influences from pre-Islamic Arab culture, the ancient Greek philosophical tradition, and above all the core religious scriptures, the Qur'an and hadith. The degree to which each of these influences asserted itself varied across different genres and works. In compendia of philosophical ethics, for example—the kind written by philosophers like Abū ʿAlī Miskawayh

(d. 1030) and Naṣīr al-Dīn al-Ṭūsī (d. 1274)—ancient philosophical ideas play a prominent role, outshining that of the scriptural sources. By contrast, in works of Sufi spirituality, which were a key vector for the development of Islamic ideals of character, the influence of these textual sources takes centre stage.

While humility (Arabic *tawāḍuʿ*) appears in works of philosophical ethics, its treatment is limited. Al-Fārābī (d. 950 or 951), for example, includes it in his *Aphorisms of the Statesman*, but has little to say about it (1971: 36). In Miskawayh's classification of the virtues in his *Refinement of Character*, humility is a conspicuous absentee. This may partly reflect the indifference to the virtue among ancient philosophers. It forms a far more important theme in texts more firmly anchored in the scriptural framework. The writers I will be focusing on populate different points of the loose philosophical–scriptural spectrum, with some (notably al-Ghazālī and al-Rāghib al-Iṣfahānī) bearing clear traces of philosophical influence and others (Ibn Qayyim al-Jawziyya) developing their ideas more independently of it. These differences are reflected in the physiognomy of their writing, particularly in the analytical depth to which they are interested in probing ideas and the level of theoretical scaffolding they seek to provide. Even among the more philosophically minded, the practical aims that shape their work mean that ideas often require unpacking to make them speak to the questions *we* might have about their subject.

Whatever their other differences, the thinkers I will be considering are united by a firm commitment to viewing the scriptural texts as a non-negotiable source of moral guidance. Both the Qur'an and the hadith show a sustained concern with moral questions about how people relate to their merits and about the right and wrong ways of doing so. "Be humble, and let none of you glory over others," one tradition describes the Prophet as urging. According to another, "Nobody will enter paradise who has the merest speck of pride (*kibr*) in his heart." The Qur'an is replete with admonitions against pride and its pernicious consequences. "How evil is the lodging of those that are proud!" (Q 40:76; compare 40:35, 16:29, 39:60). Pride is the failing of key figures in the Qur'an, including Iblis, the counterpart of Satan in the Islamic tradition. Commanded to bow to Adam after the latter's creation, Iblis refuses and haughtily retorts, "I am better than he; You created me of fire, and You created him of clay" (Q 7:12).

19.2 Humility as self-assessment

Humility, the scriptural sources suggest, is a praiseworthy trait. Yet what then *is* humility? In his influential compendium on the virtues, *The Pathway to the Noble Traits of the Law*, the eleventh-century literary and religious scholar al-Rāghib al-Iṣfahānī answers this question as follows. Humility is when "a person contents himself with a station (*manzila*) inferior to the one merited by his excellence." It is a virtue "only found among kings, grandees, and learned men and it falls under the category of gracious acts (*tafaḍḍul*), as it involves forgoing a right (*ḥaqq*)" (al-Rāghib 2007: 213).

The emphasis on social class in this statement will seem puzzlingly narrow, excluding some of the more interesting cases around which questions about humility come up, where merit is a matter of *moral* accomplishment.[1] Yet even more surprising will be the natural way of reading its main thrust: humility, it implies, has to do less with how a person *thinks* of himself than how a person *behaves*. It's not about making a low estimate of one's merits but rather of not insisting on the claims these merits would typically generate. We may think here of the magnanimous or great-souled man as described in Aristotle's *Nicomachean Ethics*, who may choose not to insist on receiving the honour due to him. The obvious implication, in Aristotle's case as in this one, is that the person has a clear understanding of what is due to him—of his moral worth. Humility here comes across as a species of magnanimity in the recognizable modern sense of the word: a gracious self-concealment and abandonment of social rewards that rests on a robust awareness of one's actual merits.

Al-Rāghib is not the only Muslim writer to frame humility in these terms, as a kind of social grace pertaining to the sphere of social behaviour.[2] Yet the more prominent formulations approach humility in terms that will be more familiar to contemporary philosophers and theologians. Humility concerns the way a person assesses their merits. And the right way of assessing one's merits is presented trenchantly, as a matter of systematic underestimation. The eleventh-century theologian Abū Ḥāmid al-Ghazālī (d. 1111) makes this stance clear in his landmark work, *The Revival of the Religious Sciences*, in the context of a *tour de force* campaign against the vice of pride. One of the many religious sayings he approvingly quotes is the following: "The higher a believer stands in God's estimate, the lower he stands in his own." The point is put even more trenchantly in another quote: "God said, 'You have worth (*qadr*) in our sight so long as you assign yourself none'" (1937–8, 11: 1943, 1959). In this part of the *Revival*, al-Ghazālī offers his readers a raft of moral exercises to help them overcome their pride. The upshot for the reader who carries them out is that he will come to "regard himself with contempt" (*yuḥaqqiru nafsahu*) and perceive "the worthlessness of his being" (*khissat dhātihi*) (1937–8, 11: 1975, 1971).[3]

The view that humility involves a programmatic underestimation of self-worth that may reach as far as wholesale denial is also conveyed by the later thinker Ibn Qayyim al-Jawziyya (d. 1350) in his spiritual compendium, *Passages of the Wayfarers*, in turn a commentary on an earlier Sufi classic, *Stations of the Journeyers*. "Humility," he reports, "is to see yourself as having no value (*qīma*)" (2010a: 613). On many occasions, this judgement is framed in absolute terms, as in the statements just cited. On others, it is framed comparatively, as exemplified by Ibn Qayyim himself in another work, *The Book of the Spirit*. Humility means "not to see yourself as superior to anyone or as having claims over anyone, and rather to see other people as superior to you and as having claims over you" (2010b: 658). Al-Ghazālī, on his part, makes this the basis of a distinction between two vices opposed to humility, pride and conceit (*ʿujb*). Both involve a high estimate of the self, but pride is individuated by the fact that this estimate is framed relative to others, as a judgement of superiority over others. Hence a person could have the vice of conceit even if she was the only human being in existence, but the same isn't true of pride (1937–8, 11: 1946–7).

In recent times, there have been a number of philosophical attempts to provide an updated and more nuanced account of what humility consists in. Humility, to take some of the best-known versions, is about not *over*-estimating our merits, about owning our limitations, or about lacking self-concern (see, e.g., the overview in Roberts and Cleveland 2016). The views of these Muslim thinkers, by contrast, appear to return us to a more traditional understanding of humility that we find in almost any dictionary we open. Humility (so the *Oxford English Dictionary*) is "the quality of … having a lowly opinion of oneself."

Taken in this form, these views will invite a question familiar to philosophers reflecting on the nature and value of humility. As a matter of fact, some people simply *are* better than others in a range of qualities, including ones of a moral and intellectual kind. Do al-Ghazālī and his peers think we ought to remain *ignorant* of this fact? Does the virtue of humility require wilful self-deception?[4] We get help toward answering these questions, and a broader perspective on Islamic attitudes to self-worth, if we ask what makes the corresponding vices problematic. Here I will take my lights from al-Ghazālī's discussion of pride and conceit in the *Revival*, supplementing it with insights provided by other writers.

Al-Ghazālī advances a number of reasons to explain why pride, taken as an attitude to the self incorporating a judgement of superiority over others, is problematic, which we could loosely distinguish into reasons of a utilitarian or forward-looking and a deontological kind. One reason of the first kind reflects a thesis we might call the "unity of the vices." Vices hang together, just like the virtues do (*al-akhlāq al-dhamīma mutalāzima*). Al-Ghazālī's argument here is that pride typically prevents us from acquiring other virtues, and naturally leads to or partners with a number of other vices, such as anger, envy, rancour, and dishonesty. It can also lead us to reject the truth, including, importantly, religious truth (on which point, more below) (1937–8, 11: 1947–8, 1951–2).

More interesting, however, is a different kind of reason, which I call "deontological" because it pivots on the notion of a right or a claim. What lends this reason its special interest is that it points to a conceptual model that provided a key framework for thinking about the life of virtue in the Islamic tradition, while at the same time revealing some of its provisos. To become virtuous, on this line of thinking, is to attempt to acquire qualities possessed by God in paradigmatic form: it is to imitate God. God's character, as al-Ghazālī suggests in one place, provides a *criterion* for what constitutes virtue or true perfection (1937–8, 13: 2335). This model has well-known precedents in the ancient tradition, notably in Plato's philosophy. In the Islamic world, it played an important role among both Sufi thinkers and philosophers.

In its ancient counterpart, it has sometimes provoked perplexity: how could God, or the gods, possess virtues like temperance or courage when they lack the bodily conditions and limitations that make gluttony or cowardice a temptation among humans (and thus their opposites virtues)?[5] In the Islamic context, the most important challenge shows up in a different place, and almost in reverse, as a question about whether qualities that are virtues in God are necessarily virtues among humans. Because God's qualities include a desire for praise, love of self-sufficiency, and a sense of greatness or superiority over other beings (*kibr, kibriyāʾ*). Yet to imitate *these* qualities, and certainly the last, is in fact to expose oneself to divine wrath, as a well-known hadith attests. Al-Rāghib is particularly forthright on this point: pride is "praiseworthy in God but blameworthy in humans" (2007: 214). God alone is entitled to pride taken as a quality that incorporates a judgement about one's greatness and superiority over other beings. It constitutes one of God's special prerogatives and exclusive claims. A human being that possesses this quality therefore antagonises and violates a divine right (al-Ghazālī 1937–8, 11: 1951; cf. Ibn Qayyim 2010b: 659, al-Makkī 2001, 2: 1042–3).

Put so simply, the force of the idea may not seem obvious. Surely we could grant that only God is entitled to judge himself absolutely great, and also comparatively greater than everyone else, while retaining our ability to make comparative judgements in the human context, and to say that certain people (including ourselves) are better than others? Judgements of worth are not a zero-sum game.

To this, al-Ghazālī and his peers would, I believe, offer a number of responses. On the one hand, it's not that such comparative judgements, on the horizontal (human) plane, couldn't be made; it's that vertical comparison renders them meaningless. Once we have set the scale for wisdom, for example, using God's wisdom, the comparison between my level of knowledge as a scholar of Renaissance literature and yours as the possessor of a mere high-school diploma is like comparing shades of grey after having looked directly at the sun, or like comparing the size of molehills around one's feet having just looked up at a sheer cliff towering hundreds of meters above. It can be done, but the comparison seems meaningless. As in the experience of the sublime (which my last example may evoke), the vision of the vertical scale has a deflationary effect (though, unlike the sublime, this effect is not superseded by a new frisson of pride).

A second response is more illuminating and decisive, though it takes a little more work to spell it out. What is wrong with human pride, and the judgements of worth it incorporates, can't be gotten at simply by examining the judgements themselves taken as pure abstract propositions. As Ghazālī explains at various points in the *Revival*, vices, like virtues, are composites made up of a number of elements. They include an element of cognition (*maʿrifa*), a phenomenology or felt emotion (*ḥāl*), and action (*ʿamal*). The bare judgement (*ruʾya* or *ʿaqīda*) that one has a superior status to another is not a sufficient condition for pride to be realised. It only becomes pride when conjoined to a particular phenomenology, which al-Ghazālī describes as a sense of "confidence, exultation, joy, and repose in this judgement" (1937–8, 11: 1946). Phenomenologically inflected this way, it then expresses itself outwardly in one's behaviour toward others.

To appreciate the force of this point, we need to see it as flagging an important link between two vices that al-Ghazālī presents as distinct but interrelated: pride and conceit. Unlike pride, as already mentioned, conceit doesn't have a comparative dimension. Instead, what individuates it is a different cognitive component. A person is conceited when they take satisfaction in a quality they possess without referring this quality to any other source than themselves. They take pleasure in it under its description as a quality that is entirely their own. The vicious cognition here is privative, and the positive cognition it excludes is the role of God's agency in making one's virtues possible. Conceit is therefore based on a false concept of ownership, and entails an equally false sense of security. The phenomenology of conceit involves a pleasured sense of confidence and repose (*rukūn*) (1937–8, 11: 1991–2; cf. Vasalou 2019: 43–4). These, of course, are the same words we just heard al-Ghazālī use to describe the phenomenology of pride. This is no accident, as conceit, in his view, is a vice that is prior to and a cause of pride. The feeling of happy self-assurance and secure possession of the valued trait is thus a shared feature in both vices.

Al-Ghazālī's response to this shared feature holds the key to explaining the problem, or one of the chief problems, with pride. Both pride and conceit can be described as vices of ignorance or self-deception, because the sense of self-assurance that constitutes them belies important facts concerning our dependence on God. This is a dependence that crucially cuts in two directions, or along two temporal lines. On the one hand, every perfection we possess in the present rests on a number of preconditions and prior causes. And all these causes, in al-Ghazālī's view, have been supplied by God in a series of undeserved acts of benefaction. We're like a servant whom a great king has had washed and combed and dressed up in his own finery. If the servant then marvels at himself, he is marvelling at the king's handiwork, not his own.[6] The servant is not responsible for his beauteous appearance and deserves no credit for it. In the same way, we are not responsible for our beauteous character and other accomplishments and any credit is due to their real author, God.

This position has an important entailment for the emotional attitudes with which we relate to our virtues. The exulting sense of self-assurance that shapes the vice of pride cannot survive the acknowledgement that we are not responsible for our virtues. Self-assurance is replaced by a trembling awareness of the fragility of virtue. This view evidently rests on the endorsement of a particularly uncompromising form of determinism, which, here at least, al-Ghazālī isn't concerned to camouflage or sugar-coat.

This acknowledgement of dependence and resulting perception of the fragility of virtue, which looks to the past, finds its natural complement in another acknowledgement that looks to the future. Because a person who at time t_1 finds herself endowed with great moral or intellectual virtue, as the result of causal chains lying outside her control, simply cannot guarantee that her virtue will endure all the way to the unknown future time t_x when death comes to her. And it is her spiritual state and spiritual performance at the moment of death, as al-Ghazālī emphasises, that determines her otherworldly destiny, whether she will be happy or unhappy (see 1937–8, 13: 2363–75).

In fact, al-Ghazālī seems prepared to go further. It's not just that we don't *know* for certain whether our present perfections will endure over time and pass the test at the final instants of our life (the *khātima*, or conclusion of life). It's that in a deeper sense we can't properly be said to *possess* particular perfections in the present time so long as the future outcome remains uncertain. This is suggested by another intervention al-Ghazālī makes on the topic of pride, explaining why it is inappropriate for humans but not God. The issue, al-Ghazālī says, is that pride must have a proper foundation; and human beings can never be certain of that foundation, since it depends on a future eventuality. "Were a person to judge that he possesses [an] attribute with a definiteness admitting no doubt," then pride

> *would* be appropriate for him and would be a virtue (*faḍīla*) with respect to him. Yet he has no way of knowing this, for this depends on the conclusion, and he does not know what the conclusion will be.
>
> *(1937–8, 13: 2415)*

This may seem like a puzzling position to take: how could what happens in the future affect what is true in the present? Surely we possess our virtues *now*, regardless of what happens at a later time? If we take a virtue in a familiar Aristotelian sense, as a stable disposition to be understood as a realised structure in psychological space, the idea may indeed appear alien. Yet, even in an Aristotelian context, virtues as dispositions cannot be separated from the expressions and performances they give rise to. Whether a person possesses a disposition is after all a judgement we make, not something we discover by looking directly into their psychological space. And how a person goes on to emote, think, and act at a future moment affects whether we still feel comfortable ascribing a certain trait to her, and may lead us to revise our earlier judgement ("She was not *really* generous after all").

This analogy is certainly relevant for making sense of al-Ghazālī's point. But it doesn't entirely capture the significance that the temporal horizon of the future possesses in al-Ghazālī's thinking and that of many of his peers. We can appreciate this more fully by considering the distinctive cognitions that constitute the mindset of the person affected by the vice of pride, as al-Ghazālī characterizes him. The person who has a (false) sense of confidence about his perfections is not simply confident about something he possesses in the present. To the extent that he is a believing Muslim, his sense of confidence about the present translates into a sense of confidence about the future, and about how he will be treated in the next life. His judgement about his merits is also a judgement about how *God* is judging his merits, and the value he attaches to his moral and intellectual *state* is intrinsically bound up with the *standing* he believes it secures with God.[7] *This* part of the proud person's mindset is no vice, but an essential (if not exhaustive) aspect of the eudaimonistic view of virtue championed in the *Revival*, which encourages us to see virtue as a necessary means to (primarily) otherworldly happiness.

In the terms of this theological economy, then, virtue looks to the future in a more fundamental way. This is what gives teeth to al-Ghazālī's critique of pride and conceit and his emphasis on the fragility of our virtues. To return to our earlier question: do al-Ghazālī and his peers think we should remain ignorant of our merits and of the differences in merit between different people? Does humility require self-deception? On the one hand, these differences will seem far less significant when measured against the scale of virtue, God himself. On the other, they will seem shorn of significance when considered against our lack of responsibility for their past production and our inability to control the future. *Real* self-deception is not when we try to pretend we don't possess a quality we in fact do; it's when we think we possess a quality while disregarding how we got there and what may still go wrong.

Yet once we have added these metaphysical "plug-ins" which undercut the objectionable attitudes of self-assurance, self-ownership, and scorn for others, this view would seem to be compatible with a type of self-knowledge that includes accurate judgements on our character, including our virtues. Such self-knowledge is after all *practically* important, and affects how we go about our efforts at self-governance and moral change. A person who can't frame the thought that she has a problematic relationship to physical enjoyments but *not* to money, or that she struggles to pass up opportunities to cheat but is easily touched by others' suffering and energised to relieve it, would not make a good planner when it comes to choosing what parts of her character to focus her efforts on. Despite the rather extreme view of the present's dependence on the future conveyed by al-Ghazālī above, al-Ghazālī himself acknowledges this practical need for self-knowledge elsewhere. At a particularly suggestive point of the *Revival*, he counsels his reader to draw up a kind of workbook or logbook (*jarīda*) and organise it by making a list of the most important virtues and vices (20 in total). When he manages to remove one of the vices from his character, he can cross it off his list and continue moving down, and he can do the same when he acquires one of the virtues (1937–8, 15: 2807).

This exercise may remind us of Benjamin Franklin's industrious 13-week plan to cultivate the virtues. What is worth underlining is the premise that evidently supports it, which is that we can assess our strengths or weaknesses in a reasonably definite way—that is, definite enough to inform our practical efforts and make us decide to stop pursuing one virtue and continue with another. Yet crucially, this assessment is embedded in a paradigm shaped by a clear awareness of one's dependencies. Once a person has succeeded in removing a vice, he must "thank God for delivering him from it and … bear in mind that this only occurred through God's assistance" (ibid). Self-knowledge, divorced from gleeful self-assurance and instead infused with a grateful acknowledgement of dependence and an anxious-but-hopeful sense of fragility, is not only possible but necessary. It is important here that self-knowledge is rooted in a practical concern, in which the self shows up as an object of practical endeavour, and not as something firmly possessed but as a work-in-progress.

19.3 Humility as moral commitment

In the above, I sketched out some of the elements of the view of humility, taken as a virtue regulating the proper attitude to the self and its merits, that emerges from the works of a number of writers, including al-Ghazālī. Humility, on this view, involves making a low estimate of one's merits. This view is situated in a field shaped by several theological presumptions, including ideas about the imitation of God (and its limits) and human dependence. Among other things, I emphasized the crucial role played by temporal concepts in Muslim thinkers' understanding of the virtues.

Yet looking at these same ethical works, one finds another conception of humility at work that cannot be entirely assimilated to this one. Rather than having a reflexive attitude (a relation to the self) at its core, the core of this other conception is a relation to authority, particularly religious or supernatural authority. Discussing pride in the *Revival*, al-Ghazālī distinguishes between three types of pride: one directed toward God, another directed toward God's human emissaries or representatives, and a third toward other human beings (1937–8, 11: 1949–52). The third is the reflexive one we considered above, and al-Ghazālī declares it the least important of the three. In fact, one of the reasons he gives for considering it a vice (in addition to the ones mentioned above) is the fact that it leads to pride in the first two senses. It makes us more likely to reject the truth claims of God's human emissaries and thereby prevents us from accepting God's authority. This point reflects the influence of the scriptures in shaping ethical discourse about this virtue. In the Qur'an, many critical references to pride occur in the context of condemning those who resist God's message (e.g. Q: 16:22, 25:21).

If al-Ghazālī puts the point with reference to the vice, pride, Ibn Qayyim frames it more directly with reference to the virtue, humility. He identifies two types of humility, which are distinguished through their object—what they are humility *to* or *before*. The first involves being humbled to or before God's greatness, and results in the kind of reflexive attitude to the self we have already seen. The second is when "a person humbles himself before [or abases himself to] God's command by obeying and before his prohibition by abstaining." He continues: "When a person holds himself to God's command and prohibition, he humbles himself before the state of servitude (*'ubūdiyya*)" (Ibn Qayyim 2010b: 658–9).

The conjunction between humility and obedience, to be sure, will not be unfamiliar. These virtues have often been drawn together across their history, not just in the Christian context, where they epitomised the ethic of monastic communities, but also in the ancient world. In one of the few seemingly positive references to humility in ancient philosophy, in Plato's *Laws*, humility is linked to adherence to justice and the divine law, while pride leads to the rejection of guidance and authority (716a–b). Ibn Qayyim, it may be noted, does not present humility as a virtue separate from obedience and *leading* to the latter. Rather, humility just *is* a form of obedience. Yet his distinction between two types of humility maps on to what *we* would be inclined to describe, as a matter of ordinary language, as a distinction between "humility" and "obedience." And having drawn this distinction, he makes clear that the first type *entails* (*yastalzimu*) the second (and *not* vice versa) (2010b: 659).

On one level, this causal link may not seem self-evident. Holding another person in high esteem and thinking poorly of yourself by comparison seems to be a very different thing from doing what that person tells you. But the gap closes up if we focus on the features that justify the feelings of esteem and admiration. If you admire a person for their creativity, that may not necessarily give you reasons to take their opinion about how you should lead your life more broadly, though you may seek out their view on occasions where you think that a knack for thinking outside the box is what's especially required. If part of what you admire in that person is their wisdom or kindness, however, you have good reasons to give serious consideration to their judgements about the choices you should make on a variety of matters.

The features you admire in a person may thus provide you with a range of different motives for accepting their judgement. Yet this account of the relations between humility-in-our-sense and obedience-in-our-sense (humility 1 and humility 2 on Ibn Qayyim's terms) is ultimately on the wrong track as a way of approaching the present case. This is clear from the fact that while this model may explain why you should "give consideration," even special consideration, to another's judgement, it is harder to see how it could be used to explain why you should *obey* them and take orders as against advice from them. The concepts of obedience and disobedience, as one Mu'tazilite theologian points out, involve a reference to *status* or *rank* (*rutba*). They presuppose that the person disobeying occupies an inferior status relative to the person being disobeyed (Mānkdīm Shashdīw 1965: 611). Hence you can disobey the king or your father, but you can't disobey a friend or a child.

The description under which you esteem or venerate God ("humility 1") and which induces obedience to his command ("humility 2") is not, in the first instance,[8] a particular attribute, such as God's wisdom or benevolence—though these attributes play a crucial role in helping you *rationally appropriate* the religious life and thereby sustain your relationship to it. ("God has good reasons for commanding me to do certain things: he knows they're good for me.") It is God's status as the sovereign or master (*rabb*) or proprietor (*mālik*) of your being, relative to whom your own status as a human being is that of a subject or subordinate (*'abd*). To acquiesce in God's command is to acknowledge this differential status and to accept one's servitude (*'ubūdiyya*). As sovereign, God has a claim to obedience that cannot be reduced to the claims created by potentially other-regarding (hence anthropocentric) attributes such as wisdom and benevolence. We might thus describe it as deontological in nature. A key condition of this kind of obedience is that we be at least *in part* unable to plumb the reasons behind God's commands and rationally appropriate them by subsuming them into our conceptions of the good (see e.g. Ibn Qayyim 2010a: 619, al-Ghazālī 1937–8, 2: 385–6).

So humility in this second sense is based on a recognition of status relations (God/human, sovereign/subject). But it is worth underlining a point that is implicit in this conception, and is already made obvious if we systematically resort to the English "obedience" to translate what is a single Arabic term in our writers. Unlike the first kind of humility we considered, which focuses on self-assessment and looks backward to existing features of the self, this kind of humility looks forward in a more fundamental way. It is a conative quality, which takes shape as a sense of commitment to adhering to a set of evaluative standards as expressed in God's Law. We see this even more clearly if we consider the vice that Ibn Qayyim opposes to humility in the *Book of the Spirit*. Ibn Qayyim's concern, interestingly, is not with the vice that represents the extreme of excessively *high* (usually populated by pride) but on the vice representing the opposite end of excessively *low*. He calls it "self-abasement" or "abjectness" (*mahāna*).[9] The idea that there could be such a thing as being *too* humble may seem to us surprising given the emphasis on radical under-estimation that shapes the attitudes to self-assessment we surveyed. Yet Ibn Qayyim's understanding of this particular vice has a tellingly different focus. The abject person, he writes, is one who "sacrifices and demeans his soul in the pursuit of its pleasures and appetites" (2010b: 658). Abjectness is thus a vice that involves failure to master inferior desires—an idea that evidently presupposes acceptance of an evaluative standard that ranks desires as inferior or superior and tells us that certain desires *ought* to be mastered. Abjectness is the failure to live up to this standard. Humility is the virtue of the one who succeeds.

In answering the question "Is there such a thing as being too humble?" Ibn Qayyim's focus, I just suggested, is not on self-assessment (on the question whether one could ever think too little of oneself) but on moral commitment and self-command. Yet a closer examination of his remarks may make us wonder whether that is entirely correct. Ibn Qayyim speaks of not "sacrificing" one's soul and of "demeaning" it. His choice of words implies an ascription of value, and it is not the value attaching to the moral standards themselves. If we wished to unpack the point, we might in fact venture to say the following. Some kind of value is being attached to the self or soul that seems to stand in an *explanatory* relation to the kind of self-mastery being more directly valorised. It is *because* we value our soul that we ought to value self-mastery and hold ourselves to these moral standards.

Here, I would suggest, we have the kernel of a more positive relation to the self that forms the counterweight of the austere view of humility found among the writers we have considered. And while we just saw it reflected in the description of a vice, it receives more direct expression in the account given by a number of writers for a positive virtue. Al-Rāghib refers to this virtue using the Arabic term *ʿizza*, while Ibn Qayyim refers to it as *sharaf al-nafs*.[10] Both terms could be translated as "a sense of dignity," "a sense of honour," or even "pride." Putting aside delicate differences between their accounts, both writers present it as a virtue that concerns self-worth, and take self-worth to be expressed in the moral standards to which a person holds himself. A sense of dignity, Ibn Qayyim writes, involves "preserving oneself from base things, vices (*radhāʾil*), and the kinds of desires that bring ruin to men, so that one exalts oneself above them" (2010b: 656). In al-Rāghib's words, it is a matter of "holding oneself above anything that inflicts a blemish upon a person" (2007: 215). Both definitions involve a distinct element of self-exaltation. It's a matter of not *stooping* to defective (immoral) actions or traits. The sense is that to do so wouldn't be *worthy* of one, and that one should value oneself higher.

Although self-assessment is evidently at stake in this virtue, it will be clear that the concept of self-worth it mobilises is rather different from the one that underpinned our earlier discussion of how Muslim thinkers approach a person's relationship to her merits. Rather than looking backward, to existing merits, it looks forward, to the acquisition of merits and indeed the avoidance of demerits. A while ago, the philosopher Elizabeth Telfer drew a distinction between two kinds of self-respect, which she called "estimative" and "conative." The former is a favourable attitude to the self that is grounded in one's "modes of conduct and qualities of character" and more broadly in the sense that one "attains at least some minimum standard." The latter is different, and is evidenced in common expressions such as "Self-respect prevented me from acting that way" or "He did it out of self-respect." Rather than being explained by past behaviour and success in meeting relevant standards, self-respect here explains behaviour and motivates efforts to uphold standards. Self-respect in this second sense is "roughly a desire not to behave in a manner unworthy oneself, or a disposition which prevents one from behaving in a manner unworthy of oneself" (Telfer 1968: 114–15).

The kind of virtue that Ibn Qayyim and al-Rāghib describe can be helpfully compared to this second concept of self-respect. This is a relationship to self-worth that achieves its highest expression in a commitment to certain standards about how one should act and about the kind of person one should be. As such, it does not involve an escape from the human condition of servitude but the fullest realisation of it. God's claim of mastery over our being takes shape as a claim that we exercise self-mastery. It is in this kind of Janus-faced mastery, which looks above (to God, accepting his governance) and below (to the self, imposing governance to its inferior parts) that human dignity is to be realized. Al-Rāghib again puts it clearly: "The dignity (*sharaf*) of created beings lies in manifesting their servitude" (2007: 214). In obedience, the truest humility and the best kind of pride coincide.

Notes

1 By contrast, the definition offered by Yaḥyā ibn ʿAdī (d. 974) in his *Refinement of Character* (1978: 88), which otherwise has much in common with al-Rāghib's, is more amenable to this broader construal.

2 Surprisingly, al-Ghazālī himself offers a view of this kind at one point in the *Revival*: al-Ghazālī 1937–8, 11: 1987–88. See Vasalou 2019: 46–7 for discussion. The same applies to Yaḥyā ibn ʿAdī (1978: 88); though a Christian, his work was influential in the Muslim context.

3 For further discussion of al-Ghazālī's view of humility, see Schillinger 2012, Vasalou 2019, part 1, and Sherif 1975: 53–6.

4 This is the question that frames Norvin Richards' discussion of humility in Richards 1988, and it made waves in the form given to it by Julia Driver in her analysis of modesty as a virtue of ignorance (Driver 2001, chapter 2).

5 I have in mind some of Nussbaum's remarks in Nussbaum 1990, chapter 15. See also Vasalou 2018.

6 My analogy is loosely based on al-Ghazālī 1937–8, 12: 2228–29. For al-Ghazālī's extended discussion of this point, see 1937–8, 11: 1992–7, and also Vasalou 2019: 43–4.

7 Cf. al-Ghazālī's telling characterisation of the pride of the learned man: "he views himself as having a higher status and greater merit than others *with God/in God's eyes*" (*ʿinda Allāh taʿālā aʿlā wa-afḍal minhum*) (1937–8, 11: 1953).

8 I add the rider because the issue is far more complex taken as a broader question about what motivates obedience of the religious Law. God's more anthropocentric ("beautiful") features partner more subtly with his self-centric ("sublime") features in answering this question. For a wedge into this nuance, see al-Ghazālī's discussion of types of obligation in 1937–38, 2: 385-86, and my discussion of the two standpoints on God in Vasalou 2016, chapter 4, esp. 176–7.

9 Compare Ibn Qayyim 2010a: 596, where humility is designated the virtuous mean relative to the vice of abjectness on the one end and pride on the other.

10 The terminological difference shouldn't be magnified; Ibn Qayyim himself juxtaposes the two terms elsewhere as if they were interchangeable. See e.g. 2010a: 597, where he focuses on *ʿizza* as the virtue term.

References

Al-Fārābī, Abū Naṣr. (1971) *Aphorisms of the Statesman/Fuṣūl muntazaʿa*. Edited by Fauzi M. Najjar. Beirut: Dar El-Mashreq.

Al-Ghazālī, Abū Ḥāmid. (1937–38 [1356–57 AH]) *The Revival of the Religious Sciences/Iḥyāʾ ʿulūm al-dīn*. 16 vols. Cairo: Lajnat Nashr al-Thaqāfa al-Islāmiyya.

Driver, Julia. (2001) *Uneasy Virtue*. Cambridge: Cambridge University Press.

Hume, David. (1975) *Enquiries Concerning Human Understanding and Concerning the Principles of Morals*. 3rd ed. Edited by L. A. Selby-Bigge, revised by P.H. Nidditch. Oxford: Clarendon.

Hume, David. (1978) *Treatise of Human Nature*. Edited by L. A. Selby-Bigge, revised by P. H. Nidditch. Oxford: Clarendon Press.

Ibn Qayyim al-Jawziyya, Muḥammad ibn Abī Bakr. (2010a) *Passages of the Wayfarers/Madārij al-sālikīn*. Edited by Shuʿayb al-Arnaʾūt. Beirut: Muʾassasat al-Risāla.

Ibn Qayyim al-Jawziyya, Muḥammad ibn Abī Bakr. (2010b [1432 AH]) *The Book of the Spirit/Kitāb al-Rūḥ*. Edited by Muḥammad Ajmal Ayyūb al-Iṣlāḥī. Mecca: Dār ʿĀlam al-Fawāʾid.

Al-Makkī, Abū Ṭālib. (2001) *Nourishment of the Heart/Qūt al-qulūb*. 3 vols. Edited by Maḥmūd bin Ibrāhīm bin Muḥammad al-Raḍwānī. Cairo: Maktabat Dār al-Turāth.

Mānkdīm Shashdīw, Aḥmad ibn al-Ḥusayn. (1965) *The Five Principles Expounded/Sharḥ al-uṣūl al-khamsa*. Edited by ʿAbd al-Karīm ʿUthmān. Cairo: Maktabat Wahba.

Nussbaum, Martha C. (1990) *Love's Knowledge: Essays on Philosophy and Literature*. New York and Oxford: Oxford University Press.

Al-Rāghib al-Iṣfahānī, Abuʾl-Qāsim ibn Muḥammad. (2007) *The Pathway to the Noble Traits of the Religious Law/Kitāb al-Dharīʿa ilā makārim al-sharīʿa*. Edited by Abuʾl-Yazīd Abū Zayd al-ʿAjamī. Cairo: Dār al-Salām.

Richards, Norvin. (1988) "Is Humility A Virtue?" *American Philosophical Quarterly*, 25, 253–59.

Roberts, Robert C. and Cleveland, W. Scott. (2016) "Humility From a Philosophical Point of View." In: *Handbook of Humility: Theory, Research, and Applications*, edited by Everett L. Worthington, Jr., Don E. Davis and Joshua N. Hook, 33–46. London: Routledge.

Schillinger, James. (2012) "Intellectual Humility and Interreligious Dialogue Between Christians and Muslims." *Islam and Christian-Muslim Relations*, 23(3), 363–80.

Sherif, Mohamed Ahmed. (1975) *Ghazālī's Theory of Virtue*. Albany, NY: State University of New York Press.

Telfer, Elizabeth. (1968) "Self-Respect." *The Philosophical Quarterly*, 18(71), 114–21.

Vasalou, Sophia. (2016) *Ibn Taymiyya's Theological Ethics*. New York: Oxford University Press.

Vasalou, Sophia. (2018) "Virtue, Human and Divine." *Renovatio*, 2(1), 17–12.

Vasalou, Sophia. (2019) *Virtues of Greatness in the Arabic Tradition*. Oxford: Oxford University Press.

Yaḥyā ibn ʿAdī. (1978) *The Refinement of Character/Tahdhīb al-akhlāq*. Edited by Nājī al-Takrītī. Beirut and Paris: Editions Oueidat.

20
BUDDHIST HUMILITY

Nicolas Bommarito

20.1 Buddhism and the context of humility

For many, it's natural to think about humility as fundamentally about a relationship between self and other. To be humble is embody a certain relationship between yourself and something else, most commonly by putting yourself below it or in some way acknowledging it as more important. This is made clear when considering humility's opposite: pride. To be proud is to adopt a standpoint of relative superiority or importance, to put yourself above other people and things.

Of course, this is a very general framework, but it's one that is quite common in philosophical writing, at least writing in English from the last few hundred years. As with any general framework, there are many details to work out. What is the something else that a humble person puts themselves below? Maybe it's other people. Or maybe it's an ideal like justice or The Moral Law. Or maybe it's a supernatural being like God or Allah. What is the nature of the relationship central to being humble? Is it intellectual, emotional, or both?

Many have noted that humility, and its cousin modesty, are opposed to a tendency many have to think too much of themselves.[1] So we find some philosophers identifying modesty with ignorance of our own good qualities.[2] Others, uncomfortable with the idea that a moral virtue might require ignorance, have suggested various alternatives. For example, some argue that what's important is that you *not overestimate* yourself.[3] Other approaches appeal to less doxastic states, making it a matter of de-emphasizing or ignoring good aspects of yourself.[4]

While these views disagree in their content, their framework is shared: humility and modesty are about placing yourself in a larger context. This framework for humility isn't assumed only in contemporary work, but by a wide range of figures in the history of philosophy in Europe. Aquinas, for example, saw humility as moderating our desires for personal excellence, while for Kant it was about checking our demands on others.[5] Later, Iris Murdoch described it as a brake on our selfish impulses.[6] Despite their differences, these figures all assume this shared framework when thinking about humility and its value.

One way to approach Buddhist humility is to think about what Buddhist thinkers might contribute *within* this framework. We might, for example, point to the practice in many Buddhist cultures of physically lowering yourself before an image of a Buddha; the importance of literally lowering yourself when faced with an important ideal. Or we can highlight texts advising a student to relate to their teacher as if they were the Buddha himself, trusting in them even when their actions don't yet make sense.[7] This kind of check on your own judgment in the face of someone with more wisdom and experience fits very well into the familiar framework of humility as a particular relation between the self and something outside the self.

Many Buddhist texts can be read within this framework. To pick a particularly famous example, consider the 8th-century Buddhist Philosopher Śāntideva. His famous text, *The Way of the Bodhisattva*, is one of the most widely studied ethical texts in the Buddhist world. In it, he presents instructions for how to become a bodhisattva, a moral and spiritual ideal in Buddhist thought. The bodhisattva ideal is a selfless one that involves, among other aspects, putting the well-being of others ahead of your own.

The bodhisattva ideal itself and much of Śāntideva's specific advice can seem to fit very nicely into the existing framework for understanding modesty and humility. Consider, for example, his advice to remain still and inactive like a log when confronted with a desire to put yourself above others:

> When the mind is wild with mockery
> And filled with pride and haughty arrogance,
> And when you want to show the hidden faults of others,
> To bring up old dissensions or to act deceitfully,
>
> And when you want to fish for praise,
> Or criticize and spoil another's name,
> Or use harsh language, sparring for a fight,
> It's then that like a log you should remain.
>
> And then you yearn for wealth, attention, and fame,
> A circle of admirers serving you,
> And when you look for honors, recognition—
> It's then that like a log you should remain.[8]

This kind of advice isn't unusual for Buddhist texts and, when read in a certain way, fits very naturally into the standard framework for thinking about humility: actions and desires that involve relative comparisons of self-superiority should be avoided. The urge to put yourself above others is often a bad one, and, when the temptation arises, it's better to do nothing than to indulge in these ways of relating to others.[9]

But passages like this are also motivated by a much deeper account of the world and our place in it, one that doesn't fit very well in the familiar terms of thinking about humility at all. This framework presupposes a certain menu of options: we can think we're better, worse, or the same as others. We can think of ourselves as occupying a starring role in the world or some cosmology or merely playing a bit part.

An important type of humility we can find in Buddhist thought is a denial of this very framework. Much of Buddhist thought involves the denial of a persisting and separate self. With this philosophical background, humility isn't about seeing yourself as having a minor role or being worse than others, but giving up relating to the world through the idea of a self at all. After all, even comparisons of relative inferiority presume there's something to be compared. Buddhist humility in this sense is less about making different comparisons than it is about giving up the underlying assumptions that such comparisons presuppose and reinforce.

20.2 Buddhist conceptions of pride

A helpful way to get at the meaning of a concept is to think about its opposites. If we want to understand the various senses of 'real' for example, it can be illuminating to think of its opposites, like 'fake' and 'nonexistent' – these various opposites shed light on the different senses of what we mean when we call something real. For humility, it can be illuminating to think about the various senses of its opposites: pride and arrogance.[10]

One term often translated into English as 'pride' is known as *māna* in Sanskrit. Like the concept of pride, *māna* is used in both positive and negative senses. In the negative sense it is a bad quality: it's included on the list of six descriptive mental states, sometimes called 'afflictions', 'defilements', or even 'stains'.[11] As we will see, it's badness has an epistemic and moral sense: it's a quality that's both morally bad, a source of suffering, and one that prevents us from seeing how the world really works.

Like pride, *māna* is used in a positive way too. Even people who would put pride on a list of sins can say things like "You should be proud of the good work you've done today" or "Being able to do the right thing yesterday filled me with pride". Śāntideva, for example, is explicit about distinguishing these two senses:

> 'I will be the victor over all;
> Nothing shall prevail and bring me down!'
> The lion-offspring of the Conqueror
> Should constantly abide in this proud confidence.
>
> Those whom arrogance and pride destroy
> Are thus defiled; they lack proud confidence.
> They fall into the power of an evil pride,
> But those with true pride will escape the enemy.
>
> When arrogance inflates the mind,
> It draws it down to states of misery,
> Or else it ruins human birth, should it be gained.
> Thus one is born a slave, dependent for one's food—
>
> Or feebleminded, ugly, without strength,
> The butt and laughingstock of everyone.
> Hapless creatures puffed up with conceit!
> If these you call proud, then tell me who are wretched?
>
> Those who would uphold pride, the enemy,
> Are truly proud, the victors in the war.
> Those who overwhelm the progress of that evil pride,
> Perfect the fruit of Buddhahood and satisfy the longings of the world.[12]

Here Śāntideva recognizes that sometimes self-confidence, a firm conviction that you can do something, is critical for moral and spiritual success. It's no accident that these verses appear in the chapter on keeping at the very hard task of working for others (sometimes translated as 'zeal' or 'perseverance'). This good pride, associated with a deep assurance in your convictions and resolve to transform into a more selfless and compassionate person, isn't to be confused with the bad kind that involves merely inflating your own self-satisfaction.

The Tibetan translation of *māna* is particularly illuminating: it is translated as *nga-rgyal* (pronounced like 'ngah gyäl' with the initial sound like the end of the word 'being'), a compound that contains the first person singular pronoun (*nga*) and the word for king (*rgyal*).[13] In the good sense, the feeling that you're a king is important if you're not to be pushed around by your own bad qualities. In the bad sense, it sometimes means thinking you're better than you really are or more important than others. But it has another negative sense that involves being *ruled by* a false sense of self.

Buddhism loves its taxonomies and pride is no exception. *Māna* or *nga-rgyal* is traditionally thought to have seven varieties.[14] These include things like thinking you're better than people who are worse than you, your peers, or even people who are really amazing. Other types include thinking you're better than you really are, that you have special qualities that you don't really have, or even being proud of qualities that are actually faults. These types fit nicely into the framework of contemporary discourse on humility and modesty—they're about how you feel about your own good qualities and comparing yourself favorably with others.

There's another type that doesn't fit so easily into the contemporary framework. It is especially important in Buddhist thought and has special relevance for understanding the different ways in which humility can operate. It's known as *the pride of the thought 'I'*.[15] This might sound like simply being self-centered. After all, when I am comparing myself to others, *I* take a central place in my mental life; other people are relevant only insofar as they're better or worse than me in some respect. In this sense, even someone who is constantly down on themselves, thinking about how much better everyone else is still has a self-centered mental life.

However, this type of pride isn't just thinking about yourself often or giving yourself pride of place in your mental life. After all, this is sometimes a feature of the kind of beneficial pride that Śāntideva endorses ("*I* will be the victor over all. Nothing shall prevail and bring *me* down!"). It instead refers to a deep-seated tendency lurking within our own thoughts, feelings, and perception. The sense that we are distinct, persisting selves. For Buddhists, there is no such self and the mind's habit of projecting this on to the world in subtle ways reinforces a false sense of how the world really is. To understand this kind of pride and why it's bad, it will be necessary to take a quick detour into Buddhist metaphysical views about the self.

20.3 Non-self: an interlude

To understand how many Buddhists think of the self, it's important to understand their views on collections in general. Buddhists are skeptical that collections are real; on a common Buddhist view there's nothing more to them than the parts that make them up and their various relations. On this view, a team is nothing more than players related in particular ways and a pot is simply bits of clay arranged in a particular way. There is no extra thing in the world that is a team or a pot – talking about a 'team' or a 'pot' just is talking about the bits and their relations.

These collections are known as *skandhas* in Sanskrit, a term that means a heap, pile, bundle, or aggregate. So just as a pile of laundry just is a collection of shirts, socks, and pants arranged in a particular way, what we think is a self is simply a collection of different physical bits and mental events. These are sometimes called the five aggregates. These categories include things like the material parts of our bodies, and instants of perception, sensations, and consciousness.

For our purposes, the details of the categories aren't important. Realizing that there's nothing to a pile of laundry beyond the clothes that make it up does not require understanding the difference between shirts and socks. What's important is this: Buddhists deny the reality of collections. There's no pile on the floor aside from all the clothes. When you clean up your bedroom you cannot see a pile of thirteen socks on the floor and complain that you must clean up fourteen things – thirteen socks and one pile.

In the same way, for many Buddhists, there is nothing more to you or me than the various mental and physical bits that make us up. There's no self beyond the five aggregates that make it up. This view, known as non-self, is the denial of a separate and persisting self, one that exists beyond the parts that we're made of.

Of course, Buddhist philosophers don't just assert this claim. There are a wide range of arguments.[16] Here's a brief taste of one famous argument for this claim. It works as a *reductio*: if we suppose that both the parts and the collection are real, we get into trouble. The trouble comes when we try to think about the relationship between them, particularly identity. If two things are real, they will either be identical or not. So, the parts and collection will either be identical or not.

But, as the argument goes, none of the options for identity between a collection and its parts seems to work very well. Consider the classical example of a chariot. The collection cannot be identical to *any particular part*; a chariot isn't a wheel or a spoke. The collection can't be identical to *all the parts*; a chariot with a single spoke removed is still the same chariot. The collection can't be identical with none of the parts either; it can't be the case that I have a chariot but all the parts have been sold. So, we should reject the supposition that both a collection and its parts are real. Since the parts are privileged in some way (they're more directly known, more causally efficacious) they're the real ones. This is in a way less radical than saying that there are collections but no parts.[17]

There are, of course, many objections and responses to this particular argument and others that aim to establish the same conclusion. In fact, many of the Buddhists I cite here accept something even more radical: that even the parts themselves lack any inherent essence, an idea known as emptiness. But this more radical idea isn't necessary to see the special kind of humility found in Buddhist thought. The point is not to set sail on the sea of metaphysics never to return, but simply that Buddhists think collections are not real and they think that *we* are such collections. This radical view has important implications for ethics in general, and for humility in particular.

It's important to keep in mind that Buddhists do not advocate for banishing words like 'pile' or 'chariot' from our speech. We can still say true things about collectives: "Watch out for that pile of socks!" or "That chariot doesn't look too safe" can both be important and useful things to say. What's important, however, is to say these things while keeping in mind what a pile of socks (or a chariot) *really* is, nothing more than a bunch of socks or parts organized in a particular way.

Though words like 'pile' or 'chariot' can be a handy shorthand for a more complicated reality, the problem is a psychological tendency to start feeling as if these things were real. The danger, then, is that we start to believe the stories we tell out of convenience. This is most dangerous when it comes to the self. The words 'I' and 'me' are useful ways to talk about a complicated and constantly changing collective, but we start to think of it as an extra thing in the world and to become intensely invested and protective of this imagined self. For Buddhists, there is a deep mistake in thinking that *the pile of socks* exists in the same way as the socks themselves. It doesn't. The socks are real and the pile is just and easy way to talk about them when they're organized in a certain way. In the same way there is also a deep mistake in thinking that I exit in the same way as the mental and physical events themselves.

Here's where the ethical relevance comes in. For Buddhists, in mistaking ourselves as separate things in the world, we make the same kind of mistake as someone who thinks they're cleaning up 14 things from their bedroom floor. This, they say, is the source of all kinds of suffering and misery in the world. It's a deeply ingrained and misleading sense of self that both produces and reinforces feelings of selfishness, alienation, and as I'll claim, pride.

20.4 What's bad about pride?

The pride of the thought 'I' isn't about *any* thoughts involving a self. After all, thoughts like "the self isn't real" or "I'm not the kind of thing I thought I was" also involve an idea of 'self' or 'I'. Instead, this kind of pride is one that reinforces, emotionally, perceptually, or cognitively, a sense of yourself as a real and separately existing thing in the world.

This is made clear in the description by Nāgārjuna, an important Buddhist philosopher from India around 200 CE. In his ethical text, *Precious Garland*, he describes this type of pride in a chapter devoted to the bodhisattva ideal:

> Consciousness grasping on to
> Those empty five aggregates
> By foolishly hanging on to the idea of 'I'
> This is called the pride of the thought 'I'[18]

This kind of pride is present in many experiences that imply a self that is separate from the five aggregates. Think of a reaction rooted in the bad kind of arrogant pride: a rich guy in a suit gets average service in a restaurant and gets angry because he thinks *he* deserved better. His pride, thinking he is better and more important than the other customers and the staff, manifests in a wide range of domains. The most obvious is behavioral – he speaks rudely to his waiter and his body language betrays his arrogance.

But his pride also touches other domains. An important one is emotional; he gets angry and frustrated and feels contempt for the people waiting on him. He might have an explicit belief that he is more important, thinking to himself, "These minimum-wage losers can't even get my burger done right." His sense of pride also affects what he notices and what he ignores; he notices things like small mistakes, messy shirts, and a working-class accent while he ignores the customer-to-waiter ratio, sincere apologies, and other mitigating factors.

This guy's pride is bad and leads to harmful emotions, thoughts, and behaviors. His thoughts about himself are self-centered and mistaken in various ways; he thinks he is more important than others and he assumes the world, or at least that restaurant, revolves around him. But if Buddhists like Nāgārjuna and Śāntideva are right, this guy's pride rests on an even deeper mistake. It rests on the assumption that he has an independent self at all, that there is a persisting self that has all of the good qualities and importance that he attaches to it.

Assuming that a pile of laundry is something separate from the items of clothing that make it up is a mistake. Talking about the 'pile' is just shorthand, a conceptual fiction and not something real. Someone who learns about the average American but then asks where exactly this person lives makes such a mistake. 'Average American' is not a real person but a conceptual fiction used to talk about a complex collection. For Buddhists, the same is true of a sense of an independent self. The guy in the restaurant isn't just wrong about his own relative importance in the world, but makes a more fundamental mistake about what *he* really is. It's not just that his comparisons are off, but he's mixed up about the very nature of the things he's comparing.

From a Buddhist perspective, he's a bit like a severely delusional person who boasts, "I am a chicken, the most powerful bird in the world!" This person is wrong on two counts – a chicken isn't the most powerful bird, but, more importantly, they're *not a chicken*. The arrogant restaurant patron is wrong that he's a more important than other customers, but this mistake rests on a deeper one. He's wrong that he's a persisting and independent self at all.

20.5 A distinctive humility

Avoiding this kind of arrogance involves a distinctively Buddhist type of humility. As we've seen, Buddhist thought acknowledges types of humility that involve a lower evaluation of yourself in the face of other sources of value in the world. But it also illuminates another, more subtle kind that involves giving up the foundations on which such evaluations rest.

Some of the most humbling experiences are those that put your own scale in perspective.[19] Seeing the Grand Canyon or arriving in a big city can make you feel small. But for Buddhists, even thinking you're very small is still taking yourself too seriously. What's really humbling is seeing that what you thought of as yourself was largely a mistake.

This kind of humility operates in a very wide range of situations. Arrogantly over-valuing yourself, your importance, or your own good qualities are ways of experiencing life through the lens of a self, but they aren't the only ones. You give a presentation and everyone applauds and tells you how great it was. You feel a warm sense of satisfaction, validated and on top of the world. Maybe it really *was* good and you deserved all that praise. Even still, Buddhists will point out that this feeling is dangerous because it deepens your investment in a sense of yourself as a separate independent thing. It might feel nice now, but it is fundamentally misleading and this sense of self will appear later in ugly and destructive ways: jealousy, insecurity, and anxiety.

Think back to Śāntideva's advice to be like a log when experiencing the desire for fame, praise, or admiration. He doesn't give this advice simply because comparative evaluations of superiority are bad but because indulging in these feelings is dangerously deceptive – they reinforce not just a sense of superiority but the sense that *you are a separate self to begin with*.

This sense of self can also appear in a depressive way, when someone continually *undervalues* themselves. Eeyore spends his days stewing on how his friends are so much better, more successful, and more talented than he is. Any time one of them does something well, he thinks "Of course, they're so much better than me." This is also a self-centered way to relate to the world. For Eeyore, everything that happens and everyone's talents have relevance only comparatively to *him* and *his abilities*. Though it takes on a depressive hue, it is an outlook that assumes the self is the more important thing and other things have relevance only when related to it.

Buddhist humility, at least this type, means giving up this way of relating to others and to life in general. Giving up a persisting self means, among other things, giving up the habit of filtering your experiences through that self. This makes humility less life-denying than it can often seem. Being humble in this Buddhist sense doesn't mean you can't think applause is nice, but you don't think that it says anything about *you* or *your ultimate worth*. This has the benefit of opening you up to fully appreciate the values around you without spoiling that benefit by getting in your own way. The restaurant customer can relate to his waiter and enjoy his food without taking things personally. Eeyore can actually appreciate the talents and good fortune of his friends without feeling like it has to say something about him.

Of course, this notion of humility exists within the practical, philosophical, and soteriological context of Buddhism. Those endorsing this idea also accept other ideas like rebirth, emptiness, and impermanence.[20] It's important to keep in mind that classical Buddhist writers are not consciously engaged in ethical theorizing; they're not primarily interested in articulating the fundamental principles that explain our ethical judgments. They're giving advice, in particular advice that assumes a particular goal and practical context.

So, as we've seen, Śāntideva does think there's a place for certain kinds of pride. This need not be contradictory if you understand that he is writing a manual with practical advice. A book about how to quit smoking might say that nicotine is bad *and* that some people should use nicotine patches. Similarly, some thoughts and feelings can be useful at certain stages of progress even if not part of the final goal.[21]

One of the most important ways to check someone's arrogance is telling them "Get over yourself". Buddhists take this advice in the most serious way possible: a supremely humble person is someone who doesn't experience life through the lens of a self at all. They're free from *nga-gyal*, no longer ruled by a sense of 'I'. It's a de-personalized humility that's not simply about letting others win or thinking you're a worse player than you really are, but giving up the game entirely (or at least giving up any personal investment in winning or losing).

One need not accept Buddhist claims about metaphysics to see this as an interesting and novel conception of humility. It's not about how you rank yourself in relation to others or what place you think you have in the world, but instead about the assumptions that underlie the impulse to rank or situate yourself at all. It's a humility that's not about changing how we compare ourselves with others, but one that challenges the assumptions about the nature of the self that underpin such comparisons. It's a humility that challenges not just our place among others, but our fundamental feeling about our own nature.

Notes

1 See, for example, Foot (1978/2002, 9), Slote (1983), and Sidgwick (1907/1981, 335).
2 See Sorensen (1988) and Driver (1989, 2001) for this claim in the context of modesty. Ben-Ze'ev (1993, 240) and Nuyen (1998, 101) take humility to involve underrating oneself.
3 Flanagan (1990) defends this for modesty and Richards (1988) for humility. See also views that associate humility with accepting one's own limitations as in Whitcomb et al. (2015) and Rushing (2013).
4 See Raterman (2006) for a reluctance account, Ridge (2000) for a de-emphasis account, and Bommarito (2013, 2018) for an attention-based account.
5 See Foley (2004) for this reading of Aquinas. Kant's comments on humility can be found in his *Doctrine of Virtue* (6:462).
6 See Milligan (2007) for more on Murdoch's understanding of humility.
7 See the Tibetan classic *The Life of Milarepa* for a famous example of this.
8 *Bodhicaryāvatāra* V.49–51 This is the Padmakara Translation Group translation.
9 For another cross-cultural take in the context of intellectual humility, see Robinson and Alfano (2016) who draw on the classical Chinese concept of *wu-wei* to argue that intellectual humility is anti-individualistic in certain ways.
10 This approach is also taken by Roberts and Wood (2003) when discussing intellectual humility. See also Tanesini (2018) who contrasts intellectual humility with intellectual servility.
11 These are known in Sanskrit as the *mūlakleśa*; the other five are often translated as ignorance, desire, anger, doubt, and wrong views.
12 *Bodhicaryāvatāra* VII.55–59. Again, the Padmakara Translation Group translation.
13 Tibetan terms are written using the Wylie transliteration system.
14 This division is standard in Tibetan presentations of *nga-rgyal*; see, for example Jamgön Kongtrul (2013, 808). For a classical Indian source see the 4th-century Indian Buddhist philosopher Asaṅga, particularly his *Compendium of Abhidharma* (Sanskrit: *Abhidharma-samuccaya*) and *Bodhisattva Stages* (Sanskrit: *Bodhisattva-bhumi*).
15 In Sanskrit *asmi-māna* and in Tibetan *nga'o-snyam-pa'i-nga-rgyal.*
16 Siderits, Thompson, and Zahavi (2011) is a good place to start of the analytically minded philosopher interested in non-self.
17 This kind of argument can be found in a text called *The Questions of King Millinda* (Sanskrit: *Milinda-pañha*), a dialogue between a Greek king and a Buddhist monk named Nagasena.
18 The Sanskrit title is *Ratnāvalī* or in Tibetan, *Rin-chen phreng-ba.* This is verse 410 (chapter V verse 10). Translation is mine from the Tibetan.
19 See Bommarito (2014) for another way perspective is relevant to Buddhist ethics.
20 See Cowherds (2015) for various contemporary philosophical takes on the relationship between Buddhist metaphysical ideas about emptiness and ethics.

21 The idea of stages on the Buddhist path is a very important one. Classic Buddhist texts like the Tibetan philosopher Tsongkhapa's *Great Stages of the Path* (Tibetan: *Lam-rim Chen-mo*) and the Indian philosopher Asaṅga's *Bodhisattva Stages* (Sanskrit: *Bodhisattva-bhumi*). See also Harvey (2000, 51).

References

Classic Sources

Asaṅga, *Abhidharma-samuccaya*.
———, *Bodhisattva-bhumi*.
Milinda-pañha.
Nāgārjuna, *Ratnāvalī*.
Śāntideva, *Bodhicaryāvatāra*.
Tsangnyön Heruka, *Mi-la-ras-pa'i rnam-thar*
Tsongkhapa, *Lam-rim Chen-mo*.

Modern Sources

Ben-Ze'ev, Aaron, 1993, "The Virtue of Modesty", *American Philosophical Quarterly*, 30(3): 235–246.
Bommarito, Nicolas, 2018, *Inner Virtue*, New York: Oxford University Press.
———, 2014, "Patience and Perspective", *Philosophy East and West*, 64(2): 269–286.
———, 2013, "Modesty as a Virtue of Attention", *Philosophical Review*, 122(1): 93–117.
Cowherds, 2015, *Moonpaths*, New York: Oxford University Press.
Driver, Julia, 2001, *Uneasy Virtue*, Cambridge: Cambridge University Press.
———, 1989, "The Virtues of Ignorance", *The Journal of Philosophy*, 86(7): 373–384.
Flanagan, Owen, 1990, "Virtue and Ignorance", *The Journal of Philosophy*, 87(8): 420–428.
Foley, Michael P., 2004, "Thomas Aquinas' Novel Modesty", *History of Political Thought*, 25(3): 402–423.
Foot, Philippa, 1978/2002, *Virtues and Vices*, Oxford: Clarendon Press.
Harvey, Peter, 2000, *An Introduction to Buddhist Ethics: Foundations, Values and Issues*, Cambridge: Cambridge University Press.
Kant, Immanuel, 1797/1996, "The Metaphysics of Morals", In: *Practical Philosophy*, Mary Gregor (trans. and ed.), New York: Cambridge University Press.
Milligan, Tony, 2007, "Murdochian Humility", *Religious Studies*, 43(2): 217–228.
Nuyen, A.T., 1998, "Just Modesty", *American Philosophical Quarterly*, 35: 101–109.
Raterman, Ty, 2006, "On Modesty: Being Good and Knowing It without Flaunting It", *American Philosophical Quarterly*, 43(3): 221–234.
Richards, Norvin, 1988, "Is Humility a Virtue?" *American Philosophical Quarterly*, 25: 253–260.
Ridge, Michael, 2000, "Modesty as a Virtue", *American Philosophical Quarterly*, 37: 269–283.
Roberts, Robert and Jay Wood, 2003, "Humility and Epistemic Goods". In: *Intellectual Virtue: Perspectives from Ethics and Epistemology*, M. DePaul and L. Zagzebski (eds.), Oxford: Clarendon Press, 257–279.
Robinson, Brian and Mark Alfano, 2016, "I Know You Are, but What Am I?: Anti-Individualism in the Development of Intellectual Humility and Wu-Wei", *Logos and Episteme*, 7(4): 435–459.
Rushing, Sara, 2013, "What is Confucian Humility?" In: *Virtue Ethics and Confucianism*, S. Angle and M. Slote (eds.), New York: Routledge, 173–181.
Siderits, M., E. Thompson and D. Zahavi eds. 2011. *Self, No Self?: Perspectives From Analytical, Phenomenological, and Indian Traditions*, New York: Oxford University Press.
Sidgwick, Henry, 1907/1981, *The Methods of Ethics*, Indianapolis: Hackett.
Slote, Michael, 1983, *Goods and Virtues*, Oxford: Clarendon Press.
Sorensen, Roy, 1988, *Blindspots*, Oxford: Clarendon Press.
Tanesini, Alessandra, 2018, "Intellectual Servility and Timidity", *Journal of Philosophical Research*, 43: 21–41.
Taye, Jamgön Kongtrul, 2013, *The Treasury of Knowledge, Book Six, Parts One and Two: Indo-Tibetan Classical Learning and Buddhist Phenomenology*, Gyurme Dorje (trans. and ed.), Boulder: Snow Lion Press.
Whitcomb, Dennis, Heather Battaly, Jason Baehr and Daniel Howard-Snyder, 2015, "Intellectual Humility: Owning Our Limitations", *Philosophy and Phenomenological Research*, 91(1): 1–31.

21
HUMILITY IN EARLY CONFUCIANISM

Alexus McLeod

The early Chinese philosophical school most focused on moral self-cultivation, Confucianism,[1] reserves an important place for humility. Interestingly, though the virtue is an important one for Confucians, they do not address it directly as an independent virtue, but rather through the consideration of related virtues. Below, I offer the general contours of the early Confucian view on humility, its link to notions of proper self-concern, and argue that Confucians do not place it as a specific separate virtue alongside the oft-discussed concepts of *ren* (humaneness), *yi* 義(righteouseness), *xiao* 孝(filiality), or other important virtues, because its primary role is to facilitate the development of these virtues and enable harmonious social interaction. I consider a number of possibilities for terms in early Confucian texts translatable as 'humility', arguing that none of them can be unproblematically translated as 'humility' across the board, even though all of them are associated with humility in a number of key ways. I argue that, for the early Confucians, humility was connected to trust, deference (to those in superior positions and with greater knowledge), and communal concern (exemplified by the concept of *ren*).

In this paper, early Confucianism is represented primarily by the *Analects* (*Lunyu*_論語·), the collected accounts of the statements of Confucius (*Kongzi* 孔子)[2] with occasional dependence on the *Xunzi*, a slightly later Confucian text.[3] Confucianism is of course far more robust than just the teachings of Confucius, and the *Analects*, while an important text in the tradition, does not enjoy the status of scripture akin to what we find in Abrahamic religions, nor can it be considered the foundational statement of Confucian ethics. It does, however, lay out themes that the later Confucian tradition adopts and develops, and can be justifiably read as offering the basic contours of the Confucian ethical tradition, including many of its core concepts.

I argue here that a Confucian conception of humility is based on the reduction of a certain kind of self-concern seen as deleterious to the social project and ultimately one's own individual thriving (which cannot ultimately be separated from that of the community), along with an augmentation of a more positive kind of self-concern that the Confucians think is instrumental in bringing about social harmony. Like views of humility found in Buddhism and in Abrahamic religious traditions, early Confucians held that the effects of certain kinds of self-concern can be corrosive, and that the development of a particularly social- and other-directed self is a necessary counterweight to the human tendency to generate a particular problematic conception of self. We can find the roots of such a view in the *Analects*, though the view is developed more fully, as I explain in the final section below, in the Confucian text *Xunzi* from the late Warring States period. In the section below, I consider a number of concepts in early Confucianism that can be associated with humility, in order to form a picture of the role of humility, and how it connects to other virtues and the issue of the harmonization of the self and community. I address the latter issue in the following sections.

21.1 Early Confucian terms for 'humility'

The closest approximation to a single term translatable in many contexts as 'humility' in early Confucian texts is *rang* 讓. The concept of *rang* is much broader than that of humility, and in many cases *rang* does not have the sense of humility, but only comes close to it in certain contexts. *Rang* most clearly indicates something like 'deference' or 'yielding', in the sense of allowing others (be they superiors or those with more knowledge) priority, whether in making decisions, initiating activity, or recognition of rank. *Rang* is most often used in the negative in connection with the individual, and often (but not always) aimed at another. The construction X *rang* Y, for example, can often be translated as something like 'X yielded/gave up/refrained from Y'. Other constructions point to the individual or thing to which one yields—one can yield or defer *to* a king, a teacher, etc. While *rang* is a broad concept, a number of early Confucian uses of the term come very close to expressing a concept of humility. Consider the following passages from the *Analects*:

> Ziqin asked Zigong: 'When the master comes to a state, he is always able to learn about its state of government. Does he ask for this, or do others give it to him?' Zigong replied: 'The master [Confucius] is warmhearted, upstanding, polite, temperate, and deferential (*rang*)—this is how he obtains information'.[4]

> The Master [Confucius] said: 'The exemplary person is not contentious. But does this extend even to archery? If one bows and yields (*rang*) to others before taking the stand, and drinks a toast on descending, then his contention is that of the exemplary person'.[5]

Here we see *rang* connected to not only characteristic actions, but also a particular kind of deferential attitude, aimed at undermining potential conflict, putting others at ease, and generating a sense of cooperation and community. Where *rang* appears as a positive feature or virtue, it appears as the proper deference to others—deference in the sense of allowing others to take credit or enjoy visibility. This deference requires a respect for the abilities and values of others, and a moderated sense of one's own comparative abilities and value. Deference is not possible without humility, in the sense of one's ability to put oneself in perspective and to recognize the possibility of one's error, subordination, or limitation. As such, deference is often connected to ritual (*li* 禮) for the Confucians, where ritual can be understood as something like moral norms that involve situating oneself with respect to the community for the benefit of the community.[6] In *Analects* 4.13, Confucius talks of the ability of a ruler to use ritual and deference (*rang*) for the benefit of the state. A passage from the *Jiyi* chapter of the *Liji* mentions the production of deference (*rang*) as one of the (intended) social effects of ritual, along with righteousness (*yi* 義), harmony in the use of resources (*he yong* 和用), and reverence toward the ghosts and spirits.[7]

Another term that can in certain contexts be accurately translated as 'humility' is *gong* 恭. Perhaps the closest English translation of the term in its broader sense is something like 'respectfulness' or 'reverence', but part of this respect is deference in a sense similar to that of *rang* discussed above. *Gong* in the *Analects* generally refers to a deferential respect involving a yielding and foregoing of one's own individual interests in order to facilitate communal harmony.

This is why *gong* is close to ritual deference, according to Confucius (*Analects* 1.13). This ritual deference is itself linked to a certain kind of 'turning away from the self' discussed in the section below—that is, with a particular kind of self-concern focused on adornment and self-aggrandizement, and opposed to communal harmony. As with all of the virtues discussed by the Confucians, *gong* must be tempered by ritual if it is to be effective in facilitating harmonious social interaction and further developing the individual. *Gong* is particularly important for the person with some level of responsibility in governing, according to the Confucians, as such a person will inevitably have greater influence on the character of the community than others.

> The master, discussing Zichan, said: 'he followed the four ways (*dao*) of an exemplary person. In his conduct, he was reverent (*gong*), in performing his responsibilities, he was respectful, in nourishing the people, he was compassionate, in ordering the people, he did what was appropriate'.[8]

21.2 Communal harmony and the self

This demonstrates an important feature shared by these concepts involving humility—the sense in which they are seen as necessary to facilitate harmonious interpersonal activity. It turns out that, for the Confucians, the *social* effect of humility is what makes it an important trait—one that facilitates the development of virtues, most of which, for the Confucian, are grounded in communal thriving. It turns out that the view of humility as primarily being a tool for facilitating harmonious social interactions is not a view limited to the Confucians, but one that finds agreement among current scholars.[9] Jin Li, in an article on contemporary Confucian conceptions of humility, summarizes much of the recent psychological literature on humility, arguing that the trait is tied to social activity, community building, and repairing damaged relationships. She writes that:

> humility promotes the formation, development, maintenance and deepening of social bonds. Humility is especially called for when social bonds are under challenge in four common situations: (1) when a person receives honor/recognition; (2) when the authority fears rebellion from the subordinate in a hierarchical relationship; (3) when empathy/respect is reduced in a conflict; and (4) when different social norms between different groups are encountered.[10]

This view of humility suggests that it should be seen as communal in nature, and primarily plays a facilitating role in supporting the operation of other virtues, as well as supporting the performance of roles, which are of central importance in early Confucianism.[11]

One of the main aims of early Confucianism—perhaps *the* main aim of early Confucianism, is the establishment of social harmony (*he* 和), understood as the proper functioning of society in terms of role exemplification and communal commitment. In a harmonious society, according to the Confucians, each member of society is committed to performing his or her proper social duties (specified by ritual) that are attached to roles. Part of the commitment to these roles is a concern for and responsiveness to others in society—particularly since a role within a community cannot be properly played without effective interaction and commitment to supporting the roles of others. A role is fundamentally community-based, and the Confucians are committed to the idea that hierarchical communities are necessary for the flourishing of humans. While different Confucians disagree about why this is,[12] all Confucians are committed to such a view.

Given that social harmony is a central concern for the Confucians, and that they saw humility as necessary for attaining such harmony, why then did the Confucians have no single term that we can unproblematically translate across contexts as 'humility'? Why did they have no single concept expressing this idea? Why didn't they speak directly and explicitly about this centrally important virtue? The main reason for this, I contend, is that humility can be understood as *part* of a host of other concepts Confucians focused on, and that humility can be captured through particular uses of the terms associated with these concepts, given the right context. As we have seen above, for example, while in certain passages, the meaning of *rang* is closer to "deference" or "yielding", in others "humility" is closer to the meaning. The conceptual overlap between humility and a number of other virtues is an important feature that explains its crucial role in the construction of virtue in general and the generation of social harmony. Looking to the particular virtues and moral features taken to be connected with humility tells us much about what humility is, what its effects are when cultivated in the individual, and how the Confucians think humility can be cultivated.

Among the virtues most often discussed by early Confucians are *ren* 仁 (humanity), *yi* 義(righteousness), *xiao* 孝(filiality), *xin*信 (honesty), and *zheng*政 (proper governance). While there are a host of other virtues discussed, those mentioned here are heavily emphasized throughout early Confucian literature, and humility plays a role in all of them. This suggests that humility has a relational or secondary function linked with other virtues, something like *phronesis* for Aristotle, or as some contemporary philosophers see it, related to the performance of other virtues.

In discussion of the numerous virtues of the early Confucian tradition, we find discussion of humility of various kinds, colored by the virtue in question. In *Analects* 12.1, the broad virtue of humanity (*ren* 仁, a term notoriously difficult to define, which even Confucius and his students struggled with)[13] is associated with 'turning away from the self and returning to ritual' (*ke ji fu li* 克己復禮). While there are a number of competing views as to what is meant here by 'turning away' (*ke*), ranging from selfish desires to self-concern (making it a statement of altruism),[14] there seems little discussion of what I think is a more critical issue—that is, just what Confucius means in 12.1 by 'self' (*ji*). On a plausible way of understanding the passage, 12.1 refers to moving away from an improper commitment to some aspect of self-regard, concern, or interest. It is in this way the diminishing of a kind of self-consideration or self-concern as a motivation for action. The humane (*ren*) person acts based on ritual propriety and righteousness, rather than out of a problematic self-concern. We see other passages reiterating this notion of the humane or exemplary person's rejection of self-concern, such as *Analects* 9.4:

> The master rid himself completely of four things: 'he was without rigid opinions, he was without inalterable imperatives, he was without stubbornness, and he was without a sense of self (*wo*)'.[15]

The problem here is that while there are a number of passages in the *Analects* and other early Confucian texts that, like *Analects* 12.1, argue that the exemplary person rejects the 'self', there are other passages that appear to endorse the exact opposite view—that the exemplary person not only has self-concern, but should have a greater self-concern than the so-called 'petty person' (*xiao ren* 小人). The humane person cannot be self-effacing or completely neglectful of the self—so this 'turning away from the self' cannot be understood as simply the undermining of all self-concern.

In a well-known (and, for many, perplexing) passage of the *Analects*, Confucius discusses the importance of fame or renown, claiming that the exemplary person (*junzi*) will constantly be concerned about making a name for themselves, or leaving a name to memory for posterity.

> The master [Confucius] said: 'The exemplary person is bothered by the prospect of his name not being spoken of by later generations after he is gone'.[16]

Note the strength of the exemplary person's concern for renown—such a person literally becomes sickened (*ji*) at the prospect of being forgotten. Part of the reason this passage is perplexing to so many is that it comes directly after a passage that seems to maintain just the opposite position, and seems to advocate humility in the sense of undermining self-concern. This passage reads:

> The master (Confucius) said: 'The exemplary person is bothered by the prospect of lacking ability—he is not bothered by the prospect of people not knowing of him'.[17]

There have been many attempts to make sense of the seeming contradiction between these two joined passages (as well as other seeming contradictions in the *Analects*).[18] One that has been relatively overlooked, however, might simply turn on a distinction between different kinds of self-concern, and different aspects of the self. The right response here seems to be that there are only certain aspects of the self (or self-concern) that the humane person, the exemplary person, will turn away from. Looking to other passages of early Confucian texts will help us discern what these aspects are.

There are a range of terms used to refer to the self in Confucianism—all reflexive terms that also have the content generally associated with personhood.[19] In Analects 1.4, Confucius' student Zengzi says that he examines himself (*wu shen* 吾身) three times daily, to make sure that he is acting consistently with moral norms. The self is the kind of thing that can be proper or improper, depending on its action. We also see passages discussing the necessity of certain kinds of concern for the *ji* (self), especially the kind of evaluative concern connected to moral development. An exemplary person, according to early Confucians, is primarily concerned with an evaluation of himself, rather than the evaluation of others, either their esteem or their character.

> The master said: 'Do not worry that people do not know of you—worry that you do not know others'.[20]
>
> The master said: 'Do not worry about being unable to stand, worry about having nothing for which to stand. Do not worry about no one knowing of you, seek instead to be worthy of being known'.[21]
>
> The master said: 'The scholars of ancient days were concerned with themselves—the scholars of today are concerned with others'.[22]

The discussions in the *Analects* and other early Confucian texts can help us make sense of the distinction between virtuous and vicious self-concern, which I distinguish below in terms of "self-adornment" (vicious) and "self-utilization" (virtuous) forms of self-concern. While humility in terms of abandonment of self-adornment is necessary for the Confucians, so is the insistence on self-concern in terms of self-utilization. Indeed, part of the Confucian commitment to the self in this latter sense is a commitment to the community of which we are part. The Confucian conception of personhood ensures that a proper commitment to the community requires a commitment to the self. Our communities, particularly our familial and ancestral communities, are embedded into our selves—we are literally constituted by aspects of our communities in this way. Each feature of oneself is not only a shared feature, but a *contributed* feature from some member or members of one's community. One's physical features come from one's parents and ancestors, for example, while one's preferences and attitudes are attributable to one's local culture. This shows that one cannot exist autonomously, but rather exists only as a relational self, made up of communal features. We can begin to see why a certain sense of self-regard or self-concern is important for the Confucians, given their commitment to social harmony (*he*) as central to human thriving. Commitment to one's self in terms of the construction of autonomy and the severing of one's natural ties to the community cuts against social harmony. In cases of concern with self-adornment, we find just such anti-communal motivation. The desire to adorn the self is the desire to be perceived as, or to believe oneself to be, different and superior (in some way or multiple ways) to others in the community, rather than a desire to integrate into and play a role in the community. The desire for self-adornment leads one to separate, to compare, to spurn—and it is thus corrosive to community. On the other hand, a self-utilization concern with the self leaves open the possibility of a self-concern without the negative implications for community.

One common contemporary way of understanding humility is that of Robert Roberts and W. Scott Cleveland, as something like 'intelligent lack of concern for self-importance, where self-importance in construed as conferred by social status, glory, honor, superiority, special entitlements, prestige, or power'.[23] This conception of humility does not map perfectly onto the early Chinese or early Confucian background. This is partly because, according to the Confucians, adequate self-concern even in the sense that we might call self-importance is necessary for moral cultivation. While special entitlements, prestige, or superiority (depending on how we understand this) may not be of particular importance to the Confucians, social status, honor, and power are important. Self-importance, as Roberts and Cleveland define it, is not a wholly negative trait according to the Confucians, and thus they do not understand humility as a 'lack of concern for self-importance'. The Confucians would agree in part with the above definition of humility. For the early Confucians, concern for self-importance in terms of social status and some sense of power is a necessary step for the requisite social influence to make changes in the world with one's virtue or potency (*de*). The Confucian exemplary person will care about making a name for themselves just because it is the wide influence of the virtue of such a person that can have a transformative effect on society. The Confucians understand the person with virtue (*de*) as having a kind of natural attractive power. Because of this, people in positions of greater power, visibility, or influence will have the opportunity to influence society much more broadly with their virtue. Thus, if the exemplary person cares about bringing about social harmony through the encouragement of virtue in the people of the community, the exemplary person will have to also care about gaining a prominent position, a measure of power, and a broad influence. This self-concern must itself be part of the cultivation of virtue. At the same time, the Confucians did worry about the negative side of self-concern, and the ways in which aspects of such concern might undermine communal commitment. Thus the Confucians made an important distinction between positive and negative forms of self-concern, associating humility with the undermining of the latter. Thus, the Confucian view disagrees with the view of humility as involving 'low self-focus', which Thomas Nadelhoffer and Jennifer Cole Wright describe as 'being hypo-egoistically decentered and aware of one's place in the grander scheme of things'.[24] Indeed, it might even be useful on the Confucian view to have an inaccurate or overinflated view of one's own importance, insofar as this may lead one to aim for the kind of social prominence necessary for gaining the influence to motivate people broadly to cultivate virtue. This inflated view of one's own importance can be consistent with humility, insofar as humility has to do with the undermining of a self-concern that is oppositional to others, other-undermining, or even neutral with respect to others.

21.3 Humility and two kinds of self-concern

One thing we see expressed throughout the *Analects* and other early Confucian literature is the view that humility, like virtues such as humanity (*ren* 仁), is difficult to attain and thus it is also rare. The difficulty of cultivating humility lies in the natural predispositions of humans. Given that attaining humility is a matter of undermining one aspect of self-concern (self-adornment) while augmenting another (self-utilization), it becomes clearer why the early Confucians found this balancing task so difficult. Though there are two aspects of self-concern, it is difficult to practically disconnect the two, and one often comes along with the other. The person who gains an understanding of their own importance in terms of assisting society can also become imperious and arrogant. Presumably this is why the term 'self-importance' in English has negative connotations connected with such arrogance. The Confucian aim is to create a sense of self-importance shorn of its antisocial aspects. According to *Analects* 12.1, we are often unable to attain humility because of the strength of our sense of self (*ji*) in this antisocial sense. The stronger this sense of self, the further we will necessarily be from humility. The proper response, then, if we aim to cultivate humility (and the broader trait of *ren* that relies on it) is to undermine the strength of this sense of self and, ideally, to eliminate it altogether.[25]

How does this negative sense of self (which I call 'self-adornment') contribute to lack of humility, according to the Confucians? This negative sense of self is associated with selfishness, grandiosity, pride, stubbornness, and unwillingness to change—a sense of self rooted in the notion of self-visibility and self-adornment as central to thriving. According to the early Confucians, such a trait is a mark of a 'petty person' (*xiao ren* 小人). The reason these traits and the sense of self of the petty person can be taken as vicious is that they manifestly cut against the interest and development of harmonious community. The petty person aims to benefit themselves alone, and the self-concern of the petty person is other-exclusive, a self-absorption that requires the exclusion of others as valuable and worthy of care to retain a view of oneself as valuable and worthy of care. Numerous discussions of the petty person in the *Analects* point to the other-excluding nature of such a person's character, where the main aim is individual comfort, enjoyment, and thriving, to the exclusion of communal concern. In numerous passages of the *Analects*, Confucius contrasts the petty person with the exemplary person (*junzi* 君子), and in almost every comparison we find the petty person associated with other-exclusive self-concern, while the exemplary person manifests other concern. Consider the following passages:

> The master said: 'the exemplary person is focused on virtue, while the petty person is focused on material goods. The exemplary person is concerned with law, while the petty person is concerned with their own benefit'.[26]
>
> The master said: 'the exemplary person is concerned with righteousness, while the petty person is concerned with profit'.[27]

The benefit (*hui* 惠) and profit (*li* 利) discussed here are self-directed.[28] The focus of the exemplary person is on moral concepts such as virtue (*de* 德) and righteousness (*yi* 義), both of which are ultimately socially directed. The concept of *de*, while most often translated 'virtue' in English (though occasionally other translations such as 'moral potency' are used), is primarily social in nature. The *de* of the exemplary person is the charismatic and persuasive power such a person has to both facilitate moral development in others, and move the community closer to the harmonious ideal at the center of the Confucian worldview. This is only possible when one's motivations are communally directed—when one attains the moral property of *ren* 仁(humanity), itself an irreducibly social property,[29] understood most simply as a commitment and responsiveness to others in one's community or communities.[30]

In *Analects* 13.23, Confucius attributes the exemplary person with the ability to harmonize (*he* 和), a central aim of the overall Confucian project. This harmonization is contrasted with "partisanship" (*tong* 同), a trait associated with the petty person. The communal interaction of the exemplary person and others is one aimed at promoting the wellbeing of the community as a whole, rather than with advancing the interests of those from whom one individually stands to gain. We can see again that this entails a certain conception of corrosive and selfish self-concern on the part of the petty person, a self-concern that ultimately undermines harmonious community. It is the *ji* (self) in this sense that the Confucians recommend one turn away from in *Analects* 12.1. The exemplary person has a commitment to the elimination of this self-concern, and has presumably made some progress on the task, but Confucius points out that not all exemplary persons are *ren* (*Analects* 14.6). While attaining *ren* is a particularly difficult task, one cannot do it without being an exemplary person—the petty person's self-concern is inconsistent with *ren*, and thus Confucius in the second part of this passage says that while an exemplary person is not necessarily *ren*, there has *never* been a petty person who is *ren*.

The self (*ji*), as noted above, is not altogether rejected by the Confucians. There are a number of passages in which the exemplary person is said to be concerned with the self in a way the petty person is not. In addition to the above-mentioned 14.24, we find this claim in *Analects* 15.21:

> The master said, 'the exemplary person seeks it in themselves, while the petty person seeks it in others'.[31]

Here, the self-concern and self-directedness of the exemplary person is ultimately a self-directedness that has the construction of virtue and communal concern as its aim. The exemplary person is motivated to develop his or her own character, despite how this might be viewed by others. That is, the reward the exemplary person seeks for their effort in moral cultivation does not come via recognition by others, nor does it come from the sense of importance of superiority one might gain through adulation of or attention from others. Rather, the exemplary person seeks the reward of development of virtue in the self, contributing to a harmonious and thriving society. The petty person, on the other hand, behaves as they do in order to win the recognition, praise of others. The petty person's self-concern is such that their motivation is primarily a bolstering of that sense of self-importance through the adulation of others.

Does this mean that the exemplary person, who is also the humble person, will lack a sense of self-importance? After all, if one is focused on development of virtue in order to assist in bringing about a harmonious society, it seems to follow that one will place a great deal of emphasis on the importance of oneself, in terms of *ji*—perhaps even more so than the petty person who only seeks attention and adulation, rather than any lofty goal like the moral transformation of society. The self-concern of the exemplary person, according to the Confucians, is an elevation of the value of purpose. Part of the reason it is so difficult to attain a sense of self-concern in the self-utilization sense is the seemingly natural human gravitation toward a concern with self-adornment. Attaining the proper kind of self-concern is neither automatic nor is it the kind of thing very many people have naturally and without effort. It takes enormous and consistent effort to develop it.

The deleterious self-adornment concern takes the self as valuable in itself and focuses on the self as the end of activity. The virtuous self-utilization concern, on the other hand, takes the self as primarily instrumental, a means to the development of the harmonious and thriving society, which also then provides one with individual thriving. While this individual thriving is not the primary aim of the activity of the person with self-utilization concern, it is additional positive effect.

In the text bearing his name, the *Xunzi*, The Confucian philosopher Xun Kuang[32] discussed the relationship between the social and personal effects of moral development (via ritual). In his discussion of ritual,[33] Xunzi argued that ritual activity has both interpersonal and intrapersonal effects.[34] Its primary aim is to facilitate social interaction and make possible social harmony. But it has a secondary effect of making it possible for individuals to satisfy their own desires. We discern these two effects of ritual, Xunzi argues, when we recognize that ritual's primary function is to limit our desires, in order to impede them from growing into vices. Desires become vices when they become so enormous that their satisfaction requires harm to the community. At the same time, such unwieldy desires will become impossible to satisfy. All such desires begin as unproblematic natural desires, but left without the limitation ritual imposes on them, all will naturally grow into vice. An example of this is the desire for material goods. This desire is part of human nature, and it is a feature of such natural human desires to augment and strengthen on their own. The desire for sufficient material goods to survive naturally grows into a desire for surplus material goods, which naturally grows eventually to an overwhelming desire for continuous material goods. This desire creates interpersonal conflict, because if one needs continuous material goods, one will require the goods held by others (or disallow others to claim open goods), such that one's own interests will necessarily clash with those of other people. The clever move Xunzi makes next, though, is partly a response to the 'why be moral?' question. Even if one does not care about social harmony (though one has plenty of reasons to care, which I won't get into here), it turns out that, without the limitations of desire imposed by ritual, the desires that become vicious are no longer capable of being satisfied. In the material goods case—if the desire has developed to the point that one requires *infinite* material goods, then the desire cannot be satisfied, no matter how plentiful the material goods one attains. Limiting the desire for material goods using ritual, then, enables us to not only avoid the social disharmony that comes from conflict over goods, but also enables us to satisfy desire for material goods, sufficiently limited that it can be satisfied.

The Confucian conception of humility, following this insight of Xunzi, can be seen as involving two aspects, connected to the two senses of self-concern outlined above. The humble person is one who both lacks the concern for self-adornment (the *ji* of *Analects* 12.1) and possesses the concern for self-utilization. The primary means to develop such traits is adherence to ritual conduct. While the operation of ritual is outside of the scope of this paper, the general idea is that the constraints on behavior involved in ritual will ultimately bring about self-constraint in terms of desires and motivations, such that the concern for self-adornment subsides with ritual adherence.

What will a person who has 'turned away from the self', in terms of abandonment of concern with self-adornment, look like? According to the Confucians, such a person will be able to develop a host of virtues that the person stuck within concern for self-adornment cannot. These include the *rang* and *gong* discussed earlier in this paper, as well as the virtues involving other concerns which, for the Confucians, are most of them. Filiality, reflectiveness, honesty—these all require humility, in the sense of an undermining of the concern with self-adornment. Such humility allows one to learn from others, as one is not only unconcerned about appearing to be the most knowledgeable or able, but is also concerned about gaining knowledge or ability in a positive sense because of their commitment to self-utilization. The virtue of humility, then, is not only the lack of concern with self-adornment, but also requires the commitment to self-utilization. This latter kind of self-concern turns out to itself be *part* of humility, rather than a necessary additional virtue. If humility is ultimately a transitional virtue facilitating social harmony involving the proper kind of self-concern, then both negative and positive self-concern play a role.

To return to contemporary psychological accounts of the role of humility, the Confucian conception of virtue seems to fit the picture of humility as facilitating social interaction. Humility is particularly important in relationships between superiors and subordinates in society, according to Confucians, not primarily to reassure the superior that the subordinate will not rebel or undermine them, but to ensure that the subordinate gains the ability to be guided by the superior. That is, humility on the Confucian view is important in such relations mainly for the benefit of the subordinate, as well as for the mutual development of the self and the community. Part of the proper self-concern of the humble person, the concern for self-utilization rather than self-adornment, insures the focus on benefit to the bearer of humility, insofar as they become able to play a crucial role in social harmonization and self-development. Thus, though the Confucian conception of humility is aimed ultimately at creating harmonious communities, it does this through the means of enhancing aspects of the self that enable a person to both be more effective at creating communal harmony and more effective at achieving individual thriving.

Notes

1 *Rujia* 儒家, more correctly translated as 'Classicist School', is more commonly known in the West as 'Confucianism', because of its strong association with the teachings of Confucius (Kongzi 孔子), one of its most influential early proponents.

2 *Kongzi* translates to 'Master Kong'—the Latinized name 'Confucius' derives from a lesser used analogue *Kong Fuzi* 孔夫子, also translating to 'Master Kong'. The full and given name of Confucius, according to tradition was Kong Qiu.

3 There have been numerous debates over the dating of the text of the *Analects*. Most scholars recognize it as a composite text, with parts potentially spanning from the mid-5th century BCE to the 1st century BCE. See Brooks and Brooks, *The Original Analects*. Some recent scholars argue for a later date of construction of the text, in the early Han Dynasty. See Michael Hunter, 'The Lunyu as a Western Han Text', as well as other papers in Hunter and Kern, eds. *Confucius and the Analects Revisited.*

4 *Analects* 1.10.

5 *Analects* 3.7.

6 Ritual, in this sense, facilitates social interaction. Chenyang Li understands ritual as what he calls a 'cultural grammar' that allows for the expression of particular virtues within the communal context associated with particular rituals. See Li, 'Li as Cultural Grammar: On the Relation Between Li and Ren in Confucius' Analects'.

7 *Jiyi* 18.

8 *Analects* 5.16. 子謂子產，「有君子之道四焉：其行己也恭，其事上也敬，其養民也惠，其使民也義。

9 Davis, et al. 'Relational Humility: Conceptualizing and Measuring Humility as a Personality Judgment', Farrell et al., 'Humility and Relationship Outcomes in Couples: The Mediating Role of Commitment'

10 Li, 'Humility in Learning: A Confucian Perspective', 149.

11 A number of scholars, most prominently Roger Ames, take Confucianism to offer what they describe as a 'role ethics.' See Ames, *Confucian Role Ethics*, Rosemont, 'Rights-Bearing Individuals and Role-Bearing Persons', Mattice, 'Confucian Role Ethics: Issues of Naming, Translation, and Interpretation'

12 The well-known debate between the later Confucians Mengzi and Xunzi on the issue of 'human nature' or 'inborn characteristics' (*xing* 性) concerned this issue.

13 *Analects* 9.1 goes so far as to say that Confucius rarely spoke about *ren*—even though it is one of the most discussed concepts in the *Analects*.

14 See John Kieschnick, 'Analects 12.1 and the Commentarial Tradition' for a number of the early interpretations of Western sinologists.

15 子絕四：毋意，毋必，毋固，毋我。

16 *Analects* 15.20. 子曰：「君子疾沒世而名不稱焉。」
17 *Analects* 15.19. 子曰：「君子病無能焉，不病人之不己知也。」
18 Some attempt to square the passages by arguing that Confucius' teachings were tailored to particular individuals who required different instruction. Amy Olberding argues that such apparent contradictions may also be resolved by considering certain of Confucius' statements 'reflective, general remarks' and others 'less studied reactions'. Olberding, 'Confucius' Complaints and the *Analects'* Account of the Good Life', 437. Some attempt to interpret 15.20 in such a way that it does not suggest that Confucius held that one should seek a reputation. This is the Han scholar Xu Gan's approach to the apparent contradiction. See John Makeham, 'Notes and Communications', *Bulletin of the School of Oriental and African Studies* 56 (3).
19 *Shen* 身 and *ji* 己 are among the terms used.
20 *Analects* 1.16. 子曰：「不患人之不己知，患不知人也。」
21 *Analects* 4.14: 子曰：「不患無位，患所以立；不患莫己知，求為可知也。」
22 *Analects* 14.24 子曰：「古之學者為己，今之學者為人。」
23 Roberts and Cleveland, 'Humility from a Philosophical Point of View' in *Routledge Handbook of Humility.*
24 Nadelhoffer and Wright, "The Twin Dimensions of the Virtue of Humility: Low Self-Focus and High Other-Focus".
25 *Wu-wei* activity (literally, 'non-action'), understood most commonly as 'non-forced' or 'non-intentional' activity, is linked to this elimination of self, whether as a result or a contributing cause. Interpretations differ on this, but for early Confucians, is appears to be a result rather than a cause. One undermines the strength of a certain kind of sense of self through moderation of desires via ritual (*Analects* 12.1).
26 *Analects* 4.11 子曰：「君子懷德，小人懷土；君子懷刑，小人懷惠。」
27 *Analects* 4.16 子曰：「君子喻於義，小人喻於利。」
28 This is also likely a shot at the Mohists, a rival philosophical school who held that the primary aim of human activity should be generation of profit (*li*) for all, in terms of material benefit.
29 Irreducibly social in the sense that it cannot be understood in terms of the individual possession of properties distinct from communal interaction, but is primarily a property of the community itself, facilitated by its members, that belongs to individuals in a secondary sense.
30 See McLeod, '*Ren* as a Communal Property in the *Analects*'.
31 子曰：「君子求諸己，小人求諸人。」
32 Xunzi ('Master Xun') lived about 200 years after Confucius, toward the end of the Warring States Period (453–221 BCE).
33 *Xunzi* ch. 19.
34 David Wong coins this way discussing the 'functions of morality' in his book *Natural Moralities* (p. 43), a distinction he also attributes to Xunzi.

References

Ames, Roger. *Confucian Role Ethics: A Vocabulary*. Hong Kong: Chinese University of Hong Kong Press, 2010.

Brooks, Bruce and Taeko Brooks. *The Original Analects: Sayings of Confucius and His Successors*. New York: Columbia University Press, 1998.

Davis, Don, Joshua Hook, Everett Worthington, Daryl Van Tongeren, Aubrey Gartner, David Jennings and Robert Emmons. 'Relational Humility: Conceptualizing and Measuring Humility as a Personality Judgment'. *Journal of Personality Assessment* 93(3), 2011., 225–234.

Farrell, Jennifer, Joshua Hook, Marciana Ramos, Don Davis, Daryl Van Tongeren and John Ruiz. 'Humility and Relationship Outcomes in Couples: The Mediating Role of Commitment'. *Couple and Family Psychology: Research and Practice* 4(1), 2015., 14–26.

Hunter, Michael. 'The *Lunyu* as a Western Han Text'. In: M. Hunter and M. Kern, eds. *Confucius and the Analects Revisited: New Perspectives on Composition, Dating, and Authorship*. Leiden: Brill, 2018.

Kieschnick, John. '*Analects* 12.1 and the Commentarial Tradition'. *Journal of the American Oriental Society* 112(4), 1992., 567–576.

Li, Chenyang. '*Li* as Cultural Grammar: On the Relation Between *Li* and *Ren* in Confucius' *Analects*'. *Philosophy East and West* 57(3), 2007., 311–329.

Li, Jin. 'Humility in Learning: A Confucian Perspective'. *Journal of Moral Education* 45(2), 2016., 147–165.

Makeham, John. 'Notes and Communications'. *Bulletin of the School of Oriental and African Studies* 56(3), 1993., 582–586.
Mattice, Sarah. 'Confucian Role Ethics: Issues of Naming, Translation, and Interpretation'. In: A. McLeod, ed. *Bloomsbury Handbook of Early Chinese Ethics and Political Philosophy*. London: Bloomsbury, 2019.
McLeod, Alexus. '*Ren* as a Communal Property in the *Analects*'. *Philosophy East and West* 62(4), 2012., 505–528.
Nadelhoffer, Thomas and Jennifer Cole Wright. 'The Twin Dimensions of the Virtue of Humility: Low Self-Focus and High Other-Focus'. In: W. Sinnott-Armstrong and C.B. Miller, eds. *Moral Psychology, Vol. 5: Virtue and Character*. Cambridge: MIT Press, 2017.
Olberding, Amy. 'Confucius' Complaints and the *Analects*' Account of the Good Life'. *Dao: A Journal of Comparative Philosophy* 12(4), 2013., 417–440.
Roberts, Robert and W. Scott Cleveland. 'Humility from a Philosophical Point of View'. In: E.L. Worthington, D.E. Davis and J.N. Hook, eds. *Routledge Handbook of Humility*.
Rosemont, Henry. 'Rights-Bearing Individuals and Role-Bearing Persons'. In: M. Bockover, ed. *Rules, Rituals, and Responsibility: Essays Dedicated to Herbert Fingarette*. Chicago: Open Court, 1991.
Wong, David. *Natural Moralities: A Defense of Pluralistic Relativism*. Oxford: Oxford University Press, 2009.

22

HUMILITY AND THE AFRICAN PHILOSOPHY OF *UBUNTU*

Thaddeus Metz

22.1 Introduction

The word '*ubuntu*' comes from the Nguni language group mainly in South Africa, and it literally means humanness, where humanness is something for a person to realize through certain positive relationships with other persons. Although the word is local, the relational approach to ethics that it signifies is much broader, being salient in many philosophies produced from the sub-Saharan African region. This chapter explores prominent respects in which humility figures into not just the relational ethic of *ubuntu*, but also the epistemic perspectives that are usually associated with it in regard to moral knowledge.

The African philosophical tradition, although long-standing, is only in its third generation when it comes to literate contributors and interpreters. Until the 1960s, sub-Saharan philosophers by and large lived in oral cultures. Whereas those in the Judeo-Christian tradition can invoke passages about humility that are at least 2000 years old (e.g., *Proverbs* 11.1–3, 16.5, 16.18–19, 18.12), as can those in the Confucian tradition (e.g., *Analects* 1.14, 14.20), there are no aged, venerable written texts to consult by those working in African philosophy.

To deal with this lack, one strategy would be to interview sages for accepted views of humility and to look for commonalities amongst indigenous African peoples (cf. Oruka 1991), or to consult proverbs about humility that can be shown to have had widespread appeal (one could consider Ibekwe 1998: 14–15, 150–151, 197; Kuzwayo 1998: 32, 34, 45, 49, 52). However, the approach of this chapter is to draw on philosophical ideas that have been published in academic fora over the past 50 years or so. They were substantially informed by the cultures of the philosophers who advanced them, and, even setting that point aside, these philosophies in themselves provide rich approaches to morality and epistemology that differ from what is salient in many other intellectual traditions and merit engagement.

Although the concept of humility has not often been explicitly invoked to make sense of African morality and epistemology in academic works, this chapter shows that it is a useful lens through which to consider key facets of these literate philosophies. In many ways, by *ubuntu* we are to be humble in respect of what an individual should claim from others and what an individual may claim to know, although no claim is made here that it is some kind of 'master virtue' for the tradition (a view often ascribed to St. Augustine in respect of Christianity).

The chapter begins by spelling out what is arguably characteristic of humility as such, whether it is a feature of how we treat others or how we come to know about the world (Section 22.2). Next, it articulates some ethical ideas associated with *ubuntu* and considers humility in the light of them (Section 22.3), after which it does so in the context of moral epistemology (Section 22.4). The chapter concludes by sketching some prominent African philosophies other than what has been advanced as *ubuntu*, and by suggesting ways in which the analyses offered here could be plausibly extended to them (Section 22.5).

22.2 An analysis of humility

In order to consider how *ubuntu* morality and epistemology may be understood to prescribe humility, one first needs some sense of what humility is. This section does not presume that there is an essence to humility, although it also does not reject that possibility (unlike Kellenberger 2010: 323–324). Instead, it advances features that are typical of a humble orientation, whether in the domains of ethics or epistemics. In emphasizing similarities between ethical and intellectual humility, the following does not strive to mark out the finer points of either one considered in isolation from the other.

The introduction spoke of making a 'claim', where one might make a claim on others' resources such as their time, or make a claim to know something about the world. Humility may be understood in these contexts to prescribe tempering claims (e.g., Roberts and Wood 2003: 258, 265–267; Kellenberger 2010). A humble person neither makes unreasonable demands to possess what others have, nor unreasonably maintains that she is in possession of certain kinds of truth. A humble person does not grasp for what is not hers to receive.

Talk of 'assumption' and cognate terms, and specifically the lack of it, is a second recurrent feature of humility. In the ethical realm, a humble agent is unassuming, relatively unconcerned that her status be greater than others (e.g., Roberts and Wood 2003: 259–261) and not wanting to impose on others without giving their interests at least due consideration (if not greater consideration than what is owed, on which see Kellenberger 2010). With regard to epistemology, a humble enquirer questions her assumptions, perhaps even when she is entitled not to doubt. She does not suppose that she knows with certainty or with too much confidence, or she accepts that there are certain topics about which she cannot know (e.g., Whitcomb et al. 2017). She judges herself to need evidence, perhaps seeking more than is sufficient. Whereas the humble agent does not take things for free from others, the humble enquirer does not take things for granted about the world. Neither is presumptuous; both accept limits.

A third term frequently associated with humility is 'extravagance', specifically the avoidance of it. An agent who is not humble might make excessive demands on others, or spend lots of resources on herself in respect of a party or an abode, perhaps ascribing to herself a value that is disproportionately great (e.g., Garcia 2006). An enquirer who lacks humility might extravagantly posit entities for which there is insufficient evidence, such as a multiverse or angels.

Putting these ideas together, a person is humble insofar as she tempers her claims, avoids being presumptuous, and eschews extravagance. It is natural to think of humility as a virtue, whether practical or intellectual (for just one instance, see Battaly 2019).[1] It is a disposition not to think too much of oneself, whether that is in relation to what goods one takes from the world or what one takes oneself to believe about it.

Of particular salience when it comes to ethics is the idea that others matter and must be given their due (and perhaps more). A proverbial Robinson Crusoe alone on a deserted island without humans or animals probably could not exhibit the moral virtue of humility, surely not to its full extent. Relatedly, the 'anti-humble' vices of arrogance, vanity, attention-seeking, selfishness, and the like could not be manifest in the absence of others.

As this volume illustrates, there is of course much more one could discuss about the nature of humility. For example, the above description has roughly focused on avoiding 'too much', but presumably humility, insofar as it is a virtue, also involves avoiding 'too little'. And any 'too' talk, as well as mention of what is 'unreasonable' and the like, beg for specifics. However, the analysis given here will be enough to make sense of certain important features of *ubuntu* as a widely shared African philosophy.

22.3 African ethics and humility

As is becoming increasingly well known around the world, the key phrase used to sum up the moral aspects of *ubuntu* is 'A person is a person through other persons'. This maxim is an overly literal translation of sayings prominent in South Africa and mirrored in much of at least southern and central Africa. This section first provides a philosophical interpretation of the maxim and then brings out how it entails humility in a variety of respects.

22.3.1 An ethical interpretation of ubuntu

To begin to understand what it means to say that a person is a person through other persons or has *ubuntu*, consider some remarks from Desmond Tutu, the influential Nobel Peace Prize winner from South Africa and former Chairperson of that country's Truth and Reconciliation Commission:

> When we want to give high praise to someone we say, '*Yu, u nobuntu*'; 'Hey, he or she has *ubuntu*'. This means they are generous, hospitable, friendly, caring and compassionate. They share what they have. It also means my humanity is caught up, is inextricably bound up, in theirs. We belong in a bundle of life. We say, 'a person is a person through other people'. It is not 'I think therefore I am'. It says rather: 'I am human because I belong'.
>
> *(1999: 34–35)*

By 'we' Tutu means indigenous African peoples, and the view he is ascribing to them is that one ought to develop one's humanity or personhood, which is constituted by the way one treats other people. One realizes humanness or lives a genuinely human way of life insofar as one exemplifies a variety of other-regarding virtues, some of which Tutu mentions.

Similar remarks appear from Yvonne Mokgoro, a former justice of South Africa's Constitutional Court who is known for having appealed to *ubuntu* in some of her judgements:

> [T]hus the notion *umuntu ngumuntu ngabantu/motho ke motho ka batho ba bangwe* [a person is a person through other persons—ed.] which also implies that during one's life-time, one is constantly challenged by others, practically, to achieve self-fulfilment through a set of collective social ideals … . Group solidarity, conformity, compassion, respect, human dignity, humanistic orientation and collective unity have, among others been defined as key social values of *ubuntu*.
>
> *(1998: 17)*

Here, too, the *eudaemonist* approach to morality is patent: one is to realize oneself by relating to others in certain supportive ways.

Philosophers are characteristically curious as to whether all the relevant *ubuntu*-constitutive virtues can be reduced to a single one. What might generosity, hospitality, friendliness, care, compassion, solidarity, respect, and unity all have in common, beyond being relational? The suggestion from Tutu, Mokgoro, and several others based in South Africa who have theoretically addressed *ubuntu* (e.g., Mkhize 2008; Metz 2014; Murove 2016)[2] is a harmonious relationship. A certain conception of harmony is plausibly foundational when it comes to the other-regarding moral virtues of *ubuntu*.

To begin to spell out what harmony involves, let us return to Tutu and Mokgoro:

> I participate, I share .... Harmony, friendliness, community are great goods. Social harmony is for us the *summum bonum* – the greatest good. Anything that subverts or undermines this sought-after good is to be avoided like the plague. Anger, resentment, lust for revenge, even success through aggressive competitiveness, are corrosive of this good.
>
> *(Tutu 1999: 35)*

> (H)armony is achieved through close and sympathetic social relations within the group.
>
> *(Mokgoro 1998: 17)*

Tutu and Mokgoro both mention two distinct ways of relating as constitutive of harmony, as do others in the literature (on which see Metz 2013 for a fuller reconstruction). One is participating or being close, which is usefully understood not merely as refraining from isolation, but also something like sustaining a common sense of self with others. So, for example, it means liking being together, taking pride in others' accomplishments, avoiding coercive, deceptive, or exploitive interaction, and realizing others' ends. Another phrase to capture this first element of harmony is 'sharing a way of life'.

The second element of harmony could be summed up as 'caring for others' quality of life'. It centrally includes doing what is at least likely to make others' lives go objectively better, i.e., in terms of their needs, and not so much their feelings or wants. These needs include the socio-moral imperative to develop one's humanness, meaning that one way to realize oneself by relating harmoniously with others is to help them realize themselves—by in turn relating harmoniously. In addition to giving to others in ways expected to improve their lives, caring for them means characteristically doing so consequent to certain positive attitudes, such out of sympathy and for their own sake.

Roughly speaking, sharing a way of life with others captures the virtues of respect, solidarity, and unity, while caring for them is what generosity, hospitality, care, and compassion have in common. And although there are still two distinct properties here, of sharing and caring, they are naturally viewed as a pair, for together they constitute what many English-speakers would call 'friendliness' or even a broad sense of 'love'. To relate in a friendly manner is more or less to enjoy a sense of togetherness, to engage in cooperative projects, to help one another, and to do so for reasons beyond self-interest.

In sum, a powerful way to understand one major strain of African thought about morality is in terms of a prescription to live in a way that prizes harmony or friendliness, or, more carefully, treats individuals with respect insofar as they are, in principle, capable of being party to such ways of relating. By this latter phrasing, a person who can by her nature be friendly and be befriended has a dignity that demands honoring, with one key way to do so being to cultivate or sustain friendly relationships with her. Although neither Tutu nor Mokgoro mentions dignity in the above quotations, a number of African philosophers have maintained that sub-Saharan peoples typically ascribe dignity to human beings (e.g., Wiredu 1996: 158; Bujo 2001: 2, 138–139, 142; Deng 2004: 501; Gyekye 2010: section 6). Often the thought has been that everyone has dignity because she is a child of God, but here the link with harmony is tightened up, so that it is roughly the capacity to love and be loved in which our dignity inheres. As Tutu suggests at one point, 'The completely self-sufficient person would be subhuman' (1999: 214). Such a relational approach to morality differs from a focus on not merely autonomy or pleasure but also care, which standardly neglects both the sharing a way of life element and the relevance of dignity.

As with the nature of humility, there is more one could say about an *ubuntu* ethic, construed as prescribing one to realize oneself by prizing harmonious or friendly ways of relating. On the one hand, many will want to know why the 'African' label is apt for this principle, beyond the fact that it is grounded on the remarks of two African intellectuals from South Africa. The brief answer, and the only one space allows for here, is that something counts as 'African' if it has been characteristic of—not necessarily unique or essential to—much of that place and for a long time in a way that differentiates it from many other locales (Metz 2015), and that harmony indeed captures a wide array of beliefs and practices salient below the Sahara desert (Paris 1995; Metz 2017a; Ejizu n.d.).

On the other hand, readers will hanker for more specifics about the nature of the ethic. Is one to relate that way only with human persons, or do some other parts of nature, such as animals, count? Does an ethic prescribing harmony categorically forbid the use of force, and, if not, under what conditions does it permit force? How is one to balance actual harmonious relationships of which one is a part with merely potential ones with strangers? These are important questions, but we do not need answers in order to make headway on the ethic's implications for humility.

22.3.2 **Ubuntu** ***and humility***

There are a number of ways in which an ethic instructing agents to respect others in virtue of their capacity for harmonious relationships, and hence characteristically to relate harmoniously, plausibly includes some form of humility, whether that means tempering claims, avoiding presumptuousness, or eschewing extravagance. This section highlights some major respects in which this is so.

The relationship between harmony and humility that is probably the most tempting to note is a causal one. That is, one naturally judges that a lack of humility, say, in the form of arrogance or self-centeredness, would likely discourage people from entering into or sustaining ties with those who manifest these traits. Instead, such attitudes can be expected to prompt discord, roughly understood as division and ill-will between people. Conversely, as Nelson Mandela (2000) has pointed out in an interview, if one is humble and so not a threat to others, then one will be in a good position not merely to avoid, but also to resolve, discord between others.

These claims are true, but they are also weak, in the sense that they ground no necessary relation between harmony and humility. *Often* haughtiness or selfishness will lead to alienation between people down the road, and is to be discouraged for that reason, but not invariably. Whether a certain attitude, or even its expression, brings about particular results or not depends on contexts that vary, for instance, on whether others have noticed it or not. If you did not hear another person gratuitously disparage you, his attitude will not on that occasion lead you to put more distance between yourself and him. Similarly, even if one is in fact humble, if people perceive one otherwise, then one's ability to resolve conflict amongst them will be hindered.

Here are some connections between harmony and humility that are stronger for being constitutive and not merely causal. To begin, consider that an ethic that ascribes a dignity to at least human persons straightforwardly forbids treating others as worth less than oneself. To have dignity is to possess superlative final value, and, by most interpretations of it these days, everyone has equal dignity if they have enough of the requisite property, in this case, the capacity to be party to harmonious relationships. Such an approach to morality rules out not only discrimination on grounds such as race or gender, but also arrogance. Having an equal worth when it comes to moral treatment easily entails a kind of humility in which one tempers one's claims on others and does not presume to impose on them (at least when it comes to non-intimates).

One way to avoid discrimination and arrogance would be to remove oneself from society. However, an ethic of harmony also forbids doing so. This ethic implies that the value of others is such as to require one to come closer to them, typically interpreted to require reconciliation between victims and those who have committed crimes against them, for instance (e.g., Tutu 1999; Krog 2008). If one were to isolate oneself, one would be failing to recognize other people's worth adequately and so failing to be humble before them. Paying attention to only oneself would amount to ascribing a certain kind of importance to oneself that one does not in fact have. It would mean that others do not matter enough for one to go out of one's way for them, but their dignity calls for more than that. If we have dignity by virtue of our ability to relate harmoniously, then the default mode of engagement (viz., with innocent parties) should be to relate in that way.

More specifically, by the present ethic, one is obligated to acknowledge the importance of others in two major ways. First, one must come closer to them by participating with them cooperatively. One must rein in one's ends so that they are at least substantially consistent with those of others, if not shared with them. One may not spend so much time, labor, money, and the like on oneself that one is left unable to advance other people's projects. Second, one should advance certain kinds of ends, ones that are at least unlikely to make people's lives objectively worse, and ideally those likely to make them better. Indeed, according to what is probably the dominant strain of thought about African morality, there is no category of supererogation, a view that is sometimes explicit (e.g., Gyekye 1997: 70–75) and other times implicit in the principles advanced (consider, say, the Golden Rule in Wiredu 1992: 198). In the African tradition, it is imperative to curb one's demands on others and instead to go out of one's way for them, especially for extended family members, to the point where, in some cultures, having slaughtered an animal and not offered some to relatives would be considered theft (Metz and Gaie 2010: 278).

There is an additional respect in which *ubuntu* as an ethic prescribes humility, which concerns not how one should treat others, a first-order virtue, but how one should regard oneself in respect of how one has treated others, a second-order virtue. In brief, one should be humble about one's having been humble.[3] It is one thing to be presumptuous in respect of others' interests and thereby lack virtue, and another to be presumptuous in respect of one's own virtue, another type of a lack of virtue. M. K. Gandhi accepts this point when he says, 'A humble person is not himself conscious of his humility .... (A) man who is proud of his virtue often becomes a curse to society' (1932: 30).[4]

How would failing to be humble about one's humility, or one's virtue more generally, show disrespect of others' ability to be party to relationships of harmony? One idea, suggested by Gandhi above, is that if one were to label oneself as 'humble' or 'virtuous', then one would rest on one's laurels and be disinclined to reflect critically on oneself. There is always room for growth as a moral person, or at the very least decline for one to ward off, both of which seem to prescribe erring on the side of underestimating the extent to which one has realized virtue. Notice, though, the 'often' in Gandhi's formulation: this rationale cannot explain why it is always a vice to some degree to fail to be humble about one's virtue, as sometimes being proud about it will not be expected to have bad consequences for others.

Reflecting on Nelson Mandela's virtue occasions awareness of other, stronger reasons for thinking that one should be humble about one's humility and, more generally, one's virtue. Mandela is famous for having illustrated humility about his moral accomplishments, and it is reasonable to think that it is a function of the *ubuntu* ethic to which he subscribed (Mandela 2012: 147, 155, 2013a: 227). Mandela would, for instance, often pay tribute to others beyond himself, such as the South African people, for major positive changes to their country's socio-political structure, and he also recommended doing so as an ideal form of leadership (Mandela 2013b). Here, it is plausible to think of sharing credit and praise with others as an instantiation of *ubuntu*; it is another way to give to others, instead of directing good things to oneself.

For another respect in which Mandela was humble about his achievements, consider that he avoided comparing them to those of others, instead being known for having referred to all the greater tasks he had yet to accomplish. In the last paragraph of his autobiography, *Long Walk to Freedom*, Mandela famously remarks, 'I have discovered the secret that after climbing a great hill, one only finds that there are many more hills to climb' (1994: 751). By focusing not on how great his achievements were relative to most people's, but instead on how many more achievements he had yet to make, Mandela respects others, in two ways. He avoids making people feel inadequate, and prompts himself to do all the more for human beings, the sole relevant achievement by an *ubuntu* morality.

22.4 African moral epistemology and humility

Whereas the previous section addressed respects in which humility is prescribed by an ethic of respect for individuals' capacity for harmonious relationships, the present one considers some ways that humility figures into the African epistemology that is the common companion to this ethic. In particular, this section notes some respects in which individuals should be humble when it comes to knowing which acts are right and attitudes are virtuous.

Very broadly speaking, the Western tradition encourages an individual to use his own rational powers to evaluate a given subject matter, including morality; methods such as *a priori* reflection and coherentist justification in the light of one's intuitions are common. In contrast, the African tradition is much less sanguine about what can be known about morality by a typical human being cogitating on his own. Roughly, although the Western tradition has recently acknowledged the importance of expert testimony as a source of knowledge, debate is ongoing about the aptness of moral testimony, and the African tradition makes reliance on epistemic authority and collective enquiry more central, and especially for moral matters.

Probably most indigenous African peoples believe in God, such that it is much too narrow to think of monotheism merely in terms of the Judeo-Christian-Islamic religions.[5] Whereas the Abrahamic faiths are revelatory, traditional African religion is not (Gyekye 1995: 129–146; Wiredu 1996: 61–77). That is, according to the Abrahamic faiths, God's benevolent and just will has been directly communicated to human beings via certain texts or prophets. If you read a certain book, or hear what a certain person has said, then you can know what God's moral purpose is. In contrast, from a characteristic sub-Saharan perspective, God is 'too big' or 'too distant' for us to be able to apprehend His mind, so that we require a mediator in order to convey God's intentions to us. For the African tradition, we must be humble in respect of knowing God's mind, including His moral commands—indeed, we have no hope of becoming directly acquainted with the thoughts of an infinite being.

As for the mediator who can become acquainted with God's will, the standard view amongst indigenous sub-Saharan peoples is that it must be an ancestor, a wise founder of a clan who has survived the death of his body, continues to reside on earth in an imperceptible realm, and instructs the clan on how to behave, which includes dishing out penalties for moral infractions. How, then, is a human being to know the mind of an ancestor? Here, again, humility is warranted on the part of a typical human person. It is not just any individual who is deemed to have the ability to access the ancestral world, but rather those who have undergone years of training in how to interpret dreams, enter trances, detect reincarnated persons, and the like.

In the African tradition, there are also less 'spiritual' mediums through which to access judgements about who did wrong and what morally should be done now. Even these more naturalist methods, however, tend to eschew reliance on individual reflection, intuition, etc. Particularly common is the thought that one should defer to the judgement of elders, and especially to consensus amongst them, about moral matters, such that moral education ought to center around apprehending, and not particularly questioning, their views (for a robust articulation and defense of this position, see Ikuenobe 2006). A young person challenging a much older one about morality would be viewed as lacking the requisite epistemic humility; specifically, the young person would be viewed as being presumptuous.

Although it is possible for an aged person not to count as an 'elder', for evincing poor judgement, the default position is that with age comes wisdom and hence the authority to speak about moral matters. The notion that some people in their 20s or 30s could reach the highest stage of moral appraisal, a view advanced by the influential American psychologist Lawrence Kohlberg (1984: 272–273), is quite out of place amongst African philosophers. Instead, as an influential Nigerian ethicist remarks of an Igbo African proverb:

> 'What an old man sees sitting down, a young man cannot see standing up' … . (A)lthough we would not have a great deal of difficulty talking about an 18-year-old mathematical giant, we would have a great deal of difficulty talking about an 18-year-old moral giant.
>
> *(Menkiti 2004: 325)*

This view is plausible insofar as an ethic of the sort analyzed in the previous section is accepted; for it takes substantial experience to learn how to navigate the complexities and challenges of interpersonal relationships (for more on the point, see Metz and Gaie 2010: 286).

Furthermore, it is common in the African tradition to maintain that moral knowledge is most likely to emerge from consensus amongst at least a group of elders, if not all those affected by the controversy, and not so much from the pronouncement of a single person. Although many indigenous African societies were led by a monarch, it was routine for him to defer to the collective judgement of a group of elders, or perhaps all those involved, about how to resolve conflicts or otherwise proceed with contentious matters. Part of the reason for being inclusionary is practical, e.g., making people more likely to enjoy a sense of togetherness, but another part is clearly epistemic, the rough idea being that two heads are better than one (one finds discussion of both in Bujo 1997: 43–57, 2001: 45–71, 2005: 427–431). If kings deem themselves unqualified to make ethical judgements on their own, so much the worse for a typical individual member of society. Instead, from this standpoint, she must be humble in respect of her own ability to determine what the best course of action is in a relational context.

22.5 Conclusion

This chapter has expounded one major strain of African thought about normative ethics, which is relational, and brought out what it means for humility in both normative ethical and moral epistemological matters. Broadly speaking, supposing that a good person, i.e., one with *ubuntu*, is one whose attitudes and actions express respect for people's dignified ability to relate harmoniously, one must not be discriminatory, arrogant, or selfish when it comes to the way one treats others, and one must consult routinely with elders about how to sustain, deepen, and otherwise honor relationships. Failing to live harmoniously would often consist of failing to manifest humility, as would believing that one can routinely ascertain how to exemplify *ubuntu* without the input of older and wiser people.

There are other accounts ofAfrican morality that contemporary philosophers have expounded that this chapter has not addressed. Instead of taking relational features to be foundational, most of the other views instead deem either vitality (e.g., Dzobo 1992; Magesa 1997) or the common good (Gyekye 1997, 2010) to be what ultimately matters for ethics (but see Wiredu 1992 for a somewhat different view). However, even by these approaches, harmonious relationships are nearly always deemed to be particularly reliable, if not essential, means by which to promote life or well-being. That is, sharing a way of life and caring for others' quality of life, even if not deemed to be relationships to pursue as ends, are thought quite likely to make other people more lively or to improve their welfare. Insofar as that is the case, the considerations about how humility figures into a relational ethic will, *mutatis mutandis*, apply with comparable force to these other African ethics. One may therefore conclude that humility is central to African moral philosophy, not merely the *ubuntu* variant on which this chapter has focused.

Notes

1 Is there an aesthetic humility that would complement the ethic and epistemic? Although the literature does not speak of one, it would be worth pursuing the idea that there is a humility possible in the realm of the beautiful, and not just in the good and the true. One thought is that, while aesthetic judgments might have an objective dimension, humility counsels against typically deeming them to be universally valid (for such a view, see Miller 1998).

2 But not only them—there are many from the rest of the continent who also place notions of harmony, cohesion, community, and the like at the heart of self-realization, just two examples of which include Paris (1995); and Ejizu (n.d.).

3 For this 'self-attribution problem', see Driver (1989); Kellenberger (2010: 328–331); and Whitcomb et al. (2017). The point is similar to the familiar idea that a person is wise (partly) insofar as she is disinclined to think of herself as wise (or at least to proclaim herself wise to others).

4 But perhaps not so much when Gandhi had earlier said, 'I claim to be a simple individual liable to err like any other fellow mortal. I own, however, that I have humility enough to confess my errors and to retrace my steps' (1926/1999: 195).

5 The rest of this paragraph borrows from Metz (2017b: 804).

References

Battaly, Heather. 2019. 'Humility'. In: LaFollette, Hugh, ed. *International Encyclopedia of Ethics*. Malden, MA: Blackwell Publishing Ltd., 1–9.

Bujo, Bénézet. 1997. *The Ethical Dimension of Community*, Nganda, C.N., trans. Nairobi: Paulines Publications.

Bujo, Bénézet. 2001. *Foundations of an African Ethic: Beyond the Universal Claims of Western Morality*, McNeil, Brian, trans. New York: Crossroad Publishers.

Bujo, Bénézet. 2005. 'Differentiations in African Ethics'. In: Schweiker, William, ed. *The Blackwell Companion to Religious Ethics*. Malden, MA: Blackwell, 423–437.

Deng, Francis. 2004. 'Human Rights in the African Context'. In: Wiredu, Kwasi, ed. *A Companion to African Philosophy*. Oxford: Blackwell, 499–508.

Driver, Julia. 1989. 'The Virtues of Ignorance'. *The Journal of Philosophy* 86(7): 373–384.

Dzobo, Noah. 1992. 'Values in a Changing Society: Man, Ancestors, and God'. In: Wiredu, Kwasi and Gyekye, Kwame, eds. *Person and Community; Ghanaian Philosophical Studies, Vol. I*. Washington, D.C.: Council for Research in Values and Philosophy, 223–240.

Ejizu, Christopher. n.d. 'African Traditional Religions and the Promotion of Community-Living in Africa'. www.afrikaworld.net/afrel/community.htm.

Gandhi, Mahatma. 1926. 'From Far-Off America'. *Young India*, 6 May 1926. Repr. in *The Collected Works of Mahatma Gandhi*, Vol. 35. New Delhi: Publications Division Government of India, 1999, 193–196, www.gandhiashramsevagram.org/gandhi-literature/mahatma-gandhi-collected-works-volume-35.pdf.

Gandhi, M. K. 1932. *From Yervada Mandir*, Desai, Valji Govindji, trans. Ahmedabad: Jitendra T. Desai, Navajivan Mudranalaya, www.mkgandhi.org/ebks/yeravda.pdf.

Garcia, J. L. A. 2006. 'Being Unimpressed with Ourselves: Reconceiving Humility'. *Philosophia* 34(4): 417–435.

Gyekye, Kwame. 1995. *An Essay on African Philosophical Thought: The Akan Conceptual Scheme*, rev edn. Philadelphia, PA: Temple University Press.

Gyekye, Kwame. 1997. *Tradition and Modernity: Philosophical Reflections on the African Experience*. New York: Oxford University Press.

Gyekye, Kwame. 2010. 'African Ethics'. In: Zalta, Edward, ed. *The Stanford Encyclopedia of Philosophy*. plato .stanford.edu/archives/fall2010/entries/african-ethics/.

Ibekwe, Patrick. 1998. *Wit and Wisdom of Africa: Proverbs from Africa and the Caribbean*. Oxford: New Internationalist Publications Ltd.

Ikuenobe, Polycarp. 2006. *Philosophical Perspectives on Communalism and Morality in African Traditions*. Lanham, MD: Rowman and Littlefield.

Kellenberger, James. 2010. 'Humility'. *American Philosophical Quarterly* 47(4): 321–336.

Kohlberg, Lawrence. 1984. *The Psychology of Moral Development*. San Francisco, CA: Harper & Row.

Krog, Antjie. 2008. '"This Thing Called Reconciliation…"; Forgiveness as Part of an Interconnectedness-Towards-Wholeness'. *South African Journal of Philosophy* 27(4): 353–366.

Kuzwayo, Ellen. 1998. *African Wisdom: A Personal Collection of Setswana Proverbs*. Cape Town: Kwela Books.

Magesa, Laurenti. 1997. *African Religion: The Moral Traditions of Abundant Life*. Maryknoll, NY: Orbis Books.

Mandela, Nelson. 1994. *Long Walk to Freedom*. London: Abacus.

Mandela, Nelson. 2000. 'The Most Humble Man Oprah Has Ever Met', www.oprah.com/world/nelson-mandela-shares-the-importance-of-humility-video#ixzz5bj4CiZu4.

Mandela, Nelson. 2012. *Notes to the Future: Words of Wisdom*, Hatang, Sello and Venter, Sahm, eds. New York: Atria.

Mandela, Nelson. 2013a. *Nelson Mandela by Himself: The Authorised Book of Quotations*, Hatang, Sello and Venter, Sahm, eds. Johannesburg: Pan Macmillan.

Mandela, Nelson. 2013b. 'The Words of Nelson Mandela (1918 – 2013) that Forever Inspire Our World'. https://jetsettimes.com/in-crowd/nelson-mandela/.

Menkiti, Ifeanyi. 2004. 'On the Normative Conception of a Person'. In: Wiredu, Kwasi, ed. *A Companion to African Philosophy*. Oxford: Blackwell, 324–331.

Metz, Thaddeus. 2013. 'The Western Ethic of Care or an Afro-Communitarian Ethic?: Finding the Right Relational Morality'. *Journal of Global Ethics* 9(1): 77–92.

Metz, Thaddeus. 2014. '*Ubuntu*: The Good Life'. In: Michalos, Alex, ed. *Encyclopedia of Quality of Life and Well-Being Research*. Dordrecht: Springer, 6761–6765.

Metz, Thaddeus. 2015. 'How the West Was One: The Western as Individualist, the African as Communitarian'. *Educational Philosophy and Theory* 47(11): 1175–1184.

Metz, Thaddeus. 2017a. 'Toward an African Moral Theory', rev. edn. In: Ukpokolo, Isaac, ed. *Themes, Issues and Problems in African Philosophy*. London: Palgrave Macmillan, 97–119.

Metz, Thaddeus. 2017b. 'African Philosophy as a Multidisciplinary Discourse'. In: Falola, Toyin and Afolayan, Adeshina, eds. *The Palgrave Handbook of African Philosophy*. New York: Palgrave Macmillan, 795–812.

Metz, Thaddeus and Gaie, Joseph. 2010. 'The African Ethic of *Ubuntu/Botho*: Implications for Research on Morality'. *Journal of Moral Education* 39(3): 273–290.

Miller, Richard W. 1998. 'Three Versions of Objectivity: Aesthetic, Moral, and Scientific'. In: Levinson, Jerrold, ed. *Aesthetics and Ethics: Essays at the Intersection*. New York: Cambridge University Press, 26–58.

Mkhize, Nhlanhla. 2008. '*Ubuntu* and Harmony'. In: Nicolson, Ronald, ed. *Persons in Community: African Ethics in a Global Culture*. Pietermaritzburg: University of KwaZulu-Natal Press, 35–44.

Mokgoro, Yvonne. 1998. '*Ubuntu* and the Law in South Africa'. *Potchefstroom Electronic Law Journal* 1(1): 15–26, www.nwu.ac.za/p-per/volume-1-1998-no-1-1#Articles.

Murove, Munyaradzi Felix. 2016. *African Moral Consciousness*. London: Austin Macauley Publishers.

Oruka, Henry Odera. 1991. *Sage Philosophy: Indigenous Thinkers and Modern Debate on African Philosophy*. Nairobi: African Center for Technological Studies Press.

Paris, Peter. 1995. *The Spirituality of African Peoples: The Search for a Common Moral Discourse.* Minneapolis, MN: Fortress Press.

Roberts, Robert C. and Wood, W. Jay. 2003. 'Humility and Epistemic Goods'. In: DePaul, Michael and Zagzebski, Linda, eds. *Intellectual Virtue: Perspectives from Ethics and Epistemology.* New York: Oxford University Press, 257–279.

Tutu, Desmond. 1999. *No Future without Forgiveness.* New York: Random House.

Whitcomb, Dennis et al. 2017. 'Intellectual Humility: Owning Our Limitations'. *Philosophy and Phenomenological Research* 94(3): 509–539.

Wiredu, Kwasi. 1992. 'Moral Foundations of an African Culture'. In: Wiredu, Kwasi and Gyekye, Kwame, eds. *Person and Community; Ghanaian Philosophical Studies, Vol. I.* Washington, D.C.: Council for Research in Values and Philosophy, 193–206.

Wiredu, Kwasi. 1996. *Cultural Universals and Particulars: An African Perspective.* Bloomington, IN: Indiana University Press.

PART 5

The epistemology of humility

23

INTELLECTUAL HUMILITY AND CONTEMPORARY EPISTEMOLOGY

A critique of epistemic individualism, evidentialism and internalism

John Greco

Let us say that "epistemic individualism" is the position that a person's epistemic standing (what she knows, what she reasonably believes, etc.) is ultimately up to her, and is in that sense independent of the epistemic standing of other people. Let us say that "evidentialism" is the position that a person's epistemic standing is entirely determined by what evidence she has. Contemporary epistemology has moved away from epistemic individualism and evidentialism, in favor of anti-evidentialist views and views that stress the importance of "social-epistemic dependence," or dependence on other persons for what one knows and reasonably believes. This paper explores how these movements in epistemology are related to the notion of intellectual humility. The central idea is that, whereas intellectual pride is characterized by ideals and illusions of self-sufficiency, intellectual humility is characterized by a realistic estimation of one's own abilities and an appreciation of one's epistemic dependence on others. My contention will be that, in moving away from internalism (to be defined below), evidentialism, and individualism, contemporary epistemology is in effect rejecting ideals of intellectual pride in favor of the virtues of intellectual humility.

The chapter is organized as follows. Section 23.1 characterises humility by contrasting it with the vice of pride. Intellectual humility and intellectual pride are then characterised accordingly. Sections 23.2 through 23.4 characterise epistemic individualism, evidentialism, and internalism, respectively, and consider how these are bound up with both ideals and illusions of self-sufficiency, as well as a conception of autonomy that juxtaposes individual autonomy with dependence on others. Section 23.4 also includes an analogy to the practical realm, where ideals of self-sufficiency have led to similar problems. Section 23.5 describes the externalist turn in epistemology. The central idea here is that an individual's epistemic standing in not entirely a function of what is internal to her own mind. Rather, it is a function of her own mind, together with how that mind is causally and otherwise related to the world. Section 23.6 argues that externalism motivates anti-evidentialism. Section 23.7 argues that externalism motivates anti-individualism. Section 23.8 describes an approach to testimonial knowledge that is externalist, anti-evidentialist, and anti-individualist. Such an approach, it is argued, illustrates how intellectual autonomy can be enabled by dependence on others rather than opposed to it.

23.1 Humility and intellectual humility characterized

A number of authors have been concerned to state necessary and sufficient conditions for the virtues of humility and intellectual humility.[1] Completing this kind of project is not necessary for present purposes. Rather, it will be sufficient to note some features that are characteristic of humility, whether definitional or not, and to note some analogous characteristic features of intellectual humility. We can do this by contrasting the virtue of humility with the vice of pride (or better, pridefulness). Likewise, we may note some characteristic features of intellectual humility by contrasting it with intellectual pride or pridefulness.[2]

In that vein, consider seven (related) characteristics of the vice of pride:

a) Overestimating one's own abilities (or underestimating one's limitations).
b) Overestimating one's own contributions to one's own successes.
c) Underestimating and thus undervaluing the contributions of others to one's successes.
d) Underestimating one's dependence on others.
e) Illusions of self-sufficiency.
f) *Ideals* of self-sufficiency (with related ideals of control and invulnerability).
g) A notion of autonomy that opposes individual autonomy to dependence on others.

If we contrast humility with pride, the virtue can be characterized in terms of a realistic estimation of one's own abilities, limitations and contributions, a realistic appreciation of the contributions of others and one's dependence on others, and the rejection of self-sufficiency as an ideal. Intellectual pride and intellectual humility can then be understood accordingly, in terms of intellectual abilities, successes, contributions, etc. In particular, the intellectually humble person rejects the ideal of intellectual self-sufficiency, is not obsessed with invulnerability to error, and embraces a notion of autonomy that sees individual autonomy as consistent with dependence on other persons.

23.2 Epistemic individualism defined

Sanford Goldberg defines *anti*-individualism this way:

> *epistemic anti-individualism* … regards the epistemic justification of a subject's … beliefs as [sometimes] depending on features of the cognitive and linguistic acts *of the subject's social peers*.

Alternatively,

> the ascription of justification and knowledge to a subject *S* sometimes depends on factors pertaining to *the cognitive lives of subjects other than S*.[3]

Epistemic individualism, then, is the thesis that the epistemic justification of a subject's beliefs *never* depends on features of the cognitive and linguistic acts of the subject's social peers. Alternatively, the ascription of justification and knowledge to a subject *S never* depends on factors pertaining to the cognitive lives of subjects other than S.

It is important to note that this is not a thesis about one's psychological development or training. It would be absurd to think that a person's epistemic standing does not in any way depend on other persons for what she has learned, what intellectual skills she has, etc. Rather, the position is about epistemic standing after such resources have been put in place. The idea, then, is something like this: A person's epistemic standing is entirely determined by how she *uses* her own epistemic resources, even if her *having* those resources is not entirely her own doing. Another way to put the idea is this: What a person knows or reasonably believes at some time *t* does not depend on what others know or reasonably believe at *t*. Rather, what a person knows or reasonably believes at a time is "up to her alone," depending only on how she uses her own evidence, abilities, etc.

To better understand the epistemic individualist's position, compare two ways of thinking about testimonial knowledge, or how one acquires knowledge from testimony. On one broad approach known as "reductionism" about testimonial knowledge, a hearer acquires testimonial knowledge by reasoning about whether she should believe a given speaker. That is, the hearer uses her own evidence regarding whether a person is knowledgeable on a given subject, whether the person is likely to be sincere, etc., and then uses that evidence to determine whether she should accept what the speaker is saying. The view is called "reductionism" because it holds that knowledge gained by testimony reduces to knowledge gained by reasoning from one's own evidence. As such, reductionism can be understood as allowing only a kind of pseudo-dependence on other persons. In this sense, reductionism embraces epistemic individualism. Compare "anti-reductionism" about testimonial knowledge. On this second broad approach, knowledge from testimony cannot be understood, at least not entirely, in terms of what is supported by one's evidence. On the contrary, anti-reductionism insists that the speaker does some epistemic work, and makes some contribution over and above what can be vetted by the hearer's own resources. As such, anti-reductionism embraces a more robust kind of epistemic dependence on other persons.[4]

It is clear enough that epistemic individualism embraces the ideal of self-sufficiency in the intellectual realm. On that position, positive epistemic status is wholly determined by the individual's own resources. Here we may consider an economic analogy. There is a sense in which any business owner "depends" on her workers. On the other hand, let us suppose that she uses her own resources to pay them, and only insofar as she evaluates their abilities and contributions as being adequate for her own purposes. Moreover, let us suppose that she is not bound to those workers in any way that does not depend on her own resources. For example, she can fire anyone who she does not evaluate as adequate, and she can recruit others as needed. This is a kind of dependence. Let's call it "pseudo-dependence," insofar as it is dependence that in turn depends upon and is subject to the individual's own resources. "Real" dependence, let us say, does not in turn depend on one's own resources. Epistemic anti-individualism embraces real dependence in the epistemic realm.

23.3 Evidentialism defined

Earl Conee and Richard Feldman define evidentialism in terms of a supervenience thesis.

> As we understand it, evidentialism is a view about the conditions under which a person is epistemically justified in having some doxastic attitude toward a proposition. It holds that this sort of epistemic fact is determined entirely by the person's evidence. In its fundamental form, then, evidentialism is a supervenience thesis according to which facts about whether or not a person is justified in believing a proposition supervene on facts describing the evidence that the person has.

Again,

> Our bedrock view is a supervenience thesis. Justification strongly supervenes on evidence.[5]

Following Connee and Feldman's characterization in terms of justification, we can define evidentialism more broadly as follows:

(E) The facts about the individual's evidence determine the facts about the individual's epistemic status (of one sort or another).

The first thing to note is that evidentialism entails epistemic individualism. In effect, epistemic individualism makes positive epistemic status (of one sort or another) supervene on the cognitive resources of the individual. Evidentialism restricts that further, making positive epistemic status (of one sort or another) supervene on the individual's evidence. Accordingly, evidentialism continues to endorse the ideal of intellectual self-sufficiency, and to reject real epistemic dependence on others.

23.4 Internalism defined

We may define internalism in epistemology as follows.

(I) The facts about an individual's epistemic status (of one sort or another) supervene on facts that are "internal" to the individual.

We get different versions of epistemic internalism depending on how the notion of "internal to the indvidual" is understood. One important version of epistemic internalism is Privileged Access Internalism.[6]

(I-PA) The facts about an individual's epistemic status (of one sort or another) supervene on facts to which the individual has privileged access.

A different way to understand the notion of "internal to the knower" is due to Conee and Feldman. Here is what Conee and Feldman say with regards to their "mentalism" about justification.

> internalism is the view that a person's beliefs are justified only by things that are internal to the person's mental life. We shall call this version of internalism 'mentalism.' A mentalist theory may assert that justification is determined entirely by occurrent mental factors, or by dispositional ones as well. As long as the things that are said to contribute to justification are in the person's mind, the view qualifies as a version of mentalism.[7]

Accordingly, we may define "Mental State Internalism" as follows:

(I-MS) The facts about an individual's epistemic status (of one sort or another) supervene on facts about the individual's mental life.

We saw that evidentialism entails epistemic individualism, and in fact further restricts the factors that determine epistemic status to the individual's *evidence*. Clearly enough, internalism also entails individualism, and does so by further restricting what resources of the individual contribute to positive epistemic status. In fact, internalism can be viewed as a kind of epistemic individualism on steroids—the only epistemic resources available to the individual (the only materials that can contribute to her epistemic status) are now those to which she has privileged access. Alternatively, they are the materials that constitute her own mental life.

Here is another way to look at it. Epistemic individualism was defined in terms of independence from *other persons*. In effect, internalism is defined in terms of independence from *the world in general*. As with individualism and other persons, the world can contribute, but only insofar as such contributions are evaluated and validated by the individual. In this sense, only pseudo-dependence on the world is allowed.

23.4.1 Internalism and scepticism

It is widely acknowledged that internalism at least threatens to be a skeptical view. Specifically, internalists incur the burden of showing how such restricted epistemic resources can account for adequate epistemic standing vis-à-vis beliefs about the external world, other minds, the past, laws of nature, etc. Sometimes the problem is characterized in terms of evidential support: How can the meager evidence that the internalist allows herself support beliefs about external objects, the past, etc. Other times the problem is characterized in terms of circularity: How can the internalist satisfy herself that her perception is reliable, without using her perception to do so? More generally, how can the internalist satisfy herself that she has any reliable grasp on external world facts, using only the resources she has allowed herself, and without falling into circularity, which validation can't tolerate?[8]

To the extent that the internalism fails to answer these worries, the non-skeptical internalist will be characterized by illusions of self-sufficiency. Suppose the internalist gives up on answering these worries and embraces skepticism. Then she will have given up the illusion of self-sufficiency, but she will still be embracing the ideal.

23.4.2 An analogy to the practical realm

In *The Fragility of Goodness*, Martha Nussbaum characterizes Greek thought as preoccupied with the vulnerability of human excellence and happiness to the contingencies of good fortune. According to Nussbaum, this preoccupation motivated a retreat in *value* to what can be guaranteed by one's own agency. For example, she argues, Platonic conceptions of virtue and happiness, centered as they are around reason and contemplation, are primarily motivated by a strategy to distance human excellence and good from what cannot be controlled. Thus, Nussbaum writes about

> the aspiration to rational self-sufficiency in Greek ethical thought: the aspiration to make the goodness of a good human life safe from luck through the controlling power of reason … What happens to a person by luck will be just what does not happen through his or her own agency, what just *happens* to him, as opposed to what he does or makes. In general, to eliminate luck from human life will be to put that life, or the most important things in it, under the control of the agent (or of those elements in him with which he identifies himself), removing the element of reliance upon the external and undependable[9]

In this regard, for example, Nussbaum cites Plato's defense in the *Phaedo* and *Republic* "of a life of self-sufficient contemplation, in which unstable activities and their objects have no intrinsic value."[10]

A similar dynamic is played out in the Kantian retreat to a realm of pure agency. Consider the following oft-cited passage from Kant's *Groundwork*.

> A good will is not good because of what it effects or accomplishes, because of its fitness for attaining some proposed end: it is good through its willing alone, that is, good in itself ... Even if, by some special disfavor of destiny ... this will is entirely lacking in power to carry out its intentions; if by its utmost effort it still accomplishes nothing, and only good will is left ... then it would still shine like a jewel for its own sake as something which has its full value in itself.[11]

This conception of the agent is both endorsed and lamented by modern-day Kantians such as Thomas Nagel. In a now-famous discussion, Nagel notes the various ways in which a human life is subject to luck, and concludes that, in this light, the sphere "genuine agency" seems to disappear.

> If one cannot be responsible for consequences of one's acts due to factors beyond one's control, or for antecedents of one's acts that are properties of temperament not subject to one's will, or for the circumstances that pose one's moral choices, then how can one be responsible even for the stripped-down acts of the will itself, if *they* are the product of antecedent circumstances outside of the will's control? The area of genuine agency, and therefore of legitimate moral judgment, seems to shrink under this scrutiny to an extensionless point.[12]

Importantly, Nagel is willing to give up the illusion of pure agency but not the ideal. Rather than rejecting a notion of agency that makes moral responsibility and moral value impossible, he accepts the skeptical conclusion.

> I believe that in a sense the problem has no solution ... as the external determinants of what someone has done are gradually exposed, in their effect on consequences, character, and choice itself, it becomes gradually clear that actions are events and people things. Eventually nothing remains which can be ascribed to the responsible self, and we are left with nothing but a portion of the larger sequence of events, which can be deplored or celebrated, but not blamed or praised.[13]

In effect, internalism does for intellectual evaluation what Plato and Kant do for practical evaluation—it retreats to a sphere, or tries to retreat to a sphere, where the agent and her success are beholden to nothing and no one. The result is that only a thin kind of agency holds value, and only a thin kind of agent gets evaluated.

23.5 The externalist turn in epistemology

We have so far defined individualism, evidentialism, and internalism in epistemology, and we have seen how both evidentialism and internalism entail individualism. We have also seen how these views are related to ideals of self-sufficiency, and how they reject any real epistemic dependence on other persons. In the remainder of the paper, I want to show how 1) externalism broadens the epistemic resources available to the individual (in effect, externalism thickens the agent and her agency), 2) externalism motivates anti-evidentialism, and 3) externalism motivates anti-individualism. That is, we will see how a) externalism rejects ideals of self-sufficiency, and b) embraces real epistemic dependence on others. This comes with c) more realistic estimations of one's own abilities and limitations, d) a greater appreciation of (in the sense of *valuing*) one's epistemic dependence on others, and e) a notion of intellectual autonomy that is consistent with social epistemic dependence and cooperation.

We defined epistemic internalism as follows:

> (I) The facts about an individual's epistemic status (of one sort or another) supervene on facts that are "internal" to the individual.

Epistemic externalism simply denies epistemic internalism. Thus, on an externalist view, the facts about an individual's epistemic status (of one sort or another) are not wholly determined by facts that are internal to the individual.

What kinds of facts might matter? Most notably, these will be causal and other modal facts, describing relations between the individual and the world. For example, facts about the reliability of one's cognitive faculties, facts about the proper functioning of one's cognition and, more generally, facts about causal and modal relations between the individual and her environment.[14] These are all paradigmatically external facts, in that they are neither facts to which one has privileged access nor are they facts about one's mental states.

Accordingly, externalism replaces the notion of a pure agent operating in a pure realm, with that of an embodied agent operating in the world. What matters for intellectual status is a function *both* of a) what goes on internal to cognition, and b) how that cognition relates to the world; e.g., whether the agent's environment is enabling or undermining. In this way, externalism makes epistemic status (of one sort or another) depend partly on an environment that is not of the agent's own making. In doing so, it also makes epistemic status, and the agent herself, vulnerable to contingencies and to what she cannot control.

23.6 An anti-evidentialist turn

The main point I want to make in this section is that externalism motivates anti-evidentialism. This is because, as we saw, externalism deems important one's causal and other modal relations to the world. For example, it makes epistemic status (of one sort or another) at least partly a matter of proper function, or reliability, or safety, or sensitivity. But once these are deemed important, it is no longer obvious why evidence is so important. That is, it is no longer obvious why evidence is important independently of its role in grounding proper function, reliability, safety, sensitivity, etc. And, in that case, a further question becomes pressing: Why should evidence be the *only* thing that can ground proper function, reliability, etc.? That is, why can't there be a variety of cognitive faculties or strategies that do the job?[15]

This line of thought, for example, opens the door to non-evidentialist accounts of perception, memory and knowledge of other minds that are more in line with contemporary cognitive science. First, consider perceptual knowledge, and the various tortured attempts in the history of philosophy to show that perceptual evidence adequately supports beliefs about the external world.[16] Evidentialist theories of perception understand perception as involving a kind of inference from experience to world, thereby inviting skeptical questions about whether any such inference is adequate to the task. By attempting to understand perception within this framework, evidentialists take reasoning as the model for perceiving. That is, they think of perception as a kind of inference from evidence to conclusions supported by that evidence. Contemporary cognitive science, on the other hand, does not try to assimilate the kind of cognitive processing in perception to the kind of processing that goes on in reasoning proper. Importantly, reasoning proper is driven by inference rules that operate on propositional structures, and operates on inputs (beliefs, assumptions, etc.) that are person-level representations. Perception of various modalities, on the other hand, is characterized by cognitive processing in which both inputs and transactions are largely on a sub-personal level, as when the visual system calculates distance from a variety of binocular and monocular cues that are not a part of conscious experience.

Similar points can be made about memory, "mind-reading" capacities, and a host of other cognitive functioning. But again, once we give up an evidentialist framework in favor of reliabilism, proper functionalism, or some other externalist view, these various sorts of cognitive function need not be understood as involving unconscious or implicit inference from good evidence, and need not be evaluated according to the norms of good reasoning. On the contrary, various cognitive functioning will be seen as epistemically valuable insofar as it places cognizers in an epistemically valuable relation to the world—i.e., relations that are reliable, safe, sensitive, etc.

23.7 Social epistemic dependence

So far, we have seen motivations for rejecting internalism and evidentialism. We have also seen how doing so allows a more realistic estimation of one's own abilities and limitations, and how doing so embraces at least a kind of epistemic dependency on the world. But all this is still consistent with epistemic individualism and its rejection of *social* epistemic dependence, or epistemic dependence on other *persons*. However, just as externalism motivates anti-evidentialism, it also motivates anti-individualism. For once we allow that epistemic status can depend on facts about the external world, it is an easy step to allow that epistemic status can depend on facts about the social world. Just as an individual's epistemic status (of one sort or another) can depend on a friendly external environment, her epistemic status can depend on a friendly social environment as well. In this regard, anti-individualism can be viewed as simply an extension of externalism into the social world.[17]

23.8 Reductionism and anti-reductionism in the epistemology of testimony

Earlier, I suggested that reductionism in the epistemology of testimony is a form of epistemic individualism. Reductionists allow that the individual can get testimonial knowledge from others, but the kind of dependence it allows here is merely a pseudo-dependence: Testimonial knowledge requires, on this view, that the speaker be adequately vetted. That is, using the non-testimonial resources that the hearer has available to her, she may extend her knowledge by means of *validated* testimony.

One way to understand anti-reductionism in the epistemology of testimony is that it insists on real epistemic dependence on other persons, as opposed to mere pseudo-dependence. Put differently, anti-reductionist views required a dependence on the speaker that is not exhausted by what can be evaluated and validated by the hearer. That is why anti-reductionist views often talk in terms of *trusting* the speaker, where this is explicitly opposed to believing the speaker on good evidence.[18]

I end by offering an example of an anti-reductionist view along such lines. The anti-reductionist position I put forward also shows how epistemic dependence on others can add epistemic value, and how individual intellectual autonomy can be advanced by means of cooperation with others.[19]

In order to present the view that I have in mind, it will be helpful to introduce the notion of an "epistemic community," understood as a group of persons who share some set of information-dependent tasks, and who share a set of norms for acquiring and distributing task-relevant information. That is, an epistemic community will have a need for *quality* information, and therefore will have norms and standards in place that are relevant for achieving that quality.

The next point to note is that the norms or standards that are appropriate for the acquisition of information will be somewhat different from the norms or standards that are appropriate for the distribution of information. That is because the different sets of norms answer to different purposes. Specifically, the primary purpose of acquisition norms is to play a kind of gatekeeping role—they are concerned with quality control regarding what information gets into the social system in the first place. The primary purpose of distribution norms, however, is to get quality information to those members of the community who need it. Here we may invoke the analogy of a military base. The standards for getting into the base are high. You have to show proper ID, perhaps answer some questions, etc. Once you get into the base, you can't just go wherever you want whenever you want, but the norms governing how you are allowed to move around will be different from those governing how you gain entry in the first place.

On the view of testimonial knowledge that I want to propose, the characteristic function of testimony is to distribute quality information within an epistemic community. That is, the primary function is to take information that has already passed the quality control test at the gatekeeping stage, and to distribute that information to those who need it. Put differently, the characteristic function of testimony is to move knowledge around within an epistemic community.

That central idea has to be qualified, however, because this characteristic function of testimony is not its sole function. In particular, testimony can be used to *acquire* information for an epistemic community as well as to *distribute* it. This happens when the speaker is not herself a member of the hearer's epistemic community, and therefore is not in the same relationship of cooperation with the hearer as are members of the same community. For example, suppose that a personnel director is interviewing a job candidate for her company. The personnel director and the job candidate are in a different relationship, governed by different norms for giving and receiving testimony, than the personnel director is in with her co-workers or with her boss. Importantly, members of the same epistemic community, cooperating in the context of shared practical tasks, can appropriately trust each other's testimony in a way that the personnel director cannot trust the testimony of the job candidate. Other examples are easy to find. For example, a police officer should approach the testimony of informants differently from the testimony of a fellow investigator. Likewise, a scientist on a research team should approach the testimony of test subjects differently from the testimony of fellow researchers.

Finally, let's make a distinction between the *generation* or *production* of knowledge for an epistemic community, and the *transmission* of knowledge within that community. The present suggestion is that the transmission of knowledge is governed by different norms and standards from the generation of knowledge. Insofar as the characteristic purpose of testimony is to transmit knowledge within an epistemic community, testimonial exchanges are (characteristically) governed by relevant norms and standards.

The current view is anti-reductionist in the sense explained above. That is, at least some testimonial knowledge is subject to its own standards and norms, and therefore not reducible to knowledge produced by inductive reasoning, or knowledge of some other kind. The view is also anti-individualist, in that the transmission of knowledge depends on both speaker and hearer playing their appropriate role in a cooperative testimonial exchange. Accordingly, the epistemic standing of the hearer—that she knows the thing she has been told—at least sometimes depends on the epistemic standing of the speaker—that she had knowledge to transmit, and did so successfully. It follows from all this that the view is also externalist in the sense explained above. That is, whether a speaker knows, and whether the speaker and hearer play their appropriate roles in a cooperative testimonial exchange, in not something that the hearer can know "by reflection alone," and is certainly not simply a matter of the hearer's own mental states.

In fact, the present approach is able to accommodate more diverse social factors and the broader social environment in its account of the transmission of knowledge. For the norms that govern relevant testimonial exchanges are often tied up with interpersonal relations, social norms and roles, institutional rules, and even positive law. In particular, all of these may contribute to successful knowledge transmission in healthy epistemic communities, and undermine transmission in unhealthy ones. And so, again, we have various ways in which the epistemic standing of individuals very much depends on features of the broader social environment.

The phenomenon I have in mind here involves the notion of what I will call "transmission channels." Much as the contours of a physical environment can promote or inhibit the movement of physical objects within it, the contours of an epistemic community can promote or inhibit the movement of knowledge. For example, imagine a social environment where there is a deficit of trust and good will, and various disincentives for cooperation. To that extent, conditions for epistemic cooperation will be limited as well, including opportunities for reliably sharing information and transmitting knowledge. Likewise, social environments that enable cooperation in general will also enable epistemic cooperation. In various cases, norms that are primarily practical or moral underwrite good epistemic practices in this regard. I will end with a few examples.

First, consider a normal, healthy relationship between parent and child. Care and love in the relationship will guide the behaviors of both parent and child in epistemically beneficial ways. For example, parents are motivated to provide their children with relevant information and to make sure that they are in a position to receive it effectively. Likewise, young children are motivated to trust their caregivers for needed information. Similar things can be said about relations among friends, which are governed by norms of care, loyalty, and mutual benefit. Various professional–client relationships also give rise to epistemically effective transmission channels, which are created and maintained not only by norms governing the professional relationship, but also by broader social factors such as professional ethics, licensing requirements, economic incentives, and even positive law. In all of these ways, the transfer of knowledge is enabled by social factors that outrun the intellectual abilities and control of the hearer.

When we consider how ubiquitous these various relationships are, the extent of real epistemic dependence on others becomes clear. What also becomes clear is that both practical and intellectual autonomy is enabled and enhanced by such dependence, rather than undermined by it. Which is to say that human agency, both practical and intellectual, is largely a social agency.

Conclusion

This chapter considered some recent trends in epistemology, and explored their relation to the notion of intellectual humility. Intellectual humility was characterized by a realistic estimation of one's own intellectual abilities and contributions, and an appreciation of one's epistemic dependence on others. In contrast, intellectual pride was characterized by both illusions and ideals of self-sufficiency in the intellectual realm. In this context, epistemic internalism, evidentialism, and epistemic individualism were criticized as embracing the ideals of intellectual pride. We ended with an approach to testimonial knowledge and knowledge transmission that embraces both the reality and value of social-epistemic dependence. As such, the view is decidedly externalist, anti-evidentialist, and anti-individualist.[20]

Notes

1 For example, see Robert Roberts and Jay Wood, "Humility and Epistemic Goods," in eds. DePaul, Michael. and Zagzebski, Linda. *Intellectual Virtue: Perspectives from Ethics and Epistemology* (New York: Oxford University Press, 2003); and Dennis Whitcomb, Heather Battaly, Jason Baehr and Daniel Howard-Snyder. (2015). "Intellectual Humility: Owning Our Limitations." *Philosophy and Phenomenological Research* 91 (1).

2 In ordinary usage, the term "pride" does not always imply viciousness. I stipulate that I am here using the term as synonymous with "pridefullness," which more explicitly marks a vice. Likewise, I am here following the literature in using "humility" to mark a virtue. If virtue hits a mean between deficiency and excess, then humility in this sense would be the mean between servility and pridefullness.

3 Goldberg, Sanford. *Anti-Individualism: Mind and Language, Knowledge and Justification* (Cambridge: Cambridge University Press, 2007), p. 134.

4 For characterizations of reductionism and anti-reductionism, see C.A.J. Coady, *Testimony: A Philosophical Study* (Oxford: Oxford University Press, 1992); Jennifer Lackey and Ernest Sosa (ed), *The Epistemology of Testimony* (Oxford: Oxford University Press, 2006); Jennifer Lackey, *Learning from Words* (Oxford: Oxford University Press, 2008); and John Greco. (2012). "Recent Work on Testimonial Knowledge," *American Philosophical Quarterly* 49, 1: 15–28.

5 Earl Connee and Richard Feldman, *Evidentialism: Essays in Epistemology* (Oxford: Oxford University Press, 2004), p. 204.

6 Cf. William P. Alston. (1986). "Internalism and Externalism in Epistemology," *Philosophical Topics* XIV: 179–221. Reprinted in Alston *Epistemic Justification* (Ithaca: Cornell University Press, 1989).

7 Earl Connee and Richard Feldman, *Evidentialism: Essays in Epistemology* (Oxford: Oxford University Press, 2004), p. 55.

8 For an extended argument that internalism entails broad skeptical results, see Greco, *Putting Skeptics in Their Place: The Nature of Skeptical Arguments and Their Role in Philosophical Inquiry* (Cambridge: Cambridge University Press, 2000). For similar worries on behalf of an internalist, see Fumerton, Richard. *Metaepistemology and Skepticism* (Lanham, Maryland: Rowman and Littlefield, 1995).

9 Martha Nussbaum, *The Fragility of Goodness: Luck and ethics in Greek tragedy and philosophy* (Cambridge: Cambridge University Press, 1986), pp. 3–4.

10 Ibid., p. 9.

11 Immanuel Kant, *Groundwork of the Metaphysics of Morals*, translated by H.J. Paton (New York: Harper and RowPublishers, 1964), p. 62.

12 Nagel, Thomas. "Moral Luck," in *Mortal Questions* (Cambridge: Cambridge University Press, 1979), p. 35.

13 Ibid., p. 37.

14 For examples of externalist views, see Goldman, Alvin. (1976). "Discrimination and Perceptual Knowledge," *Journal of Philosophy* 73: 771–791. Reprinted in Alvin Goldman, *Liaisons: Philosophy Meets the Cognitive and Social Sciences.* (Cambridge, Massachusetts: MIT Press, 1992); Goldman, Alvin. "What is Justified Belief?" in George Pappas, ed., *Justification and Knowledge.* (Dordrecht: D. Reidel, 1979), Greco, *Achieving Knowledge: A Virtue-theoretic Account of Epistemic Normativity* (Cambridge: Cambridge University Press, 2010); Plantinga, Alvin. *Warrant and Proper Function* (Oxford: Oxford University Press, 1993); Ernest Sosa, *A Virtue Epistemology: Apt Belief and Reflective Knowledge, Volume 1* (Oxford: Oxford University Press, 2007); Nozick, Robert. *Philosophical Explanations* (Cambridge, MA: Harvard University Press, 1981); and Dretske, Fred. (1970). 'Epistemic Operators,' *The Journal of Philosophy* 67, 1007–1023.

15 For more extended arguments along these lines, see my *Achieving Knowledge* op. cit.; and "Evidentialism and Knowledge," in Trent Dougherty, ed., *Evidentialism and Its Discontents* (Oxford: Oxford University Press, 2011).

16 For a nice discussion here, see Alston, W. *The Reliability of Sense Perception.* (Ithaca: Cornell University Press, 1993).

17 For discussions that emphasise social dimensions of knowledge, see Alvin Goldman. *Knowledge in a Social World.* (Oxford: Oxford University Press, 1999); Goldberg, Sanford. *Anti-Individualism: Mind and Language, Knowledge and Justification* (Cambridge: Cambridge University Press, 2007); and Sanford Goldberg. *Relying on Others: An Essay in Epistemology.* (Oxford: Oxford University Press, 2010).

18 For accounts of the role of trust in testimony, see Hinchman, Edward. (2005). "Telling as Inviting to Trust," *Philosophy and Phenomenological Research*, vol. 70, no.3, pp. 562–587; Harris, Paul. *Trusting*

What You're Told (Cambridge, MA: Harvard University Press, 2012); Faulkner, P. *Knowledge on Trust* (Oxford: Oxford University Press, 2011); McMyler, Benjamin. *Testimony, Trust, and Authority* (New York: Oxford University Press, 2011); and Greco, J. 'The Role of Trust in Testimonial Knowledge,' in Katherine Dormandy (ed) *Trust in Epistemology* (New York: Routledge, 2018). For an overview, see Benjamin McMyler and Adebayo Ogungbure (2018), "Recent Work on Trust and Testimony," *American Philosophical Quarterly* 55, 3.

19 For more detailed presentations of the view sketched below, see my "Testimonial Knowledge and the Flow of Information," in David Henderson and John Greco *Epistemic Evaluation: Point and Purpose in Epistemology* (Oxford University Press, 2015); "The Role of Trust in Testimonial Knowledge," in Katherine Dormandy (ed) *Trust in Epistemology* (New York: Routledge, 2018); and *The Transmission of Knowledge* (Cambridge: Cambridge University Press, forthcoming).

20 For helpful discussion, thanks to audiences at Biola University's Center for Christian Thought, and the Federal University of Bahia, Brazil. Research for this paper was supported by *The Philosophy and Theology of Intellectual Humility Project* at Saint Louis University, funded by a generous grant from the John Templeton Foundation.

24
HUMILITY AND SELF-KNOWLEDGE

Alessandra Tanesini

In this chapter I presuppose that humility, however it is to be characterised, is flanked by at least two vices: arrogance and self-abasement. Arrogant individuals are lacking in humility. Those who self-abase are exceedingly humble. When it is conceived in these terms, there is a close association between humility and self-knowledge. The humble individual must be cognisant of her good features or strengths to avoid belittling herself and thus losing all pride in self-abasement. She must also be aware of her bad qualities or weaknesses lest she risks becoming arrogant.

I thus follow modern sensibilities in thinking of humility as a valuable corrective to widespread arrogance and narcissism (Roberts and Wood, 2007), but also to servility and self-abasement. Humility so understood is compatible with pride in one's achievements. It does not have the association, attributed to it in traditional Christian conceptions of this virtue, with low status and unworthiness.

This close connection of humility to self-knowledge is evident in the contemporary literature on the virtue of humility, and its near-synonym: modesty. Broadly speaking, recent accounts of this character trait belong to one of three families of views. The first, initiated by Driver (1989, 1999), characterises humility as requiring ignorance of one's own good qualities. The second, inaugurated by Snow (1995), describes humility in terms of knowledge of one's own limitations. The third, embraced by Bommarito (2013), Garcia (2006), and by Nadelhoffer and Wright (2017), modifies Driver's account of humility by claiming that humility involves low self-focus rather than ignorance of one's good features.

In this chapter I discuss the role that self-knowledge plays in each of these three families of views. I highlight that none of them provides a wholly satisfactory account of the virtue of humility and of its relation to self-knowledge. In their place, I propose an account of humility as a hopeful attitude toward what self-knowledge reveals about the self.

24.1 Humility as a virtue of ignorance

In Driver's account, humility is 'a disposition to underestimate self-worth in some respect' (1999, p. 827). Hence, humility requires ignorance or underestimation of one's good qualities and achievements (1989, 1999).[1] The underestimation of strength characteristic of humility must be limited in extent and scope, since those who severely underestimate their worth or underestimate all of their good qualities are better described as self-deprecating rather than humble

(Driver, 1999, p. 830). Driver's view does not require that humble individuals have a low estimation of their abilities. They might have a good opinion of themselves. What matters, however, is that their estimate is an underestimate so that they evaluate themselves as being less worthy than they truly are (Driver, 1999, p. 828).

Driver argues that actual ignorance of one's own good qualities, rather than mere pretence in conversation with others, is necessary for humility. In her view, the person who downplays her achievements whilst being fully aware of their nature behaves in ways that are characteristic of false modesty. Interlocutors often find such behaviour patronising; it is incompatible with true modesty (Driver, 1989, pp. 377–378). True modesty thus requires that one has false beliefs about one's good qualities, or that one has no idea about what they are. Thus the surprising consequence of Driver's view is that, in order to be humble, a person must, in contravention of the Socratic maxim, not know herself.

It is often objected to Driver's view that a robust disposition to be ignorant cannot be virtuous (Flanagan, 1990). This charge is especially pressing with regard to intellectual humility (Tanesini, 2018). Intellectual virtues are usually understood as dispositions or faculties that include epistemically good motivations, such as the desire for truth or cognitive contact with reality (Zagzebski, 1996), and/or those that reliably produce good effects in the form of knowledge or true belief (Battaly, 2015; Sosa, 2007). Hence, if humility is a disposition to have epistemically inaccurate views about one's own good qualities, it cannot count as an intellectual virtue, since it does not possess either the requisite motivation or the appropriate good effects.

In response, Driver emphasises that ignorance and self-deception can in fact be valuable in limited doses (Driver, 1999). She points out that, for instance, a parent who deceives herself about her children's talents by selectively focusing her attention on evidence of their achievements, might foster improved performance through praise and thus contribute to increasing their abilities. This kind of self-deception, Driver notes, might be valuable if it has predominantly good effects (1999, p. 380). Even if we grant that ignorance might be in some limited circumstances instrumentally valuable, since some optimistic false beliefs can have the power of self-fulfilling prophecies, we can still resist conceding that ignorance can be virtuous. Driver's defence of ignorance presupposes her consequentialist account of virtue (Driver, 2001). But this is a view that we would want to resist if we think that virtues are both psychologically real and intrinsically valuable.

Be that as it may, the underestimation of one's own strengths, successes, and achievements is intuitively neither necessary nor sufficient for humility. Underestimation is not necessary for humility. Supposing that Einstein has been the greatest scientist of the first half of the twentieth century, it seems compatible with humility that he thought his scientific achievements surpassed those of his contemporaries. Driver disagrees. In her view, Einstein can humbly think of himself as a good scientist, but he could not be humble and think of himself as the best of his time (Driver, 1999, p. 827). I do not share the intuition. Sure, it would be immodest to brag about one's superiority with fellow scientists. But what makes the behaviour immodest is the bragging, rather than the conviction that one's achievements are more impressive than those notched up by others. The person who brags is above all trying to impress her interlocutors (Alfano and Robinson, 2014). She wants to impress not because she hopes to be an exemplar, but to fan her need for self-enhancement. In short, it is not knowledge of one's strengths and an awareness that these are superior to those possessed by others that makes one immodest. One lacks modesty if one adopts a self-satisfied attitude toward one's achievements, if one cares about them only because they make one feel good about oneself. It is not knowledge of success that makes one immodest; what matters is one's attitude toward those good qualities of which one is aware. If one's knowledge makes one smug, then one is not humble.

These points can be strengthened by noting that even overestimation of one's own strengths is compatible with humility. Driver appears to deny this possibility when she presents the fictional example of Roger, a reasonably successful scientist, who is fooled by his colleagues into believing that he has won the Nobel Prize. Upon learning of his error, Roger feels ashamed (Driver, 1999, p. 831). Driver concludes that Roger's shame is due to his recognition of immodesty or lack of humility. I disagree. Roger is ashamed because he recognises that his vanity has made him a fool. It is Roger's craving for honours rather than his overestimation of his own strengths that is at issue. Contrast Driver's example with the equally fictional case of Olufemi, who mistakenly overestimates the impact that his new treatment for malaria might have in affected regions. He has evidence of the treatment's effectiveness, but that evidence turns out to be misleading. Looking back, Olufemi recognises his error. He might experience regret but presumably feels no shame. Olufemi is not ashamed because he has not made a fool of himself. He has overestimated his achievement, but his is a mistake. I submit that we are not tempted to think of Olufemi as immodest despite his initially mistaken opinion about the significance of his achievement. This consideration suggests that what causes Roger to feel ashamed is not that he initially believes that he has won, but that he does so because of his susceptibility to flattery.

Underestimation of one's strengths is also not sufficient for humility. Driver acknowledges that severe underestimation is akin to self-deprecation and that it is incompatible with modesty or humility (Driver, 1999, p. 827). Hence, in her view, only limited underestimation would be required. She also adds that a person might underestimate her objective achievements without being humble because she lacks evidence of what these are. Thus, Driver refines her view by stating that modesty or humility is the underestimation of one's actual good qualities, despite having access to evidence about what they are (Driver, 1999, p. 831).

In my view, this is not sufficient (or necessary) for humility. Consider the case of Robert, who is the best rower in his club and in his town. Robert is also rather arrogant. He likes to throw his weight around. As it happens, and despite his unfortunate character, Robert is an even better rower than he thinks he is. He has both technique and strength. Robert has evidence that he is exceptionally good. He should leave his small club and town and aim to join a different outfit, face stiffer competition, and perhaps one day make the national team. But Robert likes to be the biggest fish in a small pond. He does not want to be challenged and thus ignores, out of fear of failure, evidence that he is better than he thinks. Robert is arrogant, but he also underestimates his ability, despite having access to evidence about it. All of these examples point to the conclusion that underestimation of good qualities is not what is crucial to humility.

24.2 Humility as a virtue of self-knowledge

Whilst Driver thinks that humility consists in having false beliefs about one's good qualities, a number of philosophers, starting with Snow (1995), have argued that humility presupposes self-knowledge. In particular it would require knowledge of one's limitations and other bad features. In Snow's view humility is 'the disposition to allow the awareness of and concern about [one's] limitations to have a realistic influence on [one's] attitudes and behavior' (1995, p. 210).[2] Hence, her account identifies both cognitive and affective-conative elements of humility. This virtue would require that one knows about one's shortcomings and is concerned about them.

Whilst Snow includes an affective component in her account of humility, other related views focus exclusively on knowledge of one's own limitations and ignore the different kinds of attitude that one might take to this knowledge. This approach is exemplified by Hazlett's view that intellectual humility is the disposition to adopt the correct second-order doxastic attitude toward the epistemic statuses of one's first-order doxastic attitudes such as belief, disbelief, or suspension of belief (Hazlett, 2012, p. 220). Church's view that intellectual humility is the virtue of accurately tracking the positive epistemic status of one's own beliefs provides another example of this approach (Church, 2016, p. 425). Both accounts identify intellectual humility with self-knowledge. Those who are intellectually humble know (or at least are rationally sensitive to the evidence about) how much to rely on their current views. Hence, they are able to revise them or stand firm depending on what kind of counter-evidence emerges.

The intuition underpinning these accounts is that intellectual humility is the virtue flanked by vices of over- and under-confidence in the correctness of one's opinions. If this is right, intellectual humility would involve the correct calibration of confidence in one's beliefs to the available of evidence about their epistemic status and of confidence in one's abilities to evidence of one's competence (Kidd, 2016).

These accounts are intended exclusively to apply to intellectual humility rather than humility per se. Nevertheless, since the person who is humble is presumably also intellectually humble (but not necessarily vice versa),[3] it should be impossible for someone to count as intellectually humble by these definitions and yet fail to be generically humble. Counter-examples, however, are easily generated. Imagine a Galileo figure who is a brilliant scientist. One of the reasons for his brilliance is his ability to modulate his level of confidence in his views with the available evidence. Galileo is not over- or under-confident. His confidence in his views and intellectual abilities is warranted. He is the best scientist around by any objective standards. However, Galileo is also a bully. He mocks other scientists who are not as good on their feet as he is. He also likes to let everyone know how good he is. Intuitively, this person is a jerk (James, 2014). He is also arrogant. Given the plausible assumption that it is impossible to be both arrogant and intellectually humble, this example shows that a person's confidence in one's views might be accurate without that person being intellectually humble.

I hasten to add that this fictional example might just be that: fictional. In reality, arrogant individuals tend to display overconfidence in their views and abilities (Leary et al., 2017).[4] Nevertheless, since it is at least conceivable that there might be arrogant people who mistreat others but are not overconfident, these purely doxastic accounts of intellectual humility appear to be at best incomplete. At the very least, what is required (in addition to knowledge of one's strengths, weaknesses, and well-placed confidence in one's views and abilities) is the right attitude toward that knowledge so that it is not used to put others down or merely to self-enhance.

The so-called 'limitations-owning' account of intellectual humility makes a step in this direction (Whitcomb et al., 2017). According to this view, the person who is intellectual humble knows her limitations but she also acknowledges or owns them. The intellectually humble person regrets her limitations, is concerned about them, and about their negative impact on her conduct. Hence, the view attributes both doxastic and affective-conative components to humility.

Despite all of this, in my view the limitations-owning account is not sufficiently distinct from purely doxastic views of humility. Thus, it shares some of their defects. I suspect that when Whitcomb and colleagues think of humility as requiring that one acknowledges one's limitations, what they have in mind is a person who is not in denial about these. Understood in this minimal sense, acceptance of limitations is compatible with hiding them from other people's scrutiny. Whitcomb and colleagues embrace this consequence. They argue that a person might possess the dispositions characteristic of intellectual humility whilst being wholly selfishly motivated. Such an individual would be humble but not virtuous, since he would lack the required motivation to pursue epistemic goods (2017, p. 520). They describe the case of a student who accepts her limitations and strives to improve herself, but whose behaviour is wholly driven by the desire to get good grades without any pressing concern to learn, unless that learning ultimately gets her good grades (2017, p. 521).

In my view there are many circumstances in which this hypothetical student would engage in conduct incompatible with being humble. For example, she would pretend that she knows something that she does not know, if this pretence could be instrumental in getting good grades. Thus, this student could put down other people, hide her own shortcomings, and even brag about her alleged strengths all in the interest of improving her grades. Whatever we want to say about this student, it is implausible that we wish to describe her as humble (Tanesini, 2018, p. 405). Counter-examples such as this one suggest that the 'limitation-owning' account does not give sufficient weight to the thought that to be humble it is not enough that one knows one's shortcomings; one must also relate to these in the right way, which includes owning up to them in front of other people.

In addition, the account's exclusive focus on limitations rather than strengths and weaknesses can also be questioned. This focus raises the possibility also acknowledged by Whitcomb and colleagues that a person might be humble without knowing her good qualities (Whitcomb et al., 2017, pp. 528–533). This conclusion entails that a person could be both humble and servile, or under-confident about her abilities. This result seems wrong given the intuitive understanding of humility as a virtue opposed to servility.

Finally, and this is an objection that can be raised against every account of humility discussed so far, this account fails to capture the sense in which humility is incompatible with being self-centred or highly focused on the importance of the self and of its features. This objection suggests that irrespective of whether humble individuals must have a good grasp of their strengths and shortcomings, possession of this knowledge about the self cannot be sufficient for humility. Instead, this virtue must be understood by examining how humble individuals value their own importance.

24.3 Humility as a virtue of low self-focus

The folk concept of the humble person is, plausibly, that of someone who does not think of herself and of her interests as especially important. This understanding might seem more central to the concept of humility than the idea, explored above, of a person who has an accurate appraisal of her limitations. These two conceptions of humility are related but they are different. Appreciating one's limitations might lead one to revise down one's previous estimate of one's good qualities; appreciating that one's interests and desires are not that important requires that they be framed within a larger perspective (cf., Nadelhoffer and Wright, 2017, p. 313). That said, we should expect that an appreciation of one's own limitations would be instrumental in achieving a realistic assessment of one's own importance.

The thought that humility requires, that one is not focused on the self, its importance, needs, and successes, is appealing. It has inspired philosophical accounts of humility as a virtue that consists in a disposition not to dwell on, or take delight in, one's achievements (Garcia, 2006). Along similar lines, Bommarito (2013) has defined modesty as the virtue of not attending too much to one's good qualities, or not focusing too much on their value, or alternatively as the virtue of carefully attending to the role that others' help and good luck have played in one's development of these good qualities.

These accounts of humility are different from Driver's (1989, 1999), but ultimately face similar problems. The person who does not pay attention to her good qualities or the role played by her efforts in developing them is likely to underestimate these qualities and the extent to which they are a credit to her. Humility so understood might be a corrective for arrogance but it is an impediment to the development of proper pride and self-respect in those people who are at risk of self-deprecation and self-abasement (Dillon, this volume, Chapter 5). To the extent that humility is not incompatible with proper pride, it would seem that these accounts fail to capture what is at the core of humility.

More promising in my opinion is an account of humility as the disposition to understand oneself from a viewpoint that does not put that self at its centre. Such a point of view would not focus exclusively on the interests of the self, but would instead take on others' interests into account within one's perspective. It is possible to interpret along these lines the view, defended by Nadelhoffer and Wright (2017), that humility has two dimensions: low self-focus and high other-focus. Low self-focus indicates that one does not invest the self with supreme importance; one does not think of the self as 'number one' whose interests trump all other considerations. High other-focus suggests that, within one's perspective, one invests others' interest with importance and gives due weight to their reasons within one's thinking.

So interpreted, the low self-focus account of humility does not imply that one is inattentive to the self or that one does not take pleasure in one's achievements. On the contrary, low self-focus might well require that one pays attention, and properly appreciates, one's qualities. However, one must do so from a changed perspective. Instead of evaluating oneself from a point of view that has oneself at its centre, one comes to know the worth of one's own qualities by measuring them from the viewpoint of the whole of humanity or even the whole universe. That is, this approach proposes that the humble person is the person who knows herself but whose appraisal of her own worth seeks to appreciate her significance from the viewpoint of humanity and the universe as a whole. In other words, in this view, humility is not a matter of inattention to oneself, rather it involves measuring one's worth by a meter that is not distorted by an egocentric bias.

I think of the high other-focus dimension of humility as the other face of the coin from low self-focus. The downward revision of one's own importance brings a more accurate appreciation of other people's worth in its trail. I thus disagree with the tendency to think that humility should, because of this dimension, be thought of as an interpersonal virtue. This is an idea that has recently been promoted by Wilson (2016) and by Priest (2017). Priest (2017), for instance, identifies intellectual humility with the virtue that consists in being concerned with others' intellect, and thus treats epistemic agents with the kind of respect that is due to them qua epistemic agents. Intellectual humility would, thus, be tantamount to justice.[5]

I agree with Priest that the intellectually humble person does not show disrespect to other epistemic agents. She does not steal others' credit, she is open-minded, and a good team player. That is, she engages in the range of behaviours identified by Priest. Yet, in my view, these are comportments that are likely to flow from intellectual humility but do not constitute it. Imagine a strong-minded scientist who has both a reputation for humility and bluntness. She is humble because she does not aggrandise or brag. Instead, she is a very severe critic of her own achievements. She recognises them but always expects better and more from herself. She also expects the same of others. For this reason, she can be unkind and demanding. Whilst perhaps not disrespectful or unjust toward others, she does not show a special interest in their well-being or success. She claims that her loyalty is to the truth and only the truth.

I am inclined to think that such characters can exist. They are intellectually humble, but do not demonstrate the sort of interpersonal virtue discussed by Priest. I am not suggesting here that one can be both humble and disrespectful toward others. Rather I am claiming that humility can be exemplified by some who are not especially supportive of others' endeavours. If this is right, Priest's account individuates qualities that are associated with humility but do not lie at its core.

If we think of humility as the knowledge of one's own strengths and weaknesses as measured by their significance in the context of the whole of humanity and of the universe, we can see why the humble person is likely to be sensitive to other people's reasons, needs, and interests. Looking at our seemingly pressing concerns from the viewpoint of the distant future, for example, should make us appreciate points of view other than our own. We should thus be in a better position to understand the importance of others' people interests and allow these to have some weight in our deliberations. If this is right, in ordinary circumstances we should expect low self-focus often to give rise to high other-focus. But the facilitation of generosity and justice by humility is not a forgone conclusion since one might abandon the self-centred point of view by adopting an impersonal view that assigns little importance to each and every human being.

I have argued so far that humility is not a virtue of self-ignorance or simply a virtue of especially accurate self-knowledge. A person might be humble and be mistaken about her self-worth if, for example, she has been innocently swayed by misleading evidence. Rather, humility is the virtue of evaluating one's strengths and weaknesses in a manner that is not self-centred. These appraisals are not egocentric in at least two ways. First, the standard by which one measures the worth of one's qualities and thus sorts them as strengths and weaknesses makes no reference to self-advantage. Thus, for example, the fact that a feature makes one feel good about oneself does not count as a reason to classify it as a strength. Second, one's evaluation of one's qualities by reference to non-egocentric standards is also not biased by egocentric motivations such as that to self-enhance. In short, the humble person does not measure her worth using biased weights or biased processes. Instead, she evaluates herself for her worth as it might appear from the point of view of her place within humanity as a whole.

24.4 Humility as hopeful attitude to self

I have argued so far that humility consists in adopting a range of attitudes to oneself and one's qualities that involve evaluating the self for its worth in a manner that is not biased by egocentric considerations, either in the choice of the standards against which to measure one's qualities, or in the measuring of one's features against said standards. In this account, humility is a virtue of self-knowledge and understanding. However, this is not to say that humility consists in the possession of especially accurate self-beliefs. It is possible for a person to be humble and mistaken about her qualities. What matters for humility, however, is how this person evaluates her features and the standards she employs when making these appraisals.

It might seem that humility must bring self-deprecation and nihilism in its trail. The person who assesses her significance by her contribution to humanity as a whole is bound to feel pretty insignificant. She might also think that nothing she can achieve can possibly make much difference to the course of human history. If this were true, we should refrain from thinking of humility as a virtue, since it would be contrary to the flourishing of those who possess it. I think this conclusion can be avoided by focusing on the relation between humility and hope.

Hope is an emotional orientation that includes a disposition to experience optimistic and expectant feelings, to have beliefs about the possibility of some outcome that is judged to be good, and to desire that it comes to pass.[6] Hope, when directed at one's activities, also includes a propensity to think that the outcome is achievable, even though it is beyond one's immediate ability, to desire to bring it about, and a tendency to take this combination of belief, desire, and affect as a reason to attempt to achieve the desired outcomes (Martin, 2014; Snow, 2013). Hope can be misplaced when it is directed toward outcomes that are not as a matter of fact good, or when it directed toward outcomes that cannot be achieved. Hope can also be deficient when one frequently feels or judges that achievable outcomes, which one wants to bring about, are beyond one's reach. But hope can also be well-tuned when it is directed at achievable good outcomes. Well-tuned hope is important because it supplies the motivational impetus to persevere in one's efforts to bring about desired outcomes despite the presence of obstacles in one's way.

There are important conceptual connections between hope as an emotion or attitude and the virtue of humility. The adoption of a hopeful attitude toward a good outcome presupposes that one acknowledges that that outcome is not certain and that one cannot automatically guarantee it. That is, hopefulness presupposes that there are limitations to one's abilities so that one must depend on the environment and the help of other people to secure the desired outcome. In this manner, the hopeful person must be humble in at least the limited sense that he acknowledges that he has limitations and he is not wholly self-reliant (Cobb, 2019).

Hope also presupposes an assessment of which good outcomes are possible given one's abilities. Hence, hope is predicated on evaluations of one's own strengths and weaknesses to assess the likelihood that one is capable of bringing about the desired outcome. These self-appraisals are not evaluations of the worth of one's qualities within the framework of humanity as a whole. More modestly, they are appraisals as to whether one is up to the task at hand. However, a humble outlook should in ordinary contexts promote accuracy in appraisals of this sort. The absence of egocentric biasing in evaluation, irrespective of the standards that are relevant in each case, should foster judgments about what one is or is not capable of that are more reliable than those arrived at by arrogant, and generally overconfident, people or self-abasing, and usually underconfident, individuals.

In addition, hope provides the ingredient that make a difference between humility and self-abasement, as well as pessimistic fatalism or despair. Hope can generate a sense of optimism about one's ability to achieve good outcomes. It can supply the required motivation to persevere in the face of obstacles. So understood, hope is the counterbalance required to prevent humble self-knowledge from tipping into pessimistic nihilism. If this is right, humility does not merely consists in adopting a stance of low self-focus, since that evaluative framework is compatible with nihilistic paralysis. Instead, if humility is to be a virtue, it must also involve the optimistic outlook characteristic of those who are hopeful about their abilities to bring about good outcomes.

In conclusion, I have argued that there is a special relationship between the virtue of humility and self-knowledge. I have defended the view that this special connection consists in the evaluative stance taken by humble individuals toward their own features. So understood, what is special about humility is not a remarkably accurate form of self-knowledge. It is also not a matter of ignorance or inattention to the self. Instead, humility is characterised by a self-assessment and self-knowledge that is detached from a presumption of self-importance. Finally, I have indicated that this kind of self-appraisal is supplemented with an emotional and optimistic orientation toward one's ability to succeed in one's endeavours given the results of one's evaluation of one's own qualities.[7]

Notes

1 In her work, Driver discusses modesty and false modesty rather than humility. However, she thinks that they are near-synonyms. I follow common practice in taking Driver to provide an account of humility.

2 The conception of humility as involving (but without being limited to) an accurate appraisal of one's qualities is also popular in psychology where it has been endorsed by Tangney (2000) among others.

3 I take it that the person who is humble tout court is humble in all regards, including intellectually. However, it is possible for someone to be humble intellectually without being humble in other ways. So whilst humility entails intellectual humility, the converse does not hold.

4 I emphasise this point in the final section below.

5 See Bloomfield for the view that justice rather than humility is the virtue in this neighbourhood (Bloomfield, Ch. 3).

6 I take something along these lines to be a standard view of hope. I do not wish to take a stance here on the specific details. Clearly, however, hope requires more than the belief that some outcome is possible and a desire that it comes about, since one might have both without hoping for the outcome. Recent work on hope has emphasised its heterogeneity (cf., Blöser, 2019).

7 Thanks to Mark Alfano for useful comments on the final version of this chapter. Research leading to this paper was partially funded by a subaward agreement from the University of Connecticut with funds provided by Grant No. 58942 from the John Templeton Foundation. Its contents are solely the responsibility of the author and do not necessarily represent the official views of UConn or the John Templeton Foundation.

References

Alfano, M., and Robinson, B. (2014). Bragging. *Thought: A Journal of Philosophy*, *3*(4), 263–272. doi:10.1002/tht3.141

Battaly, H. D. (2015). *Virtue*. Cambridge: Polity Press.

Blöser, C. (2019). Hope as an Irreducible Concept. *Ratio*, *32*(3), 205–214. doi:10.1111/rati.12236

Bommarito, N. (2013). Modesty as a Virtue of Attention. *Philosophical Review*, *122*(1), 93–117. doi:10.1215/00318108-1728723

Church, I. M. (2016). The Doxastic Account of Intellectual Humility. *Logos and Episteme*, 7(4), 413–433.

Cobb, A. D. (2019). Hope for Intellectual Humility. *Episteme*, *16*(1), 56–72. doi:10.1017/epi.2017.18

Driver, J. (1989). The Virtues of Ignorance. *The Journal of Philosophy*, *86*(7), 373–384. doi:10.2307/2027146

Driver, J. (1999). Modesty and Ignorance. *Ethics*, *109*(4), 827–834. doi:10.1086/233947

Driver, J. (2001). *Uneasy Virtue*. Cambridge: Cambridge University Press.

Flanagan, O. (1990). Virtue and Ignorance. *The Journal of Philosophy*, *87*(8), 420–428.

Garcia, J. L. A. (2006). Being Unimpressed with Ourselves: Reconceiving Humility. *Philosophia*, *34*(4), 417–435. doi:10.1007/s11406-006-9032-x

Hazlett, A. (2012). Higher-Order Epistemic Attitudes and Intellectual Humility. *Episteme*, *9*(03), 205–223. doi: 10.1017/epi.2012.11

James, A. (2014). *Assholes: A Theory*. New York: Anchor Books.

Kidd, I. J. (2016). Intellectual Humility, Confidence, and Argumentation. *Topoi*, *35*(2 (Special issue on Virtue and Argumentation)), 395–402. doi:10.1007/s11245-015-9324-5

Leary, M. R., Diebels, K. J., Davisson, E. K., Jongman-Sereno, K. P., Isherwood, J. C., Raimi, K. T., Deffler, S. A., and Hoyle, R. H. (2017). Cognitive and Interpersonal Features of Intellectual Humility. *Personality and Social Psychology Bulletin*, *43*(6), 793–813. doi:10.1177/0146167217697695

Martin, A. M. (2014). *How We Hope: A Moral Psychology*. Princeton: Princeton University Press.

Nadelhoffer, T., and Wright, J. C. (2017). The Twin Dimensions of the Virtue of Humility: Low Self-Focus and High Other-Focus. In: W. Sinnott-Armstrong and C. B. Miller (Eds.), *Moral Psychology: Virtues and Vices* (Vol. 5, pp. 309–371). Cambridge: MIT Press.

Priest, M. (2017). Intellectual Humility: An Interpersonal Theory. *Ergo, An Open Access Journal of Philosophy*, *4*(20191108). doi:10.3998/ergo.12405314.0004.016

Roberts, R. C., and Wood, W. J. (2007). *Intellectual Virtues: An Essay in Regulative Epistemology*. New York: Oxford University Press.

Snow, N. (2013). Hope as an Intellectual Virtue. In: M. W. Austin (Ed.), *Virtues in Action: New Essays in Applied Virtue Ethics* (pp. 152–170). New York: Palgrave Macmilllan Publishing.

Snow, N. E. (1995). Humility. *The Journal of Value Inquiry*, *29*(2), 203–216. doi:10.1007/bf01079834

Sosa, E. (2007). *A Virtue Epistemology. Apt Belief and Reflective Knowledge, Vol. I.* Oxford: Clarendon Press.

Tanesini, A. (2018). Intellectual Humility as Attitude. *Philosophy and Phenomenological Research*, *96*(2), 399–420. doi:10.1111/phpr.12326

Tangney, J. P. (2000). Humility: Theoretical Perspectives, Empirical Findings and Directions for Future Research. *Journal of Social and Clinical Psychology*, *19*(1), 70–82.

Whitcomb, D., Battaly, H., Baehr, J., and Howard-Snyder, D. (2017). Intellectual Humility: Owning Our Limitations. *Philosophy and Phenomenological Research*, *94*(3), 509–539. doi:10.1111/phpr.12228

Wilson, A. T. (2016). Modesty as Kindness. *Ratio*, *29*(1), 73–88. doi:10.1111/rati.12045

Zagzebski, L. T. (1996). *Virtues of the Mind: An Inquiry into the Nature of Virtue and the Ethical Foundations of Knowledge*. Cambridge: Cambridge University Press.

25
INTELLECTUAL HUMILITY AND EPISTEMIC TRUST

Katherine Dormandy

Intellectual humility has something important in common with trust: both, independently, help secure knowledge. But they also do so in tandem, and this chapter discusses how.

Intellectual humility is a virtue of a person's cognitive character; this means that it disposes her to perceive and think in certain ways that help promote knowledge. Trust is a form of cooperation, in which one person depends on another (or on herself) for some end, in a way that is governed by certain norms. *Epistemic* trust is trust for epistemic ends, where the one that I will focus on here is knowledge. When the parties to an epistemic-trust relationship exhibit intellectual humility, I will argue, they are in a better position than otherwise to secure knowledge. Some think that this is true trivially, on the grounds that knowledge (on their view) is *constituted by* the exercise of epistemic virtues. Whether or not this is so, I will focus on two different ways in which intellectual humility makes epistemic trust knowledge-conducive: first, it equips trusters to invest trust effectively – that is, in those who are trustworthy; second, it equips trustees to be epistemically trustworthy.

I will start by sketching epistemic trust (Section 25.1) and intellectual humility (Section 25.2). Then I will show how intellectual humility promotes effective epistemic trust in oneself (Section 25.3), and how it helps relationships of epistemic trust between two parties be effective (Section 25.4). Along the way I will draw comparisons with the epistemic vices of intellectual arrogance and intellectual servility.

25.1 Epistemic trust

Trust is a three-place relation: one person trusts another person (or herself) for some thing or end.[1] Trust involves *relying* on the trustee for the end in question. But trust is more than reliance, for you can rely on a person without trusting him. Immanuel Kant was said to be so regular in his habits that his neighbors could set their clocks to the time at which he left his house each day – but they did not *trust* him for the time. Mere reliance is a matter of planning on someone's predictable behavior, whereas trust involves a cooperative relationship with her.

This relationship has two aspects (see Dormandy 2020). First, it imposes certain norms on the truster and trustee alike (Jones 2017; Hawley 2014; Faulkner 2011; Hinchman 2017). For example, the trustee, insofar as she accepts trust, should do her best, within reason, to fulfill it; culpable failure to do so constitutes betrayal, or at least letting the truster down. As for the truster, he should allow the trustee a measure of discretion in fulfilling his trust, without nagging or micromanaging her efforts (Baier 1986).

Second, trust relationships have a characteristic psychology. The truster, for his part, works from the assumption that the trustee will respond positively to him or to the trust relationship; and the trustee – supposing that she accepts his trust – is responsive in this way. She might for instance care about the truster, be motivated by the fact that he is depending on her, aim to advance a common project, or be committed to coming through given that she has accepted his trust (Baier 1986; Jones 1996; Hinchman 2005; Faulkner 2011; Hawley 2014).

We trust people for various things, so many that trust is sometimes compared to the air we breathe – we notice it only when it is absent (Baier 1986; 234). This holds of our trust for epistemic aims. We gain a vast proportion of our knowledge by trusting people for it, ourselves as well as others.[2] We trust ourselves, for example, to perceive accurately, reason carefully, or to intuit cogently, and we trust others (parents, teachers, colleagues, friends, the media, scientists) to teach or inform us.

Epistemic trust can be *effective or ineffective*. Effective epistemic trust is trust in a trustworthy agent – that is, an agent disposed to deliver the knowledge that she is being trusted for. Ineffective trust is trust in someone who is not trustworthy, and is all the more ineffective if she is actively *un*trustworthy. Epistemic trustworthiness has two elements. One is *willingness*. This in turn has two components. The first is willingness to abide by the norms of the trust relationship: to be sincere, to do her reasonable best to provide the knowledge that she is being trusted for, and so forth. The second component is a willingness to enter into the characteristic psychology of trust: to experience the normative pull of commitment or the emotional pull of knowing that the truster is counting on her. These two aspects of willingness typically have a motivating effect: subjecting oneself to normative expectations encourages conformity to them, and responding to a truster's dependence typically involves feeling motivated to come through for him.

The second element of epistemic trustworthiness is *competence* to perform the epistemic tasks that accompany knowing and sharing one's knowledge. An epistemically trustworthy person is competent to form her own knowledge on the matter at issue: it is foolhardy to trust someone for knowledge if she is not competent to secure it. When the trustee is someone other than the truster himself (i.e., if it is not a case of self-trust), then competence has a second aspect: competence to communicate to the truster the knowledge that he needs in his context. This is important, for if a knower cannot do this, trusting her for knowledge will be of little benefit.

Epistemic untrustworthiness,[3] by contrast, involves being *unwilling* or *incompetent*. Trust in an untrustworthy person is ineffective: such a person is not apt to come through for you. The fitting attitude toward her is thus *distrust*. This is more than simply declining to trust her, which you might do simply because you do not need anything from her. Distrusting someone, by contrast, involves declining to trust her *because you regard her as untrustworthy* (Hawley 2014; D'Cruz 2019). A person can exhibit epistemic distrust in herself: she can construe herself as unwilling to subject herself to the norms of trust or to respond positively to her own epistemic needs, or as incompetent to secure the needed knowledge (Dormandy 2020). And this attitude can be fitting: a person can be unworthy of epistemic self-trust.

Epistemic trust undoubtedly has a role in *securing* knowledge. But accounts of knowledge differ about what additional role, if any, epistemic trust has in *constituting* it. One account worth mentioning here is virtue responsibilism. On this view, knowledge is true belief formed by the exercise of epistemic character virtues (Code 1987; Kvanvig 1992; Montmarquet 1993; Zagzebski 1996; Baehr 2011) such as intellectual humility. If virtue responsibilism is the right account of knowledge, then exercising intellectual humility when you form a true belief on trust can yield knowledge trivially. But I will not discuss virtue responsibilism here. For I aim to show, instead, that intellectual humility is of great value to epistemic trust even if virtue responsibilism is false. The reason is that exhibiting intellectual humility, whether or not this helps constitute knowledge, can *cause* you, if you are a truster, to direct your epistemic trust in knowledge-yielding ways; and if you are a trustee it can help you be trustworthy in your supplying of knowledge. It is this causal role of intellectual humility in securing knowledge that I will explore here, whether or not intellectual humility also has any role in constituting it.

The next step is to give a (very general) sketch of intellectual humility.

25.2 Intellectual humility

Intellectual humility is an epistemic character virtue. As such it is a stable trait of a person's cognitive character.[4] The intellectually humble agent has two features, one marking him as epistemically virtuous in general, the other as intellectually humble specifically.

The general feature is this: *the intellectually humble person is epistemically motivated* (Baehr 2011; Roberts and Wood 2003; Church 2016; Whitcomb et al. 2017; Tanesini 2018b). That is, he cares about achieving epistemic aims such as knowledge, and this is what motivates his cognitive behavior. One corollary of being epistemically motivated is that the intellectually humble person is disposed to strive for epistemic self-improvement for its own sake. This is not to say that intellectually humble agents cannot have other aims in their cognitive activities (such as career-advancement in a field that prizes epistemic prowess), only that these cannot be their sole or primary aims.

The specifically distinguishing feature of the intellectually humble agent is that *he is disposed to form largely accurate evaluations of his own epistemic strengths and weaknesses*.[5] A few clarifications are in order. First, intellectual humility is directed toward the agent himself. In this it can be contrasted with other virtues, such as epistemic charity or open-mindedness, that are directed toward others.

Second, views differ over the precise form of the epistemic self-evaluations involved in intellectual humility. Hazlett (2012) says that they are evaluative beliefs, whereas Church (2016) holds, more generally, that they involve "accurately tracking" one's epistemic state. Whitcomb et al. (2017) say that the evaluations are states of "recognition" (522), whereas Tanesini (2018) construes them as valenced attitudes, such as like or dislike, that could, but need not, be articulated in terms of evaluations. The form of the intellectually humble agent's self-evaluations will not concern us here, so I mention this issue only to pass it by.

More important for present purposes, third, is what these evaluations are evaluations of. Some views construe their objects more narrowly than others; I will follow Tanesini (2018), who construes them the most broadly, as all "aspects of the subject's cognitive agency" (410). The objects of evaluation thus include the agent's own cognitive abilities and limitations, his cognitive achievements and failures, as well as his beliefs.[6] Much of the literature reads as if intellectual humility concerns itself only with one's purely intellectual features.[7] But we must remember that knowledge acquisition is strongly influenced by our affections and volition. Their influence might be direct, supposing that emotions or desires can simply bring about beliefs; whether or not they can, they certainly exert indirect influence, as when an emotion or a desire influences what a person attends to or ignores, or "colors" his perception of some event, thereby nudging him to form a particular belief on its basis. Epistemic self-evaluation, then, must at times include emotional and volitional self-evaluation, at least insofar as these states influence one's cognition. This observation will prove important in our discussion below of the relationship between intellectual humility and epistemic trust and trustworthiness, for these, as we saw, have not only intellectual, but also emotional and volitional elements. I will refer to the objects of the intellectually humble agent's epistemic self-evaluation as his *noetic* faculties.

Fourth, the intellectually humble person's epistemic self-evaluations tend, at least in benign epistemic contexts, to be accurate (Tanesini 2018, 414; Whitcomb et al. 2017; Church 2016). That is, if she evaluates some feature of her noetic system, she does so accurately, and does not fail to evaluate any feature that matters for a given case (or at least, she does not fail to form the requisite affective attitude that would naturally give rise to an evaluation). This means, among other things, that the agent tends to recognize her noetic strengths and weaknesses, the strength of her evidence, and so forth. She is likely aware of whether she is well or poorly versed in a given topic; and if she harbors implicit racial or gender stereotypes that influence whom she trusts for knowledge, she is clued into this fact or at least to its likelihood. That said, intellectual humility does not *entail* that any given self-evaluation will be accurate, for even an intellectually humble person can be non-culpably misled (Tanesini 2018, 414).

We may contrast intellectual humility with two intellectual vices: intellectual arrogance and intellectual servility.[8] As with intellectual humility, there is one feature (I will suppose) that marks them as vices, and another singling them out as the specific vices that they are. The general feature is this: *intellectually arrogant or servile agents are not epistemically motivated.*[9] Their noetic behavior is instead motivated exclusively by other things, such as the desire to advance their career in a field that prizes knowledge. As a result, intellectually arrogant or servile agents are not disposed to strive for epistemic self-improvement, at least not for its own sake.

What makes these vices counterparts to intellectual humility is their second distinguishing feature. Like intellectual humility, both are directed toward the agent himself, specifically toward his own epistemic strengths and weaknesses. But whereas the intellectually humble agent is disposed to form accurate self-evaluations, intellectually arrogant or servile agents are disposed to form inaccurate ones. More specifically, *the intellectually arrogant agent is disposed to excessively high evaluations of her own noetic strengths in acquiring knowledge, and excessively low evaluations of her weaknesses in this area;* and *the servile agent is disposed to inaccuracy in the other direction: to an excessively low evaluation of his noetic strengths in acquiring knowledge, and a high evaluation of his relevant weaknesses.*[10] In other words, the intellectually arrogant agent is apt to think that she is better at securing knowledge than she is, whereas the servile agent is apt to think that he is worse than he is (Whitcomb et al. 2017, 526; Church 2016, 413–414; Hazlett 2012, 220; Tanesini 2018, 418;).

Because the vices of intellectual arrogance and intellectual servility have these characteristics, they tend to be epistemically detrimental in standard circumstances – that is, they tend to impede the acquisition of knowledge.

25.3 Intellectual humility and epistemic self-trust

This section and the next explore connections between intellectual humility and epistemic trust. This section discusses epistemic self-trust, the next epistemic trust in others.

As we saw, epistemic trust can be reflexive: a person can trust *herself* for the delivery of knowledge (Foley 2001, Zagzebski 2012, Lehrer 1997, Dormandy 2020). She can have normative expectations of herself, and she can rely on herself to respond positively to her own epistemic needs. Similarly, a person can be more or less worthy of epistemic self-trust: she might be more or less willing to treat herself as the norms of trust mandate, or to care about her own epistemic needs; and she might be more or less competent in acquiring the knowledge that she needs in her context.[11]

The intellectually humble person, it turns out, is in a good position to exercise effective epistemic self-trust. The reason is that she is disposed to have a good grip on her own noetic strengths and weaknesses, including those which make her epistemically trustworthy or untrustworthy. She will likely have insight into the affective and volitional states that determine how willing she is to come through for herself, and into the cognitive states that determine her level of competence (plus the affective and volitional influences on them). The intellectually humble agent, then, is well placed to tell whether trusting herself for knowledge will be effective.

If trusting herself in a given case turns out *not* to be a wise move (because she lacks the willingness or the competence), then intellectual humility confers a second benefit: it disposes a person to *grow* in epistemic trustworthiness, for it disposes her to noetically self-improve for the sake of promoting epistemic aims. This might mean working on her emotions and will, or honing the faculties that make for competence.

Intellectual humility, then, promotes effective epistemic self-trust: it helps a person know whether she is epistemically trustworthy, and when she is not, it disposes her to grow in epistemic trustworthiness.

Compare the intellectually humble self-truster with intellectually arrogant and servile ones. We saw that the intellectually arrogant person *overestimates* her noetic strengths vis-à-vis the acquisition of knowledge, and *underestimates* her noetic weaknesses in this area. In her capacity as a self-truster, then, she will tend to overestimate her own willingness or competence to secure knowledge. As a result, she will be disposed to trust herself too readily, even when doing so is not effective. This means that she will tend to form many beliefs, of which a large proportion might, unbeknownst to her, be false or unfounded. As for the intellectually servile person, we saw that he *underestimates* his noetic strengths vis-à-vis the acquisition of knowledge, and *overestimates* his relevant noetic weaknesses. In his capacity as a (potential) self-truster, then, he will tend to underestimate his willingness or competence to secure knowledge, and will thus be disposed to *distrust* himself – even when self-trust might have been effective after all. The intellectually servile person may thus form comparatively few beliefs on his own, tending instead toward tentative belief or suspension of judgment. While not conducive to false or unfounded belief, such behavior is certainly not conducive to knowledge.

Another contrast between intellectually arrogant and servile self-trusters is this: the intellectually arrogant person, at least in theory, is in a better position to epistemically self-improve. Her readiness to trust herself, though rash, means that she will have fewer qualms about putting her beliefs out there – testifying them, acting on them, and so forth. She is thus apt to receive at least some corrective feedback from the world. Of course, her arrogance may prevent her from assimilating much of it (she may for example explain it away), but at least she will often have the option. The intellectually servile person, by contrast, is in a much worse position. Because his distrust in himself prevents him from forming many confident beliefs on his own, he forfeits the opportunity to receive much feedback at all. He will thus tend to lack indications of ways in which he might epistemically self-improve. His knowledge-acquiring abilities may even atrophy to the point that his negative self-evaluations become a self-fulfilling prophecy. So whereas the intellectually arrogant person tends to be hindered by real yet unacknowledged epistemic weaknesses, the servile person tends to fall victim to imaginary or at least exaggerated ones. The intellectually humble person, in contrast to both, is in much better shape.

We have seen that intellectual humility helps make one's epistemic self-trust effective. Yet some might think that there is an even closer relationship, one of necessity, between effective self-trust and intellectual humility. Perhaps, at least in worlds similar enough to ours, intellectual humility is necessary for exercising effective self-trust. Or perhaps intellectual humility is sufficient to ensure that one's self-trust will be effective. Both entailment claims, however, are false.

First, intellectual humility is not necessary for epistemic self-trust to be effective. A person could trust herself effectively because she accurately evaluates her own noetic strengths and weaknesses – yet she might fail to be humble, because she is not motivated to promote epistemic aims for their own sake (she might wish simply to advance her career). Second, intellectual humility is not sufficient to ensure that epistemic self-trust is effective. A person could be epistemically motivated, and accurately evaluate her noetic strengths and weaknesses, yet trust herself rashly, even when those evaluations come up negative. For she might have some other epistemic vice, such as cognitive impulsiveness, that she is (on account of her intellectual humility) aware of and motivated to overcome, but is not yet in control of. So even though effective epistemic self-trust is often powered by intellectual humility, it can be found without this virtue; and even though intellectual humility tends to make for effective epistemic self-trust, it is not guaranteed to do so.

25.4 Intellectual humility and epistemic trust in others

We have seen that intellectual humility promotes effective epistemic self-trust. I will now argue that it also helps epistemic trust in other people to be effective. The paradigm case that I will focus on is a testimonial relationship, in which one person, the speaker, tells something to another, the hearer, thereby purporting to make knowledge available (Goldberg, unpublished manuscript) and inviting him to trust her for it (Hinchman 2005). The exchange might be over in an instant, as when one person tells another something that she knows off the top of her head, or it could extend over time, as when she promises to research something and get back to him. I'll argue in Section 25.4.1 that intellectual humility disposes a hearer to invest his epistemic trust effectively; in Section 25.4.2 I'll argue that it disposes a speaker to be epistemically trustworthy.

25.4.1 The intellectually humble hearer of testimony

Trusting another person for knowledge is in some ways like trusting oneself for it, and in other ways different. It is similar in that what makes it effective is the trustee's willingness and competence. It is different in that the trustee is another person, so you must gauge these things at a remove (Fricker 2006). Whereas the epistemic self-truster needs accurate evaluations of his own noetic faculties, the epistemic truster of others needs accurate evaluations of others.'[12] Intellectual humility, a virtue of self-evaluation, is tailor-made for the epistemic self-truster. But it will not help the epistemic truster of others in the same way, since evaluating others' noetic faculties is not its remit. For help in choosing which speakers to trust, he must cultivate other virtues.

Yet there are a few ways in which intellectual humility can nevertheless be useful to a prospective hearer of testimony. First, because it puts him in a good position to recognize when trusting himself for knowledge would be effective and when not, it helps him recognize when he should seek outside epistemic assistance as opposed to trusting himself.

Second, intellectual humility puts the hearer in a position to recognize his own strengths and weaknesses in assessing others' epistemic merits. That is, it helps him know when he can safely trust himself in choosing his testifiers. He might for example realize that he is better at doing this in some domains or social contexts than others, or that he is biased with regard to certain types of testifier, prompting him spontaneously to up- or down-grade their testimony.

Third, intellectual humility disposes the hearer to *improve* his testifier-selecting abilities –for example to cultivate the relevant virtues, to re-train his biases through seeking counter-instances to them, and so forth.

So even though intellectual humility cannot directly help a hearer choose his testifiers, it can help him indirectly.

Contrast this with intellectually arrogant or servile hearers. As for the arrogant hearer, we saw that such a person *overestimates* her noetic strengths at knowledge acquisition and *underestimates* her noetic weaknesses, leading to an excessive readiness to trust herself. As a hearer of testimony, this person faces two pitfalls. First, she will incline toward trusting herself when it would be wiser to trust knowledgeable others. Second, even when she does opt to delegate a cognitive task to others, her intellectual arrogance will still get in the way. For the abilities that she overestimates include *her abilities to gauge whom to trust for knowledge*, making her apt to trust herself too readily on the topic of which others to trust. She may thus wind up trusting speakers who are not in fact trustworthy. One danger is that she will trust only those whose testimony coheres with her own worldview, fostering cognitive entrenchment. Intellectual arrogance, then, is an epistemic stumbling block for a hearer of testimony.

The intellectually servile hearer has the converse problem. As we saw, this person *underestimates* his noetic strengths in knowledge acquisition and *overestimates* his noetic weaknesses, not trusting himself readily enough, and perhaps actively distrusting himself. In theory, the effects of this vice could be mitigated by compensating, other-directed, epistemic virtues that help him accurately gauge the trustworthiness of prospective speakers: the servile hearer could obtain his knowledge from them. In practice, however, any such silver lining will likely be sabotaged. For the servile hearer is also likely to underestimate his ability to reason about whom to trust for knowledge. As a result, even if he can reason well about this, he will tend to distrust himself to do so. What he is apt to do instead is to cede the choice of whom to trust to the first or loudest comer, especially if, as Tanesini (2018c) argues, servility is motivated by the desire for social acceptance. In other words, the servile hearer will tend toward gullibility: he will likely wind up, like the arrogant hearer, with a fairly large proportion of (confident) false beliefs to true ones.[13] Intellectual servility, then, leads to unwise and thus ineffective epistemic trust in others.

In summary, intellectual humility disposes someone in search of testimonial knowledge to invest his epistemic trust effectively. It does not help him assess others' epistemic merits, but it helps him recognize when he needs outside assistance, how able he is to discern whom to trust for knowledge, and it disposes him to improve his testifier-selecting abilities. Intellectual arrogance and intellectual servility, by contrast, promote ineffective epistemic trust in others.

25.4.2 The intellectually humble speaker of testimony

Let's turn to the speaker, in her capacity as trustee for knowledge. I will argue that intellectual humility fosters epistemic trustworthiness – that is, it fosters willingness and competence.

Consider first willingness, which, to recall, includes willingness to abide by the norms of the trust relationship, and willingness to experience the characteristic psychology of trust. Intellectual humility promotes both. The intellectually humble person, as we saw, is motivated to pursue epistemic aims for their own sake; this surely includes social-epistemic aims, where the person gaining knowledge is someone other than herself. So if the humble speaker knows or can find out what the hearer needs to know, she is disposed to be willing to come through for a hearer.

Let's turn to competence. Recall that this amounts to competence to form one's own knowledge on the matter at issue, and competence to communicate to the hearer the knowledge that he needs in his context. We may call these *knowledge* and *communicative* competences, respectively. Intellectual humility encourages knowledge competence: it ensures that the speaker is motivated to promote epistemic ends, with the corollary that she is motivated to epistemically self-improve for the sake of doing so. This does not guarantee that her efforts will succeed, but it certainly promotes success.

What about communicative competence? To see how intellectual humility fosters this, we need a closer look at what it involves. There are three components. One is (a) competence to testify only if one has knowledge. Since testifying is a form of asserting, this competence amounts to the speaker's being able to obey a plausible norm of assertion: to assert only what she knows (Williamson 2000, chapter 11). A speaker who cannot obey this norm cannot be trusted to refrain from asserting things that she does not know – a disaster for a hearer trusting her for knowledge. The next component of communicative competence is: (b) competence to accept the hearer's trust for knowledge only if she is willing to fulfill it; that is, willing to subject herself to the norms of trust and to experience its characteristic psychology. For example, if her jealousy toward the speaker is prone to sapping her commitment to doing her best for him, she must recognize this and perhaps decline his trust. A speaker who cannot accurately gauge her willingness to come through for a hearer is a risky bet. Finally, (c) the speaker must be competent to discern what sort of information the hearer needs in his context (Hinchman 2012, Grasswick 2018). For example, if he asks for directions to the post office and is pushing a baby carriage, she should not direct him in the way that would be simplest for someone traveling light, say, up a flight of stairs. This sort of competence involves thinking herself into the hearer's situation.

Intellectual humility fosters each of these communicative competences. (a) The intellectually humble speaker is well placed to know what she knows and does not know, and hence to testify only what she knows (Whitcomb et al. 2017, 522). This arises from the distinguishing feature of intellectual humility, the tendency to form accurate noetic self-evaluations. (b) For the same reason, the intellectually humble speaker likely has the self-insight to recognize whether she is willing to come through for the hearer, and hence whether she can in good faith accept his epistemic trust. As for the third communicative competence, (c) discerning the particular information that the hearer needs in his context, intellectual humility does not, itself, involve this. For this competence is other-directed, whereas intellectual humility (as we saw) is directed toward oneself. But because intellectual humility, being a virtue, stems from an epistemic motivation, it ensures that the speaker is motivated to develop competence in discerning hearers' epistemic needs.

In summary, intellectual humility promotes willingness in the speaker, in that it motivates her to meet the hearer's epistemic aims; and it promotes competence by equipping her to be a good knower and a good communicator.

Contrast this with intellectually arrogant and servile speakers, who have several features that make them bad bets for epistemic trustworthiness. One feature puts pressure on their willingness to come through for the hearer: neither the arrogant nor the servile speaker is characteristically motivated to achieve epistemic aims – either their own or the hearer's – for their own sake. This does not automatically mean that they will be less willing to come through for the hearer. But it does mean that they will need a substitute motivation, and that this motivation must be robust, not dependent on changeable circumstantial factors. The wise hearer, if he is to trust an arrogant or servile speaker at all, would thus do well to ensure that she has some such motivation.

But even then, arrogant and servile speakers also get low marks for competence. Consider, first, knowledge competence. The intellectually arrogant person, as we saw, is apt to form too many beliefs, of which a significant proportion could easily be false or unfounded. And the servile person is apt to form his own beliefs gullibly, as well as to miss out on corrective feedback that might otherwise sharpen his knowledge. So neither the arrogant nor the servile speaker is apt to have knowledge competence, making neither worthy of epistemic trust.

Let's turn to commitment competence. The intellectually arrogant speaker has two features that sap it. One is that she is apt to testify even in the absence of knowledge, failing with respect to aspect (a) of communicative competence, and the other is that she is apt to accept the hearer's trust even if her will to deliver for him is weak, failing with respect to aspect (b). The reason is that, because the arrogant speaker overestimates her noetic strengths and underestimates her noetic weaknesses, she is prone to thinking that she has what it takes to come through for the hearer even if she does not.

The intellectually servile speaker does not have this problem with communicative competence, for he *underestimates* his abilities. Rather than being prone to accept the hearer's trust when he shouldn't, he is prone to *declining* it when he would be competent to deliver on it after all. Because, in general, a greater proportion of his (comparatively rare) testimony is apt to constitute knowledge than the arrogant speaker's, trusting him for knowledge might be thought a less dangerous bet for the hearer than trusting an arrogant speaker. However, if servility (as Tanesini 2018c argues) is motivated by the desire for social acceptance, trusting a servile speaker may risk being told what he thinks you want to hear, whether or not it is true.

Neither arrogant nor servile speakers, then, are epistemically wise choices for prospective hearers. An intellectually humble speaker, by contrast, is in a good place to be epistemically trustworthy, so that trusting her for knowledge is likely to be effective.

25.5 Conclusion

I have considered some important areas of overlap between intellectual humility and epistemic trust. But I have left a number of topics undiscussed, including other types of situation, beside self-trust and testimony, in which epistemic trust and intellectual humility can inform each other. For example, disagreement might threaten a person's epistemic self-trust, and intellectual humility might help him navigate the appropriate response, including helping him learn from it rather than intellectually barricade himself (Whitcomb et al. 2017, 524; Dormandy 2018). And intellectual humility is surely among the epistemic virtues of a "Socratic authority" (Jäger 2016, 179), a kind of epistemic authority who, by modeling virtuous thinking, helps transmit understanding (as opposed to piecemeal knowledge). So more work is needed to build on the groundwork laid here.

Suffice it for now to summarize this groundwork. Intellectual humility promotes effective epistemic self-trust by enabling a person to assess the extent of her own epistemic trustworthiness, and by ensuring that she is motivated to epistemically self-improve should that evaluation prove negative. It also promotes effective epistemic trust in other people: it puts a hearer of testimony in a position to assess his need for epistemic assistance and his aptitude for selecting testifiers, and it puts a speaker in a position to be epistemically trustworthy. Not a bad record for a humble virtue.[14]

Notes

1 Some argue that one- or two-place trust is more basic. See e.g. Jones (2004), and Domenicucci and Holton (2017).

2 Trust, either in ourselves or others, is not *necessary* for knowledge; merely relying on ourselves or others is an option, though less effective. See Dormandy (2020).

3 It may be possible for a trustee to fail to be epistemically trustworthy without being untrustworthy; if so, then trusting either sort of person is ineffective but here I'll focus on untrustworthiness.

4 Situationists deny that people have stable character traits and thus epistemic virtues. I cannot discuss this objection here, but see (Alfano 2013, chapter 5, and Tanesini 2018, section 6).

5 This is closest to the view of Tanesini (2018), but I hope to capture at least the spirit of many other views (see footnote 5). The main outlier is Roberts and Woods's (2003) "low concern for status" view, which characterizes intellectual humility as not caring about the way in which others perceive your epistemic abilities. That said, low concern for status is often an outworking of intellectual humility as construed here (Whitcomb et al. 2017, 523).

6 Hazlett (2012) and Church (2016) limit the objects of evaluation to the epistemic statuses of the agent's beliefs, omitting other sorts of attitude and ability. Whitcomb et al. (2017) limit the objects of evalua-

tion to the agent's cognitive limitations, omitting her strengths. I adopt Tanesini's view because it is the broadest: it includes the objects of evaluation highlighted by the others.

7 For example, Tanesini says that intellectual humility might be directed at beliefs, theories, cognitive capacities, habits, or skills (2018, 411–412), including one's vision and hearing (411), memory (412), or problem-solving ability (413). See also Whitcomb et al. (2017, 516). And note the claim of Church (2016) and Hazlett (2013) that intellectual humility is directed solely at the epistemic status of one's beliefs.

8 Some characterize these two vices as the extremes between which intellectual humility is the virtuous "mean" (Church 2016, 413–414; Hazlett 2012, 220; Whitcomb et al. 2017, 516–517). But Tanesini (2018, 418) cautions against this picture on the grounds that it is psychologically unrealistic: you don't correct for servility by adding doses of arrogance until you arrive at intellectual humility. Her complex catalogue of other vices opposed to intellectual humility also speaks against a one-scale model (Tanesini 2018c).

9 Or so I suppose here, in agreement with (Zagzebski 1996; Battaly 2016; Tanesini 2018a). For contrary arguments, to the effect that intellectual vice is compatible with epistemically good motivations, see (Cassam 2016; Crerar 2018).

10 These are distinguished from a cluster of related vices, such as intellectual haughtiness and timidity, in (Tanesini 2018c).

11 On closer inspection, Foley (2001), Zagzebski (2012), and Lehrer (1997) seem to construe self-trust as mere reliance on one's faculties, rather than as trust in the richer sense discussed here (Dormandy 2020).

12 This is so regardless of whether she is required merely to respond to any defeaters against trusting others, or to seek positive reasons to trust them.

13 Another response to distrusting yourself to pick testifiers is that you decline to trust any at all, which (if you are servile and distrust yourself too) will push you toward suspension of judgment on many matters. But this tendency is arguably not proper to intellectual servility, but to the closely related vice of intellectual timidity (Tanesini 2018c).

14 Many thanks to Alessandra Tanesini for helpful comments.

References

Alfano, Mark. 2013. *Character as Moral Fiction*. Cambridge: Cambridge University Press.

Baehr, Jason. 2011. *The Inquiring Mind: On Intellectual Virtues and Virtue Epistemology*. Oxford: Oxford University Press.

Baier, Annette. 1986. "Trust and Antitrust." *Ethics* 96(2): 231–60.

Battaly, Heather. 2016. "Epistemic Virtue and Vice: Reliabilism, Responsibilism, and Personalism." In: *Moral and Intellectual Virtues in Chinese and Western Philosophy: The Turn Towards Virtue*, edited by Michael Slote, Chienkuo Mi, and Ernest Sosa. New York: Routledge.

Cassam, Quassim. 2016. "Vice Epistemology." *The Monist* 99(2): 159–80. doi:10.1093/monist/onv034.

Church, Ian M. 2016. "The Doxastic Account of Intellectual Humility." *Logos & Episteme* VII(4): 413–33.

Code, Lorraine. 1987. *Epistemic Responsibility*. Hanover, NH: University Press of New England/Brown University Press.

Crerar, Charlie. 2018. "Motivational Approaches to Intellectual Vice." *Australasian Journal of Philosophy* 96(4): 753–66. doi:10.1080/00048402.2017.1394334.

D'Cruz, Jason. 2019. "Humble Trust." *Philosophical Studies* 176(4): 933–953. doi:10.1007/s11098-018-1220-6.

Domenicucci, Jacopo, and Richard Holton. 2017. "Trust as a Two-Place Relation." In: *The Philosophy of Trust*, edited by Paul Faulkner and Thomas Simpson, 149–60. Oxford: Oxford University Press.

Dormandy, Katherine. 2018. "Does Epistemic Humility Threaten Religious Beliefs?" *Journal of Psychology and Theology* 46(4): 292–304. doi:10.1177/0091647118807186.

Dormandy, Katherine. 2020. "Introduction: Trust and Some Epistemological Applications." In: Trust in Epistemology, edited by Katherine Dormandy. New York: Routledge.

Faulkner, Paul. 2011. *Knowledge on Trust*. Oxford: Oxford University Press.

Foley, Richard. 2001. *Intellectual Trust in Oneself and Others*. Cambridge: Cambridge University Press.

Fricker, Elizabeth. 2006. "Second-Hand Knowledge." *Philosophy and Phenomenological Research* LXXIII(3): 592–618.

Grasswick, Heidi. 2018. "Understanding Epistemic Trust Injustices and Their Harms." *Royal Institute of Philosophy Supplement* 84: 69–91. doi:10.1017/s1358246118000553.

Hawley, Katherine. 2014. "Partiality and Prejudice in Trusting." *Synthese* 191: 2029–45. doi:10.1007/s11229-012-0129-4.
Hazlett, Allan. 2012. "Higher-Order Epistemic Attitudes and Intellectual Humility." *Episteme* 9(03): 205–23. doi:10.1017/epi.2012.11.
Hinchman, Edward. 2005. "Telling as Inviting to Trust." *Philosophy and Phenomenological Research* 70(3): 562–87.
———. 2012. "Can Trust Itself Ground a Reason to Believe the Trusted?" *Abstracta* 6(Special Issue VI): 47–83.
———. 2017. "On the Risks of Resting Assured: An Assurance Theory of Trust." In: *The Philosophy of Trust*, edited by Paul Faulkner and Thomas Simpson, 51–69. Oxford: Oxford University Press.
Jäger, Christoph. 2016. "Epistemic Authority, Preemptive Reasons, and Understanding." *Episteme* 13(02): 167–85. doi:10.1017/epi.2015.38.
Jones, Karen. 1996. "Trust as an Affective Attitude." *Ethics* 107(1): 4–25. doi:10.1017/S0003975605000160.
———. 2004. "Trust and Terror." In: *Moral Psychology: Feminist Ethics and Social Theory*, edited by Peggy DesAutels and Margaret Urban Walkerx, 3–18. Lanham, MD: Rowman and Littlefield.
———. 2017. "'But I Was Counting on You!'" In: *The Philosophy of Trust*, edited by Paul Faulkner and Thomas Simpson, 90–108. Oxford: Oxford University Press.
Kvanvig, Jonathan K. 1992. *The Intellectual Virtues and the Life of the Mind*. Savage, MD: Rowman and Littlefield.
Lehrer, Keith. 1997. *Self-Trust: A Study of Reason, Knowledge, and Autonomy*. Oxford: Oxford University Press.
Montmarquet, James. 1993. *Epistemic Virtue and Doxastic Responsibility*. Lanham, MD: Rowman and Littlefield.
Roberts, Robert C., and Wood, W. Jay. 2003. "Humility and Epistemic Goods." In: *Intellectual Virtue: Perspectives from Ethics and Epistemology*, edited by Michael DePaul and Linda Zagzebski, 257–279. Oxford: Oxford University Press.
Tanesini, Alessandra. 2018a. "Epistemic Vice and Motivation." *Metaphilosophy* 49(3): 350–67. doi:10.1111/meta.12301.
———. 2018b. "Intellectual Humility as Attitude." *Philosophy and Phenomenological Research* 96(2): 399–420. doi:10.1111/phpr.12326.
———. 2018c. "Intellectual Servility and Timidity." *Journal of Philosophical Research* 43: 21–41. doi:10.5840/jpr201872120.
Whitcomb, Dennis, Heather Battaly, Jason Baehr, and Daniel Howard-Snyder. 2017. "Intellectual Humility: Owning Our Limitations." *Philosophy and Phenomenological Research* 94(3): 509–39. doi:10.1111/phpr.12228.
Williamson, Timothy. 2000. *Knowledge and Its Limits*. Oxford: Oxford University Press.
Zagzebski, Linda. 1996. *Virtues of the Mind*. Oxford: Oxford University Press.
Zagzebski, Linda. 2012. *Epistemic Authority: A Theory of Trust, Authority, and Autonomy in Belief*. Oxford: Oxford University Press.

26

INTELLECTUAL HUMILITY, TESTIMONY, AND EPISTEMIC INJUSTICE

Ian M. Church

In the typical case, when a person utters or testifies that a given proposition, *p*, the goal is for someone else to come to believe or know (given that *p* is true) that *p*. Of course, this testimonial exchange can go wrong in many different ways, and various intellectual vices can contribute to this—including epistemic injustice and an absence of intellectual humility (i.e. intellectual arrogance or intellectual servility). The 21st century has seen a "social turn" within epistemology, which has led to a growing amount of exciting research on the epistemology of testimony, peer disagreement, and the general social circumstances of human knowing. Additionally, for over 35 years, virtue epistemology has played a dominant role in the epistemological literature, which has more recently lead to a flurry of interest in particular intellectual virtues like intellectual humility and vices like epistemic injustice. And, happily, more work is now being done connecting virtue-theory with this social turn in epistemology, including exciting work on group virtues (see Kallestrup, 2016). And while this has led to some fruitful dialogue about the virtues and vices at play in the epistemology of testimony—including work exploring the relationship between epistemic injustice and testimony (see Peet 2017; McKinnon 2016; Tanesini 2016)—little work has yet been done exploring how virtues like *intellectual humility* (or its corresponding vices, intellectual arrogance or intellectual servility) might influence when and why we believe what others tell us, or even how they could contribute to vices like epistemic injustice.

To see how these issues might be connected, consider the following influential case from Miranda Fricker's *Epistemic Injustice: Power and the Ethics of Knowing* (2007):

> It is the Fifties, and we are in Venice. Herbert Greenleaf, a rich American industrialist, is visiting, accompanied by a private detective whom he has hired to help solve the mystery of the whereabouts of his renegade son, Dickie. Dickie Greenleaf recently got engaged to his girlfriend, Marge Sherwood, but subsequently spent a great deal of time travelling with their 'friend' Tom Ripley—until Dickie mysteriously disappeared. Marge is increasingly distrustful of Ripley because he seems to be obsessed with Dickie and suspiciously bound up with his strange disappearance. She also knows very well that it is unlike Dickie—unreliable philanderer though he undoubtedly was—simply to do a bunk, let alone to commit suicide, which is the hypothesis that Ripley is at

> pains to encourage. Ripley, however, has all along done a successful job of sucking up to Greenleaf senior, so Marge is entirely alone in her suspicion—her correct suspicion—that Dickie has been murdered, and that Ripley is his killer ... Greenleaf is only too aware of how little he himself knows of his son ... and yet he fails to see Marge as the source of knowledge about Dickie that she manifestly is. This attitude leads Greenleaf to ignore one of Marge's key reasons for her correct hypothesis that Dickie has died at the hands of Ripley: she finds Dickie's rings at Ripley's place, one of which had been a gift from her and which he had sworn never to remove. Greenleaf ignores it, partly because he underestimates Dickie's commitment to Marge, so that in his eyes any promise to Marge on Dickie's part is virtually worthless; but mostly because Ripley successfully constructs Marge as 'hysterical'. Indeed, not only Greenleaf but also Marge's friend, Peter Smith-Kingsley, comes to perceive her that way, so that the net result is a collusion of men against Marge's word being taken seriously. The theme of knowledge ever to the fore in the dialogue, we at one point hear her off-screen, shortly after she finds the rings, her powers of expression seemingly reduced to a self-contradictory mantra, repeating emphatically to the incredulous Greenleaf, 'I don't know, I don't know, I just know it'; and it is at this point that Greenleaf replies with the familiar put-down, 'Marge, there's female intuition, and then there are facts.'[1]
>
> *(2007, pp. 86–88)*

Herbert Greenleaf wants to know what happened to his son, Dickie; after all, that's why he came to Venice and hired a private detective. Marge knows what happened to Dickie, and she is more than happy to tell Greenleaf; however, he won't listen. Greenleaf doesn't value Marge's testimony, and subsequently fails to recognize valuable information. As Miranda Fricker unpacks this story, Greenleaf is guilty of committing epistemic injustice against Marge. According to Fricker, Greenleaf has wronged Marge "in [her] capacity as a giver of knowledge" (2007, p. 7).

This seems exactly right, but we might wonder if there is another vice lurking in the conceptual neighborhood. Perhaps we could also easily think of Greenleaf as guilty of *intellectual arrogance*. In snubbing Marge's testimony, perhaps Greenleaf is unjustifiably assuming that his cognitive faculties are better positioned or equipped than Marge's. And he attributes far more positive epistemic status to his beliefs regarding his son than is actually merited. But, then again, maybe we could also easily think of Greenleaf as being guilty of *intellectual servility*. Despite Dickie's treasured rings being found at Ripley's place, Greenleaf doesn't attribute nearly as much positive epistemic status to the belief that Ripley could be the killer that he should. And, again and again, Greenleaf simply does not track the positive epistemic status of the valuable information that Marge offers him.

In this exploratory paper, I want to consider how intellectual humility and epistemic injustice might contribute to the failure of testimonial exchanges. In Section 26.1, I will briefly highlight four broad ways a testimonial exchange might fail. In Section 26.2, I will very briefly review the nature of epistemic injustice. In Section 26.3, I will explore how both epistemic injustice and intellectual humility can lead to failures in testimonial exchange, and I'll conclude by suggesting how intellectual humility and epistemic injustice might be related.

But what is intellectual humility? One account of this virtue is the doxastic account of intellectual humility, according to which intellectual humility is the virtue of accurately tracking what one could non-culpably take to be the positive epistemic status of one's own beliefs. On this view, intellectual arrogance would be the vice of overestimating the positive epistemic status of one's beliefs, and intellectual servility would be the vice of underestimating the positive epistemic status of one's beliefs. This is a view I have defended elsewhere (see, for example

Church 2016; Church and Samuelson 2017), and I won't repeat myself here. But, to be sure, there are plenty of other accounts in the literature. For example, in their seminal account, Bob Roberts and Jay Wood (2007, 2003) defined intellectual humility as having a low concern for status when pursing various intellectual goals. Dennis Whitcomb, Heather Battaly, Jason Baehr, and Daniel Howard-Snyder (2015) have argued that intellectual humility is the virtue of attending to and owning one's intellectual limitations. More recently, Alessandra Tanesini has argued that intellectual humility is "a cluster of strong attitudes (as these are understood in social psychology) directed toward one's cognitive make-up and its components, together with the cognitive and affective states that constitute their contents or bases, which serve knowledge and value-expressive functions" (2018, p. 399). All that said, however, we don't need to worry too much about the exact definition of intellectual humility here; while I will occasionally draw from or reference my favored account of intellectual humility (the doxastic account), what I say in this chapter won't hinge too much on that particular account. I'm happy to work from a general and intuitive grasp of what intellectual humility might be. I'm hoping that most of what I say in this chapter will apply regardless of how we ultimately define intellectual humility.

26.1 How testimonial exchanges can fail

Before we explore how testimony can go wrong, we should consider the basic anatomy of a testimonial exchange. For Jonathan Adler (2012), the core cases of testimonial exchange involve two strangers (with no prior engagement with each other)—one person giving the testimony (let's call this person SPEAKER) and another person receiving the testimony (let's call this person HEARER). SPEAKER's testimony involves a single assertion, *p*, and SPEAKER's testimony is solely responsible for sustaining HEARER's belief that *p*. And finally, the context of the testimony is one where there is a shared norm of truth-telling and where there are no unusual professional or institutional demands for accuracy. In sum, when we're considering the general ways that a testimonial exchange might fail, it is important that we try to think about testimonial exchanges in their most basic form; testimonial exchanges where we have one speaker making a single assertion, *p*, to a single hearer.

Now we can begin to see specific ways testimonial exchanges can go wrong. Assuming that the goal of testimony is for a given hearer to acquire knowledge through the utterance of a given speaker, testimonial exchanges go *wrong* whenever the hearer does *not* acquire knowledge from the speaker's utterance.[2] With the basic anatomy of testimony noted above, I think we can highlight four general areas where testimony can go wrong: (i) with the *hearer*, (ii) with the *speaker*, (iii) with the utterance "*p*", and (iv) with the general environment. Let's now consider an example of each.

Obviously enough, if there are significant problems with a given hearer—if, for example, the hearer is severely inebriated—then the hearer won't be able to acquire knowledge from the speaker's utterance that *p*. Consider the following case:

> BAD HEARER: HEARER is visiting Chicago. While walking down the street, she sees SPEAKER, an ostensibly normal looking stranger, and asks for directions to the Willis Tower. SPEAKER gives HEARER what sounds like plausible directions. However, given that HEARER is deeply confused about the major skyscrapers in Chicago—for example, regularly confusing the Willis Tower with the Trump Tower—it is not clear that HEARER knows how to get to the Willis Tower, since it is unclear whether or not HEARER actually knows what building 'Willis Tower' refers to.

Given HEARER's deep confusion about Chicago skyscrapers, when she asks for directions to the Willis Tower we might wonder whether or not she is really looking for the Willis Tower. And even if SPEAKER gives HEARER flawless, clear, and precise directions, it's not clear that she can acquire knowledge from these directions because she is so very confused about which buildings are which in downtown Chicago.

Additionally, if there are significant problems with a given speaker—if, for example, a given speaker is severely intoxicated or otherwise rendered sufficiently unreliable—then anyone who hears that speaker's testimony will be unable to acquire knowledge from it. Consider another case:

> BAD SPEAKER: HEARER is visiting Chicago, and wants to visit the Willis Tower. While walking down the street, she sees SPEAKER, an ostensibly normal looking stranger, and asks for directions. SPEAKER gives HEARER what sounds like plausible directions; however, SPEAKER is deeply confused about the names of Chicago skyscrapers—regularly, for example, confusing the Willis Tower for the Trump Tower. As such, it is not at all clear that HEARER can know how to get to the Willis Tower from SPEAKER's testimony, because there is a real chance that SPEAKER is confusing the Willis Tower with the Trump Tower.

Given SPEAKER's deep confusion about Chicago skyscrapers in BAD SPEAKER, any testimony about those skyscrapers—including testimony regarding how to get to them—seems undermined. SPEAKER, in this case, is not a reliable source of testimonial knowledge about Chicago skyscrapers.

Naturally enough, another way that a given testimonial exchange can go wrong is if the testimony, the assertion itself, is a bad one. Consider another case:

> BAD ASSERTION: HEARER is visiting Chicago, and wants to visit the Willis Tower. While walking down the street, she sees SPEAKER, an ostensibly normal looking stranger, and asks for directions. SPEAKER gives HEARER what sounds like plausible directions. On this occasion, however, SPEAKER—who is normally a very reliable and helpful giver of directions—decides to sow some chaos in the world and give HEARER directions to the town dump instead of directions to the Willis Tower.

Given that SPEAKER gives HEARER false information regarding the location of the Willis Tower, HEARER simply cannot acquire knowledge as to how to find the Willis Tower from SPEAKER's testimony. Speaking falsehoods, obviously enough, undermines the transferal of knowledge, given that knowledge that *p* requires that *p* be true.

How can an environment inhibit the acquisition of knowledge in a standard case of testimonial exchange? Consider the following case:

> BAD ENVIRONMENT: HEARER is visiting Chicago, and wants to visit the Willis Tower. While walking down the street, she sees SPEAKER, an ostensibly normal looking stranger, and asks for directions. Unbeknownst to HEARER, however, nine out of ten Chicagoans are deeply put off by the Sears Tower's name being changed to the Willis Tower. So much so, in fact, that if asked for directions to the 'Willis Tower,' nine out of ten Chicagoans will actually give directions to the town dump in protest. SPEAKER, as it happens, is not one of those Chicagoans who is put off by the name

change; so when SPEAKER is asked for directions to the Willis Tower, she reliably gives directions to the Willis Tower.

There's nothing wrong with HEARER or SPEAKER in BAD ENVIRONMENT. And SPEAKER gives good testimony, she gives HEARER good directions to the Willis Tower. Why should we be hesitant to grant HEARER knowledge in this case? Because, like the protagonist's belief in FAKE BARN cases, her correct belief (regarding the location of the Willis Tower) is extremely lucky. She could have very easily asked any of the other Chicagoans on the street, the majority of which would have given her directions to the town dump instead of the tower.

26.2 Testimonial injustice

In general, epistemic injustice occurs when "a wrong is done to someone specifically in their capacity as a knower." (Fricker 2007, p. 1). And this can occur in all sorts of ways. As Katherine Hawley notes, "[p]erhaps the most obvious type of epistemic injustice occurs when people are unfairly prevented from obtaining knowledge because of their lack of access to education, resources, or social networks." (2011, p. 283). In Miranda Fricker's landmark book, *Epistemic Injustice* (2007), she identifies two kinds of epistemic injustice: hermeneutical injustice and testimonial injustice. Hermeneutical injustice involves "structural prejudice in the economy of collective hermeneutical resources" (2007, p. 1). As Heidi Grasswick helpfully explains:

> Hermeneutical injustice occurs when there exists a lack of collective interpretative resources required for a group to understand (and express) significant aspects of their social experience. Fricker offers the example of the situation of women who experienced episodes of what we now identify as sexual harassment, prior to it being named and recognized as such. Without the presence of a socially recognized concept of sexual harassment, women were ill-equipped to both understand and convey these significant experiences and their harms.
>
> *(2013, sec. 4.1)*

While hermeneutical epistemic injustice is, no doubt, a useful and revealing concept—being incredibly useful in feminist approaches to epistemology, for example—the kind of epistemic injustice we're most interested in this chapter is *testimonial injustice*.

Testimonial injustice occurs when a person or group is not given the credibility that they deserve. Or, as Fricker puts it, testimonial injustice occurs when "someone is wronged in their capacity as a *giver* of knowledge" (Fricker 2007, p. 7, emphasis mine). In the typical case, this means giving a person or group *less* credibility than they deserve. For an example of this kind of epistemic injustice, think about Greenleaf's distrust of Marge's testimony in the case at the start of this paper. And some scholars simply define testimonial injustice merely along these lines.[3] However, we might also think that an epistemic injustice occurs when a person or group is given *more* credibility than they deserve.[4] Going back to the Greenleaf example, Greenleaf arguably trusts Ripley far more than he deserves simply because he's a man, which can be seen as a type of testimonial injustice as well. Is Ripley "wronged in his capacity as a knower" if he is given far more credibility than he deserves? Maybe. (Though our intuitions might be clouded in this case by the fact that Ripley is a murderer.) If so, then this is indeed another (perhaps surprising) example of testimonial injustice. But, even if Ripley isn't "wronged in his capacity as a knower" this is nevertheless something very closely related to testimonial injustice.

26.3 Epistemic injustice and intellectual humility and failures in testimonial exchange

Now, clearly enough, some failures in testimonial exchange give rise to epistemic injustice, in particular *testimonial injustice*. Greenleaf wanted to know who his son's killer was, and Marge's testimony could have told him this; however, Greenleaf doesn't believe her testimony. And, as we noted at the start of this paper, we might plausibly think that a lack of intellectual humility is at work here too. After all, Greenleaf certainly seems intellectually arrogant in his disregard of Marge's testimony. In this section, I now want to say a bit more about how these things—testimonial failure, epistemic injustice, and intellectual humility—might all hang together.

The first thing to note is that testimonial injustice only arises from failures in testimonial exchange where there is something wrong with the hearer. Again, to quote Fricker, testimonial injustice occurs when "someone is wronged in their capacity as a giver of knowledge" (Fricker 2007, p. 7). As such, we might think of testimonial injustice in terms of not giving a person or group the credibility that they deserve—in particular, when they are giving testimony. Of course, that's not to say that all failures in testimonial exchange give rise to testimonial injustice—the case BAD HEARER certainly doesn't manifest testimonial injustice—however, whenever we have a case of testimonial injustice it is going to be a case where a testimonial exchange has failed as a result of there being something wrong (viciously wrong) with the *hearer*.[5]

But, importantly, it's not just testimonial injustice that is relevant to testimony, to how testimony might fail. Instead of being a *product* of a failure of testimonial exchange, other types of epistemic injustice (like hermeneutical injustice) can *give rise* to failures of testimonial exchange. Consider a failure of testimonial exchange where something has gone wrong with the hearer. Imagine a culture where the intellectual accomplishments or achievements of women are never celebrated or even acknowledged; instead women are routinely dismissed as un-intellectual. In such a context, a woman might ask a question about Gödel's incompleteness theorem, be given a good and true answers, and yet nevertheless fail to believe what she has been told because she's convinced herself that she can't understand such things.[6] Notice, this isn't an example of *testimonial* injustice, because she's giving the testifier the creditability they deserve; nevertheless, it's still an example of *epistemic injustice*. And in this case, instead of the failure of testimonial exchange giving rise to the epistemic injustice, it is the epistemic injustice that leads to the failure in testimonial exchange.

Non-testimonial forms of epistemic injustice can lead to other types of failures in testimonial exchange. Consider a failure of testimonial exchange where something has gone wrong with the *speaker*. Again, imagine a culture where the intellectual accomplishments or achievements of women are never celebrated or even acknowledged; instead women are routinely dismissed as un-intellectual. In such a context, a woman might feel extremely sheepish about sharing an insight, or giving testimony without caveating everything she says by hedging her claims and being self-deprecating. An outsider to this culture (who doesn't share this negative view of women) might happily ask a woman for directions, but not ultimately believe what she says because of all of the hedging and self-deprecating remarks. In this situation, it's the negative attitudes toward the intellectual contributions of women that is the epistemic injustice (though not an example of testimonial injustice), and this is what can give rise to the failure of testimonial exchange.

Consider a failure of testimonial exchange where the problem lies primarily in the environment. Imagine a culture where men routinely refrain from sharing truths with women—perhaps thinking that the truth can really only be properly handled and disseminated by men to men. Because of this, let's imagine that the vast majority of men in this environment, would lie to a woman if they were asked for even basic truths (like directions). And imagine a woman from outside of this culture (who doesn't know about the "no sharing truths with women" rule) asks a man for directions. And let's say that this man is the exception to the rule in this culture, such that he is one of the very few men who doesn't mind sharing truths with everyone. And let's say he gives the outsider woman good, true directions to where she wants to go. Does she *know* how to get where she wants to go? If we think that the kind of environmental luck we find in FAKE BARN-style cases precludes knowledge, then we'd have to say, "no," she doesn't know where she's going because she could have too easily gotten bad directions from one of the other men in the local environment. Again, in this situation, it's the negative attitudes toward sharing truth with women that is the epistemic injustice (though not an example of testimonial injustice), and this is what can give rise to the failure of testimonial exchange.

The only kind of failure in testimonial exchange where it's not easy to see how epistemic injustice could cause such a failure is a failure in testimonial exchange where there is something wrong with the utterance. However, that's understandable. In talking about epistemic injustice (or intellectual humility, for that matter), we're typically talking about intellectual character traits (virtues or vices); as such, if there is an instance of epistemic injustice that we'd want to point to as leading to a bad utterance, we'd be more inclined attribute this vice to a person (be it the hearer, the speaker, or people in the environment) and not to the utterance itself. Epistemic virtue and vice are best applied to epistemic agents and not utterances.

And clearly enough, like non-testimonial epistemic injustice, a lack of intellectual humility can also lead to a given testimonial exchange failing to transmit knowledge. Of course, intellectual humility doesn't guarantee that testimony will work as it should. For example, someone can be perfectly intellectually humble and still be lied to, or someone can be perfectly intellectually humble and still find themselves in environments hostile to knowledge acquisition via testimony. And what is more, intellectual vice—namely, intellectual arrogance or intellectual servility—are not any guarantee that testimony will *fail*. Someone can be a complete, arrogant jerk and still acquire knowledge via testimony. Someone can be intellectually servile and self-deprecating and still acquire knowledge via testimony. But in any case, someone who fails to be intellectually humble might very well be more susceptible to failures in testimonial exchange than, everything else being the same, someone who *doesn't*, someone who *is* intellectually humble.

Consider the Greenleaf case again. The first place we noted where testimonial exchanges could fail is with the *hearer*—with the person receiving the testimony. It is Greenleaf, the hearer, who fails to listen to the excellent testimony of Marge, and it is Greenleaf, the hearer, who listens unreflectively to the lies and deceptions of Ricky. But if we draw from the doxastic account of intellectual humility—where intellectual humility is the virtue of accurately tracking what one could non-culpably take to be the positive epistemic status of one's own beliefs—we can easily think of the failure in Greenleaf as a failure *in intellectual humility*. After all, Greenleaf is simply not accurately tracking what he could non-culpably take to be the positive epistemic status of his belief regarding his son—the belief which is of central importance to the case. Greenleaf is intellectually arrogant in holding his belief regarding the lack of value of Marge's testimony and the value of Ricky's as strongly as he does. And, ultimately, Greenleaf is intellectually arrogant in holding his belief regarding his son's fate as strong as he does, because he has systematically (and out of prejudice) failed to track defeaters for his belief (presented by Marge).[7]

And, to be sure, this result doesn't rest on the doxastic account of intellectual humility; other accounts of intellectual humility could come to a similar verdict. Take Roberts and Wood's account of intellectual humility where intellectual humility is "a striking or unusual unconcern for social importance, and thus a kind of emotional insensitivity to the issues of status" when it comes to acquiring epistemic goods (2007, p. 239). Greenleaf, I think we can agree, is simply not sufficiently insensitive to issues of status when it comes to pursuing epistemic resources regarding his son's fate. In particular, Greenleaf seems *hypersensitive* to his and Ripley's status as men over and against Marge's status as a woman. So again, it looks like we could say that Greenleaf's failure at intellectual humility fed his prejudice and ultimately lead to a testimonial injustice.

And we can also think of cases where a lack of intellectual humility in the speaker, or a lack of intellectual humility in the local environment, can also lead to failures in testimonial exchanges. We can think of cases where a given speaker is so intellectually servile that their testimony seems understandably untrustworthy to reflective hearers. Or we can imagine an environment where nine out of ten people would give misinformation because they're far too confident in what they know. However, like non-testimonial epistemic injustice, the only kind of failure in testimonial exchange where it's not easy to see how a lack of intellectual humility could cause such a failure is a failure in testimonial exchange where there is something wrong with the utterance. But, again, I think this makes sense given that the proper objects of intellectual humility and its corresponding vices are agents (hearers or speakers) and not utterances.

Importantly, however, failures in testimony as a result of *non-testimonial epistemic injustice* don't seem to be necessarily linked in any way with failures of *intellectual humility*. It seems as though we can imagine cases where everyone in the local environment is intellectually humble, but where certain members of that environment simply don't have access to important epistemic resources. Or, we can imagine cases where someone is afflicted with anxiety and Imposter Syndrome, such that they become self-doubting and intellectually servile; this might lead to failures in testimonial exchange, but without being the product of any *non-testimonial epistemic injustice*.

Testimonial injustice, however, might be different. It seems like testimonial injustice might be *necessarily* linked with failures of intellectual humility. To be sure, someone can fail to be intellectually humble without committing testimonial injustice (just imagine an intellectually arrogant person sitting alone on a deserted island); however, all cases of testimonial injustice—where someone doesn't give someone else the credibility that they deserve—could potentially be seen as a product of either intellectual arrogance of intellectual servility.[8] Consider again Roberts and Wood's account of intellectual humility in term of "a striking or unusual unconcern for social importance, and thus a kind of emotional insensitivity to the issues of status" when it comes to acquiring epistemic goods (2007, p. 239). If testimonial injustice quintessentially involves a reliance on stereotypes concerning a stigmatized group, then perhaps this necessarily signals the kind of concern (or even hyper-concern) for social status or issues of status that Roberts and Wood see as being incompatible with intellectual humility. But the connection between testimonial injustice and intellectual humility is particularly easy to see within the doxastic account of intellectual humility: if testimonial injustice consists of not giving someone the credibility they deserve, then we might think that every instance of testimonial injustice is an instance where someone is not accurately tracking the positive epistemic status of their beliefs (because they've failed to accurately account for the epistemic value of the relevant testimony).

26.4 Conclusion

As epistemology continues to go through its "social turn," and as more and more work is done on intellectual virtues and vices, it's worth considering how these issues might be related. In this exploratory paper, I tried to suggest some ways failures in testimonial exchanges might be produced by epistemic injustice or a lack of intellectual humility. In the end, we were able to see that even non-testimonial variants of epistemic injustice are relevant to testimony and can cause failures in testimonial exchange in a number of different ways. Testimonial injustice, in contrast, doesn't cause failures in testimonial exchange, but is instead the product of a particular kind of failure, namely, failures in testimonial exchanges where the problem lies with the hearer. Vices like intellectual arrogance or intellectual servility can lead to failures in testimonial exchange as well. And while these failures are largely independent from epistemic injustice, some forms of epistemic injustice (namely, testimonial injustice) might be intimately connected with a lack of intellectual humility. There is, no doubt, a lot more to say on these issues, but hopefully these preliminary remarks can be useful for future research in these areas.[9]

Notes

1 Minghella 2000, p. 130.
2 To be sure, testimony can go wrong in all sorts of ways not captured by the basic model of testimonial exchange sketched above. For example, speakers rarely go around making utterances unprompted; as such, hearers often have to initiate the testimonial exchange by asking a question. And if their question is itself confusing or poorly articulated, then that can also pose a serious hurdle to a successful testimonial exchange. For the sake of space, however, we'll leave such complicating factors to the side and stick to the aforementioned basic model.
3 For example, Heidi Grasswick identifies testimonial injustice as occurring "when a speaker is given less credibility than deserved (suffering a credibility deficit) because of an identity prejudice held by the hearer" (2013, sec. 4.1).
4 Medina 2011 explores this possibility further. Also see Coady 2017.
5 This isn't to say that a testimonial exchange cannot fail due to a vice in the hearer that is unrelated to testimonial injustice. A testifier's membership in a stigmatized group might contribute to a failure of testimonial exchange in such a way that isn't an example of testimonial injustice. The claim that is being made here, however, is that whenever there is an example of testimonial injustice then there is necessarily something wrong (in the sense explored in 26.1) with the hearer.
6 For more on phenomena like this, see Dotson 2011, 2014
7 Of course, the testimony in the case of Greenleaf's search for his son fails for *lots* of reasons. Like the BAD ASSERTION case, Ricky's lie helps preclude viable testimonial exchange. And perhaps we could make the case that there was something wrong with the environment Greenleaf found himself in (like the BAD ENVIRONMENT case), an environment with a critical mass of liars and co-conspirators of gender prejudice. But it is worth stressing that had Greenleaf been more intellectually humble—had he done a better job accurately tracking the positive epistemic status of his beliefs (specifically his belief regarding the fate of his son and his belief regarding the value of Marge's testimony), these other treats to testimonial exchange might have been mitigated or otherwise assuaged. If Greenleaf had been a better, more intellectually humble hearer, then maybe he could have recognized Ricky's bad assertion (or later recognized he had defeaters for Ricky's assertion that he needed to address). And maybe if Greenleaf had been a better, more intellectually humble hearer, he could have recognized the poor quality of his environment and taken extra precautions. Greenleaf's failure, I propose, to accurately track the epistemic value of women's testimony (including the testimony of Marge) fed his prejudice and lead to not only a failure in testimonial exchange but also to epistemic injustice.
8 Intuitions might diverge here according to how we want to ultimately define intellectual humility. For the sake of this paper, we'll need to put debates concerning the definition of intellectual to the side; however, I hope that the above considerations show how at least a few of the proposed definitions in the contemporary literature seem to point to this connection between intellectual humility and testimonial injustice.
9 I am enormously thankful to Alessandra Tanesini for her comments and apt criticism of an earlier draft of this chapter. This research was supported in part by a grant from the John Templeton Foundation.

References:

Adler, J. (2012). Epistemological Problems of Testimony. *The Stanford Encyclopedia of Philosophy*. http://plato.stanford.edu/archives/sum2015/entriesestimony-episprob/.

Church, I. M. (2016). The Doxastic Account of Intellectual Humility. *Logos & Episteme*, 7(4), pp. 413–433.

Church, I. M., and Samuelson, P. L. (2017). *Intellectual Humility: An Introduction to the Philosophy and Science*. New York: Bloomsbury Academic.

Coady, D. (2017). Epistemic Injustice as Distributive Injustice. In: I. Kidd, J. Medina, and G. Pohlhaus Jr. eds. *The Routledge Handbook of Epistemic Injustice*. New York, NY: Routledge, pp. 61–68.

Dotson, K. (2011). Tracking Epistemic Violence, Tracking Practices of Silencing. *Hypatia*, 26(2), pp. 236–257.

Dotson, K. (2014). Conceptualizing Epistemic Oppression. *Social Epistemology*, 28(2), pp. 115–138.

Fricker, M. (2007). *Epistemic Injustice: Power and the Ethics of Knowing*. New York: OUP Oxford.

Grasswick, H. (2013). Feminist Social Epistemology. *The Stanford Encyclopedia of Philosophy*. https://plato.stanford.edu/archives/win2016/entries/feminist-social-epistemology/.

Hawley, K. (2011). Knowing How and Epistemic Injustice. In: J. Bengson, and M. A. Moffett eds. *Knowing How: Essays on Knowledge, Mind, and Action*. New York: Oxford University Press, pp. 283–299.

Kallestrup, J. (2016). Group Virtue Epistemology. *Synthese*, October 2016, pp. 1–19.

McKinnon, R. (2016). Epistemic Injustice. *Philosophy Compass*, 11(8), pp. 437–446.

Medina, J. (2011). The Relevance of Credibility Excess in a Proportional View of Epistemic Injustice: Differential Epistemic Authority and the Social Imaginary. *Social Epistemology*, 25(1), pp. 15–35.

Minghella, A. (2000). *The Talented Mr Ripley: Based on Patricia Highsmith's Novel*. London: Methuen.

Peet, A. (2017). Epistemic Injustice in Utterance Interpretation. *Synthese*, 194(9), pp. 3421–3443.

Roberts, R. C., and Wood, W. J. (2003). Humility and Epistemic Goods. In M. DePaul and L. Zagzebski eds: *Intellectual Virtue: Perspectives From Ethics and Epistemology*. Oxford: Oxford University Press, pp. 257–279.

Roberts, R. C., and Wood, W. J. (2007). *Intellectual Virtues: An Essay in Regulative Epistemology*. Oxford: Clarendon Press.

Tanesini, A. (2016). 'Calm Down, Dear': Intellectual Arrogance, Silencing and Ignorance. *Aristotelian Society Supplementary Volume*, 90(1), pp. 71–92.

Tanesini, A. (2018). Intellectual Humility as Attitude. *Philosophy and Phenomenological Research*, 96(2), pp. 399–420.

Whitcomb, D., Battaly, H., Baehr, J., and Howard-Snyder, D. (2015). Intellectual Humility: Owning Our Limitations. *Philosophy and Phenomenological Research*, 91(1), pp. 1–31.

27
FALSE INTELLECTUAL HUMILITY

Allan Hazlett

The *Oxford English Dictionary* defines "false modesty" as "affected or pretended modesty concealing pride." In this chapter, I explore a species of false modesty, which I call *false intellectual humility*. After providing an analysis of false intellectual humility (Section 27.1), I'll present an example of a species of false intellectual humility that is common in contemporary political discourse (Section 27.2). I'll then discuss the relationships between fallibilism, skepticism, and intellectual humility (Section 27.3), with the aim of showing how several familiar phenomena, despite a superficial resemblance to skepticism and fallibilism, are species of false intellectual humility (Section 27.4).

27.1 An analysis of false intellectual humility

False modesty is affected or pretended modesty concealing pride. Inspired by this definition, I propose that *false intellectual humility* is affected or pretended intellectual humility concealing intellectual arrogance. A few comments on this analysis.

I assume here no distinction between modesty and humility.[1] (Ordinary language is more subtle: "modesty" has connotations of sexual discretion and propriety; "humility" has connotations of submission and deference – thus the intuitive, if not entirely clear, connection between intellectual humility and testimony.) Thus, I assume that modesty is the same as humility, and that intellectual humility is a species of humility. (This is what is going to make it possible to say that false intellectual humility is a species of false modesty.)

More precisely, I assume that *humility* is excellence in self-attributing weakness – such that the humble person characteristically attributes weakness to themselves at the right time and in the right way – and that *intellectual humility* is excellence in self-attributing intellectual weakness – such that the intellectually humble person characteristically attributes intellectual weakness to themselves at the right time and in the right way. Intellectual weakness includes such things as uncertainty, ignorance, confusion, intellectual vice, and the lack of intellectual virtue. (This is not the ordinary sense of "weakness"; in the ordinary sense, uncertainty and ignorance per se entail no weakness.) Intellectual humility is thus manifested in admitting what you do not know or understand and those ways in which you fall short of intellectual virtue. The intellectually humble person will acknowledge what is mysterious, inexplicable, or beyond the scope of their understanding, and they will be aware of the extent to which they lack intellectual virtues, in a broad sense that includes both character traits like open-mindedness, intellectual courage, and intellectual autonomy, as well as intellectual powers like good memory, reasoning ability, and creativity.

The present account of the virtue of intellectual humility combines elements of an account I defend elsewhere (2012, 2016a) and an account defended by Dennis Whitcomb, Heather Battaly, Jason Baehr, and Dan Howard-Snyder (2015). I incorporate two ideas from Whitcomb and company: (i) that intellectual humility is concerned with intellectual weakness in general (rather than mere ignorance or unjustified belief), and (ii) that intellectual humility is concerned with a person's own intellectual weaknesses (as opposed to those of others). But I retain one idea of my own: intellectual humility is manifested in the attribution of intellectual weakness; manifestation of intellectual humility does not require "owning" said weakness, in the sense of taking responsibility for it.

Having defined humility and intellectual humility as *excellences*, it is natural to say that both, so defined, are *virtues*. And thus, following Aristotle, we can recognize the virtue of humility as a mean between two vicious extremes: the vice of *arrogance*, characterized by insufficient self-attribution of weakness (as well as excessive self-attribution of strength), and the vice of *servility*, characterized by excessive self-attribution of weakness (as well as insufficient self-attribution of strength).[2] The virtue of intellectual humility thus emerges as a mean between intellectual arrogance and intellectual servility.[3]

The vice of intellectual arrogance, which appears in our definition of false intellectual humility, is manifested in the failure to appreciate what you do not know, what you are not in a position to know, the relative strength of your intellectual powers, your biases and blind spots, and subjects about which you lack expertise. Moreover, it is manifested in the overestimation of your knowledge, of your ability to know, of your impartiality, and of the extent of your expertise.

This understanding of the virtues of humility and intellectual humility jibes with two other ideas about virtue that have been suggested by neo-Aristotelian virtue ethicists. First, we can agree that virtues are *corrective*, serving to counteract or guard against some vicious tendency.[4] In as much as you are prone to (intellectual) arrogance and (intellectual) servility, (intellectual) humility is the cure for what ails you.[5] Second, we can agree that the virtues correspond to domains or spheres of human activity or experience, such that virtues can be individuated by appeal to the various problems and situations with which human beings have to cope.[6] For each such problem or situation, the virtue ethicist wants so say, there's a virtue for that. In as much as reflective monitoring and awareness of our own (intellectual) weaknesses is, in this way, one of the things that human beings naturally do, there is a virtue for that: (intellectual) humility.

I said that false modesty "conceals" arrogance. This requires two points of clarification. First, such concealment, in the relevant sense, need not be successful. Someone's arrogance might be obvious, despite their false modesty. Second, concealment, in the relevant sense, does not require the intention to conceal. This is because falsely modest people often do not know that they are arrogant, and thus do not intend to conceal their arrogance. For the same kind of reason, we should not assume that affecting modesty or pretending to be modest is always deliberate or conscious. We are not always aware of our affectations and pretensions; it is possible to affect or pretend that you possess a trait without realizing that you are doing so.

27.2 Insincere self-attributions of ignorance

False intellectual humility in particular, and false modesty in general, find their natural home in public life, where our tendencies to arrogance inevitably run up against our socio-political needs to appear virtuous. Consider insincere self-attributions of ignorance, i.e. cases in which someone claims not to know something that they, in fact, take themselves to know. This is a pervasive feature of Donald Trump's political rhetoric – if Trump could be said to have an epistemology, it would be a skeptical one, which posits ignorance of the answers to various crucial questions about "what is going on." As a presidential candidate, Trump repeatedly insisted that "we have to figure out what's going on" when it came to various topics. For example, on then-President Barack Obama's connection to the Pulse nightclub shooting, Trump said,

> we're led by a man that either is not tough, not smart or he's got something else in mind[.] He doesn't get it or he gets it better than anybody understands. It's one or the other. … There's something going on.[7]

Implications of ignorance are part of some of Trump's most arrogant moments, such as his call for a "a total and complete shutdown of Muslims entering the United States until our country's representatives can figure out what the hell is going on."[8]

Why think that these are *insincere* self-attributions of ignorance? Trump, like a bad novel, tends to resist interpretation, but it seems like there are two possibilities here. One is that Trump is quite sure, such that he takes himself to know, that Muslims are dangerous and should be excluded from the United States – in which case he is insincere when he implies that he does not know "what the hell is going on." Another possibility is that Trump knows full well that nothing of consequence is "going on" – in which case he is also insincere when he implies that he does not know "what the hell is going on." In this second case, he follows a strategy famously employed by Hillary Clinton when she said that there was no basis, "as far as I know," for the claim that Obama was a Muslim.[9] Clinton knew full well that Obama was not a Muslim, but by hedging, she implied that she was not quite sure.

Insincere self-attributions of ignorance are standard fare when politicians seek to silence reports of sexual assault and sexual harassment. One kind of strategy resembles a kind of skepticism about the past. In connection with the Alabama Senate candidate Roy Moore, Sean Hannity maintained that "none of us knows the truth of what happened 38 years ago."[10] (As with Trump, there are two possibilities here: either Hannity is confident that Roy Moore did not sexually assault anyone 38 years ago, in which case his claim is insincere, or he is confident that Moore did sexually assault someone 38 years ago, in which case his claim is insincere.) Another strategy resembles a kind of skepticism about testimony. For example, defenders of Supreme Court nominee Brett Kavanaugh frequently cited the dearth of evidence against him, with the implication that the testimony of his victims was not evidence. This strategy exploits an ordinary-language and quasi-legal distinction between "testimony" and "evidence."[11] Appeals are sometimes made to the need for "hard" evidence, and an epistemic vocabulary borrowed from the law – "corroborating evidence," "due process," "burden of proof" – is adopted.[12] In all these ways, a politician or pundit can under-state the strength of their evidence and suggest a state of doubt. (Again, we find the same two possibilities: either the relevant testimony is being rejected or ignored, in which case the implication of doubt is insincere, or it is being accepted, in which case the implication of doubt is insincere.)

27.3 Fallibilism, skepticism, and intellectual humility

Without qualification, *fallibilism* is the view that certainty is impossible, but we can also speak of fallibilism about a particular domain, i.e. the view that certainty in that domain is impossible. We mean not mere psychological certainty – i.e. being completely sure or maximally confident – but rather *justified* or *rational* psychological certainty. Without qualification, *skepticism* is the view that knowledge is impossible, but we can also speak of skepticism about a particular domain, i.e. the view that knowledge in that domain is impossible. You might think that knowledge requires certainty; if so, fallibilism entails skepticism.

But we can also think of "fallibilism" and "skepticism" as the names of two virtues, namely, excellence in attributing uncertainty – call that the virtue of *fallibilism* – and excellence in attributing ignorance – call that the virtue of *skepticism*.[13] These virtues overlap with, but are distinct from, the virtue of intellectual humility (Section 27.1).

First, that these virtues overlap with the virtue of intellectual humility: the latter includes, as a proper part, both excellence in self-attributing uncertainty, which is also a proper part of fallibilism, and excellence in self-attributing ignorance, which is also a proper part of skepticism. Given our definitions, fallibilism entails excellence in self-attributing uncertainty (which is one part of intellectual humility) and skepticism entails excellence in self-attributing ignorance (which is another part of intellectual humility). This vindicates the historical association of fallibilism and skepticism with intellectual humility. For example, in defense of his "mitigated" or "academic" skepticism, Hume, urges dogmatists to "become sensible of the strange infirmities of human understanding," as "such a reflection would naturally inspire them with more modesty and reserve, and diminish their fond opinion of themselves, and their prejudice against antagonists."[14] For another, Pierce, articulating his fallibilism, denounces "overconfident assertion" as a "venomous error [that] assails our knowledge."[15]

Second, that the virtues of fallibilism and skepticism are distinct from the virtue of intellectual humility. For one thing, fallibilism and skepticism are concerned exclusively with uncertainty and ignorance, and not with other forms of intellectual weakness, such as epistemic vice, with which intellectual humility is concerned. For another, which is more important, the virtue of intellectual humility, given our account (Section 27.1), is concerned exclusively with *self*-attribution of intellectual weakness, and not with attribution of intellectual weakness to *others*, with which fallibilism and skepticism are concerned. This is confirmed by our image of the skeptic as a dogged interlocutor who ceaselessly challenges our assertions and claims to knowledge, which hardly manifests anything worthy of the name "humility." By stressing the "strange infirmities of human understanding," Hume not only implies his own intellectual weakness, but the intellectual weakness of human beings in general. It is the attribution of intellectual weakness to others that distinguishes skepticism, in the present sense, from mere humility. Were Hume merely intellectually humble, he might refrain from metaphysical speculation on account of the limited scope of his own intellectual powers. However, Hume the skeptic does more than that: he offers a blistering critique of *other* metaphysicians who attempt to go beyond the limited scope of *their* intellectual powers.

Moreover, since attributing ignorance sometimes entails attributing uncertainty, fallibilism and skepticism overlap, in the same sense, with each other. Given all this, we can represent the relationship between our three virtues like this:

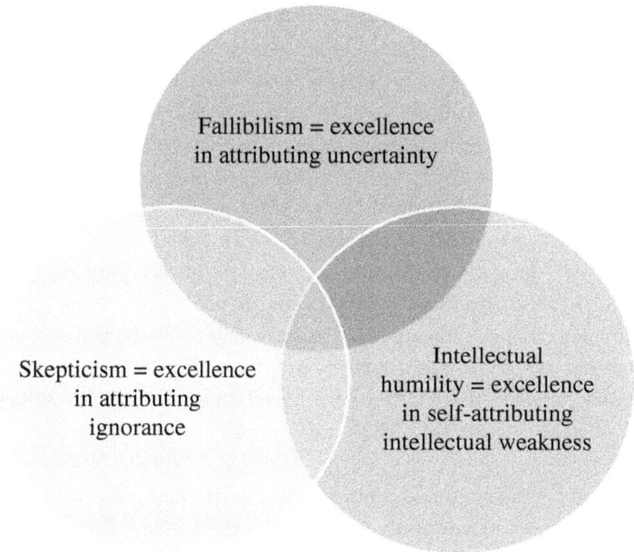

Someone who possesses the virtue of fallibilism, so defined, need not by definition accept fallibilism the view, as defined above – either without qualification or about any particular domain. For the present account of the virtue of fallibilism leaves open the possibility that excellence in attributing uncertainty sometimes requires *not* attributing uncertainty. In the same way, someone who possesses the virtue of skepticism need not by definition accept skepticism the view, either without qualification or about any particular domain, because the present account of the virtue of skepticism leaves open the possibility that excellence in attributing uncertainty sometimes requires *not* attributing ignorance. Nevertheless, it is clear why anyone attracted to fallibilism or skepticism, the views, either without qualification or about some particular domain, would be a fan of the virtue of fallibilism or the virtue of skepticism: skeptics and fallibilists are concerned about people's tendency to over-attribute certainty and knowledge – i.e. their tendency to attribute certainty and knowledge *not* at the right time – and thus will be keen to promote the virtues of fallibilism and skepticism as correctives (cf. Section 27.1).

As above (Section 27.1), we can recognize both of these virtues as means between vicious extremes: the virtue of fallibilism is a mean between a vice characterized by excessive attribution of uncertainty (as well as insufficient attribution of certainty) and a vice characterized by insufficient attribution of uncertainty (as well as excessive attribution of certainty), while the virtue of skepticism is a mean between a vice characterized by excessive attribution of ignorance (as well as insufficient attribution of knowledge) and a vice characterized by insufficient attribution of ignorance (as well as excessive attribution of knowledge). "Quietism" seems an apt name for the first in each of these pairs of vices; "dogmatism" an apt name for the second.

Historical fallibilists and skeptics seem to disagree about what their stance implies about inquiry. Hume famously insists on the "limitation of our enquiries to such subjects as are best adapted to the narrow capacity of human understanding."[16] However, Pierce rejects as another "venomous error" any insistence that "this, that, and the other never can be known," on the grounds that this necessarily "blocks the way of inquiry."[17] We could understand this as a disagreement between skepticism and fallibilism: if knowledge is impossible, then inquiry is pointless and should be closed; but if it is merely *certainty* that is impossible, then inquiry may sensibly remain open. But we could also understand this as a disagreement about the scope of fallibilism and skepticism. For Pierce, the closure of inquiry about whether p on the grounds that we cannot know whether p is rash and dogmatic, since we cannot be certain of anything, including whether we cannot know whether p; inquiry must therefore be kept open. However, for Hume, the closure of inquiry on the grounds we cannot know whether p may well be sensible and modest, since the conclusion that we cannot know whether p may well be the justified conclusion of empirical reasoning about our cognitive powers. In any event, both of these stances seem to manifest a kind of intellectual humility.[18]

Fallibilists and skeptics also associate their views with tolerance and open-mindedness. Karl Popper, articulating the "doctrine of essential human fallibility," sympathetically quotes Voltaire on tolerance, which is said to be "a necessary consequence of our humanity. We are all fallible, and prone to error; let us then pardon each other's follies."[19] And we have already encountered Hume's idea that skepticism diminishes "prejudice against … antagonists"; the problem skepticism is meant so solve is that "affirmative and dogmatical" thinkers "have no idea of any counterpoising argument … nor have they any indulgence for those who entertain opposite sentiments."[20]

A final theme from fallibilism and skepticism is a particular diagnosis of dogmatism.[21] Here is Hume on the "affirmative and dogmatical" thinkers mentioned above:

> To hesitate or balance perplexes their understanding, checks their passion, and suspends their action. They are, therefore, impatient till they escape from a state, which to them is so uneasy; and they think, that they can never remove themselves far enough from it, by the violence of their affirmations and obstinacy of their belief.[22]

And here is Pierce on those who employ the "method of tenacity" in forming beliefs:

> [T]he instinctive dislike of an undecided state of mind, exaggerated into a vague dread of doubt, makes men cling spasmodically to the views they already take. The man feels that, if he only holds to his belief without wavering, it will be entirely satisfactory.[23]

Recall the idea that the virtues are corrective and correspond to spheres or domains of human life or experience. We can put Hume and Pierce's point like this: dogmatism, i.e. insufficient attribution of uncertainty and ignorance combined with excessive attribution of certainty and knowledge, at least in a certain class of cases, is a manifestation of an inability to cope well with uncertainty and ignorance, involving an intense and unmanageable discomfort with being unsure or not knowing – an especially strong desire for certainty, or "need for closure," in the psychological jargon. Two conclusions at this point seem reasonable. First, the intellectually virtuous person will be able to *handle* uncertainty and ignorance, even when they would very much like to be certain or to know – they will not, for example, become foolishly overconfident as a way of dealing with the annoyance of not knowing or being sure. Second, the intellectually virtuous person's desires for certainty and knowledge will not entail an inability to feel comfortable or safe in their absence; the intellectual virtuous person will, in other words, can be quite happy in a state of doubt or suspension of judgment.

27.4 False skepticism and false fallibilism

I have dwelt on these affinities between the virtue of skepticism, the virtue of fallibilism, and the virtue of intellectual humility (Section 27.3) because I would like to now turn to some species of false intellectual humility (Section 27.1) which masquerade as manifestations of (the virtues of) fallibilism and skepticism. False intellectual humility is affected or pretended intellectual humility concealing intellectual arrogance. The present species of false intellectual humility all involve affected or pretended skepticism or fallibilism, but nevertheless all involve concealed intellectual arrogance. I propose three overlapping categories: conspiracy thinking, amateurism, and science denial.

27.4.1 Conspiracy thinking

By "conspiracy thinking" I have in mind the kind of thinking characteristic of those who (i) believe in a *conspiracy* (i.e. a clandestine attempt to do something wrong), (ii) the existence of which is denied by a consensus of *official sources* of information (i.e. mainstream news media, academic experts, government reports, etc.),[24] (iii) *without first-hand evidence*. Although it has been suggested that conspiracy thinking is most at home in right-wing politics,[25] it is a pervasive feature of American politics more generally: for every person who believes that the Sandy Hook massacre was a hoax, there is someone who believes that 9/11 was an inside job. Populist politicians across the political spectrum maintain that the "economy is rigged" and that liberal (for right-wingers) or capitalist (for left-wingers) elites are secretly scheming against the interests of the common man.

Knowledge denials are thus an essential part of conspiracy thinking: the conspiracy theorist must reject the claims to knowledge made by the official sources that reject the existence of the conspiracy. This accounts for the superficial resemblance between conspiracy thinking and the manifestation of the virtue of skepticism (Section 27.3) – the conspiracy theorist is rightly described as being *skeptical* of the official story. The conspiracy theorist asks whether we really *know* that the official story is true; they ask how we can be so *sure*. *Inquiry* is called for – inquiry is to be left *open*, despite the conclusion of institutional investigations and the publishing of official reports. Indeed, the conspiracy theorist often insists that others, those who accept the official story, are insufficiently committed to inquiry. The rhetoric of the conspiracy theorist resembles that of fallibilists and skeptics who insist on the perpetual continuation of inquiry (Section 27.3): the conspiracy theorist refuses to close inquiry, conducts their own investigations, and has an insatiable appetite for debate. Like Trump, the conspiracy theorist wants to know what the hell is going on.

However, these expressions of curiosity and open-mindedness are inauthentic, because the conspiracy theorist already takes themselves to know what the hell is going on: they already believe, and typically are quite sure, that the conspiracy exists. This is not to say, or at least not yet to say, that conspiracy theorists are irrational. Certainly there are conspiracies; the conspiracy theorist's characteristic belief is not necessarily false. But it is a belief, and it is typically a quite confident belief, which makes the conspiracy theorists' articulated interest in inquiry insincere.

Recall the diagnosis of dogmatism offered by fallibilists and skeptics (Section 27.3), which appeals to the dogmatist's desire for certainty. Such a desire is a familiar feature of conspiracy thinking: the need for answers, the desire to tie up loose ends, to account for complex or seemingly inexplicable events. Now, there is more than a superficial resemblance between the dogmatist's inability to cope well with uncertainty and ignorance and the virtuous person's curiosity. The difference is revealed in the results: the virtuous are led to suspension of judgment and genuine inquiry; the dogmatic are led to conviction and "sham inquiry," as Pierce calls it.

The conspiracy theorist's reluctance to inquire is a consequence of that feature identified by Popper as characteristic of pseudo-science: the refusal to accept anything as evidence *against* the existence of the alleged conspiracy. Genuine inquiry is premised on the possibility of evidence one way or another; sham inquiry is not. It might be said, in defense of conspiracy thinking, that conspiracy theorists are not insensitive to evidence in this way. Indeed, we are familiar with the way in which conspiracy theorists are able and willing to incorporate new evidence into their explanations. However, it is distinctive of conspiracy thinking that there is an non-negotiable "core" of the conspiracy theory, some basic assumption or allegation that is not genuinely open for revision, even if it is something as ambiguous and unspecific as that "something is going on" or that "the truth is out there." (This leads to a tension in some instances of conspiracy thinking, whereby it is insisted both that inquiry is needed, since we don't know the whole story, and that inquiry is pointless, because we can never know what really happened.)

It is this dogmatic commitment to the existence of a conspiracy, more than their special relationship with any particular conspiracy theory, that characterizes the intellectual arrogance of the conspiracy thinker. The reason we can level this charge of intellectual arrogance against the conspiracy thinker is that we have defined conspiracy thinking as both conflicting with a consensus of official sources of information and lacking a first-hand evidential basis. The conspiracy thinker refuses to defer to those official sources, but without the kind of evidential support that would justify doing so. By classifying conspiracy thinking as a species of false intellectual humility, we can appreciate the kind of confidence that is masked by the conspiracy thinker's would-be skeptical and fallibilistic pronouncements.

27.4.2 Amateurism

According to a familiar narrative, contemporary politics is characterized by the rise of skepticism about expertise.[26] According to the British MP Michael Gove, who argued in favor of a "Leave" vote in the UK's 2016 "Brexit" referendum, "people in this country have had enough of experts."[27] Like conspiracy thinking, this tendency can be found across the political spectrum: populists and their supporters, whether conservative or progressive, are inclined to reject what economists have to say about free trade and immigration. Academics, in particular, and professionals, in general, are suspected by such populists of bias, confusion, and ungrounded speculation.

At first glance, this could be mistaken for prudent caution about expert consensus – experts, after all, even when there is consensus among them, are often wrong. A case could be made that doubting the consensus view among experts often manifests the virtue of skepticism or the virtue of fallibilism (Section 27.3). However, the phenomenon that characterizes contemporary politics involves more than merely *doubting* the consensus view among experts. It also involves *believing* some alternative view. The "Leave" voter who rejects the standard view among economists does not *suspend judgment* about the economic consequences of the UK leaving the EU, the way someone might if they simply thought that the experts were unreliable, because that would not particularly support voting "Leave." The "Leave" voter not only *fails to believe* that leaving the EU will have negative economic consequences; they, in addition, *believe* that leaving the EU will *not* have negative economic consequences.

The phenomenon in question here, therefore, is better described as a kind of *amateurism*, rather than as "skepticism about expertise." The people who have "had enough of experts" are not going around suspending judgment, the way a skeptic might. They are going around believing the negation of what the experts say. What is distinctive of them is less their *distrust* of experts than their *trust* in alternative sources of information.

What alternative sources, exactly? In some cases, amateurism comes in the form of heightened self-trust. As Gove put it, in the same interview mentioned above, "I'm not asking the public to trust me. I'm asking them to trust themselves."[28] Amateurists are thus disposed to work things out for themselves and to draw their own conclusions. However, amateurism just as often comes in the form of deference to someone other than the experts – a politician, a pundit, a website, or an anonymous stranger on social media. Amateurists are particularly fond of intellectual iconoclasts – an especially appealing type is the "rogue" or "renegade" academic, especially if they have been censured or rebuffed in some way by the academy; ideas that have failed to survive peer review are especially exciting, and ex-academics who have been fired or resigned under pressure are particularly compelling. There is an instability in the logic of this kind of amateurism: academic credentials still mean something; but agreement with other likewise-credentialed people is grounds for suspicion.

Both of these forms of amateurism manifest intellectual arrogance, although in different ways. First, consider the amateurist who puts their trust in themselves – the voter who conducts their own economic analysis of Brexit, say. There is, we should acknowledge, something valuable about people who are prepared to put independent thought into their political decisions.[29] There is a temptation to complain that intellectual autonomy is a vice when autonomous reasoners come to different conclusions than those to which we have come. However, the value of independence and autonomy needs to be balanced against the value of truth: even if there is something good about my coming to my own conclusions, there is something bad about coming to conclusions that are uninformed, not supported by evidence, and based on fallacious reasoning. Typically, the self-trusting amateurist simply fails to recognize these costs, by overestimating their own intellectual powers and scholarly abilities, relative to the experts of whom they are suspicious. In this way, they manifest intellectual arrogance.

Second, consider the amateurist who defers to someone other than the experts. Here, there is really no question of the value of independence and autonomy, although amateurists may be tempted by the incoherent idea that, by deferring to someone outside of the mainstream, they are not being deferential. But in what way does such deference manifest intellectual arrogance? Unlike the amateurist who conducts their own research, the amateurist who defers to some "alternative" source of information has not overestimated their ability to conduct the relevant research. However, they are overestimating their ability to evaluate sources of information for the purposes of deference. There is a temptation in epistemology to think that deference involves a kind of abdication of intellectual responsibility, in which the person who defers is an entirely passive recipient of information. Perhaps in some cases. But in the case of amateurists who defer to "alternative" sources of information, deference is active: intellectual agency is exercised in the selection of such sources. (If anything, deference to expert consensus, in as much as it is standard or normal, is relatively passive.) Amateurists who defer to "alternative" sources of information take themselves to know something that others do not – and, in this way, they have an inflated opinion of their own ability to select sources of information.

As above, a desire for certainty (Section 27.3) seems to play a role here. Amateurism is appealing for someone suffering from an excessive desire for certainty, for expert explanations are often complex, invoking a plurality of factors, and hedged in probabilistic terms, such that no simple, decisive answer can be given to any question addressed by experts. Expert explanations, relative to such a desire for certainty, tend to be unsatisfying, and amateurism provides a way to avoid this, with the simple and decisive answers provided by "common sense" or "alternative" experts.

As with conspiracy thinking, we gain insight by classifying amateurism as a species of false intellectual humility, because there is a temptation to think of amateurism as something negative, involving a distinctive kind of doubt or suspicion, directed at experts and expertise. On the present analysis, amateurism is, in fact, something positive, involving a distinctive relationship of confidence or trust, directed at one's own intellectual powers.

27.4.3 Science denial

Let us consider, finally, that which is probably the most famous form of skepticism in contemporary political life, climate change skepticism. The climate change skeptic doubts that anthropogenic climate change is occurring; they argue that we do not know or cannot be sure whether it is occurring; they concede that the climate may be changing but profess not to understand why.

However, as in the case of amateurism, "skepticism" is not quite the right word here, because the climate change skeptic does not merely doubt that anthropogenic climate change is occurring; rather, they believe that anthropogenic climate change is *not* occurring. The climate change "skeptic" does not merely doubt the scientific consensus about climate change, they *deny* that consensus, by believing its negation.[30] This reveals the essential insincerity that climate change "skepticism" shares with conspiracy thinking and amateurism: belief (that anthropogenic climate change is not occurring) is combined with articulated doubt (about whether anthropogenic climate change is occurring).

The denial of climate science is part of a broader pattern of *science denial* in contemporary political life. Like conspiracy thinking and amateurism, science denial is at home both on the right (e.g. climate change "skepticism") and the left (e.g. preference for organic and GMO-free foods). Some instances of science denial manage to have bipartisan appeal despite political polarization: both conservative presidential candidate Ben Carson and progressive celebrity activist Robert DeNiro have expressed concerns about the safety of common vaccines, and suspicions about scientific bias and corruption are voiced with equal vehemence on conservative talk radio and in college humanities classrooms.

For the same reason that amateurism manifests intellectual arrogance, science denial manifests intellectual arrogance: the science denier overestimates their own intellectual powers and scholarly abilities. But the relevant contrast here is not so much with the intellectual powers and scholarly abilities of scientists, such as they are, but with the overwhelming evidential value of the scientific method and the consequent reliability of scientific consensus.[31] The science denier's arrogance is the presupposition that their methods – whatever they are – are superior to the scientific method. And this is an arrogant presupposition simply because the scientific method is the best method known to human beings for inquiring about contingent empirical questions.

As above, a desire for certainty (Section 27.3) seems involved in this species of false intellectual humility. Because science necessarily offers probability, and never certainty, the person who desires certainty will always be disappointed by what science has to say. Climate change "skeptics" are right that anthropogenic climate change hasn't been proven – but no scientific theory ever will be.

27.5 Conclusion

False intellectual humility is affected or pretended intellectual humility concealing intellectual arrogance. There are important conceptual connections between intellectual humility, fallibilism, and skepticism; one consequence of this is that several familiar species of false intellectual humility are naturally described as forms of skepticism and are naturally articulated in terms of uncertainty and doubt. It is important to recognize these as species of *false* intellectual humility, and, in particular, to recognize them as species of (concealed) intellectual arrogance, involving belief and self-confidence, rather than uncertainty and doubt. This, more than anything else, distinguishes them from fallibilism and skepticism proper.[32]

Notes

1 However, other theoretical contexts may well call for the use of the terms "modesty" and "humility" to draw some useful distinction; see e.g. Driver 2001, pp. 114–5.
2 Note that "pride," unlike "arrogance," is an apt name for a certain virtue, namely, excellence in self-attributing strength (cf. Hume, *Treatise of Human Nature*, Book III, Part III, Section II, Hazlett 2017).
3 Cf. Whitcomb et al. 2015, pp. 530–2, Tanesini 2016, 2018.
4 Cf. Foot 1978, p. 9.
5 However, we should resist the temptation to attribute such tendencies to human nature without empirical evidence: the apparent universality of a tendency for arrogance could easily be an artifact of parochial features of the kind of people we tend to think about when we theorize about humility (cf. Hazlett 2017).
6 Cf. Nussbaum 1993, pp. 244–7.
7 June 13th, 2016, on *Fox and Friends*.
8 December 7th, 2015, on donaldjtrump.com.
9 March 2nd, 2008, on *60 Minutes*.
10 November 14th, 2017, on *Hannity*.
11 Cf. Moran 2005; see also Code 1991, chapter 6.
12 Compare the way in which evidential standards are often raised in discussions of theism and atheism, e.g. the focus on proof.
13 Cf. LeMorvan 2011, Hazlett 2016a, Hazlett 2019.
14 *Enquiry concerning Human Understanding*, 12.24.
15 Pierce 1955, p. 55.
16 *Human Understanding*, 12.25.
17 Pierce 1955, p. 55.
18 Related to this is suspicion about claims that "this, that, or the other element of science is basic, ultimate, independent of aught else, and utterly inexplicable – not so much from any defect in our knowing as because there is nothing beneath it to know" (Pierce 1955, p. 55). Compare Hume's evident concern to avoid implying that a good explanation must be fundamental, e.g. the principle of custom (*Human Understanding*, §V) or the fact that utility pleases (*Enquiry concerning the Principles of Morals*, §V).
19 Popper 1963a, p. 22; cf. 1963d, p. 479.
20 *Human Understanding*, 12.24.
21 In connection with this, consider also the association of fallibilism with intellectual integrity or honesty, as manifested by the disposition for disinterested or impartial inquiry, a willingness to abandon one's beliefs in the face of counterevidence and to seek out such counterevidence, and the tendency to "follow the argument where it leads" (cf. Pierce 1955, p. 42–54, Peirce 1905/1972, p. 291, Popper 1963b, p. 68, 1963c, p. 309, p. 323, Haack 1998, pp. 8–15, 2008, pp. 195–208, Kelly 2011).
22 *Human Understanding*, 12.24.
23 Pierce 1877/1955, p. 12.
24 Cf. Keeley 1999, pp. 116–7, Coady 2003, p. 199, Harris 2018, p. 236.
25 Hofstadter, *The Paranoid Style*.
26 See e.g. Nicols 2017.
27 Mance 2016.
28 Ibid.
29 Cf. Hazlett 2016b.
30 There is, of course, a species of propaganda which aims merely to create uncertainty or confusion, which can be deployed against science (cf. Oreskes and Conway 2010). Such propaganda no doubt plays a role in sustaining climate change "skepticism." However, most of those who are called "climate change skeptics," it seems to me, are not merely unsure or confused; they positively believe the negation of the scientific consensus.
31 Cf. Hazlett 2016b, pp. 148–9.
32 Thanks to Michael Lynch for comments on a draft of this chapter.

References

Coady, D. (2003), "Conspiracy Theories and Official Stories," *The International Journal of Applied Philosophy* 17(2), pp. 197–209.

Code, L. (1991), *What Can She Know? Feminist Theory and the Construction of Knowledge* (Cornell University Press).

Driver, J. (2001), *Uneasy Virtue* (Cambridge University Press).

Foot, P. (1978), *Virtues and Vices* (Oxford University Press).

Gass, N. (2016), "Trump Attacks Obama: 'He's Got Something Else in Mind,'" *Politico*, June 13, 2016. (www.politico.com/story/2016/06/islamic-state-orlando-shooter-omar-mateen-224249).

Haack, S. (1998), "Confessions of an Old-Fashioned Prig," In: Haack, S. *Manifesto of a Passionate Moderate: Unfashionable Essays* (University of Chicago Press), pp. 7–30.

Haack, S. (2008), "The Ideal of Intellectual Integrity, in Life and Literature," In: Haack, S. *Putting Philosophy to Work: Essays on Science, Religion, Law, Literature, and Life* (Prometheus Books), pp. 195–208.

Harris, K. (2018), "What's Epistemically Wrong with Conspiracy Theorizing?" *Royal Institute of Philosophy Supplement* 84, pp. 235–57.

Hazlett, A. (2012), "Higher-Order Epistemic Attitudes and Intellectual Humility," *Episteme* 9(3), pp. 205–23.

Hazlett, A. (2016a), "The Civic Virtues of Skepticism, Intellectual Humility, and Intellectual Criticism," In: J. Baehr (ed.), *Intellectual Virtues and Education: Essays in Applied Virtue Epistemology* (Routledge), pp. 71–94.

Hazlett, A. (2016b), "The Social Value of Non-Deferential Belief." *Australasian Journal of Philosophy, 94*(1), pp. 131–151.

Hazlett, A. (2017), "Intellectual Pride," In: J.A. Carter and E.C. Gordon (eds.), *The Moral Psychology of Pride* (Rowman and Littlefield), pp. 79–98.

Hazlett, A. (2019), *The Routledge Handbook of Virtue Epistemology*, H. Battaly (ed.), (Routledge).

Keeley, B.L. (1999), "Of Conspiracy Theories," *Journal of Philosophy* 96(3), pp. 109–26.

Kelly, T. (2011), "Following the Argument Where It Leads," *Philosophical Studies* 154(1), pp. 105–24.

LeMorvan, P. (2011), "Healthy Skepticism and Practical Wisdom," *Logos & Episteme* 11(1), pp. 87–102.

Mance, H. (2016), "Britain Has Had Enough of Experts, Says Gove," *Financial Times*, June 3, 2016.

Moran, R. (2005), "Getting Told and Being Believed," *Philosopher's Imprint* 5(5), pp. 1–29.

Nicols, T. (2017), *The Death of Expertise: The Campaign against Established Knowledge and Why It Matters* (Oxford University Press).

Nussbaum, M. (1993), "Non-Relative Virtues: An Aristotelean Approach," In: M.C. Nussbaum and A. Sen (eds.), *Quality of Life* (Oxford University Press), pp. 242–69.

Oreskes, N. and Conway, E. (2010), *Merchants of Doubt: How a Handful of Scientists Obscured the Truth on Issues from Tobacco Smoke to Global Warming* (Bloomsbury Press).

Peirce, C.S. (1877/1955), "The Fixation of Belief," In: J. Buchler (ed.), *Philosophical Writings of Peirce* (Dover), pp. 5–22.

Peirce, C.S. (1955), "The Scientific Attitude and Fallibilism," In: J. Buchler (ed.), *Philosophical Writings of Peirce* (Dover), pp. 42–59.

Peirce, C.S. (1905/1972), "Issues of Pragmaticism," In: E.C. Moore (ed.), *Charles S. Peirce: Essential Writings* (Harper and Row), pp. 281–99.

Popper, K. (1963a), "On the Sources of Knowledge and Ignorance," In: Popper, K. *Conjectures and Refutations* (Routledge), pp. 3–39.

Popper, K. (1963b), "Science: Conjectures and Refutations," In: Popper, K. *Conjectures and Refutations* (Routledge), pp. 43–78.

Popper, K. (1963c), *Truth, Rationality, and the Growth of Knowledge*, pp. 291–338.

Popper, K. (1963d), "Utopia and Violence," In: Popper, K *Conjectures and Refutations* (Routledge), pp. 477–88.

Tanesini, A. (2016), "'Calm Down, Dear': Intellectual Arrogance, Silencing, and Ignorance," *Proceedings of the Aristotelian Society Supplement* 90, pp. 71–92.

Tanesini, A. (2018), "Intellectual Servility and Timidity," *Journal of Philosophical Research* 43, pp. 21–41.

Whitcomb, D., Battaly, H., Baehr, J. and Howard-Snyder, D. (2015), "Intellectual Humility: Owning Our Limitations," *Philosophy and Phenomenological Research* 94(3), pp. 509–39.

28
INTELLECTUAL HUMILITY AND ARGUMENTATION

Andrew Aberdein

In this chapter, I argue that intellectual humility is related to argumentation in several distinct but mutually supporting ways. I begin by drawing connections between humility and two topics of long-standing importance to the evaluation of informal arguments: the *ad verecundiam* fallacy and the principle of charity. I then explore the more explicit role that humility plays in recent work on critical thinking dispositions, deliberative virtues, and virtue theories of argumentation.

28.1 *Argumentum ad verecundiam*

Modern textbook treatments of informal fallacies offer "*argumentum ad verecundiam*" as an alternative name for "appeal to illegitimate authority" (for example, Copi et al., 2007, p. 51). However, "*verecundiam*" is not Latin for illegitimate authority; it is Latin for modesty, reverence, shame, or, perhaps, humility. Together with *argumentum ad hominem* and *argumentum ad ignorantiam*, *argumentum ad verecundiam* owes its name to John Locke. Locke does not explicitly characterize any of these arguments as fallacies, but he does say that they are "arguments, that men, in their reasonings with others, do ordinarily make use of, to prevail on their assent; or, at least, so to awe them, as to silence their opposition" (Locke, 1836, IV.xvii.19). As Locke explains, the trick to *ad verecundiam* argumentation,

> is to allege the opinions of men, whose parts, learning, eminency, power, or some other cause has gained a name, and settled their reputation in the common esteem with some kind of authority. When men are established in any kind of dignity, it is thought a breach of modesty for others to derogate any way from it, and question the authority of men, who are in possession of it. This is apt to be censured as carrying with it too much of pride, when a man does not readily yield to the determination of approved authors, which is wont to be received with respect and submission by others: and it is looked upon as insolence for a man to set up and adhere to his own opinion against the current stream of antiquity, or to put it in the balance against that of some learned doctor, or otherwise approved writer. Whoever backs his tenets with such authorities, thinks he ought thereby to carry the cause, and is ready to style it "impudence" in any one who shall stand out against them. This I think may be called *argumentum ad verecundiam*.
>
> *(ibid.)*

Locke diagnoses the weakness of such argumentation as taking "another man's opinion to be right, because I, out of respect, or any other consideration but that of conviction, will not contradict him" (ibid.). In modern treatments of this argument, as the fallacy of appeal to illegitimate authority, it is implicitly contrasted with a non-fallacious pattern of argument: appeal to legitimate authority, or, more commonly, appeal to expert opinion. Hence modern treatments of the fallacy are often much concerned with the recognition of legitimate expertise. In this respect, the *ad verecundiam*, like several other well-established fallacies, has somewhat drifted from its original designation. Firstly, Locke, as a good empiricist, is prepared to throw doubt on any appeal to authority. Secondly, Locke goes further than recent accounts into the psychological mechanism whereby *ad verecundiam* arguments succeed. This is the point at which humility becomes relevant. Although Locke does not directly invoke humility in his brief discussion of the *ad verecundiam*, he is clearly in the near vicinity: indeed, he does employ cognate terms, such as modesty, and antonyms, such as pride.

Ian James Kidd defends an account of intellectual humility as "a virtue for the management of intellectual confidence" (Kidd, 2016, p. 396). The intellectually humble would thereby manifest appropriate levels of intellectual confidence, avoiding both the over- and under-valuation of their intellectual circumstances (succumbing neither to the Dunning–Kruger Effect nor to Imposter Syndrome, as it were). On such an account, at least some instances of appeal to illegitimate authority may be seen as manifesting the associated vice of deficiency in deferring to someone else's arguments, since lacking confidence in your own. The corresponding vice of excess would represent overconfidence in the face of legitimate authority. This has received less attention in discussion of fallacies. However, the problems it can cause have been addressed by Michelle Ciurria and Khameiel Altamimi, who observe that standard treatments of *ad verecundiam* are silent "when an appeal to authority has been illegitimately dismissed due to the operation of epistemic injustice or epistemic irresponsibility on the part of a judge or community" (Ciurria and Altamimi, 2014, p. 451). As I have observed elsewhere, such cases may best be understood as a distinct fallacy, dual to the *ad verecundiam* (Aberdein, 2016a, p. 421). At least on Kidd's account of the virtue, instances of both the *ad verecundiam* and its dual could be attributed to their proponents' lack of intellectual humility.

28.2 Principle of charity

Thomas Aquinas maintained that "humility necessarily accompanies charity" (quoted in Overmyer, 2015, p. 658). Nonetheless, the sense in which charity is invoked in argumentation may initially seem somewhat distant from humility. As with the *ad verecundiam*, it is possible to precisely date the inception of the "principle of charity": it originates in an otherwise obscure article by the philosopher Neil Wilson, from which it was swiftly raised to much greater fame by W.V. O. Quine.[1] For Wilson, the principle of charity requires that we favor that interpretation of a word "which will make the largest possible number of [the speaker's] statements true" (Wilson, 1959, p. 532). Quine applies it to a somewhat broader purpose, as embodying the "common sense" that "one's interlocutor's silliness, beyond a certain point, is less likely than bad translation" (Quine, 1960, p. 59). In the hands of Donald Davidson, the principle of charity was to become a major methodological maxim: one that "counsels us quite generally to prefer theories of interpretation that minimize disagreement" (Davidson, 1984, p. xvii).

Unsurprisingly, the attention paid to the principle of charity in the philosophy of language soon crossed over into logic. In a useful survey, the argumentation theorist Ralph Johnson traces the earliest appeal to a principle of charity in a logic textbook to three works published in the mid-1970s. (I have been unable to find any earlier.) However, as Johnson complains, these three works already employ the principle in distinct ways. For Stephen Thomas, charity mandates that we read a passage as non-argumentative rather than ascribe bad reasoning to its author (Thomas, 1973, p. 9). Robert Baum applies the principle to the evaluation of enthymemes, and construes it as requiring us "to add whatever premises are needed to make the argument as good as possible" (Baum, 1975, p. 15). Michael Scriven offers a much more sweeping definition. For him, the "Principle of Charity requires that we make the best, rather than the worst, possible interpretation of the material we're studying" (Scriven, 1976, p. 71). He glosses this in explicitly ethical terms, as requiring fairness or justice in criticism.

Johnson's own definition hews closest to Scriven: "The Principle of Charity which governs all levels of argument analysis is that the critic should provide the best possible interpretation of the material under consideration" (Johnson, 1984, p. 5). He moderates this definition with a restriction on the circumstances in which the critic is so obligated:

> the heavy artillery of argument analysis, monitored by the requirements of the Principle of Charity, is to be pressed into service only when one confronts (i) a fully expressed argument (ii) from a serious arguer (iii) on a serious matter.
>
> *(Johnson, 1984, p. 8)*

The critical thinking theorist Richard Paul, to whose work we will shortly turn, proposes a similar definition to Johnson's, but makes the connection to humility explicit:

> We must feel *obliged* to hear [views we oppose] in their strongest form to ensure that we do not condemn them out of our own ignorance and bias. At this point we come full circle back to where we began: the need for *intellectual humility.*
>
> *(Paul, 2000, p. 170)*

Here Paul explicitly invokes humility in implicit support of a thesis familiar from Mill's *On Liberty*: "there is always hope when people are forced to listen to both sides: it is when they attend only to one that errors harden into prejudices" (Mill, 1977, p. 257). And, if we should listen to the other side, we should listen to them at their best.

As with the *ad verecundiam*, the principle of charity may be understood as a mean between complementary vices, here with respect to interpretation of another's arguments rather than acceptance of their premisses. The vice of deficiency may take the form of wilfully obtuse misinterpretation, as in the straw man fallacy; the vice of excess what Scott Aikin and John Casey have characterized as "a little noticed variety of straw man—the distortion which results in being overly charitable to someone's argument, or, as we shall call it, the iron man" (Aikin and Casey, 2016, p. 432). Once again we have uncovered an unfamiliar fallacy dual to a more familiar fallacy. In Kidd's terms, these extremes may also be seen as manifesting the under- or over-regulation of intellectual confidence, whether arrogantly twisting an argument into a straw man or obsequiously striving to reinterpret it as an iron man. Thereby each exhibits a failure of humility.

28.3 Critical thinking dispositions

Modern argumentation theory is a synthesis of several older research programmes; one of the most important of these is the critical thinking movement. From a trickle at mid century, by the 1980s this had grown into a major programme of educational reform, focused on improving the thinking abilities of schoolchildren, students, and society at large. For most theorists of critical thinking, such abilities comprise not just a skillset, but also

> tendencies, propensities, or inclinations people have to think in particular ways in particular contexts … [which] are not the same as, or reducible to, either formal rules of good thinking or specific behaviors or patterns. of behavior.
>
> *(Siegel, 1999, p. 220)*

Such dispositions are seen as essential to the successful internalization of critical thinking techniques: they present a response to the "transfer problem", that of ensuring that learners go on to use their newly acquired skills outside the classroom (Bereiter, 1995; Bowell and Kingsbury, 2015). Different theorists propose different lists of dispositions, but most such lists include "open-mindedness, fair-mindedness, independent-mindedness, an inquiring attitude, and respect for others in group inquiry and deliberation" (Bailin and Siegel, 2003, p. 183). These dispositions sound more than a little like virtues, an identity some theorists make explicit. Indeed, Sharon Bailin and Mark Battersby argue that intellectual virtues are superior to dispositions in a characterization of critical thinking, since "virtues are not psychological reifications added on to the skills of reasoning, but are inherent to the practice of inquiry and come out of appreciation of the nature of the practice" (Bailin and Battersby, 2007, p. 113). They conclude that virtues are better placed to capture the intrinsic value of reason. However, none of the virtues they propose sounds that much like humility.

Perhaps the most overt invocation of virtue language by a major proponent of critical thinking lies in the work of Richard Paul. Paul draws a distinction between weak- and strong-sense critical thinking. The latter comprises

> (a) an ability to question one's own framework of thought, (b) an ability to reconstruct sympathetically and imaginatively the strongest versions of points of view and frameworks of thought opposed to one's own, and (c) an ability to reason dialectically (multilogically) to determine when one's own point of view is weakest and when an opposing point of view is strongest.
>
> *(Paul, 1987, p. 377)*

As we saw in the previous sections, such abilities can plausibly be seen to depend, amongst other virtues, upon intellectual humility. Indeed, this is a relationship which Paul makes explicit: "To cultivate the kind of intellectual independence implied in the concept of strong sense critical thinking, we must foster intellectual (epistemological) humility, courage, integrity, perseverance, empathy, and fairmindedness" (Paul, 2000, p. 166). Paul defines intellectual humility as "a consciousness of the limits of one's knowledge, including a sensitivity to circumstances in which one's native egocentrism is likely to function self-deceptively; sensitivity to bias, prejudice and limitations of one's viewpoint" and a "lack of intellectual pretentiousness, boastfulness, or conceit, combined with insight into the logical foundations, or lack of such foundations, of one's beliefs" (ibid.).

In a helpful comparative survey of several distinct sets of critical thinking dispositions, the educational theorist Ron Ritchhart proposes six groups of dispositions: "the disposition to be open-minded, to be curious, to be metacognitive, to be strategic, and to be investigative and inquiring, and to reason and use evidence" (Ritchhart, 2001, p. 148). Paul is the only theorist in Ritchhart's survey to propose intellectual humility as a critical thinking disposition. Ritchhart classifies it as borderline between two of his categories: the dispositions to be "metacognitive" and "a truth seeker" (Ritchhart, 2001, p. 149). Paul's conception of strong sense critical thinking certainly stresses metacognitive factors: indeed questioning, or at least reflecting upon, one's own framework of thought is close to a definition of metacognition. Nor is Paul alone in linking metacognition with intellectual humility. Kidd's understanding of intellectual humility requires individuals to reflect upon their own cognition, since they must be "alert to the ways that … complex agential, collective, and deep conditions underlie and shape their intellectual confidence" (Kidd, 2016, p. 396). Some virtue epistemologists have made stronger claims for metacognition. For Jerry Green, it is a virtue in its own right (Green, 2019, p. 120). But for Christopher Lepock metacognition is a necessary component of any intellectual virtue—and specifically of intellectual humility (Lepock, 2014, p. 43). Metacognition also has much in common with Jonathan Adler's account of open-mindedness, as "an appreciation of our fallibility" that takes the form of

> a second-order (or "meta") attitude toward one's beliefs as believed, and not just toward the specific proposition believed, just as fallibilism is a second-order doubt about the perfection of one's believing, not a doubt about the truth of any specific belief.
>
> *(Adler, 2004, p. 130)*

But James Spiegel argues, I think convincingly, that Adler's account should be understood as defining humility rather than open-mindedness (Spiegel, 2012, p. 34). Without taking a stance on any of these specific claims, it does seem reasonable to conclude that the traditional virtue of intellectual humility is closely allied to metacognition, and thereby to critical thinking.

28.4 Deliberative virtues

Another argumentative context in which the virtue of intellectual humility has been explicitly invoked is the analysis of group deliberation. Scott Aikin and Caleb Clanton have argued that success in group deliberation, and thereby in democratic forms of political decision making, depends on the individual participants manifesting what they call "group-deliberative virtues" (Aikin and Clanton, 2010, p. 413). They stress that such virtues differ from epistemic virtues since they are not just truth-conducive, but also "conducive to cooperation and good sentiments among the deliberators in a group" (Aikin and Clanton, 2010, p. 421). Of course, such well-conducted deliberation may in turn be more likely to settle on the truth. One of Aikin and Clanton's virtues is deliberative humility, which they define as "the willingness to hold one's view fallibly and in such a way as to admit that one might be shown to be wrong in light of better reasons, evidence, and argument" (Aikin and Clanton, 2010, p. 419). They situate deliberative humility as a mean between two vices they term "deliberative hubris" and "deliberative insecurity": the former "the unwillingness to even consider that one's view could be refined or refuted by others", the latter "the inability to think that one could ever be on target about an issue" (Aikin and Clanton, 2010, p. 420). This approach to humility bears an obvious similarity to Kidd's confidence management account. Aikin and Clanton go further than Kidd, however, in arguing that the "epistemic norm of humility is … embedded in the very practice of holding any belief whatsoever", since to hold a belief is to be willing to defend it, and to defend it adequately is to give a fair hearing to such challenges as may be raised against it (ibid.).[2] This makes intellectual humility pivotal to the practice of group deliberation: without it deliberation cannot be expected to proceed in good faith, but with it belief in all but the safest of claims ought, at least in principle, to lead to group deliberation. The political scientist Kyle Scott takes this point further, arguing that Aikin and Clanton's seven other deliberative virtues (deliberative wit, friendliness, empathy, charity, temperance, courage, and sincerity) all critically depend on humility, which makes humility essential for group deliberation, and thereby for any feasible concept of deliberative democracy (Scott, 2014, p. 230).

There is some empirical support for these positive conclusions about the value of intellectual humility for deliberation. There is, as one recent survey has it, an embarrassment of riches in the empirical measurement of humility (McElroy-Heltzel et al., 2018). That survey compares 22 different measures, of which four are specifically measures of intellectual humility (McElroy et al., 2014; Hoyle et al., 2016; Krumrei-Mancuso and Rouse, 2016; Leary et al., 2017). Yet more such measures have been published since the data collection period of this survey (Alfano et al., 2017; Haggard et al., 2018; Porter and Schumann, 2018). For example, the psychologists Tenelle Porter and Karina Schumann have developed one of the simpler measures of intellectual humility, consisting of an inventory of nine questions, each to be answered on a seven-point Likert scale (Porter and Schumann, 2018, p. 143). This includes both positively worded questions, such as "I am willing to admit it if I don't know something" and "I like to compliment others on their intellectual strengths", and (reverse scored) negatively worded questions, such as "I feel uncomfortable when someone points out one of my intellectual shortcomings" and "I don't like it when someone points out an intellectual mistake that I made". Porter and Schumann's factor analysis suggests that this measure is one-dimensional, in contrast with some other studies (for example, Alfano et al., 2017; Haggard et al., 2018, whose studies yielded four and three factors, respectively). Porter and Schumann found that "participants who were higher in intellectual humility were more respectful of and more interested in trying to learn about opposing perspectives" both in classroom debates and on emotive public policy issues, such as gun control or same-sex marriage (Porter and Schumann, 2018, pp. 145 ff.). They also demonstrated that "those higher in intellectual humility read a greater proportion (and higher number) of opposing vs. matching reasons than those lower in intellectual humility" (Porter and Schumann, 2018, p. 153). Other studies using different measures have found similar results. For example, Elizabeth Krumrei-Mancuso and colleagues found that intellectual humility "was associated with more reflective thinking, need for cognition, intellectual engagement, intellectual curiosity, intellectual openness, and open-minded thinking" and "also associated with less social vigilantism, which may promote collaborative and cooperative learning" (Krumrei-Mancuso et al., 2020, p. 168). The results of these studies are consistent with Aikin and Clanton's conclusion that intellectual humility in participants is a crucial, perhaps indispensable, asset in group deliberation.

28.5 Virtue theories of argumentation

Although, as we have seen, virtues have been invoked for some time in theories of argument, an explicit virtue theory of argumentation (VTA) is a more recent innovation (for a brief survey, see Aberdein and Cohen, 2016). One of the difficulties that besets argumentation theory as a whole is that it is massively interdisciplinary: it brings together work from many different disciplines, including logic, epistemology, both cognitive and social psychology, communication, management, rhetoric, decision theory, law, computer science, education, economics, and others. This is, of course, a tremendous opportunity, but it also presents a massive coordination problem: it can be difficult for the minority of people in each discipline who focus on argumentation to find each other (and avoid duplicating each other's work). That problem is exacerbated for subdisciplines of argumentation theory, such as VTA, since the numbers involved are even smaller. Perhaps for this reason, VTA has mostly drawn inspiration from the familiar fields of virtue ethics and virtue epistemology; there has as yet been much less interaction with virtue jurisprudence or virtue-theoretic work in rhetoric and economics, although there is an independent interest in applying virtues (including humility) to argumentation in all of these areas (for example, de Bruin, 2013; Agnew, 2018; Amaya, 2018).

A crucial question for VTA is whether its virtues are argumentation-specific or whether it just applies generic intellectual (or moral) virtues to argumentation. For present purposes, this is to ask whether there is any such thing as argumentative humility, distinct from, or a special case of, intellectual humility. If we concede as much, perhaps we should also recognize deliberative humility and critical thinking humility as further subdivisions. We have already seen that Aikin and Clanton distinguish deliberative from epistemic virtues, since being conducive to truth need not be conducive to the optimal conduct of deliberation. In other words, deliberation and belief formation have a different telos. Elsewhere, I have argued that the telos of argumentation is the propagation of truth: "where virtuous knowers are disposed to act in a way that leads to the acquisition of true beliefs, virtuous arguers are disposed to spread true beliefs around" (Aberdein, 2010, p. 173). Katharina Stevens has a more sweeping proposal: "the good of argumentation is the bettering of belief-systems—furthering of knowledge, extension of justificatory inferences, gaining of information and understanding etc." (Stevens, 2016, p. 377). However, the same virtue may contribute to the successful pursuit of different activities with different ends. So, it need not follow that argumentation (let alone deliberation or critical thinking) requires a distinct set of virtues just because it has its own telos. On this basis, at least on Kidd's confidence-calibration account, I think it is reasonable to see intellectual humility as contributing to all of these goals.

If intellectual humility is a virtue of argument, how is it related to other such virtues—and what are these other virtues? One radical perspective would be to argue that traditional character virtues, such as intellectual humility, are all that is needed for argumentation. Against such a position, Olivier Morin maintains that "mere civil virtues (respect, humility, or honesty) do not suffice: we need virtues that specifically attach to the practice of making conscious inferences" (Morin, 2014, p. 499). I shall not attempt to adjudicate this issue here, although in my own work I follow Daniel Cohen, an early advocate of VTA, in proposing four basic virtues of argument: willingness to engage in serious argumentation; willingness to listen to others; willingness to modify one's own position; and willingness to question the obvious (Cohen, 2005, p. 64). Each of these is to be understood as a mean between a pair of vices. I complicate Cohen's typology by subdividing each of his virtues (and vices) to make room for many of the more traditional, character-based virtues and vices, especially those invoked in the responsibilist approach to virtue epistemology (Aberdein, 2010, 2016a). Specifically, I list intellectual humility as a subtype of willingness to modify one's own position. Perhaps it might with equal justice have been treated as a subtype of willingness to listen to others. Certainly, if one modifies one's own position after carefully listening to another's arguments, one has exercised humility at each step; which step took the greater humility is presumably specific to the individual case.[3] More generally, no typology of this kind can be more than suggestive, since the relationship between the virtues is too multi-dimensional to be fully captured by a simple hierarchical classification.

Some scholars argue that intellectual humility is not just *a* virtue of argument, but *the* virtue of argument—that it has a significance more profound than other such virtues. For example, Lois Agnew maintains that intellectual humility is "a guiding principle of public discourse", central to the discipline of rhetoric (Agnew, 2018, p. 335). And we have already noted Kyle Scott's argument that "humility is pivotal to the proper functioning of the other virtues" (Scott, 2014, p. 230). The concept of a higher-order virtue that is necessary for the regulation of the others is an ancient one. For Aristotle this is the virtue of phronesis, variously translated as practical wisdom or common sense. A number of virtues of argument have been proposed as candidates for a higher-order role in VTA, notably "willingness to inquire" (Hamby, 2015) and "willingness to be rationally persuaded" (Baumtrog, 2016), Elsewhere, I have suggested that intellectual humility may function in this role (Aberdein, 2016b, p. 8). We have already noted the close affinity between intellectual humility and metacognition, which is naturally implicated in any project of higher-order regulation of thinking dispositions. Moreover, the other candidates appear to be subordinate to intellectual humility: if one's level of intellectual confidence is appropriately calibrated, then one should also be both willing to inquire and willing to be rationally persuaded; but if it isn't, one won't be. Nonetheless, as just remarked, the relationship between virtues is complex and multi-dimensional. For this reason, we should be cautious about any simple assignment of priority among virtues. Anything less would be a conspicuous failure of intellectual humility.

Notes

1 It should be noted that, although the explicit invocation of a principle of charity can be dated with confidence to the 1950s, the underlying sense of charity is manifestly older: Thomas Carlyle, for one, could write of a "charitable reading" almost a century earlier (Carlyle, 1865, p. 560).

2 The rhetorician John Duffy makes a complementary point: "to provide evidence is to subject one's self to the authority and judgment of another, which is a form of humility" (Duffy, 2014, p. 220).

3 On this basis, I am unconcerned by the apparent tension between the discussion of the *ad verecundiam* fallacy above as a failure of humility, and my earlier treatment of it as primarily a failure of recognition of reliable authority, treated as a subtype of willingness to listen to others (Aberdein, 2016a, p. 420). As I argue in that paper, we should not expect fallacies to map neatly to vices: which of these vices is uppermost will turn on features of the individual fallacious argument.

References

Aberdein, Andrew. 2010. Virtue in argument. *Argumentation* 24(2): 165–179.

Aberdein, Andrew. 2016a. The vices of argument. *Topoi* 35(2): 413–422.

Aberdein, Andrew. 2016b. Virtue argumentation and bias. In: *Argumentation, Objectivity and Bias: Proceedings of the 11th International Conference of the Ontario Society for the Study of Argumentation (OSSA), May 18–21, 2016*, eds. Patrick Bondy and Laura Benacquista. Windsor, ON: OSSA.

Aberdein, Andrew and Daniel H. Cohen. 2016. Introduction: Virtues and arguments. *Topoi* 35(2): 339–343.

Adler, Jonathan E. 2004. Reconciling open-mindedness and belief. *Theory and Research in Education* 2(2): 127–142.

Agnew, Lois. 2018. Intellectual humility: Rhetoric's defining virtue. *Rhetoric Review* 37(4): 334–341.

Aikin, Scott F. and John P. Casey. 2016. Straw men, iron men, and argumentative virtue. *Topoi* 35(2): 431–440.

Aikin, Scott F. and J. Caleb Clanton. 2010. Developing group-deliberative virtues. *Journal of Applied Philosophy* 27(4): 409–424.

Alfano, Mark, Kathryn Iurino, Paul Stey, Brian Robinson, Markus Christen, Yu Feng and Daniel Lapsley. 2017. Development and validation of a multi-dimensional measure of intellectual humility. *PLoS one* 12(8): e0182950.

Amaya, Amalia. 2018. The virtue of judicial humility. *Jurisprudence* 9(1): 97–107.

Bailin, Sharon and Mark Battersby. 2007. Reason appreciation. In: *Reason Reclaimed: Essays in Honor of J. Anthony Blair and Ralph H. Johnston*, eds. H.V. Hansen and R. C. Pinto, 107–120. Newport News, VA: Vale.

Bailin, Sharon and Harvey Siegel. 2003. Critical thinking. In: *The Blackwell Guide to the Philosophy of Education*, eds. Nigel Blake, Paul Smeyers, Richard Smith and Paul Standish, 181–193. Oxford: Blackwell.

Baum, Robert. 1975. *Logic*. New York: Holt, Rinehart and Winston.

Baumtrog, Michael D. 2016. The willingness to be rationally persuaded. In *Argumentation, Objectivity and Bias. Proceedings of the 11th International Conference of the Ontario Society for the Study of Argumentation (OSSA), May 18–21, 2016*, eds. Patrick Bondy and Laura Benacquista. Windsor, ON: OSSA.

Bereiter, Carl. 1995. A dispositional view of transfer. In: *Teaching for Transfer: Fostering Generalization in Learning*, eds. Anne McKeough, Judy Lee Lupart and Anthony Marini, 21–34. New York: Routledge.

Bowell, Tracy and Justine Kingsbury. 2015. Virtue and inquiry: Bridging the transfer gap. In: *Palgrave Handbook of Critical Thinking in Higher Education*, eds. Martin Davies and Ron Barnett, 233–245. London: Palgrave.

Carlyle, Thomas. 1865. *History of Friedrich II of Prussia, Called Frederick The Great*, vol.VI. London: Chapman and Hall.
Ciurria, Michelle and Khameiel Altamimi. 2014. Argumentum ad verecundiam: New gender-based criteria for appeals to authority. *Argumentation* 28(4): 437–452.
Cohen, Daniel H. 2005. Arguments that backfire. In: *The Uses of Argument*, eds. David Hitchcock and Daniel Farr, 58–65. Hamilton, ON: OSSA.
Copi, Irving M., Carl Cohen and Daniel Flage. 2007. *Essentials of Logic*, 2nd ed. Upper Saddle River, NJ: Prentice Hall/Pearson.
Davidson, Donald. 1984. *Inquiries into Truth and Interpretation*. Oxford: Clarendon.
de Bruin, Boudewijn. 2013. Epistemic virtues in business. *Journal of Business Ethics* 113(4): 583–595.
Duffy, John. 2014. Ethical dispositions: A discourse for rhetoric and composition. *JAC* 34(1–2): 209–237.
Green, Jerry. 2019. Metacognition as an epistemic virtue. *Southwest Philosophy Review* 35(1): 117–129.
Haggard, Megan, Wade C. Rowatt, Joseph C. Leman, Benjamin Meagher, Courtney Moore, Thomas Fergus, Dennis Whitcomb, Heather Battaly, Jason Baehr and Dan Howard-Snyder. 2018. Finding middle ground between intellectual arrogance and intellectual servility: Development and assessment of the limitations-owning intellectual humility scale. *Personality and Individual Differences* 124: 184–193.
Hamby, Benjamin. 2015. Willingness to inquire: The cardinal critical thinking virtue. In: *Palgrave Handbook of Critical Thinking in Higher Education*, eds. Martin Davies and Ron Barnett, 77–87. London: Palgrave.
Hoyle, Rick H., Erin K. Davisson, Kate J. Diebels and Mark R. Leary. 2016. Holding specific views with humility: Conceptualization and measurement of specific intellectual humility. *Personality and Individual Differences* 97: 165–172.
Johnson, Ralph H. 1984. Charity begins at home. *Informal Logic* 3(3): 4–9.
Kidd, Ian James. 2016. Intellectual humility, confidence, and argumentation. *Topoi* 35(2): 395–402.
Krumrei-Mancuso, Elizabeth J., Megan C. Haggard, Jordan P. LaBouff and Wade C. Rowatt. 2020. Links between intellectual humility and acquiring knowledge. *The Journal of Positive Psychology* 15(2): 155–170.
Krumrei-Mancuso, Elizabeth J. and Steven V. Rouse. 2016. The development and validation of the comprehensive intellectual humility scale. *Journal of Personality Assessment* 98(2): 209–221.
Leary, Mark R., Kate J. Diebels, Erin K. Davisson, Katrina P. Jongman-Sereno, Jennifer C. Isherwood, Kaitlin T. Raimi, Samantha A. Deffler and Rick H. Hoyle. 2017. Cognitive and interpersonal features of intellectual humility. *Personality and Social Psychology Bulletin* 43(6): 793–813.
Lepock, Christopher. 2014. Metacognition and intellectual virtue. In: *Virtue Epistemology Naturalized: Bridges Between Virtue Epistemology and Philosophy of Science*, ed. Abrol Fairweather, 33–48. Cham: Springer.
Locke, John. 1836. *An Essay Concerning Human Understanding*. London: Tegg.
McElroy, Stacey E., Kenneth G. Rice, Don E. Davis, Joshua N. Hook, Peter C. Hill, Everett L. Worthington Jr. and Daryl R. Van Tongeren. 2014. Intellectual humility: Scale development and theoretical elaborations in the context of religious leadership. *Journal of Psychology and Theology* 42(1): 19–30.
McElroy-Heltzel, Stacey E., Don E. Davis, Cirleen DeBlaere, Everett L. Worthington and Joshua N. Hook. 2018. Embarrassment of riches in the measurement of humility: A critical review of 22 measures. *The Journal of Positive Psychology* 14(3): 393–404.
Mill, John Stuart. 1977. On liberty. In: *Collected Works of John Stuart Mill*, vol. 18, ed. J. M. Robson, 213–310. Toronto: University of Toronto Press.
Morin, Olivier. 2014. The virtues of ingenuity: Reasoning and arguing without bias. *Topoi* 33(2): 499–512.
Overmyer, Sheryl. 2015. Exalting the meek virtue of humility in Aquinas. *The Heythrop Journal* 56(4): 650–662.
Paul, Richard. 1987. Critical thinking and the critical person. In: *Thinking: The Second International Conference*, eds. David N. Perkins, Jack Lochhead and John C. Bishop, 373–404. Mahwah, NJ: Lawrence Erlbaum.
Paul, Richard. 2000. Critical thinking, moral integrity and citizenship: Teaching for the intellectual virtues. In: *Knowledge, Belief and Character: Readings in Virtue Epistemology*, ed. Guy Axtell, 163–175. Lanham, MD: Rowman & Littlefield.
Porter, Tenelle and Karina Schumann. 2018. Intellectual humility and openness to the opposing view. *Self and Identity* 17(2): 139–162.
Quine, Willard Van Orman. 1960. *Word and Object*. Cambridge, MA: MIT Press.
Ritchhart, Ron. 2001. From IQ to IC: A dispositional view of intelligence. *Roeper Review* 23(3): 143–150.
Scott, Kyle. 2014. The political value of humility. *Acta Politica* 49(2): 217–233.

Scriven, Michael. 1976. *Reasoning*. New York: McGraw-Hill.
Siegel, Harvey. 1999. What (good) are thinking dispositions? *Educational Theory* 49(2): 207–221.
Spiegel, James S. 2012. Open-mindedness and intellectual humility. *Theory and Research in Education* 10(1): 27–38.
Stevens, Katharina. 2016. The virtuous arguer: One person, four roles. *Topoi* 35(2): 375–383.
Thomas, Stephen N. 1973. *Practical Reasoning in Natural Language*. Englewood Cliffs, NJ: Prentice Hall.
Wilson, N. L. 1959. Substances without substrata. *The Review of Metaphysics* 12(4): 521–539.

29
INTELLECTUAL HUMILITY AND ASSERTION

J. Adam Carter and Emma C. Gordon

29.1 Introduction

Recent literature suggests that *intellectual humility* is valuable to its possessor not only morally, but also *epistemically*—viz., from a point of view where (put roughly) epistemic aims such as true belief, knowledge and understanding are what matters.[1] Perhaps unsurprisingly, epistemologists working on intellectual humility have focused almost exclusively on its ramifications for how we go about forming, maintaining and evaluating our own *beliefs* and, by extension, ourselves as inquirers. Less explored, by contrast, is how intellectual humility might have implications for how we should conduct our practice of *asserting*. The present entry aims to rectify this oversight by connecting these two topics in a way that sharpens how it is that intellectual humility places several distinctive kinds of demands on assertion and, more generally, on how we *communicate* what we believe and know.

Here is the plan: Section 29.2 gives a brief overview of intellectual humility and why it's valuable; Section 29.3 introduces some of the main views in contemporary debate about the epistemic norms governing assertion; Section 29.4 then develops the two key ramifications for how valuing humility might shape how we go about asserting.

29.2 Intellectual humility

Intellectual humility is typically construed as something like the virtuous mean between intellectual arrogance and intellectual diffidence. Broadly speaking, the intellectually humble person is one who accurately assesses their intellectual strengths and weaknesses, and who is aware that their beliefs could be mistaken—even when those beliefs are deeply held, and on emotive topics like religion and politics (Church and Samuelson 2017, 2). When we lack intellectual humility, we're less likely to be open to revising our beliefs in light of new evidence, and less likely to work on improving problematic aspects of our intellectual character—and, thus, more likely to be led to error in our inquiries. Consequently, as noted above, intellectual humility is valuable from an epistemic point of view, helping us to avoid falsehood and to acquire epistemic goods like truth, knowledge and understanding.

There are now a range of competing accounts of intellectual humility, all of which interpret the above core ideas in a slightly different way. On the *underestimation view* (e.g., Driver 1989), intellectual humility is chiefly about underestimating one's intellectual strengths, accomplishments, social status and entitlements. On the *low concern for status view* (e.g., Roberts and Wood 2007), intellectual humility disposes one to have low concern for one's status and social standing. The *proper belief view* (e.g., Church and Samuelson 2017), by contrast, says that intellectual humility requires valuing one's beliefs as one ought to, and holding accurate beliefs about the epistemic status of one's own beliefs. By contrast, the *interpersonal account* (e.g., Priest 2017) maintains that intellectual humility requires "not [seeing oneself] as intellectually entitled" (p. 479)—a trait that allows one to help others achieve intellectual improvement by treating their intellects with the same respect one accords to oneself.

Finally, according to what is perhaps the most well-known account of intellectual humility—and one that we'll be drawing from in several places in what follows (e.g., Section 29.4.1)—the *limitations-owning account* (Whitcomb, Battaly, Baehr, and Howard-Snyder 2015) maintains that what's central to intellectual humility is being "appropriately attentive to" and "owning" one's intellectual limitations (2015, p. 516). Connecting this account of intellectual humility with issues related to norms of assertion (as we shall do in Section 29.4.1) requires clarifying the three main concepts referred to in their account—namely, (1) being appropriately attentive, (2) owning and (3) intellectual limitations. Firstly, to be attentive in Whitcomb et al.'s sense, one has to have a disposition for one's limitations to come to mind when it's appropriate to the context—this appropriate attentiveness is to be contrasted with obliviousness to limitations on the one hand, and obsession with limitations on the other. Secondly, to own one's limitations is to be disposed to have a range of appropriate cognitive, behavioural, motivational and affective responses to the aforementioned awareness of limitations. Thirdly, the nature of the relevant limitations is illuminated by examples provided by Whitcomb et al. (p. 516)—they discuss gaps in knowledge (e.g., ignorance of the political landscape), cognitive mistakes (e.g., forgetting to meet someone), unreliable processes (e.g., poor memory), deficits in learnable skills (e.g., being bad at spelling), and intellectual character flaws (e.g., frequently jumping to conclusions).

Accordingly, on the limitations-owning account, one is intellectually humble when one is properly attentive to and owns one's intellectual limitations—and, presumably, one is *virtuously* intellectually humble when one does this because one is appropriately motivated to pursue epistemic goods (e.g., truth, knowledge and understanding).

Having summarised some of the main perspectives on intellectual humility, we now turn to the debate about the epistemic norms governing assertion. From there, we will be well placed to consider some of the demands that virtuous intellectual humility places on our practice of asserting.

29.3 Epistemic norms governing assertion

Suppose a friend asserts to you that an event you were planning to attend together has just been cancelled due to an asbestos hazard. You accordingly cancel your taxi, change into your pyjamas and stay in for the night. The next day, however, you come to find out that the event *wasn't* actually cancelled, after all! It turns out you friend had simply made it up, asbestos and all, because he was feeling too lazy to make the effort.

There are many ways in which your friend's assertion is criticisable. One of them is morally. From a perspective from which what matters are things like *being a good person* and *doing the right thing*, your friend shouldn't have asserted what he did. But let's bracket the moral shortfalls of your friend's assertion and home in on an entirely different problem, one that has to do with (put roughly) your friend's take on the *accuracy* of what he was saying.

According to one very popular view in speech act theory, in the philosophy of language, as well as in social epistemology, your friend's assertion—one that is not only false but based on no evidence whatsoever—is going to count as defective for reasons that are entirely *epistemic.*[2] On this way of thinking, assertion, *as a kind of speech act*—viz., a speech act by which a sentence is uttered in the indicative or declarative mood—is normatively constrained in the sense that one should assert something, A, only if one possesses some (to-be-specified) epistemic credential (e.g., true belief, justified belief, knowledge), with respect to A. The matter of what this credential is supposed to be is controversial. But to the extent that this general idea is on the right track, an implication is that your friend may be understood as lacking the epistemic authority to assert what he did (fabricating on the basis of no evidence whatsoever is, after all, not asserting on the basis of a very good epistemic credential).

One of the first philosophers to appreciate that assertions are subject to this kind of criticism was G.E. Moore (1944, pp. 524–5), who registered that it seems paradoxical to assert a sentence such as the following:

(1) It is raining, but I don't believe that it is raining.

Asserting (1) would certainly sound odd. But here we need to be careful. The most obvious way that an assertion can be paradoxical is if *what is asserted* is (like the liar sentence—i.e., "This sentence is false") is semantically paradoxical, viz., if it is true only if false.[3] But notice that the content of (1) isn't paradoxical in the sense that the liar sentence is. After all, suppose that, when S asserts (1), *both* conjuncts are true: it is raining *and* you don't believe that it is raining (as might be the case if one asserts (1) when inside a windowless room, when it is in fact raining outside). In such a context of utterance, what one asserts when one utters the sentence in (1) would be a *true* proposition! So, in what sense did Moore think asserting something like (1) is *paradoxical*?

In order to appreciate what's amiss with asserting a proposition like (1), it's important to think not only about *semantics* of assertion but also the *pragmatics.*[4] Put another way, we need to look not only at what is *explicitly* said when one asserts something, but also at what is presupposed and implied.

For illustrative purposes, consider by way of comparison the speech act of *questioning*. You might ask:

(2) Is it raining?

In uttering a sentence like (2) in the interrogative mood, it's of course *possible* that you already know the answer to what you are asking (you might be pretending not to know, or just asking to see whether someone else knows). However, in normal circumstances, *by* uttering (2), you are thereby *representing* yourself as not knowing whether it is raining, or more generally as being in some way epistemically impoverished or *ignorant* with respect to the matter of whether it's raining; at least, you represent yourself as in need more information to settle the matter for yourself. And that's why (for example) asking "Is it raining?" while also making explicit that you *know* whether it's raining seems so odd. It's because you are *implying* one thing (ignorance) and then immediately and explicitly contradicting what you've just implied with what you say. As Hawthorne (2004, p. 24) puts it: *ceteris paribus*, we criticise people for asking what they already know because ignorance, incompatible with knowledge, is the *norm of questioning.*[5]

Asserting is, as a speech act, a kind of 'epistemological mirror image' of questioning, at least, in a mirror that reverses how it is you represent yourself, *epistemically*, with respect to the *content* of these respective speech acts. On one simple and popular way of thinking: ignorance is the norm of questioning just as knowledge is the norm of asserting; and so asserting stands to questioning as knowledge to ignorance.[6]

Williamson and others have attempted to get a lot of mileage out of this simple idea. For one thing, it looks as though if by asserting you represent yourself as knowing, then there's a simple story for why (1) sounds so odd. Knowledge asymmetrically entails belief. And so, if knowledge is the norm of assertion, then by asserting <"*It is raining, but I don't believe that it is raining*"> you represent yourself (via asserting the first conjunct) as believing something that you then immediately explicitly commit yourself to *not* believing by (via asserting the second conjunct) claiming that you *know* it.

Here, though, a clarification is needed. If the apparent paradoxicality of 'Moore-paradoxical' sentences like (1) were all that needed expla'ining by considerations to do with how we represent ourselves, when asserting, then we might be inclined toward something *weaker* than the Williamsonian line that knowledge is the norm of assertion. After all, if the idea that *belief* is the norm of assertion were true, then this would suffice to explain why (1) seems paradoxical.

But as Moore (1962, p. 277) had also observed—and as Williamson (1996) has drawn particular attention to—sentences like (2) *also* sound paradoxical, and not just sentences like (1).[7]

(3) It is raining, but I don't **know** that it is raining.

Moreover, challenges like "*You didn't know that!*" (and not merely: "*You don't believe that!*") sound perfectly reasonable when used as challenges to assertions made in ignorance. The best explanation for this and other data about our patterns of using 'know'[8] (and more generally, of asserting as a communicative practice) recommend, according to Williamson (2000, pp. 253–5), identifying the kind of epistemic credential that's needed to warrant assertion as not merely belief, or true belief,[9] or justified belief,[10] but *knowledge*. Expressed, as it often is, as a *necessary* condition on epistemically permissible assertion, the idea is as follows:

> **Knowledge Norm of Assertion (KNA-Nec):** one is properly epistemically positioned to assert that *p* only if one knows that *p*.[11]

But there might be more to the idea that knowledge is norm of assertion. As Mona Simion (2016) puts it:

> [...] it looks as if a knowledgeable speaker *need not do more* – regarding his warrant for p – in order to be in a good enough epistemic position to transmit testimonial knowledge that p to her hearer. Thus, for the characteristic epistemic purpose associated with the practice of assertion, knowledge seems to be both necessary *and good enough*.

The idea that speakers who assert knowledgeably are beyond epistemic reproach has led Simion, along with DeRose (2002) and Hawthorne (2004) to embrace, along with KNA-Nec, a further sufficiency thesis according to which:

> **Knowledge Norm of Assertion (KNA-Suff):** one is properly epistemically positioned to assert that *p* if one knows that *p*.[12]

Here is not the place to adjudicate whether knowledge is either necessary or sufficient for epistemically proper assertion.[13] Rather, the aim has been to just briefly outline both *why* assertion is thought to be normatively constrained, epistemically and then to register 'knowledge' as popular way to think substantively about such an epistemic norm. This will provide us with the relevant background to see how intellectual humility and assertion might interact in interesting ways.

29.4 Assertion and humility

Let's now connect the previous two sections; in particular, in what follows, we outline two distinct ramifications that valuing intellectual humility might have for debates about epistemic norms governing assertion. The first concerns polarisation and KNA-Suff and the second concerns the social-epistemic value of *forbearing* from asserting.

29.4.1 First ramification

Let's assume, for the sake of argument, the Whitcomb et al. view that a central element of intellectual humility involves being "appropriately attentive to" and "owning" one's intellectual limitations (2015, p. 516).

Within the class of intellectual limitations, it will be helpful to distinguish between two varieties: *individual* intellectual limitations and *social* intellectual limitations. The former, which Whitcomb et al. are principally concerned with, include various ways that individuals fall short in their capacity as inquirers (e.g., gaps in knowledge, cognitive mistakes, unreliable processes, deficits in learnable skills, etc.). Owning our individual intellectual limitations, however, may be only part of the story for what is needed to own our intellectual limitations in a way that a characteristically intellectually humble person should aspire to. Along with intellectual limitations that impede our capacity as inquirers, we also have intellectual limitations that impede our capacity to share and exchange information or rely on others. Call these *social intellectual limitations*.

Within the class of social (rather than merely individual) intellectual limitations, some are *socially inherited* and others are *socially triggered*. In socially inherited cases such as testimonial injustice (e.g., Fricker 2007), one's being regarded as having a certain negatively perceived epistemic property (e.g., "X is a minority" "X is a woman") is (unfortunately) often enough in itself to problematically limit a thinker in her capacity to communicate and exchange information.[14] Such individuals are on account of being perceived in this way not *believed* as they should be, even if they believe (and assert) as they should.

What will be of interest for us, however, are social intellectual limitations that fall in the *socially triggered* category. These are more complicated. Consider, for example, what happens in cases of *group polarisation*, which is the tendency of groups to incline towards more extreme positions (post deliberation) than those initially held by their individual members. When one is imbedded within a polarised group, one *becomes* unable to communicate information one knows to those with opposing views, though not because of any particular perceived property of the individual *per se* (as in cases of testimonial injustice) but rather because the dynamics of group polarisation function so as to counter the persuasive force of what one is arguing.[15]

A virtuously intellectually humble person will be suitably attuned to this kind of social intellectual limitation—and to the conditions under which it's triggered in group dynamics—and not *merely* to her individual intellectual limitations. Compare: the intellectually arrogant individual *fails to appreciate* that (in contexts of group deliberation) she is socially intellectually limited as she is. Imagine here your misguided friend who is shocked to see what happens when she attempts to debate politics on Facebook. She initially expects her friends (regardless of viewpoint) to be more deferential to her own testimony, assertions and viewpoint than they are. She falsely assumes her testimony will, in *that* context, carry epistemic weight that it turns out to lack almost entirely.

This is an example of a serious kind of social intellectual limitation,[16] one whereby a subject is severely limited in her capacity to share and exchange information. Virtuously humble individuals, *by owning* this social intellectual limitation just as they might own other *individual* intellectual limitations, do not *expect* their assertions, in such contexts, to perform the function that their assertions would ordinarily perform: the function of imparting *knowledge* (see, e.g., Kelp 2018).[17] Consequently, they are better at avoiding *assertoric misfires*: assertions that fail to fulfil their function of imparting knowledge.

At this point, it is helpful to make explicit an important connection between (i) the demands of virtuous intellectual humility; and (ii) the sufficiency leg of the knowledge norm of assertion. KNA-Suff (no less than KNA-Nec) is in the business of describing one specific sense in which our assertions are normatively epistemically constrained, one where the constraint is keyed to the epistemic position of the asserter *vis-a-vis* the truth of the proposition asserted. KNA-Suff says that, in the case of *this* normative epistemic constraint, "knowledge is enough" to satisfy it.

That might well be right.[18] But to the extent that we are inclined to the plausible idea that the function of asserting is (à la Kelp) to impart knowledge in the hearer, knowledge that the propositions one asserts are true won't be enough to ensure *that* function is fulfilled. Consider again the plight of the individual engaged in a fruitless and polarising Facebook political discussion, who is (unlike many of us who know better) surprised to find that her assertions seem to carry little weight in that context; even if she is asserting (by posting) *knowledgeably*, her assertions unreliably fulfil their aim; she is mostly asserting *in vain*.

What the knowledgeable asserter lacks in the above scenario, we submit, is a very specific form of intellectual humility: one whereby one suitably owns her social intellectual limitations and, in doing so, is attuned to the way in which she is limited in her capacity to communicate and impart knowledge to others. By owning *social* and not merely individual intellectual limitations, one is better positioned to avoid assertoric misfires in contexts where the risk of such misfires is higher than average and, in doing so, becomes a *better* asserter, one whose assertions more reliably fulfil their aim *as* assertions.[19]

Cultivating intellectual humility is, accordingly, valuable to the practice of asserting in a way that is not 'swamped' by the value of complying with the norm that one should assert only when one knows. In this way, we maintain, the ramifications humility has for our practice of asserting are important and worthy of further exploration.

29.4.2 Second ramification

In this section, we outline a further way in which valuing intellectual humility has ramifications for how we should conduct ourselves as asserters. Here we take as a starting point Priest's (2017) idea that essential to intellectual humility is not seeing oneself as *intellectually entitled* (2017, 479). One way an individual might see herself as intellectually entitled is by regarding herself as deserving of what is in fact an inflated level of credibility, either relative to what would be an accurate assessment of her own capacities, or relative to others' capacities. Compare, here, the successful CEO who, at a dinner party, expects others at the table to listen attentively when they speak on matters of politics and policy, while not affording others the same respect or attention.

With respect to the doxastic triad of belief, disbelief and the withholding of judgment,[20] those who have an inflated sense of entitlement will be prone to inflated levels of *self-trust*. A consequence of this kind of self-trust is that intellectually arrogant individuals will be inclined to *believe* on the basis of their initial intellectual assessments of things when they should withhold (or disbelieve) as well as *withhold* when they should disbelieve.[21] In this respect, intellectual arrogance (viz., the lack of intellectual humility) can harm us in our capacity as inquirers.[22]

But there is a flip side to this coin. Just as one who sees herself as intellectually entitled will believe when, instead, they should withhold judgment, they will also be inclined to *assert* when they should *forbear* from asserting; both of these mistakes flow naturally from a vicious sense of intellectual entitlement, as both are different ways of manifesting a regard of oneself as deserving of an inflated level of credibility.

KNA-Nec already offers a simple explanation for why we should refrain from asserting in those cases where our epistemic position with respect to what we are asserting is impoverished; we should assert only if we know. But what about situations when our epistemic position is good enough to warrant assertion but nonetheless *not as good as someone else's*,[23] where that other individual is also a potential informant on the matter. Here, it will be helpful to consider the following case:

> CPR: Aria is lying by the pool, nonresponsive. The only person close enough to assist is her aunt Kara, who does not know what to do to apply CPR. Fortunately, there are many friends standing on the balcony above (too high to safely jump down). One of these friends is an experienced paramedic. Another is Aria's uncle Jimmy. Jimmy knows what to do to do CPR only because the paramedic had told him the night before. Kara calls up to the balcony asking for instructions, noting that time is of essence. The paramedic begins speaking, but Jimmy interrupts and begins shouting the instructions.

Cases like CPR are importantly different from cases in which the capacity to inform is not a 'zero-sum game'. Compare, for example, Jimmy's situation as an asserter in the CPR case with his situation as an asserter as, say, student in a three-hour graduate seminar when everyone has an opportunity to wax expansively. In the grad seminar, Jimmy's asserting is not *at the expense* of others' assertions; in CPR, it is.

For the present purposes, let's assume for the sake of argument that KNA-Suff is correct, and thus, that Jimmy *is* properly epistemically positioned to assert what he does precisely because he knows what he says. There is a clear sense in which, *even so*, Jimmy's assertion is criticisable; once he made it, it passes epistemic scrutiny. And yet, epistemically speaking, *he shouldn't have made it*. He should have *forbeared* from asserting, deferring in his capacity as an informant to an expert. Epistemic norms governing proper assertion, like KNA-Nec and KNA-Suff give us no guidance as to when to forbear and when to assert within the class of cases where, if we assert, our assertion will pass epistemic scrutiny. Here, intellectual humility has a special value.

What prevents Jimmy from forbearing from asserting, as he ought to, is *not* any defect he has, epistemically, with respect to the truth of what he says. He knows what he says. The problem instead lies with his sense of intellectual entitlement; he views (like the CEO at the dinner party) his assertion as deserving of an inflated weight relative to others' assertions, and this leads him to refrain from forbearing from asserting on occasions when he ought to forbear.

The antidote to Jimmy's defect as an asserter is intellectual humility. One who *lacks* the sense of entitlement the lacking of which is (on Priest's view) at the core of virtuous intellectual humility, will not be inclined to overweight her own capacity to inform *in relation to others*, especially in cases where asserting comes at the expense of blatantly silencing known experts. Here again, we find a way in which cultivating intellectual humility is valuable to the practice of asserting in a way that is not 'swamped' by the value of complying with the norm that one should assert only when one knows.

29.5 Conclusion

The value of intellectual humility has been well explored, though thus far, not yet in its connection with the practice of assertion. Meanwhile, debates about the norms governing assertion have principally concerned themselves with describing how assertion is normatively epistemically constrained, where the constraint of interest is keyed to the epistemic position of the asserter *vis-a-vis* the truth of the proposition asserted. In so far as we value asserting well, this kind of normativity is limited. We've shown two ways in which intellectual humility can make us better asserters, and in ways that won't be secured simply by (even perfectly reliable) compliance with more traditional epistemic norms, such as the norm that one should assert only when one knows. In this respect, we've signalled to what we take to be valuable avenues for future research.[24]

Notes

1 For some representative recent work, see, for example, Whitcomb et al. 2015; Church and Samuelson forthcoming; Samuelson et al. 2015; Priest 2017; Gregg and Mahadevan 2014; Kallestrup and Pritchard Forthcoming; Spiegel 2012; Tanesini 2016a; Kidd 2016; Hazlett 2012.

2 See Brown and Cappelen (2011) for a notable collection of essays.

3 For discussion, see Beall, Glanzberg, and Ripley (2017).

4 See, for example, Pagin (2016) and Stalnaker (1978).

5 For further discussion, see Turri (2016).

6 This picture is embraced by Williamson (2017).

7 See Benton (2015) for a helpful overview of Moore-paradoxicality and the knowledge norm of assertion.

8 The infelicity of asserting that one's lottery ticket is a loser, even when odds are astronomically high that this is true, is another popular line of argument in favour of a knowledge norm on assertion. See, e.g., Hawthorne (2004).

9 For a defence of the truth norm of assertion, see Dummett (1959) and Weiner (2005).

10 For proponents of the view that one should assert that p only if p is rational or justified for one, see for example Lackey (2007), Douven (2006) and Kvanvig (2009).

11 Of course, sometimes we assert things in a way that is perfectly epistemically responsible, but and yet, what we assert nonetheless falls short of knowledge. This might happen on occasions where one asserts on the basis of misleading evidence, or in cases of 'Gettiered' assertions, viz., where one's assertion is justified and true but still fall short of knowledge. While critics of the knowledge norm of assertion appeal to such cases to argue that something weaker than knowledge is the norm of assertion, proponents have a ready diagnosis for these alleged problem cases: they are examples of *blameless* norm violations. For recent discussion on this point, see Williamson (Forthcoming).

12 For criticisms of the sufficiency leg of the knowledge norm of assertion, see for example Lackey (2011) and Carter and Gordon (2011).

13 Note that a further position one who accepts the KNA-Nec and KNA-Suff pair might embrace is that being subject to these norms is that it is *constitutive* of something's being an assertion that it is governed by the (relevant) knowledge norms. This is Williamson's (2000) own position. One needn't embrace the further constitutive claim by simply embracing KNA-Nec and KNA-Suff. For recent criticism of the position that there is one and only one norm that is constitutive of assertion, see Kelp and Simion (2016).

14 Consider, for instance, testifiers from marginalised groups whose assertions are not given appropriate evidential weight. Such individuals, in virtue of having a kind of unjust credibility deficit, are intellectually limited; such a perceived credibility deficit limits their ability to share and exchange information normally. It's debatable whether and to what extent one with virtuous intellectual humility should *own* this particular form of limitation, apart from simply recognising it. For social and moral reasons, the normative background within which this kind of marginalisation takes place should plausibly be strongly resisted.

15 It is debatable within social psychology what explains group polarisation. There are three principal views here. These include pervasive arguments theory, social comparison theory and social identity

theory. For an overview of these differing accounts of the mechanisms of group polarisation, see Broncano-Berrocal and Carter (2020).

16 To be clear, this kind of intellectual limitation described here is not an example of an *individual* intellectual limitation, as we've defined it earlier. One might be, individually, operating perfectly well despite being severely limited in her capacity to share and exchange information. Nonetheless, we submit that having one's capacity to share and exchange information subverted or undermined (including by environmental factors) is a kind of *social intellectual* limitation.

17 See, for example, Kelp (2018) for a sustained development of the view that the etiological function of assertion is to impart knowledge.

18 We have elsewhere challenged this idea, e.g., in Carter and Gordon (2011, 2016b, 2016a) and Carter (2017), though taking issue with KNA-Suff substantively is beyond the scope of what we aim to do here.

19 It's worth noting that not all failures to own this particular kind of social intellectual limitation implicate arrogance, even if owning them corresponds with a kind of intellectual humility. After all, one might potentially simply misjudged (albeit, in a responsible way) the group dynamics at play. Thanks to Alessandra Tanesini for raising this point.

20 See Feldman (2006); cf., Turri (2012).

21 Note that withholding, with respect to some proposition, *p*, might not be best described as a mere *absence* of any positive or negative epistemic attitude toward *p*; on some views, e.g., Friedman (2017), withholding, or suspending, judgment is a distinctive kind of inquiring attitude in its own right, one that is important to positive inquiry.

22 We are using 'intellectual arrogance' here simply as a contrast point to intellectual humility understood along Priest's (2017) lines. For some positive discussions of intellectual arrogance and what it might involve, see for example Tanesini 2016a; 2016b; Goldberg 2016; Gregg and Mahadevan 2014; Tiberius and Walker 1998.

23 This is a case of what Lackey (2011) calls *isolated second-hand knowledge*. Lackey appeals to cases of isolated second-hand knowledge to argue against KNA-Suff. Crucial to Lackey's argument is the idea that certain institutional roles carry with them certain epistemic expectations on the part of the asserter which are such that merely possessing second-hand knowledge will not always suffice to satisfy. In the present case, these kinds of considerations are not relevant, and for that matter, we are not appealing to the case in an attempt to challenge KNA-Suff. We are, however, sympathetic to Lackey's argument in this case (see, e.g., Carter and Gordon 2011). For opposition to the line that cases of isolated second-hand knowledge undermine KNA-Suff, see Simion (2016) and Benton (2014).

24 Thanks to Alessandra Tanesini for helpful feedback on a previous version of this chapter.

References

Beall, J.C., Michael Glanzberg, and David Ripley. 2017. 'Liar Paradox'. In: *The Stanford Encyclopedia of Philosophy*, edited by Edward N. Zalta, Fall 2017. Metaphysics Research Lab, Stanford University. https://plato.stanford.edu/archives/fall2017/entries/liar-paradox/.

Benton, Matthew A. 2014. 'Expert Opinion and Second-Hand Knowledge'. *Philosophy and Phenomenological Research*, 1–17. doi:10.1111/phpr.12109.

———. 2015. 'Knowledge Norms'. *Internet Encyclopedia of Philosophy*. www.iep.utm.edu/kn-norms/#SH1d.

Broncano-Berrocal, Fernando, and J. Adam Carter. 2020. *The Philosophy of Group Polarization*. London: Routledge.

Brown, Jessica, and Herman Cappelen. 2011. *Assertion: New Philosophical Essays*. Oxford: Oxford University Press.

Carter, J. Adam. 2017. 'Assertion, Uniqueness and Epistemic Hypocrisy'. *Synthese* 194(5): 1463–1476. doi:10.1007/s11229-015-0766-5.

Carter, J. Adam, and Emma C. Gordon. 2011. 'Norms of Assertion: The Quantity and Quality of Epistemic Support'. *Philosophia* 39(4): 615–635. doi:10.1007/s11406-011-9317-6.

———. 2016a. 'Objectual Understanding, Factivity and Belief'. In: *Epistemic Reasons, Norms and Goals*, 423–442, edited by M. Grajner and P. Schmechtig. Berlin: De Gruyter.

———. 2016b. 'Knowledge, Assertion and Intellectual Humility'. *Logos & Episteme*, 1 November 2016. doi:10.5840/logos-episteme20167444.

Church, Ian, and Peter Samuelson. 2016. *Intellectual Humility: An Introduction to the Philosophy and Science*. London: Bloomsbury Publishing.

Church, Ian M., and Peter L. Samuelson. Forthcoming. *Intellectual Humility: An Introduction to the Philosophy and Science*. London: Bloomsbury Academic.
DeRose, Keith. 2002. 'Assertion, Knowledge, and Context'. *Philosophical Review* 111(2): 167–203.
Douven, Igor. 2006. 'Assertion, Knowledge, and Rational Credibility'. *Philosophical Review* 115(4): 449–485.
Driver, Julia. 1989. 'The Virtues of Ignorance'. *The Journal of Philosophy* 86(7): 373–384. doi:10.2307/2027146.
Dummett, Michael. 1959. 'Truth'. *Proceedings from the Aristotelian Society* 59(1): 141–162.
Feldman, Richard. 2006. 'Epistemological Puzzles About Disagreement'. In: *Epistemology Futures*, edited by S. Hetherington, 216–236. Oxford: Oxford University Press.
Fricker, Miranda. 2007. *Epistemic Injustice: Power and the Ethics of Knowing*. Oxford: Oxford University Press.
Friedman, Jane. 2017. 'Why Suspend Judging?' *Noûs* 51(2): 302–326. doi:10.1111/nous.12137.
Goldberg, Sanford C. 2016. 'II—Arrogance, Silence, and Silencing'. *Aristotelian Society Supplementary Volume*, 90: 93–112. Oxford University Press.
Gregg, Aiden P., and Nikhila Mahadevan. 2014. 'Intellectual Arrogance and Intellectual Humility: An Evolutionary-Epistemological Account'. *Journal of Psychology and Theology* 42(1): 7–18.
Hawthorne, John. 2004. *Knowledge and Lotteries*. Oxford: Oxford University Press.
Hazlett, Allan. 2012. 'Higher-Order Epistemic Attitudes and Intellectual Humility'. *Episteme* 9(3): 205–223.
Kallestrup, Jesper, and Duncan Pritchard. Forthcoming. 'From Epistemic Anti-Individualism to Intellectual Humility'. In: Res Publica, edited by John Greco and Eleanore Stump, London: Philosophy and Theology of Intellectual Humility.
Kelp, Christoph. 2018. 'Assertion: A Function First Account'. *Noûs* 52(2): 411–442. doi:10.1111/nous.12153.
Kelp, Christoph, and Mona Simion. 2016. 'The C Account of Assertion: A Negative Result'. *Synthese*: 1–13.
Kelp, C., and Simion, M. 2020. 'The C Account of Assertion: A Negative Result'. *Synthese* 197: 125–137. doi:10.1007/s11229-018-1760-5.
Kidd, Ian James. 2016. 'Intellectual Humility, Confidence, and Argumentation'. *Topoi* 35(2): 395–402.
Kvanvig, Jonathan L. 2009. 'Assertion, Knowledge and Lotteries'. In: *Williamson on Knowledge*, edited by P. Greenough and D. Pritchard. Oxford: Oxford University Press.
Lackey, Jennifer. 2007. 'Norms of Assertion'. *Noûs* 41(4): 594–8211.
———. 2011. 'Assertion and Isolated Second-Hand Knowledge'. In: *Assertion: New Philosophical Essays*, edited by Jessica Brown and Herman Cappelen, 251–276. Oxford: Oxford University Press.
Moore, George Edward. 1944. 'Russell's "Theory of Descriptions"'. *Journal of Symbolic Logic* 9(3): 78–78.
Moore, George Edward, and Casimir Lewy. 1962. *Commonplace Book 1919–1953*. London/New York: George Allen & Unwin/Macmillan.
Pagin, Peter. 2016. 'Assertion'. In: *The Stanford Encyclopedia of Philosophy*, edited by Edward N. Zalta, Winter 2016. Metaphysics Research Lab, Stanford University. https://plato.stanford.edu/archives/win2016/entries/assertion/.
Priest, Maura. 2017. 'Intellectual Humility: An Interpersonal Theory'. *Ergo, An Open Access Journal of Philosophy* 4: 463–480.
Roberts, Robert C., and W. Jay Wood. 2007. *Intellectual Virtues: An Essay in Regulative Epistemology*. Oxford: Oxford University Press.
Samuelson, Peter L., Matthew J. Jarvinen, Thomas B. Paulus, Ian M. Church, Sam A. Hardy, and Justin L. Barrett. 2015. 'Implicit Theories of Intellectual Virtues and Vices: A Focus on Intellectual Humility'. *The Journal of Positive Psychology* 10(5): 389–406.
Simion, Mona. 2016. 'Assertion: Knowledge Is Enough'. *Synthese* 193(10): 3041–3056.
Spiegel, James S. 2012. 'Open-Mindedness and Intellectual Humility'. *School Field* 10(1): 27–38.
Stalnaker, Robert C. 1978. 'Assertion'. In: *Pragmatics*, vol. 9, edited by P. Cole, 315–332. Syntax and Semantics. Cambridge, MA: Academic Press.
Tanesini, Alessandra. 2016a. 'Intellectual Humility as Attitude'. *Philosophy and Phenomenological Research* 93(1): 399–420.
———. 2016b. 'I—"Calm Down, Dear": Intellectual Arrogance, Silencing and Ignorance'. *Aristotelian Society Supplementary Volume* 90(1): 71–92. doi:10.1093/arisup/akw011.
Tiberius, Valerie, and John D. Walker. 1998. 'Arrogance'. *American Philosophical Quarterly* 35(4): 379–390.
Turri, John. 2012. 'A Puzzle about Withholding'. *The Philosophical Quarterly* 62(247): 355–364.
———. 2016. *Knowledge and the Norm of Assertion: An Essay in Philosophical Science*. Cambridge: Open Book Publishers.
Weiner, Matthew. 2005. 'Must We Know What We Say?' *The Philosophical Review* 114(2): 227–251.
Whitcomb, Dennis, Heather Battaly, Jason Baehr, and Daniel HowardSnyder. 2015. 'Intellectual Humility: Owning Our Limitations'. *Philosophy and Phenomenological Research* 91(1).

Whitcomb, D., Battaly, H., Baehr, J., and Howard-Snyder, D. 2017. 'Intellectual Humility: Owning Our Limitations'. *Philosophy and Phenomenological Research*, 94: 509–539. doi:10.1111/phpr.12228.

Williamson, Timothy. 2000. *Knowledge and Its Limits*. Oxford: Oxford University Press on Demand.

Williamson, Timothy. Forthcoming. *Justifications, Excuses, and Skeptical Scenarios*, edited by Julien Dutant and Fabian Dorsch. The New Evil Demon. Oxford: Oxford University Press.

———. 1996. 'Knowing and Asserting'. *The Philosophical Review* 105(4): 489–523.

———. 2017. 'Acting on Knowledge'. In: *Knowledge First: Approaches in Epistemology and Mind*, edited by J. Adam Carter, Emma C. Gordon and Benjamin Jarvis, 163–181. Oxford: Oxford University Press.

30

HUMILITY, CONTINGENCY, AND PLURALISM IN THE SCIENCES

Ian James Kidd

30.1 Introduction

Humility is a complex concept with many meanings. The term 'science' is a complex umbrella term for a deeply pluralistic array of activities, institutions, and projects. This means that any discussion of humility in relation to science must be appropriately sensitive to these respective complexities. In this chapter, I start by sketching a general framework for thinking about the forms and roles for epistemic humility in the sciences, and then turn to two debates in the contemporary philosophy of science—contingency and pluralism—with implications for our ways of thinking about epistemic humility in relation to the sciences. If so, then humility and science can be related in a double sense. First, humility can be understood as an aspect of good scientific practice, maybe as an epistemic virtue of scientists, individually or collectively, or an epistemic norm guiding enquiry. Humility, of certain sorts, is essential to the proper conduct of scientific enquiry. Second, science can be a source of humility, in the sense that the deliverances of scientific enquiry could help to encourage a certain humility, if that's the right term, about our origins and significance, relative to the wider natural order as disclosed by scientific enquiry. Cashing this out is a delicate task, since much turns on how we define existentially complex matters about the meaning of human life. Some see science as a challenge to the religious traditions that, for them, confirm a sense of the meaningfulness of human life—something challenged by what critics, like Heidegger, have criticised as the 'disenchanting' scientific picture of the world. Some take the rival view, that the sciences provide an account of our origins and status that emphasises our particularity, of the sort captured in Stephen Jay Gould's sense that an appreciation of our evolutionary history can feed a 'deep humility for our status as a tiny and accidental twig on [the] luxuriating branching tree of life' (2011: 267). Others are prone to see needless excess in such existentially charged language of 'cosmic significance', arguing that science simply induces a sensible sense of epistemic humility, without any deep implications for the meaning and purpose of human lives.

Such existential forms of humility are not my concern in this paper, which focuses on the more tractable set of issues concerning epistemic humility—broadly stated, the reflective sense of the stability, contingency, and limitations of the knowledge and understanding made available through forms of scientific enquiry. Across all of its forms, the scientific enterprises that developed during the early modern period of European history were construed as having essential epistemic aims—to acquire epistemic goods, such as knowledge, or, ideally, truth of the origins, structure, and organisation of the natural, empirical world.

Cashing out that complex set of claims has been a matter of ongoing epistemological and metaphysical debate ever since, much of which has used a vocabulary of humility and its opposing traits, such as dogmatism and hubris. Philip Kitcher warns of the tensions between the 'epistemological modesty' of a properly fallible, reticent scientific enterprise and the scientific anti-realists' charges of 'metaphysical hubris' (Kitcher 2001: 22). Such philosophical tensions can have repercussions at the cultural level. Within forms of life that incorporate the sciences, they can generate destructive patterns of 'overconfidence' and 'disappointment', which Kitcher (2012: chapter 1) includes among the main drivers of the current 'erosion of scientific authority'.

30.2 Some initial characterisations

The sciences have contributed many images and metaphors that help us to conceive of the nature of humility. The more popular are exploratory metaphors of 'discovery', an 'ongoing quest for knowledge', 'pushing the frontiers of human understanding', and so on. Such images and slogans affirm both our current epistemic limitations and the possibility of overcoming or transcending them—a joint commitment to assess and, if possible, exceed our limits, which is constitutive of certain sort of active humility. Consider, in this respect, two famous images of humility, furnished by two distinguished English physicists.

Sir Isaac Newton offered a now-famous image of the humble scientist, 'standing on the shoulders of giants', a humble builder upon the greater work of earlier generations (quoted in Turnbull 1959: 416). Although insincere in Newton's own case, the image nicely expresses an *intergenerational conception of humility*: a sense of one's own dependence on the efforts of earlier generations, cooperatively building on the contributions of their predecessors, in an ennobling process of progressive, cumulative achievement. This stirring image informed the sociologist of science Robert K. Merton's famous 'norms of scientific enquiry', who devoted an entire book to tracing the history of the 'shoulders of giants' phrase (Merton 1942, 1965).[1]

Second, there is a beautiful image of epistemic humility offered by Joseph Priestley, the Victorian theologian, chemist, and natural philosopher, that of a growing circle of light which represents our ever-growing knowledge: '[t]he greater is the circle of light, the greater is the boundary of the darkness by which it is confined', such that 'the more light we get, the more thankful we ought to be' (Priestley 1790, 1: xviii–xix). With this image, Priestley conveys what we might call a *dynamic conception of humility*, an active sense that current limitations to our knowledge and understanding arise from contingent features of our investigative systems in ways that could be overcome with sustained investment and ingenuity. Humility of an active sort does not acquiesce in existing limitations, but encourages efforts to overcome them, the determination to do so being a main ennobling feature of scientific enquiry.

The 'shoulders of giants' and 'circle of light' images are powerful ways of conveying a sort of active humility, encouraging the scientific community to actively build upon achievements inherited and to gradually expand that circle of light. Within academic and popular discourses about science, this sense of active humility is perhaps most familiar from a sense of *progress*, of the sort built explicitly into conceptions of the natural sciences since Sir Francis Bacon and supercharged, during the 19th century, by Auguste Comte's 'Doctrine of the Three Stages'. If the sciences are properly performed, resourced, and respected, they will reliably deliver the goods, epistemically and practically.

Within the philosophy of science, the relationship of humility to science seems to have been articulated in at least three main ways. The first is that the epistemic imperatives of the scientific enterprise are grounded in a deep sense of humility, of the current limitations of our knowledge and understanding of the origins, structure, and processes of the empirical world, at the micro and macro scales. Our everyday experience affords some degree of knowledge and understanding about the nature of our world, although only to a very limited degree and, in any case, everyday experience is only an imperfect guide. Quite how much knowledge and understanding we can gain about the nature of reality is a central theme of the debates about scientific realism and anti-realism, underlying much of which is a latent vocabulary of humility—of the sort seen in the names of modern positions in that debate, such as 'modest realism' and 'perspectival realism' (Kitcher 2001: chapters 1–5, Massimi 2012).

Second, forms of humility have been regarded as integral to the epistemic discipline of scientific enquiry, therefore, to the individual and collective practice of scientific enquiry. This reflects the historical influence of the Christian tradition upon the European natural sciences, which were shaped by postlapsarian anxieties about the corrupted epistemic capacities of we 'fallen' creatures—a history well told by Peter Harrison (1990) and Sorana Corneanu (2011). If humility involves acceptance of our epistemic frailties, then the discipline of methodological enquiry offers a means of transforming ourselves for the better. Probably the most developed expression of this was Sir Francis Bacon's analysis of the 'Idols of the Mind', the set of intrinsic and acquired epistemic vices and failings which, on his account, had systematically impeded earlier projects of enquiry into nature (*Novum Organum* §§ 38–44).

A third way of articulating the relationship of humility to science is more epistemological, since it plays on the delicate balance within scientific enquiry of concepts such as certainty, dependence, fallibility, tentativeness, and the revisability of established truths. Much of the focus of 20th-century philosophy of science plays on these epistemological concerns, as one sees, for instance, in Karl Popper's vision of science as the fallible, self-correcting process of 'problem-solving', proceeding by 'conjectures and refutations' aimed at the 'falsification' of tentatively advanced hypotheses (Popper 1959, 1963),[2] or in Thomas Kuhn's (1962) argument that a pragmatic attitude of 'dogmatism' about current convictions is vital to scientific enquiry, as long as the possibility of periodic 'revolutionary' revisions is accepted, Consider, too, newer forms of the realism debate, such as the problem of unconceived alternatives, central to which is the insistence that entrenched epistemic limitations of scientific communities will forever prevent the identification of robust alternatives to existing fundamental theories (see Stanford 2006, and Bhakthavatsalam and Kidd 2019). In these and other debates, a vocabulary of humility plays a central role in critical, systematic thinking about the nature and possibilities of scientific enquiry.

30.3 Some broad claims

Based on these remarks, we can make some broad claims about science and humility. First of all, humility takes many *forms* in the sciences, although typically the focus is on *epistemic humility*. Historically, however, the sciences necessarily invoked concerns about other forms of ethical, existential, and spiritual humility, which is one reason that thinking about humility and science requires careful engagement with history of science. Second, humility operates at many different *levels* in the sciences, from the stances of scientific practitioners right through to multigenerational collectives to the wider scientific enterprise. Individual failures of humility, for instance, can be mitigated at the group level, by artful management of the composition and organisation of the community—this being one of the ways proposed by social epistemologists to operationalise individual epistemic vices, like dogmatism, within scientific communities (see Rowbottom 2011).

A third point is that humility in the sciences is typically *dynamic*, in a double sense. One is that the forms and means of scientific enquiry are constantly refined, for instance as new theoretical and technological developments offer new ways of extending, enhancing, or augmenting our individual and collective epistemic capacities (see Humphreys 2004). Second, the deliverances of the sciences are constantly changing as researchers offer new theories, discoveries, models, styles of reasoning, data sets, and so on. Consistent with the idea of active humility, these developments point to constant adjustments to the epistemic limits of scientific enquiry. All of these can transform estimates of the scope and stability of our current epistemic achievements and alter our sense of what count as tenable ambitions of enquiry.

A fourth point is that the relationship between science and humility is *problematic* and *contested*, as one sees very clearly in the ongoing epistemological and metaphysical debates about the sciences. Indeed, the existence of the philosophy of science is premised on the persistence and significance of those debates, most clearly when it comes to debates about scientific realism. We can distinguish two main sorts of challenge. First, *internal challenges*, inspired by reflections on the history, practice, and social organisation of the sciences as they have developed, which give grounds for critically rethinking our epistemic attitudes towards scientific practice and theory. A short list of internal challenges would include the pessimistic meta-induction (Wray 2015), the problem of unobservable entities, the underdetermination of theory by data, and scepticism about inference to the best explanation (see Chakravartty 2017: §§3–4).

Second, there are *external challenges*, from those who question the general epistemic ambition to provide what Bernard Williams called an 'absolute conception', an account of 'what there is *anyway*' (Williams 1978: 245). External challenges are diverse—Kantian arguments about our inability to transcend the structures of sensibility and experience, arguments about the fundamentality of metaphysics relative to natural science (Lowe 2006), phenomenological arguments that see scientific accounts of the world as prescinding from a more fundamental, taken-for-granted sense of 'being-in-the-world' that is presupposed by, and cannot be explained in terms of, scientific enquiry (Cooper 2002: chapters 8–10, Ratcliffe 2013)—to name just a few. The upshot of these challenges is genuine, substantive disagreement about the epistemic successes and ambitions of the sciences, and the range, kind, and fixity of the limitations relevant to enquiry.

30.4 Levels of humility in science

We can think about epistemic humility in the sciences as fundamentally involving efforts to respond appropriately to the multiply *conditioned* nature of epistemic confidence—the ways that the availability of certain materials, artefacts, and technologies structures the epistemic attitudes, activities, and ambitions available to scientific enquirers, and therefore affect what can be known and understood. To be epistemically confident is to stand in a certain relation to the attitudes, activities, and ambitions one has adopted or is considering adopting—a relation characterised by the expectation of the stability and efficacy of one's capacities, of the rightness of one's epistemic goals, the tenability of one's ambitions (where their successful realisation is anticipated) or their worthwhileness (where failure is a tangible possibility), coupled with the anticipation of success and a trust in one's ability to respond well to possible disruptions and contingencies (Kidd 2016a).

This conception of epistemic humility has a pragmatist character. To be epistemically confident is to be free of what Charles Sanders Peirce (1992: §4) famously called the 'irritation of doubt', which motivates *enquiry*: the active 'struggle' for 'settlement', a state marked by a felt sense of the relative stability of our commitments and the likely efficacy of our activities. Such settlement is a precondition for the styles of smooth, unanxious epistemic comportment which make for the most effective sorts of enquiry. I suggest that epistemic humility in the sciences ought to be conceived of as an active, reflective responsiveness to the contingent, conditioned character of our epistemic capacities and our wider epistemic activities, projects, and ambitions. (Note my terminological preference for *conditioned* over *limited*.) There are a variety of things that can condition the forms, scope, stability, and strength of our epistemic confidence, which can include *material conditions* (e.g. the availability of essential investigative technologies) to *social conditions* (e.g. the existence of a supportive community of peers) to *intellectual conditions* (e.g. the availability of suitably complex conceptual resources). Call these *confidence conditions*.

An advantage of this account of humility as a reflective appreciation of the conditioned status of our individual and collective epistemic life is that exposes certain attractive features of the scientific enterprise. We can think about the sciences as systematic efforts to develop and implement receptive material, social, and intellectual conditions for increasingly complex forms of enquiry. Within the Western tradition, this conception of science goes back to Bacon, whose proposals for the methodological disciplining of science and the collective direction of enquiry was intended to provide systematic means for nullifying our individual failings and to maximise the effectiveness of our pooled epistemic capacities and resources. Of course, there are legitimate worries about the extent to which the sciences, historically and in their current forms, actually deliver on this ideal: our scientific practices, communities, and institutions are shot through with gendered biases, suspect political and ideological influences, and other deliberate and contingent suboptimalities. Crucially, then, a proper sense of humility needs active acknowledgement of existing suboptimalities and appropriate ameliorative responses.

When applying this model of humility to the sciences, focus on *confidence conditions*. We can think about these as operating at three main *levels*—the *agential*, *collective*, and *deep*—with the provisos that these levels are interpenetrating, such that changes at one level can effect consequent changes at the others. Some of these conditions can be overcome, quickly and easily—for instance, uncertainty about the chemical composition of a substance will act to condition the confidence of a chemist tasked with its identification, but that can be solved by performing a straightforward laboratory test. In other cases, the confidence conditions will be harder to fulfil, due to practical, financial, epistemic, or other reasons The absence of a certain fossil conditions an archaeologist's confidence in a palaeontological hypothesis, which could only be fulfilled by the discovery of that fossil—something that cannot be guaranteed, given the practical expense of excavation and the enormous gaps in the fossil record. In some cases, fulfilment of the relevant conditions could be practically impossible, in ways that act as a perpetual constraint on one's epistemic confidence.

Consider the following examples of epistemic confidence at the three levels:

A. *Agential humility* is that that exercised by individual scientists, as they adopt, amend, or reject certain *epistemic attitudes*, or perform and reject certain *epistemic actions*, or accept, amend, or reject certain *epistemic ambitions*. Such agential confidence can be conditioned by, *inter alia*, the subject's cognitive, bodily, and perceptual capacities; the education and training available to them; the variety and degree of their practical skills and competences; the self-esteem and epistemic self-trust they have developed; and so on.

B. *Collective humility* is that exercised by scientific collectives, such as research teams or, at a larger level, the disciplinary communities characteristic of modern 'Big Science' (Galison and Hevly 1992). It includes confidence in shared values and norms; systems such as peer review and data-sharing; the integrity of the disciplinary community, and so on. Such collective condition is conditioned by the quality, stability and complexity of the structures of local and transnational scientific communities. As those conditions change, the confidence one can reasonably invest in the collective changes, too—the replication crises in psychology and biomedicine, for instance, are often described as 'crisis of confidence' (e.g. Pashler and Wagenmakers 2012).

C. *Deep humility* is motivated by the recognition that individual and collective epistemic activities depend for the intelligibility and salience on something beyond themselves. Objects of deep confidence could be a certain project of enquiry, an intellectual inheritance that provides shape and direction to a research agenda, or a metaphysical vision that provides what Heidegger (1977: 118f) called a 'ground-plan' for enquiry, that stipulates in advance the sorts of entities allowable for investigation. Such deep confidence is often sustained by wider cultural projects, too. Consider Husserl's (1970: 48) remark that 'science is [an] accomplishment which presupposes' a *Lebenswelt*, a 'surrounding world of life'. In these cases, what *counts* as humility is determined relative to a certain metaphysical vision or worldview (Kidd 2018a: §§ IV–VI).

Proper humility about science ought to attend to all of these levels, though not necessarily at each level at all times. The dynamics of agential confidence might be highly complex, while changes in the objects of deep confidence in science change very slowly, for instance, due to the influence of radical philosophical developments. Consider the ways that deep confidence in the capacity of human beings to describe the nature of reality was profoundly challenged by Kant's 'Copernican Revolution' (on this example, and others, see Kidd 2017a). Moreover, an estimation of the degree of confidence one can invest, at whatever level, is often subject to uncertainty and contestation. Kant's transcendental idealism, Nietzsche's genealogy, and the 'historical' and 'sociological' turns of the middle-third of the 20th century each challenged the prevailing forms of deep confidence in science, even if their pertinence and force was subject to vigorous counter-challenges.

Humility, then, depends on current conceptions of science, the nature and grounds of the confidence invested in science, and the types of critical challenge considered salient within a given cultural period.

30.5 Epistemic humility within the philosophy of science

The theme of epistemic humility will look different when considered in relation to different debates or topics. Contemporary philosophy of science offers a variety of candidates, of which I want to survey two—*contingency* and *pluralism*—each of which can inflect our conceptions of epistemic humility.

30.5.1 Contingency and science

Acceptance of the importance of engagement with the methods and results of the history of science is an established feature of the philosophy of science. Studying the ways that sciences have developed over time matters for all sorts of reasons, of course, although one of the more neglected reasons is that an historical sensibility discloses a deeper feature of the sciences—their *contingency*.

Taken broadly, contingency refers to the fact that the emergence, development, and entrenchment of the sciences was and continues to be shaped by various contingent events and processes—material, social, intellectual, cultural, and technological. These are contingent in the sense that they might not have occurred or might have occurred differently to the way that they did. Put that way, talk of contingency seems a historical banality, but during the last century, a variety of philosophers began to argue that reflection on contingencies motivates important changes in our epistemic attitudes towards the science. Crucially, contingency can reveal that our scientific inheritance is a product of social and historical accidents, rather than deliberations and decisions that vindicate *that* inheritance over its alternatives.

There are two broad styles of 'contingentist' argument, popular among some groups of philosophers, which are worth noting because they are popular, but ineffective. First, there are *constructionist* arguments, popular among sociologists of science from the 1980s onwards, which emphasise the socially constructed nature of scientific theories, which are presented as the products of personal ambitions, institutional politics, and much else (classic examples of such work are Pickering 1984 and Latour 1987). Second, a '*Baconian*' style of argument, according to which the modern sciences are fundamentally animated by the goals of mastery of nature, or, more broadly, to dominate nature, women, and aboriginal peoples (a classic is Merchant 1980). The force of these arguments is contested, with critics accusing them of using *non sequiturs*, or of exaggerating the role of contingent personal, social, and other factors (see, for instance, Hacking 1999 and, more polemically, Koertge 1998). In general, the contemporary debate is focused on a newer set of arguments, many of which play on connections between a properly epistemically humble attitude towards the sciences and an appreciation of their historical contingency.

30.5.2 The modern contingency debate

The most comprehensive treatment of the modern contingency debate is provided by Léna Soler (2008a, 2015a). She lays out a range of positions on a spectrum between *inevitabilism* and *contingentism* which are distinguished by their different answers to the guiding question of whether the sciences could have developed in ways different to how they did actually develop and still count as successful. A contingentist, for instance, can argue that a non-genic biology could have emerged and in principle been as successful, explanatorily, as the biology that did actually emerge (Radick 2005), for instance, or that phlogiston theory could have become entrenched in chemistry instead of oxygen theory (Chang 2009). In each case, what's often most in dispute is what Katharina Kinzel (2015: §4) calls the *challenge of decidability*—how, if at all, can claims about putative alternative developments of the sciences be decided in any principled way?

To see the connection of the challenge of decidability to humility, consider a standard objection to contingentist claim about the possibility alternative successful developments. It owes to Ian Hacking (1999, 2000), who calls it the 'put-up-or-shut-up' objection—PUSU. Put bluntly, it is a challenge to those make contingentist claims: 'put up or shut up. Show us an alternative development' (Hacking 2000: 67 and Soler 2015b: 55). More fully, a contingentist should either substantiate this talk by 'putting up' some relevant alternative to an established scientific theory—such as oxygen theory or Big Bang cosmology—or, if they cannot, to 'shut up' about them. The problem is that a contingentist is typically unable to actually provide for consideration a sufficiently well-developed alternative development, for the good reason that no one possesses the epistemic capacities required to conceive, articulate, and detail a range of alternatives developments, and then to compare them with the sciences which did actually emerge (Cooper 2002: chapter 8, Kidd 2016). The collective epistemic agency cannot be simulated by any lone theorist, given the scale and complexity of the necessary epistemic work, which, as Emiliano Trizio puts it, thereby forbids 'any private reconstruction of the entire edifice of knowledge' (Trizio 2008: 258). To hope or suppose otherwise is to exaggerate one's epistemic powers in a way that constitutes a failure of humility.

At the same time that a contingentist cannot 'put up' the well-articulated alternatives to existing scientific developments, a parallel concern about failures of humility arise for their inevitabilist rivals who issue the PUSU challenge. In their case, the problem is the difficulty of their being able to warrant claims about the *inevitability* of specific scientific outcomes. There is a general sense in which certain scientific outcomes become inevitable at a certain point in their histories—for instance, entrenchment of the Copenhagen interpretation of quantum mechanics was all but inevitable in the 1950s, unlike ten years before (Cushing 1994, Pessoa 2001). But the inevitabilist goes further by claiming that the range of possible developmental trajectories is sufficiently determined that we ought only to accept scientific theories broadly similar to those which did actually emerge (French 2008, Sankey 2008). The usual arguments invoke metaphysical considerations, although that is robustly challenged by the majority of participants in the contingency debate (an overview of which is provided by Soler 2018b and 2015b).

An impasse is reached, since neither the contingentist nor the inevitabilist can warrant their respective claims, in each case because they lack the necessary epistemic capacities to either put up their claims about the possibility of alternative development possibilities or the inevitability of the scientific theories and results which did, as a matter of historical fact, come to be entrenched. The impasse is noted by participants in the contingency debate, often in a vocabulary of humility. Hacking describes his own discussions of contingency and inevitability in science as 'deliberately non-conclusive' (2000: 58), for instance, while Trizio speaks of our epistemic predicament as being one where we must

> accept the existing science, without being able to rule out the possibility that it would have been different if the decisions of our predecessors had been different. And there is no way to prove that our predecessors had no choice, but to do what they did.
>
> *(2008: 258)*

Humility is therefore a fundamental theme that sustains the contingency debate since it concerns the limits of our abilities to warrant robust confidence in the deliverances of the sciences which came to be (see Aylward 2019, Tambolo forthcoming).

30.5.3 Deep contingency

A further and more radical form of humility can be encouraged by some philosophers who emphasise what might be called *deep contingency*, not of specific theories or outcomes, but rather of the scientific worldview or scientific 'picture of the world' (Kidd 2016). Historically, sensitivity to the deep contingency of science is clearest in Heidegger's (1977) remarks on the contingent 'ways of revealing' that made possible the development of our scientific 'world-picture' and Husserl's (1970) reflections on the 'crisis of the European sciences', to interesting remarks scattered through the later writings of Ludwig Wittgenstein (1980) and Paul Feyerabend (1999). What these authors share is a sense that, had history and culture gone other ways, a very different worldview or Weltbild could have emerged and become entrenched—one too different, in its ontology and laws, to count as a natural scientific account of any sort recognisable today.

The fullest account of this argument, which draws on the aforementioned philosophers, has been developed by David E. Cooper in his 2002 book, *The Measure of Things*, which has complex reflections on hubris and humility:

> [T]he failure of any rival to the scientific image to become our entrenched view was not due to the recognition, after patient and prolonged investigation, that the entities

> and processes postulated by the rivals did not pass muster in comparison with those proposed by physics [.] The fact is that no one has ever tried, in detail, to develop the 'research programmes' indicated by such rival images of reality, or to compare them, in terms of explanatory scope, with those of the natural sciences.
>
> *(Cooper 2002: 194)*

Against insistence that any rivals were doomed to fail, Cooper argues that the confidence expressed in their judgments could only be legitimate if the critic had epistemic capacities which they patently lack—those needed to 'survey such rivals, to work out their implications, to compare them with one another and with our entrenched scientific account', which no one does or could possess, and 'to pretend that we not only could, but actually do, is to be lacking in humility.(Cooper 2002:195).

Similar arguments are there in Wittgenstein and Feyerabend, as reconstructed by Cooper (2017) and Kidd (2017c), respectively. Their general form is that our confidence in our most fundamental sense of what the world is like is at least partly a product of a contingent set of historical developments, rather than of a careful chain of deliberation and decisions. Appreciation of that deep contingency ought to affect that background confidence by adjusting our attitudes, for instance, towards those putative alternatives—a sense that Feyerabend conveys poetically in terms of a proactive sense of the 'abundance' and 'richness' of ways of conceiving of and engaging with the world. Such deep humility, on his account, acts as a guard against a natural drift into more dogmatic attitudes towards the scientific pictures of the (see Feyerabend 1993, 1999; Oberheim 2006).

The current contingency debate in philosophy of science tends to play down talk of the deep contingency of science, although it does creep, for instance in Soler's suggestion that attending to it could help 'foster a profound change of spirit regarding science', not least by motivating deeper, more critical reflection on 'our scientifically based form of life' (2015a: 42). I have argued that acceptance of deep contingency is necessary if one wants to take up a radically critical stance on the sciences, since it compels us to consider extremely different ways that science could have been (Kidd 2013a, 2017c). But this brings us to a second theme—*pluralism*.

30.5.4 Pluralism

Contemporary philosophy of science is currently experiencing a 'pluralist turn', the turn to a descriptive and normative vision of the sciences as plural—theoretically, methodologically, axiologically. Starting from a rejection of the monism promoted by Thomas Kuhn (1962) and other early to mid-20th-century philosophers of science, several major developments within the discipline contributed to a revitalising perception of the pluralistic character of sciences. Some standout examples were the 'historical' and 'sociological' turns, which made clear the plurality to be found within actual scientific practice, and the array of normative arguments for pluralism developed by feminist philosophers of science. By the 1990s, the 'disunity' and 'plurality' of science was increasingly accepted (see, *inter alia*, Dupre 1993, Galison and Stump 1996, Kellert, Longino, and Waters 2006, and Mitchell 2003).

There are several ways that pluralism connects with the theme of humility. I focus on the *active normative epistemic pluralism* developed by Hasok Chang (2012: chapter 6), since he is most explicit about the constitutive connections of pluralism and humility. He distinguishes two forms of pluralism. First, *tolerant pluralism*, a weaker stance of tolerance for multiple systems of practice, each of them making its own distinct contributions, without any need for the systems to ever interact with one another. Tolerant pluralists accept the existence of alternative systems, forswear monistic ambitions to subsume them, and affirm the limitations of their own preferred systems (Chang 2012: § 5.2.2). Second, a stronger stance of *interactive pluralism*, which actively facilitates interaction between the different systems of practice, cultivating and mutually enriching them to maximise their individual and collective benefits. This interactive pluralist is motivated by a sense that the ontological complexity of the world can only be captured by a plurality of partial, overlapping, changing, and interacting systems (Chang 2012: § 5.2.3).

Chang's account of active normative epistemic pluralism arguably builds in a range of different forms of humility, each of which span the three levels described in Section 30.4. These include a reasonable humility about human epistemic capacities (2012: xx), acceptance of the limitations inherent to any epistemic practice (2012: 148), appreciation of human epistemic fragility and fallibility (2012: 238), an expectation that any successful system of practice will run up against its limitations sooner or later (2012: 258), a sense that reality is more abundant and complex than our minds can grasp through simple schemes (2012: 292), and a conviction that the fundamental nature or structure of reality is unknowable (2015: 363).

Gathering these points together, Chang makes explicit the significance of humility to his form of pluralism:

> The most fundamental motivation for pluralism is *humility*: we are limited beings trying to understand and engage with an external reality that seems vastly complex, apparently inexhaustible, and ultimately unpredictable. If we are not likely to find *the* perfect system of science, it makes sense to foster multiple ones, each of which will have its own unique strengths.
>
> *(Chang 2012: 255)*

Other pluralists add other connections, as when Dupré talks of pluralism as a 'therapy' against the 'monopoly of epistemic authority sustained by science' (1993: 262–263) and a check against attitudes, such as 'the lure of the simplistic' (2002), a determined preference for reductive, mono-causal responses to complexity. Others regard epistemic pluralism as one way of guarding against the monistic excesses found, for instance, in many forms of scientism (Dupré 2003: 112 and Kidd 2013b, 2018b).

Much work remains to be done articulating these and other connections between humility and pluralism, and, more widely, to contingency and other themes in philosophy of science. A humble appreciation of the role of a long chain of contingencies can encourage an active humility about our epistemic attitudes those achievements, perhaps by encouraging us to be less confident in their inevitability in ways that might encourage a more pluralist stance—the sort of humility encouraged in those images of standing on the shoulders of giants and the expanding circles of light.

Related topics

Chapters 0000

Biographical note

Ian James Kidd is an assistant professor of philosophy at the University of Nottingham, UK. His research interests include social and character epistemology, the philosophy of science, and the later work of Wittgenstein, Heidegger, and Husserl. He co-edited *Wittgenstein and Scientism* (2017, with Jonathan Beale), *The Routledge Handbook to Epistemic Injustice* (2017, with Gaile Pohlhaus, Jr. and José Medina) and co-edited *Vice Epistemology* (with Heather Battaly and Quassim Cassam 2020). His website is www.ianjameskidd.weebly.com.

Notes

1 Interestingly, the phrase was in standard use from at least the 12th century (Merton 1965: 293).
2 A good study of Popper's critical rationalism is Rowbottom (2010).

References

Aylward, A. (2019) "Against Defaultism and Towards Localism in the Contingency/Inevitability Conversation: Or, Why We Should Shut up about Putting-Up", *Studies in History and Philosophy of Science* 74: 30–41.

Bhakthavatsalam, S. and I.J. Kidd (eds.) (2019) *Unconceived Alternatives and Scientific Realism*, *Synthese* 196(10): 3911–3993.

Bowler, P.J. (2013) *Darwin Deleted: Imagining a World without Darwin* (Chicago, IL: University of Chicago Press).

Chakravartty, A. (2017) "Scientific Realism". In: E.N. Zalta (ed.), *The Stanford Encyclopedia of Philosophy*. https://plato.stanford.edu/entries/scientific-realism/.

Chang, H. (2009) "We Have Never Been Whiggish (About Phlogiston)", *Centaurus* 51(4): 239–264.

Chang, H. (2012) *Is Water H20? Evidence, Realism, and Pluralism* (Dordrecht: Springer).

Chang, H. (2015) "Cultivating Contingency: A Case for Scientific Pluralism". In: L. Soler, E. Trizio and A. Pickering (eds.), *Science as It Could Have Been: Discussing the Contingency/Inevitabilism Problem* (Pittsburgh, PA: University of Pittsburgh Press), 352–389.

Cooper, D.E. (2002) *The Measure of Things: Humanism, Humility, and Mystery* (Oxford: Clarendon Press).

Cooper, D.E. (2017) "Superstition, Science, and Life". In: J. Beale and I.J. Kidd (eds.), *Wittgenstein and Scientism* (London: Routledge), 28–38.

Corneanu, S. (2011) *Regimens of the Mind: Boyle, Locke, and the Early Modern Cultura Animi Tradition* (Chicago, IL: The University of Chicago Press).

Cushing, J.T. (1994) *Quantum Mechanics: Historical Contingency and the Copenhagen Interpretation* (Chicago, IL: University of Chicago Press).

Dupré, J. (1993) *The Disorder of Things: Metaphysical Foundations of the Disunity of Science* (Harvard, MA: Harvard University Press).

Dupré, J. (2002) "The Lure of the Simplistic", *Philosophy of Science 69/3, Supplement: Proceedings of the 2000 Biennial Meeting of the Philosophy of Science Association. Part II: Symposia Papers*, S284–S293.

Dupré, J. (2003) *Human Nature and the Limits of Science* (Oxford: Oxford University Press).

Faraday, M. (1834) "Experimental Researches in Electricity, Seventh Series", *Philosophical Transactions of the Royal Society* 124: 77–122.

Feyerabend, P. (1975) *Against Method: Outline of an Anarchistic Theory of Knowledge* (London: New Left Books).

Feyerabend, P. (1993) *Against Method*, 3rd ed. (London: Verso).

Feyerabend, P. (1999) *Conquest of Abundance: A Tale of Abstraction versus the Richness of Being*, ed. B. Terpstra (Chicago, IL: University of Chicago Press).

French, S. (2008) "Genuine Possibilities in the Scientific Past and How to Spot Them", *Isis* 99(3): 568–575.

Galison, P. and B. Hevly (1992) *Big Science: The Growth of Large-Scale Research* (Stanford, CA: Stanford University Press).

Galison, P. and D. Stump (eds.) (1996) *The Disunity of Science: Boundaries, Contexts, and Power* (Stanford, CA: Stanford University Press).

Gould, S.J. (2011) *The Lying Stones of Marrakech: Penultimate Reflections in Natural History* (Cambridge, MA: The Balknap Press of Harvard University Press).

Hacking, I. (1999) *The Social Construction of What?* (Cambridge, MA: Harvard University Press).

Hacking, I. (2000) "How Inevitable Are the Results of Successful Science?" *Philosophy of Science* 67: 58–71.

Harrison, P. (2007) *The Fall of Man and the Foundations of Science* (Cambridge: Cambridge University Press).

Heidegger, M. (1977) *The Question Concerning Technology and Other Essays*, trans. W. Lovitt (New York: Harper & Row).

Hookway, C. (2002) *Truth, Rationality, and Pragmatism: Themes from Peirce* (Oxford: Oxford University Press).

Humphreys, P. (2004) *Extending Ourselves: Computational Science, Empiricism, and Scientific Method* (Oxford: Oxford University Press).

Husserl, E. (1970) *The Crisis of European Sciences and Transcendental Phenomenology*, trans. D. Carr (Evanston, IL: Northwestern University Press).

Kellert, S., H. Longino and C.K. Waters (eds.) (2006) *Scientific Pluralism, Minnesota Studies in the Philosophy of Science*, Vol. XIX (Minneapolis, MN: University of Minnesota Press).
Kidd, I.J. (2013a) "Science and the Making of Modernity", *Annals of Science* 70: 105–107.
Kidd, I.J. (2013b) "Historical Contingency and the Impact of Scientific Imperialism", *International Studies in the Philosophy of Science* 27(3): 317–326.
Kidd, I.J. (2016) "'Inevitability, Contingency, and Epistemic Humility", *Studies in History and Philosophy of Science* 55: 12–19.
Kidd, I.J. (2016a) "Intellectual Humility, Confidence, and Argumentation", *Topoi* 35(2): 395–402.
Kidd, I.J. (2017a) "Confidence, Humility, and Hubris in Victorian Scientific Naturalism". In: H. Paul and J. van Dongen (eds.), *Epistemic Virtues in the Sciences and the Humanities: Boston Studies in the Philosophy and History of Science* (Dordrecht: Springer), 11–25.
Kidd, I.J. (2017b) "Reawakening to Wonder: Wittgenstein, Feyerabend, and Scientism". In: J. Beale and I.J. Kidd (eds.), *Wittgenstein and Scientism* (London: Routledge), 101–115.
Kidd, I.J. (2017c) "Other Histories, Other Sciences", *Studies in History and Philosophy of Science Part A* 61: 57–60.
Kidd, I.J. (2018a) "Deep Epistemic Vices", *Journal of Philosophical Research* 43: 43–67.
Kidd, I.J. (2018b) "Is Scientism Epistemically Vicious?" In: J. de Ridder, R. Peels and R. van Woudenberg (eds.), *Scientism: Prospects and Problems* (Oxford: Oxford University Press), 222–249.
Kinzel, K. (2015) "State of the Field: Are the Results of Science Contingent or Inevitable?", *Studies in History and Philosophy of Science* 52: 55–66.
Kinzel, K. (2016) "Counterfactuals, Causes, and Contingency in the History of Science", *Studies in History and Philosophy of Biological and Biomedical Sciences* 60: 92–96.
Kitcher, P. (2001) *Science, Truth, and Democracy* (Oxford: Oxford University Press).
Kitcher, P. (2012). *Science in a Democratic Society* (New York: Prometheus).
Koertge, N. (ed.) (1998) *A House Built on Sand: Exposing Postmodernist Myths About Science* (Oxford: Oxford University Press).
Kuhn, T.S. (1962) *The Structure of Scientific Revolutions* (Chicago, IL: University of Chicago Press).
Latour, B. (1987) *Science in Action: How to Follow Scientists and Engineers Through Science* (Cambridge, MA: Harvard University Press).
Longino, H. (2001) *The Fate of Knowledge* (Princeton, NJ: Princeton University Press).
Lowe, E.J. (2006) *The Four-Category Ontology: Metaphysical Foundations for Natural Science* (Oxford: Oxford University Press).
Massimi, M. (2012) "Scientific Perspectivism and Its Foes", *Philosophica* 84: 25–52.
McDowell, J. (1998) *Mind, Value, and Reality* (Cambridge, MA: Harvard University Press).
Merchant, C. (1980) *The Death of Nature: Women, Ecology, and the Scientific Revolution* (New York: Harper and Row).
Merton, R.K. (1942) "Science and Technology in a Democratic Order", *Journal of Legal and Political Sociology* 1: 115–126.
Merton, R.K. (1965) *On the Shoulders of Giants: A Shandean Postscript* (Chicago, IL: University of Chicago Press).
Mitchell, S. (2003) *Biological Complexity and Integrative Pluralism* (Cambridge: Cambridge University Press).
Oberheim, E. (2006) *Feyerabend's Philosophy* (Berlin: Walter de Gruyter).
Pashler, H. and E.J. Wagenmakers (2012) "Editors' Introduction to the Special Section on Replicability in Psychological Science: A Crisis of Confidence?" *Perspectives on Psychological Science* 7(6): 528–530.
Peirce, C.S. (1992) "The Fixation of Belief" [1877]. In: N. Hauser and C. Kloesel (ed.), *The Essential Peirce: Selected Philosophial Writings: Volume 2 (1867–1893)* (Bloomington, IN: Indiana University Press).
Pessoa, O. (2001) "Counterfactual Histories: The Beginning of Quantum Physics", *Philosophy of Science* 68(S3): S519–S530.
Pickering, A. (1984) *Constructing Quarks: A Sociological History of Particle Physics* (Chicago, IL: The University of Chicago Press).
Popper, K.R. (1959) *The Logic of Scientific Discovery* (London: Hutchinson).
Popper, K.R. (1963) *Conjectures and Refutations: The Growth of Scientific Knowledge* (London: Routledge).
Priestley, J. (1790) *Experiments and Observations on Different Kinds of Air, and Other Branches of Natural Philosophy, Connected with the Subject*, vol. 3, 2nd ed. (Birmingham: Thomas Pearson).
Radick, G. (2005) "Other Histories, Other Biologies". In: A. O'Hear (ed.), *Philosophy, Biology, and Life* (Cambridge: Cambridge University Press), 21–47.
Radick, G. (2008) "Counterfactuals and the Historian of Science", *Isis* 99(3): 547–584.

Ratcliffe, M. (2013) "Phenomenology, Naturalism, and the Sense of Reality", *Royal Institute of Philosophy Supplement* 72: 67–88.
Rowbottom, D.P. (2010) *Popper's Critical Rationalism: A Philosophical Investigation* (New York: Routledge).
Sankey, H. (2008) "Scientific Realism and the Inevitability of Science", *Studies in History and Philosophy of Science Part A* 39(2): 259–264.
Soler, L. (2015a) "Introduction. The Contingentist/Inevitabilist Debate: Current State of Play, Paradigmatic Forms of Problems and Arguments, Connections to More Familiar Philosophical Themes". In: L. Soler, E. Trizio and A. Pickering (eds.), *Science as It Could Have Been: Discussing the Contingency/Inevitabilism Problem* (Pittsburgh, PA: University of Pittsburgh Press), 1–42.
Soler, L. (2015b) "Why Contingentists Should Not Care about the Inevitabilist Demand to 'Put-Up-Or-Shut-Up'". In: L. Soler, E. Trizio and A. Pickering (eds.), *Science as It Could Have Been: Discussing the Contingency/Inevitabilism Problem* (Pittsburgh, PA: University of Pittsburgh Press), 45–98.
Soler, L. (ed.) (2008a) "The Contingentism versus Inevitabilism Issue", *Studies in History and Philosophy of Science* 39.
Soler, L. (2008b) "Are the Results of Our Science Contingent or Inevitable?" *Studies in History and Philosophy of Science Part A* 39(2): 221–229.
Soler, L., E. Trizio and A. Pickering (eds.) (2015) *Science as It Could Have Been: Discussing the Contingency/Inevitabilism Problem* (Pittsburgh, PA: University of Pittsburgh Press).
Stanford, K.P. (2006) *Exceeding Our Grasp: Science, History, and the Problem of Unconceived Alternatives* (Oxford: Oxford University Press).
Trizio, E. (2008) "How Many Sciences for One World? Contingency and the Success of Science", *Studies in History and Philosophy of Science* 39: 253–258.
Turnbull, H.W. (ed.) (1959) *The Correspondence of Isaac Newton*, vol. 1 (Cambridge: Cambridge University Press).
Williams, B. (1978) *Descartes: The Project of Pure Enquiry* (Harmondsworth: Penguin).
Wittgenstein, L. (1980) *Culture and Value*, trans. P. Winch (Oxford: Blackwell).
Wray, K.B. (2015) "Pessimistic Inductions: Four Varieties", *International Studies in the Philosophy of Science* 29(1): 61–73.

31
HUMEAN HUMILITY AND ITS CONTEMPORARY ECHOES

James Van Cleve

My source for "Humean Humility" is section 1.4.4 of Hume's *Treatise of Human Nature*, the section in which he gives his critique of "the modern philosophy." Hume contends that the world according to the modern philosophy—a world with primary qualities but no secondary qualities—is a world of which we can form no conception. There are echoes of Hume's premises (if not his conclusion) in two contemporary foci of philosophical attention: Russellian Monism, which agrees with Hume that there would be something defective in a world without anything like the traditional secondaries, but then, unlike Hume, goes on to attribute such qualities to the world, and Ramseyan Humility, which agrees with Hume that there must be more to any conceivable world than just structure with no underlying intrinsic or nonrelational properties, then goes on to argue that we could never know what these intrinsic properties are. In what follows, I examine all three views, as well as the merits of several possible lines of reply to them, of which the most prominent is causal structuralism.

31.1 Hume's critique of the modern philosophy

Hume's critique occurs in Book 1, Part 4, Section 4 of the *Treatise of Human Nature* (T 1.4.4), mainly in paragraphs 3 through 10 (T 1.4.4.3–10). Here is my reconstruction of Hume's argument, along with commentary on each of the premises:

1. *There are no colors or other secondary qualities in bodies* (paragraphs 3 and 4).

   Colors, sounds, and so on are only impressions in the mind, resembling nothing in bodies. This is the first main tenet of the modern philosophy. Some readers may think Hume is assuming it only as a premise for a *reductio ad absurdum*, but Hume rehearses the standard arguments for it and pronounces them "as satisfactory as can possibly be imagin'd" (T 1.4.4.4). For example, the distant mountain looks blue in the haze (it presents me with a blue impression), but when I get close enough to hike on it, I see that it is mostly green (it presents me with green impressions). Since the mountain itself did not change as I approached it, not all my color impressions resemble it, and the modern philosophy concludes that none do.

2. *Bodies have no properties but the primary qualities—extension, motion, and solidity (and others that entail one or more of these, such as figure)* (paragraph 5).

   This is the second main tenet of the modern philosophy, telling us what remains once the secondary qualities are removed.

   What is now to be shown is that if there are no secondary qualities in bodies, we cannot conceive of bodies as having primary qualities, either—in which case we cannot conceive of bodies at all (paragraph 6).

   We need to distinguish between two things that might be meant by saying such and such is not conceivable. On the one hand, it might mean that we can form no concept of such and such—in Hume's terms, that we have no idea of it. In his philosophy, this is most often the case when we have no impressions from which the idea might be derived. On the other hand, it might mean that some state of affairs is inconceivable in the sense that Hume takes to imply the impossibility of it—the sense that figures in his maxims that what is inconceivable is impossible and what is conceivable is possible (T 1.2.2.8 and many other places in the *Treatise*). It should be clear that something's being inconceivable in the first sense (inconceivability$_1$) need not imply its being inconceivable in the second sense (inconceivability$_2$). A blind man cannot conceive of the color red, but no one should conclude that it is impossible for there to be red things. To anticipate, Hume's conclusion is going to be that under the modern philosophy, bodies are inconceivable$_1$.

3. *We can conceive of bodies only if we can conceive of them as having (some of) the properties they actually have.*

   Hume does not explicitly state this premise, but there is a hint of it in T 1.4.4.10, and it is required for the validity of his argument. The alternative to admitting it would be very strange—it would be to hold that there are things we can conceive of only by putting them in a false light (or by not attributing any properties to them at all).

4. *We can conceive of bodies only if we can conceive of them as having one or more of the primary qualities—motion, extension, solidity.*

   This step, presupposed throughout Hume's argument, follows from 2 and 3. He is not forgetting other primary qualities such as shape—shapes are ways of being extended and cannot be conceived without extension.

5. *We can conceive of a body as moving only if we also conceive of it as extended or solid* (paragraph 7).

   Hume argues for this premise as follows:

   > [Motion] is a quality altogether inconceivable alone, and without a reference to some other object. The idea of motion necessarily supposes that of a body moving. Now what is our idea of the moving body, without which motion is incomprehensible? It must resolve itself into the idea of extension or of solidity.
   >
   > *(T 1.4.4.7)*

   Why not of color? Because, as the next paragraph reminds us, color is excluded from bodies by the modern philosophy.

6. *We can conceive of a body as extended only if we also conceive of it as either colored or solid*, that is, conceive of it as colored or conceive of it as solid (paragraph 8).

   In support of this premise Hume cites his own analysis of extension, given most explicitly at T 1.2.3.4–5. An extended thing is an array of indivisible points, and if these points are to be more than non-entities and amount to anything through their aggregation, they must be either colored or solid.

7. "*Color is excluded from any real existence*" (paragraph 8).

   This is just a reaffirmation of the first tenet of the modern philosophy. Colors belong only to impressions and ideas in our minds, not to any external bodies. The same goes for heat and cold and any other secondary qualities through which we might attempt to get a purchase on the extendedness of bodies.

8. *We can conceive of a body as extended only if we also conceive of it as solid* (paragraph 8). As Hume puts it, "The reality, therefore, of our idea of extension depends upon the reality of that of solidity, nor can the former be just while the latter is chimerical."

   At first glance, it may seem that 8 follows from 6 and 7, perhaps with the help of 3. On closer inspection, however, there is a non sequitur, which I am not sure how to repair. We would need a premise stronger than 3—one implying that we can conceive of a body as colored only if it actually *is* colored. But that is too strong—wouldn't Hume allow that we can *conceive* of bodies as colored, even if the modern philosophy is correct in arguing that they are *not* colored? Alternatively, we could make it a premise that we can conceive of bodies as colored only if it is *possible* for them to colored, adding that the modern philosophy rules out that possibility.[1] But I doubt that Hume credits the argument from independent variability with that much power—it only shows that bodies are not in fact colored, not that they could not be. I leave the proper rationale for 8 as an unsolved problem.

9. *We can conceive of bodies only if we conceive of them as solid.*

   This follows from 4, 5, and 8. Solidity is a property without which we cannot get any mental grip on what bodies are. Many of the moderns, including Locke, Reid, and Kant, would have agreed with Hume on this point.

10. *There is no way to understand solidity but this: to be solid is to resist penetration by other solid things* (paragraph 9).

    Hume equates solidity with impenetrability: "The idea of solidity is that of two objects, which being impell'd by the utmost force, cannot penetrate each other; but still maintain a separate and distinct existence." The equation was common in Hume's day. For Locke, solidity may have been the categorical basis of impenetrability rather than being identical with it,[2] but it was still a property that could only be understood in terms of impenetrability, which is all Hume's argument requires.

    Hume does not say in the sentence I quoted that to be solid is to be impenetrable by other *solid* things, but he arrives at that claim in short order. How are we to conceive of the other bodies by which a given body is impenetrable? Not by way of any secondary qualities, since these are excluded from bodies. By way of motion or extension, then? But according to premises 5 and 8, that would require that we conceive of those other bodies as being solid. Thus we can understand solidity only as a relation to other solid things.

11. *If 10 is true—if we can understand solidity only in terms of solidity—we do not understand solidity at all.*

    So what if we can understand solidity only in terms of itself, some may ask at this point—that just shows it is a primitive concept. Relatedly, there are sometimes small circles of mutually definable concepts where there is no prospect of a definition taking us outside the circle. That does not mean that no concept in the circle is understood; it just means that they are understood only if at least one is understood without need for definition. But Hume would deny that that is our situation here. It really is true that we can understand solidity only if we have a prior grasp of body or some other bodily mark, and that we can understand body only if we have a prior grasp of solidity. If that is the case, we do not understand either of them. As Hume puts it:

'Tis impossible, therefore, that the idea of solidity can depend on either of them. For that wou'd be to run in a circle, and make one idea depend on another while at the same time the latter depends on the former.

(T 1.4.4.9)

12. *'Our modern philosophy, therefore, leaves us no just nor satisfactory idea of solidity; nor consequently of matter'* (paragraph 9).

This is the conclusion I am entitling Humean Humility. It is not the thesis that it is inconceivable$_2$, that there be bodies, but the thesis that we can form no satisfactory conception of what they are. We should contrast this conclusion with two other conclusions that Hume sometimes seems to draw, one weaker and one stronger.

In announcing his conclusion at the start of the argument, he says that by depriving external objects of their primary qualities, "we reduce ourselves to the opinions of the most extravagant skepticism concerning [external objects]" (T 1.4.4.6). If by skepticism is meant the doctrine that we cannot *know* that external objects exist, this gloss is an understatement. Humean Humility is not a doctrine about what we can know, but about what we can even conceive of or entertain. It is conceptual skepticism rather than epistemic skepticism. Hume offers reasons for epistemic skepticism elsewhere (e.g., in T 1.4.2), but the upshot of 1.4.4 is conceptual skepticism.[3] His next sentence gets it right: "If colours, sounds, tastes, and smells be merely perceptions, nothing we can conceive is possest of a real, continu'd, and independent existence; not even motion, extension and solidity, which are the primary qualities chiefly insisted on" (T 1.4.4.6). Since having a continued and distinct existence is the mark of body in T 1.4.2, he is saying we cannot conceive of bodies.

The final sentence of the section gives another gloss of his conclusion, this one overstating it: "When we exclude these sensible qualities there remains nothing in the universe, which has [continu'd and independent existence]."

(T 1.4.4.15)

Here he advances beyond skepticism of either variety to nihilism: there are no bodies. This sentence is probably best taken as exaggeration for dramatic effect.

31.2. Russellian Monism

There are strong echoes of Hume's 1.4.4 in contemporary philosophy. "How can there be a world in which objects have primary qualities, but no secondary qualities?" ask J.J.C. Smart (1963), D.M. Armstrong (1961), and Simon Blackburn (1993), all seeing the question as a problem for the scientific realism they would otherwise like to defend. Smart and Armstrong credit Berkeley and Hume with having raised the question before them, Smart citing 1.4.4 as well as Berkeley's *Principles* 10 (Berkeley 1975, 92–93)

As Smart and Armstrong develop the problem, a critical aspect of it is that science seems to ascribe to objects relational properties only. Electrons have mass, charge, and spin, says Smart, but these are all relations—"What is the electron in itself?" (72). And Armstrong says, "If we look at the properties of physical objects that physicists are prepared to allow them such as mass, electric charge, or momentum, these show a distressing tendency to dissolve into relations that one object has to another" (1968, 74–75). But if something has relational properties, must it not have intrinsic properties, too?

Blackburn raises a distinct but similar problem. In his case, the problem is that science ascribes to objects nothing but dispositional properties (255). But if things have dispositional properties, must they not also have categorical properties to ground the dispositions? The concern looms that the worldview of science is at best incomplete and at worse inconceivable.

None of these authors believes that the problem they raise is insoluble. They believe either that a world of nothing but relations or dispositions is possible after all or, if not, that purely physical properties can fill the apparent gaps. But some recent authors have not been so sanguine. Under the banner "Russellian Monism," they advocate a cluster of views I enumerate as follows, guided by Alter and Nagasawa 2015b:

(1) Physics tells us only about the structural properties of the world. It ascribes no properties to fundamental things except relational and dispositional properties.
(2) Nothing can have relational and dispositional properties alone. Things with relational properties must also have intrinsic properties, and things with dispositional properties must also have categorical properties.
(3) Therefore, there must be properties of external things unknown to physics. Because they are unknown to physics, they are sometimes called *inscrutables*, even though on some views we are acquainted with them as properties of our own percepts, which according to Russell are the only intrinsic properties we know.

Tenet (1) is defended in various of the writings of Bertrand Russell from 1927 on.[4] It is defended by many philosophers of science today under the name "epistemic structural realism" (Ladyman 2016).

The twin tenets in (2), though contested, are defended by many metaphysicians. There is a tendency in discussions of our topic to roll them together: dispositional properties get equated with relational properties and categorical properties with intrinsic properties. The equations are mistaken. There are relations that are not dispositions, even if they imply dispositions: I am seated at my desk, and that is something that is occurring right now. Conversely, there are dispositions that are not relational; sugar has the disposition to dissolve in water, and that might be true even of a cube of sugar that was the only thing in the universe. Moreover, the thesis that dispositions must have a categorical basis is sometimes equated with the thesis that dispositions must have an intrinsic basis, and that equation is also mistaken. An object might be visible right now because it is placed against a dark background and bathed in bright light—to say that is to ground a disposition in categoricals, but not in intrinsics.

The dependence of dispositions on categoricals is typically held as a thesis of grounding: any disposition of a thing must be grounded in a categorical property, as the disposition to roll if released on a hill is grounded in roundness. The dependence of relations on intrinsic properties could also be advanced as a thesis of grounding, as it was by Leibniz (relations are grounded in qualities of the relata), but it need not be. One could hold that the relata of any relation must have intrinsic properties just because everything must have them—no concrete thing can have relational properties only.

If tenets (1) and (2) are both admitted, tenet (3) is the almost inevitable result:[5] there must be properties unknown to physics. What might they be? Alter and Nagasawa canvass four candidates. (a) They might be phenomenal properties or qualia, such as we experience in seeing a splash of red or hearing the F above middle C. (b) They might be proto-phenomenal properties, properties that are not themselves phenomenal, but are capable of compounding somehow into phenomenal properties. (c) They might be properties that are neither mental nor physical, but neutral. (d) They might be physical properties of a special sort, unknown to physics but physical nonetheless.

Option (a) verges on panpsychism, a view often thought extravagant, but taken seriously by some contemporary philosophers, including David Chalmers (1996, 297–299) and Galen Strawson (2019). Whether it would really be panpsychism depends in part on the relation of qualia to consciousness. If qualia are either modifications of conscious states or items that exist only as objects of conscious states, then consciousness would have to be present at a very fundamental level in the physical world. An advantage sometimes claimed for this possibility is that it not only provides us with the intrinsic properties missing from the worldview of physics, but makes it easier to comprehend how consciousness could arise in complex organisms—it is already present in some form in the basic building blocks.[6]

Option (b), proto-phenomenal properties, is advanced by Chalmers (1996, 127 and 154). It is hard to say much about it until it is more explicitly worked out. Option (c), neutral properties, has some overlap with the view Russell espoused under the name "neutral monism." He said that the properties we are aware of in introspection are by themselves neither mental nor physical, but are properties some constellations of which constitute minds and other constellations of which constitute matter. This is one reason why Russellian Monism is so called, but it need not be developed in this direction. On option (d), the inscrutables are physical properties, but properties of a special sort unknown to physics. This has been advocated by Derk Pereboom (2015).

It should now be clear in what ways Russellian Monism is and is not an echo of Hume. "The modern philosophy" and modern physics both describe a world that has primary or structural qualities only, and Hume and the Russellian Monists both say *nothing can be conceived as being like that*. For Hume, this is a case of inconceivability$_1$: we can form no conception of the modern philosopher's world, no "just idea" of it. For the Russellian Monists, it is a case of inconceivability:$_2$ we cannot see how a world could exist merely as described by science—all relation and no quality, all disposition and no basis, all form and no filling—or perhaps more strongly, we positively see that things could not be that way. The Russellian Monists fix the problem by positing properties not found in physics textbooks—perhaps phenomenal properties, akin to the secondary qualities Hume says are not there; perhaps inscrutable physical properties, of which Hume would say we have no idea because we have no resembling impression.

31.3. Ramseyan Humility

Rae Langton (1998) has offered a new reading of Kant's thesis that we have no knowledge of things in themselves. According to her, the thesis does not mean there is a class of things behind the scenes about which we know utterly nothing; rather, it means we have no knowledge of the intrinsic properties of the things we encounter every day—no knowledge of how they are "in themselves," though we may have knowledge of their relational properties. This is the thesis she calls Kantian Humility. David Lewis (2009) has taken over something like the thesis Langton attributes to Kant, given a new argument for it, and given it a new name: Ramseyan Humility.

In the statement "we have no knowledge of the intrinsic properties of bodies" there is an apparent echo of Hume, but there are two differences worth noting. First, in one way Lewis's thesis is more modest. As noted above, the skepticism affirmed by Hume is *conceptual* skepticism—we cannot even form a good conception of what bodies might be. The skepticism affirmed by Lewis is *epistemic* skepticism—he allows that we can conceive of various intrinsic properties of bodies, but argues that we cannot know which of these properties are actually instantiated by bodies. Second, in another way Lewis's thesis is more radical. Hume allows that we can know the intrinsic properties of *some* things—for example, the colors and shapes of our own impressions. But Lewis maintains that "humility spreads," making us ignorant even of the intrinsic properties of our own qualia.[7]

Lewis's argument for Ramseyan Humility consists of three premises—the Ramsey premise, combinatorialism, and quidditism.

To state the first premise, we must briefly review Ramsey's method for dealing with theoretical terms, which I shall do with a made-up example of a simple theory for explaining the tastes of apple and lemon juice. The theory may be written like this:

> Lemon juice contains negative particles, and whatever contains negative particles is sour; apple juice contains positive particles, and whatever contains positive particles is sweet.

The theory contains observational terms, such as "lemon juice" and "sour," which we understand because we are acquainted with the things or properties they stand for. It also contains theoretical terms, such as "positive particle," which stand for things or properties we are not acquainted with. How, then, are we to understand the theory? Ramsey proposed that we replace all the theoretical terms by variables and then write out the existential generalization of the resulting formula with respect to every variable, as follows:

> ∃F∃G(Lemon juice contains Fs, and whatever contains Fs is sour; apple juice contains Gs, and whatever contains Gs is sweet).

Gone now are the theoretical terms. We can understand the resulting formula—the Ramsey sentence for the theory—if we understand the observational terms plus logic.[8]

Now for Lewis's Ramsey premise. It is provable that a theory and its Ramsey sentence have all the same observational consequences, so two theories with the same Ramsey sentence have all the same observational consequences. Lewis assumes that any evidence we have for a theory must consist in its record of predictive success—in its observational consequences that come out true; hence that no amount of observation will tell us whether a given theory or another theory with the same Ramsey sentence is true; hence that we could never know which is true.[9] This is the epistemological premise in his argument, which combines with the other two premises to yield Humility as the conclusion.[10]

The second premise in Lewis's argument is combinatorialism. This is the principle that if the elements (including the properties and relations) in any possible situation are taken apart and rearranged (for example, one n-place relation switched with another), the result is again a possible situation. As applied to our toy theory, it implies that if the original was possible, so is the proposition expressed by

> Lemon juice contains positive particles, and whatever contains positive particles is sour; apple juice contains negative particles, and whatever contains negative particles is sweet.

To get from the original to the above, we have simply permuted the terms "positive particle" and "negative particle"—or, as Lewis also says, permuted the properties themselves in the realization of the original theory.[11] As Lewis notes, combinatorialism implies that the laws of nature are contingent. If it were necessary that positive particles make for sweetness, our permuted theory would not express a possibility.

The third premise is quidditism. Quidditism tells us that the result of permuting properties is not only a possibility, but a possibility distinct from the one we started with. "Two different possibilities can differ just by a permutation of fundamental properties" (209). The import of this will be better appreciated when we consider below structuralist views that deny it. It can also be appreciated by its analogy with haecceitism—the view that you can permute the individuals in a situation and get a distinct possibility.[12]

We can now see how the three premises come together to yield Ramseyan Humility. By combinatorialism, the properties of being positive and negative could change places. By quidditism, if they did, the result would be a possibility distinct from what we started with. And by the Ramsey premise, we could never know that one rather than the other of these possibilities was actual. This is one of countless cases in which we could not know which intrinsic properties are possessed by the particles composing this or that stuff.

How Humean are Lewis's premises? Lewis presents the combinatorial premise as a development of Hume's dictum that there can be no necessary connections among distinct existences. As for quidditism, Hume would agree if the permuted properties were observable properties, but in Lewis's argument they are theoretical properties, in which case the question may not arise for Hume. Insofar as the properties are theoretical, Hume would say they are properties of which we have no idea because no relevant impressions. What, finally, of the Ramsey premise? It is in the spirit of Hume's empiricism to say that if two theories have all the same observational consequences, we cannot know that one rather than the other is true; but that may only be because Hume would not allow any content to a theory over and above its observational consequences.

The main point of affinity between Lewis and Hume is that they both make assumptions that would be challenged by proponents of structuralism, to be examined in the next section.

31.4 Responses to Humean Humility, Russellian Monism, and Ramseyan Humility

A crucial premise in the argument for Humean Humility is the contention that if there are certain concepts that cannot be understood except in terms of each other, then they cannot be understood at all. In this section I discuss several challenges to this contention, all involving strategies for understanding concepts despite their interdependence or perhaps even in virtue of it.

31.4.1 Holistic understanding

According to a traditional argument for the existence of self-evident beliefs, when we inquire what justifies a belief, what justifies the justifier, and so on, there are only four possibilities: the series goes on forever, it runs around in a circle, it stops with items that are unjustified, or it stops with items that are self-evident (or epistemically basic). If the first three options are considered untenable, it follows that no beliefs are justified unless some beliefs are self-evident.

A response on the part of some coherence theorists is that the "run around in a circle" alternative has been two narrowly and simplistically conceived. It has taken justification to be *linear* (A is justified by B, which is in turn justified by C, which is in turn justified by D, … , which is in turn justified by A). But instead it should be regarded as *holistic*: A is justified by B and C and various other items in one's system of beliefs; B is justified by A and D and various other items; more generally, each item is justified not by any single other item but by some combination of them. A web of mutual support of this sort is supposed not to incur the objection to simple circularity.

We might adopt a similar model to defend the idea of holistic understanding—a coherence theory of concepts, as it is sometimes called. We understand concept F in terms of concepts G and H among others, G in terms of F and K, and so on; we understand each by knowing its relation to the rest. To make this work in the case of concern to Hume, we might have to add a few more concepts to body and solidity.

The holistic strategy may sound promising, but in the end I think it is no better off than the more simple-minded strategy. We may see this by restating its claims in terms of the relation of partial grounding. To say that P is partly grounded in Q is to say that for some item R, P is wholly grounded in Q and R. Restating the coherence theory above in these terms, we have it that our understanding of F is partly grounded in our understanding of G and that our understanding of G is partly grounded in our understanding of F. But nearly all contemporary theorists of grounding take as one of its axiomatic properties that it is *strongly asymmetrical*, in the sense that not only can two things not be wholly grounded in each other, but neither can two things even be *partially* grounded in each other (see Rosen 2010, 115–116). Understanding solidity and body each just partly in terms of the other would in that case be out of the question.

31.4.2 Reid's definition of straightness

Thomas Reid, though a pioneer of non-Euclidean geometry in his work on visual space, tried over a period of years to vindicate Euclid by showing that the parallel postulate of Euclidean geometry is provable from the other postulates. He thought we could do this if we used a better definition than Euclid's of straightness. Here is one of his own definitions crafted for the purpose:

> D1. Right line is that which cannot meet another Right line in more points than one, otherwise they perfectly coincide, and are one and the same.[13]

This definition turned out to be inadequate for the job, but that is not my topic. As Reid acknowledged, his definition is not of the standard form for definitions. In the standard form, we would say "L1 is straight iff ___." In this form, we say "L1 and L2 are both straight iff ___."

Can we use a similar strategy to define solidity? If we did, we would say

D2. B1 and B2 are both solid iff neither one can penetrate the other.

Hume's complaint was that solidity in one body could be understood only in terms of solidity in another, making for a circular definition. In this definition, we seem to be circumventing that difficulty by defining the joint solidity of two bodies; there is no need to mention solidity on the right.

It is a consequence of Reid's definition that if two lines intersect in more than one point, they cannot both be straight; at least one of them must be curved. But Reid's definition will not tell us *which* line is curved, and to that extent it may be regarded as not giving us a full understanding of straightness. Similarly, it is a consequence of D2 that if two items interpenetrate, at least one of them must not be solid.[14] But D2 will not tell us *which* of two interpenetrating things fails to be solid, and to that extent it does not give us a full understanding of solidity.

31.4.3 Causal structuralism

In an influential article, Sidney Shoemaker has advanced the view that properties are individuated by the causal powers they bestow on their bearers (1980). The Shoemaker view, dubbed causal structuralism by John Hawthorne (2001), can be developed in a way that challenges Humean Humility, Russellian Monism, and Ramseyan Humility all three.

Here is one of Shoemaker's formulations of his view:

> What makes a property the property it is, what determines its identity, is its potential for contributing to the causal powers of the things that have it. This means, among

> other things, that if under all possible circumstances properties X and Y make the same contribution to the causal powers of the things that have them, X and Y are the same property.
>
> *(Shoemaker, 212)*

He goes on to claim the following consequences for the view: the causal potentialities of a property are essential to it; properties having the same causal potentialities are identical; causal laws hold necessarily when they hold at all.

Shoemaker's view is antithetical to two of the premises in Lewis's argument for Ramseyan Humility. The combinatorial premise says that if a world is possible in which chilling water hardens it and heating water vaporizes it, so is a world in which heating and chilling have the opposite effects. This is not so if causal laws are necessary. The quidditism premise says that when you permute certain pairs of properties, you get a possibility distinct from the possibility you started with. This is not so if properties are individuated by their causal roles; if P plays a certain causal role at one time and Q at another, Q and P are the same property.

Shoemaker's view is also antithetical to Russellian Monism. The Russellian Monist insists that things must have intrinsic properties and therefore posits properties not yet known to physics. As pointed out in Langton and Lewis (1998), Shoemaker's view greatly reduces the number of intrinsic properties. One might think initially that the property of being an ellipsoidal star is intrinsic. But if the laws of nature are necessary truths, and if they permit a star to be ellipsoidal only if it orbits another star, then no star could be ellipsoidal unless there were another star. This would violate one of Langton and Lewis's conditions for being an intrinsic property, namely, that a solitary thing could have it. Shoemaker's view arguably also implies the stronger result that there are *no* intrinsic properties. This follows if we use one of Langton's further conditions for an intrinsic property: an intrinsic property is one that a thing could have even in the absence of laws (Langton, 119). Thus if sugar would no longer dissolve in water if certain laws were suspended, its water-solubility is not an intrinsic property. By this standard, no properties are intrinsic for Shoemaker, since none could be had in the absence of laws. Properties are what make the laws.

The respects in which Shoemaker is at odds with Ramseyan Humility and Russellian Monism are also respects in which he is at odds with Hume. Shoemaker would challenge Hume's contention that causal laws are contingent, as well as Hume's view that the redness of an impression is intrinsic to it. Shoemaker is also opposed to Hume in another way, which will be easier to see if we first consider his reply to an objection to causal structuralism by John Hawthorne.

Hawthorne's objection is that causal structuralism identifies properties we should regard as distinct. To see this, let us first state causal structuralism by reference to Ramsey sentences. Let causal laws be written in the form *AnB*, meaning that having property A nomologically necessitates having property B. Now take the conjunction of all the laws and construct its Ramsey sentence: replace all property constants by variables and form the existential generalization that contains quantifiers for each of these variables. Finally, define each property as the property that satisfies the open sentence that results if you delete "its" quantifier (that is, the quantifier containing the variable that replaced the constant for that property). In effect, this is to define each property as the property that plays a certain causal or nomic role. It is a consequence of this style of definition that each property bears the causal relations it does to all other properties essentially: if A did not nomically necessitate B, A and B would not be the properties they are.

Suppose now that there is a world containing just four properties, A, B, C, and D, related by just three law, AnC, BnC, and (A&B)nD. Here A and B must be regarded as distinct properties, for as Hawthorne notes, "Their coinstantiation has different effects (the addition of D to the world) than is produced by either being instantiated alone" (224). But A and B have the same definition in terms of Ramsey sentences. A is defined as the property F such that ∃G∃H∃K[FnH & GnH & (F&G)nK]. B is defined as the property G such that ∃F∃H∃K[FnH & GnH & (F&G) nK]. By rewrite of bound variables, the second definiens is equivalent to "the property F such that ∃G∃H∃K[GnH & FnH & (G&F)nK]," which is equivalent to the first definiens by commutation of conjuncts. The two definitions are so closely equivalent that they define the same property, in which case structuralism identifies properties that are intuitively distinct.

In a postscript to his article, Hawthorne notes that Shoemaker has said in reply that he had not envisioned defining properties in terms of Ramsey sentences in the manner described above. Instead, he proposes defining them as follows: Do not replace *all* property constants in the book of laws by variables, but only the constant A, the one you wish to define. Then say "A is the property V (a variable) such that VnC, BnC, and (V&B)nD." This does not merely say that A is the property that necessitates C and, along with some C necessitator, necessitates D; that would be equally true of B. It says that A is the property that necessitates C and, *along with B*, necessitates D. That is not true of B, so the distinction between A and B has been upheld.

But notice at what cost. If we defined B in the same manner, we would say that B is the property V such that AnC, VnC, and (A&V)nD—defining B in terms of A. We are defining A as the property that (among other things) couples with B to produce D, and we are defining B as the property that (among other things) couples with A to produce D. By mentioning the properties in the definientia by name rather than simply referring to them by quantified variables, we are committing a circularity—precisely the circularity thoroughly Ramsified functional definitions are supposed to avoid. It is also precisely analogous to the circularity Hume complains of in the attempt to define solidity in terms of bodies and bodies in terms of solidity.[15]

So we need to come to grips with the question whether defining each of two properties in terms of the other is a vice. It must be conceded that such definitions considered simply as identities might be totally true—for instance, A might indeed be the property that couples with B to produce D while B is the property that couples with A to produce D. But given the larger purposes the definitions are meant to subserve, the circularity does turn out to be vicious.

In Hume's case, the definitions are essential routes to our understanding of the concepts defined. If we understand what bodies are, it is because we understand what solidity is, and if we understand what solidity is, it is because we understand what bodies are. It follows that we do not understand either concept. If we did, we would understand each because we understand the other, which violates the asymmetry of "because."

In Shoemaker's case, the definitions are supposed to tell us what "makes a property the property it is." They are meant not merely to give us necessary truths about properties, but to give the essence of these properties in a more than merely modal sense—essence in a sense that might be spelled out by saying the property is the property it is *because* it is related thus and so to other properties. There is that "because" again, which must needs be asymmetrical. So the circularity Shoemaker proposes, like the one Hume exposes, turns out to be vicious, and Hume's case for Humility stands against the challenge from Shoemaker.

31.5 Conclusion

"If the world is as described by the modern philosophy (or in a way not going beyond physics), we cannot conceive of it." I side with Hume and the Russellian Monists—and against causal structuralists—in affirming that conditional statement. But should we then go on to affirm the antecedent or deny it? Here, I side with the Russellian Monists against Hume—the world has intrinsic properties after all, perhaps analogous to colors as naively conceived.[16]

Notes

1 The following counterpart of the argument from 6 and 7 to 8 is valid in modal logic: (6') N(Bx & Ex → Cx v Sx); (7') N(Bx → ~Cx); therefore, (8') N(Bx & Ex → Sx). (6') would be delivered by 'It is inconceivable$_2$ that a body be extended, yet neither colored nor solid' (a possible reading of 6) together with the principle that what is inconceivable$_2$ is impossible. And together with the converse principle that whatever is impossible is inconceivable$_2$, (8') would deliver 'It is inconceivable$_2$ that a body be extended, yet not solid' (a possible reading of 8). But nothing plausible would deliver (7'), as I point out in the text.

2 Locke says he uses the term Solidity "because it carries something more of positive in it, than *Impenetrability*, which is negative, and is, perhaps, more a consequence of *Solidity*, than *Solidity* itself" (1975, 2.4.1, 123).

3 For more on these two varieties of skepticism, both of which Thomas Reid found in Hume, see Van Cleve 2015, 53–56.

4 See Russell 1927 and the excerpts from Russell in Alter and Nagasawa 2015a.

5 But not logically inevitable unless (1) is read strongly as implying that physics ascribes no intrinsic and no categorical properties to things. It must be read as excluding the possibility, allowed by the twin tenets in (2), that every dispositional property is grounded in a categorical relational property and every relational property in an intrinsic dispositional property in an endlessly alternating downward sequence.

6 My own favorite argument for panpsychism proceeds from the need for simple substances to have intrinsic properties rather than from the need to solve the mind–body problem. It is an argument attributed by Kant to Leibniz and reconstructed in Van Cleve 1988.

7 Lewis's thesis is also more radical than Langton's insofar as it implies that in many cases we cannot know which of several candidate *relations*—not just which of several intrinsic properties—is instantiated by things.

8 The original presentation is Ramsey 1931; a good exposition is Psillos 2004. One of the artificialities of my toy example is that there is no sentence in the theory saying how the theoretical entities or properties are related to each other; to remedy that, we could add a sentence saying (for instance) that at certain distances, positives attract negatives.

9 For discussion of epistemological strategies that would let us know that one of the theories rather than the other is true despite their observational equivalence, see Schaffer 2004 (pro) and Locke 2009 (contra).

10 Some authors see Ramsey sentences as one way of articulating the "structure" that according to Russell is all that physics can tell us. See Psillos 2004 for critical discussion.

11 There is a serious typo in the version of Lewis's article in Braddon-Mitchell and Nola. In the fourth sentence of the second paragraph of section 4, the first occurrence of "F1" should be "F2."

12 As it happens, Lewis denies haecceitism despite accepting quidditism; he devotes several paragraphs of 2009 to defending this asymmetry.

13 Quoted in Wood 1998, p. 31.

14 What manner of thing might the nonsolid item be? Two possibilities are places themselves in the philosophy of Newton and extended souls in the philosophy of Henry More.

15 Above, I characterized Hume's circle as defining solidity in terms of solidity, but this small circle follows from the larger circle (solidity in terms of bodies and bodies in terms of solidity) by transitivity.

16 A longer version of this chapter, containing among other things discussions of dispositional monism, naïve realism, and the relations of bodies to places, is available on my USC website. I thank Matt Davidson, Janet Levin, and Adam Pautz for helpful discussion.

References

Alter, Torin, and Yujin Nagasawa (eds.). 2015a. *Consciousness in the Physical World: Perspectives on Russellian Monism*. New York: Oxford University Press.

Alter, Torin, and Yujin Nagasawa (eds.). 2015b. "What is Russellian Monism?" In *Consciousness in the Physical World: Perspectives on Russellian Monism*, edited by T. Alter and Y. Nagasawa, 422–451.

Armstrong, D.M. 1961. *Perception and the Physical World*. London: Routledge and Kegan Paul.

Armstrong, D.M. 1968. *A Materialist Theory of the Mind*. London: Routledge and Kegan Paul.

Berkeley, George. 1975. *Philosophical Works*, edited by Michael R. Ayers. London: J.M. Dent.

Blackburn, Simon. 1993. "Filling in Space." In *Essays in Quasi-Realism*, 255–258. Oxford: Oxford University Press.

Braddon-Mitchell, David, and Robert Nola (eds.). 2009. *Conceptual Analysis and Philosophical Naturalism*. Cambridge, MA: MIT Press.
Chalmers, David. 1996. *The Conscious Mind*. New York: Oxford University Press.
Hawthorne, John. 2001. "Causal Structuralism." *Philosophical Perspectives*, 15:361–378.
Hume, David. 2000. *A Treatise of Human Nature*, edited by David Fate Norton, and Mary J. Norton. Oxford: Oxford University Press. Cited as (e.g.) T 1.1.1.1 (for book, part, section, and paragraph numbers).
Ladyman, James. 2016. "Structural Realism." In *The Stanford Encyclopedia of Philosophy* (Winter 2016 Edition), edited by Edward N. Zalta. https://plato.stanford.edu/archives/win2016/entries/structural-realism/.
Langton, Rae. 1998. *Kantian Humility: Our Ignorance of Things in Themselves*. Oxford: Clarendon Press.
Langton, Rae, and David Lewis. 1998. "Defining 'Intrinsic'." *Philosophy and Phenomenological Research*, 58(2):333–345.
Lewis, David. 2009. "Ramseyan Humility." In *Conceptual Analysis and Philosophical Naturalism*, edited by D. Braddon-Mitchell and R. Nola, 203–222.
Locke, Dustin. 2009. "A Partial Defense of Ramseyan Humility." In *Conceptual Analysis and Philosophical Naturalism*, edited by D. Braddon-Mitchell and R. Nola, 223–241.
Locke, John. 1975. *An Essay Concerning Human Understanding*, edited by Peter H. Nidditch. Oxford: Clarendon Press.
Pereboom, Derk. 2015. "Consciousness, Physicalism, and Absolutely Intrinsic Properties." In *Consciousness in the Physical World: Perspectives on Russellian Monism*, edited by T. Alter and Y. Nagasawa, 330–323.
Psillos, Stathis. 2004. "Ramsey's *Ramsey-Sentences*." In *Cambridge and Vienna: Frank P. Ramsey and the Vienna Circle*, edited by Maria Carla Galavotti, 67–90. Dordrecht, The Netherlands: Springer.
Ramsey, Frank. 1931. "Theories." In *The Foundations of Mathematics and Other Essays*, edited by R.B. Braithwaite. London: Routledge and Kegan Paul.
Rosen, Gideon. 2010. "Metaphysical Dependence: Grounding and Reduction." In *Modality: Metaphysics, Logic, and Epistemology*, edited by Bob Hale, and Aviv Hoffmann, 109–135. Oxford: Oxford University Press.
Russell, Bertrand. 1927. *The Analysis of Matter*. London: Kegan Paul.
Russell, Bertrand. 2015. "Excerpts from *Analysis of Matter* (1927), *Human Knowledge: Its Scope and Limits* (1948), *Portraits from Memory* (1956), and *My Philosophical Development* (1959)." In *Consciousness in the Physical World: Perspectives on Russellian Monism*, edited by T. Alter and Y. Nagasawa, 29–57.
Schaffer, Jonathan. 2004. "Quiddistic Knowledge." In *Lewisian Themes: The Philosophy of David K. Lewis*, edited by Frank Jackson, and Graham Priest, 210–230. Oxford: Clarendon Press.
Shoemaker, Sidney. 1980. "Causality and Properties." In *Time and Cause*, edited by Peter van Inwagen, 109–135. Dordrecht, Holland: Reidel. Reprinted in Sydney Shoemaker *Identity, Cause, and Mind* (Cambridge: Cambridge University Press, 1984); my page references are to this volume.
Smart, J.J.C. 1963. *Philosophy and Scientific Realism*. New York: Humanities Press.
Strawson, Galen. 2019. "What Does 'Physical' Mean? A Prolegomenon to Physicalist Panpsychism." In *The Routledge Handbook of Panpsychism*, edited by William Seager, 317–339. New York: Routledge.
Van Cleve, James. 1988. "Inner States and Outer Relations: Kant and the Case for Monadism." In *Doing Philosophy Historically*, edited by Peter H. Hare, 231–247. Buffalo, NY: Prometheus Books.
Van Cleve, James. 2015. *Problems from Reid*. Oxford: Oxford University Press.
Wood, Paul. 1998. "Reid, Parallel Lines, and the Geometry of Visibles." *Reid Studies*, 2:27–41.

PART 6

The psychology of humility

32

HUMILITY IN PERSONALITY AND POSITIVE PSYCHOLOGY

Peter L. Samuelson and Ian M. Church

32.1 Introduction

Though "humble" might not be the first character trait to describe philosophers, a case could be made that the practice of philosophy demands a certain humility, or at least an intellectual humility, requiring such traits as inquisitiveness, openness to new ideas, and a shared interest in pursuing truth. All of these traits are markers of intellectual humility, and, while the pursuit of the truth may involve the practice of humility simpliciter, we feel that a volume on the Philosophy of Humility would be best served by a better understanding of intellectual humility and, as such, this will be the focus of this chapter.[1]

Moreover, there are a few theoretical reasons for focusing on intellectual humility as opposed to humility more broadly. Of course, we typically and naturally (and reasonably!) assume that intellectual humility is a subset of humility; after all, it's easy to assume that if we are talking about *intellectual* humility we're talking about a specific kind of humility. But we might at least wonder if humility could be viably understood as a subset of intellectual humility; perhaps, for example, humility is just being intellectually humble about how someone conceives of themselves. If this is correct, then perhaps the most parsimonious way to understand humility is by way of intellectual humility. Indeed, in a seminal theoretical piece in the psychology literature, Tangney (2000) grounds the definition of humility in two realms: a proper understanding of the self (accurate assessment, keeping one's abilities/accomplishments in proper perspective, low self-focus) and a certain intellectual disposition (acknowledging mistakes, intellectual openness). Various measures of humility have also reflected these dimensions (Davis et al. 2011; Landrum 2011; Rowatt et al. 2006). The honesty–humility dimension in the HEXACO, a trait assessment measure, assesses only accurate self-understanding (modesty, Ashton and Lee 2008). Perhaps some of the problems that have been encountered in the measurement of humility could find resolution if humility was seen as a component of intellectual humility. But even if we fall understandably shy of this fairly radical proposal, a weaker thesis might nevertheless suit our purposes for this chapter: that our understanding of the philosophy of humility could be significantly informed and developed by considering the emerging literature on *intellectual* humility.

We will begin with a discussion of intellectual humility as a character trait. The study of both humility and intellectual humility has been grounded in the methods and approach of personality psychology, specifically the examination of these virtues as traits. We will take a look at various well-known traits in the personality psychology literature, discussing the "Big 5" as they relate to intellectual humility, as well as other key traits related to cognition and the search for the truth. In this initial examination of intellectual humility as a trait, we use the terms "character trait" and "personality trait" interchangeably, though we recognize there is a case for making a distinction between the two (Miller 2014). We then examine the role of situations in the expression of intellectual humility, and for the interaction of "situation" and "trait." In the final analysis, it is the interaction of trait with situation that provides the most robust understanding of the psychology of any virtue, including humility and intellectual humility.

32.2 Intellectual humility as a character trait

The recent interest in studying virtues and character has been inspired by the positive psychology movement, but largely informed by the methods and approach of personality psychology. Peterson and Seligman (2004) in their seminal work *Character Strengths and Virtues* declare "the stance we take toward character is in the spirit of personality psychology and specifically trait theory" (p. 10). In their conception, virtues are core characteristics that are universally valued across cultures (wisdom, courage, humanity, justice, temperance, and transcendence) whereas character strengths (traits) are "the psychological ingredients – processes or mechanisms – that define the virtues" (p.13). Personality psychology defines a trait as an attribute of a person that is relatively long-lasting and stable (Funder 2010). Philosophers use similar language about character traits defining them as "relatively long-term stable disposition to act in distinctive ways" (Harman 1999). The key to the definition is that these characteristics, traits, and dispositions are expressed over the long term and are relatively stable across situations (Funder 2010).

Personality psychologists are interested in individual differences between people regarding the relative expression of traits. In this way the studies are often comparative, measuring how much a given trait influences an individual's thought and behavior compared to others who share the same trait. For example, when measured on the Big 5 personality traits (extraversion, agreeableness, conscientiousness, neuroticism, and openness), individuals show high or low levels of each trait relative to other people. Each trait is orthogonal; that is, a high or low score on any one trait does not influence the score on the other traits (McCrea and Costa 1987). Intellectual humility may, or may not, work in the same way. It may also have orthogonal characteristics relative to other character traits such that, for example, being high in intellectual humility may not impact how high or low a person is in courage or persistence. However, as with the Big 5, some character traits and virtues may show some kind of correlative relationship. For example, just as people who score low on neuroticism often score high on agreeableness and conscientiousness (Funder 2010), those high in intellectual humility may be high in forgiveness or prudence. It is also possible that intellectual humility may have different characteristics than personality traits, especially in regards to how to measure it or in the relative comparison of the trait between people. Unlike personality traits, it may have a moral standard to which it can be compared (per Miller 2014). We take no position as to if or how character strengths and virtues are distinct from personality traits, our initial interest is simply to understand the unknown (intellectual humility, a virtue with trait-like qualities) by comparison with the known (personality traits).

In this spirit, there may also be correlations between intellectual humility and existing traits related to information seeking, curiosity, and other epistemic pursuits. In this section, we highlight them in more detail: the need for cognition, (Cacioppo and Petty 1982), the need for closure (Kruglanski 1990), those traits from factor models of personality that relate to intellectual humility (The Big 5, HEXACO, and the Big 2), and the role of emotion and cognition.

32.3 Need for cognition

One of the individual differences that lends itself to the kind of open-minded thinking characteristic of intellectual humility is the "need for cognition," which is defined as "a stable individual difference in people's tendency to engage in and enjoy effortful cognitive activity" (Cacioppo et al. 1996, p. 198). People high in need for cognition expend more effort analyzing the content and quality of arguments (Haugtvedt, Petty and Cacioppo 1992), consider arguments central to the issue rather than peripheral features (Petty, Cacioppo and Goldman 1981), enjoy complex cognitive tasks (Cacioppo and Petty 1982), and are more attracted to messages that appeal to rational argument than emotion (Haddock et al. 2008). As with any trait, the preferences identified as "need for cognition" exist in people as a matter of degree, some showing low preference for this approach, others a high preference. Those with a high need for cognition use what Petty et al. (1981) call the "central" route of analysis which employs deliberative, rational processes whereas those with a low need for cognition take the "peripheral" route which relies on heuristics and attends to surface features (Haugtvedt et al. 1992). It is important to note that those high in need for cognition are more susceptible to context bias demonstrated in mood priming and primacy-recent effects. Cacioppo et al. (1996) aver that this is because those high in need for cognition form stronger initial attitudes compared to those low in need for cognition. When perceived biases are obvious or detectable, however, individuals high in need for cognition are more likely to make the cognitive effort necessary to correct their judgments and consider all the evidence.

Since those high in need for cognition are more curious, open-minded, and enjoy the search for knowledge, it may be one of the important characteristics that makes up intellectual humility (Cacioppo et al. 1996; Stanovich and West 1997). It reflects an intrinsic motivation for effortful cognition that is more process than results oriented, which can be developed and can change over time (Cacioppo et al. 1996). However, little research has been done on the development of the need for cognition. Although there may be a heritable component, some of the antecedent experiences that would contribute to its development would be those that reinforce a love of learning, experiences of mastery over subjects, a sense of control over one's learning, and experiences of coping with interpersonal problems through reason and verbal competence. Need for cognition is correlated with many important skills for optimal development.

32.4 Need for closure

Another extensively studied motivational characteristic that could have bearing on the psychology of intellectual humility is the need for closure (Kruglanski 1990; Kruglanski et al. 2009; Webster and Kruglanski 1994). "Closure," in this conception, means the need to make a decision, to have an issue *closed*. The concept is part of a general framework for the formation of all kinds of knowledge called lay epistemic theory (Kruglanski et al. 2009). This theory has as a fundamental assumption that knowledge is derived from evidence. Evidence can come from all sources, but a special category of evidence in lay epistemic theory comes from the testimony of other people (other people's opinions). Lay epistemic theory has noted individual differences in the process of hypothesis testing and evidence gathering. Individuals high in need for closure will take in and process less information before making a judgment and give preference to information met early in the decision-making process. Because of the early closure in the epistemic process they also have higher confidence in their judgments than those with a high need to avoid or postpone closure. They tend to be influenced in their judgment of people and their actions by preexisting stereotypes and prejudices, paying less attention to situational or individuating information. People high in need for closure will, for the most part, look to compare to those of similar mind and to reject or devalue others who do not share their perspectives and judgments (Kruglanski 1990). These attributes hold for what lay epistemic theory calls "non-specific" closure, which is a need for a firm answer to any question in order to avoid confusion and ambiguity. This need to avoid confusion and ambiguity may lead to a preference to "seize and freeze" early in the judgment process on information that is easily accessible and affords closure. A search for "specific" closure, by contrast means a person is looking for a particular answer to a specific question. A person high in this need (for specific closure) may actually postpone closure until a desirable answer that might bolster self-esteem or be more positive or optimistic can be found (Kruglanski et al. 2009). By closing off the gathering of evidence too early (non-specific closure) or by searching only for evidence that yields a desirable answer (specific closure) those who are high in need for closure are more susceptible to numerous cognitive biases (such as the availability heuristic or the confirmation bias). Using virtue language, they may be more susceptible to intellectual arrogance (and therefore less intellectually humble).

Lay epistemic theory affords a unique look at the issue of the self-centered nature of heuristics and biases. Heuristics and biases are those mental shortcuts we all make in order to navigate the world in order to not waste precious cognitive resources on processing routine or previously known experiences, or simply to reduce our cognitive load in everyday life (Kahneman 2011; Kahneman and Frederick 2002; Stanovich 1999; Evans and Stanovich 2013). While both the need for closure and the use of heuristic rules that preference easy to process evidence favor the self as a source of knowledge (i.e. figuring things out for oneself), as opposed to sources external to the self (e.g. relying on other people), the theory introduces another influence on the judgment process: epistemic authority. Kruglanski et al. (2009) define the concept of epistemic authority as "encompassing a combination of perceived expertise and trustworthiness … it addresses the extent to which an individual is prepared to rely on a source's information and to accept it as evidence for the veracity of the source's pronouncements" (p. 175). The key to the function of epistemic authority is in the comparison of the self to another. The decision to rely on the authority of another may depend in part on the perceived gap in epistemic authority between the other and the self. In combination with a need for closure, this could either lead to an over-reliance on the self as epistemic authority (intellectual arrogance) or a denigration of the self as an epistemic authority and an over-reliance on others (gullibility or "group think"). Intellectual humility in the context of lay epistemic theory may lie in a proper balance of a need for closure with an openness to new information and a tolerance for ambiguity, along with a capacity to discern when the self is enough of an epistemic authority or when others need to be sought out and relied upon.

32.5 Intellectual humility and personality: The Big 5

Considering intellectual humility within the framework of conceptions of personality such as the Five-Factor Model (The Big Five, McCrae and Costa 1987, 1997) and the HEXACO (Lee and Ashton 2004) leads in a promising direction. We can imagine that high levels of the Openness to Experience factor might correlate with high intellectual humility, especially when we look at specific facets of the Openness construct. The facet "openness to ideas," for example, seems to capture an element of curiosity we would expect to find in the intellectually humble; the "values" facet might figure into whether someone is willing to really consider an opposing political or religious view with charity. Similar corollaries of intellectual humility might exist within some facets of Agreeableness, Conscientiousness, and even Emotional Stability.

Along these lines, special attention might be given to the HEXACO model of personality which adds the dimension of Honesty–Humility (H) to the factors mentioned above (Ashton and Lee 2005). A connection between the H dimension and socially important criteria such as sincerity, fairness, and modesty has already been demonstrated (Ashton and Lee 2008). Additionally, the H factor has been negatively correlated with particularly vicious personality traits (e.g.: narcissism, psychopathy, Machiavellianism, materialism, and power-seeking) that we would expect to find somewhere opposite of intellectual humility (Ashton and Lee 2005, 2007): a finding which lends some support to the understanding of intellectual humility as involving a lack of concern for one's status. Not surprisingly, the H factor has also been used to show that the trait of humility is linked to higher social relationship quality (Peters, Rowatt and Johnson 2011).

Despite these helpful leads in the personality literature, it seems important to avoid oversimplified association of intellectual humility with certain personality traits. Even traits that seem to track with intellectual humility could have their own special hazards. For example, a trait like Openness could easily be an impediment to intellectual virtue if it leads to a kind of non-committal intellectual paralysis. And a person scoring high in Agreeableness might be too compromising, sacrificing intellectual honesty for likability.

As the psychology of intellectual humility is developing, various measures and constructs of intellectual humility are being tested against the Big 5 and the HEXACO in order to assess construct validity. Because of its epistemic dimension, Openness to Experience is often shown to correlate with measures of intellectual humility. Tenelle Porter (2015) tested her measure of intellectual humility with two different samples of adults and found significant correlations ranging from .26 to .40 with Openness to Experience. She also found significant correlations in both samples between her measure and Agreeableness and Conscientiousness, and in one sample with Extraversion. Krumrei-Mancuso and Rouse (2016), using a slightly different measure for Openness, also found a robust correlation between their measure of general intellectual humility and Openness (.40). They did not measure other constructs from the Big 5 but did find significant correlations between intellectual humility and general humility, open-mindedness, and tolerance. Price et al. (2015) tested their construct of "Open-Minded Cognition," a key component of intellectual humility, and found significant positive correlations with a variety of personality traits including openness to experience, agreeableness, emotional stability (the obverse of neuroticism) and conscientiousness. Leary et al. (2015) also found positive correlations with openness, along with measures of epistemic curiosity, and existential quest.

32.6 Intellectual humility and personality: The Big *2*

A recent development in personality and social psychology is a growing discernment of the importance of two main dimensions that are useful in guiding the description of personality traits, how those traits are perceived and judged in individuals, groups, and cultures: namely, agency and communion (Abele and Wojciszke 2007). Sometimes called the "Big Two" (Abele and Wojciszke 2013; Bruckmüller and Abele 2013), they are based on two "fundamental modes of existence" (Bakan 1966) that reflect two intuitive categories of social information processing: perspectives on the self and perspectives of other people. Thus, agency is related to what Able and Wojciszke (2007) call the "goal-pursuit of the self," while communion is related to "consideration of others" (p. 751). Each is identified by their differential focus, that is, agency as individual striving with its dimensions of competence, instrumentality, and power, and communion as social relatedness characterized by warmth, morality, expressiveness, and affiliation (Abele and Wojciszke 2013). These two categories can also be used as themes to organize the Big 5 traits with agency reflecting the personal growth dimensions of the traits (Extraversion and Intellect) and communion reflecting the socialization dimensions (Agreeableness, Conscientiousness, and Emotional Stability, Digman 1997).

Since agency is characterized by pursuing personal goals and exhibiting skills and accomplishments (traits such as competence, intellectual goodness, or dominance); and communion is related to forming and maintaining social connections (traits such as warmth, morality, social goodness, or nurturance, Bruckmüller and Abele 2013), intellectual humility, with its epistemic and social dimensions might fall in with either dimension of the Big Two. The intellectual dimension, with its focus on the pursuit of truth, might align it more on the agentic side, while the social dimension, with its emphasis on the social skills required for collaborative pursuit of knowledge, might land it more on the communal side (Samuelson et al. 2014).

Gregg, Mahadevan, and Sedikides (2017) used a cross-sectional design to examine patterns of relations that might occur between agency and communion on the one hand, and measures of intellectual arrogance and intellectual humility on the other. They operationalized communion (C) and agency (A) on three different levels: socially, as inclusion (C) and status (A); dispositionally, as warmth (C) and competence (A), and behaviorally, as amiability (C) and assertiveness (A) using self-report scales and items developed in previous research. Intellectual humility and intellectual arrogance were measured by novel instruments developed by the researchers. They found that the higher an individual's communal traits were (inclusion, warmth, and amiability) the more that person exhibited aspects of intellectual humility (were more rationally objective), while the opposite was true for those with higher agentic traits (they were less rationally objective). In addition, the higher an individual scored on the measures of agency, the more an individual showed a tendency toward intellectual arrogance (higher BIAS scores). Their conclusion was that high agency and low communion predicts high intellectual arrogance.

32.7 Both trait and situation in intellectual humility

We have been discussing intellectual humility as a trait with a certain expectation that, as a trait, it is fairly stable; that is, it will determine a person's behavior in most situations, except for some kind of reasonable response to changing circumstances. This gives us a basis by which we can describe a person as intellectually humble and so, depending on the efficacy of the measure used to determine whether or not any given person has what it takes to be intellectually humble, once we have made such a determination we might also have a basis on which to predict their behavior. We may even be able to correlate intellectual humility with some important life outcomes, especially in the interpersonal realm, like has been done with other traits like the Big 5 (Ozer and Benet-Martínez 2006).

There is some controversy in the field of social and personality psychology about the power of personality traits to influence behavior. People are not consistent in their behavior across situations (Fleeson 2004). For example, a person at wedding reception A is observed going from table to table, greeting each guest, laughing, and generally being the life of the party, while that same person, at wedding reception B is observed sitting alone most of the time, talking only to a handful of people. What is the difference? At wedding A he is the father of the bride and the "host" of the party. At wedding B he is a guest at the wedding of a distant relative and knows hardly anyone. Is this person an introvert or an extrovert? The answer is: it depends. The situation seems to be the determining factor. Or, to return to the example of the caricature of the arrogant philosopher: does philosophy attract people with intellectual arrogance or do the situations that philosophers are routinely found in call for the expression of that trait? What is important to study is not how traits make people behave in a certain way, but how people's perceptions of situations and their reactions to them make people behave in a certain way (Fleeson 2004, Funder 2010). We would describe such an approach as "interactionist," which recognizes that situations do have great influence in determining behavior but that the truth is that both come into play. Fleeson (2004) provides an apt description of the interactionist approach:

> The same person changes his or her behavior quite rapidly and frequently, presumably in response to changing situation … Although this within-person variance is large and presumably due to individuals adapting to situations, it is possible that individuals adapt such that they nonetheless maintain their relative position compared with others in the same situations.
>
> *(p. 85)*

There have been recent studies that take this interactionist approach to intellectual humility that have yielded fruitful insight. We highlight a few here.

Since the study of intellectual humility is still in its early stages, the first tasks in these investigations is to create measures of traits that are related to intellectual humility and then test them in different situations. Victor Ottati and his colleagues (Price et al. 2015; Ottati et al. 2015) have developed a trait measure for Open Minded Cognition which they describe as a "cognitive style … marked by a willingness to consider a variety of intellectual perspectives, values, attitudes, opinions or beliefs; even those that contradict the individual's prior opinion" (Price et al. 2015, p. 3). They take an interactionist approach, conceiving of Open Minded Cognition as comprised of both trait-like (dispositional) and situational components. Therefore, an individual's average level of open-mindedness across situations would be indicative of "an individual's chronic level of open-mindedness" (p. 5). By the same token, situations may merit increased or decreased levels of open-mindedness, depending on the reaction the situation demands. Price et al. (2015) explore open-minded cognition in three conditions: general open-minded cognition (OMC-G), political open-minded cognition (OMC-P), and religious open-minded cognition (OMC-R). They developed a measure to test for each. The six items of the measure are nearly identical. Three assess a person's openness to different or new opinions, arguments, and viewpoints, and three assess a person's resistance or "closedness" to arguments, ideas, or messages, especially those with which they disagree. The difference is the political measure inserts the word "political" before the words argument, ideas, opinions, etc., and the religious measure inserts the word "religious," while the general measure has no qualifier (e.g. I try to reserve judgment until I have a chance to hear arguments from both sides of an [political/religious] issue).

The evidence for trait expression in different situations in this study comes from the differential correlations of the three measures with other trait measures. For example, the general and political scales show a significant negative correlation with dogmatism, but the religious scale does not, whereas the religious scale correlates significantly with humility, while the other scales do not. A similar pattern is shown in relation to the Conscientiousness, Neuroticism, and Agreeableness subscales of the Big 5. All three measures correlate with three of the four subscales of Stanovitch and West's (2007) measure of Active Open-Minded Thinking, but only the political measure correlates with the "counter-factual thinking" subscale. From these results we see that across individuals, different contexts tap different kinds of characteristics and traits. Moreover, their results show that, within individuals, a person can have a high level of Open-Minded Cognition in one area, for example, politics, while having a low level in another, like religion.

Ottati and his colleagues (Ottati, Wilson and Price 2016) further examined the interaction of disposition and situation in Open-Minded Cognition. They constructed a model, called the Flexible Merit Standard Model, that can account for both disposition and situation in the expression of Open-Minded Cognition. They surmised that in any given situation, a person determines how much Open-Minded Cognition is merited, that is, across situations the standard by which one should be open-minded is flexible. That determination, of course, is influenced by how chronically open-minded that person is across situations. Therefore, the Flexible Merit Standard Model accounts for a trait x situation interaction in the expression of Open-Minded Cognition. From the results of this study they report:

> Clearly, *both* dispositional and situational forces are at play when individuals adopt a particular level of Open-Mindedness in a specific situation. In many situations, the dispositional and situational forces function as separate and independent sources of norm activation that produce additive effects (*Additive* Postulate). In some situations, however, individuals high in dispositional Open-Mindedness may be more responsive to the situation than individuals low in dispositional Open-Mindedness (*Discerning Open-Mindedness* Postulate).
>
> *(p. 30)*

Ottati et al. (2015) call this the "Joint Influence Hypothesis" and it confirms what Fleeson (2004) and others have asserted that neither dispositional tendencies or situation forces are adequate in explaining a person's behavior at any given time, but it is the interaction of the two in specific contexts that will determine how a person acts and reacts. This is an especially important insight for intellectual humility. As Price et al. (2015) show, there are differences even within a person depending on whether the situation is politics or religion. Knowing how important the interaction of situation and personality to human encounters could help us develop more civil ways of discourse, especially in politics and religion.

Mark Leary, Rick Hoyle, and their colleagues (Leary et al. 2015; Hoyle et al. 2016) took a similar interactionist approach to their study of intellectual humility. First, they devised and tested a general measure of intellectual humility (Leary et al. 2015) and tested it in a variety of situations. They wondered how intellectually humble people would act in a situation of disagreement (e.g. religion and politics). In one of their studies (Leary et al. 2015), they sorted the participants into two groups, those scoring low on their general intellectual humility scale and those who scored high. They then determined how religious individuals were within those two groups. Finally, participants were randomly assigned to read one of three essays on the effects of religion on individuals and society, one pro-religious, one anti-religious, and one offering a balanced view. Participants then rated how much they agreed with the essay, the accuracy of the beliefs of the writer, the impression they had of the writer on a number of personal qualities (e.g. warm or cold, moral or immoral), how they felt while reading the essay, and finally, answered a question on religion's effect on society on a positive to negative scale and how certain they were about their own personal religious views. They found that the higher people scored in the intellectual humility measure, the less certain they were of their views and the less they thought their views were superior to others. Moreover, though the majority of participants disagreed with the anti-religious essay, only those high in intellectual humility were more open to it. They preferred the balanced view and not those that were one-sided. The other situation they examined was people's reaction to politicians who change their minds. Those high in intellectual humility were more willing to vote for a candidate who changed positions on an issue than those who were low in intellectual humility.

Hoyle et al. (2015) hypothesized that people will be less intellectually humble the more specific the issue. Thus, while a person might be intellectually humble about politics in general, they may not be as intellectually humble about gun control, and may show even less intellectual humility about background checks for gun purchases. They found that, while there was a modest overlap between a person's scores on the general intellectual humility measure and the measures of specific intellectual humility, the correlation did not necessarily weaken as the issues became more specific. However, what they did find was that the more extreme a person's view on a specific issue (the more the strongly agreed or disagreed with an issue, such as "physician-assisted suicide should be legal in all states," the lower their specific intellectual humility. They also found that the method by which people came to their views had an impact on specific intellectual humility. Those whose opinions were formed by their own exploration and study were less intellectually humble than those who formed opinions by other means (e.g. from experts, anecdotal evidence, non-experts, "gut feelings," common knowledge, common sense, religious teachings, emotions, or evaluating facts and reasoning carefully).

32.8 Conclusion

In this chapter we have explored the situational and dispositional determinants of intellectual humility. We began first by positioning the study of intellectual humility in the tradition of personality psychology and examining those qualities of intellectual humility that appear relatively long-lasting and stable, therefore making intellectual humility look much like a personality trait. We proposed that, because intellectual humility is a complex phenomenon with many facets, it is likely composed of many traits and attributes already measured in social and personality psychology, such as some of the Big 5 (Openness to Experience, Agreeableness, Conscientiousness, and even Emotional Stability, McCrae and Costa 1987, 1997) as well as the Big 2 (agency and communion, Abele and Wojciszke 2007). We also looked at epistemic traits such as the need for cognition (Cacioppo et al. 1996) and the need for closure (Kruglanski 1990). Scholars have begun to define and measure intellectual humility (e.g. Porter 2015; Krumrei-Mancuso and Rouse 2016; Leary et al. 2015) and related traits (Open-Minded Cognition, Price et al. 2015) to examine its stability and expression across time and situations.

It has become clear that intellectual humility is also influenced by situations. We have seen an interactionist approach to the study of intellectual humility, measuring its expression in general and in specific situations (Ottati et al. 2015; Price et al. 2015; Hoyle et al. 2015; Leary et al. 2015). Ideas like the "Joint Influence Hypothesis" (Ottati et al. 2015) and studies that show differences in the expression of intellectual humility depending on the subject matter (Hoyle et al. 2015; Leary et al. 2015), demonstrate that no simple trait measure will suffice in determining how intellectually humble a person might be in any given situation.

So what are we to conclude? Is intellectual humility a stable and long-lasting trait or blown about by the winds of the situation? The answer is it is both. About the trait vs. situation debate, Fleeson (2004) concludes:

> There is no longer any need for debate because large within-person variability and the sensitivity of behavior to situations are not a threat to the viability of traits, and the power of traits is not a threat to the need to explain the considerable amount of within-person behavioral variability. It is time for the study of personality to go forward with both approaches.
>
> *(p. 86)*

We believe this holds true for intellectual humility as well. Measures that assess the relative disposition of intellectual humility in people are necessary to understanding this important intellectual virtue. Examining the situations that either promote or inhibit the expression of intellectual humility is also a critical line of investigation. Testing the trait of intellectual humility in various situations will yield critical knowledge of how intellectual humility plays out. The later line of research – the trait × situation interaction – may be most informative in promoting conditions for more civil discourse, especially in areas of disagreement. Learning how to exchange ideas in an intellectually humble way, and the situations which might promote such exchange, would make a positive impact on the field of philosophy in particular, and on our society in general.

Note

1 In addition, most of our work has been in the philosophy and science of intellectual humility, and we feel that we have the most to contribute to this volume with a focus on that topic. See, for example, Church 2016, 2017; Samuelson and Church 2014; Samuelson et al. 2015; Church and Samuelson 2017; Church and Barrett 2017.

References

Abele, A. E. and Wojciszke, B. (2007). Agency and communion from the perspective of self versus others. *Journal of Personality and Social Psychology*, 93(5), pp. 751–763. doi: 10.1037/0022-3514.93.5.751

Abele, A. E. and Wojciszke, B. (2013). The big two in social judgment and behavior. *Social Psychology*, 44(2), pp. 61–62. doi: 10.1027/1864-9335/a000137

Ashton, M. C. and Lee, K. (2005). Honesty-humility, the big five, and the five-factor model. *Journal of Personality*, 73(5), pp. 1321–1353. doi: 10.1111/j.1467-6494.2005.00351.x

Ashton, M. C. and Lee, K. (2007). Empirical, theoretical, and practical advantages of the HEXACO model of personality structure. *Personality and Social Psychology Review*, 11(2), pp. 150–166. doi: 10.1177/1088868306294907

Ashton, M. C. and Lee, K. (2008). The HEXACO model of personality structure and the importance of the H factor. *Social and Personality Psychology Compass*, 2(5), pp. 1952–1962. doi: 10.1111/j.1751-9004.2008.00134.x

Bakan, D. (1966). *The Duality of Human Existence. An Essay on Psychology and Religion*. Chicago, IL: Rand McNally.

Bruckmüller, S. and Abele, A. E. (2013). The density of the Big Two: How are agency and communion structurally represented? *Social Psychology*, 44(2), pp. 63–74. doi: 10.1027/1864-9335/a000145

Cacioppo, J. T. and Petty, R. E. (1982). The need for cognition. *Journal of Personality and Social Psychology*, 42(1), pp. 116–131. doi: 10.1037/0022-3514.42.1.116

Cacioppo, J. T., Petty, R. E., Feinstein, J. A. and Jarvis, W. B. G. (1996). Dispositional differences in cognitive motivation: The life and times of individuals varying in need for cognition. *Psychological Bulletin*, 119(2), pp. 197–253. doi: 10.1037/0033-2909.119.2.197

Church, I. M. (2017). The limitations of the limitations-owning account of intellectual humility. *Philosophia*, 45(3), pp. 1–8.

Church, I. M. (2016). The doxastic account of intellectual humility. *Logos & Episteme*, 7(4), pp. 413–433. doi: 10.5840/logos-episteme20167441

Church, I. M. and Barrett, J. L. (2017). Intellectual humility. In E. L. Worthington Jr., D. E. Davis and J. N. Hook eds., *The Routledge Handbook of Humility*. New York: Routledge, pp. 62–75.

Church, I. M. and Samuelson, P. L. (2017). *Intellectual Humility: An Introduction to the Philosophy and Science*. New York: Bloomsbury Academic.

Davis, D. E., Hook, J. N., Worthington, E. L., Van Tongeren, D. R., Gartner, A. L., Jennings, D. J. and Emmons, R. A. (2011). Relational humility: Conceptualizing and measuring humility as a personality judgment. *Journal of Personality Assessment*, 93(3), pp. 225–234. doi: 10.1080/00223891.2011.558871

Digman, J. M. (1997). Higher-order factors of the Big Five. *Journal of Personality and Social Psychology*, 73(6), pp. 1246–1256. doi: 10.1037/0022-3514.73.6.1246

Evans, J. T. and Stanovich, K. E. (2013). Dual-process theories of higher cognition: Advancing the debate. *Perspectives on Psychological Science*, 8(3), pp. 223–241.

Fleeson, W. (2004). Moving personality beyond the person-situation debate: The challenge and the opportunity of within-person variability. *Current Directions in Psychological Science*, 13(2), pp. 83–87. doi: 10.1111/j.0963-7214.2004.00280.x

Funder, D. C. (2010). *The Personality Puzzle*. 5th ed. New York: W. W. Norton and Co.

Gregg, A. P., Mahadevan, N. and Sedikides, C. (2017). Intellectual arrogance and intellectual humility: Correlational evidence for an evolutionary-embodied-epistemological account. *The Journal of Positive Psychology*, 12(1), pp. 59–73. doi: 10.1080/17439760.2016.1167942

Haddock, G., Maio, G. R., Arnold, K. and Huskinson, T. (2008). Should persuasion be affective or cognitive? The moderating effects of need for affect and need for cognition. *Personality and Social Psychology Bulletin*, 34(6), pp. 769–778. doi: 10.1177/0146167208314871

Harman, G. (1999). XIV-Moral philosophy meets social psychology: Virtue ethics and the fundamental attribution error. *Proceedings of the Aristotelian Society*, 99(3), pp. 315–331. Retrieved online at www.filosofia.unimi.it/~zucchi/NuoviFile/harman.pdf.

Haugtvedt, C. P., Petty, R. E., and Cacioppo, J. T. (1992). Need for cognition and advertising: Understanding the role of personality variables in consumer behavior. *Journal of Consume Psychology*, 1(3), pp. 239–260. doi: 10.1016/s1057-7408(08)80038

Hoyle, R. H., Davisson, E. K., Diebels, K. J. and Leary, M. L. (2016). Holding specific views with humility: Conceptualization and measurement of specific intellectual humility. *Personality and Individual Differences*, 97, pp. 165–172.

Kahneman, D. (2011). *Thinking, Fast and Slow*. New York: Farrar, Straus and Giroux.

Kahneman, D. and Frederick, S. (2002). Representativeness revisited: Attribute substitution in intuitive judgment. In T. Gilovich, D. Griffin and D. Kahneman eds., *Heuristics and Biases: The Psychology of Intuitive Judgment*. New York: Cambridge University Press, pp. 49–81.

Kruglanski, A. W. (1990). Lay epistemic theory in social-cognitive psychology. *Psychological Inquiry*, 1(3), pp. 181–197. doi: 10.1207/s15327965pli0103_1

Kruglanski, A. W., Dechesne, M., Orehek, E. and Pierro, A. (2009). Three decades of lay epistemics: The why, how, and who of knowledge formation. *European Review of Social Psychology*, 20(1), pp. 146–191. doi: 10.1080/10463280902860037

Krumrei-Mancuso, E. J. and Rouse, S. V. (2016). The development and validation of the Comprehensive Intellectual Humility Scale. *Journal of Personality Assessment*, 98(2), pp. 209–221. doi: 10.1080/00223891.2015.1068174

Landrum, R. E. (2011). Measuring dispositional humility: A first approximation. *Psychological Reports*, 108(1), pp. 217–228. doi: 10.2466/02.07.09.pr0.108.1.217-228

Leary, M. R., Diebels, K. J., Davisson, E. K., Isherwood, J. C., Jongman-Sereno, K. P., Raimi, K. T., Deffler, S. A. and Hoyle, R. A. (2015). Cognitive and interpersonal features of intellectual humility. *Personality and Social Psychology Bulletin*, 43(6), pp. 793–813. doi: 10.1177/0146167217697695

Lee, K. and Ashton, M. C. (2004). Psychometric properties of the HEXACO personality inventory. *Multivariate Behavioral Research*, 39(2), pp. 329–358. doi: 10.1207/s15327906mbr3902_8

McCrae, R. R. and Costa, P. T. (1987). Validation of the five-factor model of personality across instruments and observers. *Journal of Personality and Social Psychology*, 52(1), pp. 81–90. doi: 10.1037/0022-3514.52.1.81

McCrae, R. R. and Costa, P. T., Jr. (1997). Personality trait structure as a human universal. *The American Psychologist*, 52(5), pp. 509–516. doi: 10.1037/0003-066x.52.5.509

Miller, C. B. (2014). *Character and Moral Psychology*. New York: Oxford University Press.

Ottati, V., Wilson, C. and Price, E. D. (2016). *Open Minded Cognition in Social Context*. Unpublished manuscript.

Ottati, V., Wilson, C., Price, E. D. and Sumaktoyo, N. (2015). When self-perceptions of expertise increase closed-minded cognition: The earned dogmatism effect. *Journal of Experimental Social Psychology*, 61, pp. 131–138.

Ozer, D. J. and Benet-Martínez, V. (2006). Personality and the prediction of consequential outcomes. *Annual Review of Psychology*, 57, pp. 401–421. doi: 10.1146/annurev.psych.57.102904.190127

Peters, A., Rowatt, W. C. and Johnson, M. K. (2011). Associations between dispositional humility and social relationship quality. *Psychology*, 2(3), pp. 155–161. doi: 10.4236/psych.2011.23025

Peterson, C. and Seligman, M. E. P. (2004). *Character Strengths and Virtues: A Handbook and Classification*. Washington, DC: American Psychological Association, Oxford University Press.

Petty, R. E., Cacioppo, J. T. and Goldman, R. (1981). Personal involvement as a determinant of argument-based persuasion. *Journal of Personality and Social Psychology*, 41(5), pp. 847–855. doi: 10.1037/0022-3514.41.5.847

Porter, T. (2015). *Intellectual Humility, Mindset, and Learning*. Unpublished dissertation. Palo Alto, CA: Stanford University.

Price, E. D., Ottati, V., Wilson, C. and Kim, S. (2015). Open-minded cognition. *Personality and Social Psychology Bulletin*, 41(11), pp. 1488–1504.

Rowatt, W. C., Powers, C., Targhetta, V., Comer, J., Kennedy, S. and Labouff, J. (2006). Development and initial validation of an implicit measure of humility relative to arrogance. *The Journal of Positive Psychology*, 1(4), pp. 198–211. doi: 10.1080/17439760600885671

Samuelson, Peter L. and Church, Ian M. (2014). When cognition turns vicious: Heuristics and biases in light of virtue epistemology. *Philosophical Psychology*, 28(8), pp. 1095–1113. doi: 10.1080/09515089.2014.904197

Samuelson, P. L., Jarvinen, M., Paulus, T. B., Church, I. M., Hardy, S. A. and Barrett, J. (2015). "Implicit theories of intellectual virtues and vices: A focus on intellectual humility." *The Journal of Positive Psychology*, 10(5), pp. 389–406. doi: 10.1080/17439760.2014.967802

Stanovich, K. E. (1999). *Who Is Rational?: Studies of Individual Differences in Reasoning*. Mahwah, NJ: Lawrence Erlbaum Associates Publishers.

Stanovich, K. E. and West, R. F. (1997). Reasoning independently of prior belief and individual differences in actively open-minded thinking. *Journal of Educational Psychology*, 89(2), pp. 342–357. doi: 10.1037/0022-0663.89.2.342

Stanovich, K. E., and West, R. F. (2007). Natural myside bias is independent of cognitive ability. *Thinking and Reasoning*, 13(3), pp. 225–247. doi:10.1080/13546780600780796

Tangney, J. P. (2000). Humility: Theoretical perspectives, empirical findings and directions for future research. *Journal of Social and Clinical Psychology*, 19(1), pp. 70–82. doi: 10.1521/jscp.2000.19.1.70

Webster, D. M. and Kruglanski, A. W. (1994). Individual differences in need for cognitive closure. *Journal of Personality and Social Psychology*, 67(6), pp. 1049–1062. doi: 10.1037/0022-3514.67.6.1049

33
PSYCHOLOGICAL MEASUREMENT OF HUMILITY

Rick H. Hoyle and Elizabeth Krumrei Mancuso

Humility has long been a topic of interest and inquiry for philosophers and theologians, resulting in a deep and rich literature on the virtue. Around the turn of the century, the topic began to attract the attention of psychological scientists, owing in part to the emergence of positive psychology with its emphasis on positive human functioning. Since the publication of Tangney's (2000) influential review, in which she described humility as "a neglected virtue in the social and psychological sciences," (p. 70) interest in the topic from psychological scientists has grown steadily. A search of articles published in journals indexed by PsycINFO found only four articles including the term *humility* in 2001. In contrast, 123 articles including the term were published in 2018, continuing a trend of more than 100 such articles published per year, starting in 2014.

A key concern for psychological scientists, who rely primarily on empirical methods of inquiry, is how to operationally define abstract concepts such as humility. One approach to operationally defining such concepts is the development and use of measurement instruments and strategies that capture individual differences in their expression. Noting the necessity of measurement for empirical research on humility, Tangney (2000) observed that, "Work in this area would be greatly enhanced by the development of theoretically informed measures of humility" (p. 70) and that, "psychologists' expertise in the area of measurement would be especially welcome" (p. 71). Psychological scientists have answered Tangney's call, resulting in the development of numerous empirical methods for measuring humility. In fact, the number of humility measures and measurement strategies has expanded to the point that the need has arisen to review, summarize, and synthesize the available options. Several such reviews have recently appeared in print (e.g., Card, 2018; Hill et al., 2017; McElroy-Heltzel et al., 2019; Nielsen and Marrone, 2018; Worthington and Allison, 2018).

Drawing on two decades of empirical research on humility, our goal in this chapter is to extend recent reviews of psychological measures of the concept by offering a framework for choosing among extant measures and developing new measures of humility. The framework takes into account the motivating research question and chosen research strategy. Although our focus is psychological measurement, conceptualizations of the concept and, in some cases, the measures themselves have been informed by philosophical and theological inquiry on humility. Thus, our framework is relevant for philosophers and theologians interested in integrating findings from empirical research by psychological scientists into their conceptual models or developing their own empirical studies of humility. We refer to specific extant measures as examples of different measurement approaches, but do not recommend one over another apart from emphasizing the importance of fit between measure, research question, and research strategy. Rather, we suggest that, at this early point in the history of empirical research on humility, and given the specific challenges involved in measuring the concept, the availability and routine use of multiple measures is warranted.

33.1 Themes in the conceptualization of humility as reflected in its measurement

Effective measurement of a concept such as humility requires careful consideration of two separate but intertwined considerations: *what* the concept is and *how* it is to be measured. Owing to the long history of inquiry by philosophers and theologians, psychological scientists began empirical inquiry on humility with access to well-specified conceptual models of the construct (e.g., Richards, 1988; Roberts and Wood, 2003). Thus, the "what" of humility, though not always amenable to measurement or observation, is better specified than most concepts of interest to psychological scientists in the general area of positive human functioning. As context for discussing considerations relevant to the "how" of empirical research on humility, we briefly review conceptual definitions and models that underlie contemporary measures of humility.

Although rigorous and detailed descriptions of humility have been provided by philosophers, there is no widely endorsed definition of humility within the empirical research literature. As a result, extant measures of humility differ from one another on the basis of their underlying conceptualizations. These differences have important implications for inferences related to key research questions about the causes and consequences of humility, as different operational definitions of humility will be associated with different antecedents, cognitions, emotions, and action tendencies (e.g., Weidman, Cheng and Tracy, 2018).

Despite widespread use of the term and implicit understanding of its meaning in everyday language, humility as an object of empirical inquiry has proven challenging to define. Psychological scientists have observed that humility may be easier to conceptualize by what it is not than by what it is (Peterson and Seligman, 2004). Yet, there is an emerging consensus among researchers that humility is not simply the absence or even the opposite of dispositions such as arrogance and narcissism. Rather, the core of humility is often conceptualized in terms of what it is. Specifically, it is often described as reflecting one or more of four characteristics related to views of oneself and others: a low view of self; an accurate view of self; the forgetting of self; and a focus on others.

These themes are, to varying degrees, evident in extant measures of humility, though they are often accompanied by idiosyncratic features that reflect the lack of a tight and clear definition of the concept. In the most extensive review of humility measures to date, McElroy-Hetzel et al. (2019) examined items in 22 self-report measures, coding each item according to the feature of humility it reflects. They found that current measures of humility and its subdomains reflect combinations of eight features: openness, or lack of superiority; being other-oriented, or unselfish; admitting to mistakes, or teachability; interpersonal modesty; accurate view of self; global humility; spiritual humility; and regulating need for status. Being other-oriented is assessed by items in the most measures (assessed by 16 out of 22 measures), followed by openness (assessed by 15 out of 22 measures). Although there is evidence of overlapping content across measures, there is also clear evidence of measure-specific content reflecting alternative conceptualizations of the construct. These alternative conceptualizations, in most cases, can be traced to different conceptual treatments, to which we now turn.

A fundamental question about humility is whether it is a favorable or unfavorable quality. Researchers of humility are quick to point out that the root of the word humility is the Latin *humilis*, meaning "low," and that dictionary definitions of humility tend to emphasize a low view of oneself. Nevertheless, most assessments of humility developed by psychological scientists are built on a conceptualization of humility as an accurate view of oneself or a positive focus on others, which is somewhat of a departure from the historical understanding of humility. The pre-Christian Greco-Roman conceptualization of humility was mostly negative, with the subsequent Christian conceptualization of humility as a valued virtue representing a radical, counter-cultural shift (Foulcher, 2015). Later, 18th- and 19th-century philosophers rejected humility as either unnatural or as a hindrance to individual and political advancement. In addition, views of humility as a virtue were amenable to use by those in authority to enforce low positions in the social hierarchy. For this reason, feminists critiqued a conceptualization of humility that facilitated the control of the weak by the strong.

This history may initially make the positive conceptualization of humility within the contemporary empirical literature seem surprising. However, the favorable view of humility is understandable, given that measurement has been motivated primarily out of an interest in assessing and promoting beneficial qualities. In particular, humility research has often fit within the positive psychology field, within which humility has frequently been studied as a virtue. This has left psychologists to grapple with conundrums such as the implications of the current science of humility for the oppressed. A few authors have promoted the idea that humility may function as a virtue under some circumstances, but not others. For example, Owens, Rowatt and Wilkins (2012) differentiated virtuous humility from non-virtuous humility, following the Aristotelian conceptualization of a virtue as a golden mean between extremes. On this basis, they conceptualized virtuous humility as a balance between arrogance and low self-esteem, indicating that humility becomes a virtue when it is accompanied by self-respect and self-worth. Some have emphasized that humility as a virtue practiced at the wrong time can do harm (Davis and Hook, 2014), whereas others have emphasized that an otherwise virtuous trait practiced at the wrong time is not a virtue at all. Specifically, Whitcomb, Battaly, Baehr and Howard-Snyder (this volume) define the trait of humility as being attentive to and owning one's limitations. They argue that, defined as such, humility becomes a virtue when it is paired with *phronesis*, or a person's ability to judge when, toward whom, and how to properly attend to and own their limitations. Finally, some recent work has focused on the value of measuring humility in both appreciative and self-abasing forms (Weidman et al., 2018).

The question of how best to operationally define humility also involves deciding whether to assess cognitions, emotions, behaviors, or motivations reflective of the construct. The answer to this question is determined in part by whether humility is conceptualized as involving intrapersonal qualities, interpersonal qualities, or both. Almost all researchers attempt to get at some aspect of *intra*personal humility in their assessments. Including *inter*personal aspects of humility within assessments is somewhat common but not universal. Specific interpersonal content differs across measures, and may include being oriented toward others, respecting others, and lacking a sense of superiority (Davis and Hook, 2014). Davis et al. (2011) argue that the interpersonal component of humility is crucial because it defines whether the intrapersonal aspects of humility exist for other-oriented motivations, which they consider foundational for defining humility as a virtue. The distinction between intrapersonal and interpersonal features of humility is reflective of the discussion of whether modesty, often defined as an interpersonal behavioral style related to how one presents oneself to others, falls within or outside of the conceptual boundaries of humility. This debate is important to the measurement of humility, given that many widely used measures of humility assess modesty content. Davis, McElroy et al. (2016) offered theoretical and empirical support for considering modesty to be a subdomain of humility, whereas Kruse, Chancellor and Lyubomirsky (2017) emphasized theoretical and empirical differences between these two closely related constructs. Leary and Banks (in press) offered a novel definition of humility that implies modesty—the belief that one should not be treated as special in recognition of accomplishments outside the domain of the accomplishments. Where one falls on these important questions of what is or is not humility, and what should be emphasized in a measure, will dictate both the content of a measure and, as described below, the approach to measurement.

As this brief and selective review of conceptual treatments suggests, the measurement of humility is not unlike aiming at a moving target. The burgeoning empirical literature has benefited from participation by scholars working from different assumptions about the construct. However, those assumptions are, as we have shown, sometimes contradictory, resulting in a lack of clarity about what exactly constitutes the core of the humility construct. It is not our goal to attempt a resolution to these contradictions or an integration of the different conceptualizations. Yet, we feel it is important to acknowledge the current unfolding state of the literature focused on *what* humility is before offering a framework for considering *how*, for a given study, it should be measured. It is to this set of considerations that we now turn.

33.2 Dimensions on which psychological measures of humility vary

Most measures of humility are multi-item, self-report scales. However, the potential approaches to measuring humility are varied and many. Given the varied manifestations of the multiple features of humility summarized in the previous section, alternatives to self-report scales hold promise for strengthening our understanding of the concept and its relevance for behavior and well-being (Davis and Hook, 2014; Davis, Worthington and Hook, 2010). In this section, we present a general measurement typology that highlights the dimensions on which psychological measures of humility may vary and the types of measures that result from different combinations of those dimensions. The value of considering the full array of alternatives with respect to measuring humility is that (1) research to date has relied almost entirely on trait-level, self-report measurement, and (2) humility may neither evince the stability of a trait nor be subject to valid self-reports (cf. Davis, Worthington and Hook, 2010; Davis et al., 2011; Tangney, 2000). Concretely, researchers must decide whether to measure a particular instance of humility (e.g., ask respondents to recall a particular experience in which they felt humble), humility as a state (e.g., ask respondents to respond about the moment in which they are completing the measure), humility as a trait (respondents' general levels of humility across situations and contexts), or humility as a personality judgment (how individuals are viewed by others across the situations and contexts in which the rater has observed the individual). Fortunately, the typical approach to measuring humility through self-reports is but one of a number of potential approaches that reflect combinations of distinctions on four characteristics of psychological measures: the source of information on the participants' level of humility; the form in which that information is expressed; the presumed stability of the participant's level of humility; and the degree to which the participants' level of humility is assumed to generalize across all settings, topics, and forms of humility.

33.2.1 Source

Although the humility score that is assigned to a research participant is assumed to reflect his or her level of humility, that score does not have to be based on information provided by the participant. Alternatives to self-report, outlined below, when considered alongside self-reports define the first dimension on which approaches to the measurement of humility may vary: source. Essentially, reports on research participants' humility can come either from the participants themselves in the form of self-reports or from someone else in the form of informant reports. Within the latter category, sources may range from informants who know well the participant on whom they are reporting, to informants who are unacquainted with the participant. The principal question to be addressed with respect to source is who is in the best position to provide valid information about the target's standing on humility?

A fundamental question to be considered with respect to self-reports of humility is whether people have insight into their levels of humility. Do humble people realize they are humble? Or might humility make people more sensitive to recognizing and admitting instances in which they do not think, feel, or behave humbly (Peterson and Seligman, 2004)? If humility involves less-than-normal amounts of self-focus, humble people may not attend to their humble qualities as much, decreasing their ability to report their own levels of humility (Rowatt et al., 2006). In addition, even if humble people are aware of their humility, being humble may make them modest in reporting their levels of humility (Davis et al., 2010). For all these reasons, people who are more humble may appear less humble on self-reports.

Whereas people who are humble may display a modesty effect, those who are less humble may enhance their report of humility (Rowatt et al., 2006). This reflects a social desirability bias, which is common to the measurement of many constructs in psychology, but is compounded in the case of humility by the fact that the presence and extent of self-enhancement differs on the basis of levels of the construct being measured. Davis et al. (2010) detail how the combination of modesty and self-enhancement effects within a sample can muddy the waters when using self-reports to assess humility (see their Figure 1). Furthermore, the fact that some research has shown informant reports, described below, to provide higher scores and some research has shown informant reports to provide lower scores on humility in comparison to self-reports, suggests that the modesty and self-enhancement effects on self-reports are present to different extents across samples.

In recent years, concerns voiced about the validity of self-reported humility have been somewhat attenuated (e.g., Davis and Hook, 2014; Worthington and Allison 2018). Scores on self-report measures of many constructs studied by psychological scientists can be consciously manipulated by respondents, but this does not necessarily invalidate these measures. Particularly in anonymous or confidential low-stakes research contexts, respondents have little incentive to fake their responses on self-report humility scales (de Vries, Zettler and Hilbig, 2014). Moreover, Ashton, Lee and de Vries (2014) have noted that there is sufficient support for the construct validity of self-reports of humility, including similar score distributions to personality factors; moderately high agreement between self-reports and reports by close acquaintances; and weak loadings on a factor representing social desirability bias. Importantly, shared variance between measures of humility and social desirability may, in fact, result from measures of social desirability validly tapping into substantive traits, including modesty (de Vries et al., 2014). Nonetheless, to be cautious, some researchers have taken measures to minimize potential social desirability bias, such as avoiding the word humility and its derivatives in items on self-report instruments of humility (Kruse et al., 2017).

A separate, though no less troublesome, concern about self-reports of humility is whether respondents are *able* to judge how humble they are. This concern is not about a motivated bias but rather a lack of adequate insight (Nisbett and Wilson, 1977). Lacking such insight about their own standing, particularly on intrapersonal features of humility, respondents may rely more on lay theories of humility in people like them as opposed to valid accounts of their own thought, feelings, and motives. Unfortunately, this validity threat is more difficult to detect than threats such as social desirability bias; however, it should be evident in discrepancies between self- and informant-reports on features of humility that are evident to informants.

Informants are people who make judgments about the dispositions, preferences, or other characteristics of a target person, in whom evidence of those characteristics is believed to be apparent to others. Informants may base their judgments on direct observation of the target at the time judgments are provided; observation of video recordings of the target; or, if they are acquainted with the target, a history of interacting with target. The advantage of direct observation and observation of video recordings is that they can be staged to give evidence of the characteristic being judged. For example, judges of humility might see the target telling someone about their strengths and weaknesses. The advantage of judgments by informants who know the target is that they will be informed by knowledge of the target's reactions and behaviors across many situations.

A key consideration when using informant reports is who should be enlisted as informants. We have already highlighted the important distinction between informants who know the target versus those who do not. Whereas the former might be able to offer a summary judgment with reasonable validity without significant training or instructions, the latter will need instructions or training that provide clear criteria. If ratings are to be more specific than present–absent, then information about degree will need to be provided for each criterion. For example, Bell et al. (2019) developed a set of criteria on which judgments were made by clinicians based on observations during clinical interviews of clergy candidates. For each of seven criteria (e.g., "acknowledged and owned personal strengths and limitations") these researchers provided clinician informants sufficient information to rate targets on 1-to-5 scales. Although the clinician informants did not know the targets, they learned a great deal about them in the clinical interviews and were provided detailed instructions for expressing judgments. In contrast, Meagher et al. (2015) had university students interact with 3–5 fellow students with whom they were not acquainted for about 20 minutes then rate them on four items indicative of intellectual humility (e.g., "Open to criticism of ideas."). There was no evidence of consensus between informants ratings. A follow-up study obtained judgments from students who had worked together in groups throughout a semester. Although consensus was reached on ratings of humility, scores were not correlated with self-ratings of humility. These findings suggest that strangers with limited exposure to targets are not good judges of their humility. Moreover, though consensus across informants is evident when informants have even a brief history of interacting with targets, the lack of convergence with self-ratings of humility is a puzzle yet to be solved. Minimally, the findings clearly indicate that source matters in measures of humility.

Before turning to other dimensions relevant for measuring humility, we note a special, relatively unexplored research circumstance for which source is likely to matter a great deal—research on children. In such cases, self-reports, unless they focus on explicit behaviors, are unlikely to be useful. For similar reasons, peer informants are not likely equipped to provide useful judgments. Parents, teachers, and adult caregivers may be the only sources available for reliable and valid information about humility in children.

33.2.2 Expression

Regardless of the source of information about a target's level of humility, the means by which that level is expressed or captured may vary. The primary forms of expression are verbal reports of humility, humility as evidenced in behavior, and humility in cognitive or physiological responses to relevant stimuli. These categories, in theory, cross-cut the source dimension such that both self and informants could be sources of information expressed as verbal reports, behavior, or responses to stimuli; however, informants are likely to have limited access to information about responses to stimuli, which may not be observable.

Verbal reports are expressed through responses to questions or statements about one's preferences or tendencies, or narrative responses to open-ended queries designed to elicit descriptions that can be coded for correspondence to different levels of humility. Verbal reports, whether from self or informants, make two assumptions that may not hold for humility and similarly abstract concepts: (1) Valid verbal expressions of the concept can be generated or detected. (2) Respondents or informants are capable of determining whether the feature of the concept targeted by statements or open-ended queries apply. Meeting the first assumption requires that the conceptualization of humility is sufficiently detailed and clear to provide a basis for generating questions or statements or coding open-ended responses. Meeting the second assumption may be possible when the expression is social or behavioral but not when it is cognitive, metacognitive, or affective. If either assumption does not hold, then alternative forms of expression are likely to be more valid for use in assessment.

Apart from verbal reports, humility may be expressed as behavior or as responses to stimuli designed to elicit reactions consistent or not with humility. Although humility has implications for behavior, it is rarely defined with explicit reference to behavioral manifestations as is, for example, conscientiousness as measured by the Behavioral Indicators of Conscientiousness (Jackson et al., 2010). The closest conceptual treatments are those that involve an explicit interpersonal focus. Whether motivated by a behavior-oriented conceptualization or assuming that humility should be evident in behavior, several attempts have been made to measure humility as expressed in behavior. For example, Van Tongeren et al. (2014) operationalized humility as the ability to regulate defensiveness in response to being challenged by another person. Other behavioral indicators of humility discussed in the literature include how a person behaves when given the opportunity to share credit (e.g., when accomplishing a task or receiving praise or an award), when vying for power in a group, in interpersonal conflict, when making a mistake or hurting someone, and in relationships involving power differentials (e.g., Chancellor and Lyubomirsky, 2013; Davis et al., 2011; Van Tongeren et al., 2014). The challenge of relying on behavioral measures is that behaviors consistent with humility may or may not be driven by humility. That is, people may engage in behaviors consistent with humility for other reasons, such as following social norms or out of a desire to appear humble to others (Peterson and Seligman, 2004).

Although behavioral expressions of humility would typically be captured by informants (which may include experimenters), research participants may be valid sources of information about their behavior under certain conditions. In particular, ecological momentary assessment (EMA) studies may repeatedly over short periods of time ask participants to indicate whether they have engaged in certain concrete behaviors within the past few minutes. These reports can be elicited in ways that do not involve subjective judgments. Perhaps because most models of humility do not specify specific behavioral indicators of the concept, EMA studies that capture behavior indicative of humility in the moment are not yet evident in the empirical literature on humility.

In addition to behavior, humility may express as reactions to stimuli designed to elicit responses consistent with high or low humility. For example, Rowatt et al. (2006) developed an implicit association test of humility, comparing the reaction times of pairings of self with humility to pairings of self with arrogance. Implicit assessments are difficult to control deliberately, and thereby sidestep potential concerns about response biases. Implicit measures may prove useful, particularly if they are updated in response to progress in the science of humility. However, concerns about a potential lack of awareness about one's levels of humility that have been expressed about self-reports carry through to implicit assessments, as do problems related to self-deceived narcissists or others low in humility who truly view themselves as humble. In such cases, neither self-report nor implicit assessments would prove particularly useful. Physiological correlates of humility have also been explored, but are subject to interpretation and therefore only as valid as their theoretical backing. For example, one might examine physiological responses to ego threat as an indicator of humility (Peterson and Seligman, 2004). However, would a lack of physiological arousal to an ego threat induction be indicative of humility, or would behaving humbly in the face of physiological arousal be a closer approximation of humility? Furthermore, would levels of physiological arousal to ego threat depend on a person's trait level of humility? For example, Worthington has argued that the presence of true ego strain is essential to developing humility (e.g., Worthington and Allison, 2018). However, if the biomarkers of humility are different depending on the degree to which a person has developed the skill or virtue of humility, then using such physiological data for the purpose of determining levels of humility is problematic.

In summary, verbal reports, for which critical assumptions related to validity may never be met, are far and away the expression of choice in empirical research on humility. Alternative expressions that make fewer assumptions may be viable, but relatively little research to date has attempted to use them. The primary obstacle to consulting potential alternative expressions such as behavior and reactivity is that conceptual models of humility have not yet developed to the point that the relevant behaviors or physiological reactions are clear. Better or more creative approaches to measurement of humility are constrained by underspecified conceptual accounts of the concept.

33.2.3 Specificity

With respect to measurement, specificity concerns whether a concept is reflected in a single score assumed to represent the concept in full, or is reflected in a single score that reflects the concept in part or multiple scores that correspond to specific features or manifestations of the concept. As with the expression dimension, standing on the specificity dimension is, to some degree, dictated by conceptual models of the concept. Those models may provide information about specificity of two types. As noted earlier in the chapter, models of humility often specify particular features of the construct. Examples include being other-oriented and holding an accurate view of oneself. Alternatively, they may suggest different domains across which humility may vary. Examples include relational humility and intellectual humility. These domains may be quite specific. For example, relational humility may be further subdivided into humility with respect to family, friends, and romantic partners. Intellectual humility may be considered with respect to politics or religion or, even more specifically, particular political or religious issues. Humility measures that are specific in focus allow for specificity matching when the outcomes of interest also are specific in focus. Poor specificity matching is typical of individual differences research, including research on humility, typically taking the form of the prediction of specific behaviors or performances from a general or global form of the individual difference (Hoyle and Leary, 2009). Such research likely underestimates the influence of humility on specific outcomes because people are able to function and interact with humility in some settings and not others, or in interactions with some people or with reference to some areas of knowledge but not others.

Although some models of humility are global and unidimensional (e.g., Leary and Banker, in press), most are multifaceted. Indeed, in the seminal treatment of humility as a psychological construct, Tangney (2000) proposed six "elements" of humility—accurate self-assessment, ability to acknowledge mistakes, openness to new ideas, keeping ones' accomplishments in perspective, relatively low self-focus, and appreciation of the value of others' contribution. Although these facets of humility were adjusted, replaced, or supplemented in subsequently articulated conceptual models, nearly all models pose a similar set of dimensions. Reflecting this feature of conceptual models, most current measures of humility include between three and six subscales corresponding to posited features of the construct.

The other form of specificity with implications for measurement—domain specificity—has been less evident in conceptual treatments of humility. In fact the most prominent form of domain-specificity with respect to humility, intellectual humility, has spawned its own set of models (e.g., Leary et al., 2017) and a research literature that has little connection to the literature on general humility. Unlike hierarchical models of personality and other individual differences, wherein facets (e.g., personality traits) or domains (e.g., self-concept) are assumed to be specific variants of higher-order concepts, it is not clear, for example, that intellectual humility can be fully understood as a specific variant of general humility as conceptualized by most models. Nevertheless, specificity matching, by which specific forms of humility, such as intellectual humility, are used instead of general humility to predict reactions or behavior in the same domain (e.g., willingness to consider political perspectives that differ from one's perspective), increases the likelihood of detecting effects of humility on multiply determined behaviors. Unlike individual differences such as self-concept (Marsh and Shavelson, 1985) and self-esteem (Harter, Whitesell and Junkin, 1998), for which domains are well-specified, the full array of humility domains and the nature of their relations with general humility remain unspecified. Nonetheless, some attention has been given to humility in selected domains, including intellectual, spiritual, relational, and cultural humility (e.g., Davis and Hook, 2014; Davis, Rice et al., 2016; Worthington and Allison, 2018).

In the same way that a widely accepted conceptualization of humility would likely hasten scientific progress in understanding the concept and its implications for behavior and well-being, an agreed-upon set of domains would promote progress. In developing a more comprehensive set of domains, researchers might look to the outcomes for which humility might be relevant as has been done with self-concept and self-esteem. That kind of analysis gave rise to the limited set currently considered, but a more systematic and wide-ranging analysis would no doubt point to others. Development on this front would strengthen both conceptual models and predictive validity of humility.

33.2.4 Stability

A relatively unexplored feature of humility with relevance for how it is measured is its stability across time and place. Humility is typically assessed in a manner that assumes it is a trait; that is to say, peoples' level of humility varies little from one time or context to another. To the extent that humility demonstrates such stability it might reasonably be positioned in personality space as a facet of a broader personality domain (e.g., Ashton et al., 2014) or as a cross-cutting trait that manifests features of multiple personality domains (like, for example, sensation seeking). Alternatively, it might be the case that humility reliably varies across contexts and short periods of time, in which case referencing structural models of personality as a means of embellishing models of the concept might not prove useful. Rather, conceptualizing the concept as a state that characterizes the person with respect to context and time may prove truer to the concept as it manifests "in the wild." Humility might evidence properties of both traits and states (as, for example, do anxiety and other forms of affect), suggesting the need for models and measures that capture both stable and varying manifestations of the concept. Indeed, at the outset of contemporary empirical research on humility, Tangney (2000) referred to "two levels of interest, two levels of questions," and discussed the merits of conceptualizing and measuring humility as "dispositional" and "situational."

Two prominent models of personality process offer a theoretical rationale for developing conceptual models and measures of humility that characterize it as both trait and state. Fleeson (2001) proposed a resolution of the apparent contradiction between state and trait forms of individual differences in the form of density distributions of behaviors reflective of those individual differences. Fleeson observed that, when personality-relevant behaviors are assessed using EMA methods across several days, most participants report behaviors that span the continuum of typical personality traits, thus showing evidence of variable personality states. Yet the within-person density distributions, characterized by mean and standard deviation of behavior over time and place, are stable, suggesting trait-like consistency. Applied to humility, Fleeson's approach suggests value in research that identifies behaviors indicative of humility, assesses them at the momentary level using EMA methods, and examines within-person density distributions. Such work is likely to reveal that (1) expressions of humility vary across situation, (2) the central tendency and range of people's distributions are stable across situations, and (3) people vary in how variable their expressions of humility are across situations. This pattern would support an inference that humility has both trait and state manifestations, each of which warrants measurement and study.

Cognitive-affective processing system (CAPS) theory offers an alternative perspective that accounts for both variability and consistency in personality (Mischel and Shoda, 1995). The theory asserts that, although people's behavior is contingent on features of situations and therefore state-like, they develop patterns of responses to situational features such that they behave similarly in a given situation as they encounter it repeatedly across time. Consistency in behavior is found in the if-then contingencies that develop between situations and behaviors. Coherent sets of stable if-then contingencies reflect personality, which is both consistent and variable. Operating from a set of principles specified in CAPS theory, researchers have identified the personality signatures for narcissism, characterizing the trait as a stable set of cognitive, affective, and interpersonal processes associated with specific features of situations (Morf and Rhodewalt, 2001). A similar analysis of humility would likely highlight the person-situation contingencies that underlie trait-level humility and contribute to its situated expression.

The preponderance of research on humility has used trait measurement, resulting in relatively little information about the dynamics of humility in daily life. A promising line of research by Kruse and colleagues resulted in the development of a measure of state humility and a set of studies suggesting that variability in state humility is associated with variability in other states over short periods of time (Kruse et al., 2017; Kruse et al., 2014). Kruse et al. (2017) identified a dozen themes that emerged from statements provided by research participants' asked to reflect on what humble people are like, including things they might say or believe. They incorporated themes most clearly reflective of humility in six self-report items, to which respondents were instructed to indicate "how you feel right this moment." A key validation strategy for the measure was an examination of its covariation with a "stress test" of humility, which involved imagining someone angry with them and providing an attribution and indicating their likely responses. Responses were rated by two sets of judges, one referencing their own definition of humility and the other using the state humility scale items. Both sets of ratings were moderately to highly correlated with self-reports of state humility. In a separate set of studies using their conceptualization and measure of state humility, Kruse et al. (2014) showed that state humility is responsive to experiences of gratitude and, when both are assessed daily, state gratitude and humility are mutually reinforcing. These findings suggest that humility states can be measured with reliability and validity, and provide hints at processes that influence state humility and may, over time, contribute to stability and change in levels of humility.

33.3 Choosing a measurement approach

Although the empirical literature on humility is dominated by verbal descriptions of stable levels of general humility captured by self-report, we have described multiple alternative measurement approaches that could be used and would be more appropriate for some research questions and designs. If each of the measurement dimensions we described were treated as binary, the result would be 16 distinct approaches to measuring humility. Some combinations are likely to be more fruitful than others, but all merit consideration as researchers consider how best to measure humility for a given study or what measures might be developed to spur new research on humility. To that end, we shift the focus to research questions and strategies and address the question, Which measurement approach is best suited for different research questions and strategies?

We first note the interdependence between how humility is measured and how it is studied. If the only approach to measurement is self-report questionnaires, then the primary approach to studying humility will be large-sample surveys and correlation-based analytic methods. Thus, one benefit to an investment in alternative approaches to measuring humility is that doing so will lead to the use of a wider array of research strategies and data-analytic methods. More generally, extending measurement of humility to other approaches will facilitate broader exploration of the antecedents and consequences of humility as well as the processes by which it influences behavior and well-being and, potentially, how it can be changed through intervention.

When designing new studies of humility, four questions should guide researchers' choice of measurement approach.

- **Is there reason to believe that members of the population of interest are willing and able to provide valid information about their own level of humility?** Children, and perhaps even adolescents, are not likely able to do so. Adults are perhaps able to do so but, for reasons discussed early in the chapter, may not be willing to do so. If participants are willing and able, then self-report is a viable approach to measuring humility. If they are either unable or potentially unwilling to do so, then the use of informants may be required.
- **Is the form of humility that is to be studied amenable to verbal expression?** Put differently, can research participants or informants judge humility by providing ratings of statements in which it is described? If not, then capturing alternative expressions of humility, such as behavior or reactions to relevant stimuli, will be required. Despite the appeal of these alternative expressions, relatively little work has examined them with reference to humility. The empirical literature on humility would benefit from a better of understanding of how humility is evidenced in behavior and reactions to people and situations for which humility is relevant.
- **Is the interest general humility, particular features of general humility, or humility as evidenced in specific domains?** When humility is included in a larger set of correlates or predictors, then a single score representing general humility may be sufficient to evaluate the position of humility in a network of variables or set of predictors. However, the specificity-matching principle highlights the fact that such measures are likely to underestimate associations involving humility unless correlates or outcomes are similarly general (e.g., subjective well-being). If the correlates or outcomes are specific then, to the extent possible, the measure of humility should be specific to the domain of variables with which its association will be estimated. When the motivating research questions concern the nature of humility, information on particular features of humility may be important, necessitating a measure that produces subscale scores reflecting the features of interest.
- **Does the question of interest concern the degree of humility research participants evidence most of the time in most situations, or does it concern humility**

as evident at specific times and places? Basic questions about trait-level humility are important for positioning the concept among the range of traits that characterize people's self-construal, motives, and behavior. Questions about when and how humility affects in-the-moment self-construals, motives, and behaviors are also important and, in order to study them, state-level measurement is required. Initial attempts at measuring state humility are promising, but more options are needed. Specifically, measures suitable for ecological momentary assessments would allow for further study of the dynamics of humility in everyday life.

Although each of these questions points to a class of measures, it is the intersection of responses to the questions that points to a specific measurement approach for a specific study. For example, determining that state-level measure is required to address the research question of interest does not address questions about specificity, expression, or source. Each new study of humility would benefit from answering each of these questions in search of the optimal measurement approach. Also, ongoing efforts to improve measurement of humility would do well to focus on particular combinations for which measures are lacking.

33.4 Conclusion

Empirical research on humility in the tradition of psychological science has relied too heavily on an approach to measurement characterized by verbal self-reports of a stable and general characteristic. As outlined in this chapter, many alternative approaches could be used, potentially to substantial benefit. Broadening the types of measurement approaches used in research on humility would suggest new avenues of research, the results of which would deepen our understanding of the concept. More thoughtful decisions about how to measure humility for specific populations and research questions would likely produce evidence of stronger associations with important outcomes than is evident at this time. The fundamental importance of measurement to progress in research on humility underscores the need for greater diversity and creativity in measures of the concept.

Acknowledgement

The writing of this chapter was generously supported by the John Templeton Foundation, Grant No. 60622, "Developing Humility in Leaders."

References

Ashton, M. C., Lee, K. and de Vries, R. E. (2014). The HEXACO honesty-humility, agreeableness, and emotionality factors: A review of research and theory. *Personality and Social Psychology Review*, 18(2), pp. 139–152.

Bell, C. A., Dumitrascu, N., Sandage, S. J. and Waldheter, M. (2019). *Development of a Clinician Rating of Clergy Candidate Humility During Psychological Assessment*. Unpublished study.

Card, N. A. (2018). Meta-analyses of the reliabilities of measures of forgiveness and humility. *Research in Human Development*, 15(1), pp. 72–87.

Chancellor, J. and Lyubomirsky, S. (2013). Humble beginnings: Current trends, state perspectives, and hallmarks of humility. *Social and Personality Psychology Compass*, 7(11), pp. 819–833.

Davis, D. E. and Hook, J. N. (2014). Humility, religion, and spirituality: An endpiece. *Journal of Psychology and Theology*, 42(1), pp. 111–117.

Davis, D. E., Hook, J. N., Worthington, E. L., Jr., Van Tongeren, D. R., Gartner, A. L., Jennings, D. J. and Emmons, R. A. (2011). Relational humility: Conceptualizing and measuring humility as a personality judgment. *Journal of Personality Assessment*, 93(3), pp. 225–234.

Davis, D. E., McElroy, S. E., Rice, K. G., Choe, E., Westbrook, C., Hook, J. N., Van Tongeren, D. R., DeBlaere, C., Hill, P., Placares, V. and Worthington, E. L., Jr. (2016). Is modesty a subdomain of humility? *The Journal of Positive Psychology*, 11(4), pp. 439–446.

Davis, D. E., Worthington, E. L., Jr. and Hook, J. N. (2010). Humility: Review of measurement strategies and conceptualization as personality judgment. *The Journal of Positive Psychology*, 5(4), pp. 243–252.

de Vries, R. E., Zettler, I. and Hilbig, B. E. (2014). Rethinking trait conceptions of social desirability scales: Impression management as an expression of honesty-humility. *Assessment*, 21(3), pp. 286–299.

Fleeson, W. (2001). Toward a structure- and process-integrated view of personality: Traits as density distributions of states. *Journal of Personality and Social Psychology*, 80(6), pp. 1011–1027.

Foulcher, J. (2015). *Reclaiming Humility: Four Studies in the Monastic Tradition*. Collegeville, MN: The Liturgical Press.

Harter, S., Whitesell, N. R. and Junkin, L. J. (1998). Similarities and differences in domain-specific and global self-evaluations of learning-disabled, behaviorally disordered, and normally achieving adolescents. *American Educational Research Journal*, 35(4), pp. 653–680.

Hill, P. C., Laney, E. K., Edwards, K. J., Wang, D. C., Orme, W. H., Chan, A. C. and Wang, F. L. (2017). A few good measures: Colonel Jessup and humility. In: E. L. Worthington Jr., D. E. Davis and J. N. Hook, eds., *Handbook of Humility: Theory, Research, and Applications*. New York: Routledge/Taylor & Francis Group, pp. 119–133.

Hoyle, R. H. and Leary, M. R. (2009). Methods for the study of individual differences in social behavior. In: M. R. Leary and R. H. Hoyle, eds., *Handbook of Individual Differences in Social Behavior*. New York: Guilford Press, pp. 12–23.

Jackson, J. J., Wood, D., Bogg, T., Walton, K. E., Harms, P. D. & Roberts, B. W. (2010). What do conscientious people do? Development and validation of the Behavioral Indicators of Conscientiousness (BIC). *Journal of Research in Personality*, 44(4), pp. 501–511.

Kruse, E., Chancellor, J. and Lyubomirsky, S. (2017). State humility: Measurement, conceptual validation, and intrapersonal processes. *Self and Identity*, 16(4), pp. 399–438.

Kruse, E., Chancellor, J., Ruberton, P. M. and Lyubomirsky, S. (2014). An upward spiral between gratitude and humility. *Social Psychological and Personality Science*, 5(7), pp. 805–814.

Leary, M. R. and Banker, C. (in press). A critical examination and reconceptualization of humility. In: J. Wright, ed., *Humility*. New York: Oxford University Press.

Leary, M. R., Diebels, K. J., Davisson, E. K., Jongman-Sereno, K. P., Isherwood, J. C., Raimi, K. T., Deffler, S. A. and Hoyle, R. H. (2017). Cognitive and interpersonal features of intellectual humility. *Personality and Social Psychology Bulletin*, 43(6), pp. 793–813.

Marsh, H. W. and Shavelson, R. (1985). Self-concept: It multifaceted, hierarchical structure. *Educational Psychologist*, 20(3), pp. 107–123.

McElroy-Heltzel, S. E., Davis, D. E., DeBlaere, C., Worthington, E. L. and Hook, J. N. (2019). Embarrassment of riches in the measurement of humility: A critical review of 22 measures. *The Journal of Positive Psychology*, 14(3), pp. 393–404.

Meagher, B. R., Leman, J. C., Bias, J. P., Latendresse, S. J. and Rowatt, W. C. (2015). Contrasting self-report and consensus ratings of intellectual humility and arrogance. *Journal of Research in Personality*, 58, pp. 35–45.

Mischel, W. and Shoda, Y. (1995). A cognitive-affective system theory of personality: Reconceptualizing situations, dispositions, dynamics, and invariance in personality structure. *Psychological Review*, 102(2), pp. 246–268.

Morf, C. C. and Rhodewalt, F. (2001). Unraveling the paradoxes of narcissism: A dynamic self-regulatory processing model. *Psychological Inquiry*, 12(4), pp. 177–196.

Nielsen, R. and Marrone, J. A. (2018). Humility: Our current understanding of the construct and its role in organizations. *International Journal of Management Reviews*, 20(4), pp. 805–824.

Nisbett, R. and Wilson, T. (1977). Telling more than we can know: Verbal reports on mental processes. *Psychological Review*, 84(3), pp. 231–259.

Owens, B. P., Rowatt, W. C. and Wilkins, A. L. (2012). Exploring the relevance and implications of humility in organizations. In: G. M. Spreitzer and K. S. Cameron, eds., *Oxford Handbook of Positive Organizational Scholarship*. New York: Oxford University Press, pp. 260–272.

Peterson, C. and Seligman, M. E. P. (2004). *Character Strengths and Virtues: A Handbook and Classification*. Washington, D.C.: American Psychological Association and New York: Oxford University Press.

Richards, N. (1988). Is humility a virtue? *American Philosophical Quarterly*, 25(3), pp. 253–259.

Roberts, R. and Wood, J. (2003). Humility and epistemic goods. In: M. DePaul and L. Zagzebski, eds., *Intellectual Virtue: Perspectives from Ethics and Epistemology*. Oxford: Clarendon Press, pp. 257–279.

Rowatt, W. C., Powers, C., Targhetta, V., Comer, J., Kennedy, S. and Labouff, J. (2006). Development and initial validation of an implicit measure of humility relative to arrogance. *The Journal of Positive Psychology*, 1(4), pp. 198–211.

Tangney, J. P. (2000). Humility: Theoretical perspectives, empirical findings and directions for future research. *Journal of Social and Clinical Psychology*, 19(1), pp. 70–82.

Van Tongeren, D. R., Green, J. D., Hulsey, T. L., Legare, C. H., Bromley, D. G. and Houtman, A. M. (2014). A meaning-based approach to humility: Relationship affirmation reduces worldview defense. *Journal of Psychology and Theology*, 42(1), pp. 62–69.

Weidman, A. C., Cheng, J. T. and Tracy, J. L. (2018). The psychological structure of humility. *Journal of Personality and Social Psychology*, 114(1), pp. 153–178.

Whitcomb, D., Battaly, H., Baehr, J. and Howard-Snyder, D. (in press). The puzzle of humility and disparity. In: M. Alfano, M. P. Lynch and A. Tanesini, eds., *Routledge Handbook on the Philosophy of Humility*. New York: Routledge.

Worthington, E. L., Jr. and Allison, S. T. (2018). *Heroic Humility: What the Science of Humility Can Say to People Raised on Self-Focus*. Washington, D.C.: American Psychological Association.

34

THE MORAL PSYCHOLOGY OF HUMILITY

Epistemic and ethical alignment as foundational to moral exemplarity

Jennifer Cole Wright

34.1 What is humility?

> Although humility is often equated in people's minds with low self-regard and tends to activate images of the stoop-shouldered, self-deprecating, weak-willed soul only too willing to yield to the wishes of others, in reality humility is the antithesis of this caricature.
>
> *(Emmons, 1998, p. 33)*

Strikingly, most accounts of humility share a similar feature—namely, a sort of "shrinking" of the self. Or, more specifically, a shrinking of the *value, esteem, care*, or *prioritization* that is given to it. That said, there are also a number of important differences between the various accounts of humility on offer. In this chapter, I will restrict the discussion to two main approaches (though for a more thorough discussion of them, see Nadelhoffer and Wright, 2017, Nadelhoffer, Wright, Echols, Perini, and Venezia, 2017). Historically, for example, one approach to humility has been to view it as a form of self-denigration, deprecation, or abasement, a recognition of one's own lowliness and insignificance—especially in relation to God's greatness (Aquinas II–II, Q. 161, Art. 1, ad. 2, 1274/1972; see also Baxter, 1830; Horneck, 1651; Kempis, 1441/1940; Maimonides, 1972; St. Bernard of Clairvaux, 1942). Contemporary versions of this view exist—for example, the view that the humble person is someone "who accepts his lowly position as due him" (Taylor, 1985, p. 17; see also Klein, 1992; Knight and Nadel, 1986; Langston and Cantor, 1989; Weidman, Cheng, and Tracy, 2016; Weiss and Knight, 1980), that humility is "having a lowly opinion of oneself; meekness, lowliness ... the opposite of pride or haughtiness" (McArthur, 1998), or being "of little worth, unimportant ... having a sense of insignificance, unworthiness, dependence, or sinfulness" (Funk and Wagnall, 1963).

Others, critical of this view, have either rejected humility entirely as a legitimate moral capacity or virtue (Hume 1777/1960; Nietzsche 1886/1966; Sidgwick, 1874/2011; Spinoza, 1677/1955), or they have tried to salvage it, while retaining the essential "self-shrinking" feature. In this alternative approach, people argue that humility does not require self-deprecation, etc. at all. Instead, what it requires is only that one "keep one's accomplishments, traits, abilities ... in perspective, even if stimulated to exaggerate them" (Richards, 1988, p. 256; see also Snow, 1995). According to this approach, we are not required to hold ourselves in low regard, but simply to not be overly centered upon, or enamored with, ourselves—as C.S. Lewis (1952/1980) is credited with saying that a truly humble man "will not be thinking about humility: he will not be thinking about himself at all". Thus, while this approach still involves a shrinking of the self, so to speak, it looks like more of a *decentering* than a decreasing—more of a *quieting* than a reducing (Leary, Adams, and Tate, 2006; Leary and Guadango, 2011; Leary and Terry, 2012)—of the self.[1]

This more positive approach underlies two related strategies for defining humility. The first of these defines humility in terms of certain *intrapersonal* attributes—for example, arguing that it involves qualities and capacities such as having an accurate assessment of one's talents and achievements, an open-minded willingness to admit one's mistakes, imperfections, and limitations, an openness to new ideas and advice, an appreciation for other people's ideas, beliefs, and values, and a relative lack of self-preoccupation or desire to "self-enhance" or make oneself look or feel better, and so on (Baumeister and Exline, 2002; Emmons, 1999; Hwang, 1982; Peterson and Seligman, 2004; Rowatt, Ottenbreit, Nesselroade, and Cunningham, 2002; Sandage, Wiens, and Dahl, 2001; Tangney, 2000, 2009; Templeton, 1997).

The second strategy defines humility more in terms of certain *inter-personal* qualities—for example, the possession of empathy, gentleness, gratitude, respect for others, and the recognition of the equality, autonomy, and value of others (Emmons and Kneezel, 2005; Halling, Kunz, and Rowe, 1994; Means, Wilson, Sturm, Bion, and Bach, 1990; Sandage, 1999; Tangney, 2000, 2009), as well as a willingness (even desire) to share credit with other for one's accomplishments (Exline and Geyer, 2004; Tangney, 2000, 2009; Vera and Rodriguez-Lopez, 2004), an appreciation of and compassion for other's welfare (LaBouff, Rowatt, Johnson, Tsang, and Willerton, 2012) that allows one to balance the needs of self and others (Davis, Worthington, and Hook, 2010). Yet others speak of it as a willingness to surrender to God, a higher being, or some transcendent power (Emmons and Kneezel, 2005; Murray, 2001; Powers, Nam, Rowatt, and Hill, 2007)—as Gerber (2002) maintains, "humility stems from a person's relationship with something greater" (p. 43).

While my colleagues and I are strongly supportive of the more positive approach to humility, nonetheless we have elsewhere argued that these various strategies for defining humility are problematic insofar as they run the risk of confusing whatever capacities and qualities actually *constitute* humility with those that are simply *related to* it—whether as a precursor, a parallel process, or a downstream consequence (Nadelhoffer and Wright, 2017, Wright, Nadelhoffer, Ross, and Sinnott-Armstrong, 2018). After all, as we have pointed out, while it is certainly the case that humble people may possess and express all (or a subset) of these intra- and inter-personal capacities and qualities, and they may even do so because they are humble, this does not show that these capacities and qualities *are* humility. Thus, while these different strategies have likely succeeded in identifying important intra- and inter-personal preconditions and consequences of humility, they may have nonetheless failed to capture humility itself.

34.2 The core of humility: epistemic and ethical alignment

> Everything in my own immediate experience supports my deep belief that I am the absolute center of the universe; the realest, most vivid and important person in existence.
>
> *(Wallace, 2005, online)*

As this quote suggestion, all human beings are naturally structured in such a way as to experience themselves as the organizing center of a consciousness—a "self" that stands at the phenomenological center of their experiences, weaving these experiences together into the coherent structure of a *life*. And they experience this life as real and substantial—as something that they are not only living, but feel compelled to live. It is thus not surprising that in a world filled with different needs and interests, it is the ones that they experience as *their own*—as emanating out from the life for which they are the center—that most strongly demand their attention, and in a world filled with different beliefs and values, it is their own that most strongly demand their allegiance.

In other words, those needs, desires, interests, beliefs, goals, and values (hereafter needs, etc.) that we experience as our own have a natural "gravitational pull", making it seem natural and unproblematic to privilege and favor them over the needs, etc. of others. We naturally expend more energy, dedicate more resources, give more thought, and allocate more time to our own lives—to satisfying our own needs, looking out for our own interests, pursuing and defending our own beliefs, values, and goals, etc.—often without realizing that we are doing so.

Yet, as natural as this centeredness feels, it is problematic. After all, the fact that our values and beliefs are our own does not make them more likely to be actually true or appropriate; just because we experience our own needs and interests more strongly, does not mean that they actually matter more, objectively speaking.[2] And the ethical life "is a life in which you encounter yourself as one person among others, all equally real" (Johnston, 2009, p. 89). Therefore, some sort of corrective process is needed to create a more balanced state of awareness. And this is where humility comes in.

Johnston (2009) points out that all major religions agree that any corrective process "crucially requires overcoming the centripetal force of self-involvement, in order to orient one's life around reality and the real needs of human beings as such" (p. 23). What this highlights is that the problem with our centeredness is that it generates both *epistemic* and *ethical* distortion. That is, it interferes with our ability to accurately perceive, and fully engage with *the world* and with *the other living beings around us* as they actually are.

The position that we have argued for at length elsewhere is that, at its core, humility is a state of awareness free of the epistemic and ethical distortion generated by our centeredness (Nadelhoffer and Wright, 2017, Nadelhoffer, Wright, Echols, Perini, and Venezia, 2017; Wright, Nadelhoffer, Perini, Langville, Echols, and Venezia, 2017, Wright, et al., 2018). More specifically, humility is a state of epistemically and ethically aligned awareness—one in which we have escaped the centripetal force of self-involvement and experience ourselves in true relation to all else (everything and everyone), thereby allowing us to experience those relations, and their objects, objectively.[3]

Because humility facilitates a realistic, unbiased appraisal of ourselves, it removes the need to inflate or deflate our own—or others'—value or significance, resulting in a more balanced, "unencumbered", encountering of self and others. And while, as a state of awareness, humility is something that we can "come into and go out of" (i.e., temporary states of humility), as a virtue it becomes stabilized into a standing disposition, or trait, that continuously informs and influences our cognition, affect, and behavior.

In a state of *epistemic alignment* (i.e., being oriented toward reality), we understand and experience ourselves as we, in fact, are—e.g., as a finite, fallible, imperfect beings that are but an infinitesimal part of a vast universe, and so have a necessarily limited and incomplete perspective or grasp on the "whole", which is infinitely larger and greater than ourselves. Many experience this spiritually, as a connection to God or some higher source, though others experience it as a heightened awareness of their place in, and connection to, the natural world and/or cosmos (a state of "existential awareness"). In this way, humility is a corrective to our natural tendency to seek social praise, status, acclaim, and influence over others—and to have undue attachment to our needs, etc. simply because they are ours.

In a state of *ethical alignment* (i.e., oriented toward the real needs of human beings as such), we understand and experience ourselves as only one among a host of other morally relevant beings, whose interests are as legitimate, and as worthy of attention and concern, as our own (a state of "extended compassion"). In this way, humility is a corrective to our natural tendency to prioritize and privilege—to seek "premium treatment" for—our own needs, etc., even at significant cost to others, simply because they are ours.

Humility quiets the pull of our own needs, etc., not because they matter less, but because we no longer experience them *in isolation*—as separate, in conflict, or in competition, with those of others. Instead we experience them as connected and shared, as bonded and interwoven with the needs, etc. of others. Thus, humility involves both a shrinking and an expansion of the self. Through humility, we become *more*, not less.

34.3 Why humility matters: healthy moral functioning

Should we consider humility important for our moral functioning? There is a solid body of evidence that suggests we should. Indeed, years of research provide strong support for the view that humility is positively connected to healthy moral functioning. For example, humility (measured by the HEXACO, Ashton and Lee, 2008) has been found to strongly correlate with lower rates of infidelity and other moral transgressions (Hilbig, Moshagen, and Zettler, 2015). People high in humility are more cooperative and more fair in their economic allocations (Ashton and Lee, 2008; Zettler, Hilbig, and Heydasch, 2013) and are more likely to refrain from exploiting others in economic exchanges for their own benefit, even when they have the chance to do so (Hilbig and Zettler, 2009). Humility was also found to negatively correlate with the intention to commit premeditated vengeful acts, to engage in retaliation or displaced aggression (Lee and Ashton, 2012), as well as right-wing authoritarianism, social dominance orientation, and hierarchy-oriented values (Lee, Ashton, Ogunfowora, Bourdage, and Shin, 2010; for an overview, see Ashton et al., 2004).

Davis et al. (2011) found humility to be positively related to forgiveness and empathy. And higher levels of perceived humility were related to greater attributions of both warmth-based and conscientiousness-based virtues. Kruse, Chancellor, Ruberton, and Lyubomirsky (2014) found that humility and gratitude to be mutually reinforcing. People who wrote a letter expressing their gratitude showed higher humility than those who performed a neutral activity and people's baseline humility predicted the degree of gratitude felt after writing the letter.

In my own research, my colleagues and I have found humility to be positively related to a wide range of morally important capacities—e.g., empathy, benevolence, civic responsibility, gratitude, humanitarian-egalitarian attitudes, positive moral identity, integrity, universalistic values, mindfulness, conscientiousness, and the tendency to feel guilt for bad behavior and seek to repair wrong-doing. We also found it to be positively related to intrinsic religiosity and faith maturity, as well as negatively related to sadism, psychopathic tendencies, and economic and social greed (Wright, et al., 2018). Relatedly, we found humility to correlate with several important markers of psychological wellbeing, such as optimism, hope, achievement values, positive life-regard, secure attachment, positive growth, personal relationships, decisiveness, comfort with ambiguity, and openness to experience (Wright, Nadelhoffer, and Ross, 2019).

We also found that people's humility was reflected in the way they expressed themselves. Specifically, we asked people to reflect on their relationship with (or to) the surrounding universe or cosmos, God or a higher power, the earth and the environment, and their fellow human beings, and found that when describing these relationships people higher in humility used more *inclusive* language (e.g., "we", "us", "our", as well as "all", "together", "everything"), whereas those lower in humility used more *exclusive* language (e.g., "they", "them", "people", "my own", "some", etc.). Those higher in humility also used "and" much more frequently, compared to those low in humility, who more frequently used "or". In summary, we found that people high in humility more frequently used language intended to break down boundaries and hierarchies, to maintain equality, and to emphasize connection, whereas those low in humility more frequently used language designed to express skepticism, impose judgment, assert superiority, and emphasize distance and disconnection (Perini, Langville, Wright and Nadelhoffer, 2019).

And finally, we found that humility predicted people's behavioral responses to conversational partners who disagreed with them. Specifically, we found that people high in humility exhibited little behavioral change (measured in terms of the distance they placed between themselves and those partners) when having a conversation with someone who strongly agreed with them and someone who strongly disagreed with them. People low in humility, on the other hand, acted differently toward—that is, they sat significantly further away from—those who disagreed with them, compared to where they sat when having a conversation with someone who agreed with them.

In sum, our own and others' research clearly shows a close connection between humility and numerous positive moral and social capacities, character strengths, and behaviors, suggesting that humility is a powerful virtue with psychological, moral, and social benefits.

But, elsewhere I have argued (Wright, 2019) that the importance of humility goes deeper than this—that, beyond normal, everyday moral capacities, humility is foundational to mature virtue and moral functioning—e.g., moral exemplarity.

34.4 Why humility matters: Moral exemplarity

Whenever we hear about the good deeds of moral exemplars, it is hard not to stand in awe of their brave and/or compassionate actions. These are individuals who dedicate significant time and energy, who even risk their lives, to save the lives of others and to protect and promote their wellbeing; individuals who fight for justice and work tirelessly to create a saner, more humane, more compassionate world.

What makes such exemplarity possible, psychologically speaking? The position I've argued for elsewhere (Wright, 2019) is that humility is foundational to mature virtue and moral functioning—and thus, to moral exemplarity. To see this, consider: humility allows for the (at least temporary) transcendence of our natural centeredness. And in escaping the centripetal force of our own needs, etc. we become able to genuinely *experience* the pull of the others' needs, etc. as they truly are—as being on par with our own. Thus, we become genuinely connected to the living beings around us, and to humanity as a whole; we become committed to and responsible for their wellbeing.

This is exactly the sort of life-long connection and commitment to, and responsibility for, others that we see demonstrated in the lives (and actions) of moral exemplars (Colby and Damon, 1992; Monroe, 2004, 2011; Oliner, 2003; Oliner and Oliner, 1988). And research on exemplars has revealed that at the heart of this connection and commitment is their experience of what has been referred to as "enlightened self-interest" (Frimer and Walker, 2009; Frimer, Walker, Dunlop, Lee, and Riches, 2011)—the synergistic integration of their self and other-oriented values. That is, exemplars report experiencing the benefitting of others and of themselves as *complementary facets* of their larger life values/goals, rather than as contradictory values that have to be chosen between, creating competition, internal tension, and guilt. In other words, exemplars experience their own needs, etc. as essentially woven into the needs, etc. of those around them, of their communities (Frimer, et al., 2011; see also Colby and Damon, 1992;

Monroe, 2004, 2011)—so when they act on the behalf of those individuals and communities, they are acting on their own behalf as well.

My own research has found a significant relationship between people's humility (as measured by our Dual-Dimension Humility Scale, Wright, et al., 2018) and the integration of their self and other-oriented values, expressed both explicitly in value statements and implicitly in life narratives and in their actions toward others in a competitive activity. Specifically, people high in humility expressed a deep investment in the lives and wellbeing of others, rather than being merely absorbed with the satisfaction of their own needs, etc. And they more frequently opted to share a portion of their winnings with their competitors, rather than keep them only for themselves (Wright, Goya-Tocchetto, Beck, Kutty-Falls, Sweat, and Swett, 2019).

Importantly, it is their experience of a deep and abiding connection with, commitment to, and responsibility for, others that empowers exemplars to dedicate themselves to saving lives, fighting injustices, caring for the sick and hungry, and protecting the weak, vulnerable, and oppressed, even when there is great potential risk to themselves. They do not feel alone, but rather grounded by and embedded in—both supporting and supported by—the inter-connected web of humanity, and of living beings more generally, of which they are a part (Brooks, 2015; Colby and Damon, 1992; Monroe, 2004, 2012; Oliner, 2003; Oliner and Oliner, 1988).

What is more, in order to be able to appropriately and consistently engage with and advocate for the needs, etc. of others across a range of situations, moral exemplars must be able to identify and evaluate the relevant information, decide what to do, and then implement their decision successfully, ideally in a way that is in sync with the situation itself. This means that: 1) they must be able to perceive, identify, understand, and properly evaluate the facts with respect to what to do (or not do), 2) they must be able to properly weigh the needs, desires, interests, beliefs, goals, and values of everyone involved in determining what to do (or not do), and 3) they must be able to carry it out without having to fight against internal conflict or "corruption".

Among other things, all of this requires moral exemplars to cognitively and affectively experience and appreciate the significance of many different features of the situation, *as they actually are*, in order to determine the appropriate response. And this requires the absence—the "quieting"—of anything that might bias, distort, or otherwise interfere with this process.

Central among these influences are those that arise from our natural centeredness. While certainly not the source of every potential bias and distortion, many are likely to originate from this source, and they are arguably often some of the more powerful and pernicious distorting influences—especially since they are generated by our natural default setting. And these are the influences most effectively (and perhaps only) combated—and ultimately quieted—through humility. It is thus arguably the core catalyst for the transformation undergone by moral exemplars.[4] It is also foundational to mature moral functioning and the ability to generate appropriate moral responses more generally.

34.5 Conclusion

In this chapter, I have presented the view (argued for by my colleagues and I elsewhere, see Nadelhoffer and Wright, 2017, Nadelhoffer, et al., 2017; Wright, et al., 2017, 2018) that humility is an epistemically and ethically aligned state of awareness. Humility's epistemic alignment orients us toward reality, allowing us to experience and evaluate things as they actually are. Humility's ethical alignment orients us toward others, allowing us to deeply understand and experience the needs, etc. of other morally relevant beings. Thus, humility is a state of awareness free from the many centeredness generated biases that distort and/or otherwise interfere with our ability to perceive, identify, understand, and properly evaluate the significance of the facts, as well as to properly weigh the needs, desires, interests, beliefs, goals, and values of others, in determining what we ought (or ought not) do. It also silences the internal conflict or "corruption" that would otherwise interfere with us acting on those determinations. This makes humility foundational to mature virtue and moral functioning, and moral exemplarity.

Notes

1 While my colleagues and I are also highly critical of the self-abasement view of humility, we have nonetheless found evidence for a limited potential role for self-abasement in humility development (Nadelhoffer and Wright, 2017, Nadelhoffer, Wright, Echols, Perini, and Venezia, 2017). Specifically, we found evidence that the experience of being humbled, of being "brought down" to see oneself as "lowly", of being humiliated in the eyes of another (and/or of oneself) may sometimes play an crucial role in the initial shifting of one's psychological positioning relative to other living beings and the larger universe. Thus, while self-abasement may be problematic as the centerpiece of humility, it may nonetheless have something to offer at the early stages of humility development.

2 This is not to say that morality cannot (or should not) accommodate agent-centric motivations and reasons—for example, something might be morally appropriate to do at least in part because it contributes to your own wellbeing, or the wellbeing of those closest to you.

3 This is a view my we have argued for both theoretically and empirically—for example, our analysis of people's folk concept of humility provided support for this view, showing that children, adolescents, and adults are sensitive to both the epistemological and ethical alignment features of humility (Nadelhoffer, et al., 2017). I also found support for this view cross-culturally, interviewing people across five countries in SE Asia (Wright, 2019).

4 Interestingly, it also suggests that while moral exemplars are likely to differ in many respects from one another, to have very different personalities, the one thing that they will all share is humility.

References

Aquinas. (1274/1972). *Summa Theologiae*, vol. 44, trans. Thomas Gilby. Cambridge, UK: Blackfriars, 1972, (p. 105, 107).

Ashton, M. C., and Lee, K. (2008). The HEXACO model of personality structure and the importance of the H factor. *Social and Personality Psychology Compass*, *2*(5), 1952–1962. doi:10.1111/j.1751-9004.2008.00134.x.

Ashton, M. C., Lee, K., Perugini, M., Szarota, P., de Vries, R. E., Di Blas, L., Boies, K., and De Raad, B. (2004). A sixfactor structure of personality-descriptive adjectives: Solutions from psycholexical studies in seven languages. *Journal of Personality and Social Psychology*, *86*(2), 356–366.

Baumeister, R. F., and Exline, J. J. (2002). Mystical self-loss: A challenge for psychological theory. *International Journal for the Psychology of Religion*, *12*(1), 15–20. doi:10.1207/S15327582IJPR1201_02.

Baxter, R. (1830). Christian directory. In: William Orme (Ed.), *The Practical Works of the Reverand Richard Baxter*. London: James Duncan.

Brooks, D. (2015). *The Road to Character*. New York: Random House Press.

Colby, A., and Damon, W. (1992). *Some Do Care: Contemporary Lives of Moral Commitment*. New York: Free Press.

Davis, D. E., Hook, J. N., Worthington, E. J., Van Tongeren, D. R., Gartner, A. L., Jennings, D. J., and Emmons, R. A. (2011). Relational humility: Conceptualizing and measuring humility as a personality judgment. *Journal of Personality Assessment*, *93*(3), 225–234. doi:10.1080/00223891.2011.558871.

Davis, D. E., Worthington, E. J., and Hook, J. N. (2010). Humility: Review of measurement strategies and conceptualization as personality judgment. *The Journal of Positive Psychology*, *5*(4), 243–252.

Emmons, R. A. (1998). The psychology of ultimate concern: Personality, spirituality, and intelligence. Unpublished manuscript, University of California at Davis.

Emmons, R. A. (1999). Religion in the psychology of personality: An introduction. *Journal of Personality*, *67*(6), 873–888.

Emmons, R. A., and Kneezel, T. T. (2005). Giving thanks: Spiritual and religious correlates of gratitude. *Journal of Psychology and Christianity*, *24*(2), 140–148.

Exline, J. J., and Geyer, A. L. (2004). Perceptions of humility: A preliminary study. *Self and Identity*, *3*(2), 95–114.

Frimer, J. A., and Walker, L. J. (2009). Reconciling the self and morality: An empirical model of moral centrality development. *Developmental Psychology*, *45*(6), 1669–1681.
Frimer, J. A., Walker, L. J., Dunlop, W., Lee, B., and Riches, S. (2011). The integration of agency and communion in moral personality: Evidence of enlightened self-interest. *Journal of Personality and Social Psychology*, *101*(1), 149–163.
Funk and Wagnail's. (1963). *Standard College Dictionary*. New York : Hardcourt, Brace, and World, Inc.
Gerber, L. (2002). Standing humbly before nature. *Ethics and the Environment*, 7(1), 39.
Halling, S., Kunz, G., and Rowe, J. O. (1994). The contributions of dialogical psychology to phenomenological research. *Journal of Humanistic Psychology*, *34*(1), 109–131. doi:10.1177/00221678940341007.
Hilbig, B. E., Moshagen, M., and Zettler, I. (2015). Truth will out: Linking personality, morality, and honesty through indirect questioning. *Social Psychological and Personality Science*, *6*(2), 140–147. doi:10.1177/1948550614553640.
Hilbig, B. E., and Zettler, I. (2009). Pillars of cooperation: Honesty-humility, social value orientations, and economic behavior. *Journal of Research in Personality*, *43*(3), 516–519. doi:10.1016/j.jrp.2009.01.003.
Horneck, A. (1651). *The Happy Ascetic*. London: Gale Ecco.
Hume, D. (1960). *An Enquiry Concerning the Principles of Morals*. La Salle, IL: The Open Court Publishing Company (original published in 1777).
Hwang, C. (1982). Studies in Chinese personality- A critical review. *Bulletin of Educational Psychology*, *15*, 227–242.
Johnston, M. (2009). *Saving God: Religions after Idolatry*. Princeton, NJ: Princeton University Press.
Kempis, T. A. (1940). *Of the Imitation of Christ*, trans. A. Croft, and H. Bolton, Milwaukee, WI: The Bruce Publishing Company (original publication in 1441).
Klein, D. C. (1992). Managing humiliation. *The Journal of Primary Prevention*, *12*(3), 255–268.
Knight, P. A., and Nadel, J. I. (1986). Humility revisited: Self-esteem, information search, and policy consistency. *Organizational Behavior and Human Decision Processes*, *38*(2), 196–206.
Kruse, E., Chancellor, J., Ruberton, P. M., and Lyubomirsky, S. (2014). An upward spiral between gratitude and humility. *Social Psychological and Personality Science*, *5*(7), 805–814. doi:10.1177/1948550614534700.
LaBouff, J. P., Rowatt, W. C., Johnson, M. K., Tsang, J., and Willerton, G. M. (2012). Humble persons are more helpful than less humble persons: Evidence from three studies. *The Journal of Positive Psychology*, 7(1), 16–29.
Langston, C. A., and Cantor, N. (1989). Social anxiety and social constraint: When making friends is hard. *Journal of Personality and Social Psychology*, *56*(4), 649–661.
Leary, M. R., Adams, C. E., and Tate, E. B. (2006). Hypo-egoic self-regulation: Exercising self-control by diminishing the influence of the self. *Journal of Personality*, *74*(6), 1803–1832.
Leary, M. R., and Guadagno, J. (2011). The role of hypo-egoic self-processes in optimal functioning and subjective well-being. In: K. M. Sheldon, T. B. Kashdan, M. F. Steger (Eds.), *Designing Positive Psychology: Taking Stock and Moving Forward* (pp. 135–146). New York: Oxford University Press.
Leary, M. R., and Terry, M. L. (2012). Hypo-egoic mindsets: Antecedents and implications of quieting the self. In: M. Leary, J. P. Tangney (Eds.), *Handbook of Self and Identity* (pp. 268–288). New York: Guilford Press.
Lee, K., and Ashton, M. C. (2012). Getting mad and getting even: Agreeableness and Honesty-Humility as predictors of revenge intentions. *Personality and Individual Differences*, *52*(5), 596–600. doi:10.1016/j.paid.2011.12.004.
Lee, K., Ashton, M. C., Ogunfowora, B., Bourdage, J. S., and Shin, K. (2010). The personality bases of socio-political attitudes: The role of Honesty–Humility and Openness to Experience. *Journal of Research in Personality*, *44*(1), 115–119. doi:10.1016/j.jrp.2009.08.007.
Lewis, C. S. (1952/1980). *Mere Christianity*. New York: Harper Row.
Maimonides (Moses Ben Maimom). (1972). *A Maimonides Reader*, ed. Isadore Twersky, New York: Behrman House, Inc.
McArthur, T. (1998). *Oxford English Dictionary. Concise Oxford Companion to the English Language*. Retrieved January 09, 2015 from Encyclopedia.com: www.encyclopedia.com/doc/1O29- oxfordenglishdictionary.html.
Means, J. R., Wilson, G. L., Sturm, C., Biron, J. E., and Bach, P. J. (1990). Humility as a psychotherapeutic formulation. *Counselling Psychology Quarterly*, *3*(2), 211–215. doi:10.1080/09515079008254249.

Monroe, K. (2004). *The Hand of Compassion: Portraits of Moral Choice during the Holocaust.* Princeton, NJ: Princeton University Press.

Monroe, K. (2012). *Ethics in an Age of Terror and Genocide: Identity and Moral Choice.* Princeton, NJ: Princeton University Press.

Murray, A. (2001). *Humility: The Journey Toward Holiness.* Bloomington, MN: Bethany House.

Nadelhoffer, T., and Wright, J. C. (2017). The twin dimensions of the virtue of humility: Low self-focus and high other-focus. In: W. Sinnott-Armstrong, C. Miller (Eds.), *Moral Psychology: Volume 5: Virtues and Happiness.* Cambridge: MIT Press.

Nadelhoffer, T., Wright, J. C., Echols, M., Perini, T., and Venezia, K. (2017). The varieties of humility worth wanting: An interdisciplinary investigation. *Journal of Moral Philosophy, 14*(2), 168–200. doi:10.1163/17455243-46810056.

Nietzsche, F. (1966). *Beyond Good and Evil*, trans. W. Kaufmann. New York: Random House, Inc. (original publication in 1886).

Oliner, S. (2003). *Do Unto Others: Extraordinary Acts of Ordinary People.* Cambridge, MA: Basic Books.

Oliner, S., and Oliner, P. (1988). *The Altruistic Personality: Rescuers of Jews in Nazi Europe.* New York: Free Press.

Perini, T., Langville, A., Wright, J. C., and Nadelhoffer, T. (2019). *Humble Speech: Textual Analysis of the Writing of Humble vs. Non-Humble People.* Manuscript in preparation.

Peterson, C., and Seligman, M. P. (2004). *Character Strengths and Virtues: A Handbook and Classification.* Washington, D.C.; New York: American Psychological Association.

Powers, C., Nam, R. K., Rowatt, W. C., and Hill, P. C. (2007). Associations between humility, spiritual transcendence, and forgiveness. *Research in the Social Scientific Study of Religion*, 18, 1875–1894.

Richards, N. (1988). Is humility a virtue? *American Philosophical Quarterly, 25*(3), 253–259.

Rowatt, W. C., Ottenbreit, A., Nesselroade, K. J., and Cunningham, P. A. (2002). On being holier-than-thou or humbler-than-thee: A social-psychological perspective on religiousness and humility. *Journal for the Scientific Study of Religion, 41*(2), 227–237.

Sandage, S. J. (1999, January). An ego-humility model of forgiveness: A theory-driven empirical test of group interventions. *Dissertation Abstracts International, 59*, 3712.

Sandage, S. J., Wiens, T. W., and Dahl, C. M. (2001). Humility and attention: The contemplative psychology of Simone Weil. *Journal of Psychology and Christianity, 20*(4), 360–369.

Sidgwick, H. (2011). *The Method of Ethics*, ed. J. Bennett. www.earlymoderntexts.com. (original 1874).

Snow, N. (1995). Humility. *Journal of Value Inquiry, 29*(2), 203–216.

Spinoza, B. (1677/1955). *The Ethics*, tran. R. H. M. Elwes. New York: Dover.

St. Bernard of Clairvaux. (1942). *Sermon 42 on Canticle 6*, tran. George Bosworth Burch in his *Introduction to Bernard's The Steps of Humility.* Cambridge: Harvard University Press.

Tangney, J. P. (2000). *Humility:* Theoretical perspectives, empirical findings and directions for future research. *Journal of Social and Clinical Psychology, 19*(1), 70–82. doi:10.1521/jscp.2000.19.1.70.

Tangney, J. P. (2009). Humility. In: S. J. Lopez, C. R. Snyder, S. J. Lopez, C. R. Snyder (Eds.), *Oxford Handbook of Positive Psychology* (2nd ed., pp. 483–490). New York: Oxford University Press.

Taylor, G. (1985). *Pride, Shame, and Guilt.* Oxford: Clarendon Press.

Templeton, J. M. (1997). *Worldwide Laws of Life: 200 Eternal Spiritual Principles.* Philadelphia, PA: Templeton Press.

Vera, D., and Rodriguez-Lopez, A. (2004). Strategic virtues: Humility as a source of competitive advantage. *Organizational Dynamics, 33*(4), 393–408. doi:10.1016/j.orgdyn.2004.09.006.

Wallace, D. F. (2005). https://web.ics.purdue.edu/~drkelly/DFWKenyonAddress2005.pdf.

Weidman, A. C., Cheng, J. T., and Tracy, J. L. (2016). The psychological structure of humility. *Journal of Personality and Social Psychology.* doi:10.1037/pspp0000112.

Weiss, H. M., and Knight, P. A. (1980). The utility of humility: Self-esteem, information search, and problem-solving efficiency. *Organizational Behavior and Human Performance, 25*(2), 216–223.

Wright, J. C., Goya-Tocchetto, D., Beck, E., Kutty-Falls, S., Sweat, S., and Swett, M. (2019). Humility as a form of value integration: The expression of enlightened self-interest. Manuscript under review.

Wright, J. C., Nadelhoffer, T., Perini, T., Langville, A., Echols, M., and Venezia, K. (2017). The psychological significance of humility. *The Journal of Positive Psychology, 12*(1), 3–12. doi:10.1080/17439760.2016.1167940.

Wright, J. C., Nadelhoffer, T., Ross, L., and Sinnott-Armstrong (2018). Be it ever so humble: Proposing a dual-dimension account and measurement for humility. *Self and Identity, 17*(1), 92–125.

Wright, J. C. (2019). The folk concept of humility in SE Asia. Manuscript in preparation.

Wright, J. C., Ross, L., and Wensing, J. (2019). Humility, psychological functioning, and personality. Manuscript in preparation.

Zettler, I., Hilbig, B. E., and Heydasch, T. (2013). Two sides of one coin: Honesty–humility and situational factors mutually shape social dilemma decision making. *Journal of Research in Personality*, 47(4), 286–295. doi:10.1016/j.jrp.2013.01.012.

35

THE ROLE OF KNOWLEDGE CALIBRATION IN INTELLECTUAL HUMILITY

Nicholas Light and Philip Fernbach

The state of current public discourse is troubling. Groups fail to listen to one another, questions go unanswered, and responses are often incomplete or unhelpful. Even more worrisome is the degree to which people hold entrenched attitudes about complex issues that they do not understand well (Caplan, 2011; Sloman and Fernbach, 2017). The pervasive lack of intellectual humility is a barrier to productive discourse on important societal, political, and scientific issues. But what is intellectual humility? In laying out the challenge for researchers interested in addressing this issue, the organizers of this handbook define intellectual humility as "being aware of our own cognitive limitations and biases, and being responsive to the evidence" ("John Templeton Foundation – Intellectual Humility in Public Discourse," n.d.). We believe that in order to understand the scope of the challenge of making humans aware of their cognitive limitations, we first need to understand how human knowledge works.

People use their knowledge to make sense of the world around them, deal with uncertainty, and make decisions (Craik, 1943; Long, Fernbach, and de Langhe, 2018). They assess what they think they know about objects, people, issues, environments, and processes to make many kinds of judgements and choices (Alba and Hutchinson 2000; Fernbach, Sloman, et al. 2013; Hadar, Sood, and Fox 2013; Heath and Tversky 1991; Long, Fernbach, and de Langhe 2018; Wood and Lynch 2002). Skilled gamblers use their knowledge of the probabilities in a game to act when they believe the game is in their favor, judges use their knowledge of law to affect appropriate legal outcomes, and campers use their knowledge of wild animals to avoid encounters with predators. This is a rational behavioral pattern: it makes good sense to call on and use as much information as possible from past experiences in order to decide on the right courses of action in subsequent situations. The discouraging news for humans is that drawing on our accumulated knowledge in order to make decisions can lead us astray because self-assessments of knowledge are frequently inaccurate (Alba and Hutchinson, 2000; Moorman, 1999).

In this chapter, we explore the topic of intellectual humility and its counterpart, overconfidence, through the lens of knowledge calibration. First, we review common examples of overconfidence and knowledge miscalibration, and explore theories of why humans often lack intellectual humility. We discuss unique challenges with respect to knowledge miscalibration, providing examples from several streams of research. We then discuss both positive and negative implications of human overconfidence, and conclude by mentioning recent work on potential interventions to increase intellectual humility, as well as opportunities for future research.

35.1 Knowledge miscalibration and its origins

Miscalibration of knowledge is directional and is often manifested as overconfidence (Alba and Hutchinson 1987; Fischhoff, Slovic, and Lichtenstein 1977). People tend to overestimate—rather than underestimate—their knowledge, and findings from several different research areas suggest that overconfidence is common. We do not mean to suggest that all overconfidence is driven by miscalibration of knowledge. A boxer who has been training more intensely than ever before may believe that he is a better boxer than he really is, and that he is better than others, but his overconfidence has little to do with knowledge of boxing. Moore and Healy (2008) categorize overconfidence into three types: overestimation, overplacement, and overprecision. Because knowledge miscalibration can take all three forms, we believe it is one of the most important drivers of overconfidence. Take, for example, someone who believes they know more about financial investing than they really do. They may exhibit all three types of overconfidence by thinking they are better at choosing investments than they really are (overestimation), by thinking they are better than others at investing (overplacement), and by believing that their investment picks have a higher probability of success than they do in reality (overprecision).[1]

Rozenblit and Keil (2002) demonstrated that people systematically overestimate their knowledge of even simple things, suffering from an "illusion of explanatory depth" (IOED). In these studies, subjects were first asked to evaluate how well they understood simple mechanical objects such as a zipper or toilet, on a 1-to-7 scale. In the next step, the experimenters asked subjects to write step-by-step causal explanations for how these items work. Finally, subjects were asked to re-rate their understanding. The result was that they significantly reduced their reported levels of understanding compared to their initial levels. The difficulty of the step-by-step explanation task made it salient to subjects that their initial mental models were impoverished and overly simple. Separate research on judgment and decision making has used the difference between people's average confidence ratings for their answers to fact-based questions and their number of correct answers to demonstrate that people are overconfident (Fischhoff et al., 1977; Yates, Lee, and Bush, 1997; Yates, Lee, and Shinotsuka, 1996).

There are several plausible explanations for why knowledge overconfidence is pervasive. First, it may be socially adaptive to be confident. Confident people are perceived to be more competent by their peers, and achieve higher status in their groups (Anderson, Brion, Moore, and Kennedy, 2012; Tetlock and Gardner, 2015). When evaluating others, people tend to use a "confidence heuristic," inferring that those with more confidence possess greater knowledge, and liking experts who project more certainty (Gaertig and Simmons, 2018; Price and Stone, 2004). Not only is confidence socially adaptive—it may be evolutionarily adaptive. An individual's confidence in their social status enables positive risk-taking such as seeking necessary support from others in response to social negativity (Baumeister, Heatherton, and Tice, 1993; Park and Maner, 2009). Self-confidence can also signal social dominance, which is sexually attractive to potential mates (Bernstein, 1980; Ellis, 1995).

We suggest that another major contributing factor to overconfidence is the way in which people mentally represent and store knowledge. In Rozenblit and Keil's (2002) IOED studies overestimation of knowledge appears to have been driven by a neglect of underlying complexity. Subjects reduced their reported levels of understanding compared to their initial levels because the difficulty of the step-by-step explanation task made it salient that the domains or objects in the experiment were much more complex than they originally thought. The IOED is also consistent with separate work arguing that knowledge overconfidence is driven by a tendency to focus on known information and neglect unknowns (Walters, Fernbach, Fox, and Sloman, 2017). Importantly, this miscalibration is particularly dramatic for knowledge of explanations, which is distinguished by a structure of more *causal* complexity compared to knowledge of facts, procedures, or narratives (Keil, Rozenblit, and Mills, 2004). This is important to note for the current discussion because topics on which there is heated discourse (and a lack of intellectual humility) are frequently those with high levels of complexity, such as the causes and consequences of climate change, changes in the U.S. healthcare system, vaccination, and immigration policy, for example.

If knowledge miscalibration is at least partially driven by underestimation of complexity, it is useful to consider why humans systematically underestimate complexity. Although we may prefer to think otherwise, relative ignorance is a default human state; the world is so complex that no individual can truly understand very much of it (S. A. Sloman and Fernbach, 2017). Trying to understand and remember millions of causally inter-related details, processes, and potential outcomes is impossible because the human mind evolved to act effectively *in spite* of pervasive ignorance (Keil, 2006; S. A. Sloman and Fernbach, 2017). A common way humans cope with the overwhelming complexity of the world is to outsource knowledge to others (Rabb, Fernbach, and Sloman, 2019; Wegner, 2011). They frequently underestimate complexity because most people function normally without ever truly having to deal with it.

This shared nature of human knowledge makes it difficult for people to separate their own knowledge from what their communities know and believe (S. A. Sloman and Fernbach, 2017; S. A. Sloman and Rabb, 2016). This introduces a barrier to intellectual humility because people overestimate their understanding by virtue of simply being part of a community, and get a lift in their sense of understanding just from the knowledge that others have some understanding. For example, merely telling people that scientists have explained a newly discovered natural phenomenon—without saying anything about what the explanation is—causes people to increase their assessment of their own understanding (S. A. Sloman and Rabb, 2016). People even get a boost in their perceived understanding and think they have more knowledge in their heads when they have access to information on the internet (Fisher, Goddu, and Keil, 2015; Ward, n.d.), and fail to remember more information when they think it is being saved by a computer (Sparrow, Liu, and Wegner, 2011). Because people outsource knowledge and fail to recognize it, their mental models are often oversimplified and incorrect. When individuals fail to adequately check their understanding, unjustified attitudes may become entrenched in a community, perpetuating a dangerous cycle of ignorance.

35.2 The challenge of knowledge miscalibration

Lack of intellectual humility, manifested as knowledge miscalibration and overconfidence, is a particularly difficult issue to tackle. Higher perceptions of understanding are associated with higher reported certainty about one's attitudes (Fernbach, Rogers, Fox, and Sloman, 2013; Long et al., 2018). In the absence of salient information disproving what is perceived to be high knowledge, perceived high knowledge can lead to even more overconfidence, a phenomenon Alba and Hutchinson (1987) call "a cycle of self-delusion." It is also more difficult for people with objectively lower knowledge of a domain (or who are novices) to assess what it is they do not know, and as a result, they are poorer at evaluating their knowledge compared to individuals with objectively higher knowledge (or who are experts) (Dunning, 2011; Kruger and Dunning, 1999). According to Dunning and Kruger, "people who are unskilled in these domains suffer a dual burden: Not only do [they] reach erroneous conclusions and make unfortunate choices, but their incompetence robs them of the metacognitive ability to realize it" (Kruger and Dunning, 1999, p. 1121).

Independent of someone's expertise (or lack thereof) in a domain, knowledge miscalibration is a pervasive challenge. Recent research on information processing and judgment formation has found that people believe that they and others sample and consider more evidence before making up their minds on goods, services, and people than they do in reality (Klein and O'Brien, 2018). Klein and O'Brien (2018) argue that because people consume far less information than expected before evaluating things, they misjudge how quickly impressions form and change, which means that significant time, money, words, and effort is wasted on people who have already made up their minds. Beyond what could be called innocent scenarios of limited information processing, there are also less innocent ones: sometimes people deliberately choose to be ignorant in order not to feel the emotions associated with some information, maintain fairness, or avoid liability, for example (Hertwig and Engel, 2016).

35.3 Consequences of overconfidence

There are many negative consequences of knowledge miscalibration for both individual and societal wellbeing. As we have stated, people tend to be overconfident in their knowledge, know less than they think, underestimate or neglect true underlying complexity, and confuse exterior knowledge and information for their own. Research from decision affect theory has shown that this overconfidence can lead to real affective consequences for decision makers. In two studies where recreational basketball players made predictions about their shooting accuracy, McGraw et al. (2004) showed that overconfidence leads to less pleasure in response to predicted successes (because they are less surprising) and more pain in response to unexpected failures (because they are more surprising). These affective consequences were the result of overconfidence in a trivial task, but overconfidence and knowledge miscalibration can also lead to underestimation of risks, with significant material consequences. Research on consumer financial decision making has shown that higher self-assessments of financial knowledge lead to higher likelihoods of people making risky investments, and are correlated with lower subjective ratings of risk (but not objective risk) (Hadar et al., 2013; Long et al., 2018; Ward, Grillo, and Fernbach, 2019). For most, losing money as a result of underestimating financial risk would be affectively painful on its own, and could potentially cause additional stress if paying for bills becomes difficult.

Overconfidence among people with objectively high levels of knowledge is often manifested as excessive attitude certainty. Instead of overestimating their knowledge, they rely too heavily on it or reject external information that may be relevant or helpful. Wood and Lynch (2002) found that people with high prior product knowledge committed memory encoding errors and had lower motivation to search for new information, caused by superficial information processing. These findings are consistent with work by Alba and Hutchinson (1987) who argued that overconfidence can lead experts to shorten the search for answers, find false causal connections, and misinterpret objective facts. In the domain of medical decision making the consequences of overconfidence can be a matter of life and death. Dawes, Faust, and Meehl (1989) argued that medical experts make poorer choices than simple computer programs based on those experts' decision processes, which, they posit, is partially a consequence of the human propensity to overattend to information consistent with hypotheses and underattend to contradictory information (Greenwald, Pratkanis, Leippe, and Baumgardner, 1986). Among political and military leaders, overconfidence can lead to initiation of too many wars, military overcommitment, and loss of life (D. D. P. Johnson, 2004). These phenomena are important due to the connection between higher perceptions of knowledge and the tendency to rely on the knowledge (Krosnick and Petty, 1995).

There are also several streams of research pointing to extremity of beliefs as a consequence of knowledge miscalibration. When people overestimate their knowledge they are more likely to hold extreme views and fail to realize that they do not have enough knowledge required to justify their extreme positions (Fernbach, Rogers, et al., 2013). In three experiments, Fernbach et al. (2013) showed that asking people to explain policies in detail reduced subjective perceptions of understanding and led to more moderate political attitudes, which suggests that political polarization is at least partially caused by people's overestimation of their knowledge of the issues (also D. R. Johnson, Murphy, and Messer, 2016; but see Crawford, n.d.).

People also hold more complex cognitive representations of their own groups than of others, which leads them to evaluate others more extremely (Linville 1982). In this literature on the relationship between complexity and extremity of evaluations (see also Linville 1985, 1987), complexity is operationalized as the perceived number of non-redundant features or dimensions of people, objects, or issues—the more perceived dimensions, the higher perceived complexity. Linville (1982) manipulated the complexity of knowledge structures: participants in one study were instructed to think of either two (simple condition) or six (complex condition) attributes of a cookie before rating it. The participants in the simple condition gave higher ratings to the cookies they liked and lower ratings to the cookies they disliked, while participants in the complex condition gave more moderate ratings for all cookies. The fact that the complexity–extremity effect is present when people evaluate policies, people, and simple objects suggests that it is broadly generalizable and is a product of how humans mentally represent and store knowledge. The mechanism for these extremity effects is that it is more difficult for someone to think of any person, object, or issue in black and white when cognitively representing them with more dimensionality. With increasingly more labels to attach to something, the weight each label can possibly contribute to an overall evaluation mathematically decreases.

Because both knowledge overconfidence and extreme beliefs are at least partially caused by oversimplified mental models, lack of intellectual humility and extreme beliefs often coincide. Additional evidence for the link comes from work on opposition to applications of genetic engineering. Fernbach, Light et al. (2019) examined the relationship between self-assessed knowledge, objective knowledge, and extremity of participants' opposition to two applications of genetic engineering (on which there are scientific consensuses of safety): genetically modified foods and gene therapy. For both issues, they found that the most extreme opponents thought they knew the most about genetically modified foods (or gene therapy), but actually knew the least, scoring the lowest on a battery of true–false science and genetics questions. Similar patterns of results have been found in the domains of anti-establishment voting in the Netherlands (van Prooijen and Krouwel, 2018), and opposition to vaccination (Motta, Callaghan, and Sylvester, 2018). More generally, work on metacognition showed that participants with extreme political beliefs exhibited less insight into the correctness of their assessments of simple visual displays (Rollwage, Dolan, and Fleming, 2018). These examples suggest that extreme views often reflect low objective knowledge paired with high self-assessments of knowledge. This is doubly problematic, since gaining knowledge frequently has the effect of revealing nuance and complexity to those who gain it (Rozenblit and Keil, 2002), which in turn reduces extremity of belief.

Taken together, these findings suggest that overconfidence can lead to inaccurate predictions, lost money, wasted time, dissatisfaction, and entrenched false beliefs. We believe they also underscore an underappreciated obstacle: those who are the most overconfident or miscalibrated in their knowledge are the most likely to hold extreme views and the most in need of humility-inducing knowledge, but also the least likely to be receptive to learning. As previously discussed, knowledge overconfidence is correlated with decreased openness to new information (Wood and Lynch, 2002), and people are more likely to reconsider their positions on policies or issues when they have less confidence in their knowledge (Krosnick and Petty, 1995). To make matters worse, increasing the difficulty of a task or decision process has also been shown to increase overconfidence (Larrick, Burson, and Soll, 2007), so people may be most likely to overestimate their understanding and make judgement errors in the most complex and critical situations. This suggests that a necessary condition for increasing intellectual humility is getting people to realize gaps in their knowledge.

35.4 Benefits of overconfidence

When it comes to intellectual humility, the news is not all bad. As we suggested previously, overconfidence can be beneficial. Entrepreneurs famously tend to be more confident and tolerant of risk than others. Cooper, Woo, and Dunkelberg (1988) found that entrepreneurs exhibited unrealistic confidence about their businesses' chances of success given observed odds of business success. Entrepreneurs are also poor at recognizing the limits of their knowledge, overestimate the extent to which their actions can increase performance, and sample a limited amount of information to draw conclusions (M. Simon, Houghton, and Aquino, 2000). In a context of high levels of competition and low chances of success, however, these positive illusions can increase motivation, raise aspiration levels, and strengthen coping mechanisms in response to adversity (Taylor and Brown, 1988). These benefits can also create halo effects, encouraging the formation of lasting connections and increasing resiliency (Fredrickson, 2001; Tugade and Fredrickson, 2004).

Knowledge overconfidence can also lead people to undertake efforts they normally would not if they knew the true scale of their ignorance, such as embarking on a risky voyage, starting a new business, or trying to remodel the kitchen without professional help (S. A. Sloman and Fernbach, 2017). As long as failures (or low-quality successes) in these undertakings do not cause incapacitation or death, they may lead people to learn new skills or information that can be passed on. If attempts are successful against the odds, they may give rise to solutions or outcomes that are better than the pre-attempt status quo. Although success comes at a cost, the world may need overconfidence in order to grow and improve.

Not only are there benefits to individual overconfidence, which is the symptom, there are benefits associated with the root cause of knowledge miscalibration: the way in which humans mentally represent and store knowledge. As we have mentioned, ignorance is not only pervasive; it is a natural human state because the world is nearly infinitely complex. To deal with that complexity, humans draw seamlessly on knowledge contained not just in our own brains, but in our bodies, the environment, and especially in other people (S. A. Sloman and Fernbach, 2017). Humans are inherently social animals who benefit from the collaboration of many individuals guided by a division of cognitive labor (S. A. Sloman and Rabb, 2016). In many ways, this is a good thing. Although knowledge miscalibration can be viewed as an error, it may simply be one byproduct of an adaptive way humans try to understand the world around them. The feeling of understanding or knowing that is associated with overconfidence may be an indirect signal to individuals that they can stop explaining or seeking more explanations for an event, because the causes are now understood (Trout, 2003). Alternatively, it may also give humans a level of insight sufficient enough to seek out appropriate experts for more information (Keil et al., 2004). This is beneficial because dealing with complexity and evaluating the validity of new information requires cognitive effort, which is aversive (Payne, 1976; Shah and Oppenheimer, 2008; H. A. Simon, 1990). Because humans try to conserve cognitive effort, there are diminishing returns to seeking additional information and explanations. Without simplified mental models, people would spend all of their time trying to find better and better explanations, causes, and courses of action, which would interfere with making decisions and ultimately taking necessary action.

35.5 Underconfidence

People are not universally overconfident. Several researchers have pointed out situations in which people are underconfident, though these situations tend to be more about practical skill than knowledge. For example, people believe that they are below average at riding a unicycle and computer programming, and think they have lower-than-average chances of living past 100 years of age (Kruger, 1999; Kruger and Burrus, 2004). Moore and Cain (2007) argue that people believe that they are worse than average at difficult skill-based tasks because they have more information about themselves and thus make judgments for others closer to their beliefs about what is average. When difficulty is increased for both parties in a competitive scenario, for example in a negotiation via added time constraints, both parties believe that they will be hurt more by the added difficulty than their competitors (Moore, 2005), which reflects underconfidence in the ability to deal with adversity, compared to others. With respect to knowledge specifically, Keil et al. (2004) have speculated that the root causes of knowledge overconfidence should also predict instances of knowledge underconfidence when explanations for outcomes are "highly, but not obviously, constrained," meaning when they are actually less complex than they seem.

35.6 Efforts to increase intellectual humility

If lacking intellectual humility is caused in part by lacking knowledge, an intuitive recommendation for mitigating knowledge overconfidence might be to simply educate people about important issues on which their knowledge is lacking. In the public understanding of science literature, support has been growing for the idea that people hold strong positions on scientific issues such as genetically modified organisms, climate change, and vaccination, despite incredibly limited understanding of the issues (NSF, 2016; Ranney and Clark, 2016). The traditional approach to bringing individuals' beliefs closer to the scientific consensus, the "deficit model," appeals to the notion of missing information (Bodmer, 1985). The thinking is that if people are too ignorant to appreciate the other side of an issue, their ignorance can lead to reliance on the most vociferous personalities, polarization of attitudes, and further failure to understand. The standard method for trying to overcome these informational deficits and change attitudes is to simply educate people. Unfortunately, the deficit model has been questioned on the grounds that educational interventions rarely succeed in meaningfully changing beliefs (Allum, Sturgis, Tabourazi, and Brunton-Smith, 2008; Miller, 2001).

There is another seemingly intuitive approach to mitigating intellectual overconfidence in the domain of public acceptance of science. The thinking is that if teaching people the facts that they lack does not cause meaningful attitude change, maybe simply communicating that there are scientific consensuses on these important issues (and what those consensuses are) will make an impact. Recent research has tested this approach in a randomized online survey experiment (Landrum, Hallman, and Jamieson, 2019). Specifically, this work tested the effect of different messages on subjects' evaluations and acceptance of the scientific consensus on the safety of genetically modified organisms. Two of the messages communicated that there is a consensus that genetically modified organisms are safe for humans to consume, but neither meaningfully reduced subjects' initial levels of concern, even though research suggests that safety concerns are a dominant driver of opposition (Fernbach et al., 2019). Communicating a consensus appears to be no more successful at changing minds than teaching missing facts.

These attempts and the previously mentioned findings regarding the prevalence of high self-assessments of knowledge paired with low objective knowledge among extremists suggest that the challenge of improving intellectual humility may not just be a matter of informing people about facts, but of encouraging them to appreciate that issues are complex, and they know less about them than they think. There have been some initial inroads along these lines. One team of researchers explored the connection between knowledge and perceived absoluteness of information surrounding contentious topics. Their findings show that people shift their understanding of the nature of truth to match certain goals in interactive scenarios (Fisher, Knobe, Strickland, and Keil, 2017). Specifically, Fisher et al. (2017) found that people view the truth of contentious issues as less absolute when adopting a goal to learn when arguing, but more absolute when adopting a goal to win the argument (or with no experimentally manipulated goal at all). Because the authors found no significant differences in their dependent measure between the argue-to-win and control conditions, they concluded that a learning goal in an argument caused participants to develop a more subjective view of incoming information. The authors cited previous work showing that goal-directed cognitive processes are more likely to acted upon when a corresponding goal is active (Xu and Wyer, 2008), and proposed that the mechanism for their overall findings is that a learning goal causes people to place higher information value on incoming messages. They also suggested that adopting a learning goal may drive additional "open" responses, of which perceived subjectivity is just one.

We believe that the way in which humans store and access knowledge provides additional evidence for why argument goal interventions may be promising for increasing intellectual humility surrounding contentious issues. Evaluating the validity of incoming information about processes, domains, or truth in general entails evaluating and drawing on one's own knowledge to use as a comparison (Hofer, 2017). Fox and Tversky (1995) found that people avoid options about which they know less in a joint evaluation, but do not when options are evaluated separately. This finding suggests that people may be led to realize their ignorance of a topic if assessing their knowledge in comparison with another topic about which they know comparatively more ("comparative ignorance" Fox and Tversky, 1995). Assessments of knowledge are also fundamentally social (Chinn, Buckland, and Samarapungavan, 2011; S. Sloman and Fernbach, 2017). Evidence for this comes from the previously mentioned idea that knowledge miscalibration is partially driven by people confusing their access to others' knowledge for their own internally held knowledge, which allows them to deal with a world of infinitely deep complexity by outsourcing it to others (Keil et al. 2004). Knowledge is also inherently goal-directed (Chinn et al., 2011; Sandoval, 2017). People seek knowledge in order to do things, and rarely obtain knowledge for its own sake. If humans are hardwired to use others to store knowledge and expertise, and seek knowledge in order to achieve goals, it makes sense that adopting a learning goal in an argument—with an explicit aim of receiving previously outsourced knowledge from others to be put to use—would positively affect people's openness to new information and perceptions of their own knowledge.

In terms of interventions designed to increase intellectual humility and decrease knowledge miscalibration, we have discussed education attempts, appeals to expert consensus, and goal interventions. We believe that the nature of human knowledge provides researchers with another promising approach to mitigating knowledge miscalibration: mechanism interventions. One such intervention attempting to increase acceptance of the scientific consensus on climate change provided subjects with a clear step-by-step account of how climate change works, and was successful at increasing acceptance across the liberal–conservative spectrum (Ranney and Clark, 2016). This supports the notion that what is important about mechanistic interventions is forcing people to make a metacognitive evaluation in which previously underestimated complexity is revealed.

In addition to these interventions that have already been tested, we believe that several others may be promising. The first potential intervention is to attempt to draw people's attention to the distributed nature of knowledge (e.g., by asking them to identify who has specific pieces of knowledge). Experimental subjects could be asked to indicate who has—and where they would find—the information necessary to make the most informed decision regarding a specific policy, technology, topic, etc. A more abstract version of this type of intervention would be to simply remind people that they may not know as much as they think about particular issues, but that, in a real situation, they would have access to broad expertise. In both cases, experiments would measure perceived understanding and attitude strength after the interventions in order to test their effectiveness at making subjects more humble and less extreme in their positions.

Given that the IOED manipulations reduce perceptions of understanding/knowledge but would be difficult to implement on a larger scale outside of a lab setting, our second proposed direction would be to design similar mechanism and analogy interventions that target specific false beliefs. In these studies, we would collect individual difference measures that indicate the categories of concerns that drive attitudes, and customize interventions to address those concerns. Our hope is that this type of intervention would make people more open to new information, increase awareness of the complexity of the mechanisms, and support more productive discourse.

We also believe that there is a broader opportunity to design interventions that manipulate subjects' perceptions of complexity. Specifically, there may be promise in using manipulated complexity to make domains, technologies, or issues seem more or less similar to each other by experimentally equating them on number of dimensions, attributes, or themes. Evers, Inbar, and Zeelenberg (2014) found that people prefer sets of items that are less complex (with products within sets perceived to be more similar to each other) than more complex sets (with products perceived to be less similar to each other), even if the more complex set contains a more preferred item. These studies suggest that the constructs of complexity and similarity are highly negatively correlated. As a result, complexity manipulations could help encourage the realization of the complexity of contentious scientific policies or technologies by equating them on complexity with more accepted complex issues. On the other hand, complexity manipulations could be deployed to encourage the belief that an issue or technology is not similar to others that are unpopular with specific groups.

35.7 Conclusion

In this chapter we have focused on the human propensity to overestimate knowledge and underestimate complexity, which we believe to be significant hurdles in efforts to promote intellectual humility. Knowledge miscalibration is a particularly difficult overconfidence challenge to address because we believe it is the product of an adaptive way in which humans seek to understand the world around them. The world is just too complex for any individual to understand in much detail. The paradox is that, in order to promote openness to new knowledge, people might first need to be made aware of their ignorance and generally oversimplified models of the world. Of course, when it comes to our own understanding of the complexities of human cognition, intellectual humility, and encouraging more productive public discourse, we have just begun to scratch the surface.

Note

1 It should be noted that Moore and Healy argue that there is a negative overall relationship between overestimation and overplacement because the difficulty of a task affects the two phenomena in opposite ways.

References

Alba, J. W., and Hutchinson, J. W. (1987). Dimensions of consumer expertise. *Journal of Consumer Research, 13*(4), 411. doi:10.1086/209080

Alba, J. W., and Hutchinson, J. W. (2000). Knowledge calibration: What consumers know and what they think they know. *Journal of Consumer Research, 27*(2), 123–156. doi:10.1086/314317

Allum, N., Sturgis, P., Tabourazi, D., and Brunton-Smith, I. (2008). Science knowledge and attitudes across cultures: A meta-analysis. *Public Understanding of Science, 17*(1), 35–54. doi:10.1177/0963662506070159

Anderson, C., Brion, S., Moore, D. A., and Kennedy, J. A. (2012). A status-enhancement account of overconfidence. *Journal of Personality and Social Psychology, 103*(4), 718. doi:10.1037/a0029395

Baumeister, R. F., Heatherton, T. F., and Tice, D. M. (1993). When ego threats lead to self-regulation failure: Negative consequences of high self-esteem. *Journal of Personality and Social Psychology, 64*(1), 141. doi:10.1037/0022-3514.64.1.141

Bernstein, I. (1980). Dominance: A theoretical perspective for ethologists. In D. R. Omark, F. F. Strayer, and D. G. Freedman (Eds.), *Dominance Relations: An Ethological View of Human Conflict and Social Interaction* (pp. 71–84). New York: Garland Press.

Bodmer, W. F. (1985). The public understanding of science. *Royal Society*, 1–43. doi:10.1038/340011a0

Caplan, B. (2011). *The Myth of the Rational Voter: Why Democracies Choose Bad Policies (New Edition).* Princeton and Oxford: Princeton University Press.

Chinn, C. A., Buckland, L. A., and Samarapungavan, A. (2011). Expanding the dimensions of epistemic cognition: Arguments from philosophy and psychology. *Educational Psychologist, 46*(3), 141–167. doi:10.1080/00461520.2011.587722

Cooper, A. C., Woo, C. Y., and Dunkelberg, W. C. (1988). Entrepreneurs' perceived chances for success. *Journal of Business Venturing, 3*(2), 97–108. doi:10.1016/0883-9026(88)90020-1

Craik, K. J. W. (1943). *The Nature of Explanation.* Cambridge: Cambridge University Press.

Crawford, J. T. (n.d.). *Puncturing the Illusion of Understanding Does Not Reduce Political Extremism: A Replication of Fernbach.* Rogers: Fox, and Sloman.

Dawes, R. M., Faust, D., and Meehl, P. E. (1989). Clinical versus actuarial judgment. *Science, 243*(4899), 1668–1674. doi:10.1126/science.2648573

Dunning, D. (2011). The Dunning–Kruger effect. In *Advances in Experimental Social Psychology* (Vol. 44, pp. 247–296). doi:10.1016/B978-0-12-385522-0.00005-6

Ellis, B. J. (1995). The evolution of sexual attraction: Evaluative mechanisms in women. In J. H. Barkow, L. Cosmides, and J. Tooby (Eds.), *The Adapted Mind: Evolutionary Psychology and the Generation of Culture* (pp. 267–288). New York and Oxford: Oxford University Press.

Evers, E. R. K., Inbar, Y., and Zeelenberg, M. (2014). Set-fit effects in choice. *Journal of Experimental Psychology: General, 143*(2), 504–509.

Fernbach, P. M., Light, N., Scott, S. E., Inbar, Y., and Rozin, P. (2019). Extreme opponents of genetically modified foods know the least but think they know the most. *Nature Human Behaviour, 3*(3), 251–256.

Fernbach, P. M., Rogers, T., Fox, C. R., and Sloman, S. A. (2013). Political extremism is supported by an illusion of understanding. *Psychological Science, 24*(6), 939–946. doi:10.1177/0956797612464058

Fernbach, P. M., Sloman, S. A., Louis, R. St., and Shube, J. N. (2013). Explanation fiends and foes: How mechanistic detail determines understanding and preference. *Journal of Consumer Research, 39*(5), 1115–1131. doi:10.1086/667782

Fischhoff, B., Slovic, P., and Lichtenstein, S. (1977). Knowing with certainty: The appropriateness of extreme confidence. *Journal of Experimental Psychology: Human Perception and Performance, 3*, 552–564. doi:10.4324/9780203141939

Fisher, M., Goddu, M. K., and Keil, F. C. (2015). Searching for explanations: How the internet inflates estimates of internal knowledge. *Journal of Experimental Psychology: General, 144*(3), 674. doi:10.1037/xge0000070

Fisher, M., Knobe, J., Strickland, B., and Keil, F. C. (2017). The influence of social interaction on intuitions of objectivity and subjectivity. *Cognitive Science, 41*(4), 1119–1134. doi:10.1111/cogs.12380

Fox, C. R., and Tversky, A. (1995). Ambiguity aversion and comparative ignorance. *The Quarterly Journal of Economics, 110*(3), 585–603. doi:10.2307/2946693

Fredrickson, B. L. (2001). The role of positive emotions in positive psychology: The broaden-and-build theory of positive emotions. *The American Psychologist, 56*(3), 218–226. doi:10.1037/0003-066X.56.3.218

Gaertig, C., and Simmons, J. P. (2018). Do people inherently dislike uncertain advice? *Psychological Science, 29*(4), 504–520. doi:10.1177/0956797617739369

Greenwald, A. G., Pratkanis, A. R., Leippe, M. R., and Baumgardner, M. H. (1986). Under what conditions does theory obstruct research progress? *Psychological Review, 93*(2), 216. doi:10.1037/0033-295X.93.2.216

Hadar, L., Sood, S., and Fox, C. R. (2013). Subjective knowledge in consumer financial decisions. *Journal of Marketing Research, 50*(3), 303–316. doi:10.1509/jmr.10.0518

Heath, C., and Tversky, A. (1991). Preferences and beliefs: Ambiguity and competence in choice under uncertainty. *Journal of Risk and Uncertainty, 4*(1), 5–28. doi:10.1007/BF00057884

Hertwig, R., and Engel, C. (2016). Homo ignorans: Deliberately choosing not to know. *Perspectives on Psychological Science, 11*(3), 359–372. doi:10.1177/1745691616635594

Hofer, B. K. (2017). Identifying the role of epistemic cognition and metacognition in conceptual change. In T. G. Amin, and O. Levrini (Eds.), *Converging Perspectives on Conceptual Change: Mapping an Emerging Paradigm in the Learning Sciences* (pp. 191–196). New York: Routledge.

John Templeton Foundation. (n.d.). *Intellectual Humility in Public Discourse.* https://www.templeton.org/grant/intellectual-humility-in-public-discourse

Johnson, D. D. P. (2004). *Overconfidence and War: The Havoc and Glory of Positive Illusions.* Cambridge: Harvard University Press. doi:10.1111/j.1468-2508.2006.00382_13.x

Johnson, D. R., Murphy, M. P., and Messer, R. M. (2016). Reflecting on explanatory ability: A mechanism for detecting gaps in causal knowledge. *Journal of Experimental Psychology: General, 145*(5), 573–588. doi:10.1037/xge0000161

Keil, F. C. (2006). Explanation and understanding. *Annual Review of Psychology, 57*, 227–254. doi:10.1146/annurev.psych.57.102904.190100.Explanation

Keil, F. C., Rozenblit, L., and Mills, C. M. (2004). What lies beneath? Understanding the limits of understanding. In D. T. Levin (Ed.), *Thinking and Seeing: Visual Metacognition in Adults and Children* (pp. 227–249). Cambridge: MIT Press.

Klein, N., and O'Brien, E. (2018). People use less information than they think to make up their minds. *Proceedings of the National Academy of Sciences of the United States of America, 115*(52), 13222–13227. doi:10.1073/pnas.1805327115

Krosnick, J. A., and Petty, R. E. (1995). Attitude strength: An overview. In R.E. Petty and J. A. Krosnick (Eds.), *Attitude Strength: Antecedents and Consequences (pp. 1-24).* New York and London: Psychology Press.

Kruger, J. (1999). Lake Wobegon be gone! The "below-average effect" and the egocentric nature of comparative ability judgments. *Journal of Personality and Social Psychology*, 77(2), 221–232. doi:10.1037/0022-3514.77.2.221

Kruger, J., and Burrus, J. (2004). Egocentrism and focalism in unrealistic optimism (and pessimism). *Journal of Experimental Social Psychology, 40*(3), 332–340. doi:10.1016/j.jesp.2003.06.002

Kruger, J., and Dunning, D. (1999). Unskilled and unaware of it: How difficulties in recognizing one's own incompetence lead to inflated self-assessments. *Journal of Personality and Social Psychology*, 77(6), 1121–1134. doi:10.1037/0022-3514.77.6.1121

Landrum, A. R., Hallman, W. K., and Jamieson, K. H. (2019). Examining the impact of expert voices: Communicating the scientific consensus on genetically-modified organisms. *Environmental Communication, 13*(1), 51–70. doi:10.1080/17524032.2018.1502201

Larrick, R. P., Burson, K. A., and Soll, J. B. (2007). Social comparison and confidence: When thinking you're better than average predicts overconfidence (and when it does not). *Organizational Behavior and Human Decision Processes, 102*(1), 76–94. doi:10.1016/j.obhdp.2006.10.002

Linville, P. W. (1982). The complexity-extremity effect and age-based stereotyping. *Journal of Personality and Social Psychology, 42*(2), 193–211.

Linville, P. W. (1985). Self-Complexity and Affective Extremity: Don't Put All of Your Eggs in One Cognitive Basket. *Social Cognition, 3*(1), 94–120.

Linville, P. W. (1987). Self-Complexity as a Cognitive Buffer Against Stress-Related Illness and Depression. *Journal of Personality and Social Psychology, 52*(4), 663–676.

Long, A. R., Fernbach, P. M., and de Langhe, B. (2018). Circle of incompetence: Sense of understanding as an improper guide to investment risk. *Journal of Marketing Research, 55*(4), 474–488.

McGraw, A. P., Mellers, B. A., and Ritov, I. (2004). The affective costs of overconfidence. *Journal of Behavioral Decision Making, 17*(4), 281–295. doi:10.1002/bdm.472

Miller, S. (2001). Public understanding of science at the crossroads. *Public Understanding of Science, 10*(1), 115–120. doi:10.1088/0963-6625/10/1/308

Moore, D. A. (2005). Myopic biases in strategic social prediction: Why deadlines put everyone under more pressure than everyone else. *Personality and Social Psychology Bulletin, 31*(5), 668–675. doi:10.1177/0146167204271569

Moore, D. A., and Cain, D. M. (2007). Overconfidence and underconfidence: When and why people underestimate (and overestimate) the competition. *Organizational Behavior and Human Decision Processes, 103*(2), 197–213. doi:10.1016/j.obhdp.2006.09.002

Moore, D. A., and Healy, P. J. (2008). The trouble with overconfidence. *Psychological Review, 115*(2), 502–517. doi:10.1037/0033-295X.115.2.502

Moorman, C. (1999). The functionality of knowledge illusions. In *Paper presented at the Association for Consumer Research Conference*, Columbus, Ohio.

Motta, M., Callaghan, T., and Sylvester, S. (2018). Knowing less but presuming more: Dunning-Kruger effects and the endorsement of anti-vaccine policy attitudes. *Social Science and Medicine, 211*, 274–281. doi:10.1016/j.socscimed.2018.06.032

NSF. (2016). *Science and Engineering Indicators 2016*. National Science Board. doi:10.1002/ejoc.201200111

Park, L. E., and Maner, J. K. (2009). Does self-threat promote social connection? The role of self-esteem and contingencies of self-worth. *Journal of Personality and Social Psychology, 96*(1), 203. doi:10.1037/a0013933

Payne, J. W. (1976). Task complexity and contingent processing in decision making: An information search and protocol analysis. *Organizational Behavior and Human Performance, 16*(August), 366–387. doi:10.1016/0030-5073(76)90022-2

Price, P. C., and Stone, E. R. (2004). Intuitive evaluation of likelihood judgment producers: Evidence for a confidence heuristic. *Journal of Behavioral Decision Making, 17*(1), 39–57. doi:10.1002/bdm.460

Rabb, N., Fernbach, P. M., and Sloman, S. A. (2019). Individual representation in a community of knowledge. *Trends in Cognitive Sciences*,23(10), 891–902.

Ranney, M. A., and Clark, D. (2016). Climate change conceptual change: Scientific information can transform attitudes. *Topics in Cognitive Science, 8*(1), 49–75. doi:10.1111/tops.12187

Rollwage, M., Dolan, R. J., and Fleming, S. M. (2018). Metacognitive failure as a feature of those holding radical beliefs. *Current Biology: CB, 28*(24), 4014–4021. doi:10.1016/j.cub.2018.10.053

Rozenblit, L., and Keil, F. (2002). The misunderstood limits of folk science: An illusion of explanatory depth. *Cognitive Science, 26*(5), 521–562. doi:10.1016/S0364-0213(02)00078-2

Sandoval, W. (2017). Situating practices of epistemic cognition. In T. Amin, and O. Levrini (Eds.), *Converging Perspectives on Conceptual Change: Mapping an Emerging Paradigm in the Learning Sciences* (pp. 210–215). Cambridge: MIT Press.

Shah, A. K., and Oppenheimer, D. M. (2008). Heuristics made easy: An effort-reduction framework. *Psychological Bulletin, 134*(2), 207–222. doi:10.1037/0033-2909.134.2.207

Simon, H. A. (1990). Invariants of human behavior. *Annual Review of Psychology, 41*(1), 1–20. doi:10.1146/annurev.psych.41.1.1

Simon, M., Houghton, S. M., and Aquino, K. (2000). Cognitive biases, risk perception, and venture formation: How individuals decide to start companies. *Journal of Business Venturing, 15*(2), 113–134. doi:10.1016/S0883-9026(98)00003-2

Sloman, S., and Fernbach, P. (2017). *The Knowledge Illusion: Why We Never Think Alone*. New York: Riverhead Books.

Sloman, S. A., and Rabb, N. (2016). Your understanding is my understanding: Evidence for a community of knowledge. *Psychological Science, 27*(11), 1451–1460. doi:10.1177/0956797616662271

Sparrow, B., Liu, J., and Wegner, D. M. (2011). Google effects on memory: Cognitive consequences of having information at our fingertips. *Science, 333*(6043), 776–778. doi:10.1126/science.1207745

Taylor, S. E., and Brown, J. D. (1988). Illusion and well-being: A social psychological perspective on mental health. *Psychological Bulletin, 103*(2), 193–210. doi:10.1037/0033-2909.103.2.193

Tetlock, P., and Gardner, D. (2015). *Superforecasting: The Art and Science of Prediction*. New York: Crown Publishers.

Trout, J. D. (2003). Scientific explanation and the sense of understanding. *Philosophy of Science*, *69*(2), 212–233. doi:10.1086/341050

Tugade, M. M., and Fredrickson, B. L. (2004). Resilient individuals use positive emotions to bounce back from negative emotional experiences. *Journal of Personality and Social Psychology*, *86*(3), 320–333. doi:10.1037/0022-3514.86.2.320

van Prooijen, J.-W., and Krouwel, A. P. M. (2018). Overclaiming knowledge predicts anti-establishment voting. In *SPSP 2018 (conference presentation)*. Atlanta.

Walters, D. J., Fernbach, P. M., Fox, C. R., and Sloman, S. A. (2017). Known unknowns: A critical determinant of confidence and calibration. *Management Science*, *63*(12), 4298–4307. doi:10.1287/mnsc.2016.2580

Ward, A. F. (2013). *One with the "Cloud": Why People Mistake the Internet's Knowledge for Their Own*. Unpublished doctoral dissertation. Cambridge, MA: Harvard University.

Ward, A. F., Grillo, T. H., and Fernbach, P. M. (2019). *From Novice to Know-It-All: Online Financial Search and Financial (Over)Confidence*.

Wegner, D. M. (2011). Transactive memory: A contemporary analysis of the group mind. In *Theories of Group Behavior* (pp. 185–208). New York: Springer. doi:10.1007/978-1-4612-4634-3_9

Wood, S. L., and Lynch, J. G. (2002). Prior knowledge and complacency in new product learning. *Journal of Consumer Research*, *29*(3), 416–426. doi:10.1086/344425

Xu, A. J., and Wyer, R. S. (2008). The comparative mind-set: From animal comparisons to increased purchase intentions. *Psychological Science*, *19*(9), 859–864. doi:10.1111/j.1467-9280.2008.02169.x

Yates, J. F., Lee, J. W., and Bush, J. G. G. (1997). General knowledge overconfidence: Cross-national variations, response style, and "reality." *Organizational Behavior and Human Decision Processes*, *70*(2), 87–94. doi:10.1006/obhd.1997.2696

Yates, J. F., Lee, J. W., and Shinotsuka, H. (1996). Beliefs about overconfidence, including its cross-national variation. *Organizational Behavior and Human Decision Processes*, *65*(2), 138–147. doi:10.1006/obhd.1996.0012

PART 7

Humility

Applications to the social world

36
HUMILITY AND TERRORISM STUDIES

Quassim Cassam

36.1

In a memoir published a decade after the 9/11 attacks on New York and Washington, former U.S. Defense Secretary Donald Rumsfeld reflected on an aphorism with which he will forever be associated.[1] According to Rumsfeld, there are known knowns, things we know we know; known unknowns, things we know we don't know; and unknown unknowns, things we don't know we don't know. The category of unknown unknowns points to gaps in our knowledge that we don't know exist. Prior to 9/11, Rumsfeld claimed, 19 hijackers using commercial aircraft as guided missiles was an unknown unknown. Recognising that there are things we don't know we don't know can be regarded as a form of intellectual humility. This is how Rumsfeld puts it:

> The idea of known and unknown unknowns recognizes that the information those in positions of responsibility in government, as well as in other human endeavors, have at their disposal is almost always incomplete. It emphasizes the importance of intellectual humility, a valuable attribute in decision making and in formulating strategy.
>
> *(2011: xvi)*

In support of this approach, Rumsfeld quotes Socrates' assertion that the beginning of wisdom is the realization of how little one truly knows. In Rumsfeld's eyes, Rumsfeldian humility is Socratic humility. Of course, we know nothing about any specific unknown unknown but that doesn't prevent us from justifiably believing in the existence of particular truths that we don't know we don't know: 'there are things of which we are so unaware, we don't even know we are unaware of them' (Rumsfeld 2011: xvi).

Rumsfeldian humility pertains to the ability of governments to predict future terrorist attacks, but a different form of intellectual humility concerns our understanding of what makes terrorists tick. It is often claimed that terrorists are evil and irrational. From this, some have concluded that 'one cannot – and indeed should not – know them' (Stampnitzky 2013: 189).[2] The types of knowledge at issue in such formulations include knowledge of (a) the root causes of terrorism and (b) terrorists' motives and objectives. It has been argued that in order to acquire knowledge of these things, especially (b), one would have to engage with what Zulaika calls the 'desires and subjectivities' (2012: 53) of terrorists.[3] This is what some scholars regard as problematic, especially in relation to the so-called 'new' terrorism, a form of terrorism with supposedly 'unlimited and non-negotiable' ends and 'incomprehensible and amorphous' aims (Crenshaw 2011: 54).[4] The perpetrators of 9/11 were 'new' terrorists. Members of the IRA and other such organisations were 'old' terrorists, people with negotiable and limited goals.

The notion that new terrorism is incomprehensible has had a range of negative impacts on the study of terrorism. Even if it is false, the belief that we cannot know the answer to certain questions can make it harder to know the answer to those questions. Pessimism about the extent of our knowledge can be self-fulfilling, even if it is motivated by intellectual humility. Since intellectual humility is widely regarded as an intellectual virtue, it would be both surprising and disappointing if this epistemic posture gets in the way of knowledge, perhaps by encouraging us to abandon the pursuit of certain types of knowledge. Intellectual virtues are supposed to be epistemically beneficial, to abet rather than obstruct knowledge. It is therefore important to decide whether Rumsfeldian humility and its variants are expressive of genuine intellectual humility. If not, why not? If so, then either it is false that Rumsfeldian humility has negative epistemological consequences, or intellectual virtues are not always epistemically beneficial. Is it possible that the study of terrorism is a domain in which intellectual humility gets in the way of knowledge?

Intellectual humility has been described as 'self-centred' (Tanesini 2018: 408). The force of this description can be brought out by noting that humility involves self-acceptance. Humility, as Tanesini notes, is 'importantly concerned with human limitations in general and one's own limitations in particular' (2018: 404). Intellectual humility has also been seen as a matter of having the right stance towards one's intellectual limitations, of being 'appropriately attentive to them and to *own* them' (Whitcomb et al. 2017: 516). These limitations include gaps in our knowledge and restrictions in our ability to know certain truths. These gaps can be explained in two different ways. If a person S fails to know that P, this might say more about S than about P. For example, if P is knowable by S without excessive cognitive labour, then S's ignorance may have more to do with S than with P. In this case, S's ignorance is avoidable. A different case is one in which S's ignorance has more to do with the nature of P. It could be that S doesn't know that P because P is unknowable, either by S or more generally. In acknowledging and owning this gap in her knowledge, S would be acknowledging her *unavoidable* ignorance. Since there is no way for S to close this gap in her knowledge she can't fairly be criticised for her ignorance.

A particular form of avoidable ignorance is *wilful ignorance*.[5] S may fail to know whether P, not because she can't know but because she doesn't want to know. Even if S is happy to 'own' this gap in her knowledge, one might be reluctant to regard this as genuine intellectual humility.[6] Another case is one in which it is possible for S to know whether P, but she makes no effort to know because she unjustifiably believes it is impossible to know. S owns what she sees as her intellectual limitations with respect to P, but these limitations aren't genuine. In this case, S is guilty of a form of what might be called *false humility*. A different form of false humility consists in claiming not to know whether P, even though one does know. The result is *unacknowledged knowledge* or an '*unknown known*' (Jackson 2012).[7]

Do any of these descriptions apply to Rumsfeldian humility? When students of 'new' terrorism proclaim their ignorance of its motives and causes, is their ignorance genuine? If so, is it avoidable or unavoidable ignorance? While genuine intellectual humility is essential for the effective study of terrorism, it is arguable that the intellectual humility on display in some influential accounts of terrorism is false. How is this false humility to be accounted for? One hypothesis is that false humility, especially in relation to Islam-related terrorism, is rooted in a desire to provide an intellectual justification for contentious anti-terrorist policies. Another is that pointing to the unknowability of a particular form of terrorism is a highly effective means of emphasising the radical alienness of those responsible for it. The 'othering' of some forms of terrorism but not others can, according to this hypothesis, only be properly understood by reference to the tenets of what Edward Said calls 'Orientalism'.[8]

The next sections will be divided as follows: Section 2 will expose the extent to which the study of terrorism has been shaped by wilful ignorance and false humility. The discussion will also bring into focus difficulties in understanding the claim that intellectual humility involves owning one's intellectual limitations. As will also become apparent, the notion of an intellectual limitation is far from straightforward. Section 3 will explore the relations between false humility and othering. Finally, Section 4 will argue that proper intellectual humility in the study of terrorism requires acknowledging and owning *genuine* limitations in our ability to comprehend terrorism, while refraining from representing avoidable ignorance as unavoidable. One such limitation will be identified and discussed.

36.2

In her account of the evolution of terrorism studies Lisa Stampnitzky analyses what she calls the 'politics of anti-knowledge' (2013: 187). This consists in an active refusal to seek knowledge of the motives or root causes of terrorism.[9] As an epistemic posture, anti-knowledge can be explained and understood in two different ways. On one interpretation, the point is not that knowledge of terrorism and terrorists is impossible, but that one ought not to seek it. This can in turn be understood as a moral or as a political 'ought'. Either way, it is a matter of choice or decision not to address certain questions about terrorism. On a different interpretation, an anti-knowledge posture is a reasonable response to the fact that it is impossible to explain or understand terrorism. On this view, terrorism is not subject to rational understanding so trying to understand it is futile.

An example of the first approach can be found in the work of Alan M. Dershowitz. He argues that terrorism works because its perpetrators take it to be an effective means of drawing attention to their grievances. They are encouraged in this belief by the fact that governments have been receptive to suggestions that, in order to respond effectively to terrorism, they must first understand it. In contrast, Dershowitz recommends a policy of never responding to acts of terrorism by attending to terrorists' grievances, real or otherwise, or to the supposed root causes of terrorism. The clear message to terrorists should be:

> even if you have legitimate grievances, if you resort to terrorism as a means toward eliminating them we will simply not listen to you, we will not try to understand you, and we will certainly not change any of our policies toward you.
>
> *(2002: 25)*

There is no suggestion here that terrorism is incapable of being understood. Dershowitz's argument for wilful ignorance is fundamentally political or strategic rather than epistemological.[10]

The ethical argument for wilful ignorance is 'we ought not to seek to know terrorists, for such knowledge is potentially contaminating' (Stampnitzky 3013: 189). One concern is that any serious attempt to understand the motivations of terrorists will require a degree of empathy that might be seen as morally problematic. Without empathy there is little chance of engaging with the subjectivity of terrorists, and without doing that we are unlikely to grasp their motives.[11] Empathy is 'emotionally charged perspective-taking' (Bailey 2018: 143). It involves 'using one's imagination to "transport" oneself' and consider someone else's situation as though one were occupying their position (Bailey 2018: 143). On this account, empathising is closely relating to sympathising. This explains why some argue that we should be very reluctant to empathise with individuals, such as the 9/11 hijackers, who were guilty of mass murder. Refusing to empathise means refusing to understand, but there is no alternative to wilful ignorance if one wishes to avoid contamination or 'moral confusion' (Jones and Smith 2006: 1083).

There are several questions about the merits of these approaches. English argues, in opposition to Dershowitz, that if we have any serious interest in curtailing terrorism we *do* need to understand it: 'understanding something is a necessary part of effectively fighting against it' (2009: 28). In addition, the risks of moral contamination are exaggerated by ethical arguments for wilful ignorance. One can empathise with some aspects of the motivations of terrorists with genuine grievances without approving of what they do in pursuit of their objectives. There need be no moral confusion in an inquiry into the root causes of terrorism. It is also doubtful whether it is possible, in practice, to avert one's eyes from the motives of terrorists who make it plain why they act as they do. One might take the view that the explanations and justifications of their actions offered by terrorists are bogus but this means engaging with the very questions of explanation and motivation that those who recommend a policy of wilful ignorance wish to avoid.

Dershowitz's view is unusual among terrorism scholars. Most argue not that we *should not* understand terrorism but that we *cannot* understand it, at least if the terrorism in question is of the newer variety. We cannot understand it because it is not *subject* to rational understanding. Accepting this is therefore a case of acknowledging an unavoidable gap in our knowledge. For example, in his *The New Terrorism*, Walter Laqueur describes new terrorists as 'divorced from rational thought' (1999: 5).[12] Indeed, this is one of the bases on which 'new' terrorism is distinguished from 'old' terrorism. Those who subscribe to this distinction see old terrorism as rational and realistic and new terrorism as megalomaniacal, paranoid and delusional. On this account, new terrorists have 'an altogether different logic' (Sprinzak 2001: 73) from their predecessors and this is what makes them so hard to fathom. It is not a matter of being 'anti-knowledge' but of being realistic and accepting genuine limitations in our ability to understand people who are capable of such actions as beheading a hostage with a butcher's knife or massacring 50 worshippers in a mosque in New Zealand.

To what extent, if any, is wilful ignorance an expression of intellectual humility? One issue is how to understand the notion of an 'intellectual limitation' in accounts of this type of humility. Examples of intellectual limitations include gaps in knowledge, cognitive mistakes, unreliable cognitive processes, deficits in learnable skills and intellectual character flaws.[13] Suppose that wilful ignorance results in a gap in a person's knowledge or understanding of terrorism. There is no reason to deny that the wilfully ignorant subject is aware of the gap in her knowledge and is in this sense attentive to an intellectual limitation. She therefore satisfies at least one condition on intellectual humility. Does she also satisfy the further condition that she *owns* her limitation? It would seem so. Like Dershowitz, she might even be *proud* of her ignorance to the extent that that she sees it as a political or ethical necessity. It has been argued that fully 'owning' one's intellectual limitations means, among other things, viewing them with 'regret or dismay' on the basis that they have negative outcomes (Whitcomb et al. 2017: 519). There is also the idea that owning a limitation means caring enough about it to be motivated to overcome it if at all possible. However, while the wilfully ignorant subject doesn't regret her lack of knowledge, she rejects the assumption that her ignorance is undesirable.[14] If there are desirable gaps in knowledge, or intellectual limitations that have positive outcomes, then it should be possible to own such limitations without regretting them or seeking to overcome them.

Despite these considerations, there are good reasons not to regard ownership of gaps in knowledge that result from wilful ignorance as genuine intellectual humility. One is that, as suggested above, those who recommend wilful ignorance in response to terrorism exaggerate the political and ethical benefits of this epistemic posture. It is also worth noting that, when intellectual humility is described as requiring ownership of one's intellectual limitations, it is generally assumed that the limitations in question aren't voluntary or self-imposed. Acceptance of intellectual limitations is not genuine humility if they are taken to be ones that could easily be overcome by subjects who care to know. Not caring to know is not humility, intellectual or otherwise. Furthermore, trying not to understand the root causes of terrorism, or the motives of terrorists, won't result in *actual* gaps in knowledge if those causes and motives are all too obvious. One can adopt the policy of refusing to take such considerations into account, but that is a different matter from genuinely not knowing. If there is no actual gap in one's knowledge then there is, at least in this sense, no intellectual limitation for one to own or accept. Talk of intellectual humility in this context is disingenuous.

It is a different matter if the intellectual limitations that a person purports to own are ones they take to be involuntary and a reflection of the inherent difficulty of the subject matter, rather than the result of a policy of wilful ignorance. Acknowledging and regretting what one sees as insuperable cognitive obstacles to acquiring knowledge of a given subject matter sounds more like intellectual humility.[15] Yet, even here, much depends on whether the belief that the obstacles to knowledge are insuperable is itself a justified belief. If not, then the result is false intellectual humility rather than the real thing. It is false humility to insist that it is not possible for one to know whether P, when it is possible to know and the belief that it is not possible to know is, in the circumstances, unreasonable. *Genuine* intellectual humility is a matter of acknowledging and owning *genuine* intellectual limitations. It is incompatible with laying claim to intellectual limitations that one ought to know are spurious.

The case for detecting false humility in some branches of terrorism studies is a strong one. The difficulties begin with the distinction between 'old' and 'new' terrorism. As Martha Crenshaw notes, an examination of the objectives, methods and structures of what is said to be new and what is said to be old terrorism 'reveals numerous similarities rather than differences'. Accordingly, 'it cannot really be said that there are two fundamental types of terrorism' (2011: 66). 'New' terrorists have been described as apolitical, 'megalomaniacal hyperterrorists' (Sprinzak 2001: 73) for whom killing is an end in itself. Yet there is ample evidence that, just like 'old' terrorists, such individuals are politically motivated and see violence as a means to a political end. On a politico-rational interpretation, terrorism is 'a form of political behavior resulting from the deliberate choice of a basically rational actor' (Crenshaw 2011: 66). For example, Osama bin Laden's stated goal was the expulsion of American forces from Muslim territories. His reasoning might have been flawed but it was not patently illogical, given such historical precedents as the American defeat in Vietnam and the expulsion of Soviet forces from Afghanistan.[16] There is no indication that new terrorists operate with an altogether different logic.

The collapse of the distinction between old and new terrorism calls into question any notion that terrorism scholars and policy-makers face a special problem identifying the motives and root causes of new terrorism. While it is possible that people are deluded about their own motives, one would need to have a special reason for rejecting terrorists' accounts of their own motives. One report suggests that between 2006 and 2009, US drone strikes in Pakistan killed just 14 Al-Qaeda leaders but as many as 700 civilians in the same area.[17] A 2007 UN report concluded that US air strikes were 'among the principle motivations for suicide bombers in Afghanistan' (Sluka 2011: 72). A survey of 42 Taliban fighters revealed that 12 had seen family members killed in air strikes and 6 had joined the insurgency as a direct result of this.[18] It would be perverse and an example of false humility to insist that we cannot know the motivations of such individuals. This is not to say that a desire for vengeance motivates all forms of terrorism.

As English notes, 'the vital importance of ideological conviction .... must be taken into account when explaining why so many people act in the extreme manner characteristic of terrorists' (2009: 49). The person responsible for the New Zealand mosque massacre emailed an ideological manifesto to the office of the Prime Minister before opening fire. Many other terrorists have been motivated by ideological convictions. The fact that these convictions are deeply flawed does not make the motives of such individuals impossible to understand.

It is no more plausible that the root causes of terrorism are unfathomable, though it is undeniable that the issue is a complex one. To the extent that it is possible to generalise about the causes of terrorism, it would seem that what English calls a 'multi-causal' approach is called for.[19] Not surprisingly, there isn't a single cause but a multiplicity of causal factors. Contrary to what one might have expected, 'poverty is not a root cause of terrorism' (Silke 2014: 46). More relevant factors are political repression, lack of political representation and 'catalyst events' (Silke 2014: 55) that create martyrs to be avenged.[20] Important work has also been done on the role of kinship and friendship networks in persuading some individuals to turn to political violence. As Marc Sageman has shown, a terrorist group can be a "bunch of guys" bonded to one another by more than just politics.[21]

When Rumsfeld emphasizes the importance of intellectual humility he is specifically concerned with humility regarding our knowledge of the mode and timing of terrorist attacks. It is hard to argue with the suggestion that our knowledge of the specifics of terrorist attacks is limited, but it is also important not to exaggerate these limits. A month before the 9/11 attacks, President Bush received an intelligence briefing regarding bin Laden's determination to strike in the U.S.[22] The precise date of such an attack was unknown, but this was a known unknown rather than an unknown unknown. While the use of commercial aircraft as missiles was unprecedented, there were indications of individuals of investigative interest attending flight schools in Arizona.[23] No doubt there are unknown unknowns, but there is also plenty that is knowable and known about terrorist attacks, including their methods and approximate timing. When attacks like 9/11 come as a complete surprise, the surprise is more often due to failures in the collection and processing of intelligence than to deep obstacles to knowledge.

To sum up: despite numerous references to our unavoidable ignorance of the motives, causes and specifics of terrorism, a great deal about these matters is known. It is hard to justify a policy of wilful ignorance in relation to terrorism and just as hard to justify the belief that knowledge of these matters is, for us, unattainable. The "humility" of terrorism scholars who are impressed by how little is known and knowable about their subject matter is therefore false rather than true humility. Above all, it is perverse to insist that terrorism is beyond rational comprehension. It is possible, in theory, that it isn't widely known how much is known about terrorism. In Jackson's terminology, this would make terrorism an unknown known. In reality, however, false humility is more likely to be the result of an unwillingness to *acknowledge* how much is known rather than by a failure to *know* how much is known. This raises a question: how is such unacknowledged knowledge to be explained? More generally, what accounts for false humility in the study of terrorism? This is the next question to be addressed.

36.3

In the world of *realpolitik*, claims about how much or little is knowable about terrorism have as much to do with the policy objectives of governments as with epistemological reality. For example, the Bush administration was warned by intelligence professionals that its 2003 invasion of Iraq would strengthen the hand of anti-American terrorist organisations based in the Middle East. These warnings were ignored, and false humility played a significant role in the adminis-

tration's approach. It represented the relationship between Iraq and Al-Qaeda as unknown and took military action against Iraq to pre-empt the possibility of Iraqi weapons of mass destruction falling into the hands of Al-Qaeda. In reality, Iraq had no weapons of mass destruction and no working relationship with Al-Qaeda. These things could and should have been known by policy-makers in Washington, but they concentrated instead on pressuring the intelligence community to come up with evidence that supported their assumptions.[24] In place of evidence-based policy, the administration relied on policy-based evidence.

According to what came to be known as the 'Cheney doctrine', 'even if there's just a one per cent chance of the unimaginable coming true, act as if it is a certainty' (Suskind 2007: 62). While it is hardly unimaginable that weapons of mass destruction will one day fall into the hands of terrorists, the real purpose of the doctrine was to suggest that, in order to be justified in taking pre-emptive military action against Iraq, it wasn't necessary to *know* or have *evidence* that there was a real threat of such a thing happening in Iraq. In effect, the administration's pre-emptive action was based on its supposed *ignorance* of the threat, by what it insisted with false humility was a gap in its knowledge. The rationale for its Iraq policy was what Stampnitzky calls a 'logic of pre-emption' (2013: 174), one that was rooted in the administration's militant anti-knowledge posture.

Pointing to the unknowability of a particular form of terrorism is not just a way to justify certain types of pre-emptive action. It is an effective means of underlining the alienness of its perpetrators. A useful concept in this connection is that of *othering*. This has been defined as 'the attribution of relative inferiority and/or radical alienness to some other/ out-group' (Brons 2015: 83). When an in-group 'others' an out-group, it is usually through the identification of a desirable characteristic that the in-group has and the out-group lacks. One such characteristic might be rationality. Othering sometimes implies the inferiority of the out-group. In other cases, the other is rendered 'not so much (implicitly) inferior, but *radically alien*' (Brons 2015: 72). Othering can be more or less crude. In crude othering, the out-group is partly defined by reference to its lack of one or more desirable characteristics.

An example of othering is the Orientalist myth of the contrast between the rational (and therefore superior) West and the irrational and inferior East. In Said's words, Orientalism is 'a style of thought based upon an ontological and epistemological distinction made between "the Orient" and (most of the time) "the Occident"' (2003: 2). Its essence is 'the ineradicable distinction between Western superiority and Oriental inferiority' (2003: 42). It is a political vision of reality that promotes the difference between 'the familiar (Europe, the West, "us") and the strange (the Orient, the East, "them") (2003: 43). The Orientalist attitude was one to which Rudyard Kipling gave expression when he wrote that 'You'll never plumb the Oriental mind' and that 'if you did, it isn't worth the toil' (Kipling 1942: 69).[25] The connection between this attitude and false humility in the study of terrorism might not be obvious, but it is nevertheless real. It is striking that the varieties of terrorism that are most commonly represented as beyond rational comprehension tend to be of Middle Eastern ('Oriental') rather than European origin. 'Oriental' terrorism is unknowable because it is illogical, irrational and fanatical, and the effect of applying these epithets to an individual or organisation is to emphasise its alienness and inferiority.[26]

On this account, it is no accident that Western terrorist organisations such as the IRA were rarely said to be irrational or unknowable. Their methods and objectives might have been objectionable but they were hardly ever seen as beyond rational comprehension. The terrorism of the IRA was Occidental rather than Oriental and therefore in the space of reason. As Jackson notes, groups such as the IRA and ETA 'were considered to be epistemologically predictable – at least in retrospect' (2015: 43) and could therefore be studied without Rumsfeldian humil-

ity. To emphasise a special need for such humility in the study of Islam-related terrorism is to imply a lack of predictability that is, in turn, a reflection of a lack of rationality. Emphasising the unpredictability and unknowability of Islam-related terrorism isn't an expression of intellectual humility but a form of othering, rooted in Orientalist stereotypes about the Oriental mind. It is *false* humility because, like Orientalist stereotypes more generally, it has no basis in reality.

As well as being hard to reconcile with what is known about Islam-related terrorism, the othering of some terrorists is also problematic on conceptual grounds. As argued by Donald Davidson, there are conceptual limits to how much irrationality an interpreter can attribute to others while continuing to regard them as thinkers.[27] The possibility that individuals like the 9/11 hijackers were incapable of thought has not so far been contemplated, even by the most ardent proponents of Rumsfeldian humility. It is also noteworthy that, in a speech to Congress just after the 9/11 attacks, President Bush asked why 'they' hate 'us' and suggested that the hijackers acted as they did because 'they hate our freedoms', including freedom of religion and freedom of speech.[28] As has often been noted, there is very little evidence for this interpretation. What is more relevant in the present context is that there is no suggestion in the President's remarks that 'we' can't understand 'them', or that it is impossible to know the true motives of the Orientals who hate 'us'. This points to more than a little ambivalence about the extent to which it is possible to plumb the Oriental mind.

The real challenge for policy-makers and political leaders who wish to acknowledge how much is known about terrorism is that doing so may be politically unpalatable. It has been deemed politically unacceptable by many Western governments to admit that their own policies in the Middle East might have bolstered support for terrorist organisations in the region, even though the evidence that this is the case is overwhelming. Given the choice between frankly acknowledging what is known about these matters and maintaining the fiction that we cannot understand what terrorists do and why they do it, many Western governments take the second option. In the longer term, however, the consequences of wilful blindness and false humility are problematic. By refusing to engage with the reality of terrorism, governments are less likely to develop effective and realistic counterterrorism strategies. Humility does have its place in the study of terrorism, but only proper intellectual humility. The remaining question is how such humility should be understood.

36.4

It should go without saying that proper intellectual humility requires a willingness to acknowledge and own actual limitations and gaps in our knowledge of terrorism. By the same token, it requires us to refrain, for political reasons or otherwise, from exaggerating the extent of our ignorance. However, there are other aspects of proper intellectual humility that may be less obvious. One aspect presupposes a distinction between 'generalist' and 'particularist' approaches to terrorism.[29] Generalism and particularism are responses to a fundamental question posed by Marc Sageman: what leads people to turn to political violence?[30] For the particularist, there is no general answer to this question because people who turn to political violence are historically specific particulars with their individual trajectories and interactions with different environmental factors. Pathways to terrorism are not unknowable but, they are, as Heath-Kelly notes, 'individualised and disconnected' (2017: 300). One person's turn to political violence might be understandable, at least in retrospect, in the light of his biography, but what makes his turn to violence intelligible may have little or no bearing on another person's turn to political violence. There is, as Andrew Silke puts it, 'no one path into terrorism' (2003: 34).

Generalists are much more optimistic about providing a general answer to Sageman's question. They are confident that different individuals' pathways to terrorism have enough in common to justify the construction of general theories of how people become terrorists. Judicious abstraction from irrelevant individual differences is a part of all theorising, and there is no *a priori* reason to suppose that Sageman's question can't be answered.[31] So, for example, one particularly influential form of generalism claims that people become terrorists because they have been 'radicalised', that is, acquired extremist beliefs and values, usually by interacting with other extremists. Other theories explain the turn to violence by reference to situational factors, or as a 'collectively rational strategic choice' (Crenshaw 2011: 112).[32]

The debate between generalism and particularism can't be resolved here. A case has been made elsewhere for a moderate form of particularism that strikes a balance between the particular and the general.[33] Suppose that this is taken as read. The question that then arises is this: to the extent that pathways to terrorism *are* individualised and disconnected, what type of understanding is it possible to achieve of a given individual's turn to violence? Even if there are some things of a general nature that can be said about why *people* make this turn, there is still the question why a specific person ended up as a terrorist. For example, many terrorists belong to aggrieved minorities, but few members of aggrieved minorities become terrorists. The question, then, is: 'why did these particular individuals engage in terrorism when most of their compatriots did not?' (Silke 2003: 33). This cannot be answered without extensive biographical knowledge of the individuals in question and a willingness to engage with their desires and subjectivities. This is the emotionally charged perspective-taking described above. When all goes well it results in a biographical rather than scientific understanding of the terrorist subject. Instead of applying scientific laws to their subjects, biographers try to get into their subjects' heads in an effort to sense of them.[34] To the extent that it is possible to do this with individual terrorists it should be possible to answer Silke's question.

How realistic is this? This is the point at which issues of intellectual humility come to the fore once again. The discussion so far has been relatively optimistic. In an effort to resist the exaggerated pessimism of the anti-knowledge perspective on terrorism it has been argued above that both the causes and motivations of terrorism are knowable to a considerable extent and that, in general, terrorism is not beyond rational comprehension. Yet it cannot be denied that some forms of terrorism and certain specific acts of terrorism are hard to understand, even with the best will in the world, and a serious effort to achieve a biographical understanding of their perpetrators. *Some* acts of terrorism come close to defying rational comprehension even if the majority do not.

This difficulty can be illustrated by Tarak Barkawi's comment that 'we need to find the requisite empathy to understand why men dedicated to the betterment of their peoples and willing to sacrifice their lives, found it necessary to fly jet aircraft into buildings' (2004: 37). Even if one sets aside moral qualms about empathising with the 9/11 hijackers, or doubts about the idea that 'the betterment of their peoples' was their objective, the challenge is that it is extraordinarily difficult *in this case* to achieve the understanding that Barkawi describes. Whatever the grievances and personal histories of Mohammed Atta and his fellow 9/11 terrorists, it is almost literally beyond comprehension that they did what they did in pursuit of their objectives. In this case, it is not Orientalism that makes 'othering' inevitable, but the nature of the act. The same might be said about the actions of ISIS. There sometimes comes a point at which intellectual humility requires the frank admission that we cannot understand. However, the existence of such extreme cases should not blind us to the extent to which terrorism in its less pathological forms is not beyond rational comprehension.[35]

Notes

1 Rumsfeld 2011, author's note.
2 This is not Stampnitzky's own view but rather a description of what she sees as the root of the politics of anti-knowledge.
3 For a defense of this claim, see not only Zulaika 2012 but also Ilardi 2004, Jackson 2015 and Cassam 2018.
4 Crenshaw herself is highly critical of the distinction between 'old' and 'new' terrorism. See below.
5 For an account of wilful ignorance in terrorism studies see Jackson 2015.
6 Can one be said to 'own' a gap in one's knowledge if one has no desire to fill it? Yes, if one regards the gap as desirable, or at least not undesirable. Whitcomb et al. assume that one must take one's limitations to be problematic, but this is not always the case. See below for more on this.
7 For Jackson, unknown knowns are examples of what he calls 'subjugated knowledge', that is, knowledge which is 'wilfully ignored or suppressed' (2015: 35).
8 Said 2003. On 'othering', see below and Brons 2015.
9 Or, as Stampnitzky puts it, it is 'an active refusal of explanation itself' (2013: 187).
10 Dershowitz is not a lone voice on this side of the argument. Jones and Smith also object to focusing on the root causes of terrorism. As they see it, 'casting terrorism in terms of root causes determines it in a form that both reduces its significance and explains it away' (2006: 1085).
11 On the role of empathy in engaging with another person's subjectivity, see Cassam 2018. Engaging with another person's subjectivity can be more or less demanding. In its least demanding form, it might simply be a matter of listening to what they have to say. Yet, as Jackson notes, 'with only a few notable exceptions, little effort has been made by terrorism experts and officials to try and understand terrorist motivations by listening to their own words and messages' (2015: 45). Jackson attributes this to the counterterrorist's passion for ignorance. This is especially noticeable in relation to Al-Qaeda, where Osama bin Laden's voice remained largely unheard by Western audiences despite 'a vast corpus of open letters, interviews, propaganda videos and statements' (Jackson 2015: 45). See also Ilardi 2004.
12 Or, as Zulaika and Douglass put it, 'Terrorists are kooks, crazies, demented, or at best misguided. Contact with them is polluting; dialogue is pointless since terrorists are, by definition, outside the pale of reason' (1996: x). This might sound like a parody but fits a number of remarks in Lacqueur 1999. See, for example, Lacqueur 1999: 230–231.
13 This list is from Whitcomb et al. 2017: 516.
14 One's desire not to know may or may not be conscious. It is more straightforward to think of a person's ignorance as wilful when the desire not to know is conscious.
15 Even this might be disputed since what one sees as an insuperable cognitive obstacle might be no such thing.
16 Crenshaw also makes this point. See Crenshaw 2011: 57.
17 See Sluka 2011: 73 and Zulaika 2012: 54–56.
18 Sluka 2011.
19 English 2009: 52.
20 As Crenshaw puts it, 'a regime thus encourages terrorism when it creates martyrs to be avenged' (2011: 47).
21 Sageman 2004.
22 This was the President's Daily Brief dated 6 August 2001. The title of the brief was 'Bin Ladin (sic) Determined to Strike in U.S.'.
23 As reported in July 2001 by an FBI agent based in Phoenix. The so-called 'Phoenix memo' was extensively discussed after 9/11.
24 For a compelling account of all this see Bamford 2005 and Suskind 2007.
25 These words are from Kipling's poem 'One Viceroy Resigns'.
26 On the idea of the 'terrorist Other', see Zulaika and Douglass 1996: x. They argue that 'it is one of the tenets of counterterrorism that any interaction with the terrorist Other is violation of a taboo'.
27 Davidson 2001.
28 A full transcript of the speech is available via: www.washingtonpost.com/wp-srv/nation/specials/attacked/transcripts/bushaddress_092001.html
29 This distinction is explained in Cassam 2018.
30 See Sageman 2017: ix. Not all political violence is terrorism. For present purposes this can be ignored.

31 Silke claims that 'after nearly four decades of research it is now appreciated that there are a number of relatively common factors in the backgrounds of terrorists' (2003: 34).
32 These varieties of generalism are further analysed in Cassam, forthcoming.
33 See the exposition and defence of 'Moderate Epistemic Particularism' in Cassam 2018.
34 For some interesting reflections on the nature of biographical understanding see chapter 1 of Holmes 2017. Holmes describes biography as 'a simple act of complex friendship' (2017: 17). This would explain the reluctance of terrorism researchers to seek a biographical understanding of terrorists.
35 I thank Alessandra Tanesini for helpful comments on an earlier draft of this paper.

References

Bailey, O. (2018) Empathy and Testimonial Trust. *Royal Institute of Philosophy Supplement*. 84, 139–160.
Bamford, J. (2005) *A Pretext for War: 9/11, Iraq and the Abuse of America's Intelligence Agencies*. New York, Anchor Books.
Barkawi, T. (2004) On the Pedagogy of Small Wars. *International Affairs*. 80(1), 19–37.
Brons, L. (2015) Othering, an Analysis. *Transcience*. 6(1), 69–90.
Cassam, Q. (2018) The Epistemology of Terrorism and Radicalisation. *Royal Institute of Philosophy Supplement*. 84, 187–209.
Cassam, Q. (2020) The Epistemologies of Terrorism and Counterterrorism Research. In L. Gearon (ed.) *The Routledge Handbook of Universities, Security and Intelligence Studies*. 303–311. Abingdon, Routledge.
Crenshaw, M. (2011) *Explaining Terrorism: Causes, Processes and Consequences*. London and New York, Routledge.
Davidson, D. (2001) Radical Interpretation. In D. Davidson *Inquiries into Truth and Interpretation*. Oxford, Clarendon Press, 125–140.
Dershowitz, A. (2002) *Why Terrorism Works: Understanding the Threat, Responding to the Challenge*. New Haven, Yale University Press.
English, R. (2009) *Terrorism: How to Respond*. Oxford, Oxford University Press.
Heath-Kelly, C. (2017) The Geography of Pre-Criminal Space: Epidemiological Imaginations of Radicalisation Risk in the UK Prevent Strategy, 2007–2017. *Critical Studies on Terrorism*. 10(2), 297–319.
Holmes, R. (2017) *This Long Pursuit*. London, William Collins.
Ilardi, G. J. (2004) Redefining the Issues: The Future of Terrorism Research and the Search for Empathy. In A. Silke (ed.) *Research Terrorism on: Trends, Achievements and Failures*. Abingdon, Routledge, 214–228.
Jackson, R. (2012) Unknown Knowns: The Subjugated Knowledge of Terrorism Studies. *Critical Studies on Terrorism*. 5(1), 11–29.
Jackson, R. (2015) The Epistemological Crisis of Counterterrorism. *Critical Studies on Terrorism*. 8(1), 33–54.
Jones, D. M. and Smith, M. L. R. (2006) The Commentariat and Discourse Failure: Language and Atrocity in Cool Britannia. *International Affairs*. 82(6), 1077–1100.
Kipling, R. (1942) One Viceroy Resigns. In *Rudyard Kipling's Verse: Definitive Edition*. London, Hodder & Stoughton.
Lacqueur, W. (1999) *The New Terrorism: Fanaticism and the Arms of Mass Destruction*. Oxford, Oxford University Press.
Rumsfeld, D. (2011) *Known and Unknown: A Memoir*. New York, Sentinel.
Sageman, M. (2004) *Understanding Terror Networks*. Philadelphia, University of Pennsylvania Press.
Sageman, M. (2017) *Turning to Political Violence: The Emergence of Terrorism*. Philadelphia, University of Pennsylvania Press.
Said, E. (2003) *Orientalism*. London, Penguin.
Silke, A. (2003) Becoming a Terrorist. In A. Silke (ed.) *Terrorists, Victims and Society: Psychological Perspectives on Terrorism and Its Consequences*. Chichester, John Wiley & Sons, 29–53.
Silke, A. (2014) *Terrorism: All That Matters*. London, Hodder & Stoughton.
Sluka, J. (2011) Death from above: UAVs and Losing Hearts and Minds. *Military Review*, May–June, 70–76.
Sprinzak, E. (2001) The Lone Gunmen. *Foreign Policy*. 127(127), 72–73.
Stampnitzky, L. (2013) *Disciplining Terror: How Experts Invented "Terrorism"*. Cambridge, Cambridge University Press.
Suskind, R. (2007) *The One Per Cent Doctrine: Deep Inside America's Pursuit of Its Enemies Since 9/11*. New York, Simon & Schuster.

Tanesini, A. (2018) Intellectual Humility as Attitude. *Philosophy and Phenomenological Research*. 96(3), 399–420.
Whitcomb, D. et al. (2017) Intellectual Humility: Owning Our Limitations. *Philosophy and Phenomenological Research*. 94(3), 509–539.
Zulaika, J. (2012) Drones, Witches and Other Flying Objects: The Force of Fantasy in US Counterterrorism. *Critical Studies on Terrorism*. 5(1), 51–68.
Zulaika, J. and Douglass, W. (1996) *Terror and Taboo: The Follies and Faces of Terrorism*. London, Routledge.

37

'KNOWLEDGE IS POWER'

Barriers to intellectual humility in the classroom

Lani Watson

37.1 'Knowledge is power'

Francis Bacon is usually credited with first delivering to us the notion that 'knowledge is power' in his collection of religious meditations published in 1597 entitled the *Meditationes Sacrae*.[1] Bacon had strong ties to early Empiricism and was influential in the establishment of experimental methods in the sciences. In this Enlightenment context, the claim that knowledge is power can be understood as reflecting Bacon's reverence for major advances in our knowledge of the natural world that were made during his lifetime and which represented, for him, a previously unrealised power. Today, the claim that 'knowledge is power' has become something of an aphorism. As with all good aphorisms, it has been adopted as a pithy marketing tool. Two recent appearances are worth noting. In 2012, the claim appeared on a billboard advertisement for a new Volkswagen pick-up truck – the Amarok. More recently, PlayStation have assumed it as the title of a "brilliantly entertaining quiz show game", launched in 2017. These contemporary appropriations of the claim that knowledge is power reflect something interesting about what it has come to mean in the twenty-first century. They indicate, in the first place, that we still recognise and engage with this idea. Moreover, the familiarity of the aphorism and its use as a marketing tool suggest that it has broadly positive connotations. These connotations can no doubt be attributed, at least in part, to the Enlightenment context in which the idea originated. Knowledge is still power. Francis Bacon would be proud.

I take this Enlightenment idea as a starting point for the following discussion. In particular, I am interested in the impact that this idea has had in the context of a twenty-first century education. How does the idea that knowledge is power play out in our schools and universities? How does it feature in our education systems and how does it impact upon the intellectual characters of students? Specifically, how does the pervasiveness of this idea in our schools and classrooms affect students' willingness and ability to be *intellectually humble*? I suggest that this idea presents itself in contemporary classrooms as a barrier to the development and exercise of intellectual humility. Simply put, when we equate knowledge with power, we make it harder to be intellectually humble. In its most prevalent manifestation, this barrier arises in the form of *answer-oriented* education. I will spend the majority of the paper outlining the nature and impact of answer-oriented education. Towards the end, I will suggest one way to remove this barrier by shifting from answer-oriented to *question-oriented* education. The latter, I argue, warrants further attention in philosophical and educational research.

37.2 Winning by knowing

To begin, it will be useful to examine contemporary appropriations of the idea that knowledge is power in more detail. What do these tell us about what this idea means today. The Volkswagen billboard offers an insight. The image above the slogan is, unsurprisingly, of the Amarok itself. The truck is covered with a series of complex mathematical equations suggestive of the extensive technical understanding that is required in the design and construction of an automobile. Drawing our attention to this fact is Volkswagen's way of highlighting how clever their trucks really are. The image serves as an indication of the knowledge that has gone into the design and manufacture of the Amarok: a knowledge that Volkswagen has and that you, as the consumer, can acquire. Ultimately, the aim of the advertisement is to make the truck appear desirable to the target market. According to the marketing teams at Volkswagen, it is the knowledge that has gone into the development of this new model that renders it desirable, leading to the image and choice of slogan. Power, it is assumed, is something that we want and knowledge is power. As long as we identify power with knowledge and knowledge with Volkswagen, then buying Volkswagen gets us something that we want. Hence Volkswagen can sell us pick-up trucks on the basis of this famous Enlightenment adage. It is difficult to imagine what Bacon would make of this bold endorsement by one of the twenty-first century's largest automobile manufacturers. Given his ties to Empiricism, we might imagine him taking pride in the show of scientific and technological prowess implied by the advertisement. At any rate, we can conclude, at least as far as Volkswagen is concerned, that knowledge represents a certain kind of value. And it can be used to sell pick-up trucks. Knowledge has selling power, one might say.

The PlayStation game – 'Knowledge is Power' – offers another insight. In this quiz-show style game, players select a character and answer a series of questions to progress through the rounds in competition with fellow players. A player wins by consistently selecting the correct answers to the questions faster than the other players in the game. Winning can, one imagines, be loosely construed as some form of power in the context of a PlayStation game. At least, this is one easy way to make sense of the company's choice to adopt the claim that knowledge is power as the title of the game. Noticeably, in this case, knowledge is not so much selling power (although there is perhaps some sense in which that notion is operating in the background). Rather, knowledge is winning, and winning is power. In this sense, the PlayStation game offers a virtual representation of the real-world game that Volkswagen is playing in the marketing of its pick-up truck. In both cases, knowledge is positioned as having a certain kind of value. That value is attached to power, through the use of the Enlightenment claim. And power, it is assumed, is something that we want. Whether it be the power one briefly wields by beating one's friends and family to the top of the leaderboard in a PlayStation game, or by driving away from the Volkswagen dealership in a shiny new pick-up truck. Either way, these seemingly unrelated and innocuous uses of the claim that knowledge is power shed light on the idea that underlies that claim in the twenty-first century. In the post-Enlightenment world in which we live, knowledge can and does position one in a power relation with others. Put simply, as in the PlayStation game, *you win by knowing*. I believe that this idea is pervasive in contemporary society, throughout public and private life. We find it in our scientific endeavours, our politics, our media discourse, and in our educational institutions.

37.3 Answer-oriented education[2]

How does the Enlightenment idea that knowledge is power present itself within contemporary education? My claim is that we find it in the pervasive answer-orientation of the education system. Broadly speaking, an answer-oriented education system is one in which the emphasis is placed on *student answers*. Students are taught to answer questions from their earliest schooling until the point at which they exit formal education. As such, much like in the PlayStation game, students 'win' at the game of being educated in an answer-oriented education system by providing correct answers to the questions they are asked. In other words, they succeed or not on the basis of what they know, understand, or remember, *in the form of answers*. Hence, knowledge is power in an answer-oriented education system, insofar as succeeding in one's formal education is empowering (which it often, if not typically, is).

What reasons do we have for thinking that the education system is answer-oriented. I have identified four basic aspects of any education system that can be examined in order to reveal (or not) its answer-orientation. First and foremost, this orientation can be seen in the *aims* of the education system and in particular, in the *assessment practices* used to measure those aims. Secondly, in common *teaching practices* and approaches to *curriculum design*. Thirdly, in the *theory* that informs teaching practices and curriculum design. Lastly, in the *behaviours and roles* that students adopt within the classroom. In order to form a more comprehensive picture of answer-orientated education, I will look at each of these aspects in more detail. Note that, from hereon, when I refer to 'the education system' I am referring to the education system, or systems, operating at present in the UK and the US. These are the contexts in which the data discussed below has been collected and in which I am most confident in my understanding of educational theory and practice. The extent to which education systems elsewhere in the world, particularly non-Western education systems, are answer-oriented remains an open question, although I suspect that a similar case can be made.

37.3.1 Assessment practices

The answer-orientation of the education system reveals itself, perhaps most conspicuously, in the assessment practices used to evaluate students and, ultimately, to measure the success of the system through student results. In this regard, the system is noticeably answer-oriented: students are predominantly assessed throughout their formal education on their ability to answer questions. Exams, tests, assessments, both formative and summative, from primary school right through to university finals, are presented in the format of question–answer. Students are presented with questions and given a set amount of time in which to answer them. Indeed, this format is surprisingly uniform when one considers the diverse educational stages and subject areas that comprise 10–15 years of education.[3] Moreover, this question–answer format has not changed significantly in at least four decades of research into the use of questions in education. In an extensive 1970 review of empirical studies, Meredith Gall notes that "students are exposed to many questions in their textbooks and on examinations" (p.707). This conclusion is reiterated 36 years later by Barbara Gayle, Raymond Preiss, and Mike Allen (2006) in their review of empirical studies in which they observe "the pervasive use of educational questions … Written questions are common in handouts, assignments, projections, Web content, and study guides" (p.279).

These observations highlight the use of the question–answer format even in non-exam based forms of assessment, such as essays and project-work. In these cases, students are typically presented with a question or problem and assessed on their ability to answer or respond to it. At times, students may be permitted or actively encouraged to generate their own questions.

However, even on these occasions, students are usually still assessed on their ability to answer their questions, not on the questions themselves. Students may also be assessed through measures such as attendance or participation, particularly in higher education. However, these are typically not summative measures, or else make up a marginal proportion of a student's final grade. Contemporary formal assessment practices in education are heavily weighted towards evaluating student answers, revealing one significant aspect of the answer-orientated education system.

37.3.2 Teaching practices

A second aspect of the answer-oriented education system reveals itself in teaching practices. In particular, this manifests in the prevalence of teacher questioning in the classroom. Research on teacher questioning gained attention in education theory in the 1970s and has continued to be a subject of interest for both education theorists and practitioners to the present day (Dillon 1981, 1982; Gall 1970, 1984; Dantanio and Paradise 1988; Grow-Maienza, Hahn, and Joo 2001). This research focuses on several dimensions of teacher questioning, including the numbers of questions asked by teachers, the types of questions asked, and the cognitive level of teachers' questions, this latter measure informed in part by the development of Bloom's taxonomy in the 1950s (Kleinman 1965; Wright and Nuthall 1970; Riley 1981; Miller and Pressley 1989; Martin and Pressley 1991).

From this research one can derive the conclusion that teacher questioning is a common form of pedagogy in the classroom. James Dillon (1982), for example, draws precisely this conclusion in his survey of a number of empirical studies measuring teacher questioning, including his own, from the 1970s and 1980s. He writes, "It is a well-documented fact that teachers traditionally ask a lot of questions" (p.127). Over two decades later, in their 2006 survey of the updated literature on teacher questioning, Gayle, Preiss, and Allen (2006) once again echo this conclusion, noting that "teachers frequently ask questions in their classrooms" (p.281). There is consensus among researchers writing and studying questions in education across several decades that teachers ask a lot of questions in their classrooms. This reveals a second significant dimension of the answer-orientated education system. The focus on student answers is not only present in the question–answer format of assessments but, perhaps unsurprisingly, is mirrored in the teaching practices that teachers adopt in their classrooms on a daily basis.

37.3.3 Education theory

A third dimension of the answer-orientation of education in the UK and the US is evident when one surveys the education theory that supports teaching and learning in these settings. Alongside empirical studies on teacher questioning in the classroom, a significant body of literature has emerged over the course of several decades dedicated to offering practical guidance for teachers on how to incorporate questions into their teaching (Aschner 1961; Hunkins 1972; Hollingsworth 1982; Farrar 1983; Guthrie 1983; Brualdi 1998; Sachen 1999). This literature indicates that educational theorists in general regard teacher questioning in the classroom as good pedagogy. An early comment by the theorist Mary Jane Aschner (1961) reflects this when she writes that questions are "one of the basic ways by which the teacher stimulates student thinking and learning" (p.44). Similarly, the theorist Paul Hollingsworth (1982) commented in an article in the 1980s that "The use of appropriate questions can enhance classroom learning for every child" (p.352).

More compelling than these comments in isolation, however, is the extensive and growing production of instructional resources for teachers providing guidance on how to use questions in the classroom. A selective representation of such resources produced in the last six years alone includes Esther Fusco's (2012) *Effective Questioning Strategies in the Classroom: A Step-by-Step Approach to Engaged Thinking and Learning*, Gordon Pope's (2013) *Questioning Technique Pocketbook*, Mike Gershon's (2013) *How to use Questioning in the Classroom: The Complete Guide*, and Robert Marzano and Julia Simms' (2014) *Questioning Sequences in the Classroom*. This focus on teacher questioning in training and pedagogy illustrates, once again, the pervasive answer-orientation of the education system. This focus, moreover, has the potential to disguise the answer-orientation of the system in a problematic way by indicating a central role for questioning in educational theory and practice. Importantly, however, this role is restricted to *teacher*, not student, questioning. This has a direct impact on the answer-orientation of the education system. We can observe this by examining educational research that focuses on student, rather than teacher questioning in the classroom.

37.3.4 Student behaviour

Dillon is one of a small number of education researchers whose work focuses on student questioning in the classroom. Dillon's research throughout the 1980s looks at numbers and types of student questions and their relationship to teacher questions (1978, 1981, 1982, 1988). He presents his own empirical studies as well as reviewing a selection of other studies which also focus on student questioning, beginning as early as 1938 (Houston 1938; Corey 1940; Fahey 1942; Johns 1968; Susskind 1969, 1979; Tizard et al. 1983). The results of these studies are as conclusive as those of the studies on teacher questioning, finding across the board that students ask very few questions in the classroom. Dillon summarises his findings unambiguously: "No one has ever gone into a sample of classrooms and found a lot of student questions ... investigators can scarcely find any student questions" (1988, p.199). In his own study (1988), involving recordings of 27 discussion classes in six schools, Dillon reports an average of 2 questions per hour from all the students in each class, compared with 84 questions per hour from the teacher. Earlier research conducted by Edwin Susskind (1969) found approximately the same average in a study of primary school classes and reports even starker results in a study, 10 years later, involving 32 social studies classes. Summarising these later findings, Susskind states unequivocally "our data indicate that children do not ask questions in school (1979, p.103).

The empirical findings reveal that students adopt the role of answerers in the classroom. The studies, moreover, indicate a negative correlation between teacher and student questions: a higher rate of teacher questions correlates with a lower rate of student questions. On the basis of this correlation, Susskind (1979) comments, "Clearly, the teacher is the primary initiator, while the student adopts a responsive role: the teacher questions, the student replies" (p.103). Likewise, Tizard et al. (1983) comment, "children seem to learn very quickly that their role at school is to answer, not to ask questions" (p.279). Dillon also picks this up, referring to "classroom discourse as a series of three-part exchanges, principally a teacher question, a pupil response, and a teacher comment—plus a further question" (1982, p.128). Dillon (1982) cites socio-linguistic research that refers to this dynamic as "'an exponential law of successive questioning', whereby the chances at any point are two to one that a teacher will ask a question" (p.128). A study by the psychologist Elliott Mishler (1975), for example, based on recordings of 4 primary classrooms across the course of a school year found that in 85% of the exchanges between teachers and students, teachers were heard to ask a further question after a student had responded to an initial question and in 67% of exchanges teachers were heard to respond to student questions by asking another question. Simply put, teachers ask questions and students answer them.[4]

This conclusion, and the results of the studies above are not surprising when one considers the answer-orientation of the education system. Students are continually assessed on their ability to answer questions, teachers ask numerous questions of their students throughout the day, and educational theorising endorses teacher questioning as pedagogical practice through a cottage industry of instructional resources. As a result, students are consistently placed in the position of answerers in their daily classroom interactions. Their success within the system depends, in no small part, on their ability to adapt to this role: students win, in an answer-oriented education system, by knowing the answers. We can now return to the question posed in Section 37.1: how does this affect students' willingness and ability to be intellectually humble.

37.4 Answer-oriented education as a barrier to intellectual humility

I have argued that the education system is answer-oriented. What, if any, effect does this have on students' intellectual character and, in particular, on their willingness and ability to be intellectually humble? I argue that the answer-oriented education system presents a barrier to intellectual humility. More specifically, it prevents students from practising and refining a key form of intellectual humility, namely questioning. The discussion in Section 37.3 has already gone some way towards establishing this. We have seen that educational theory and practice consistently places students in the position of answerers, as opposed to questioners. Responding to this, students quickly adopt the role of answerers in the classroom and learn to practice and refine their answering, as opposed to questioning skills. As a result, students are observed to ask very few questions. The answer-oriented education system is a barrier to student questioning.

In order to show that answer-oriented education presents a barrier to intellectual humility, however, I need to establish the sense in which student questioning functions as a form of intellectual humility. By 'form' of intellectual humility I mean that student questioning is one way in which intellectual humility is expressed. This can also be said of other modes of expression, such as assertions, actions, and answers. All of these can be expressions, or forms, of intellectual humility. Moreover, none of these, including questions, are necessary for intellectual humility nor will they always be intellectually humble. Questions can be arrogant or servile, for example. Nonetheless, I argue that in the context of an answer-oriented (or perhaps more precisely, answer-*dominated*) education system, student answers operate as a barrier to intellectual humility, while student questions can function as a powerful expression of intellectual humility. As such, student questions represent a potentially rich pedagogical resource for cultivating students' willingness and ability to be intellectually humble.

37.4.1 Questioning and intellectual humility

A significant body of research on the nature and value of intellectual humility has emerged in recent years, particularly within virtue epistemology (Roberts and Wood 2007; Hazlett 2012; Kidd 2015; Whitcomb et al. 2017). Scales for measuring and assessing intellectual humility have been developed in conjunction with this literature (Alfano et al. 2017; Haggard et al. 2018). One of the most prominent recent accounts of intellectual humility is the Limits-Owning account developed by Dennis Whitcomb et al. (2017), along with the associated Limits-Owning Intellectual Humility Scale, developed by Haggard et al. (2018). On this account, intellectual humility "consists in proper attentiveness to, and owning of, one's intellectual limitations" (2017, p.520). This characterisation of intellectual humility offers a particularly clear insight into the relationship between intellectual humility and questioning.

Firstly, questions often, if not typically, represent a gap in the questioner's knowledge or information; their ignorance about a certain thing. Whether that's the price of milk, the speed of light, or who wrote *The Adventures of Huckleberry Finn*. Thus, in order to ask a question based on one's ignorance, one must first notice that one is lacking the information that one needs or wants; that one is indeed ignorant about this or that. If we think of ignorance, at least in some more or less descriptive sense, as an intellectual limitation, the questioner, much like the intellectually humble person, exhibits "a disposition to be aware (even if just implicitly) of [her] limitations" (2017, p.516). As such, questioning frequently involves the questioner in a key aspect of intellectual humility: attentiveness to intellectual limitations.

Secondly, questioning often, if not typically, involves an interpersonal interaction. By asking a question, the questioner exposes her ignorance to others. Just as "in owning her intellectual limitations, the person with IH is disposed to admit them to others, and more generally, to act as the context demands" (2017, pp.517–518), so too the questioner publicly admits to and acts upon her ignorance. Indeed, arguably the act of asking a question neatly captures the sense in which a person 'owns' her intellectual limitations, according to the Whitcomb et al. account. One might nod in agreement when a colleague asserts that 'the author of Huckleberry Finn' was an excellent writer but an unfortunate entrepreneur. Or one might ask 'who was the author of Huckleberry Finn'. Acknowledging privately to oneself that one doesn't know who the author of Huckleberry Finn is will not suffice for intellectual humility on the Limits-Owning account. Rather, it is by asking the question, as in the second instance, that one owns one's ignorance and so exercises intellectual humility. As such, questioning frequently involves the questioner in a second key aspect of intellectual humility: owning her intellectual limitations.

The questioner both attends to and owns her intellectual limitations by identifying a gap in her knowledge and attempting to fill it. She can be counted among the "people who easily accept or expose their ignorance rather than deny or cover it up" (2017, p.510). There is a close alignment between questioning and intellectual humility.[5]

37.4.2 Student questions as a form of intellectual humility

A close conceptual alignment between questioning and intellectual humility is significant, but not sufficient for my central claim. The *context* of a question is also central to understanding whether and in what sense it expresses intellectual humility. Whether a question is intellectually humble depends, at least in part, on the pre-existing power relations in operation in the context in which it is asked. In any number of situations where there exists a real or perceived expectation that one already does know this or that, exposing the fact that one does not, by asking a question, can be considered an expression of intellectual humility. This is especially so when one is operating under a system that values knowing things highly. One in which knowledge is power. The answer-oriented education system is a system like this; one in which knowledge is power. My claim, therefore, is that the context in which students are placed is one in which the pre-existing power relations mean that student questions can and often do express intellectual humility. At the same time, however, these power relations – manifested in the answer-orientation of the education system – act as a barrier to student questioning, and so to intellectual humility.

Indeed, the relationship between questioning and intellectual humility is, I think, particularly clear in the classroom. Rightly or wrongly, students often feel under pressure to have the 'right answers' at their immediate disposal, and can be especially unwilling to expose the fact that they do not know or understand something to their teachers or peers. This is, at least in part, a result of the expectations placed on students in their position as answerers and their ensuing lack of familiarity with the process of asking questions. One teacher expressed this well in an online discussion forum which I took part in, as part of a Harvard School of Education course aimed at helping teachers to teach student questioning:

> I think there can be a pride element, almost, that prevents us from asking Qs; some of my 6th graders said in their reflections that they were initially afraid to disclose some Qs for fear of the Qs being weak in some way with the result that this could reflect something not good about themselves.
>
> *(Rich Pierog, Technology and Design teacher, Daegu International School, South Korea)*

As this teacher puts it, the students in his class were 'afraid' of asking questions for fear of 'being weak'. If a student is afraid that asking a question will expose her as weak – or, in the Limits-Owning vernacular, expose her limitations – and she asks it anyway, I think that it is correct to say that the student expresses intellectual humility (as well as a not-insignificant degree of intellectual courage). When students are systematically placed in the position of answerers, however, they are denied such rich opportunities to expose, and become comfortable with exposing, their limitations in this way. As such, students are denied the opportunity to practice and refine intellectual humility. The answer-oriented education system is a barrier to intellectual humility in the classroom.

37.5 Question-oriented education

If we are invested in the project of educating for intellectual character, and for intellectual humility in particular, then this conclusion should generate cause for concern. One solution may be to shift from an answer-oriented to a question-oriented education system. I will not discuss this solution in detail here (I have discussed it in more detail in Watson 2018). An outline will suffice to offer an indication of what a question-oriented system has to offer, and how it may serve the goal of educating for intellectual humility.

What would a question-oriented education system look like. In essence, it is one in which student questions are at least as important as student answers. Note that the claim is not that we should prefer an education system in which student answers are given no space at all. It is, of course, possible and desirable to cultivate intellectual character by teaching students to know, articulate, and defend answers to the questions that they are asked. Indeed, there may be certain intellectual virtues, for example, rigour, that are better served by a focus on student answering. Moreover, students can learn to exercise intellectual humility in giving answers, as well as in asking questions. Thus, the suggestion is not that we replace answering questions with asking them in any wholesale manner. Rather, we should aim for an education system in which there is a more even balance between cultivating the knowledge and skills to ask questions and the knowledge and skills to answer them. In order to achieve this, the key factors discussed in Section 37.3 would each need to be reoriented towards questioning.

Perhaps most significantly, a question-oriented education system requires a means by which to assess student questions. Without this, it is hard to see how pedagogy and/or curriculum design alone will truly reorient the system. Teachers will naturally be motivated to teach the skills which allow their students to succeed within the system, and students will be motivated to learn these skills. As long as students are predominantly assessed on their answers, teachers and students have good reason to focus on answering, rather than questioning skills: assessment practices drive teaching practices. This point is often made critically by education theorists and practitioners but it can also be viewed as a valuable tool. If it is the case, then assessments geared towards student questions will drive teaching practices geared towards student questions. This is, I think, perhaps *the* key feature of a truly question-oriented education system.

Alongside assessments, question-oriented education requires pedagogy that teaches students (not just teachers) to ask good questions, and curricula designed with that aim in mind. There are promising indications of these question-oriented approaches towards both pedagogy and curriculum design in contemporary education theory and practice. 'Inquiry-based learning', 'problem-based learning', 'case-based learning', and 'phenomena-based learning' all represent relatively new initiatives in curriculum design and delivery geared towards student-led classroom learning. Insofar as these approaches aim at inspiring students to pursue their own curiosity and take on roles as autonomous learners, there is a clear role for student questions. 'Socratic Teaching' and 'Dialogical Teaching' also provide an opening for student questioning in the classroom. Another specific pedagogical technique designed to help students ask their own questions is found in the Question Formulation Technique developed by the *Right Question Institute*. This latter is currently being used by over 300,000 educators globally and can be incorporated into the curriculum-based strategies listed above.[6] These approaches provide a useful indication of what the shift towards a question-oriented system might look like.

How then would a question-oriented education system affect students' willingness and ability to be intellectually humble. Simply put, teaching students to ask questions in the classroom provides them with immediate and tangible opportunities to practice and refine this form of intellectual humility. It requires them to attend to gaps in their knowledge and understanding, to acknowledge their own ignorance about this or that, and to expose this ignorance to their teachers and peers. Over time, this process should not only help students to practice and refine the owning of their intellectual limitations, but to become comfortable and confident in doing so. As the teacher quoted above goes on to say:

> having that really supportive environment that allows for Qs to be asked without fear, to allow the students to risk, seems to me to be very important.
>
> *(Rich Pierog, Technology and Design teacher, Daegu International School, South Korea)*

A question-oriented education system would provide multiple opportunities for teachers to cultivate intellectual humility in the classroom. In fact, I think the question-oriented system would provide opportunities for the cultivations of many others of the intellectual virtues, and for the development of intellectually virtuous character in general (Watson 2018). But for the purposes of this paper, I restrict myself to the conclusion that a reorientation within education away from answers and towards questions would have a positive impact on students' willingness and ability to be intellectually humble.

This conclusion is especially salient if the education system truly is answer-oriented in the way I have described. If knowing the answers is the key, the only key, to formal success in a twenty-first century education, then what incentive do students have for attending to their own ignorance or exposing it to others? If knowledge is power, then it is *disempowering* not to know. The answer-oriented system is a barrier to intellectual humility. Philosophers and education theorists invested in the project of educating for intellectual humility should, therefore, pay attention to the shift towards a question-oriented education system in which the skills involved in asking good questions are taught and assessments, teaching practices, and curricula are developed with this aim in mind.

Acknowledgments

Many thanks to Mark Alfano, Emma Gordon, and Michael Lynch for useful comments, as well as audiences who attended presentations of this paper as part of the John Templeton Foundation Humility and Conviction in Public Life project. The paper has been made possible by the Leverhulme Trust, grant no. R444. The opinions expressed in this publication are those of the author and do not reflect the views of the John Templeton Foundation or the Leverhulme Trust.

Notes

1 The Latin phrase "ipsa scientia potestas est" ('knowledge itself is power' or 'knowledge is His power'), occurs towards the end of the essay 'Of Heresies' in the *Meditationes Sacrae* (1597). The phrase "scientia potentia est" ('knowledge is power') appears for the first time in Latin in the 1668 version of *Leviathan* by Thomas Hobbes, who was Bacon's secretary for a period as a young man.

2 Some of the empirical data discussed in this section is also presented and discussed in a recent paper (Watson 2019).

3 Notable exceptions include performance-based subjects such as music, theatre, and dance where a performance element is included, often alongside a question–answer exam.

4 One might wonder if this is, indeed, too simple. If one thinks of teaching as emulative, for example, teacher questioning inside the classroom could be regarded as a model for student questioning outside the classroom. I have argued elsewhere that there is reason to be cautious here and, at the very least, that more empirical data is needed in order to fully understand the effects of teacher questioning on student questioning (Watson 2019). At present, the data indicates that teacher questioning inside the classroom leads to student answering inside the classroom.

5 A prominent alternative to the Limits-Owning account, presented by Roberts and Wood (2007) characterises intellectual humility as an absence of the vices of pride. While I am focusing on the Limits-Owning account here, I think an argument could be made for understanding questioning as (sometimes) an absence of a certain type of pride, and so as a form of intellectual humility in the Roberts and Wood sense. More generally, the claim that questioning is sometimes a form of intellectual humility does not turn on which account of intellectual humility one adopts.

6 https://rightquestion.org/ [Accessed 13 May 2019]

References

Alfano, M., Iurino, K., Stey, P., Robinson, B., Christen, M., Yu, F., and Lapsley, D. (2017) "Development and validation of a multi-dimensional measure of intellectual humility." *PloS one* 12(8): e0182950.

Aschner, M. J. (1961) "Asking questions to trigger thinking." *NEA Journal* 50: 44–46.

Bacon, F. (1996/1597) *Meditationes Sacrae and Human Philosophy*. Whitefish, MT: Kessinger Publishing.

Brualdi, A. (1998) "Classroom questions." *Practical Assessment, Research and Evaluation* 6(6): 1–3.

Corey, S. M. (1940) "The teachers out-talk the pupils." *The School Review* 48(10): 745–752.

Dantanio, M., and Beisenherz, P. (2001) *Learning to Question, Questioning to Learn: Developing Effective Teacher Questioning Practices*. London: Pearson.

Dantanio, M., and Paradise, L.V. (1988) "Teacher question-answer strategy and the cognitive correspondence between teacher questions and learner responses." *Journal of Research and Development in Education* 21(3): 71–75.

Dillon, J. (1978) "Using questions to depress student thought." *The School Review* 87(1): 50–63.

Dillon, J. (1980) "Curiosity as a non sequitur of Socratic questioning." *Journal of Educational Thought* 14: 17–22.

Dillon, J. (1981) "To question and not to question during discussion." *Journal of Teacher Education* 32(6): 15–20.

Dillon, J. (1982) "The effect of questions in education and other enterprises." *Journal of Curriculum Studies* 14(2): 127–152.

Dillon, J. (1988) "The remedial status of student questioning." *Journal of Curriculum Studies* 20(3): 197–210.

Fahey, G. (1942) "The extent of classroom questioning activity of high-school pupils and the relation of such activity to other factors of pedagogical significance." *Journal of Educational Psychology* 33(2): 128–137.

Farrar, M. T. (1983) "Another look at the use of oral questions for comprehension." *The Reading Teacher* 36: 370–375.
Fusco, Esther. (2012) *Effective Questioning Strategies in the Classroom: A Step-by-Step Approach to Engaged Thinking and Learning, K-8.* New York: Teachers College Press.
Gall, M. (1970) "The use of questions in teaching." *Review of Educational Research* 40(5): 707–721.
Gall, M. (1984) "Synthesis of research on teacher's questioning." *Educational Leadership* 40: 40–47.
Gayle, B., Preiss, R., and Allen, M. (2006) "How effective are teacher-initiated classroom questions in enhancing student learning?" In Gayle, B., Preiss, R., Burrell, N., and Allen, M. (eds.) *Classroom Communication and Instructional Processes: Advances Through Meta-Analysis.* Hillsdale, NJ: Lawrence Erlbaum Associates, 279–293.
Gershon, M. (2013) *How to Use Questioning in the Classroom: The Complete Guide.* Mike Gershon: Self-published.
Grow-Maienza, J., Hahn, D. D., and Joo, C. A. (2001) "Mathematics instruction in Korean primary schools: Structures, processes, and a linguistic analysis of questioning." *Journal of Educational Psychology* 93(2): 363–376.
Guthrie, J. T. (1983) "Questions as teaching tools." *Journal of Reading* 26: 478–479.
Haggard, M. et al. (2018) "Finding middle ground between intellectual arrogance and intellectual servility: Development and assessment of the limitations-owning intellectual humility scale." *Personality and Individual Differences* 124: 184–193.
Hazlett, A. (2012) "Higher-order epistemic attitudes and intellectual humility." *Episteme* 9(3): 205–223.
Hollingsworth, P. M. (1982) "Questioning: The heart of teaching." *The Clearinghouse* 55(8): 350–352.
Houston, V. M. (1938) "Improving the quality of classroom questions and questioning." *Educational Administration and Supervision* 24: 17–28.
Hunkins, F. P. (1972) *Questioning Strategies and Techniques.* Boston, MA: Allyn & Bacon.
Johns, J. (1968) "The relationship between teacher behaviors and the incidence of thought-provoking questions by students in secondary schools." *The Journal of Educational Research* 62(3): 117–122.
Kidd, I. (2015) "Educating for intellectual humility." In Baehr, J. (ed.) *Intellectual Virtues and Education: Essays in Applied Virtue Epistemology.* New York: Routledge, 54–70.
Kleinman, G. (1965) "Teachers' questions and student understanding of science." *Journal of Research in Science Teaching* 3(4): 307–317.
Martin, V. L., and Pressley, M. (1991) "Elaborative-interrogation effects depend on the nature of the question." *Journal of Educational Psychology* 83(1): 113–119.
Marzano, R. and Simms, J. (2014) *Questioning Sequences in the Classroom.* Bloomington: Marzano Research Laboratory.
Miller, G., and Pressley, M. (1989) "Picture versus question elaboration on young children's learning of sentences containing high- and low-probability content." *Journal of Experimental Child Psychology* 48(3): 431–450.
Mishler, E. (1975) "Studies in dialogue and discourse. II: Types of discourse initiated by and sustained through questioning." *Journal of Psycholinguistic Research* 4(2): 99–121.
Pearson, J., and West, R. (1991) "An initial investigation of the effects of gender on student questions in the classroom: Developing a descriptive base." *Communication Education* 40(1): 22–32.
Pope, G. (2013) *Questioning Technique Pocketbook.* Alresford: Teachers' Pocketbooks.
Riley, J. P. (1981) "The effects of preservice teacher's cognitive questioning level and redirecting on student science achievement." *Journal of Research in Science Teaching* 18(4): 303–309.
Roberts, R., and Wood, J. (2007) *Intellectual Virtues: An Essay in Regulative Epistemology.* Oxford: Oxford University Press.
Sachen, J. B. (1999) "Instructing the instructor: Effective questions." *Fire Engineering* 52: 130–134.
Susskind, E. (1969) "The role of question-asking in the elementary school classroom." In Kaplan, F., and Sarason, S. B. (eds.) *The Psycho-educational Clinic.* New Haven, CT: Yale University Press.
Susskind, E. (1979) "Encouraging teachers to encourage children's curiosity: A pivotal competence." *Journal of Clinical Child Psychology* 8(2): 101–106.
Tizard, B., Hughes, M., Carmichael, H., and Pinkerton, G. (1983) "Children's questions and adults' answers." *Journal of Child Psychology and Psychiatry, and Allied Disciplines* 24(2): 269–281.
Watson, L. (2018) "Educating for good questioning: A tool for intellectual virtues education." *Acta Analytica* 33(3): 353–370.
Watson, L. (2019) "Educating for inquisitiveness: A case against exemplarism for intellectual character education." *Journal of Moral Education* 48(3): 303–315.

Whitcomb, D., Battaly, H., Baehr, J., and Howard-Synder, D. (2017) "Intellectual humility: Owning our limitations." *Philosophy and Phenomenological Research* 94(3): 509–539.
Wilen, W. W., and Clegg, A. A. (1986) "Effective questions and questioning: A research review." *Theory and Research in Social Education* 14(2): 153–161.
Wright, C., and Nuthall, G. (1970) "Relationships between teacher behaviors and pupil achievement in three experimental elementary science lessons." *American Educational Research Journal* 7(4): 477–491.

38
HUMILITY IN LAW[1]

Amalia Amaya

38.1 Introduction

Humility has been claimed to be a virtue that is relevant to a variety of legal scholarly discussions.[2] However, the most prominent use that humility has been put to in law is as an adjudicative virtue that favors judicial restraint. The first section of this paper examines this prevalent conception of humility and argues that it is grounded on a problematic view of humility as an assertion of one's poor epistemic standing. Contrary to what views of humility as judicial restraint hold, the value of humility in law is hardly restricted to the judiciary – let alone to it providing an argument for judicial deference. Humility, understood as a relational virtue that is a mean between self-aggrandizement and self-deprecation, is exceedingly relevant for all the legal professions. More specifically, I will argue that humility has an important impact on the organizational dimensions of the legal profession (Section 38.3); it is critical for excelling in professional legal practice (Section 38.4); and it is also central to professional development (Section 38.5). Section 38.6 suggests some ways in which legal education and professional training could foster this valuable trait. I conclude (in Section 38.7) with a few reflections on the political implications of giving an important role to humility within the legal professions.

38.2 Humility as an adjudicative virtue

Humility has been primarily employed in law in the context of adjudication, that is to say, as a judicial virtue. Judicial humility is mostly understood as a trait of character that leads judges to exercise judicial restraint, i.e., not to overpass what are taken to be the proper functions of the judicial role. Judicial restraint is at the core of a number of doctrines, such as deference to legislative and administrative decision-making, respect for precedent, a textualist approach to statutory interpretation, doctrines of standing and mootness, the requirement that judges should avoid deciding political questions, the presumption of constitutionality of statutes, and the presumption of legitimacy of legislative and executive motives (Daley: 2000). In this view, humility is a valuable trait of character for judges to have insofar as it instills in them a disposition to restrain themselves in the exercise of the judicial function. Judicial humility has been invoked to justify an attitude of restraint in constitutional review (Gewirts [1996] and Gely and Caron [2004]), rule following (Schauer: 2012), deference to popular opinion (Sunstein: 2009), restraint in granting summary judgment (Stempel: 2012), deferential rulings that leave contentious social issues to the democratic process (Myers: 2015), as well as to argue against constructivism about constitutional interpretation (McConnell: 1997) and in favor of a theory of fidelity in constitutional interpretation (Lessig: 2019). This use of humility to support doctrines of restraint is mediated by a very specific view of what humility amounts to, namely, a view of humility as a trait of character that makes its possessor acutely aware of his own cognitive limitations and that leads him to recognize that others are better positioned to take some decisions – and thus, that deference is in order.

This view of judicial humility is quite problematic. As I have argued elsewhere, it unduly reduces humility to its intellectual dimensions, defines it in a way that makes it incompatible with intellectual autonomy, and limits its reach to it being an argument against judicial activism, which is a claim that would need a political, rather than an epistemic, justification (Amaya: 2018). Humility, however, far from being a mere rhetorical instrument at the service of arguments in support of judicial restraint, is a very valuable trait of character in the context of adjudication for several reasons. First, humility is a virtue that is associated with a number of epistemic virtues that are of high consequence in adjudication, such as open-mindedness to alternative viewpoints, a disposition to listen carefully to the views of others, and a willingness to reassess previous positions (Scharffs: 1998; Gerhardt: 2007, 44). These intellectual dispositions are not only exceedingly important to individual judicial decision-making, insofar as they enable judges to examine the merits of the case in a way that appropriately takes into account different perspectives, but are particularly needed (more on this in Section 38.5) for judges who sit on multi-member courts.

Secondly, humility is also related to some moral virtues that are critical in adjudication, such as gentleness, kindness, compassion, and service (Amaya: 2018). Humility brings with it an attitude of proper care and respect for the well-being of others and disposes those who possess it to avoid boastful behavior that might make others feel inferior or unworthy, as well as cause harm, hatred, and resentment. A humble judge is thus more likely to adopt a respectful attitude toward the parties, not to abuse power, empathize with the parties' and victims' plight, be compassionate in the exercise of the judicial function, and understand the judicial role as one of service to the people (Scharffs: 1998). Therefore, humility's well-known social benefits are critical to foster a courtroom environment that properly exemplifies the kind of social relationships (i.e., egalitarian relations of mutual care and respect) that are distinctive of a democratic polis.

Third, humility in judges is also of fundamental importance in contexts of adjudication that require collaboration across jurisdictions, as well as cases in which more than one legal order is relevant (Borrows: 2016). The multiplicity of relevant legal orders may result from the coexistence of different legal orders within the state, e.g., an indigenous law and a state law, regional integration, e.g., European Union law and state law, as well as from the interaction of global law with domestic law. Humility is pivotal in multi-juridical legal contexts, insofar as it involves an appreciation of different viewpoints, enables the judge to relate to the diverse normative orders that are relevant in the case in a way that shows respect for the other and avoids privileging one's legal perspective.

In order for humility to perform these central roles, something other than a 'thin' conception that reduces it to awareness of one's poor epistemic standing compared to others is called for. Indeed, alongside the dominant view of judicial humility as judicial restraint, 'thick' views of humility that avoid overtones of self-deprecation are also being articulated and defended in legal scholarship. In Berger's account, humility is a virtue that is based on 'awareness of one's role and position in respect of power and willingness to accept the burdens of responsibility that flow from this' (Berger: 2018). In the context of the judicial role, humility requires that the judge be keenly aware of his role and responsibilities in a web of relationships that are much broader than those between the judiciary and other branches of government. Humility, claims Berger, does not urge judges to be 'smaller,' but rather to take 'the appropriate amount of space' by fully discharging their duties toward others and accepting the burdens of judgment.

A focus on the relational aspects of humility is also at the core of Borrow's conception of judicial humility. In her view, 'humility is a state of positioning oneself in a way that does not favor one's importance over another. It is a condition of being teachable. Humility allows us to recognize our dependence upon others and to consider their perspectives along with our own' (Borrows: 2016, 154). In the judicial context, humility requires working across differences by engaging with different perspectives, especially in cases where age, religion, gender, race or indigenousness are at stake. Critically, the humble judge would make an effort to step out of his own viewpoint, accept the 'healthy discomfort' that comes with encountering difference, and assert other perspectives as equally worthy of respect.

A commitment to equality is, in my own account, at the core of judicial humility. Humility requires that a person has a profound appreciation of the equality of all human beings, avoiding both self-aggrandizement, in which one asserts one's superiority, and self-abasement, in which one asserts one's inferiority. Humility prevents one from holding that one is superior to others on the grounds that one is better than others with respect to some features or qualities (e.g., wealth, status, ability, etc.). In the context of the judicial role, it requires that judges view themselves as equal to the parties and actors involved in the trial process, regardless of the differences that there might be in prestige, professional or social status, and power (Amaya: 2018).

These thick views of judicial humility emphasize different components of the virtue of humility, namely, its connection to responsibility, diversity and inclusion, and equality. Despite differences, they all focus on the socio-relational aspects of humility, rather than on the self-evaluation of one's own epistemic abilities. That is to say, they take humility to be a matter of how one positions oneself *vis a vis* other people, rather than how one stands *vis a vis* one's merits or capacities. In contrast to thin views of judicial humility as restraint, they view humility as a relational, other-directed disposition, instead of a self-referencing quality. In addition, these conceptions of humility take humility to be a mean between excess and defect, thereby avoiding arrogance (in which one makes oneself 'bigger') and servilism (in which one makes oneself 'smaller'). On this point, they significantly depart from views of judicial humility as restraint that focus, almost exclusively, on the ways in which humility helps those who possess it to avoid having too grand a view of themselves and take it to be a trait of character that issues in deference and submission. Last, thick views of judicial humility anchor it to core legal and political values, especially to its potential to contribute to building a community in which citizens properly assume their own responsibilities in their encounters with others, respond in an inclusive and respectful way to the facts of pluralism, and relate to each other on an egalitarian basis, beyond the narrow political aim of counteracting judicial activism. A thick conception of humility not only allows us to give a broader account of the reach of judicial humility, but it also enables us to explain the benefits of humility beyond the judicial role, to encompass, more broadly, the legal professions. In the next three sections, I explore the consequences of humility for the legal professions in a way that includes, but is not reduced to, the judicial function.

38.3 Humility and professional organization

Humility has an important positive impact on the functioning of legal professional organizations, such as corporate law firms, government agencies, prosecuting offices, international organizations, public interest law firms, and public defender offices. There are several ways in which humility is relevant to the organizational dimensions of the legal professions. First, humility helps to foster an egalitarian ethos at the work place. As argued, the virtue of humility involves a commitment to relate to others on an egalitarian basis. Given the hierarchical structure that is characteristic of most work environments in the legal professions, the egalitarian stance that humility brings in is central to promote collegiality among people across levels within the organization. The egalitarianism that is at the core of the virtue of humility is particularly important in the context of public institutions, for the way in which public officials relate to others (i.e., co-workers, but also those in need of legal counsel or service, victims, parties, etc.) manifests how the state treats people and sets an example for how citizens should treat each other.

Second, humility has been associated with a number of pro-social values that are extremely consequential in the context of organizations (Nielsen and Marrone: 2018; Owens et al., 2011; Wallace et al., 2017).[3] There is robust empirical evidence for the connection between humility and other-oriented behavior that is altruistic, generous, cooperative, and helpful; higher levels of empathy, benevolence, forgiveness, and gratitude; making decisions that are non-exploitative of others; and lower levels of power-seeking (Krumrei-Marcuso: 2017; Davis et al., 2012; Wright et al., 2017). This connection between humility and a number of pro-social values and behaviors results in highly beneficial outcomes for legal professional organizations. To begin with, humility has important positive effects on team work, especially with regard to team integration and team performance (Owens et al., 2011; Nielsen and Marrone: 2018, 817; Wallace et al., 2017, 251). The positive impact of humility on teams is not only relevant for the well-functioning of legal organizations but, as I will argue below, is particularly significant for collective legal decision-making. In addition, humility results in strong social bonds, increased group cohesiveness, and a higher level of employee retention (Nielsen and Marrone: 2018, 816), all of which are very valuable for legal organizations.

Third, there is a substantive body of empirical research that shows that humility is a predictor of emotional well-being (Nielsen and Marrone: 2018, 815). Specifically, humility decreases depressive symptoms, positively correlates with subjective well-being and self-reported health, and is associated with more positive emotions (such as gratitude and love) and less negative emotions (i.e., shame and mistrust) in contexts in which the humble person is receiving assistance or help from others. These findings are particularly relevant in the context of legal professional organizations, in light of sustained critiques of the dehumanization of the legal profession, the high levels of distress and anxiety facing legal professionals, and the challenges of leading a successful career and a satisfactory personal life in the legal professions (especially, albeit not exclusively, in corporate law firms and legal services in the banking and finance sector) (Schiltz: 1999 and Rothstein: 2007).

Fourth, humility has been shown to be connected with high performance and innovation in the context of business organizations (Vera and Rodriguez-Lopez: 2004; Owens et al., 2011; Nielsen and Marrone: 2018). The positive impact of humility on performance and innovation is the outcome of a number of different mechanisms: (i) humble people have a better awareness of strengths and weaknesses, which leads to a better distribution of time and work; (ii) humility influences performance insofar as it is a key characteristic of effective leadership (Collins: 2005); (iii) humility enhances social learning (through imitation of role models), which results in better individual performance and higher organizational outcomes (more on this in Section 38.5); (iv) humility helps innovation and performance insofar as it enables an open attitude to new paradigms and promotes experimentation, learning by trial and error, and risk-taking; and (v) humility also has a positive impact on performance insofar as it increases an organization's resilience, i.e., the organization's capability to adapt to change and improve performance in the long run, insofar as humble people are more receptive to feedback after failure and avoid self-complacency after success. These results may arguably be indicative of the significance of humility for bolstering organizational outcomes in the legal professions.[4]

Last, humility is a trait of character that enhances one's capacities to work in transcultural environments, which is critical in the context of legal professional organizations (Foronda et al., 2016; Hamman: 2017). Cultural diversity is a central characteristic of some legal organizations, like international organizations, NGOs, and international courts. Besides, given that contemporary societies are highly diverse, and the impact of globalization in the legal sector, domestic legal professional contexts are also increasingly marked by cultural diversity. This makes humility essential for legal professionals to collaborate across cultural barriers as well as interact with clients, victims, defendants, and people in need of legal services of any kind in a way that is respectful of cultural difference.

In sum, humility is valuable to legal professional organizations in that it generates an egalitarian work environment, strengthens social bonds within the organization, is positively related to emotional well-being, enhances performance and innovation, and is a valuable resource for organizations to function in highly diverse contexts.

38.4 Humility and professional practice

Not only is humility relevant to the organizational dimensions of the legal professions, but it is also essential to achieve excellence in legal practice. Law is, first and foremost, an argumentative enterprise. Argumentation is the backbone of legal practice, be it at a courtroom, the classroom, a public defender office, executive agency, state legislature or union, law is in the business of reasoned decision-making. Humility has been claimed to be a deliberative virtue, i.e., a trait of character that facilitates the attainment of the goals of deliberation (Aikin and Clanton: 2010). It is also a valuable trait in deliberative settings insofar as it is associated with other deliberative virtues such as open-mindedness and curiosity (Scott: 2014; Krumrei-Marcuso et al., 2019). In addition, humility is related to argumentative virtues, such as the willingness to modify one's position and the willingness to listen to others (Kidd: 2016, 401; Aberdein, this volume). In light of humility's direct (as a deliberative virtue in its own right) and indirect (via its relation to other virtues) contribution to reasoned decision-making, it is an essential trait of character for jurists to possess.

The virtue of humility is particularly relevant in group deliberation and decision-making. This importantly adds to its value in the context of the legal professions, given that some of the most important legal decisions are taken by collective bodies (i.e., by multi-member courts, the jury, executive committees, etc.). Humility enhances group-deliberation in law in a variety of ways. First, humility contributes to generating the background conditions needed to enable a productive deliberation. To begin with, it helps generate an egalitarian ethos among the members of the deliberating group which increases the likelihood that group deliberation will reach better decisions than those that would be reached by its individual members, as it makes it more likely that all views are heard and taken seriously. In addition, insofar as it enhances cooperativeness, humility would also promote information-sharing within the group, which also augments group synergy. Last, humility, as explained earlier, favors inclusiveness, and is thus critical to prevent information from being undisclosed (more on this below) or under-valued for reasons that are unrelated to its credibility or warrant, i.e., because it is sourced from a member of a minority or disadvantaged group.[5]

Second, in addition to promoting an egalitarian, cooperative, and inclusive deliberative environment, humility aids members of deliberating bodies to tackle disagreement. The person with the virtue of humility would respond to disagreement by 'reflecting in the nature of their evidence … considering the other person's reasons for thinking otherwise, being willing to respectively discuss the issue further, and all the time showing a willingness to change her mind' (Pritchard: 2018). These dispositions, which are absent in the arrogant, enable a genuine collective deliberation and help deliberators face disagreement in ways that avoid obtuse self-encroachment in their respective positions and antagonism. It is critical to note that humility does not demand that, in cases of peer disagreement, the person downgrades his epistemic assessment of the issue under discussion (Pritchard: 2018). Quite the contrary, straightforwardly lowering one's epistemic assessment of the contested issue in light of disagreement would signal a lack of humility. The virtue of humility demands that, when disagreeing, one be willing to listen to other's people´s views and to seriously consider conflicting evidence, which may or may not result in a change in view. To respond to disagreement by holding one's views as less justified, by the sheer fact of the disagreement, or lowering one's commitment in them to the point of withdrawing them and surrendering to someone else's position would manifest intellectual diffidence or servility, rather than humility.

Last, humility also helps group deliberation by preventing some well-known failures of group deliberation from arising.[6] Phenomena that distort group deliberation include amplification of individual cognitive biases; homogenization, i.e., the reduction of the variety of information available within the group; polarization, i.e., the adoption by members of the group of a more extreme version of their own pre-deliberative positions, and domination, i.e., the shifting of attitudes within the group toward those hold by its socially advantaged members (Sunstein and Hastie: 2015 and Luskin et al., 2015). There are two main reasons that help explain these deliberative failures: informational influences, so that people who are in a minority position self-silence on the grounds that their own judgment must be wrong; and social influences, for fear of social sanctions may lead people to silence themselves. Humility helps address the two main forces driving deliberative distortions. The proper self-confidence that is characteristic of the intellectually humble would prevent minority members from thinking that their beliefs are wrong by the mere fact that they contradict the majority position. Informational influences would thus be counteracted and minority beliefs shared, which results in an increase of the cognitive diversity within the group that importantly enhances group deliberation. Humility also helps contain social influences. Humility, as argued, contributes to generating an egalitarian, cooperative, and inclusive deliberative environment, which makes it less likely that those who hold a minority position or are members of a minority group self-silence for fear of being ridiculed, rejected, or harmed in their reputation.

Humility may also be helpful in reducing the specific failings involved in some of these deliberative failures.[7] 'Group polarization' may be reduced if deliberators show some of the dispositions that are associated with humility and that help deal with disagreement in a productive way, such as openness to other's people viewpoints, willingness to modify one's positions, and a disposition to change one's mind. Humility may also be helpful in mitigating the cascade effects (i.e., when people follow the statements previously made, ignoring their private knowledge) and 'common knowledge' effects (i.e., when shared information crowds out information held by one or few members) that result in 'homogenization.' An appraisal of oneself as a cognitive agent that avoids both self-aggrandizing and, critically for these cases, self-diminishing, is useful for avoiding a tendency to simply follow the lead of predecessors or adhere to shared views within the group. 'Domination' may also be mitigated when deliberators have the virtue of humility and are thereby committed to an egalitarian stance, which would prevent social disadvantage from translating into loss of credibility or lack of participation.

38.5 Humility and professional development

Humility is critical for professional development as well. A main venue for legal professionals to transit from novice to expert is the imitation of exemplary jurists, i.e., those legal professionals who possess and display a large share of the virtues necessary to excel at the legal practice. Witnessing excellent others gives rise to admiration, which may trigger a process of emulation that may lead to the acquisition of the professional virtues. There are, however, several ways in which this process of emulation of admirable models may go wrong (Amaya: 2019). Humble people, I would argue, are less likely to divert from the path that leads to professional development via the imitation of admirable jurists.

To begin with, witnessing excellence in others may fail to generate admiration, and thus, to put in place a process of emulation that may result in virtue development. Other emotional responses when faced with exemplary models include indifference, reluctance to admire, or an outright rejection of admiration (Zagzebski: 2017, 50–59). When experienced, exposure to exemplars will fail to deliver virtue. Inflated views of oneself or arrogance favor these kind of emotional reactions toward the excellence of others. In fact, there is psychological evidence that supports the view that an excessive self-esteem undermines inspiration by outstanding models (Lockwood and Kunda: 1999). Thus, lack of humility by excess seems to stand in the way of properly admiring someone and, thus, is an obstacle to learning by example.

Conversely, lack of humility by defect, i.e., self-abasement, or insufficient self-esteem or self-affirmation, may distort the emotional response to excellent others by replacing admiration with awe and adoration.[8] In these cases, models are perceived as idols, and the process of imitation, which is meant to involve the autonomous acquisition of admirable traits of character, degenerates into worshipping. The critical engagement with models of virtue that imitation requires at its best gives way to an unexamined devotion and servile deference, which are the marks of fetishism. Rather than relating – as humility would require – to the model on an equal footing, those who mistake models for idols engage in processes of copycatting that attempt to replicate superficial features of the model. In contrast to admiration, which triggers a process of imitation that aims at a genuine transformation of the self, adoration moves agents to mindlessly become 'like' the model in ways that tend to efface, rather than develop, their own subjectivity.

In addition to triggering the right emotional response to models of excellence, thereby avoiding both indifference and adoration, humility is also needed to have an appropriate motivational response to admiration. A desire to emulate is central in the motivational profile of admiration; that is to say, admiration typically motivates the agent who experiences it to emulate the model in the admired respect. However, a desire to imitate is not always the appropriate response to admiration (Archer: 2019). If there is a vast distance between the model and the person who admires it, in terms of capacities, expertise, resources, or achievements, then imitation of the exemplar might not be the best way to go. This is not to say that admiration in these cases is motivationally inert. Admiration of these truly exceptional exemplars may be inspirational, moving us to improve, and it may also motivate us to enhance their reputation, praise the values they embody, and promote them in a variety of ways. Thus, attainability of the model – which the humble person is well-positioned to assess – is a key factor that is relevant to determining what the appropriate response to admiration should be.[9]

On the one hand, a judgment of attainability, which involves an accurate assessment of one's (current) capacities as compared to those of the exemplar, is critical to avoid 'over-stretching'; that is, to attempt to imitate in ways that do not take into account one's limitations (Kristjansson: 2018, 179). This 'shooting for the stars' is not merely likely to be ineffective in terms of professional improvement, but it may also be harmful as it may result in worse outcomes than those that would have been reached if one had more fitting goals in mind. While the source of the misrepresentation of the distance that separates oneself from the model may be simply due to mistakes or ignorance, a potential cause for over-stretching may be a lack of humility by excess. Those who have a self-aggrandizing view of themselves are prone to misjudge the attainability of the model, as they fail to see the extent to which the exemplar is beyond what they may currently achieve. Moreover, insofar as a person who has an excess of self-esteem does not have her limitations in the focus of attention (Bommarito: 2013), she is likely to engage in imitation without having even considered first whether the model is within her reach.

On the other hand, the path that goes from witnessing excellence in others to developing admirable traits of character may be impeded when admiration is not accompanied by a desire to emulate in cases in which such desire, given the attainability of the model, is the correct motivational response. In these cases, the person feels paralyzed, rather than energized, by witnessing excellent others, as he feels unworthy or incapable of approximating the model.[10] A lack of proper self-esteem and self-affirmation may lead the person to magnify the model and perceive the distance between his own capacities and those of the model as insurmountable. The model is perceived as being so above oneself that admiration fails to propel a process of imitation, or even to motivate the agent to take steps toward professional improvement, which may allow him to eventually succeed at emulating the model.

Thus, humility is central to instilling in legal professionals the emotional and motivational dispositions necessary for learning by example. The virtue of (intellectual) humility has also been shown to be associated with attitudes that contribute to knowledge acquisition (Krumrei-Mancuso et al., 2019). Specifically, it is associated with less claiming of knowledge that one does not have, more reflective thinking, need for cognition, intellectual engagement, curiosity, open-minded thinking, and less social vigilantism, which promotes collaborative learning. Hence, humility not only facilitates learning by example, but, more generally, it is positively related to traits, motivations, and patterns of thinking and behavior that promote learning. As such, it is a virtue that importantly helps law students and early legal practitioners to acquire the knowledge, capacities, and understanding of the values embedded in the professional practice that are characteristic of experts and to actively continue learning through their professional careers.

38.6 Enhancing humility in the legal professions

Humility, I have argued, is highly relevant to legal organizations, legal practice, and professional development. Given the relevance of humility to the legal professions, it is worth asking which steps may be taken to develop it among law students, legal scholars, and practitioners. How could we reconceive legal education and professional training so that it fosters humility? A first way in which the virtue of humility may be inculcated is through exposure to exemplars. As argued, humility enables social learning through example, but, like any other virtue, it can also be cultivated through imitation (Tangley: 2012).[11] Exposing students to exemplary jurists who possess humility to a high degree and exercise it in their legal professional role, combined with critical discussion of such models, may be a productive path to developing this virtue. In a similar vein, given that leaders are important role models within their organizations, selecting humble leaders and praising humility in leadership in the diverse contexts of the legal professions may have a positive impact in humility development, as the distinctive way in which humble leaders relate to others and engage professionally permeates through the different levels of the organization (Vera and Rodriguez: 2004).

A second way in which humility could be cultivated in the legal professions is through the study of comparative and international law or the inclusion of a comparative element in the study of the different branches of domestic law. Exposure to different cultures have been claimed to foster humility (Tangley: 2012). Similarly, the engagement with a diversity of legal cultures and perspectives that comparative and international law enables may arguably help law students and legal professionals in training to develop the virtue of humility. Likewise, it could be argued that diversity in different work environments, from the bench to law firms or public offices, is also beneficial for the purposes of inculcating humility in legal professionals (Nava: 2010).

An additional third way to promote humility in the legal profession could be through its explicit inclusion in strategies and professional codes of conduct. Just as it may be beneficial to include humility as an element in a firm's strategy and culture (Vera and Rodriguez: 2004), arguably, humility could be fostered by explicitly recognizing its value in the strategies of law schools, law firms, and public legal institutions. Likewise, professional codes may also be useful for promoting humility in law. Even though professional codes of conduct are limited instruments for inculcating the virtues, they still play an important role in conveying the values that the profession takes to be relevant, in providing standards for assessing professional conduct, as well as enabling criticism and discussion of core professional values. In this sense, the explicit inclusion of humility in professional legal codes may help highlight the relevance of humility for the legal professions and motivate law students and professionals to cultivate it.

A fourth venue for the development of humility is institutional design. Organizational structures and procedures, space design, and normative frameworks may foster (or be an obstacle to) virtuous behavior (Anderson: 2012). More modestly, one may attempt to nudge virtue, that is to say, to trigger behavior that is in accordance with virtue, through institutional design. For example, one could bring about open-mindedness in legal decision-making by asking jurists to overshoot on the side of charity in interpreting arguments (Aikin and Casey: 2016, 439) or indirectly promote impartiality by instructing jurors to seriously consider alternative views (Simon: 2004). Even if such behaviors would fall sort of virtue, as they do not arise out of virtuous motivations, still they may be a step toward development of (genuine) virtue. It is thus important to examine the normative, organizational, and spatial features of the context in which legal professionals work with a view to determining the extent to which they promote (or hinder) humility (or, at least, behavior that is in accordance with humility).

Several interventions to promote humility have been proposed in the field of positive psychology, and they may provide a (fifth) way in which humility in the legal professions may be fostered. Lavelock et al. (2014) administered an intervention which involved completing a workbook with several multi-modal exercises designed to promote humility and found that participants in the humility condition reported greater increases in humility across time than those in the control condition. Building on those results, Wright et al. (2017) have argued that humility could be fostered by developing primes and writing assignments that incorporate and promote the 'semantic signature' of humility, i.e., the text features that, they found, are characteristic of humility, such as inclusive language, as well as language that maintains equality and emphasizes connectedness. The incorporation of interventions such as these (tailored to the legal professional context) in legal training could perhaps be an effective means for fostering humility among legal professionals.

Sixth, argumentation has been claimed to be conducive to the cultivation of (intellectual) humility (Kidd: 2016). Given the centrality of argumentation in legal practice, argumentation may afford a particularly suitable means of developing humility among legal professionals. Engaging in argumentation, however, only contributes to the development of humility if it is conceived as an edifying discipline. If the mode of argumentation and the conduct of those involved is aggressively adversarial, abusive, and fiercely competitive, rather than enhancing humility, it encourages pedantic attitudes in the 'winners' and may seriously damage self-confidence in the 'losers' (Kidd: 2016, 400–401). Thus, the argumentative nature of law places legal professionals in an advantaged position to develop humility, but only if legal education and culture advice against the employment of forms of legal argument that may have corrupting, rather than positive, effects on character formation.

Last, legal education could promote humility by endorsing a style of teaching that informs law students about the complexity of knowledge, highlights the partiality of their perspectives, communicates to them respect for the discipline and the achievements of those who have contributed to shaping it, and engages them into practices such as dialectical exchange, receiving criticism, responding to feedback, revising their own views, and listening to alternative viewpoints (Kidd: 2017). Legal education could also enhance humility by helping students regulate their appraisals of their own weaknesses and strengths, and, correspondingly, their ambitions, as well as their attitudes toward others (i.e., students, legal professionals, and members of other professions who play important roles in law), collectives, and legal traditions (Kidd: 2017). Gaining knowledge has been claimed to promote (intellectual) humility, for a higher level of education is associated with appreciating the complexity of knowledge, its tentative nature, and the limits of one's knowledge (Krumrei-Marcuso et al., 2019). However, a higher level of education could also arguably lead to arrogance, bigotry, and pedantry. Hence, it seems critical that legal education wholeheartedly endorses a teaching style that helps develop the kind of attitudes and behaviors that are characteristic of humility.

38.7 Conclusions

In this paper I have argued that humility, far from being (as is mostly defended in legal scholarship) a judicial virtue that favors restraint in the exercise of the judicial function, is a trait of character that is highly valuable for the legal professions broadly conceived. Humility is critical for professional organizations, professional practice, and professional development in law. Its political value, moreover, is hardly restricted to it being an argument against judicial activism, but it importantly fosters democratic values in that it contributes to establishing egalitarian, cooperative, and inclusive social relations within the legal professions, enhances practices of group deliberation in law, and promotes legal professional development through social learning. Arguably, given the central role that legal professionals (especially those in public service, but also in the private law sector) play in shaping legal and political culture, the democratic effects that the cultivation of humility in law brings about extend beyond the legal profession to reach the society at large. The important implications of humility for the legal profession and beyond make its cultivation among law students and legal professionals highly desirable. I have also offered some suggestions about how humility could be fostered in the context of the legal professions, which I hope could provide food for thought about how to best design legal education, professional legal training, and legal institutional structures with a view to enhancing humility.

Notes

1 I am grateful to Alessandra Tanesini, Pablo de Larrañaga, and Iris van Domselaar for valuable comments on an earlier draft.

2 Such as constitutional law (Gerhardt: 2007; Lessig: 2019), legal theory (Sherry: 2017, Amaya: 2018); criminal law (Strang: 2017 and Sigler: 2018), evidence law (Haddad: 2015); law teaching (Noah: 2018) and legal theology (Fronnen: forthcoming and Marshall: 2017).

3 It is worth noting, however, that in addition to the well-documented association between humility and pro-social and affiliative feelings of appreciation for others, a recent study also shows that humility has another dimension which involves more anti-social, withdrawal-oriented feelings of self-abasement. Further empirical work would be needed to explain the complexity of the emotional experiences involved in humility. See Weidman, Cheng and Tracy (2018).
4 If this is on the right track, then worries about the potential tensions that there might exist between fostering humility in the legal professions and the current commercialization and competitiveness that these professions are undergoing, especially in the corporate sector, may be put to rest. I thank Iris Van Domselaar for raising this point.
5 Thus, the virtue of humility is arguably a tool to combat epistemic injustice.
6 Other virtues are, of course, also useful for preventing deliberative distortions in group deliberation. See (Amaya: forthcoming).
7 Cf. Alfano and Sullivan's and Levy's chapter, in this volume.
8 On the differences between admiration and adoration, see Schindler et al. (2013).
9 The attainability of the model has also an important impact in its effectiveness. See Han et al. (2017). The point also holds in the context of professional organizations, see Moberg (2000).
10 For a discussion of the energizing vs. paralyzing effects of admiration, see Onu, Kessler and Smith (2016).
11 Humility in novices would thus be valuable in that it would help them to learn by example and humility in exemplars would be valuable in that it provides models that novices may imitate in order to develop humility. This picture, however, would be complicated if, as Nadelhoffer and Wright have suggested, humility were the 'most stable shared attribute across moral exemplars (…) and the most stable unshared attribute between moral exemplars and moral novices.' If validated, these claims would mean that humility would be a characteristic of exemplarity, thereby making it easier to develop this virtue through imitation, but it would also make it more difficult for imitation to be a general mechanism for virtue development if, as argued, humility in novices enables social learning. See Nadelhoffer and Wright (2017).

References

Aberdein, Andrew. Forthcoming. Intellectual Humility and Argumentation. In *The Routledge Handbook of Philosophy of Humility*, edited by Mark Alfano, Alessandra Tanesisi and Michael Lynch. Routledge: London.

Aikin, Scott F. and Casey, John P. 2016. Straw Men, Iron Men and Argumentative Virtue. *Topoi* 35 (2), 431–440.

Aikin, Scott F. and Clanton, J. Caleb. 2010. Developing Group-Deliberative Virtues. *Journal of Applied Philosophy* 27(4), 409–424.

Alfano, Mark and Sullivan, Emily. Forthcoming. Humility in Social Networks. In *The Routledge Handbook of Philosophy of Humility*, edited by Mark Alfano, Alessandra Tanesisi and Michael Lynch. London: Routledge

Amaya, Amalia. 2018. The Virtue of Judicial Humility. *Jurisprudence* 9(3): 1–11.

Amaya, Amalia. 2019. Admiration, Exemplarity and Judicial Virtue. In *Virtue, Emotion and Imagination in Law and Legal Reasoning*, edited by Amalia Amaya and Maksymilian del Mar. Oxford: Hart Publishing, 26–45.

Amaya, Amalia. Forthcoming. Group-Deliberative Virtues and Legal Epistemology. In *Evidential Reasoning in Law*, edited by Jordi Ferrer and Carmen Vazquez. Cambridge: Cambridge University Press.

Anderson, Elisabeth. 2012. Epistemic Justice as a Virtue of Social Institutions. *Social Epistemology* 26(2), 163–173.

Archer, Alfred. 2019. Admiration and Motivation. *Emotion Review* 11(2), 140–150.

Berger, Benjamin. 2018. What Humility Isn't: Responsibility and the Judicial Role. In *The Chief: Essays in Honor of Chief Justice Beverley McLachlin*, edited by Daniel Jutras and Marcus Moore. Toronto: LexisNexis.

Bonmarito, Nicolas. 2013. Modesty as a Virtue of Attention. *Philosophical Review* 122(1), 93–117.

Borrows, Lindsay. 2016. Dabaadendiziwin: Practices of Humility in a Multi-Juridical Legal Landscape. *Windsor Yearbook of Access to Justice* 33(1), 149–165.

Collins, Jim. 2005. Level 5 Leadership: The Triumph of Humility and Fierce Resolve. *Harvard Business Review* 18(2), 95–109.

Daley, John. 2000. Defining Judicial Restraint. In *Judicial Power, Democracy and Legal Positivism*, edited by Tom Campbell and Jeffrey Goldsworthy. Aldershot: Ashgate, 279–314.

Davis, Don E., Worthington, Everett L., Hook, Joshua, N., Emmons, Robert A., Hill, Peter C., Bollinger, Richard A. and Van Tongeren, Daryl R. 2012. Humility and the Development and Repair of Social Bonds: Two Longitudinal Studies. *Self and Identity* 2012, 1–20.

Foronda, Cynthia, Reinholdt, Maren M. and Ousman, Kevin. 2016. Cultural Humility: A Concept Analysis. *Journal of Transcultural Nursing* 27(3), 210–217.

Frohnen, Bruce, P. Forthcoming. Augustine, Lawyers and the Lost Virtue of Humility. *Catholic University Law Review*.

Gely, Rafael and Caron, Paul L. 2004. Affirmative Refraction: Grutter v. Bollinger Through the Lens of the Case 'The Case of Speluncean Explorers.' *Constitutional Commentary* 21, 63–106.

Gerhardt, Michael J. 2007. Constitutional Humility. *University of Cincinnati Law Review* 76, 23–54.

Gewrits, Paul. 1996. On I Know It When I See It. *Yale Law Review* 105(4), 1023–1047.

Haddad, Pedro. 2015. La virtud de la humildad y sus aportes a la actividad probatoria. *Quaestio Iuris* 8(4), 2402–2923.

Hamman, Evan. 2017. Culture, Humility and the Law: Towards a More Transformative Teaching Framework. *Alternative Law Journal* 42(2), 156–161.

Han, Hyemin, Kim, Jeongmin, Jeong, Changwoo and Cohen, Geoffrey L. 2017. Attainable and Relevant Moral Exemplars Are More Effective than Extraordinary Exemplars in Promoting Voluntary Service Engagement. *Frontiers in Psychology* 8(1): 283.

Kidd, Ian J. 2016. Intellectual Humility, Confidence and Argumentation. *Topoi* 35(2), 395–402.

Kidd, Ian J. 2017. Educating for Intellectual Humility. In *Intellectual Virtues and Education*, edited by Jason Baehr. New York: Routledge, 54–71.

Kristjansson, K. 2018. *Virtuous Emotions*. Oxford: Oxford University Press.

Krumrei-Marcuso, Elizabeth. 2017. Intellectual Humility and Prosocial Values: Direct and Mediated Effects. *The Journal of Positive Psychology* 12(1), 13–28.

Krumrei-Marcuso, Elizabeth J., Haggard, Megan C., Labouff, Jordan P. and Rowatt, Wade C. 2020. Links between Intellectual Humility and Acquiring Knowledge. *The Journal of Positive Psychology* 15(2), 155–170. DOI: 10.1080/17439760.2019.1579359

Lavelock, Caroline R., Worthington, Everett, Davis, J., Don, E., Griffien, Brandon J., Reid, Chelsea A., Hook, Joshua N. and Van Tongeren, Daryl R. 2014. The Quiet Virtue Speaks: An Intervention to Promote Humility. *Journal of Psychology and Theology* 42(1), 99–110.

Lessig, Lawrence. 2019. *Fidelity and Constraint: How the Supreme Court Has Read the American Constitution*. Oxford: Oxford University Press.

Levi, Neil. Forthcoming. Arrogance and Servility Online: Humility Is Not the Solution. In *The Routledge Handbook of Philosophy of Humility*, edited by Mark Alfano, Alessandra Tanesisi and Michael Lynch. London: Routledge.

Lockwood, Penelope and Kunda, Ziva. 1999. Increasing the Salience of One's Best Selves Can Undermine Inspiration by Outstanding Role Models. *Journal of Personality and Social Pscyhology* 76(2), 214–228.

Luskin, Rorbert C., Sood, Gaurad, Firshkin, James S. and Hahn Kyu, S. 2015. Deliberative Distorsions? Homogenization, Polarization and Domination in Small Group Deliberation, Annual Meeting of the American Political Science Association.

Marshall, Ellen O. 2017. Theological Humility in the World of Law. *Journal of Law and Religion* 32(1), 93–97.

McConnell, Michael W. 1997. The Importance of Humility in Judicial Review: A Comment on Ronald Dworkin's 'Moral Reading' of the Constitution. *Fordham Law Review* 65(4), 1269–1293.

Moberg, Dennis J. 2000. Role Models and Moral Exemplars: How Do Employees Acquire Virtues by Observing Others? *Business Ethics Quarterly* 10(3), 675–696.

Myers, Richard S. 2015. The Virtue of Judicial Humility. *Ave Maria Law Review* 13(2), 207–218.

Nadelhoffer, Thomas and Wright, Jennifer C. 2017. The Twin Dimensions of the Virtue of Humility: Low Self-Focus and High Other-Focus. In *Moral Psychology, Volume 5: Virtue and Character*, edited by Walter Sinnott-Armstron and C. Miller. Cambridge: MIT Press, 309–343.

Nava, Michael. 2010. The Servant of All: Humanity and Judicial Diversity. *Golden Gate University Law Review* 38(2), 175–194.

Nielsen, Rob and Marrone, Jennifer A. 2018. Humility: Our Current Understanding of the Construct and Its Role in Organizations. *International Journal of Management Reviews* 20(4), 805–824.

Noah, Barbara A. Teaching Bioethics: The Role of Empathy and Humility in the Teaching and Practice of Law. *Health Matrix* 28, 201–216.

Onu, Diana, Kessler, Thomas and Smith, Joanne R. 2016. Admiration: A Conceptual Review. *Emotion Review* 8(3), 218–230.

Owens, Bradely P., Rowatt, Wade C. and Wilkins, Alan L. 2011. Exploring the Relevance of Humility in Organizations. In *The Oxford Handbook of Positive Organizational Scholarhsip*, edited by Kim Cameron and Gretchen Spretizer. Oxford: Oxford University Press.
Pritchard, Duncan. 2018. Intellectual Humility and the Epistemology of Disagreement. *Synthese* 190(6), 1079–1098.
Rothstein, Laura. 2007. Law Students and Lawyers with Mental Health and Substance Abuse Problems: Protecting the Public and the Individual. *University of Pittsburgh Law Review* 69(3), 531–566.
Scharffs, Brett. 1998. The Role of Humility in Exercising Practical Wisdom. *University of California Davis* 32, 129–199.
Schauer, Frederick. 2012. Must Virtue be Particular? In *Virtue, Law and Justice*, edited by Amalia Amaya and Ho Hock Lai. Oxford: Hart Publishing.
Schilnder, Ines, Zink, Veronika, Windrich, Johannes and Menninghaus, Winfried. 2013. Admiration and Adoration: Their Different Ways of Showing and Shaping Who We Are. *Cognition and Emotion* 27(1), 85–118.
Schiltz, Patrick J. 1999. On being a Happy, Healthy, and Ethical Member of an Unhappy, Unhealthy, and Unethical Profession. *Vanderbilt Law Review* 52, 871–951.
Scott, Kyle. 2014. The Political Value of Humility. *Acta Politica* 49(2), 217–233.
Sherry, Suzanne. 2008. Judges of Character. In *Virtue Jurisprudence*, edited by Colin Farrelly and Lawrence B. Solum. New York: Palgrave Macmillan, 88–106.
Sigler, Mary. 2018. Humility, No Doubt: A Reply to Adam Kolber. *University of Illinois Law Review*, 158–167.
Simon, Dan. 2004. A Third View of the Black Box: Cognitive Coherence in Legal Decision-Making. *The University of Chicago Law Review* 71, 511–586.
Stempel, Jeffrey. 2012. Taking Cognitive Illiberalism Seriously: Judicial Humility, Aggregate Efficiency, and Acceptable Justice. *Loyola University of Chicago Law Journal* 43, 627–687.
Strang, Dean. 2017. Humility in Criminal Justice: What It Might Invite Us to Reconsider. *Marquette Law Review* 100(4), 1433–1444.
Sunstein, Cass. 2009. *A Constitution of Many Minds*. Princeton: Princeton University Press.
Sunstein, Cass and Hastie, Reid. 2015. *Wiser: Getting Beyond Groupthink to Make Group Smarter*. Cambridge: Harvard Business Review Press.
Tandgley, June P. 2012. Humility. In *The Oxford Handbook of Positive Psychology*, edited by Shane L. Lopez and C. R. Snyder. Oxford: Oxford University Press.
Vera, Dusya and Rodriguez-Lopez, Antonio. 2004. Humility as a Source of Competitive Advantage. *Organizational Dynamics* 33(4), 393–408.
Wallace, Angela, Chiu, Chia-Yen (Chad) and Owens, Bradley P. 2017. Organizational Humility and the Better Functioning Business Nonprofit and Religious Organizations. In *Handbook of Humility: Theory, Research, and Applications*, edited by Everett L. Worthington, Jr., Done E. Davis and Joshua N. Hook. New York: Routledge.
Weidman, Aaron C., Cheng, Joey T. and Tracy, Jessica L. 2018. The Psychological Structure of Humility. *Journal of Personality and Social Psychology* 114(1), 153–178.
Wright, Jennifer C., Nadelhoffer, Thomas, Perini, Tyler, Langville, Amy, Echols, Matthew and Venezia, Kelly. 2017. The Psychological Significance of Humility. *The Journal of Positive Psychology* 12(1), 3–12.
Zagzebski, Linda. 2017. *Exemplarist Moral Theory*. New York: Oxford University Press.

39
EXTENDED COGNITION AND HUMILITY

Duncan Pritchard

39.1 Extended cognition

Extended cognition is the thesis that a subject's cognitive processes can extend beyond the brain and central nervous system of the subject; indeed, can extend beyond her skin and skull. In particular, it is the thesis that features of the subject's cognitive environment, such as technology, can in the right conditions become genuine, proper parts of the subject's cognitive processes.[1] Extended cognition has in recent years become a very influential research programme in the cognitive sciences, with its philosophical implications developed and explored by philosophers of mind and cognitive science.

Putative examples of extended cognition are legion, and uniformly controversial. The canonical example, due to Andy Clark and David Chalmers (1998), concerns a subject, Otto, who is losing his memory and so begins to use a notebook to compensate for his memory loss. The question is whether Otto's use of the notebook can eventually count as an extended cognitive process—i.e., as a kind of extended memory, on a par with his biological memory. Clark and Chalmers claim that it can. In particular, they appeal to the following parity principle:

> If, as we confront some task, a part of the world functions as a process which, were it done in the head, we would have no hesitation in recognizing as part of the cognitive process, then that part of the world is [...] part of the cognitive process.
>
> *(Clark and Chalmers 1998, 29)*

Applied to Otto and his notebook, the rationale in play is that, so long as the notebook functions just like his 'internal' onboard memory, then we should treat it as a genuine part of an extended cognitive process. That is, Otto's use of the notebook is not to be understood as simply an agent employing an instrument, but rather as an integrated part of his cognitive processes, and thus cognitively equivalent to his (biological) memory.[2]

The crucial element in this thought experiment is, of course, whether Otto's use of the notebook could ever be on a functional par with his use of his biological memory. In particular, the latter tends to have an immediacy and a distinctive kind of phenomenology that goes along with its usage that seems very different to how one might employ a notebook. For example, one can employ one's memory in one's reasoning in such a seamless fashion that one might not even be consciously aware that this is what one is doing. Could one's use of a notebook ever be seamless in this fashion? In particular, won't the use of the notebook always involve a kind of intellectual distance, just like that present when one uses an instrument?

Still, even if one is not convinced that the parity principle is satisfied in this case, one might think that there are cases that are more plausible in this regard. Indeed, for the purposes of this article we can just stipulate a kind of technology that would fit the bill, and leave it an open question as to whether such technology yet exists. Elsewhere I have referred to such technology as *neuromedia*, which I described as follows:

> information processing technology that is so seamlessly integrated with one's on-board cognitive processes that the subject is often unable to distinguish between her use of those on-board processes and the technology itself. The subject's relationship to the technology is consequently no longer one of subject-to-instrument, but rather 'feels' like a technological extension of her normal cognitive processes.
>
> *(Pritchard 2018d, 328)*[3]

So understood, neuromedia would clearly satisfy the parity principle. Moreover, even if one is not convinced that there is any technology available just now that would count as neuromedia in this specific sense, I think it is undeniable that those who are developing new technologies of the relevant kind are aiming to create something along just these lines. For example, couldn't we easily imagine a time when consulting the internet for information is so automatic and phenomenologically immediate that it is no different from consulting one's memory (to the extent that one might not ordinarily be able to tell the difference)?[4] If so, then this would be neuromedia, and hence a plausible case of extended cognition, in virtue of its satisfaction of the parity principle.[5]

Notice, too, that neuromedia would also clearly manifest a further feature that is often thought to be entailed by the parity principle, which is that cognitively extended processes need to be sufficiently integrated into one's wider cognitive system that their employment leads to rich feedback loops. The information one gains from one's neuromedia could mesh in substantive ways with information from other sources (memorial, perceptual, and so on), such that they collectively guide action, leading in turn to new information-processing that employs both extended and onboard cognitive resources. This kind of cognitive integration is important to any claim about functional equivalence between the extended and the corresponding onboard cognitive processes, given that one's onboard cognitive processes are clearly cognitively integrated. Think, for example, about how one's feeling of coldness meshes with one's memorial and perceptual knowledge of one's environment (seeing that it is night time, remembering how cold it gets at night in these parts, and so on), with each reinforcing the other and guiding action accordingly (seeking out one's jumper, for example).[6]

Of course, one might dispute the parity principle, not just in terms of the detail (e.g., whether it entails cognitive integration, and to what extent) but more broadly as a test for extended cognition. Indeed, one might be suspicious of the very idea that there can be extended cognition, and hence the possibility of neuromedia would be neither here nor there.[7] For our purposes, however, we will take it as given that there could be such a thing as extended cognition, and that were it to exist then neuromedia would be an instantiation of it. The question we will be engaging with is what implications the extended cognition thesis might have for humility.

38.2 Cognitively extended humility

One challenge facing any discussion of the relationship between extended cognition and humility is that the former, but not the latter, specifically concerns cognitive processes. There are many conceptions of humility in the literature, but while they all involve a cognitive element (which we will come to in a moment), none of them consider humility to be exclusively a cognitive process. Indeed, it is standard in this regard to distinguish between humility in general and a particular type of humility that *is* geared towards cognitive ends—*viz.*, *intellectual humility*. If, as is common, we think of humility as a virtue, and thus treat intellectual humility as a specifically intellectual virtue, then we capture this point by noting that while the general manifestation of humility involves a motivational state directed towards the good, the manifestation of intellectual humility involves the specific motivation towards the intellectual good—i.e., truth.[8]

Nonetheless, we will begin by considering what bearing extended cognition might have for humility in general (we will be considering intellectual humility in its own right in the next section). Even though virtues in general, as opposed to intellectual virtues, are not specifically cognitive traits, they do employ cognitive traits. Being virtuous is not simply a matter of wanting to be a certain way (having good motives, and so on), but rather also involves being reliable at attaining certain virtuous outcomes, at least in the right conditions. Accordingly, there are cognitive skills involved in manifesting virtues even if the virtues themselves are not geared towards specifically cognitive goals. With this in mind, we can ask whether the manifestation of the virtue of humility could essentially involve extended cognitive processes.

On the face of it, there seems no inherent reason why this shouldn't be so. Indeed, it might be that one could help someone both acquire and maintain this virtue by employing extended cognitive processes. In particular, there seems no inherent reason why technology cannot be employed to assist the cognitive processes that underlie the successful manifestation of virtue, and, if that is right, so long as this technology becomes suitably cognitively integrated, we should be able to think of these cognitive processes as extended in the relevant sense.

For example, accounts of humility characteristically regard this virtue as demanding, *inter alia*, that one doesn't regularly overestimate one's importance. There would thus be a cognitive trait underlying this virtue that involved making judgements about one's importance that don't inaccurately overstate that importance.[9] On the face of it, technology ought to be useful in assisting subjects in this regard. One could imagine, for example, a subject employing a device that is designed to pick-up on the use of certain phrases (in the subject's speech and writing, say) that are indicative of non-humble attitudes (arrogance, and so on). The device could then be programmed to remind the subject (in a suitably evocative manner) that one shouldn't overestimate one's importance. In this way, a general motivation to be humbler could be more effectively realised via the subject's continued employment of this technology.

Imagine now that this device is employed not as mere technology, but is instead cognitively integrated such that it becomes neuromedia. Perhaps, for example, rather than consciously using this device, such that one is aware of it as an external instrument, one is fitted with it in some unobtrusive way, such that on a day-to-day basis one is not even aware of its presence. Relatedly, the way that it works, on suitable occasions, to generate thoughts that stimulate humility is such that the thoughts engineered by the device are not noticeably different from the various thoughts that pop into one's head during a normal day. We would thus have an example of neuromedia, in that the subject's use of this technology would be as seamlessly integrated into their cognitive processes as their entirely onboard cognitive processes, with a consequently similar associated phenomenology.

Interestingly, one would think that this device, *qua* neuromedia, would be even more effective at promoting humility than its unextended counterpart. One would simply find oneself becoming humbler without even being aware of the role of the technology in this regard. In contrast, being aware of the technology and its role in one's beliefs could serve to undermine its effectiveness, since it naturally prompts the subject to reflect on the input from the technology *qua* the bearer of 'external' advice, rather than as 'internal' monitoring. For example, one might be inclined to downgrade the external input when it comes to guiding one's actions (i.e., what one will say or write next) precisely because it is external, preferring instead one's own internal judgement. In contrast, if the 'external' monitoring is not noticeably different from the 'internal' monitoring, such that the two are seamlessly merged, then the potential for the kind of intellectual distance required to downgrade the former over the latter simply doesn't arise.

Should one then conclude that it would be better for the technology that we employ to promote humility to be neuromedia where possible? One reason why we might pause here concerns the fact that virtues seem to demand a high level of cognitive ownership on the part of the subject. One does not acquire and maintain one's virtues passively, but rather actively, through conscious effort, emulation of the virtuous, reflection on one's performance to cultivate that virtue, and so on. The reason why this is relevant is that it suggests that there is a limit to the extent to which one can thoughtlessly manifest a virtue, which means that there is a sense in which one doesn't want one's employment of the cognitive processes that underlies the virtue to be *too* seamless. Accordingly, if it is in the nature of neuromedia that it is technology that is employed in a way such that one is unaware of employing it (at that moment at any rate), then one might think that this is a bar to it forming part of the cognitive basis for the manifestation of the virtue.

In order to see the import of this point, compare one's use of the unextended virtue-enhancing technology with one's use of the corresponding extended virtue-enhancing neuromedia. When one uses the unextended technology, one is consciously taking responsibility for the development of one's virtue of humility. After all, one is actively employing the technology to enhance one's humility, and so there is a very real sense in which the technology is merely a tool for one's own cultivation of the virtue. Accordingly, one is able to take cognitive responsibility for the use of this technology in cultivating one's virtue. How does one's use of the neuromedia fare in this regard? The issue of cognitive responsibility is unclear when it comes to the use of neuromedia precisely because of how the technology is so seamlessly (and thus unreflectively) employed. Doesn't that suggest that one isn't now cultivating one's virtue at all, but is rather passively relying on the technology to engineer the relevant responses?

Another way of putting this point is in terms of where the causal attribution of responsibility naturally flows in each case. Where one is simply using technology as (unextended) technology in the usual way, then one's enhancement of the relevant virtue-associated behaviours naturally flows to the agent rather than to the technology, since the latter is merely being put into service by the former. But once the technology becomes neuromedia, then the relevant attribution of responsibility becomes much more muddled. In particular, if the responsibility for virtue-associated behaviours flows to the technology rather than to the agent, then it ceases to be straightforward that this behaviour is sufficiently creditable to the agent to qualify as the manifestation of virtue.

One could push back on this thought by emphasising that extended cognitive processes are simply parts of the extended cognitive subject, of her cognitive character.[10] Accordingly, the idea that the virtue-associated behaviours are creditable to the technology rather than the subject is simply incoherent, as the technology is now part of the cognitive subject in the relevant sense. Whether this kind of push-back is credible depends on what counts as neuromedia. Where the subject actively incorporates neuromedia into her cognitive life with the expressed purpose of enhancing virtue, then it does seem very plausible to suppose that the unreflective use of the technology later in time is no less creditable to her agency for being employed without any conscious awareness of its use on the part of the subject. After all, part of what is involved in developing virtue is ensuring that the relevant behaviours and associated motivations become second nature, and hence one can hardly impugn one's choice to employ neuromedia in this fashion on the grounds that it leads to unreflective behaviour, as manifestations of virtue are ideally meant to be (in the moment at least) unreflective.

The more interesting case, however, is surely neuromedia that doesn't essentially involve any original conscious deliberation on the part of the subject. Although more controversial as an example of extended cognition than the type of neuromedia just described (whereby the subject does consciously choose to extend their cognitive processes in this way), it nonetheless is a plausible variety of *bona fide* extended cognition. Imagine, for example, a future world where everyone is automatically cognitively augmented from birth with certain kinds of neuromedia. Now consider an agent who is unaware of the nature of this cognitive augmentation, but nonetheless unthinkingly employs it in her everyday life. Insofar as we are inclined to treat neuromedia as a genuine extended cognitive process at all, then wouldn't we likewise be inclined to treat this subject as exhibiting extended cognition?[11] But if the subject has never consciously endorsed this use of technology, then in what sense would it be appropriate to treat the virtue-apt behaviours that result from the use of this technology as attributable to her agency (such that they could count as a genuine virtue)?

38.3 Cognitively extended intellectual humility

These issues about virtue and responsibility in the context of extended cognition become even more vexed once we turn our attentions from a general virtue like humility, and focus instead on the potential role of extended cognitive processes with regard to the specifically intellectual virtue of intellectual humility. As noted above, since the intellectual virtues are themselves a kind of cognitive trait, then the issue is not merely whether the cognitive bases of the virtue can be extended, but whether the intellectual virtue itself can be cognitively extended. As we will see, the reasons why we should be cautious about thinking of a virtue like humility as even *involving* an extended cognitive process become even more pressing once we turn to the more ambitious idea of intellectual humility as actually *being* an extended cognitive process.

Indeed, building on our previous point about the virtues more generally and extended cognition, there seem to be good reasons for supposing that no intellectual virtue could be an extended cognitive process. If that's right, then at most the cultivation of intellectual humility could be in part aided via the employment of extended cognitive processes; it could never be the case that intellectual humility could itself be an extended cognitive process. For comparison, let's start with this latter, weaker claim, in order to bring out what is problematic about the former, stronger claim.

Just as we can imagine an agent making use of technology to aid her development of humility, even to the extent that the technology qualifies as neuromedia (though this is more controversial, as we saw above), so we can also imagine an agent making use of technology to aid her development of intellectual humility. As before, the exact manner in which this occurs will depend on what one holds intellectual humility to be, but in keeping with our remarks earlier we could treat it as relatively uncontroversial that intellectual humility at least demands that one doesn't regularly overestimate one's intellectual abilities and achievements.[12] Accordingly, we can imagine technology that encourages a healthy mindfulness in this regard, and in the process enables one to be more intellectually humble. Moreover, if this technology is developed along the right lines, then it may qualify as neuromedia, due to our seamless interactions with it and its cognitive integration with our other cognitive capacities. We thus have a case of the intellectual virtue of intellectual humility being supported by neuromedia, and thus incorporating the use of an extended cognitive process.

The interesting question, however, is whether we can move from this kind of claim to the stronger thesis that the intellectual virtue of intellectual humility can itself consist in an extended cognitive process, as opposed to merely incorporating such processes in its cultivation. We can see the implausibility of this suggestion by outlining what it might involve in particular cases. For example, suppose we fitted subjects with neuromedia from birth such that they exhibited behaviour associated with intellectual humility. No matter how cognitively integrated this neuromedia became with the subject's other cognitive processes, would there be any temptation to treat this behaviour as the manifestation of an intellectual virtue (rather than just the product of the technology)?

We can bring this point into sharper relief by imagining two groups of subjects, where the first group is trained up to be intellectually humble in the usual way (through regular emulation of intellectually humble exemplars, say), while the second group is simply fitted with the neuromedia to ensure that they end up exhibiting intellectually humble behaviour. Even if the behaviours ultimately exhibited by the two groups are identical (and in fact it is likely that the second group would exhibit the intellectually humble behaviours much more quickly), it only seems to be the former group who are genuinely manifesting intellectual humility. The crux of the matter is that intellectual virtues seem to be in part characterised by the essentially reflective manner of their acquisition and cultivation, such that even if they can be exhibited on particular occasions in an unreflective manner (as manifestations of one's second nature, whereby via habituation the exercise of virtue has become automatic), it nonetheless remains that no virtue, properly speaking, can be completely manifested unreflectively. And yet that is exactly what the idea of neuromedia as a cognitively off-loading of intellectual virtue implies.[13]

One can imagine various kinds of critical push-back against this line. If cognitive abilities in general can become extended cognitive processes, then why not the specific kinds of cognitive abilities at issue when it comes to the intellectual virtues? (But then it has often been the case that the intellectual virtues have been explicitly contrasted with mere cognitive skills, just as the virtues in general are typically distinguished from mere skills.)[14] Or, if one grants that there can be such a thing as extended cognitive abilities, then doesn't it follow that there can be an extended cognitive character? Accordingly, why not hold that the lines of cognitive responsibility do genuinely thread back to the extended cognitive agent, and hence that there is the relevant degree of cognitive responsibility involved on the part of the subject when neuromedia is in play that is needed for the manifestation of an intellectual virtue like intellectual humility? (But isn't the reality rather that a divide opens up between two kinds of cognitive responsibility: the lower-grade sort that is applicable to an extended cognitive character, and the higher-grade sort that is applicable to the intellectual virtues.)

38.4 Concluding remarks

This is not the place to settle these issues, but it is important to note that there are standing questions regarding the extent to which extended cognitive processes can be part of the manifestation of both the general virtue of humility and the specific intellectual virtue of intellectual humility. We have seen that there is some plausibility to the idea that the cognitive traits that underlie the general manifestation of virtue involved in humility could be extended. But we have also seen that there may be some limitations to the extent to which a virtue can rely on extended cognitive traits, due to the kind of cognitive responsibility involved in the manifestation of a genuine virtue. Moreover, this issue becomes more acute once we consider the question of whether intellectual humility could itself be an extended cognitive process.[15]

Notes

1 Note that, for the purposes of this article, I will be setting to one side a particular kind of extended cognition—sometimes called *distributed* or *socially extended cognition*—where the cognitive extension involves other agents. For some useful discussions of distributed cognition, see Giere and Moffat (2003), Theiner et al. (2010), and Gallagher (2013). For specific discussion of the epistemological ramifications of distributed cognition, see Palermos and Pritchard (2016) and Carter et al. (2018).

2 Note that Clark and Chalmers (1998) are less interested in arguing for extended cognition than for the more specific thesis of the *extended mind*—*viz.*, roughly, that minds can extend beyond the skill and skull of the subject. Whether the extended mind thesis is a more demanding thesis than the extended cognition thesis—as Clark and Chalmers (1998) clearly believe—depends on further factors, such as whether one treats the cognitive as the mark of the mental. In any case, our concern here is with the extended cognition thesis rather than the extended mind thesis. For Clark's more considered take on extended cognition (/mind), see Clark (2008).

3 Note that the 'neuromedia' terminology is not my invention, but since this terminology is used in varied ways it is important that it is understood along the specific lines set out here. For a philosophical discussion of neuromedia that is relevant to our current concerns (but which uses this terminology in a slightly different manner), see Lynch (2014; 2016).

4 Note that it might be important to the technology that the subject *can* tell the difference, if only in principle, perhaps for legal reasons. But it would still be significant that there could exist technology of this kind where ordinarily the subject could not tell the difference.

5 Interestingly, one way in which neuromedia might be developed could be as devices that are fitted beneath the skin and skull of the subject. Indeed, if one is aiming for the technology to be as seamlessly integrated into one's cognitive character as much as possible, such that one isn't even normally aware of it as technology, then it would make sense to have it as hidden from view as much as possible. If neuromedia is developed in this way, however, then it is in a certain sense an 'internal' form of extended cognition (even though it is still 'external' in the manner that is relevant to extended cognition, as it is external the biological cognitive processes that the subject has under her skin and skull).

6 For further discussion of cognitive integration in the context of extended cognition, see Palermos (2014a; 2014b).

7 For two prominent critiques of extended cognition—and also the related extended mind thesis (see endnote 2)—see Adams and Aizawa (2008) and Rupert (2009).

8 That's the standard way of thinking about the intellectual good at any rate—see, for example, Zagzebski's (1996) influential account of the intellectual virtues in this regard—though some might wish to substitute a more elevated epistemic standing like knowledge, understanding or wisdom. (For what it is worth, I think that this would be a mistake—see Pritchard [2014; 2016]).

9 I leave it as an open question whether this cognitive trait would be compatible with one making *inaccurate* judgements that regularly *under*estimate one's importance—this would depend on further features of one's account of humility.

10 For a development of the idea of an extended cognitive character, see Alfano and Skorburg (2016).

11 I discuss a case of this kind, whereby the extended cognitive process is never consciously endorsed by the subject, but where it nonetheless seems to count as a *bona fide* instance of extended cognition, in Pritchard (2010).

12 There are a range of different accounts of intellectual humility in the contemporary literature. For some key recent discussions in this regard, see Tanesini (2016), Whitcomb et al. (2017), and Priest (2017). For my own take on these issues, see Pritchard (2018c; 2019).

13 I develop this idea in Pritchard (2018a; 2018b; 2018d).

14 For some recent treatments of virtues, including intellectual virtues, as being a kind of skill—which is, of course, compatible with the idea that intellectual virtues might be more demanding cognitive traits than other kinds of (mere) cognitive skills—see Annas (1995; 2011) and Stichter (2018).

15 I am grateful to Mark Alfano for detailed comments on an earlier version of this paper.

References

Adams, F., and Aizawa, K. (2008). *The Bounds of Cognition*, Oxford: Blackwell.

Alfano, M., and Skorburg, G. (2016). 'The Embedded and Extended Character Hypotheses'. *Routledge Handbook of Philosophy of the Social Mind*, ed. J. Kiverstein, 465–78, London: Routledge.

Annas, J. (1995). 'Virtue as a Skill'. *International Journal of Philosophical Studies* 3(2), 227–43.

———. (2011). *Intelligent Virtue*, Oxford: Oxford University Press.

Carter, J. A., Clark, A., Kallestrup, J., Palermos, S. O., and Pritchard, D. H. (2014). 'Varieties of Externalism'. *Philosophical Issues* 24(1), 63–109.

———. (Eds.). (2018). *Socially Extended Epistemology*, Oxford: Oxford University Press.

Clark, A. (2008). *Supersizing the Mind: Embodiment, Action, and Cognitive Extension*, Oxford: Oxford University Press.

Clark, A., and Chalmers, D. (1998). 'The Extended Mind'. *Analysis* 58(1), 7–19.

Gallagher, S. (2013). 'The Socially Extended Mind'. *Cognitive Systems Research* 25/26, 4–12.

Giere, R., and Moffat, B. (2003). 'Distributed Cognition: Where the Cognitive and the Social Merge'. *Social Studies of Science* 33(2), 1–10.

Lynch, M. P. (2014). 'Neuromedia, Extended Knowledge, and Understanding'. *Philosophical Issues* 24(1), 299–313.

———. (2016). *The Internet of US: Knowing More and Understanding Less in the Age of Big Data*, New York: W. W. Norton & Co.

Palermos, S. O. (2014a). 'Knowledge and Cognitive Integration'. *Synthese* 191(8), 1931–1951.

———. (2014b). 'Loops, Constitution, and Cognitive Extension'. *Cognitive Systems Research* 27, 25–41.

Palermos, S. O., and Pritchard, D. H. (2016). 'The Distribution of Epistemic Agency'. *Social Epistemology and Epistemic Agency: De-Centralizing Epistemic Agency*, ed. P. Reider, 109–26, Lanham, Maryland: Rowman & Littlefield.

Priest, M. (2017). 'Intellectual Humility: An Interpersonal Theory'. *Ergo, an Open Access Journal of Philosophy* 4. doi:10.3998/ergo.12405314.0004.016.

Pritchard, D. H. (2010). 'Cognitive Ability and the Extended Cognition Thesis'. *Synthese* 175(S1), 133–51.

———. (2014). 'Truth as the Fundamental Epistemic Good'. *The Ethics of Belief: Individual and Social*, eds. J. Matheson, and R. Vitz, 112–29, Oxford: Oxford University Press.

———. (2016). 'Epistemic Axiology'. *Epistemic Reasons, Epistemic Norms, and Epistemic Goals*, eds. M. Grajner, and P. Schmechtig, 407–22, Berlin: DeGruyter.

———. (2018a). 'Extended Knowledge'. *Extended Epistemology*, eds. J. A. Carter, A. Clark, J. Kallestrup, S. O. Palermos, and D. H. Pritchard, 90–104, Oxford: Oxford University Press.

——— (2018b). 'Extended Virtue Epistemology'. *Inquiry* 61(5–6), 632–47.

——— (2018c). 'Intellectual Humility and the Epistemology of Disagreement'. *Synthese*. (Online First, doi:10.1007/s11229-018-02024-5).

——— (2018d). 'Neuromedia and the Epistemology of Education'. *Metaphilosophy* 49(3), 328–49.

———. (2019). 'Disagreement, Intellectual Humility, and Reflection'. *Thinking about Oneself: The Place and Value of Reflection in Philosophy and Psychology*, ed. W. Da Silva Filho, chapter 5, Dordrecht, Holland: Springer.

Rupert, R. D. (2009). *Cognitive Systems and the Extended Mind*, Oxford: Oxford University Press.

Stichter, M. (2018). *The Skillfulness of Virtue: Improving Our Moral and Epistemic Lives*, Cambridge: Cambridge University Press.

Tanesini, A. (2016). 'Intellectual Humility as Attitude'. *Philosophy and Phenomenological Research* (Online First, doi:10.1111/phpr.12326).

Theiner, G., Allen, C., and Goldstone, R. (2010). 'Recognizing Group Cognition'. *Cognitive Systems Research* 11(4), 378–95.

Whitcomb, D., Battaly, H., Baehr, J., and Howard-Synder, D. (2017). 'Intellectual Humility: Owning Our Limitations'. *Philosophy and Phenomenological Research* 94(3), 509–39.

Zagzebski, L. (1996). *Virtues of the Mind: An Inquiry into the Nature of Virtue and the Ethical Foundations of Knowledge*, Cambridge: Cambridge University Press.

40

ARROGANCE AND SERVILITY ONLINE

Humility is not the solution

Neil Levy

It is widely held that the rise of social media has led to a degradation in public debate. We substitute invective for argument online, trolls hijack our few attempts at reasoned argument, and fake news proliferates. We talk and listen only to those who are like us in our beliefs, inhabiting echo chambers in which prior attitudes are reinforced and genuine problems pass undetected. Social media leaves us epistemically vulnerable. It leaves us vulnerable to the acquisition of false, or at least unjustified, beliefs. It leaves us vulnerable to accepting wild conspiracy theories. It leaves us vulnerable to manipulation by nefarious actors, who want to sell us stuff or undermine our democracies.

It is tempting to think that epistemic humility offers us the solution to these problems. We are not epistemically humble online. Sometimes we are not epistemically humble because we are arrogant: we shut ourselves off from other voices, or denigrate them if they happen to slip through. Sometimes we are not epistemically humble not because we are arrogant but because we are servile. We take the word of Fox News, or The Intercept, or our Facebook friends without checking and without skepticism. We often seem to adopt an attitude of default trust toward information on the internet (Lynch 2016; but see Rini 2017 for important qualifications). This excessive trust is not humble, because humility is the mean between servility and arrogance.[1] If we were more humble – if we trusted to the extent we ought to and were skeptical to the extent we ought to – then we would engage respectfully with other points of view (to the extent that doing so was warranted) and treat unreliable stories with the skepticism they deserve. If social media is the problem, epistemic virtue (along with other virtues) is the solution.

In this chapter, I will argue that epistemic humility is not the solution to the problems of social media. In fact, neither the apparent arrogance nor the servility we see online are well understood as epistemic vices. Rather, they are the manifestations of dispositions that are typically knowledge-conducive. Being more humble will not bring it about that our beliefs are more accurate or better justified. My argument is not specific to social media: it applies to the exchange of information much more broadly than that.

In passing, I hope to shed some illumination, too, on what has come to be called the situationist challenge to epistemic virtue. According to the situationist challenge, agents lack stable character traits. But if they lack stable character traits, they cannot in fact develop the corresponding virtues.[2] Our traits may be too sensitive to irrelevant contextual features to count as virtues. I will argue that what seemed a bug is actually a feature, at least with regard to the putative epistemic virtue of humility. Our sensitivity to features of the context does (indeed) entail that we are not epistemically humble, in the way that proponents of the virtue would want. In some contexts, the epistemic dispositions we do and *should* manifest are more arrogant than humble; in others, they are more servile than humble. We should aim to approximate the mean between servility and arrogance only occasionally. I will argue that these dispositions, and the context-sensitivity that causes us to oscillate between them, are epistemically adaptive: they allow us to track significant truths.

40.1 The background: Deeply social epistemology[3]

Despite some small steps in the direction of a recognition of the extent to which cognition is divided and distributed, virtue epistemology remains heavily individualistic.[4] For the mainstream, virtues are dispositions of agents, supervening on their internal states; knowledge is the possession of individual agents, and so on. Most importantly, whether an agent knows a proposition depends on facts about her alone: is it the upshot of her virtuous activity? This approach seriously underplays the extent to which knowledge is dependent on other agents and the environment for its generation, acquisition, and for its maintenance. For a large range of significant propositions, agents have true beliefs because of the way they are embedded in networks of other agents, and because of the way the environment they come to inhabit is structured.

Consider the knowledge (as I think it deserves to be called) that allows indigenous people across the world to flourish in very harsh environments. Much of that knowledge is the product of *cumulative culture*: innovations acquired and gradually built on for generations (Richerson and Boyd 2005; Laland 2017). Cumulative culture has for centuries provided us with tools for the acquisition of knowledge that no individual could discover for themselves (at least before the advent of modern science), because the relevant data is too noisy for distinguishing signal from noise. Cumulative culture allows us to detect environmental changes that are generations long, for example (Shea 2009). It also allows for the accumulation of innovations that build on one another; again something that no individual can do for herself, because life is simply too short.

There are some well-known and spectacular examples of how well-equipped and prepared individuals were unable to acquire the knowledge they needed to survive in environments in which indigenous people were flourishing. In 1846, two ships commanded by Sir John Franklin, on an expedition to chart the Northwest passage, became stuck in sea ice in the Canadian Arctic. The entire crew perished. But the area was regarded by the local Inuit people as being rich in resources. Despite their training and the resources of the wealthiest empire the world had ever seen, which had ensured the expedition was well-provisioned, they were unable to acquire the skills they needed to survive. A few decades later, Roald Amundsen spent two winters in the same region. He relied on the help of the Netsilik Inuit for his survival (Boyd, Richerson and Henrich 2011). The fate of the Burke and Wills expedition to cross the Australian continent also illustrates the wisdom of relying on indigenous knowledge and the folly of rejecting it (Burcham 2008). Running low on food, members of the expedition accepted the gift of cakes made from the Nardoo plant for sustenance. However, apparently as a consequence of unease with being reliant on people they saw as inferior, they spurned further assistance and attempted to make the cakes themselves. They ground the seeds into a powder, mixed it with water and baked it. Unbeknownst to them, the local people roasted the seeds prior to grinding. This step is required to remove toxins from the plant. Because they missed it, the explorers did not receive the nutrients they needed from the Nardoo cakes. There was only one survivor: he accepted further aid from the Yandruwandha people.

The Netsilik Inuit and the Yandruwandha were reliant on cumulative culture for the knowledge of how to survive in harsh environments. But reliance on cumulative knowledge is common, not a strategy for harsh environments alone (Henrich 2017). Edible plants frequently evolve toxins that must be removed prior to consumption, and across the world indigenous people have gradually developed techniques for their removal. These techniques are often counterintuitive and complex, and the very need for them may not be obvious (because it may take years for ill-health to develop as a result of eating the foods). Individuals do not hit upon these techniques by themselves; they emerge from (literally) centuries of tinkering and innovation.

It is worth stressing one other way in which this knowledge cannot be understood as an individual possession. Not only does it owe its existence to previous generations, but it is often ill-understood by those who deploy it. Consider, for example, the practice of several indigenous groups in the Americas of mixing ash with cornmeal prior to cooking. This is adaptive in regions which rely on corn as a staple, because ash is alkaline and releases the niacin that is otherwise chemically bound in corn. Failing to introduce a base (whether derived from wood ash or seashells, as with some coastal groups) leads to pellagra, which is a serious and sometimes fatal illness. When corn was exported to the old world and became a staple in the United States, pellagra became a serious problem, the causes of which weren't understood by the scientific community until well into the 20th century. Indigenous peoples overcame the problems arising from a diet reliant on corn centuries before Western science was able to solve the problem. But individual members of these indigenous cultures possessed the knowledge that Western science sought only in an attenuated sense.

Asked *why* it is necessary to mix wood ash with cornmeal, indigenous people may have no more to say than "it is our custom" (Henrich 2017). They may not know *that* it is adaptive, let alone *why* it is adaptive. They may even have false beliefs about their adaptive practices. Food taboos, for instance, are typically justified on supernaturalistic grounds, though they are maintained in the group because they are (naturalistically, of course) adaptive (Henrich and Henrich 2010). Those people who adopt these practices do not know central facts about why they do the things they do. In this respect, it is worth noting, they may not be as different from Western scientists as we'd like to think. Science produces knowledge, including knowledge of the causes of pellagra. But when knowledge is deeply social, much of it is not the property of any one individual. Contemporary scientific research routinely involves multiple individuals, with different disciplinary backgrounds and expertise working together (for example, work in neuroimaging may involve neurologists, physicists and statisticians, as well as neuroscientists – and 'neuroscientist' may fragment again, such that different individuals have different ranges of skills). Some of the authors of a paper may have little interest in, or capacity to assess, its main claims. Cutting-edge medical research may take this very much further, involving (literally) thousands of people in research, at multiple locations around the world (from primary physicians to epidemiologists to bench scientists). None of them may be in a position to understand, let alone assess, every claim made in the resulting paper (Kukla 2012). *A fortiori*, they – like the indigenous people who rely on corn as a staple – are not in a position "to take … reflective responsibility for their true beliefs" (Pritchard 2005); for many the *sine qua non* of the possession of intellectual virtue. Socially distributed knowledge production may produce irreducibly social knowledge: knowledge that is the possession of the group and not of any of the individuals who compose it.

Equally, blind imitation remains an important part of science. As Shea (2009) notes, when scientists perform a well-established protocol, whether to replicate it or to build on it, they may have little idea of the causal contribution (if any) of every step of the protocol. Why *that* amount of a solvent, rather than 5ml more, or 5ml less? Why *that* amount of time in the centrifuge? Especially if the experiment is expensive to run (in terms of resources required or time commitment), scientists have little incentive to attempt the kind of trial-and-error experimentation that would be required to discover whether certain steps might be dropped or shortened. Unless they have a particular interest in some step, they are likely to simply stick to the protocol. As Shea puts it, "all sorts of techniques and steps are copied without any appreciation of whether or why they are necessary to achieve the goal – following an experimental protocol can feel rather like following a magic spell" (2434).

40.2 Deeply social knowledge and epistemic humility

Does social knowledge production require epistemic humility? Epistemic humility is typically conceived of as the mean between epistemic arrogance and servility. But the dispositions appropriate to cumulative culture seem more servile than humble. Cumulative culture is transmitted from generation to generation largely by way of imitation: we are disposed selectively to imitate the behavior of models. Children, who come to the world preadapted for culture,[5] imitate the actions of others to a far greater extent than other primates (Tomasello 1999). Other primates attempt to discern why a behavior is successful and copy only those aspects of it that explain its success; children are much more prone to copy the entire sequence, even those aspects that seem causally irrelevant. This disposition to copy seems to increase, not diminish, with age. We are also subject to the *prestige bias* (Henrich and Gil-White 2001; Chudek, Heller, Birch and Henrich 2012) and the *conformist bias* (Henrich and Boyd 1998); that is, we imitate the behavior of successful individuals, and we imitate the behavior of the majority. All of these strategies are adaptive in environments that are causally opaque: in which it is difficult to discern what aspects of behavior are adaptive. Prestigious individuals are successful individuals, but what underlies their success? If we can't tell, we may do better to imitate all their behavior, without asking whether it contributes to success or not. Similarly, if our group owes its capacity to flourish in the local environment to cumulative culture, and cumulative culture is the repository of generations of innovations the point of which is often inscrutable to the individual, we do well to copy the majority behavior.

Of course, human beings are clever animals, and we also innovate, invent, and probe. But successful innovations tend to build on the platform provided by cumulative culture, because this platform embodies knowledge the adaptive value of which it is almost impossible to replicate *de novo*. The dispositions to copy, to accept testimony, to adopt the local way of doing things seem more servile than humble. Even in the contemporary laboratory, we take a great deal on trust. Scientists are inculcated into scientific paradigms they cannot justify for themselves, in a very significant part, and which contain elements they will never fully understand. They make their contributions to the advancement of science as members of a team, with no member fully able to grasp the contribution the other members make.

Much of our most adaptive epistemic behavior therefore seems to manifest epistemic servility, not humility. The role for epistemic humility seems more circumscribed than is usually thought. On this basis, we may think that only in our innovations do we abandon servility sufficiently to be in the humility game. In fact, the scope for epistemic humility is more circumscribed still: when we are not servile, we are often – appropriately – arrogant, rather than humble. Perhaps surprisingly, I contend that we display epistemic arrogance not in counterbalance to our deeply social knowledge generation and acquisition, but in the service of social knowledge acquisition.

There is extensive evidence that when we do deliberate (rather than acquire ways of going on by imitation), groups do much better than individuals, at least under a variety of conditions (Mercier and Sperber 2017). Consider our performance at reasoning tasks, like the Wason selection task. Though the task is logically simple, most people do badly at it: around 10% of people select the right cards on the task. But *groups* of individuals do very much better, and transcripts of exchanges within groups indicate that success is explained by the exchange of reasons (rather than, say, the recognition that one individual is smarter than the others). Indeed, groups of deliberators may exhibit the *assembly bonus effect*, where the group performs better than the best individual within it. Even deliberation at its best is often social.

But, notoriously, groups have a bad name (think of books with titles like *Popular Delusions and the Madness of Crowds*). We badly underestimate the extent to which groups outperform individuals on many reasoning cases; we often think they will do worse, rather than better. Academic psychologists with a specialism in human reasoning, who are well aware of the dismal performance of individuals on the Wason selection task, underestimate the benefits of group deliberation on a given task to the same extent as laypeople do. Managers of teams, individuals from East Asia and WEIRD people, all alike underestimate the benefits of group deliberation (Mercier, Trouche, Yama, Heintz and Girotto 2015).

We are, it seems epistemic individualists who are reliant on social networks and culture for our epistemic success. Why are we epistemic individualists? Group deliberation is powerful, but is subject to characteristic limitations and pathologies. Information cascades can overwhelm the group; powerful individuals can carry disproportionate weight and people may self-silence in the face of prejudice or anxiety. All of these problems can be mitigated if people are epistemically arrogant: if they are disposed to give their private information and their individual deliberation greater weight than it deserves in group deliberation.

Information cascades (Bikhchandani, Hirshleifer and Welch 1992) occur when people deliberate sequentially, and information about previous decisions is available to each. In this situation, each may rationally discount their own private information, because the public information outweighs it. A situation may arise in which the publicly available evidence is highly misleading, while many individuals are in possession of private information that would correct the picture. The problem of information cascades can be reduced if individuals are overconfident: if they take their private information to have a weight greater than it ought, relative to public information. It seems intellectually arrogant to think that one's own private information or one's opinion should be given greater weight than the apparent information of several (or many) individuals who are one's epistemic peers, but this kind of intellectual arrogance can be conducive to group deliberation.

If it is intellectually arrogant to place greater weight on one's own opinions than those of one's epistemic peers, it is even more arrogant to prefer one's own opinions to those of epistemic *superiors*. But the disposition to do so may be epistemically fruitful, because self-silencing by those who recognize their inferiority may also lead to 'hidden profiles'; information relevant to deliberation going unshared. In fact, groups may benefit from what looks like the intellectual arrogance of intellectual inferiors, even when the information they insist on turns out to be misleading (Surowiecki 2004). Again, the apparent individual vice of epistemic arrogance may be a virtue at the level of the group. Mercier and Sperber (2017) have argued that some of our individual-level reasoning pathologies may be adaptations for collective deliberation: the confirmation bias, for example, which leads us to overvalue evidence in favour of hypotheses we are well disposed to and undervalue evidence contrary to these hypotheses, may conduce to the division of epistemic labor. Similarly, I suggest, our epistemic individualism – our disposition to under-weigh the views of others and to think that group deliberation brings few or no benefits over that of the individual – may be an adaptation *for* collective deliberation (Levy 2019).

I have suggested that we owe our success very significantly to collective and cultural mechanisms of knowledge generation. The mechanisms whereby cumulative culture is generated are very heavily dependent on an epistemic deference so thoroughgoing that it often looks more like epistemic servility than humility. Moreover, our collective mechanisms of knowledge generation may require epistemic arrogance. If something like this picture is accurate, then epistemically well-functioning agents do not exhibit anything like the virtue of epistemic humility; not, at any rate, in much of their most important epistemic activity. Instead, they are disposed to oscillate between different dispositions: dispositions to servility (in blind deference and imitation), to arrogance (preferring their own views to those of acknowledged experts and numerous dissenting peers) and – no doubt – to humility, as the situation demands it.[6]

40.3 Whence the virtue?

Virtue epistemologists have seen in situationism a threat to their framework. They have worried that if our dispositions are sensitive to features of context, then we do not have the kind of stability of character required for epistemic virtue. Sometimes, virtue epistemologists have attempted to befriend the threat, suggesting that the right response was to enlist the context: in appropriately structured environments, an agent can display stable characters and (therefore) epistemic virtue (Alfano and Skorburg 2017). I agree that enlisting the context is the appropriate response, but I will argue that an appropriately structured environment does not bring agents to manifest stable dispositions. Rather, it will cue shifts between epistemic arrogance, humility and servility, as appropriate to the context.[7]

What cues shift the dispositions of agents from context to context? We know quite a lot about the cues to which agents are sensitive when they defer and when they imitate. Many of the cues to which we're sensitive are cues about other agents and *their* dispositions. Starting in early childhood, and increasing with age, agents are more likely to accept the testimony of those who evince signs of benevolence and of competence (Mascaro and Sperber 2009; Sperber et al. 2010). Perhaps because political orientation is a proxy for benevolence toward us (Levy 2019), we are sensitive to cues that others share our political views (Nyhan and Reifler 2013). We are often critical recipients of testimony, but these cues tend to trigger epistemic deference in us.

Of course, message content matters. But our assessment of the message is heavily influenced by information about the testifier. Maoz, Ward, Katz and Ross (2002) found that whether a peace proposal was presented as having been put forward by Palestinians or Israeli Jews was a significant predictor of attitudes toward it among their Palestinian and Israeli Jewish subjects. Indeed, information about the attitudes of other agents may trump message content. Cohen (2003) found that information about whether welfare policy proposals were supported by House Democrats or Republicans overwhelmed policy content when it came to support. These patterns of deference might be best understood in the context of the conformity bias: we defer to those we identify with, because doing so effectively allows us to distinguish signal from noise.

In the absence of cues that other agents are like or unlike us, or in addition to them, there is evidence that numbers matter. Of course, that's unsurprising: multiple sources of independent testimony constitute evidence in favor of a hypothesis that is stronger than a single source (other things equal). It is also unsurprising that we may be influenced by sheer numbers inappropriately, when we fail to recognize that the sources are not properly independent of one another. The range of cues for widespread agreement to which we are sensitive is much more surprising. For instance, the familiarity of a claim is a cue for acceptance, probably because familiarity is usually the product of repeated previous exposure, and such exposure is a proxy for widespread agreement. But, of course, familiarity is not always a reliable proxy for widespread agreement. Repetition of a claim increases familiarity, whether the claim is repeated by many different voices or the same one repeatedly (Weaver, Garcia, Schwarz and Miller 2007). In fact, repetition of a claim explicitly in the service of debunking it increases familiarity and may backfire (Schwarz, Sanna, Skurnik and Yoon 2007).

Apparent consensuality, cues that the source shares our political values, and cues of competence (even in unrelated domains and even evidence that the person *takes themselves*, rightly or wrongly, to be competent; Martens and Tracy 2013) are all triggers for epistemic deference. What triggers epistemic arrogance? The myside bias is triggered when the hypothesis under consideration is unfavorable in some way to the person (Sharot and Garrett 2016). A hypothesis might be unfavorable to someone in multiple ways: because its truth conflicts with their self-image, because it would predict bad consequences for them, or simply because they have staked something (their reputation, say) on its being false. These kinds of circumstances set the stage for motivated reasoning, whereby evidence against the view we defend is less likely to come to mind at all, and is systematically discounted when it cannot be ignored.

Importantly, the cues for acceptance – for servility – are epistemically adaptive. We *should* be sensitive to cues of consensuality. We *should* be sensitive to cues of prestige. We should care about the benevolence and competence of others: knaves may try to epistemically exploit us and fools may unwittingly deceive us. Raising and lowering our epistemic defenses in response to these cues is how we ought to behave, in the service of knowledge.

Once again, content matters too.[8] We are more likely to accept claims that cohere with our own beliefs, for instance. We should not think that we exhibit only epistemic servility and arrogance: no doubt much of the time we behave in the kinds of ways those who value epistemic humility would applaud. I have no idea how to assess the proportion of the time we are epistemically arrogant, servile or somewhere in-between (no doubt, it is very context dependent). However, given that our success as deliberators is and remains very heavily dependent on group deliberation at a time and cumulative culture over time, and that epistemic arrogance and servile deference are plausibly adaptations for cumulative culture and group deliberation (respectively), these dispositions are not marginal features of human cognition. They are central. Accordingly, we should not expect calls for us to be epistemically humble to be either easy to conform to or to provide a panacea to our epistemic problems. Epistemic humility is risky: it risks some of our most important epistemic practices.

40.4 Epistemic humility and social media

As mentioned in the introduction, social media is often regarded as an epistemically dysfunctional arena because (inter alia) it is an echo chamber: because we friend those who are similar to us, we tend to hear only from those who share our political views and do not hear evidence against them. As a consequence, we come to have an unwarranted degree of credence in a variety of shibboleths repeated by our side; perhaps worse, our insulation from dissent leave us vulnerable to fake news. There is good reason to think that there is *something* to this story.[9] As we have seen, we are disposed to take evidence that a claim is widely held, or is held by those who share our political orientation, as cues for deference. Social media is an epistemic environment unlike any to which we are adapted, and these differences may drive a degree of deference that overwhelms our epistemic defenses. In echo chambers, we may (for instance) think that a claim is consensual, when in fact it is widely contested.

On the other hand, there is a widespread worry that when we encounter dissent online, we may not engage with it in a way that gives it due weight. Again, we have seen that the empirical evidence suggests that there is *something* in this claim. As we have seen, when we are disposed toward a claim, we engage in motivated reasoning and are subject to the myside bias. We dismiss opinions because of their source, rather than their content, and without adequately considering that content.

We best avoid these twin ills, it would seem, if we calibrate our trust to the environment. We are apt to defer to a greater extent than we should in relation to claims that stem from 'our' side and should instead be more critical. We are apt to unthinkingly reject claims that stem from the other side, and should instead be more humble. We should strike the Aristotelian mean between servility and arrogance. We should be epistemically humble.

But if servility and arrogance are both epistemically adaptive – if, as I have suggested, together they play a large role in explaining our most impressive epistemic achievements – prescribing that individuals attempt to reign in these dispositions is risky (assuming, rather implausibly, that it succeeds). This is most obvious with regard to the suggestion that we cease to be arrogant. If the claim that epistemic arrogance is an adaptation for group deliberation is correct, then it is far from apparent that we *should* be more receptive to the claims of others. Perhaps the arrogance we display on social media is epistemically appropriate. Perhaps it is actually truth conducive; we probably tend, on the whole, to garner mainly true beliefs from social media (and it is far from obvious that we would do better, on average, to avoid it).[10] To the extent to which it is not truth conducive, moreover, it is far from obvious that altering our dispositions is either possible, or that if it is possible it would not have more costs (measured in the social generation of knowledge) than benefits.

Perhaps the epistemic servility we display with regard to claims that seem to stem from 'our' side, or that support our existing beliefs, can usefully be addressed by a little more care in accepting claims. Given the extent of our epistemic reliance on others, however, and our inability to check more than a tiny fraction of the claim we are presented with for ourselves, however, such servility may be required for good epistemic functioning. Time constraints, too, make epistemic dependence essential. Finite beings like us can't do better than defer, most of the time, on most issues. When the issue is morally inflected, deference to our side – to those who weigh values in the way we do – may be a reliable guide to what we would think were we able to take the time to reflect on the issue. Of course, all kinds of factual questions are morally inflected (and this is true whether or not we accept cognitivism about morality), in part perhaps because different attitudes to risk or to value (the value of individuals versus groups; the value of non-human animals; the value of the citizen versus the stranger, and so on) tend to correlate with moral attitudes, and in part because on politicized issues we have good reason to suspect that biases occlude accurate perception. Again, we have good reason to suspect that deference to those on our side is an epistemically adaptive strategy. My fellow partisans tend to get normative questions right, by my lights (Rini 2017), and the domain of the partly normative is extensive.

Even if we decide that we would do better to display less servility in some contexts, and less arrogance in others, it is difficult to see how we may realistically expect agents to calibrate their trust in ways that would filter *in* the right array of claims while filtering *out* the wrong. It is worth noting that the view I am urging here seems to imply that one obvious, and oft-promoted, way of addressing the problem has limitations that usually pass unperceived. It is often suggested that we should avoid the echo chamber by ensuring a diversity of voices (perhaps Facebook might implement algorithms that ensure that every conversation of more than a certain length or with more than a certain number of contributors, which features only like-minded voices, be visible to others who are not on their side, so that they can chime in). But contrary voices may tend to trigger the confirmation bias, flipping us from epistemic servility to epistemic arrogance (rather than humility). Indeed, there is evidence that adding a diversity of voices leads to biased assimilation of information (Corner, Whitmarsh and Xenias 2012) not necessarily to more accurate beliefs.[11]

If epistemic humility is not the solution to the epistemic problems of social media, what is? Addressing that question is beyond the scope of this chapter. I will allow myself just a few remarks. First, it is not apparent to me that there is a special problem here. No doubt fake news reaches a broader audience today than previously, but that doesn't entail that on average people have less accurate or fewer well-justified beliefs today than previously. Accurate reports also reach a broader audience today than at previous times. It is not apparent to me that debate is really less rational than before. Nor is it apparent that the close-mindedness and servility we see online are, on balance, really epistemically vicious.

If there is a problem, however, it is probably best addressed in the way we best address all epistemic matters: socially. Perhaps the epistemic environment is not well structured to scaffold knowledge generation and dissemination. Perhaps we need to regulate it better. As we have seen, though cues for deference and for triggering the myside bias are typically well calibrated for epistemic success, false positives and false negatives certainly exist. We may, for instance, be taken in by an illusion of consensuality. To the extent there is a problem, I suspect it is best addressed by ensuring that networks are structured and information is filtered so that the cues for deference are better calibrated. We are deeply social animals, in our epistemic dispositions as much as anywhere else, and individualistic approaches, such as those that would have each of us cultivate virtue, ill fit with how we function.[12]

Notes

1 While accounts that understand the virtues as the mean between excess and deficiency are common, a number of theorists of epistemic virtue reject such views. However, I don't think I beg any questions against them by describing epistemic humility as a mean between servility and arrogance. These theorists hold that we cannot define the virtue like that. They do not deny that whatever the nature of the virtue, manifestations of it exhibit dispositions that are too self-effacing to be arrogant but not so self-effacing as to be servile.

2 The situationist challenge was originally levelled at the moral virtues, by philosophers like John Doris and Gilbert Harman (1999). Its extension to virtue epistemology is due in particular to Mark Alfano (2012).

3 The following section draws on material in Levy and Alfano (forthcoming).

4 For steps in the direction of anti-individualism, see Kallestrup and Pritchard (2012; 2016), Palermos (2016). The anti-individualism countenanced by these epistemologists is explicitly weak; stronger forms of anti-individualism are rejected. Alfano and Skorburg (2017) are rare defenders of a stronger anti-individualism.

5 Heyes (2018) dissents from the claim that children are preadapted for culture: she suggests that the dispositions that underlie the acquisition of cumulative culture are themselves the product of cultural evolution.

6 Of course, virtue epistemologists accept that, as contexts change, the virtuous agent will alter her response. Just as the courageous agent must recognize when it would be foolhardy to take a risk rather than be courageous, so the epistemically humble agent must recognize when she should defer to others, when she should discount their claims and how much weight to give to them in those situations where she should neither (completely) defer nor (completely) discount. But the kinds of contextual shifts we've discussed are nothing like those traditional virtue epistemologists envisage. Blind deference seems no virtue, from their perspective, but it is something that looks alarmingly like such deference that underlies cumulative culture in an important way. Similarly, there seems to be a good case for calling the kind of behavior that minimizes hidden profiles epistemic arrogance (indeed, Samuelson and Church 2015 are explicit that epistemic humility is incompatible with the confirmation bias).

7 Insofar as virtue theory requires stability of response, this seems to me like bad news for the approach. Of course, there are obvious responses available. One would be to deny that what look like arrogance or servility are any such thing: the person who insists on his opinion, in the presence of dissenting epistemic superiors, say, does not manifest epistemic arrogance *because* his doing so is conducive to collective deliberation. There are two problems with this response. First, at the individual level, his behavior may count as epistemically arrogant on any plausible account. It certainly need not be conducive to

knowledge *for him*. Second, the response risks emptying the virtue theoretical approach of all content, by identifying the virtues with whatever response might be appropriate in a context. Another possible response turns on issues related to the so-called *generality problem*: can we appropriately identify virtues with fine-grained dispositions? Perhaps we should say that an agent possesses the virtue of epistemic humility if she is disposed to exhibit it in that narrow slice of contexts in which it is genuinely appropriate.

8 Though it should be recognized that some of the ways in which content matters can make us worse off epistemically. Our content biases include a disposition to accept and repeat emotionally arousing claims (Peters, Kashima and Clark 2009); that disposition likely plays a role in the way in which consume and spread fake news.

9 There is a danger of exaggerating the extent to which social media is liable to echo chambers. Guess and colleagues have found less evidence of selective exposure to a one-sided diet of voices than we might have expected (Guess, 2018; Guess, Nyhan, Lyons, and Reifler, 2018). We might even hope that social media could serve to harness the wisdom of crowds, leading to better justified beliefs. Sullivan et al. (forthcoming) suggests that that hope is yet to be realized, at least with regard to vaccination messages on Twitter.

10 It should be acknowledged that this might be true of some populations (perhaps 'digital natives') and not others. Guess, Nagler and Tucker (2019) found that the over 55s shared nearly 7 times as much fake news as the youngest. This may not be an indication of greater arrogance in this group, however, so much as greater credulity.

11 Here I take issue with Nguyen (2018), who suggests that adding a diversity of voices pops our epistemic bubble in a way that leads to better justified or more accurate beliefs, except when other voices are systematically denigrated. Nguyen reserves the term 'echo chamber' for epistemic spaces in which rival views are denigrated, calling those that simply happen to be closed to other voices epistemic bubbles. The evidence suggests, however, that the kind of vociferous and systematic denigration characteristic of his echo chambers is not required for triggering the myside bias and subsequent belief polarization. As we have seen, our filters on testimony are not the problem, and popping epistemic bubbles is not the solution.

12 I am grateful to Mark Alfano for his helpful comments on this paper. This work was supported by a generous grant from the Australian Research Council.

References

Alfano, M. 2012. Expanding the Situationist Challenge to Responsibilist Virtue Epistemology. *The Philosophical Quarterly* 62(247): 223–249.

Alfano, M. and Skorburg, J.A. 2017. The Embedded and Extended Character Hypotheses. In J. Kiverstein (ed.), *The Routledge Handbook of Philosophy of the Social Mind*. New York: Routledge.

Bikhchandani, S., Hirshleifer, D. and Welch, I. 1992. A Theory of Fads, Fashion, Custom, and Cultural Change as Informational Cascades. *Journal of Political Economy* 100(5): 992–1026.

Boyd, R., Richerson, P.J. and Henrich, J. 2011. The Cultural Niche: Why Social Learning Is Essential for Human Adaptation. *Proceedings of the National Academy of Sciences of the United States of America* 108(Supplement 2): 10918–10925.

Burcham, P.C. 2008. Toxicology Down Under: Past Achievements, Present Realities, and Future Prospects. *Chemical Research in Toxicology* 21(5): 967–970.

Chudek, M., Heller, S., Birch, S. and Henrich, J. 2012. Prestige-Biased Cultural Learning: Bystander's Differential Attention to Potential Models Influences Children's Learning. *Evolution and Human Behavior* 33(1): 46–56.

Cohen, G.L. 2003. Party over Policy: The Dominating Impact of Group Influence on Political Beliefs. *Journal of Personality and Social Psychology* 85(5): 808–822.

Corner, A., Whitmarsh, L. and Xenias, D. 2012. Uncertainty, Scepticism and Attitudes Towards Climate Change: Biased Assimilation and Attitude Polarisation. *Climatic Change* 114(3–4): 463–478.

Guess, A. 2018. (Almost) Everything in Moderation: New Evidence on Americans' Online Media Diets. Working Paper. Retrieved from https://webspace.princeton.edu/users/aguess/Guess_OnlineMediaDiets.pdf.

Guess, A., Nagler, J. and Tucker, J. 2019. Less than You Think: Prevalence and Predictors of Fakenews Dissemination on Facebook. *Science Advances* 5(1): eaau4586.

Guess, A., Nyhan, B., Lyons, B. and Reifler, J. 2018. Avoiding the Echo Chamber About Echo Chambers: Why Selective Exposure to Like-Minded Political News is Less Prevalent than You Think. Knight Foundation White Paper. Retrieved from https://kf-site-production.s3.amazonaws.com/media_elements/files/000/000/133/original/Topos_KF_White-Paper_Nyhan_V1.pdf.

Harman, G. 1999. Moral Psychology Meets Social Psychology: Virtue Ethics and the Fundamental Attribution Error. *Proceedings of the Aristotelian Society* 99: 316–331.

Henrich, J. and Boyd, R. 1998. The Evolution of Conformist Transmission and between-Group Differences. *Evolution and Human Behavior* 19(4): 215–242.

Henrich, J. and Gil-White, F. 2001. The Evolution of Prestige: Freely Conferred Deference as a Mechanism for Enhancing the Benefits of Cultural Transmission. *Evolution and Human Behavior: Official Journal of the Human Behavior and Evolution Society* 22(3): 165–196.

Henrich, J. and Henrich, N. 2010. The Evolution of Cultural Adaptations: Fijian Food Taboos Protect against Dangerous Marine Toxins. *Proceedings of the Royal Society B: Biological Sciences* 277(1701): 3715–3724.

Henrich, J. 2017. *The Secret of Our Success*. Princeton: Princeton University Press.

Heyes, C. 2018. *Cognitive Gadgets: The Cultural Evolution of Thinking*. Harvard: Harvard University Press.

Kallestrup, J. and Pritchard, D. 2012. Robust Virtue Epistemology and Epistemic Anti-Individualism. *Pacific Philosophical Quarterly* 93(2): 84–103.

Kallestrup, J. and Pritchard, D. 2016. From Epistemic Anti-Individualism to Intellectual Humility. *Res Philosophica* 93(3): 533–552.

Kukla, R. 2012. Author TBD: Radical Collaboration in Contemporary Biomedical Research. *Philosophy of Science* 79(5): 845–858.

Laland, K.N. 2017. *Darwin's Unfinished Symphony*. Princeton: Princeton University Press.

Levy, N. 2019. Due Deference to Denialism: Explaining Ordinary People's Rejection of Established Scientific Findings. *Synthese* 196(1): 313–327.

Levy, N. and Alfano, M. Forthcoming. Knowledge from Vice: Deeply Social Epistemology. *Mind*.

Lynch, M.P. 2016. *The Internet of Us*. New York: W.W. Norton.

Maoz, I., Ward, A., Katz, M. and Ross, L. 2002. Reactive Devaluation of an 'Israeli' vs. 'Palestinian' Peace Proposal. *Journal of Conflict Resolution* 46(4): 515–546.

Martens, J.P. and Tracy, J.L. 2013. The Emotional Origins of a Social Learning bias does the Pride Expression Cue Copying? *Social Psychological and Personality Science* 4(92): 492–499.

Mascaro, O. and Sperber, D. 2009. The Moral, Epistemic, and Mindreading Components of Children's Vigilance Towards Deception. *Cognition* 112(3): 367–380.

Mercier, H., Trouche, E., Yama, H., Heintz, C. and Girotto, V. 2015. Experts and Laymen Grossly Underestimate the Benefits of Argumentation for Reasoning. *Thinking and Reasoning* 21(3): 341–355.

Mercier, H. and Sperber, D. 2017. *The Enigma of Reason*. Harvard: Harvard University Press.

Nguyen, C.T. 2018. Escape the Echo Chamber. *Aeon*. Retrieved from https://aeon.co/essays/why-its-as-hard-to-escape-an-echo-chamber-as-it-is-to-flee-a-cult.

Nyhan, B. and Reifler, J. 2013. *Which Corrections Work? Research Results and Practice Recommendations*. Washington, D.C.: New America Foundation, Media Policy Initiative.

Palermos, S.O. 2016. Spreading the Credit: Virtue Reliabilism and Weak Epistemic Anti-Individualism. *Erkenntnis* 81(2): 305–334.

Peters, K., Kashima, Y. and Clark, A. 2009. Talking about Others: Emotionality and the Dissemination of Social Information. *European Journal of Social Psychology* 39(2): 207–222.

Pritchard, D. 2005. *Epistemic Luck*. Oxford: Oxford University Press.

Richerson, P.J. and Boyd, R. 2005. *Not by Genes Alone*. Chicago: University of Chicago Press.

Rini, R. 2017. Fake News and Partisan Epistemology. *Kennedy Institute of Ethics Journal* 27(S2): E-43-E64.

Samuelson, Peter L. and Church, Ian M. 2015. When Cognition Turns Vicious: Heuristics and Biases in Light of Virtue Epistemology. *Philosophical Psychology* 28(8): 1095–1113.

Schwarz, N., Sanna, L.J., Skurnik, I. and Yoon, C. 2007. Metacognitive Experiences and the Intricacies of Setting People Straight: Implications for Debiasing and Public Information Campaigns. *Advances in Experimental Social Psychology* 39: 127–161.

Sharot, T. and Garrett, N. 2016. Forming Beliefs: Why Valence Matters. *Trends in Cognitive Sciences* 20(1): 25–33.

Shea, N. 2009. Imitation as an Inheritance System. *Philosophical Transactions of the Royal Society B* 364(1528): 2429–2443.

Sperber, D., Clément, F., Heintz, C., Mascaro, O., Mercier, H., Origgi, G. and Wilson, D. 2010. Epistemic Vigilance. *Mind and Language* 25(4): 359–393.

Sullivan, E., Sondag, M., Rutter, I., et al. Forthcoming. Can Real Social Epistemic Networks Deliver the Wisdom of Crowds? In Tania Lombrozo, Joshua Knobe and Shaun Nichols (eds.), *Oxford Studies in Experimental Philosophy*.

Surowiecki, J. 2004. *The Wisdom of Crowds*. New York: Doubleday.

Tomasello, M. 1999. *The Cultural Origins of Human Cognition*. London: Harvard University Press.

Weaver, K., Garcia, S.M., Schwarz, N. and Miller, D.T. 2007. Inferring the Popularity of an Opinion from Its Familiarity: A Repetitive Voice Can Sound Like a Chorus. *Journal of Personality and Social Psychology* 92(5): 821–833.

41
HUMILITY IN SOCIAL NETWORKS

Mark Alfano and Emily Sullivan

41.1 Introduction

In recent years philosophers have begun to theorize, and psychologists have begun to measure, a suite of related dispositions:

- modesty (Bommarito 2013; Wilson 2016),
- humility (Driver 2001; Saucier 2009; Lee and Ashton 2018),
- intellectual humility (Roberts and Wood 2007; Hazlett 2012; Samuelson et al. 2015; Krumrei-Mancuso and Rouse 2015; Alfano et al. 2017; Leary et al. 2017; Whitcomb et al. 2017; Haggard et al. 2018), and
- open-mindedness (Riggs 2010; Baehr 2011; Madison forthcoming; Kwong 2017).

At the same time, philosophers and psychologists have addressed a range of dispositions that, in one way or another, seem to oppose these dispositions, including:

- vanity (Egan and McCorkindale 2007; Roberts and Wood 2007),
- narcissism (Egan and McCorkindale 2007; Paulhus and Williams 2002; Roberts this volume),
- arrogance (Haggard et al. 2018, Tanesini 2016a, 2016b),
- pride (Roberts and Wood 2007; Tracy et al. 2009; Carter and Gordon 2017; Roberts this volume),
- myside bias (Taber and Lodge 2006; Westen et al. 2006; Stanovich and West 2007; West and Stanovich 2008; Wolfe and Britt 2008; Levy and Alfano 2019),
- dogmatism (Cassam 2016), and
- intellectual insouciance (Cassam 2018).

The first family of dispositions seems, at least at first blush, to encompass intellectual virtues, while the latter seems to be a rogues' gallery of intellectual vices. That said, there have been a number of contrarian positions defending, for example, closed-mindedness, staked out by Battaly (2018) and Fantl (2018).

In this chapter, we address a problem internal to the suite of dispositions referred to as modesty, humility, intellectual humility, and open-mindedness. For the sake of brevity, we will refer to them collectively as *h-traits*. The problem is this: if someone who embodies h-traits spends the bulk of their time, attention, and engagement with a homogeneous ingroup, they are liable to overcome myside bias (closely related to the broader phenomenon of confirmation bias) at a significant social epistemic cost. Myside bias is a disposition to seek out, interpret, prize, and remember information in a way that supports my side of an argument in an interpersonal dispute. Consider a different bias, which we might call *ourside bias*. This is a disposition to seek out, interpret, prize, and remember information in a way that supports our side of an argument in an intergroup conflict. Our contention is that, in many real-world contexts, the h-traits forestall myside bias at the cost of exacerbating ourside bias. For example, humbly conciliating about practical values with one's ingroup can, in some circumstances, lead to even starker practical conflict with outgroups. And humbly conciliating about what one believes or accepts as epistemically rational with one's ingroup is liable to lead to even starker epistemic conflict with outgroups. Ourside bias thus has both practical and epistemic import. So, to the extent that it is exacerbated by the h-traits, we should be leery of cultivating and recommending them.

If this is on the right track, then people who embody h-traits are especially liable to participate in a process of group polarization (Brady et al. 2017; Van Bavel and Pereira 2018; Sunstein 2017) that leads to the development of "filter bubbles" and "echo chambers" (Pariser 2011; see also Nguyen forthcoming). Avoiding this effect may require them either to develop different dispositions from the h-traits, or to rewire their networks of trust so that their h-traits function more appropriately. Our claim is that the evaluative character of h-traits—whether they should be considered epistemically good or not—depends on the structure of the social networks in which agents find themselves. This idea could be given a strong interpretation, according to which epistemic virtues are partly constituted by the material, social, and political environment, or a weaker interpretation, according to which epistemic virtues are essentially embedded in material, social, and political environments. Alfano and Skorburg (2017) call these positions the extended and embedded character hypotheses, respectively. We contend that unless one's social network is structured in a way that many real social networks are *not* (Sullivan et al. forthcoming; Alfano et al. 2018), one's h-traits may fail to qualify as virtues. For instance, recent simulations suggest that even ideally rational Bayesian agents are guaranteed to polarize in their opinions unless the patterns of epistemic trust and distrust that connect them are structured in the right way (Pallavicini et al. forthcoming). These structures in the *topology* of social networks can be analyzed and sometimes ameliorated at both the local and global level (Alfano 2016).

The tension between myside and ourside bias is a problem because the h-traits are—ideally—supposed to forestall both individualistic manifestations of vanity, undue pride, and so on, *and* groupish manifestations of these vices such as "racism, sexism, ethnic hatred, religious hatred, and homophobia" (Spezio et al. 2018; see also Christen, Alfano, and Robinson 2017; Christen, Robinson, and Alfano 2014). We thus need to reconsider how people can best ensure that h-traits are expressed in appropriate attitudes not only toward members of their own communities (a topic that has been addressed in the literature) but also toward those who belong to other communities (a topic that has been largely neglected).

Here is the plan for this paper: in Section 1, we argue that h-traits plausibly correct or ameliorate myside bias. Next, in Section 2 we argue that, given how people's social networks are typically structured, h-traits can be expected to lead to ourside bias. Finally, in Section 3 we explore three approaches to resolving the dilemma we've diagnosed. The first involves restructuring one's social network so that ourside bias is not exacerbated by h-traits. The second involves emulating the Socratic figure of the gadfly. And the third involves the Nietzschean virtue of solitude.

41.2 H-traits and myside bias

Myside bias is a manifestation of a broader phenomenon referred to as confirmation bias (McKenzie 2004). It is tempered in social contexts when the group is decentralized and contains a diversity of opinions (Surowiecki 2004; see also Masterton et al. 2016, 2017, 2018 and Zollman 2013). In such groups, each individual's myside bias is harnessed in a way that leads to a better overall outcome. In particular, Mercier and Sperber (2019) argue that that the people who are sympathetic to *p* will tend to find and emphasize all the relevant evidence and arguments in favor of *p*, while those who are unsympathetic to *p* will tend to find and emphasize all the relevant evidence and arguments against *p*. Together, then, they manage to take into account all the evidence and arguments *both* in favor of and against *p*. Such a division of cognitive labor seems to be essential to many human cognitive successes. Social scientists have institutionalized it in the form of adversarial collaborations (Mellers et al. 2001). If one is good enough at role-playing, one can even form an adversarial collaboration with oneself (Alfano 2018).

The h-traits plausibly assist in these processes. For example, Baron (2008) argues that actively open-minded thinking opposes myside bias. Presumably, people high in open-mindedness are more disposed to engage in actively open-minded thinking (else, the construct lacks what social scientists call face validity).[1] If this is right, then open-mindedness can be expected to undercut the disposition to myside bias.

Likewise, someone high in modesty would presumably engage more effectively with people with whom she disagrees than someone low in modesty. According to Bommarito (2013), modesty is a virtue of attention: it involves actively attending to things other than oneself and one's own qualities and excellences. Doing so should obscure what my side of an argument or dispute even is, making it less likely that I manifest myside bias.

Next, consider humility. In the HEXACO personality inventory (Lee and Ashton 2018), humility is measured by agreement with the following two items: "I am an ordinary person who is no better than others," and "I wouldn't want people to treat me as though I were superior to them." It is also indicated by disagreement with the following two items: "I think that I am entitled to more respect than the average person is," and "I want people to know that I am an important person of high status." The division of cognitive labor mentioned above only works when people are able to take seriously those with whom they disagree, and to continue engaging with them over a period of time. Someone who scores high on the humility scale would, presumably, do just that. For these reasons, humility should also help someone overcome myside bias.

Finally, intellectual humility seems especially suited to helping its bearer overcome myside bias. Theorists characterize intellectual humility in terms of very low concern for one's intellectual reputation and entitlements (Roberts and Wood 2007), openness to others' views and engagement with those who disagree (Alfano et al. 2017), and owning one's intellectual limitations (Whitcomb et al. 2017). All of these dispositions make one more likely to take seriously evidence that runs contrary to one's beliefs and expectations, and thus to overcome or forestall myside bias.

41.3 H-traits and ourside bias

Most research on intellectual humility and other h-traits focuses only on individual traits and peer-disagreement, with little attention to group membership and the inter-group conflict that so easily arises given the all-too-human tendency to form coalitions and engage in partisan competition and conflict (Van Bavel and Pereira 2018). This is problematic because the h-traits could be practiced or expressed in a partial and partisan way, which has the potential to exacerbate inter-group arrogance that manifests in "racism, sexism, ethnic hatred, religious hatred, and homophobia" (Spezio et al. 2018). For example, Brady et al. (2017) have found that moral-emotional language is especially likely to go viral in polarized networks, and that it may drive the poles further and further apart. Appealing to what is valued by the ingroup (whether it is genuinely valuable or not) may come at the cost of inter-group understanding.

Thus, despite what we've just said in favor of the h-traits in relation to myside bias, we fear that they may have the opposite evaluative valence in relation to ourside bias. Recall that we have defined ourside bias as a disposition to seek out, interpret, prize, and remember information in a way that supports our side of an argument in an intergroup conflict. There are several reasons to think that someone who embodies the h-traits *and* spends the bulk of their time, attention, and engagement with their ingroup is especially liable to exhibit ourside bias.

First, someone is especially likely to consider those who are fellow members of their ingroup to be epistemic peers. This notion of peer-hood coupled with embodying h-traits leads to conciliatory behavior in the face of peer-disagreement, especially in cases where someone has a minority opinion compared to the rest of the ingroup. Over time, this may lead to group convergence on a set of shared opinions and evidence. Importantly, group convergence comes out of cultivating h-traits and conciliating in a way that is often called for in the case of peer-disagreement (Christensen 2007). In light of group convergence, conciliation in the face of disagreement with members of one's *out*group is not obvious. One could argue that one's interlocutor does not qualify as a peer because of the differing group membership, or one might become steadfast in the face of the disagreement. For example, Zagzebski (2012) and Pasnau (2015) argue that self-trust is an important factor to consider in cases of peer-disagreement. They argue that there are cases where conciliating is not epistemically required because self-trust is epistemically basic. It is our contention that h-traits that cultivate ingroup conciliation, cultivate *ingroup-trust*. In the face of ingroup-trust, steadfastness toward outgroup members appears epistemically virtuous. Thus, the very h-traits that help people overcome myside bias set them on the path to ourside bias. More precisely, the h-traits can be expected to do this if, like most people's, the agent's social network is structured around a relatively homogeneous and homophilic ingroup.

Here, one might object that treating *anyone* as a member of an outgroup is inconsistent with the h-traits. Perhaps the genuinely intellectually humble person agrees with the Roman poet Terence in thinking, "I am human; nothing human is alien to me." We think that this is too extreme a constraint to put on the h-traits. Almost everyone enjoys a sense of community with a small subset of the full human population (Dunbar 1993). While cosmopolitanism of a sort is valuable, that does not mean that people should be expected not to form partial attachments, involving trust, with small groups. What is at issue, then, is how one's community of trust is formed, shaped, structured, and modified over time, as well as one's disposition toward those who are not already part of one's community. In the next section, we turn to such processes of forming, shaping, structuring, and modification.

If our arguments in this section are on the right track, they run contrary to Rini's (2017) claim that "partisanship-in-testimony-reception is sometimes compatible with epistemic virtue," and to Levy's (2017) argument that the best thing to do in many cases is to go out of one's way to avoid testimony that one regards as prima facie fake news. Walling oneself off in an enclave of like-minded thinkers may be comfortable and cozy, but it risks aggravating ourside bias—especially in those who embody h-traits.

41.4 Rescuing h-traits via the gadfly, curiosity, and solitude

Just as generosity without thrift or honesty without tact can fail to be fully virtuous, so ingroup-oriented h-traits without outgroup-oriented h-traits (and vice versa) can fail to be fully virtuous. However, philosophers and psychologists have paid little attention to balancing ingroup and outgroup h-traits. Much of trait psychology focuses on pan-situational dispositions. Even research on social dominance theory (Pratto et al. 1994) tends to treat the social dominance orientation as pan-situational. This is especially troubling because the deep-seated conflicts that are readily apparent in many contemporary societies embody a tension between ingroup and outgroup h-traits. In addition, while the cultivation of virtuous dispositions is no doubt part of the solution, the structure of social networks is likely to play just as big a role. If the voice of one's community is amplified while outsiders are silenced, one is likely to end up with an arrogant attitude toward outsiders. Deferring to members of one's ingroup is liable to intensify conflicts with outgroups, but criticizing one's ingroup runs the risk of appearing or being intellectually arrogant and can lead to social exclusion.

How should we respond to the antinomy between myside and ourside biases? We believe the answer resides in a joint understanding of both the h-traits themselves and the social structures in which they are embedded. In this section, we canvass three mutually-compatible strategies: the gadfly, curiosity, and solitude.

41.4.1 H-traits and the gadfly

One approach to reducing ourside bias relies on the Socratic figure of the gadfly.[2] In Plato's *Apology* 30e, Socrates famously compares himself to a gadfly and his community (Athens) to a sluggish horse. Here we quote at length:

> [I]f you kill me you will not easily find another like me. I was attached to this city by the god—though it seems a ridiculous thing to say—as upon a great and noble horse which was somewhat sluggish because of its size and needed to be stirred up by a kind of gadfly. It is to fulfill some such function that I believe the god has placed me in the city. I never cease to rouse each and every one of you, to persuade and reproach you all day long and everywhere I find myself in your company.

The idea behind this metaphor is that, despite the pain he causes to his ingroup, Socrates manifests an other-regarding moral and intellectual virtue. He systematically and repeatedly provokes members of his ingroup to examine not only their own lives and values, but also the values of their shared community. He forces them to consider the extent to which they understand their own motives, customs, and norms, as well as the rationale for these motives, customs, and norms. He prompts them to reconsider whether their own local customs are indeed best. Furthermore, he approaches only members of his ingroup in this way. Socrates does not play the role of the devil's advocate (to use a more recent metaphor) with every interlocutor he encounters; instead, he focuses his critical energies on the most (over-)confident members of his ingroup: adult male citizens of Athens. In so doing, he undermines their confidence (sometimes) and makes them less secure in their own parochial smugness. This is the sort of thing that should have a salutary effect in reducing ourside bias, since it makes the ingroup default less appealing and seemingly obvious.

However, being a Socratic gadfly—someone disposed to turn a critical eye to their own community's conventional wisdom in order to goad the community into reflection and reform—is challenging and risky. It can easily shade over into contrarianism for its own sake. And a community composed entirely of gadflies would hardly be a community at all. Socrates here assumes that there is a division of moral and intellectual labor in his community: the vast majority together are represented by the figure of the horse, whereas he alone is the gadfly. This prompts the question whether there might be dispositions other than that of the gadfly that are worth cultivating and manifesting in other parts of a community. In addition, as the case of Socrates demonstrates, the community is liable to become defensive and even violent against the gadfly. For these reasons, it may sometimes be more prudent to adopt other strategies. We now turn to two such strategies: curiosity and solitude.

41.4.2 · H-traits and curiosity

If we ignore social context, it might seem that there is nothing in the h-traits to worry about. After all, wouldn't someone who embodies humility, modesty, and intellectual humility be just as disposed to defer to or conciliate with an ingroup member as an outgroup member? The problem only arises because humans tend to cluster socially into groups of like-minded and like-valued individuals, a process known as homophily (Centola et al. 2007). Even if I am equally likely to conciliate and defer in each particular encounter, if most of my encounters are with people who share a common set of opinions and values, I will end up gravitating toward their views.

This is where curiosity, understood as a drive to encounter new people, places, things, and ideas, comes into play (Alfano 2013; Iurino et al. 2018; Inan et al. 2018). Someone who manages to combine curiosity with the h-traits will make a point of learning about the opinions, values, customs, and norms of people who do not belong to their ingroup. Such a person will be attracted to novelty and strangeness. As a stranger they will, in Hamlet's words, give it welcome. In so doing, they employ a social strategy to put themselves in a position to encounter information and testimony that they might not otherwise have encountered. Unlike someone in the grip of confirmation bias, then, they actively seek out those whose views are liable to differ from their own.

From the point of view of social network theory, curious agents can be understood as those who go out of their way to establish heterophilic connections, i.e., to connect with those who do not belong to their ingroup. This does not mean that they necessarily shun their ingroups, just that they make a point of engaging with, learning about and from, and attending to people who belong to other groups. In so doing, they temper the ourside bias that arises in more closed-off social networks. Unlike the gadfly, then, which is primarily an other-regarding virtue, curiosity is a self-regarding virtue. It may not do much to help the community avoid ourside bias, but it should help its bearer to do so.

41.4.3 H-traits and solitude

The problem of ourside bias arises from the ratio between homophilic and heterophilic connections. If someone has vastly more homophilic than heterophilic connections, they are liable to suffer ourside bias. An extremely imbalanced ratio can be solved either by addition or subtraction. Whereas curiosity helps rescue the h-traits by leading its bearer to establish new heterophilic connections, the Nietzschean virtue of solitude helps by leading its bearer to sever or weaken homophilic connections.[3]

Solitude is a complex disposition that involves someone taking a distant and elevated perspective on their own community and ingroup. It protects it's bearer's psychology from being overwhelmed by the pressures and expectations of their community, from conciliating too easily and too often with their ingroup. And it prevents its bearer from provoking too much easily internalized disapprobation from their community (this is why Nietzsche frequently associates solitude with politeness). Finally, it makes possible a collective version of the self-contempt that Nietzsche associates with both the pathos of distance and having a sense of humor. Whereas the latter two dispositions make it possible for someone to improve their character through criticism of the *I*, solitude makes it possible for someone to improve their community through criticism of the *we*—that is to say, through cultural criticism.

When Nietzsche talks about solitude, he typically has in mind emotional rather than physical distance. For example, in *Human, All-too-human* Assorted Opinions and Maxims 386, he declares that "wisdom is the whispering of the solitary [*Einsamen*] to himself in the crowded marketplaces." Solitude is the drive to get away from, and often above, one's ingroup or local community, to view that community and its values critically, and to divorce oneself from aspects of the community that one might otherwise adopt uncritically and by default. Just as the ability to laugh at oneself is an important part of self-criticism and self-improvement, so the ability to look from a distance or at a height down on one's community is an important part of cultural critique. Solitude thus opposes precisely the vices of collective arrogance: chauvinism, narrow-mindedness, and cozy cultural smugness.

For Nietzsche, solitude is a penchant for challenging the doxastic and axiological truisms of one's community, for "indict[ing] the people's favorites" (*Ecce Homo* Books.UM2). Likewise, Nietzsche congratulates himself for writing books that "contain snares and nets for unwary birds and in effect a persistent invitation to the overturning of habitual evaluations and valued habits." (*Human, All-too-human* Preface 1). Solitude is a sort of instinctual aversion to the familiar and an attraction to the strange and new. In a later passage (*Beyond Good and Evil* 212), Nietzsche points to an important philosophical precedent for his sort of solitude: Socrates the gadfly, who, as a philosopher, "*needed* to be at odds with his today: his enemy has always been the ideal of today." Philosophers tend to feel like "disagreeable fools and dangerous question-marks." Gadflies like Socrates are "the bad conscience of their age [who apply] a vivisecting knife directly to the chest of the *virtues of the age*."

But solitude differs from the gadfly in being more selective. Solitude is practiced not in the marketplace but in the library. It is therefore less liable to instigate the kind of collective punishment that ended Socrates's philosophical career (and his life). In terms of social network theory, whereas curiosity is about establishing new, heterophilic connections, solitude is about severing or weakening extant, homophilic connections.

We believe that the gadfly, curiosity, and solitude all have a role to play in rescuing the h-traits from the antinomy between myside bias and ourside bias. They seem prima facie consistent with one another, and they answer to different aspects of the problem. For these reasons, it is likely that cultivating all three and knowing which to use when is the right approach to take if one wants to avoid ourside bias.

Notes

1 Face validity is a property of a psychometric instrument. When an instrument is valid "on its face" that means it intuitively taps into the construct that it allegedly measures. For example, an intelligence test that in no way required someone to solve a problem, answer a question, draw an inference, or exhibit a skilled behavior would lack face validity. Likewise, a psychometric test of open-mindedness that in no way tapped into actively open-minded thinking would lack face validity.

2 There is some controversy about how to translate *μυ'ω*, which could also reasonably be rendered as 'spur' in this context (Marshall 2017). For our purposes, either translation makes sense, and spur may even be more appropriate, as it implies a pedagogical function rather than merely causing annoyance.

3 See Alfano 2019, chapter 10 for a fuller account and interpretation of Nietzsche on solitude.

References

Alfano, M. (2013). The most agreeable of all vices: Nietzsche as virtue epistemologist. *British Journal for the History of Philosophy*, 21(4): 767–90.

Alfano, M. (2016). The topology of communities of trust. *Russian Sociological Review*, 15(4): 30–56.

Alfano, M. (2018). Nietzsche's affective perspectivism as a philosophical methodology. In: P. Loeb and M. Meyer (eds.), *Nietzsche's Metaphilosophy*. Cambridge: Cambridge University Press.

Alfano, M. (2019). *Nietzsche's Moral Psychology*. Cambridge: Cambridge University Press.

Alfano, M., Cunningham, S., Meulemans, W., Rutter, I., Sondag, M., Speckmann, B., and Sullivan, E. (2018, October). Social network epistemology. In *2018 IEEE 14th International Conference on e-Science (e-Science)*, pp. 320–321. Amsterdam: IEEE.

Alfano, M., Iurino, K., Stey, P., Robinson, B., Christen, M., Yu, F., and Lapsley, D. (2017). Development and validation of a multi-dimensional measure of intellectual humility. *PloS one*, 12(8): e018250.

Alfano, M. and Skorburg, J. A. (2017). The embedded and extended character hypotheses. In: J. Kiverstein (ed.), *Handbook of Philosophy of the Social Mind*, pp. 465–78. New York: Routledge.

Baehr, J. (2011). The structure of open-mindedness. *Canadian Journal of Philosophy*, 41(2): 191–213.

Baron, J. (2008). *Thinking and Deciding*, 4th edition. Cambridge: Cambridge University Press.

Battaly, H. (2018). Can closed-mindedness be an intellectual virtue? *Royal Institute of Philosophy Supplement*, 84: 23–45.

Bommarito, N. (2013). Modesty as a virtue of attention. *Philosophical Review*, 122(1): 93–117.

Brady, W., Wills, J., Jost, J., Tucker, J., and Van Bavel, J. (2017). Emotion shapes the diffusion of moralized content in social networks. *Proceedings of the National Academy of Sciences of the United States of America*, 114(28): 7313–18.

Carter, J. A. and Gordon, E. (2017). *The Moral Psychology of Pride*. New York: Rowman & Littlefield.

Cassam, Q. (2016). Vice epistemology. *The Monist*, 99(2): 159–80.

Cassam, Q. (2018). Epistemic insouciance. *Journal of Philosophical Research, 43, 1-20.* .

Centola, D., González-Avella, J. C., Eguiluz, V. M., and Miguel, M. S. (2007). Homophily, cultural drift, and the co-evolution of cultural groups. *Journal of Conflict Resolution*, 51(6): 905–29.

Christen, M., Alfano, M., and Robinson, B. (2017). A cross-cultural assessment of the semantic dimensions of intellectual humility. *AI and Society*, 34(4), 785–801.

Christen, M., Robinson, B., and Alfano, M. (2014). The semantic neighborhood of intellectual humility. *Proceedings of the European Conference on Social Intelligence*, pp. 40–9.

Christensen, David. (2007). Epistemology of disagreement: The good news. *Philosophical Review*, 116(2): 187–218.

Driver, J. (2001). *Uneasy Virtue*. Cambridge: Cambridge University Press.

Dunbar, R. (1993). Coevolution of neocortical size, group size and language in humans. *Behavioral and Brain Sciences*, 16(4): 681–735.

Egan, V. and McCorkindale, C. (2007). Narcissism, vanity, personality and mating effort. *Personality and Individual Differences*, 43(8): 2105–15.

Fantl, J. (2018). *The Limitations of the Open Mind*. Oxford: Oxford University Press.

Haggard, M., Rowatt, W., Leman, J., Meagher, B., Moore, C., Fergus, T., Whitcomb, D., Battaly, H., Baehr, J., and Howard-Snyder, D. (2018). Finding middle ground between intellectual arrogance and intellectual servility: Development and assessment of the limitations-owning intellectual humility scale. *Personality and Individual Differences*, 124: 183–93.

Hazlett, A. (2012). Higher-order epistemic attitudes and intellectual humility. *Episteme*, 8(3): 205–23.

Inan, I., Watson, L., Whitcomb, D., and Yigit, S., eds., (2018). *The Moral Psychology of Curiosity*. New York: Rowman and Littlefield.

Iurino, K., Robinson, B., Christen, M., Stey, P., and Alfano, M. (2018). Constructing and validating a scale of inquisitive curiosity. In: I. Inan, L. Watson, D. Whitcomb, and S. Yigit (eds.), *The Moral Psychology of Curiosity*. New York: Rowman & Littlefield.

Krumrei-Mancuso, E. and Rouse, S. (2015). The development and validation of the comprehensive intellectual humility scale. *Journal of Personality Assessment*, 98(2): 209–21.

Kwong, J. (2017). Is open-mindedness conducive to truth? *Synthese*, 194(5): 1613–26.

Leary, M., Diebels, K., Davisson, E., Isherwood, J., Jongman-Sereno, K., Raimi, K., Deffler, S. A., Hoyle, R. (2017). Cognitive and interpersonal features of intellectual humility. *Personality and Social Psychology Bulletin*, 43(6): 793–813.

Lee, K. and Ashton, M. (2018). Psychometric properties of the HEXACO-100. *Assessment*, 25(5): 543–56.

Levy, N. (2017). The bad news about fake news. *Social Epistemology Review and Reply Collective*, 6(8): 20–36.

Levy, N. and Alfano, M. (2019). Knowledge from vice: Deeply social epistemology. *Mind*, fzz017.

Madison, B. (forthcoming). Is open-mindedness truth conducive? *Synthese*.

Marshall, L. (2017). Gadfly or spur? The meaning of *μυ'ωψ* in Plato's *Apology of Socrates*. *Journal of Hellenic Studies*, 137: 163–74.

Masterton, G., Olsson, E. J., and Angere, S. (2016). Linking as voting: How the condorcet jury theorem in political science is relevant to webometrics. *Scientometrics*, 106(3), 945–966.

Masterton, G. and Olsson, E. J. (2017). From impact to importance: The current state of the wisdom-of-crowds justification of link-based ranking algorithms. *Philosophy and Technology*, 31(4), 593–609.

Masterton, G. and Olsson, E. J. (2018). PageRank's ability to track webpage quality: Reconciling Google's wisdom-of-crowds justification with the scale-free structure of the web. *Heliyon*, 4(11): 1–34.

McKenzie, C. (2004). Hypothesis testing and evaluation. In: D. J. Koehler and N. Harvey (eds.), *Blackwell Handbook of Judgment & Decision Making*, pp. 200–19. Blackwell.

Mellers, B., Hertwig, R., and Kahneman, D. (2001). Do frequency representations eliminate conjunction effects? An exercise in adversarial collaboration. *Psychological Science*, 12(4): 269–75.

Mercier, H. and Sperber, D. (2019). *The Enigma of Reason*. Harvard University Press.

Nguyen, C. T. (forthcoming). Echo chambers and epistemic bubbles. *Episteme*: 1–21.

Pallavicini, J., Hallsson, B., and Kappel, K. (forthcoming). Polarization in groups of Bayesian agents. *Synthese*, 1–55.

Pariser, E. (2011). *The Filter Bubble: What the Internet Is Hiding from You*. Penguin.

Pasnau, Robert. (2015). Disagreement and the value of self-trust. *Philosophical Studies*, 172(9): 2315–39.

Paulhus, D. and Williams, K. (2002). The dark triad of personality: Narcissism, Machiavellianism, and psychopathy. *Journal of Research in Personality*, 36(6): 556–63.

Pratto, F., Sidanius, J., Stallworth, L. M., and Malle, B. F. (1994). Social dominance orientation: A personality variable predicting social and political attitudes. *Journal of Personality and Social Psychology*, 67(4): 741–63.

Riggs, W. (2010). Open-mindedness. *Metaphilosophy*, 41(1–2): 172–88.

Rini, R. (2017). Fake news and partisan epistemology. *Kennedy Institute of Ethics Journal*, 27(S2): 43–64.

Roberts, R. (this volume). *Humility and Human Flourishing*, in Alessandra Tanesini, Michael Lynch & Mark Alfano (eds.), *The Routledge Handbook of the Philosophy of Humility*. New York: Routledge.

Roberts, R. and Wood, J. (2007). *Intellectual Virtues: An Essay in Regulative Epistemology*. Oxford: Oxford University Press.

Samuelson, P., Jarvinen, M., Paulus, T., Church, I., Hardy, S., and Barrett, J. (2015). Implicit theories of intellectual virtues and vices: A focus on intellectual humility. *The Journal of Positive Psychology*, 10(5): 389–406.

Saucier, G. (2009). Recurrent personality dimensions in inclusive lexical studies: Indications for a big six structure. *Journal of Personality*, 77(5): 1577–614.

Spezio, M., Peterson, G., and Roberts, R. (2018). Humility as openness to others: Interactive humility in the context of l'Arche. *Journal of Moral Education*.

Stanovich, K. and West, R. (2007). Natural myside bias is independent of cognitive ability. *Thinking and Reasoning*, 13(3): 225–47.

Sullivan, E., Sondag, M., Rutter, I., Meulemans, W., Cunningham, S., Speckmann, B., and Alfano, M. (forthcoming). Can real social epistemic networks deliver the wisdom of crowds? In: T. Lombrozo, J. Knobe, and S. Nichols (eds.), *Oxford Studies in Experimental Philosophy*, vol. 2. Oxford: Oxford University Press.

Sunstein, C. (2017). *#Republic: Divided Democracy in the Age of Social Media*. Princeton: Princeton University Press.

Surowiecki, J. (2004). *The Wisdom of Crowds*. New York: Anchor.

Taber, C. and Lodge, M. (2006). Motivated skepticism in the evaluation of political beliefs. *American Journal of Political Science*, 50(3): 755–69.

Tanesini, A. (2016a). "Calm down, dear": Intellectual arrogance, silencing and ignorance. *Aristotelian Society Supplementary Volume*, 90(1): 71–92.

Tanesini, A. (2016b). Teaching virtue: Changing attitudes. *Logos and Episteme*, 7(4): 503–27.

Tracy, J., Cheng, J., Robins, R., and Trzesniewski, K. (2009). Authentic and hubristic pride: The affective core of self-esteem and narcissism. *Self and Identity*, 8(2–3): 196–213.

Van Bavel, J. and Pereira, A. (2018). The partisan brain: An identity-based model of political belief. *Trends in Cognitive Sciences* 22(3), 213–224.

West, R. and Stanovich, K. (2008). On the failure of cognitive ability to predict myside and one-sided thinking biases. *Thinking and Reasoning*, 14(2): 129–67.

Westen, D., Blagov, P., Harenski, K., Kilts, C., and Hamann, S. (2006). Neural bases of motivated reasoning: An fMRI study of emotional constraints on partisan political judgment in the 2004 U.S. Presidential election. *Journal of Cognitive Neuroscience*, 18(11): 1947–58.
Whitcomb, D., Battaly, H., Baehr, J., and Howard-Snyder, D. (2017). Intellectual humility: Owning our limitations. *Philosophy and Phenomenological Research*, 94(3): 509–39.
Wilson, A. (2016). Modesty as kindness. *Ratio*, 29(1): 73–88.
Wolfe, C. and Britt, M. (2008). The locus of myside bias in written argumentation. *Thinking and Reasoning*, 14(1): 1–27.
Zagzebski, Linda. (2012). *Epistemic Authority: A Theory of Trust, Authority, and Autonomy in Belief.* New York: Oxford University Press.
Zollman, K. (2013). Network epistemology: Communication in epistemic communities. *Philosophy Compass*, 8(1): 15–27.

INDEX

Page numbers in **bold** indicate tables. Page numbers in *italic* indicate figures.

For Product Safety Concerns and Information please contact our EU
representative GPSR@taylorandfrancis.com
Taylor & Francis Verlag GmbH, Kaufingerstraße 24, 80331 München, Germany

www.ingramcontent.com/pod-product-compliance
Ingram Content Group UK Ltd.
Pitfield, Milton Keynes, MK11 3LW, UK
UKHW050231200926
475702UK00020B/2964
* 9 7 8 0 3 6 7 5 0 2 6 4 5 *